Introduction to Political Theory

Visit the *Introduction to Political Theory* Companion Website at **www.pearsoned.co.uk/hoffman** to find valuable **student** learning material including:

- Original theory text extracts
- Case studies
- 'How to be a Theorist' guide
- Links to relevant sites on the web

We work with leading authors to develop the strongest educational materials in politics, bringing cutting-edge thinking and best learning practice to a global market.

Under a range of well-known imprints, including Longman, we craft high quality print and electronic publications which help readers to understand and apply their content, whether studying or at work.

To find out more about the complete range of our publishing, please visit us on the World Wide Web at: www.pearsoned.co.uk

Introduction to Political Theory

John Hoffman
University of Leicester

Paul Graham
University of Glasgow

PEARSON
Longman

Harlow, England • London • New York • Boston • San Francisco • Toronto • Sydney • Singapore • Hong Kong
Tokyo • Seoul • Taipei • New Delhi • Cape Town • Madrid • Mexico City • Amsterdam • Munich • Paris • Milan

Pearson Education Limited
Edinburgh Gate
Harlow
Essex CM20 2JE
England

and Associated Companies throughout the world

Visit us on the World Wide Web at:
www.pearsoned.co.uk

First published 2006

© Pearson Education Limited 2006

ISBN: 978-0-582-47373-7

British Library Cataloguing-in-Publication Data
A catalogue record for this book is available from the British Library

Library of Congress Cataloging-in-Publication Data
A catalog record for this book is available from The Library of Congress

10 9 8 7 6 5 4 3 2
10 09 08

Typeset in Sabon 10/12 by 59

Printed by Ashford Colour Press Ltd., Gosport

The publisher's policy is to use paper manufactured from sustainable forests.

Brief Contents

Part 4   Contemporary Ideas

Contents

Part 3 Contemporary Ideologies

Chapter 13 Feminism 324

Part 4   Contemporary Ideas

Supporting resources

Visit **www.pearsoned.co.uk/hoffman** to find valuable online resources

Companion Website for students
• Case studies
• Student guide to studying Political Theory
• Links to relevant sites on the web

For instructors
• Original theory text extracts
• Multiple choice questions for the original theory text extracts
• Instructor guide with teaching ideas for tutorials and case studies from the book

Also: The Companion Website provides the following features:

• Search tool to help locate specific items of content
• E-mail results and profile tools to send results of quizzes to instructors
• Online help and support to assist with website usage and troubleshooting

For more information please contact your local Pearson Education sales representative or
visit **www.pearsoned.co.uk/hoffman**

Guide to Features

Test Cases

Biography Boxes

Ideas and Perspectives Boxes

How To Read Boxes

Influences and Impact Boxes

Guided Tour

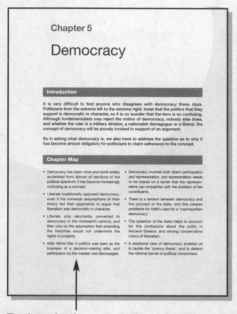

Test cases focus on interesting and contentious real-life examples and are accompanied by questions to challenge your own views.

The **Introductions** concisely set the scene at the start of each chapter and **Chapter Maps** summarise the key points that will be covered.

The lives and achievements of the most important theorists are fully covered in **Biography** boxes throughout the text.

Ideas and Perspectives boxes focus on detailed issues.

Margin **cross references** emphasise the linkages between thinkers and ideas throughout the book.

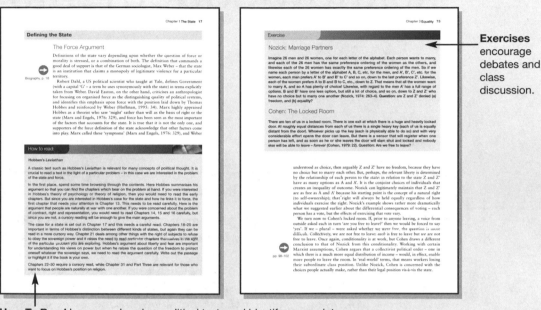

Exercises encourage debates and class discussion.

How To Read boxes analyse key political texts and identify core points.

Summaries pull together the fundamental concepts presented in the chapter

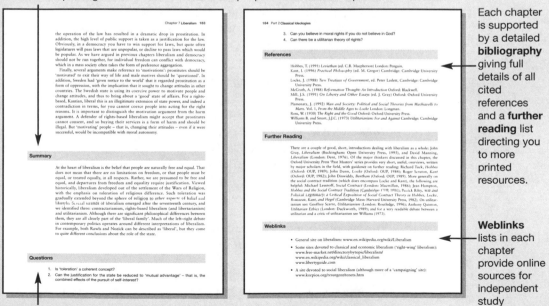

Each chapter is supported by a detailed **bibliography** giving full details of all cited references and a **further reading** list directing you to more printed resources.

Weblinks lists in each chapter provide online sources for independent study

Each chapter ends with **Questions** to test your understanding of the topics covered, reflect on the theories presented and to formulate your own opinions.

Publisher's Acknowledgements

We are grateful to the following for permission to reproduce copyright material:

Figures 3.2 and 3.3 reprinted by permission of Sage Publications Ltd. from Laver, M. (1997) *Private Desires, Political Actions*, Copyright © Sage, 1997.

Photographs: p15 (©CORBIS), p18 (AKG Images), p19 (©Bettmann/CORBIS), p39 (Rex Features), p41 (©CORBIS), p61 (©Charles Gupton Photography/CORBIS), p83 (©Getty/Tim Boyle), p85 (Harvard News Office/Jane Reed), p92 (Harvard News Office/Jane Reed), p98 (Joseph Raz), p105 (©Faleh Kheiber/Reuters/CORBIS), p108 (©Bettmann/ CORBIS), p110 (©Classic Image/Alamy), p129 (Rex Features), p133 (©CORBIS), p142 (Popperfoto), p163 (©Brooklyn Productions/CORBIS), p171 (©Getty/Hulton Archive), p176 (©Bettmann/CORBIS), p187 (©Jim Bourg/Reuters/ CORBIS), p192 (©Christie's Images/CORBIS), p194 (©Bettmann/CORBIS), p198 (London School of Economics & Political Science), p202 (University of Chicago), p209 (©Bettmann/ CORBIS), p213 (©Getty/Hulton Archive), p214 (Topfoto), p215 (©Getty/Hulton Archive), p218 (©Michael Nicholson/CORBIS), p219 (©Getty/ Hulton Archive), p222 (Topfoto), p223 (©Getty/Hulton Archive), p229 (Topfoto), p239 (©REUTERS/Dylan Martinez), p263 (©Getty/Peter Adams), p287 (Rex Features), p294 (©Bettmann/ CORBIS), p299 (©Hulton-Deutsch Collection/CORBIS), p311 (Camera Press/Hutchinson/ RBO), p325 (©Black Box RF/Alamy), p330 (©Lebrecht Music & Arts Photo Library/ Alamy), p351 (Empics/EPA), p371 (©Getty/ Peter Adams), p376 (©CORBIS), p379 (Vesa Lindqvist Matti Hurme/norden.org), p393 (©REUTERS/Mahfouz Abu Turk), p419 (Empics), p422 (Rex Features/SIPA Press), p437 (Punchstock/Brand X), p461 (Empics), p465 (©Rune Hellestad/ CORBIS), p475 (Rex Features/Everett Collection), p511 (©Ira Nowinski/CORBIS).

Glossary extracts reprinted by permission of Sage Publications Ltd from John Hoffman, *Citizenship Beyond the State*, © John Hoffman, 2004.

In some instances we have been unable to trace the owners of copyright material, and we would appreciate any information that would enable us to do so.

Authors' Acknowledgements

We are very grateful for the help received from Morten Fuglevand and David Cox of Pearson Education. David Cox read and commented on drafts with great enthusiasm and acumen and was an endless source of lively and interesting ideas. Morten and David's commitment to the book was inspiring and sustaining. In addition, the anonymous referees made invaluable, if at times painful, observations and have played an important part in improving the quality of the book. We are also grateful to Julie Knight for all her help.

We found working together on this book a stimulating and enjoyable experience. Both of us are committed to making political theory more accessible and lively and have tried to write a book that is stimulating, provocative and interesting.

John Hoffman

I would like to thank the publishers of the *Cambridge Dictionary of Sociology*, Cambridge University Press, for permission to draw upon entries submitted to this project. I am also very grateful to Edinburgh University Press for permission to use material that has also been submitted to a *Political Glossary* dealing with political theory, and to Sage Publications Ltd. who have kindly allowed me to draw upon *Citizenship Beyond the State* that appeared last year.

I have been supported by my partner, Rowan Roenisch, and my son, Fred and daughter, Frieda. All three have encouraged me in the project.

Paul Graham

Edinburgh University Press kindly granted permission to draw upon an essay from *Political Concepts: a Reader and Guide* (edited by Iain Mackenzie), as did OneWorld Books for use of material from *Rawls* (forthcoming).

I would like to express my gratitude to my parents, Douglas and Heather Graham, for their support and encouragement, and to my colleagues in the Department of Politics at Glasgow University, for providing a stimulating intellectual environment in which to work.

About the Authors

John Hoffman has taught in the Department of Politics, University of Leicester since 1970. He is currently Emeritus Professor of Political Theory, having retired at the end of September 2005. He has written widely on Marxism, feminism and Political Theory, with his most recent book being *Citizenship beyond the State*, published by Sage in 2004. He is currently working on John Gray and the problem of utopia.

Paul Graham is a Lecturer in Political Theory at Glasgow University. He teaches and researches in German and Anglo-American political thought, with a special focus on multiculturalism, human autonomy and rationality, freedom, and distributive justice.

Introduction

Students of politics often believe that politics can be studied without theory. They take the view that we can focus upon the facts without worrying about general ideas. In everyday life, however, we are guided by notions of right and wrong, justice and injustice, so that everything we do is informed by concepts. Politicians are similarly guided. It is not a question of *whether* political animals follow theory, but a question of *which* theory or concept is supported when they present policies and undertake actions. We can argue as to whether the British prime minister or the US president acts according to the right political concepts, but it is undeniable that their actions are linked to theory. Humans in general cannot act without ideas: indeed it is a defining property of human activity that we can only act when we have ideas in our head as to what we should do.

In discussing ideas about the state or democracy or freedom in this book, we are talking about ideas or concepts or theories – we use the terms interchangeably – that guide and inform political action. The state is particularly important in Part 1 and readers should tackle this topic at an early stage. It is a great pity that theory is sometimes presented as though it inhabits a world of its own: as though it can be discussed and analysed in ways that are not explicitly linked to practical questions and political activity. This is, indeed, something this book seeks to address.

Theory as Abstraction

We accept that all theory by definition involves abstraction. The very words we use involve a 'standing back' from specific things so that we can *abstract* from them something that they have in common. To identify a chair, to use a rather corny example, one needs to abstract the quality of 'chairness' from a whole range of objects, all of which differ in some detail from every other. Take another example. The word 'dog' refers both to particular dogs and dogs in general. If we define a dog as a mammal with four legs, it could be said that a dog is the same as an elephant. So our definition is too abstract. We need to make it more particularistic. A dog is a four-legged mammal with fur. But does this mean that all dogs are poodles? Such a view is too particularistic: we need to argue that 'dogness' is more abstract than just being a poodle.

The point is that we are abstracting all the time, whether we like it or not! This is the only way to understand. Thus, in an analysis of the recent war in Iraq, we might use a whole host of abstractions to make sense of what we see: 'war', 'violence', 'law', 'armies', the elusive 'weapons of mass destruction' etc. Particular things are injected with a conceptual dimension, so that references to 'democracy' or 'terrorism' (for example) reflect interpretations as well as physical events.

Political theory, however, seems rather more abstract than say an analysis of the Iraq war, because it considers the notion, for example, of 'violence' beyond any particular instance, asking what violence is in every circumstance that we can imagine. This apparent remoteness from specific instances creates a trap and gives rise to a pejorative use of the term 'abstract'. For thousands of years theorists have believed that the abstraction is somehow independent of reality, or even worse, that it creates reality. Because we cannot act without ideas, the illusion arises that ideas are more important than, and are even independent of, objects. We can, therefore, talk about democracy or the state, for example, without worrying about particular states or specific kinds of democracies. Understandably students may find it bewildering to be asked 'what is power?' or 'what is democracy?' without this being related to, for example, the power which Mao Zedong exerted over the Chinese people before he died in 1976 or the question of whether the inequalities of wealth in contemporary Britain have a negative impact upon the democratic quality of its political institutions.

We believe that this link between theory and recognisable political realities is essential to an understanding and appreciation of the subject. What gives concepts and theories a bad name is that they are all too often presented abstractly (in the pejorative sense). Thinkers may forget that our thoughts come from our experience with objects in the world around us, and they assume that political thought can be discussed as though it is independent of political realities. It is true that a person who is destitute and asking for money in the street is not necessarily conscious of whether he is acting with freedom and what this concept means; but it is equally true that a theorist talking about the question of freedom may not feel the need to relate the concept of freedom to the question of social destitution. It is this act of 'abstraction' that makes many students feel that theory is a waste of time and is unrelated to the world of realities. What we are trying to do in this book is to show that general ideas can help rather than hinder us in getting to grips with particular political events.

The Distinction between Facts and Values

One of the common arguments that aggravates theory's abstractness (unless otherwise stated, we will use the term 'abstraction' in its pejorative sense), arises when people say that theory is *either* empirical *or* it is normative. In fact, it is always both. Facts and values interpenetrate, so that it is impossible to have one without the other.

Are facts the same as values? To answer this, we turn to a concrete example. It is a fact that in Western liberal societies fewer and fewer people are bothering to vote. George Bush was elected in 2000 in a situation in which only about half of the electorate turned out to vote. This fact has an implicit evaluative significance, because historically, democracy has implied participation, and this fact suggests either that Western liberal societies are minimally democratic, or that the notion of democracy has to be revised. The implicitly evaluative dimension of this fact is evidenced in the way it is challenged, or at least approached. It might be said that low voter participation is only true of *some* Western liberal societies (the United States in particular), and it might be said that voting is not the only form of political participation that counts – people can participate by joining single-issue organisations such as Greenpeace or Amnesty International.

The point about facts is that they are generally agreed upon, and can be verified in ways that are not particularly controversial. They are accepted much more widely than explicit value judgements. Evaluation, on the other hand, refers to the relationships that are only implicit in the fact. Thus the interpretation of the fact that fewer and fewer people in Western liberal societies vote raises the question of why. Does the reason for this arise from a relationship with poverty, lack of self-esteem, education, disillusionment, or is it the product of a relationship to satisfaction? The explanation embodies the evaluative content of the fact much more explicitly, since the explanation offered has obvious policy implications. If the reason for apathy is poverty, etc., then this has very different implications for action than an argument that people do not vote because they are basically satisfied with what politicians are doing in their name.

Therefore we would argue that although facts and values are not the same, they are inherently linked. In our view it is relationships which create values, so that the more explicit and far-reaching these relationships the more obviously evaluative is the factual judgement. The fact that the earth goes round the sun is not really controversial in today's world, but it was explosively controversial in the medieval world, because the notion that the earth was the centre of the universe was crucial to a statically hierarchical world outlook.

The idea that facts and even ideas can be value free ignores the linkage between the two. Not only is this empiricist view (as it is usually called) logically unsustainable, but it is another reason why students may find theory boring. The more you relate political ideas to political realities (in the sense of everyday controversies), the more lively and interesting they become. David Hume (1711–76) argued famously that it would be quite rational to prefer the destruction of the whole world to the scratching of my finger (1972: 157), but we would contest this scepticism. Reason implies the development of humans, and this is why political theory matters. Of course, what constitutes the well-being of people is complex and controversial, but a well-argued case for why the world should be preserved and its inhabitants flourish is crucial for raising the level of everyday politics.

The Problem with the Contestability Thesis

As we see it, all theories and concepts are contestable, by which we merely mean that they are part of an ongoing controversy (Hoffman 1988). Thus, democracy is contestable because some identify democracy with liberal parliamentary systems that already exist such as the British or French or Indian systems, while others argue that democracy implies a high level of participation so that a society is not democratic if large numbers are not involved in the process of government.

But there is a more specialist use of the notion of 'contestability' associated in particular with a famous essay by Gallie (1955: 188–93). Gallie argued, first, that only some political concepts are contestable (democracy was his favoured example), and that when concepts are essentially contestable we have no way of resolving the respective methods of competing arguments. We can note the rival justifications offered (they are mere emotional outpourings), but we cannot evaluate them in terms of a principle that commands general agreement.

But this implies that evaluation is only possible on matters about which we all agree. Such an argument stems from a misunderstanding of the nature of politics. For politics arises from the fact that we all have different interests and ideas, and the more explicit the difference between us is, the more explicit the politics. It therefore follows that a political concept is always controversial and it cannot command general agreement. Where an issue ceases to be controversial, it is not political. In this case differences are so slight that conflict is not really generated. Let us assume that chattel slavery – the owning of people as property – is a state of affairs which is so widely deplored that no one will defend it. Slavery as such ceases to be a political issue, and what becomes controversial is whether patriarchal attitudes towards women involve a condoning of slavery, or the power of employers to hire and fire labour gives them powers akin to a slave-owner. We think that it is too optimistic to assume that outright slavery is a thing of the past, but it is used here merely as an example to make a point.

All political concepts are inherently contestable, since disagreement over the meaning of a concept is what makes it political. But does it follow that because there is disagreement we have no way of knowing what is true and what is false? It is crucial not to imagine that the truth has to be timeless and above historical circumstance. But this rejection of ahistorical, timeless truth does not mean that the truth is purely relative. A relativist, for example, might argue that one person's terrorist is another person's freedom fighter. But this would make an 'objective' definition of terrorism (to pursue our example) impossible.

To argue that something is true is not to banish all doubt. If something is true, this does not mean that it is not also false. It simply means that *on balance* one proposition is more true or less false than another. To argue otherwise is to assume that a phenomenon has to be one thing or another. Philosophers call this a 'dualistic' approach. By dualism is meant an unbridgeable chasm, so that in our example, a dualist would assume that unless a statement is timelessly true, it is absolutely false. In fact, to say that the statement 'George W. Bush is a good president' is *both* true and false. Even his most fervent admirers would admit (we hope!) that he is deficient in some regards, and even his fiercest critics ought to concede that he has some positive qualities.

Take the question of freedom, as another example. What is freedom for Plato (427–347BC) differs from what freedom is for Rousseau (1712–78), and freedom for Rousseau differs from what we in the twenty-first century normally mean by freedom. So there is an element of relativity: historical circumstances certainly affect the character of the argument. But we can only compare and contrast different concepts of freedom if we have an absolute idea as to what freedom is. The absolute notion of freedom refers to some kind of absence of constraint, but this absolute idea can only be expressed in one historical context rather than another, and it is this context that gives an absolute idea its relativity. As a consequence, there is *both* continuity (the absolute) *and* change (the relative).

There is a distinction between the absolute and the relative, but not a dualism, for we cannot have one without the other. The same is true of the distinction between the general and the particular, and the subjective and the objective. In our arguments in this book we strive to make our ideas as true as possible – i.e. we seek to make them objective, accurate reflections of the external world – but because they are moulded by *us,* and we live in a particular historical context, an element of subjectivity necessarily comes in.

What we think of freedom today will necessarily be refined by the events of tomorrow. We are only now becoming aware of how, for example, sexual orientation affects the question of freedom, and there is understandable concern about increasing freedom for people with disabilities. Health, physical and mental, also affects freedom, and all we can say is that our conception of freedom will inevitably alter in the future. But the change that will take place is not without its continuity with past concepts. Freedom is still an absolute concept, although it can only be identified in relative form.

The contestability thesis must, in our view, be able to address not merely the controversial character of political concepts, but how and why we can prefer some definitions in relation to others. Otherwise the thesis becomes bogged down in a relativism that merely notes disagreements, but has no way to defend preferences. A belief that the recent elections in Iraq will advance democracy is not an arbitrary assertion: it is the argument which can be defended (or challenged) with evidence and information to establish how much truth it contains.

Structure of the Book

In our view, a work on political theory should address itself to the kind of issues that politicians and the media themselves raise, and which are part and parcel of public debate. In the first part of this work we seek to investigate the classical concepts. These are the ones that readers are likely to be more familiar with, if they have already read some political thought, and they represent the 'staple diet' of courses on political theory. This is our justification for dealing with these concepts first. We aim to explain even the older ideas as clearly as possible so that those who have had no contact with political theory at all will not feel disadvantaged.

Of course, the fact that these concepts are traditional does not mean that our treatment of them will be traditional. We seek to make them as interesting and contentious as possible, so that readers will be stimulated to think about the ideas in a new and more refreshing way. We aim to combine both exposition and argument to enable readers to get a reasonable idea of the terrain covered by the concept, and to develop a position on the concept, often in opposition to the one we adopt. The fact that this work is written by two people means that differences will manifest themselves in the way that ideas and ideologies are analysed.

The ideas that we deal with are interlinked so that, for example, the argument about the state (and its problematic character) has a direct bearing on democracy. It is impossible to discuss the issue of citizenship without, for instance, understanding the argument about justice. Of course, it is always possible to choose to present ideas differently. In some texts, for example, 'sovereignty' is dealt with as a separate topic. In making sense of ideas and ideologies, it is crucial to say something about the key thinkers and the key texts. Our biography boxes seek to show the background and wider interests of key thinkers, and the exercises will try to emphasise why the ideas in the chapter are so relevant to understanding significant events. We have tried to make political theory challenging and enjoyable, and to deal with more detailed issues in special sections entitled 'Ideas and Perspectives'. The use of arrows is intended to cross-reference both thinkers and ideas so as to emphasise linkages between them.

The second part will tackle ideologies and we will say more about the nature of ideology and its relation to political theory at the beginning of Part 2. Here we would only say that we follow the logic of Part 1 by dealing with the classical and more traditional ideologies such as nationalism, conservatism, fascism and liberalism first, before turning to more recent developments with ideologies such as feminism and multiculturalism. We have thought it appropriate to say something general about these new ideologies in terms of a discussion about new social movements. These contemporary ideologies naturally draw upon the more traditional ones, so that feminism, for example, builds upon liberalism and socialism, and fundamentalism has a particular relationship to conservatism.

In Part 4 we look at some of the contemporary concepts – such as difference, human rights and terrorism – where the problems that these concepts address have either developed recently or have been given a new urgency by contemporary events. Sometimes it is difficult to decide what the distinction is between an idea and a movement. Is terrorism a movement, an ideology or a concept? We have treated it as a concept, but clearly it could be regarded as an ideology. We feel on balance that it raises sufficient thorny conceptual problems to be treated as an idea, but we are conscious that a respectable case could be made for dealing with it as an ideology.

Thus the outline of the book is as shown in the box.

Part 1 – classical ideas (state, freedom, equality, justice, democracy, citizenship)

Part 2 – classical ideologies (liberalism, conservatism, socialism, anarchism, nationalism, fascism)

Part 3 – contemporary ideologies (feminism, multiculturalism, ecologism, fundamentalism)

Part 4 – contemporary ideas (difference, human rights, civil disobedience, terrorism, victimhood)

It might be thought that the newer ideas and ideologies relate more specifically to political controversies, and of course it is true that recent debates have raised these questions acutely. But the classical ideologies and ideas have not lost their relevance. Think of the debate about smoking, for example. Arguments about whether to ban smoking in public places revolve around contradictory interpretations of freedom, and it is hard to make sense of US elections without a knowledge of liberalism and conservatism, and the different ways these ideologies are defined.

All the ideas and ideologies, whether contemporary or classical, are treated in ways that relate them to ongoing controversies, and show why an understanding of theory is crucial to an understanding of political issues.

Questions

1. Is it possible to devise political concepts that have no normative implications, and are thus value free in character?
2. Can one make a statement about politics without theorising at the same time?
3. Should political theory embrace or seek to avoid controversy?
4. Do teachers of political theory make practical political judgements?
5. Is the use of logic and the resort to factual evidence ethically neutral?

References

Gallie, W. (1955) 'Essentially Contested Concepts' *Proceedings of the Aristotelian Society,* 56, 167–98.
Hoffman, J. (1988) *State, Power and Democracy* Brighton: Wheatsheaf.
Hume, D. (1972) *A Treatise of Human Nature* Books 2 & 3 London: Fontana/Collins.

Part 1   Classical Ideas

What is Power?

As indicated in the *Introduction* the structure of the book is as shown in the box.

Part 1	classical ideas (Ch. 1 state, Ch. 2 freedom, Ch. 3 equality, Ch. 4 justice, Ch. 5 democracy, Ch. 6 citizenship)
Part 2	classical ideologies (Ch. 7 liberalism, Ch. 8 conservatism, Ch. 9 socialism, Ch. 10 anarchism, Ch. 11 nationalism, Ch. 12 fascism)
Part 3	contemporary ideologies (Ch. 13 feminism, Ch. 14 multiculturalism, Ch. 15 ecologism, Ch. 16 fundamentalism)
Part 4	contemporary ideas (Ch. 17 difference, Ch. 18 human rights, Ch. 19 civil disobedience, Ch. 20 terrorism, Ch. 21 victimhood)

In introducing the concepts of the state, freedom, equality, justice, democracy and citizenship here, we need to find an idea that underpins them all, and indeed, politics in general. In our view, this is power.

We are always talking about power. Do ordinary people have any? Do prime ministers and presidents have too much? Do people decline to vote because they feel they have no power? The question of power inevitably merges into the question of authority. Is might right? Are those who have power entitled to exercise it? When we raise questions such as these we are in fact asking whether power is the same as, or different from, authority. No one can really dispute the fact that after Operation Iraqi Freedom in Iraq, the United States has power, or considerable power, in Iraq, but does that mean that it is entitled to exercise this power? The critics of US policy would argue that it lacks authority. Does this mean that it will be frustrated in its exercise of power?

It is not difficult to see that when we talk about power and its relation to authority we are also implicitly raising issues that have a direct bearing on the classical concepts of Part 1.

The Link with Other Concepts

The definition of the state which we will adopt is that of the famous German sociologist Max Weber (1864–1920), who defined the state as an institution claiming a monopoly of legitimate force. How does the notion of 'legitimate force' connect to the notion of power? Is the use of force the same as power? We will try to argue that while the two ideas sound similar, in fact power requires compliance, whereas force does not. Of course, it is easy to think of examples where the two come very close to one another. In the proverbial case of the person with a gun who demands your money or life, you have a 'choice' in a technical sense, but the 'power' exercised involves a threat of credible force, so that in reality your choice is illusory. In this case we would prefer to speak of coercion rather than power.

One of the most frequently debated topics is the question of whether **force** can be legitimate, and by legitimacy we mean force that has been authorised and limited. Clearly a soldier or a member of the police can use force, and usually this force has been authorised by parliament and, therefore, ultimately by those who can vote and hold parliament accountable. Does this make the force legitimate and, thus, an act blessed by authority? And if the act of state force is authoritative, in whose eyes does it have authority? Those who are subject to this force (let us say protesters in a demonstration that is deemed to get out of hand), or those who are not part of the demonstration and approve of the action of the police? These are difficult questions, and we introduce them here in order to show why in a discussion of the state it is important to involve questions of power and its relation to authority.

Consider the question of freedom or liberty. We usually think of a person being free if she can exercise power, thus changing herself and her surroundings. But if freedom is defined 'negatively', it may simply mean that you are free when no one deliberately interferes with you. Being free in this case is merely being left alone, not actually exercising power. On the other hand, if freedom is defined 'positively', it relates to a person's capacity to do something, so that, for example, freedom of speech is concerned with the power of a person to speak his mind, not the restrictions that may be placed on someone's right to do so. When does a person's freedom become an act of power that should be accepted or tolerated, and when should it be curbed? Clearly, a person who had no power at all could not (say) smoke, but should smoking be banned from public places on the grounds that it is a form of power that is harmful? It is impossible to discuss these issues and the famous argument raised by the British liberal thinker, John Stuart Mill (1806–73), without having some kind of idea about power and authority and that is what Chapter 2 of this book sets out to do.

Equality and justice rest upon ideas of 'rightness'. Some people see a conflict between equality and freedom on the grounds that redistributing wealth through high taxation prevents individuals from being rewarded according to their merits. The state has too much power and the **individual** too little. This, it is argued, undermines the authority of the state: people pay their taxes because they have to, not because they want to. Egalitarians, on the other hand, link equality with justice, and argue that everyone should be treated equally. We should aim to spread power so that one person or group cannot tell another individual or group what to do, and governments should implement policies that move in this direction. People have the same rights, and therefore exercise similar power. Bill Gates, the billionaire owner of Microsoft, has rather more power than Josephine Bloggs who cleans his office or Willhelm Peter who removes some of the 4 million emails that Bill Gates receives every day. Is this just? Equality and justice rely, as we have already commented, upon the question of rightness, and can it be right that some individuals have so much more power than others?

Indeed, one definition of democracy is the 'power of the people'. Historically, the objection to democracy was precisely that the wrong kind of person would exercise power, and nineteenth-century liberals such as Lord Macaulay feared that democracy would enable the poor to plunder the rich. On the other hand, left-wing critics of liberal democracy complain that the right to vote does not in itself give a person power to influence the course of events and that material resources must be available to people if they are to exercise power. The authority of liberal democracy rests upon equal rights rather than equal power so that the notion of power is indissolubly tied to debates about democracy.

The same is true with the concept of citizenship. Being a **citizen** gives you power. But does it give you enough? Is the housewife a citizen? She may have the right to vote and stand for parliament, but at the same time she may feel compelled to do what her husband tells her, and have limited power over her own life. Nancy Hartsock, a US academic, wrote a book entitled *Money, Sex and Power* (1985). Yet one of the most central questions in the debate about citizenship is whether the unequal distribution of resources distort the power that people exercise. Are we already citizens or can we only become citizens if resources are more evenly spread both within and between societies? It is not difficult to see why the question of **power**, how we define it, identify it and analyse it is central to this (as to other) classical political ideas.

Power and Authority: an Indissoluble Link?

Power, as defined here, is a social concept. By this we mean that power is concerned with human relations and not with the mere movement of inanimate objects.

Power and authority are often contrasted. The police have power (power comes from the barrel of a gun, the former Chinese leader Mao Zedong is supposed to have said) whereas the late Queen Mother in Britain had authority (she inspired love and warmth – at least among some). A simple definition to start with would be to argue that power involves dominating someone or some group, telling them what to do, whereas authority is concerned with the rightness of an action. A person has to be pressured into complying with power, whereas they will obey authority in a voluntary way.

Alas, things are not so simple, because power and authority always seem to go together. This problem particularly bothers Jean-Jacques Rousseau, the great French eighteenth-century thinker (1712–78). On the one hand, might can never be transformed into right, since 'force is a physical power; I do not see how its effects could produce morality' (1968: 52). On the other hand, Rousseau famously insists that people must obey the **law**. The social contract would be worthless unless it could ensure that those who refuse to abide by the general will must be constrained to do so. Dissenters must, in that most celebrated of phrases, be 'forced to be free' (1968: 64).

Power and authority contradict each other, and yet there is an indissoluble link between them.

Our problem can be presented as shown in the diagram.

Power implies	Authority implies
constraint	consent
force	morality
subordination	will
dependence	autonomy

This is the problem of the 'two levels'. Power and authority appear to exclude one another, but they are never found apart.

Does a Broad View of Politics Help?

It might be argued that the problem of power and its relationship to authority is not a serious one. All we need to do is point to a state that rests purely on power, and one that rests solely upon authority, and the problem is solved!

But April Carter in her *Authority and Democracy* concedes that in the political sphere, 'authority rarely exists in its pure form', and she says that even a constitutional government acting with great liberalism would still lack 'pure authority' since, as she puts it, such a government 'relies ultimately upon coercion' (1979: 41; 33). Political authority (defined in statist terms) is paradoxical – a contradiction in terms – since no state, however benevolent, can wholly abstain from the use of force. Pure authority turns out to be a pure abstraction, at least as far as politics is concerned, and Carter demonstrates that rigorous definition and common sense cannot avoid the problem of paradox. Power and authority may be mutually exclusive, but it seems impossible to effect a clean divorce.

This is why Barbara Goodwin in her *Using Political Ideas* (1997) argues that the attempt to distinguish rigorously between power and authority is 'doomed to failure. In any normal political situation, and in every state institution, they co-exist and support each other' (1997: 314). It might be objected that politics is far broader than the state, and involves social relations between individuals. Surely here, at least, we can find a sharp separation between power and authority.

Taylor, who is interested in anthropological material on stateless societies, argues that a society without any form of coercion is 'conceivable' (1982: 25), and the New Left theorist, C.B. Macpherson (1911–87), takes the view that in a simple market model in which every household has *enough* either to produce goods and services for itself or to exchange with others, then we have an example of cooperation without coercion – or in our terminology, authority without power.

But it could be objected that the market mechanism constrains and Marx argues under capitalism, 'the dull compulsion of economic relations' subordinates the labourer to the capitalist (1970: 737). Even the independent producers of commodities suffer what Marx calls 'the coercion exerted by the presence of their mutual interests' (1970: 356).

But what about social examples that not only avoid the state, but do not involve the market either? What of the relationship between parent and child, teacher and student, doctor and patient? Are these not spheres in which we *can* (although do not always) witness the kind of respect that is essential for authority but which excludes power? However, J.S. Mill raises a problem that calls this analysis into question. In *On Liberty* Mill champions the right of the individual to think and act freely. In his argument he contrasts the physical force of the state to what he calls 'the moral coercion of public opinion' (1974: 68). Morality itself is seen as constraining, and we would contend that the very notion of a **relationship** subverts the idea that power and authority can be spliced apart. If all relationships are governed by norms (i.e. morality) of some kind, how then can any relationships be free from pressures of a constraining kind?

Negative and Positive Power

We have assumed that power and authority are contrasting concepts. But a distinction is often made between power as a negative and power as a positive concept. This, as we will see, has important implications for the concept of authority.

Power is negative in the sense that it relates to my ability to get you to do things that you would not otherwise do. The negative view of power is associated with the liberal tradition, and centres around the capacity of the individual to act freely and take responsibility for their actions. It is a notion deeply rooted in our culture and, in our view, forms a necessary part of any analysis of power. People who exercise power can and should be punished (or helped) when they exercise this power in ways that harm others or, indeed, irreversibly harm themselves. By this latter point, we mean a situation in which people cannot change their minds because, as with serious self-abuse, or taking addictive drugs, it is too late! This notion emphasises the differences between people and their conflict of interests. Each individual is separate, and we are all capable of exercising negative power.

In contrast, power is deemed *positive* when it is expressed as empowerment. Empowerment occurs when one person helps ('empowers') themselves or another, or when a group or community enables people to develop. Contrary to what people may think, the notion of power as negative is a modern one; while the ancients took the view that power was always expressed positively within communities. The idea of power being exercised to strengthen our relations with others is a very old one.

Positive power is seen as the ability to do things by the discovery of our own strength – a capacity – a power *to* – as opposed to negative power that is seen as a power *over* – a domination. The conventional view sees power in negative terms, linked to the state, and force or the threat of force. Elshtain distinguishes between *potestas* – which relates to control, supremacy, domination, and *potential* – which relates to ability, efficacy and potency, especially that which is 'unofficial and sinister' (Elshtain, 1992: 117).

However we distinguish them, it is impossible to separate negative and positive power in an empirical sense. It is clear from Lukes's (2005) commentary that positive power broadly corresponds to what has sometimes been called authority, and negative power expresses the conventional view of power. Defining power in a way that separates out logically the negative from the positive does not resolve the power/authority problem and, like power and authority, negative and positive power always go together. It is impossible to think of a relationship in which one exists without the other.

Negative and Positive Power as a Relationship

The reason why negative and positive power cannot be divorced is that all relationships contain both. It is true that earlier notions of power were predominantly positive in character, but the problem, historically, is that this power has in practice been repressively hierarchical: the power of fathers, of lords, of priests, of kings. Positive power has been exercised in the past by people who claim (somewhat implausibly) to be acting on behalf of everyone else – men acting on behalf of women and children, lords for their serfs, priests for parishioners, sovereigns for subjects.

As liberals rightly object, 'negative power' is smuggled in through the back door. The holders of positive power see themselves as chastising others for their own good. The master may imagine that he is acting in the slave's interests – but when the slave is thought of as an individual, then things seem rather different! Power must be both positive and negative. It is important that we do not reject the individual focus of negative power, but seek to build upon it. We must come up with the proposition that if I am to exercise power as an individual, then I must allow you to exercise power as an individual. In other words, to sustain negative power, it must be exercised in terms of a *relationship* – or positively – so that I exercise power in a way that enables you to exercise power.

Power implies mutuality – but it can only be mutual if it is both positive and negative. If it is positive 'on its own', as it were, it stresses unity at the expense of separation, the community at the expense of the individual, so that (as liberals suspect), it becomes oppressive and hypocritical. Positive power exercised 'on its own' is as one-sided as negative power when the latter is conceived in an abstract manner, because when negative power is exercised on its own separation is expressed at the expense of unity. One individual exercises power in a way that prevents another from doing the same.

If the notion of 'negative' power is crucial for a person's freedom and individuality, it is not enough. 'On its own', it presents power in what is sometimes called a 'zero sum game', i.e. I have power because you do not. I exercise power *over* you – if I win, you lose. I am separate from you, and therefore my power differentiates me from you. Normally when people think of power they think of power in negative terms.

Why is this notion a problem? It assumes – as its classical liberal roots reveal – that individuals can exist in complete isolation from other individuals, whereas in fact, as any parent can tell you, we only acquire our sense of individuality (and thus separateness) in conjunction with others. Logically, if each person is to exercise power, then this negative power must take account of the right of each individual to be the same as everyone else. In other words, power can only be consistently 'negative' if it also has a social, positive and what we want to call a 'relational' attribute.

Three-dimensional Power and the Problem of Power and Authority

Lukes argues that power can be divided into three dimensions. The one-dimensional view identifies power as decision making, the two-dimensional view argues that power can be exercised beyond the decision-making forum as in a situation where certain issues are excluded from an agenda and people feel that their interests are not being met. Three-dimensional power arises when people express preferences that are at variance with their interests: they support a system through a consciousness that is 'false'.

Lukes's argument is that the first dimension is highly superficial. He is sharply critical of Dahl's defence of power as decision making in *Who Governs* (1961) on the grounds that those taking decisions may not exercise decisive power at all. The second dimension is an improvement but still confines itself to observable activity: we have to be able to show that groups outside the decision-making forum are consciously exercising power, while three-dimensional power is deemed the most subtle of all. People do not protest precisely because they are victims of a power system that creates a phoney consensus, and those exercising power (such as the media or educational system) may do so unintentionally. An example of three-dimensional power could be taken to be the Great Leap Forward in China that was supported by many who believed that through their heroic will-power the arrival of a communist society would be hastened. They certainly did not want the famine that followed.

But how can Lukes prove the existence of a 'latent' conflict, a potential event and a non-existing decision? How can he demonstrate an exercise of power when nothing takes place? The gulf between interests and preferences can, it seems, be demonstrated if it can be shown that with more information people's preferences would have changed, and that interests only come into line with preferences when no further unit of information would cause any further change. Lukes has indicated that at least under some circumstances (for example where partial information leads to people in the town of Gary, Indiana not campaigning for an air pollution ordinance), power can be exercised which *appears* authoritative. Power and authority seem to go together but in fact the authority is an illusion. Power is being exercised all along.

But has this really resolved the power/authority problem? It certainly points to the way in which unintended circumstances pressure people to do things they otherwise would not have done. But the fact is that the separation remains because when power is expressed in a situation without observable conflict the authority is simply a propagandist illusion – an idealised mystification of the reality of power. Indeed, Lukes seems to be saying that where people are fully informed, there is authority; where information is blocked even unintentionally, there is power. The problem is still not resolved.

Accounting for the 'Indissoluble Link'

Long after liberals rejected the notion of a state of nature in which individuals live in splendid isolation from one another, they continue to write as though individuals can be conceived in the absence of relationships through which they in fact discover their identity.

Constraint is unavoidable since no agent can exist except through a structure: these structures are both natural and social. You have to obey the laws of gravity and you have relationships with your family and friends whether you like it or not. Constraint should not be confused with force, although classical liberals and anarchists use the terms as though they were synonyms. Although we know of many societies that were or (in the case of international society) are, stateless in character, we know of no society in which there is an absence of constraint. Consensus arises when people can 'change places' and show empathy with one another's point of view, and this necessarily involves constraining pressures. Force, on the other hand, disrupts consensus and relationships, since when force is used the other party ceases to be a person, and becomes a 'thing'.

To see how this translates into the argument about power and authority, the chart as shown can be drawn up.

Power	Authority
Necessity	Freedom
Circumstances	Rational consciousness
Negative power	Positive power
Pressure	Will
Constraint	Autonomy

All relationships involve constraints (power) and entitlements (authority). Remove one side of the power /authority equation, and the other crumbles. Take two diametrically opposed examples by way of illustration. In a master/slave relationship, power is obvious and manifest. Not only are there constraints, but there is also a threat of credible force. But at the same time unless slaves (however reluctantly or under whatever duress) 'acknowledge' or 'accept' their slavery, then the relationship between them and their masters is impossible, and they will die or escape. Relationships are mutual: being a slave obviously limits your freedom, but so too does *having* one, even if, in one case, the constraint causes pain and in the other, pleasure. To put the point *in extremis:* slave owners who simply kill their slaves or fail to keep them in service destroy the basis of their own power. Even the slave, in other words, makes some input in this most repressive of relationships, and it is this input that gives the relationship its (minimally) authoritative character. In this case, we would want to say that slave owners exercise 'much' power and 'little' authority.

Let us turn to a relationship at the other end of the political spectrum, that between doctor and patient (or if you prefer, between teacher/pupil; priest/ parishioner, etc.). In this case, it seems that only authority exists, and there is no power. People normally go to the doctor because they want to, and if they accept the advice offered it is because there is a communication of a persuasive or potentially persuasive kind. Authority predominates, but power also exists. Doctors communicate with their patients by pointing to constraints. If the advice they offer is not taken, highly unpleasant circumstances will follow! In these circumstances a person may have as much or as little freedom to choose as in a situation where they are threatened with force, since what choice does a chronically ill person have when told of the need for a dangerous operation, if the alternative is a swift and certain death? In this case, we have a relationship in which there is 'much' authority, but there is by no means a complete absence of power.

What has to be excluded from power and authority is the use of force itself, since this makes compliance impossible and is therefore a violation not merely of authority, but of power as well. Obviously the more authority predominates, the better, but even a purely consensual relationship involves some element of constraint.

Let us conclude by giving an example of a member of the police seeking to persuade football supporters who have been unable to obtain tickets to go home. Initially, mild pressures would be invoked: 'it would be a good idea not to hang around but to go home'. If this does not work something stronger might be tried, such as: 'I would like you to go home – it would be silly not to'. If this does not work, a command follows: 'I am ordering you to go home'. Then – a threat: 'if you don't go home, I will arrest you' and black marias around the corner are indicated. If the police authority has to actually seize the protester, then force is used and both power and authority have failed. But the point is that even in the most authoritative statement, power is also implied, and in the sternest expression of power, authority is also present. The two always go together, and unless they are linked, no relationship is possible.

There is therefore a difference between what are conventionally called democratic and authoritarian states. The latter rely far more upon power and the former have much more authority. But the two concepts always go together, even though they are different, and it is a sobering thought that for those subject to force neither power nor authority can be said to exist.

Power is not merely a crucial but the central concept of politics. It underpins, as we have tried to show, the other ideas that are elaborated in Part 1 and hence it deserves a separate (and fairly extended) treatment of its own by way of prefacing this section of the book.

References

Bock and James (eds) (1992) *Beyond Equality and Difference* London and New York: Routledge.
Carter, A. (1979) *Authority and Democracy* London: Routledge and Kegan Paul.
Dahl, R. (1961) *Who Governs?* New Haven: Yale University.

Elshtain, J. (1992) 'The Power and Powerlessness of Women' in G. Bock and S. James (eds) *Beyond Equality and Difference* London and New York: Routledge.

Goodwin, B. (1997) *Using Political Ideas* 4th edn Chichester and New York, *et al.*: John Wiley and Sons.

Hartsock, N. (1985) *Money, Sex and Power* Boston, Mass.: Northeastern University Press.

Lukes, S. (2005) *Power: A Radical View* 2nd edn Basingstoke: Palgrave.

Marx, K. (1970) *Capital* Vol. 1 London: Lawrence & Wishart.

Mill, J.S. (1974) *On Liberty* Harmondsworth: Penguin.

Rousseau, J.J. (1968) *The Social Contract* Harmondsworth: Penguin.

Taylor, M. (1982) *Community, Anarchy and Liberty* Cambridge: Cambridge University Press.

Chapter 1

The State

Introduction

If you asked the average person to identify the state, they might look at you in astonishment, and say that they were not aware of living under a state, unless by that you meant the 'government'. Indeed, some writers have spoken of Britain and the United States as state less societies, although this is to confuse what people think about the state, and what the state really is. In tackling this question, we shall also try to deal with the problem: does the state really exist?

Chapter Map

- The history of the concept of the state so as to decide whether the state is purely modern;

- Various definitions of the state, and our own definition;

- The link between the state and conventional notions of sovereignty; and

- The argument that holds that it is possible to look beyond the state provided certain conceptual distinctions are put in place.

Changing States: Hitler's Rise to Power

Adolf Hitler salutes a huge crowd of Hitler Youth, Nuremberg, Germany ca.1930s.

With the end of World War I the Weimar Republic was established and soon things began to deteriorate. War reparations, totalling £6.6 billion, had completely crippled the economy. France and Belgium occupied the Ruhr in response to alleged defaults in Germany's repayments. A general strike was called across the entire country.

It was in this climate that a group of right-wing ex-army officers attempted to seize power in Munich. One of the ringleaders, Adolf Hitler, was imprisoned, and on his release the Nazis began a programme of violence towards the left, calculated to drive the bourgeoisie towards Nazism. In the 1928 elections the party won 800,000 votes.

Wealthy Germans, fearing for their lives and property, began to donate generously to the Nazis. The Wall Street Crash of 1929 had a further disastrous effect on the economy and within a year the price of a loaf of bread jumped from 163 marks to 200,000,000,000 marks.

As a result of such upheaval, extreme political polarisation between the right and left occurred. The presidential elections of 1932 saw the Nazi Party gain 13.5 million votes. A decision was taken to appoint Hitler as the Chancellor of Germany. The Cabinet believed that the Nazis would soon be revealed as unequal to the task of government and hoped that Hitler would be easily controlled by the non-Nazis in the Cabinet.

This decision proved to be a fatal error. In just over a year Hitler became the undisputed dictator of Germany, ruling over a fascist state astonishing in its ruthless totalitarianism and violent anti-Semitism.

Germany in the inter-war years is a real laboratory for identifying and conceptualising politics and the state, as it changed from a liberal to a fascist state with amazing speed.

- How inevitable was World War II, and how could the state have worked to prevent it?
- What are your thoughts on the question of whether or not Nazism is distinctively German. Compare those characteristics associated with a fascist regime to issues such as high unemployment, inflation and humiliation after war that could occur in any society.

How Modern is the Concept of the State?

The question of what the **state** is is linked to the question of when the state emerges historically. T.H. Green (a nineteenth-century British political philosopher) believed that state have always existed, since families and tribes require an ideal of what is right, and right is the basis of the state (1941). Hegel (who was a nineteenth-century German philosopher) took the view that tribal societies had neither state nor history. Lacking reason, they cannot be understood (1956: 61).

More common, however, is the argument that the state is a modern institution since its 'forms' are as important as its 'content'. The state, in one account, is defined in terms of five attributes (Dunleavy and O'Leary, 1987: 2).

1. **A public institution separated from the private activities of society**. In ancient Greek **society**, the polis (wrongly called, Dunleavy and O'Leary argue, the city state) did not separate the **individual** from the state, and in a feudal society kings and their vassals were bound by oaths of loyalty that were both public and private. Certain sections of society, such as the clergy, had special immunities and privileges, so that there was no sharp separation between members of society, on the one hand, and the polity on the other.

2. **The existence of sovereignty in unitary form**. In a feudal society, for example, the clergy, the nobility, the particular 'estates' and 'guilds' (merchants, craftsmen, artisans, etc.) had their particular courts and rules, so that the only loyalty which went beyond local attachments was to the Universal Church, and in Europe this was divided between pope and emperor. **Laws** confirmed customs and social values – they were not made by a particular body that had a united '**will**'.

3. **The application of laws to all who live in a particular society**. In the ancient Greek polis, protection was only extended to citizens, not slaves, and even a stranger required patronage from a **citizen** to claim this protection. Under feudalism, protection required loyalty to a particular lord. It did not arise from living in a territory, and the ruling political system could not administer all the inhabitants.

4. **The recruitment of personnel according to bureaucratic as opposed to patrimonial criteria**. Whereas the state selects people for an office according to impersonal attributes, earlier polities mixed the office-holder with the job, so that offices belonged to particular individuals and could be handed to relatives or friends at the discretion of the office holder. Imagine the vice-chancellor of a university deciding to name his or her own successor!

5. **The capacity to extract revenue (tax) from a subject population**. In pre-modern polities, problems of transport and communication meant that this was limited, and rural communities in particular were left to their own devices.

The argument is that only the state is sovereign, separate from society, can protect all who dwell within its clearly demarcated boundaries, recruits personnel according to bureaucratic criteria and can tax effectively. These are seen not merely as the features of a modern state but of the state itself. We will later challenge this argument but it is very widely held.

Defining the State

The Force Argument

Biography, p. 18

Definitions of the state vary depending upon whether the question of **force** or **morality** is stressed, or a combination of both. The definition that commands a good deal of support is that of the German sociologist, Max Weber – that the state is an institution that claims a **monopoly** of legitimate violence for a particular territory.

Robert Dahl, a US political scientist who taught at Yale, defines **Government** (with a capital 'G' – a term he uses synonymously with the state) in terms explicitly taken from Weber. David Easton, on the other hand, criticises an anthropologist for focusing on organised force as the distinguishing quality of political systems, and identifies this emphasis upon force with the position laid down by Thomas Hobbes and reinforced by Weber (Hoffman, 1995: 34). Marx highly appraised Hobbes as a theorist who saw 'might' rather than will as the basis of right or the state (Marx and Engels, 1976: 329), and force has been seen as the most important of the factors that accounts for the state. It is true that it is not the only one, and supporters of the force definition of the state acknowledge that other factors come into play. Marx called these 'symptoms' (Marx and Engels, 1976: 329), and Weber

How to read:

Hobbes's *Leviathan*

A classic text such as Hobbes's *Leviathan* is relevant for many concepts of political thought. It is crucial to read a text in the light of a particular problem – in this case we are interested in the problem of the state and force.

In the first place, spend some time browsing through the contents. Here Hobbes summarises his argument so that you can find the chapters which bear on the problem at hand. If you were interested in Hobbes's theory of psychology or theory of religion, then you would need to read the early chapters. But since you are interested in Hobbes's case for the state and how he links it to force, the first chapter that needs your attention is Chapter 13. This needs to be read carefully. Here is the argument that people are naturally at war with one another. If you were concerned about the problem of contract, right and representation, you would need to read Chapters 14, 15 and 16 carefully, but since you are not, a cursory reading will be enough to give the main arguments.

The case for a state is set out in Chapter 17 and this needs a careful read. Chapters 18–20 are important in terms of Hobbes's distinction between different kinds of states, but again they can be read in a more cursory way. Chapter 21 deals among other things with the right of subjects to refuse to obey the sovereign **power** and it raises the need to read particular chapters themselves in the light of the particular problem you are exploring. Hobbes's argument about liberty and fear are important for understanding his views on power but when he raises the question of the freedom to protect oneself whatever the sovereign says, we need to read the argument carefully. Write out the passage or highlight it if the book is your own.

Chapters 22–30 require a cursory read, while Chapter 31 and Part Three are relevant for those who want to focus on Hobbes's position on religion.

Max Weber (1864–1920)

German economist and sociologist. Born in Saxony of a prosperous middle-class family. Weber initially studied the history of commercial law at the University of Heidelberg. Here he took a chair in political economy in 1897 and co-founded the first sociological journal, *Archiv für Sozialwissenschaft und Sozialpolitik (Journal for Social Science and Politics)* (1903). Weber was variously a lawyer, historian, economist, philosopher, political scientist and sociologist!

A personal breakdown in 1898 led to his withdrawal from teaching. He continued writing. He was initially concerned with the impact of capitalism on the agricultural estates east of the Elbe, and this led to a wider study of capitalism and its relation to the Protestant religion, *The Protestant Ethic and the Rise of Capitalism* (1904–5). Here he argued that the impulse to accumulate far beyond the needs of personal consumption was grounded in the 'worldly asceticism' of reformed Christianity, and this ethic led the believer to demonstrate salvation through the accumulation of wealth.

Weber became interested in exploring modern Western rationalism, and he argued that only in modern societies has the conscious linkage of ends to means become central to a goal-maximising calculation. Reason was crucial to the scientific assumption that the world could be subject to human control. Whereas legitimacy (or the entitlement to rule) was based upon hereditary lords or monarchs in traditional societies, in the modern world legitimacy is rooted in a rationalised administration ruled by professionals, who are selected according to merit.

Although he took repressive hierarchy for granted, he was concerned about restricting bureaucracy through energetic political leaders who had been elected. He was a member of the German Social Democratic Party, a member of the German delegation to the Armistice settlement following World War I and one of the authors of the Weimar Constitution that existed until the Nazis came to power.

himself specifically stated that force is not the only attribute of the state. Indeed his definition makes it clear that the force of the state has to be 'legitimate', monopolised and focused on a particular territory. Nevertheless, as Weber himself says, force is a 'means specific to the state' (1991: 78, 134).

The other factors are important but secondary. Force is central to the state, its most essential attribute.

The Centrality of Will

Those who see morality or right as the heart of the state are often called 'idealists' because they consider 'ideas' rather than material entities to be central to reality. Hegel, perhaps the most famous of the idealist thinkers, described the state as the realisation of morality – the 'Divine Idea as it exists on Earth' (1956: 34).

T.H. Green argued that singling out what he called 'supreme coercive power' as the essential attribute of the state undermines the important role that morality plays in securing a community's interests (1941: 121). Green acknowledges the role of Jean-Jacques Rousseau, an eighteenth-century French writer, in arguing that morality, **right** and duty form the basis of the state. Green does not deny that what he calls 'supreme coercive power' is involved in the state, but crucial to the state are the moral ends for which this power is exercised. This led Green's editor to sum up his argument with the dictum that 'will, not force, is the basis of the state' (Hoffman, 1995: 218–19).

More recently, writers such as Hamlin and Petit have argued that the state is best defined in terms of a system of rules which embody a system of rights – this is crucial to what they call a 'normative analysis of the state' (1989: 2).

The State as a Mixture of Will and Force

Others argue that the state does not have a 'basis' or central attribute, but is a 'mixture' of both force and morality. It is wrong to regard one of these as more important than the other.

Antonio Gramsci, an Italian Marxist, traced this view of the state back to Machiavelli's *The Prince*. Machiavelli, writing in the sixteenth century, declared that there are two means of fighting: 'one according to the laws, the other with force; the first way is proper to man, the second to beasts', but because, Machiavelli argued,

Biography — **Georg Wilhelm Friedrich Hegel (1770–1831)**

Born in Stuttgart. He studied philosophy and classics at the University of Tübingen, and became a private tutor in Berne and then in Frankfurt.

His first work (only published posthumously) was *The Spirit of Christianity and Its Fate*, but in 1801 he returned to the study of philosophy at the University of Jena. In 1806 he completed a very serious systematic study of philosophy entitled *Phenomenology of the Mind* – just in time to flee Jena from the approaching French armies. In 1816 he became a professor at the University of Heidelberg, and in 1817 *The Encyclopaedia of the Philosophical Sciences* followed. Two years later he became a professor at the University of Berlin, where he remained until his death in 1831.

In 1821 he published his major political work, *Philosophy of Right*. In this Hegel argued that while society consists of laws which are necessary for the good life, man (and by 'man' Hegel means biological men!) also possesses a free conscience. It is necessary to balance the need for a legal order and a realm of responsible personal freedom. The danger is that one tendency will prevail over another, so that the state will be either a legal tyranny or an anarchy of human wilfulness. Hegel took modern constitutional monarchy as it evolved out of the French Revolution and the French Restoration as the state form most likely to realise freedom.

After his death his lecture notes were compiled into a number of publications: *Philosophy of Religion* (1832), *History of Philosophy* (1833–6), *Philosophy of Fine Art* (1835–8), and *Philosophy of History* (1837).

Biography · Antonio Gramsci (1891–1937)

Born in Sardinia. He had a physical deformity (he was hunchbacked) and his father was imprisoned for corruption. Despite a wretched childhood, he won a scholarship to the University of Turin. Here he specialised in linguistics and fell under the influence of the Hegelian, Benedetto Croce. Gramsci joined the Italian Socialist Party in 1913, supported the Russian Revolution (which he saw as a triumph of the 'will' over circumstances) and in a socialist weekly, the *Ordine Nuovo* (New Order), he championed the factory council movement.

After World War I he opposed what he saw as the passivity of the Socialist Party and became a founding member of the Italian Communist Party. In 1924 he became its general secretary and was elected to parliament. However, this did not protect him from being tried and sent to prison during Mussolini's rule.

Here he wrote his magnum opus the *Prison Notebooks* (1929–35), which dealt with a wide range of topics from the theatre to the state. He considered classical Marxist theory too deterministic and concentrated a good deal on moral and intellectual factors in politics. He regarded Bolshevik strategy as inappropriate for conditions in the West and argued the case for what he called 'a war of position' that would take full account of cultural as well as economic circumstances.

He was released from prison in 1937, as a result of an international campaign but in extremely poor health and died shortly afterwards.

the first is often not sufficient, 'it becomes necessary to have recourse to the second' (1998: 58). The state was seen as analogous to the mythical creature, the centaur, which was half-human and half-beast. Gramsci embraced this argument. The state is linked to force, but equally important is law, morality and right (1971: 170). The state in this argument has a dual character, and although Gramsci subscribed to the Marxist argument that the state would wither away, he argues that what disappears is force, and an 'ethical state' remains (Hoffman, 1996: 72).

It has become very common to contend that theories which argue that the essential property of the state is either morality or force are 'essentialist' or 'reductionist'. By this is meant an approach that highlights one factor as being crucially relevant. Just as it is wrong to ignore the part of the state that imposes force upon those who will not voluntarily comply with the law, so it is wrong to downgrade the 'civilising' aspects of the state – the aspects of the state which regulate people's lives in ways that make them healthier and happier. The notion of a 'welfare state' captures this amalgam, since it is argued that the state is *both* negative and positive – a mixture of force and 'will'. Your local hospital is part of the National Health Service and funded from taxes that people *have* to pay. But the staff there are trained to help you with healthcare. The hospital is part of a state that is both negative and positive in its role.

Force and the Modernity Argument

Those who stress the centrality of force argue that the state is far older than the 'modernists' assume. It is true that earlier states are different from modern ones and lack the features described by Dunleavy and O'Leary. Force is regarded as the defining attribute of the state. Feudal and ancient polities may have been more partisan and less effective than the modern state, but they were state nevertheless. They sought to impose supreme power over their subjects. We come back to Weber's definition of the state as an institution that claims a monopoly of legitimate force for a particular territory. Does this mean that only the modern state is really a state, or do all post-tribal polities act in this way (albeit less efficiently and more chaotically), and therefore deserve to be called states as well?

Proponents of the force argument contend that differences in 'form' should not be allowed to exclude similarities. Once we argue that only modern state can be called state, we ignore the problem of defining totalitarian state (such as Iraq under Saddam Hussein). Are they not state because they are corrupt and violate in all sorts of ways bureaucratic criteria for recruiting functionaries and the **public/private** distinction as elaborated above?

The danger with the 'modernist argument' (as we call it) is twofold. It assumes that state have to be liberal in character, and that modern state live up to the forms which are prescribed for them. But even liberal states that consider themselves democratic do not always practise what they preach, and are plagued with corruption (think of the role played by money in the election process in the United States), so that criteria for appointments are violated and the rule of law is breached. Is the Italian state not a 'real' state for example, because it fails to live up to the 'ideals' of the state? If it is not a state, then what is it? It would be much better to identify states in terms of the supreme force that they exercise (albeit in different ways) over subjects. Weber's definition applies to all (post-tribal) polities for roughly the last 5,000 years.

Exercise

List the features that make the state modern.

Are these features enough to bolster the argument that the modern state is the state, and that earlier polities should not be called states at all?

T. H. Green called the Tsarist state a state by courtesy (1941: 137). Would you call the following states?

- Iraq under Saddam Hussein

- (contemporary) Yugoslavia

- apartheid South Africa

- the United States

- Afghanistan.

Make two columns, one headed 'Difference in Degree', the other 'Difference in Kind'. Now list the features that differentiate modern states from pre-modern states, or the state from earlier (but post-tribal) polities under what you see as the appropriate column.

The Argument against the Concept of the State

Three bodies of argument contend that the state is not a suitable concept for political theory, since it is impossible to define it. The state has been described as one of the most problematic concepts in **politics** (Vincent, 1987: 3) and it has been seen as so problematic as to defy definition at all.

The Behaviouralist Argument

The first group to subscribe to what might be called the 'indefinability thesis' was developed by political scientists who worked in the United States in the 1960s but whose influence was not confined to that country alone. It extended throughout Europe. This group is generally known as the *behaviouralists.*

The founding father of behaviouralism is considered to be Arthur Bentley, who argued that the state was afflicted with what he called in 1908 'soul stuff' – an abstract and mystical belief that the state somehow represents the 'whole' of a community. Much better, Bentley argued, to adopt a process view of politics that contends that the state is no more than one government among many (1967: 263).

The term 'behaviour' coined by the behaviouralists was intended to capture the fact that humans, like animals, *behave*, and hence the approach denied that human society is different in kind from animal society or the activity of other elements in nature. This led to a view that the study of politics was like a **natural** science, and behaviouralists argued that as a science, it must not make value judgements. Just as biologists would not describe a queen bee as 'reactionary' or 'autocratic', so the political scientist must abstain from judgements in analysing the material she studies. Behaviouralists believe that a 'science' of politics should not defend particular values, and instead should draw up testable hypotheses by objectively studying political 'behaviour'.

The Argument of David Easton

A leading figure of the behavioural political scientists was David Easton, who examined the theoretical credentials of the state in his *Political System* (1953, 2nd edn 1971). He argues that the state is a hopelessly ambiguous term. Political scientists cannot agree on what the state is or when it arose. Some define the state in terms of its morality, others see it as an instrument of exploitation. Some regard it as an aspect of society, others as a synonym for government, while still others identify it as a unique and separate association that stands apart from social institutions such as churches and trade unions. Some point to its **sovereignty**, others to its limited power.

What makes the state so contentious, Easton argues, is that the term is imbued with strong mythical qualities, serving as an ideological vehicle for propagating national sovereignty against cosmopolitan and local powers. Given this degree of contention and controversy, there is no point, Easton argues, in adding a 'definition of my own' (1971: 106–15). If political theory is to be scientific, then it must be clear, and clarity requires that we abstain from using the concept of the state altogether.

For around three decades after World War II the state, conceptually at any rate, appeared in the words of one writer to have 'withered away' (Mann, 1980: 296). Yet in 1981 Easton commented that a concept which 'many of us thought had been polished off a quarter of a century ago, has now risen from the grave to haunt us once again' (1981: 303). What had brought the state back into political science? Easton noted the following:

- the revival of interest in **Marxism**, which places the state at the heart of politics;
- a conservative yearning for stability and authority; a rediscovery of the importance of the **market** so that the state is important as an institution to be avoided;
- a study of policy which found the state to be a convenient tool of analysis.

Easton is however still convinced that the state is not a viable concept in political science. He recalls the numerous definitions that he had noted in 1953, and argues that 'irresolvable ambiguities' have continued to proliferate since then. To make his point, he engages in a hard hitting and witty analysis of the work of a Greek Marxist, Nicos Poulantzas (who was much influenced by the French theorist, Louis Althusser). Poulantzas, Easton tell us, concludes after much detailed and almost impenetrable analysis that the state is an 'indecipherable mystery'. The state is 'the eternally elusive Pimpernel of Poulantzas's theory' – an 'undefined and undefinable essence' (1981: 308). All this confirms Easton's view that the concept of the state is obscure, empty and hopelessly ambiguous. It should be abandoned by political science.

David Easton's Concept of the Political System

If the concept of the state should be pushed to one side by political theorists, what do we put in its place? Easton argues that at the heart of our study of politics lies, not the idea of the state, but rather the concept of the political system. This Easton defines as 'the authoritative allocation of values for society as a whole' (1971: 134). Politics, he contends, is far better defined in this way. Such a definition avoids the ambiguity of the state-concept, but at the same time it is not so broad that it considers all social activity to be political. After all, a political system refers to the allocation of values for society *as a whole*. It, therefore, confines the term 'political' to public matters, so that, as far as Easton is concerned, the pursuit of power which may take place in trade unions, churches, families and so on is not part of politics itself.

The notion of a political system makes it possible to differentiate sharply the political from the social. It also resolves historical problems that afflict the concept of the state. Whereas the state only arose in the seventeenth century (in Easton's view), the concept of the political system can embrace politics as a process existing not only in medieval and ancient times, but in tribal societies that had no significant concentrations of power at all. Once we free politics from the state we can also talk about a political system existing at the international level, authoritatively allocating values for the global community.

In his later work, Easton contends that a political system can persist through change so that one could argue that a system continues to allocate values authoritatively while its structures change dramatically. Thus it could be said, for example, that a political system persisted in Germany while the imperial order fell to the Weimar Republic, which yielded to the Nazi regime that was replaced by a very different order after World War II (1965: 83).

Easton's concept of the political system is, he claims, superior to the concept of the state. The latter is ambiguous, limited and ideological. Even though Robert Dahl is critical (as we will see) of Easton's particular definition, he too prefers to speak of a 'political system' that can exist at many levels, and which he defines as any persistent pattern of human relationships involving, to a significant extent, control, influence, power or **authority** (1976: 3).

The Linguistic and Radical Argument

The **linguistic analysts** were a philosophical school fashionable in the 1950s and 1960s in Britain and the United States. Their doyen, T.D. Weldon, wrote an extremely influential book called *The Vocabulary of Politics* in 1953 in which he argued that analysts are only competent to tackle what linguistic analysts called 'second order' problems. This referred to the words politicians use, and not the realities to which these words are supposed to refer. The concept of the state is (Weldon argued) a hopelessly muddled term, frequently invested with dangerously misleading mystical overtones. Practical political activists use it but it is an unphilosophical 'first order' term that has imported into political theory its confusions from the world of practice. Whereas we all know (as citizens) that the United States and Switzerland are state whereas Surrey and the United Nations are not, the term has no interest for political philosophers (1953: 47–9).

We refer to the radical argument as one that is in favour of radical **democracy** and sees the concept of the state as a barrier to this end. Why conceive of politics in statist terms when we want people at all levels of society to participate in running their own affairs? Radicals come in many forms. Some see the term guilty of a kind of monopolisation of politics, so that political activity outside the state is downgraded. Others argue that the term is so complex that it is fruitless to try and define it. Richard Ashley, a postmodernist or post-structuralist in international relations, takes the view that it is impossible to 'decide what the state is' (1988: 249), while Pringle and Watson quote the words of the French postmodernist, Michel Foucault, that 'to place the state above or outside society is to focus on a homogeneity which is not there' (1992: 55). The state, says Foucault, is 'a mythical **abstraction** whose importance is a lot more limited than many of us think' (Hoffman, 1995: 162). Pringle and Watson, for their part, find the state too erratic and disconnected to evoke as an entity (1992: 63), while a feminist, Judith Allen, takes the view that the state is too abstract, unitary and unspecific to be of use in addressing the disaggregated, diverse, specific or local sites which require feminist attention (Allen, 1990: 22).

The radicals agree with the linguistic analysts and the behaviouralists that the concept of the state should be abandoned. Their particular argument is that the notion discourages participation and involvement at local levels and in social institutions, and is therefore an unhelpful term.

Ideas and Perspectives:

Behaviouralism

Not to be confused with behaviourism – a psychological theory – **behaviouralism** developed in the United States after World War II as an intellectual concept that stressed precision, systems theory and pure science. The idea is that all living things behave in regular ways and it is possible to see them as adjusting to their environment as a result of the inputs they receive and the outputs they produce. Generalisations can be made that can be verified through methods that have no ethical implications. Theory must be scientific in the sense that no values are involved, and the social sciences do not involve any special approaches which are not relevant to the natural sciences. Indeed, the notion of behaviour makes it possible to examine all living things since the human will express itself in regularities that can be scientifically investigated. The behavioural 'revolution' (as its supporters called it) reached its height in the 1960s but was accused of taking the politics out of politics by its critics, who felt that the methods of natural science were not appropriate to the social sciences, and that the notion anyway that science could be value free is naive and superficial.

Problems with the Argument against the State

Many of the points that the critics of the concept of the state make are useful. It is certainly odd to identify politics with the state and, therefore, to take the view that families, tribes, voluntary organisations from cricket clubs to churches and universities, and international institutions are not political because the state is either not involved at all, or at least directly at any rate, in running their affairs.

But it does not follow from this that we cannot define the state or that the state is not an important concept and institution for political scientists to study. Indeed we will argue that it is impossible to ignore the state, and that unless one can contend that the state no longer exists it can and must be defined.

The Argument of David Easton

At no point does Easton suggest that the state does not exist, and Dahl, his fellow behaviouralist, speaks explicitly of the state as 'the Government' (1976: 10). In a more recent book, Easton identifies with those who argue that the state has never really been left out (1990: 299n).

Nevertheless, we must consider Easton's argument that the concept of the political system is a much clearer and more flexible idea than the concept of the state, Easton's notion might seem ingenious but in fact it has serious difficulties of its own. Easton's argument is that, when we define a political system as the author-itative allocation of values for society as a whole, we can say that the **conflict** within a tribe which leads to secession of one of its clans is 'exactly similar' to conflicts between states in international institutions (1971: 111). But what is the meaning of 'society as a whole'?

Easton defines society as a 'special kind of human grouping' in which people develop 'a sense of belonging together' (1971: 135). When secession occurs within a tribe or war between states takes place, there would seem to be the absence, not the presence, of that sense of belonging together which Easton defines as a society. To say that tribes and international orders that involved warring states are 'genuine societies' (1971: 141) seems to empty the term society of any content. The same problem afflicts his argument that a political system can persist through change even though (in the case of Germany, for example) the authorities and the regimes not only change drastically, but are divided until 1991 into two warring halves. The political system appears to be a shadowy abstraction that could only perish if all popular participants were physically obliterated. It could be argued that Easton's 'political system' seems no less mysterious than Poulantzas's elusive state.

In later definitions, Easton speaks of the political system not as a 'something' that authoritatively allocates values for society as a whole, but as that which takes decisions 'considered binding by most members of society, most of the time' (1990: 3). But this does not solve his problem. Indeed, in an early review of *The Political System*, Dahl raises the problem of Easton's definition, by asking how many have to obey before an 'allocation' is deemed binding. Criminals, as Dahl points out, do not believe that criminal statutes must be obeyed (Hoffman, 1995: 28). The point is a good one, and it is not answered by saying that most of the members of society, most of the time have to consider allocations binding. What happens if the order is an authoritarian one in which relatively few people support the regime? Moreover, what counts as genuine support as opposed to compliance based upon fear? Think of 'popular support' in Nazi Germany, Stalinist Russia or in Saddam Hussein's Iraq. How useful is it to say that people considered the allocations binding? This is a real problem, and what it shows is that Easton has not done away with the ambiguities and elusiveness that characterise the state.

Indeed it has been argued that Easton can only bring his political system down to earth by making it synonymous with the state, so that we can give some kind of empirical purchase to the notion of society as a whole. And once we return to the state, then the problem of ambiguity and abstractness remain. The substitution of the political system for the state has not solved any of the problems that led Easton to reject the concept of the state in the first place.

The Question of Existence

Moreover, Easton's argument suffers from the same difficulty that confronts all who argue that the state cannot be defined. We have to ask: does the state exist? None of the critics of the concept of the state suggest that the state as a real-life institution has disappeared. Easton tries to adopt a sceptical position to the effect that political life has no 'natural' coherence so that we could, for argument's sake, construct a political system out of the relationship between a duckbilled platypus and the ace of spades. But he does insist that a conceptually 'interesting' idea must have 'empirical status' (1965: 33; 44), and this seems to suggest that there must be something in the world out there which corresponds to the political system. Such an institution is the state.

Neither behaviouralists, nor linguistic theorists or radicals argue that the state does not exist. If states do exist, then the challenge is surely to define them. Weber's notion of the state as an institution that claims a monopoly of legitimate force for a particular territory is a useful definition: as we see it, it is rather silly to talk about the state and then deny that it can be defined.

Force and Statelessness

The value of highlighting force as the central attribute of the state is that it focuses upon a practice that is extraordinary: the use of force to tackle conflicts of interest. It is true that states defined in a Weberian way have been around for some 5,000 years, but humans have been in existence for much longer, and therefore an extremely interesting question arises. How did people secure order and resolve disputes before they had an institution claiming a **monopoly** of legitimate force?

Most anthropologists would dispute Green's argument that states have always existed. They argue that in tribal societies, political leaders rely upon moral pressures – ancestor cults, supernatural sanctions, the threat of exclusion – to maintain social cohesion and discipline. Although many of these sanctions would strike us today as being archaic and unworkable, the point about them is that they demonstrate that people can live without a state.

International relations writers have also become aware of how international society regulates the activities of states themselves, without a super or world state to secure order. Moral and economic pressures have to be used to enforce international law, and as the recent conflict in Iraq has demonstrated, there is nothing to prevent states from interpreting international law in conflicting ways.

The Distinction between Force and Constraint, State and Government

When we define the state in terms of force, we are naturally curious about the political mechanisms in societies without a state. But to understand how order is maintained in societies without institutions claiming a monopoly of legitimate force, we need to make two distinctions that are not usually made in political theory.

The first is the distinction between force, on the one hand, and constraint, on the other, and the second (which we will come to later) is the distinction between state and government. If stateless societies exert discipline without having an apparatus that can impose force, how do we characterise this discipline? In our view, it is necessary to distinguish between force and **constraint**. The two are invariably lumped together, particularly by classical liberal writers who often use the terms force and constraint synonymously. Yet the two are very different.

Force imposes physical **harm**, and it should be remembered that mental illnesses such as depression create physical pain so that causing depression counts as force. **Coercion** we take to be a credible threat of force: a two-year-old with a plastic gun cannot be said to coerce because the force 'threatened' is not credible. Thus, in the standard example of 'your money or your life' demand, what causes you to comply is the knowledge that force will be used against you if you do not.

It is true that coercion can be defined in a much broader way. Here coercion is seen not as the threat of force, but moral and social pressures that compel a person to do something that they otherwise would not have done. It is better, however, to describe these pressures as 'constraints': constraints certainly cause you to do something you would not have done otherwise, but these pressures do not involve force or the credible threat of force. Constraint may involve pressures that are unintentional and informal.

Take the following example. You become religious and your agnostic and atheist friends no longer want to have coffee with you. You are cycling on a windy day and find that you have to pedal considerably harder. Constraints can be natural or social and, when moral judgements are made about a person's behaviour, these constraints are 'concentrated' in ways that are often unpleasant. But the point about these constraints, whatever form they take, is that they are impossible to avoid in a society. They do not undermine our capacity for choice. On the contrary, they are conditions that make choice both possible and necessary.

This distinction between force and constraint translates into the second distinction we want to discuss, that between state and government. The latter two are not the same, even though in state-centred societies it may be very difficult to disentangle them. The term 'governance' is often used but the argument is better expressed if we stick to the older term. Government, it could be argued, involves resolving conflicts of interest through sanctions that may be unpleasant but do not involve force. Families, schools, clubs and voluntary societies govern themselves with rules that pressure people into compliance but they do not use force. States, on the other hand, do use force. It is true that states do not always act as states. In other words, they may in particular areas act 'governmentally', as we have defined it: in these areas they can be said to constrain, rather than resort to force. Of course in real life institutions in state-centred societies these two dimensions are invariably mixed up. The NHS in Britain is a good example of an institution that is mostly governmental in that its rules do not have force attached to them, but rely upon social pressures – naming and shaming, embarrassing and using verbal sanctions – to enforce them. On the other hand, it cannot be said that the state (strictly defined) does not play a role as well. After all, the NHS is tax funded, and if people refuse to pay taxes they are likely to be subject to more than moral pressures to pay up!

The distinction between state and government is important, first because it explains how stateless societies have rules and regulations that make order possible, and why people conform or dissent through pressures which most of the time are non-statist in character. You may try to get to the doctor's on time – not because you are fearful of being arrested and put in prison – but because it seems discourteous and improper not to do so. The distinction separates force (or violence) – the terms seem to boil down to the same thing in this context – from human nature, pointing to the fact that force comes into play only in situations in which moral and economic pressures do not work.

The Argument So Far...

- We have argued that the state is not just a modern institution even though the 'modern state' does have features that distinguish it from more traditional states.

State, Politics and Government

Is there a case for distinguishing between politics and the state? List all the things in your life that you would call 'political' and see whether it can be said that the state is directly involved.

The following is sometimes argued:

- the family is political
- the church is political
- sport is political
- relations between people are political.

Do you agree, and if so, what makes these institutions political?

How would you counter the argument that if 'everything is political, then nothing is political'?

Do you see government as a synonym for politics; is there a distinction between government and the state? List the institutions that have governments, starting with yourself (do you govern your own life?).

Consider the following institutions: are they inherently statist in character, or could they be run without the state?

- the National Health Service
- the prisons
- the post office
- the army and police.

- We have defended Max Weber's 'force argument'. Although force is not the only attribute of the state, it is the central attribute so that the state is distinguished from other social institutions because it uses 'legitimate force' to address conflicts of interest. The police, the army and the prisons are the distinctive attributes of the state.
- We have assumed that the state is an important concept in political theory. But there are those who argue that the state is too vague, elusive, divisive and ambiguous to merit attention. We have identified these critics as behaviouralists, linguistic analysts and radicals. Their arguments are rejected on the grounds that since states clearly exist in the real world it is important to try and define them, however difficult this task might be.
- States have not always existed. In fact throughout most of human history, people have resolved conflicts without relying upon a special institution that claims a monopoly of legitimate force. Even today state are (usually) bound by

international law and treaties even though there is no world state to maintain order. These facts make it important that we distinguish between constraints of a diplomatic kind (relying upon economic pressures, self-interest, ostracism, etc.) and force as such, just as we need to distinguish between the state and government.

State and Sovereignty

It is impossible to talk about the state without saying something about sovereignty. This is the aspect of the state that relates to its supreme and unchecked power. Hence sovereignty is commonly regarded as an attribute of states. But here agreement ends since some argue that only modern states are sovereign, others that all states are sovereign. Does claiming a *monopoly* of legitimate force mean that this monopoly endows the state with sovereignty?

Sovereignty as a Modern Concept

It is argued by Justin Rosenberg, for example, that sovereignty only arises when the state is sharply separated from society. His argument is that only under **capitalism** do we have a sharp divide between the public and the private, and this divide is necessary before we can speak of the *sovereign* state (1994: 87).

Rosenberg takes the view that sovereignty is a modern idea just as the state is a modern institution. F.H. Hinsley, on the other hand, argues that while the state can be broadly defined as a modern as well as an archaic institution, sovereignty cannot, since sovereignty requires a belief that absolute and illimitable power resides in the 'body politic' which constitutes a 'single personality' composed of rulers and ruled alike (1986: 125). This means effectively that rulers and ruled must be deemed 'citizens' – a modern concept. Even the celebrated theory of Jean Bodin's (*c.* 1529–96), that sovereignty as unconditional and unrestrained power is, for Hinsley, undermined by the assumption that the holder of sovereignty is limited by divine and natural law. With Hobbes, however, law in all its forms is the creation of the sovereign, so that there is no distinction to be made between sovereign and subject. The sovereign is simply the individual writ large.

In Hinsley's view, therefore, the state can take a pre-modern form but sovereignty cannot. This is also the position taken by Murray Forsyth in his entry on the state in *The Blackwell Encyclopaedia of Political Thought*.

Sovereignty as a Broad Concept

It is perfectly true that the concept of sovereignty was not known 'in its fullness' before the fifteenth and sixteenth centuries (Vincent, 1987: 32). Like the state, it was only explicitly formulated in the modern period, but that does not mean that it did not exist in earlier times. The Roman formulation – 'whatever pleases the prince has the force of law' – demonstrates not only that the notion of sovereignty existed in pre-modern periods, but that formulations such as these clearly influenced the modern conception. The idea that God rather than secular rulers exercised sovereignty still expressed the notion of absolute and illimitable power, and although sovereignty was more chaotic in pre-modern times, it clearly existed. One writer has spoken of the 'parcellised sovereignty' of the medieval period (Hoffman, 1998: 35–6) so that those who define the state broadly often define sovereignty broadly as well.

Alan James argues that states have always been sovereign, and that sovereignty is best defined as constitutional independence: a sovereign state is a state that is legally in control of its own destiny (1986: 53). Although he is preoccupied with states in the modern world, the notion of sovereignty applies to all states, whether ancient, medieval or modern.

Problems with the Theories of State Sovereignty

Those who assume that sovereignty is about the power of the state are mistaken. They take the view that the state is capable of exercising absolute power whereas it has been argued that in fact the state only claims this sovereign power, because others – terrorists, criminals, etc. – challenge it. In other words, the state claims something that it does and cannot have, so that the notion of the state as sovereign imports into the notion of sovereignty the problem of the state itself.

Difficulties with the Modernist Conception

The idea that sovereignty is purely modern confuses formulation with institution. It is true that sovereignty is only explicitly formulated by modern writers, but the notion of supreme power is inherent in the state.

The modernist notion misses the ironic part of Weber's definition: that a monopoly can be *claimed*, not because it exists, but precisely because it does not. The sovereign state claims an absolute power that it does not and cannot have. Unless criminals and terrorists also exercise some of this 'supremacy', it cannot be claimed. In other words, the notion of sovereignty merely brings into the open the problem that has existed all along. Like the state itself, the idea of state sovereignty has severe logical difficulties associated with it.

On the one hand, sovereignty is unitary in its scope. It is absolute and unlimited. In modern formulations, rulers and ruled are bonded together as citizens. On the other hand, there has to be a sharp **division** between the public and the private, the state and society, before modern sovereignty can be said to exist. There is a clear contradiction here since we can well ask, how can an institution have absolute power, and yet be clearly limited to a public sphere? Sovereignty allows the state to have a hand in everything – and yet we are told that it is confined to the public sphere and must not interfere in private matters! The formulation of **state sovereignty** in the modern period serves only to highlight its absurd and contradictory character.

It is true that in 'normal' times the sovereign character of the state is not obvious to the members of a liberal society. But if there is a crisis or emergency – as when war breaks out between states – the capacity of the state to penetrate into all aspects of life becomes plain. During World War II the British state told its citizens what they must plant in their back gardens, and today, for example, the state tells us through advertising about safe sex, that we should conduct the most private of activities with adequate protection. The British Cabinet even had a discussion in the early 1980s about the importance of parents teaching children how to manage their pocket money (*The Guardian*, 17 February 1983).

We are told that state sovereignty needs to be limited and restricted. Yet it is clear from the practice of state even in 'normal' times that sovereignty is seen as a power which can penetrate into the most private spheres of life.

The Broad View of State Sovereignty

Realists in international relations define sovereignty in terms of states, whether these state are ancient or modern. But it is not difficult to see that state sovereignty is a problematic concept, however the state is defined.

James's theory of state sovereignty is a case in point. James regards sovereignty as an attribute of any state, ancient or modern, and defines it as a state's legal claim to constitutional independence. Sovereignty, James argues, is a formal attribute: a state is sovereign no matter how much it may in practice be beholden to the will of other states. But his argument comes to grief over the question of identifying sovereignty in situations when it is explicitly contested.

James contends that sovereignty expresses a legal, not a physical reality. Yet this position is contradicted by the position he takes on Rhodesia (today, Zimbabwe). In 1965 Ian Smith, a right-wing white Rhodesian leader, announced a 'unilateral declaration of independence' to prevent Britain from pushing the country into some kind of majority rule. However, James argues that the Smith regime was a sovereign state, even though it came about in what he concedes was an unlawful manner. What is the basis for arguing that the Smith rebel regime was sovereign? Because, James tells us, it was able to keep its enemies at bay – to defend itself through force of arms.

This implies that it is not legality that ultimately counts but physical effectiveness. In another of James's examples, he argues that the country Biafra (which broke away from federal Nigeria in the late 1960s) did not become a sovereign state because it was defeated by the superior strength of the federal state of Nigeria (after a long and bloody civil war). James makes it clear that sovereignty is ultimately the capacity of a state to impose its will through force. But if this is what sovereignty is, then it suffers from the same problem that afflicts states in general: the problem of asserting a monopoly that it does not have. James speaks of sovereignty as a statist effectiveness that rests upon 'a significant congruence between the decisions of those who purport to rule and the actual behaviour of their alleged subjects' (Hoffman, 1998: 27–9). But this congruence, in the case of Smith's Rhodesia – a state that lasted only 14 years – was met with massive resistance from those who challenged this sovereignty and sought to achieve a sovereignty of their own.

In other words, the absolute and illimitable will is shared with wills that have a power of their own. State sovereignty is as illogical and problematic as the state itself.

Rescuing the Idea of Sovereignty

The idea of sovereignty is too important to be chewed to pieces by those who uncritically embrace the concept of the state. We will suggest a way in which the notion can be reinstated without the problems that inhere in the state.

The classical liberals saw individuals as sovereign, and they were right to do so. But the problem with classical liberals is that they assumed that individuals could enjoy their supreme power in complete isolation from one another, and indeed, for this reason, depicted individuals as living initially in a 'natural' condition outside of society. This assumption runs contrary to everything we know about individuals. The individual who has not been 'socialised' cannot speak or think, and certainly cannot identify herself as an individual! Individuals acquire their identity through their *relations* with others – they are social beings. Our life develops through an infinity of relationships – with parents, friends, teachers, and more abstractly, with people we read about or see and hear in the media.

Sovereignty is an attribute that individuals enjoy, and which enables us to govern our own lives. This definition frees sovereignty from the problems that blight it when it is linked to the state. Not only is the search for self-government developed in our relations with others, but it involves an infinite capacity to order our own lives. We aspire to sovereignty, but we never reach a situation in which we can say that no further progress towards sovereignty is possible. The fact that sovereignty is individual does not mean that it is not organisational, for individuals work in multiple associations at every level – the local, regional, national and global. Each of these helps us to develop our sovereignty– our capacity to govern our lives.

Ironically, therefore, the idea of state sovereignty gets in the way of individual sovereignty as we see from the way in which states often resist **human rights** on the grounds that they, states, should be entitled to treat their inhabitants as they see fit. The Chinese authorities object when their policies are criticised, and the US administration considers that it is entitled to continue incarcerating prisoners in Guantanamo Bay. But when we define sovereignty as self-government, we place the rights of humans above the power of the state, and argue that only by locating sovereignty in the individual can it become consistent and defensible as a concept.

Moving to a Stateless World

Why are most people so sceptical about the possibility of a world without the state? Part of the reason, it could be argued, is that people think of government as being the same as the state, but if we make a sharp distinction (as we have above) between government and the state, then it can be seen that a stateless society is not a society without government, but rather a society in which an institution claiming a monopoly of legitimate force becomes redundant. What prevents this from happening?

People, it seems to us, can settle their conflicts of interest through moral and social pressures where they have a common interest with their opponents: when they can, in other words, imagine what it is like to be 'the other'. This does not mean that people have to be the same in every regard. On the contrary, people are all different, and these **differences** are the source of conflict. But it does not follow that because people are different and have conflicting interests that they cannot negotiate and compromise in settling these conflicts. It is only when they cannot do this that force becomes inevitable, and even if this force begins outside the state, the state will soon be involved, since the state claims a monopoly of legitimate force, and is concerned (quite rightly) about the force of private individuals. We are not, therefore, suggesting that we should not have a state in situations where people resort to force to tackle their conflicts.

But instead of taking this force for granted, as though it was part and parcel of 'human nature' (as Hobbes does), it could be argued that force arises where people lack what we have called 'common interests'. Policies that cement and reinforce common interests help to make government work. There is a case for resorting to force where this is the only way of implementing policies that will strengthen common interests. The debate around the war in Iraq revolved around the question of whether the use of force, in the form of a war, was the only way to defeat Saddam Hussein's regime, and whether the use of force could lead to a democratic reconstruction of the country.

It is true that force can never really be legitimate since it necessarily deprives those whom it targets of their **freedom**. But it can be justifiably used if it is the only way to provide a breathing space for policies that will cement common interests. For example, it could prove impossible to involve residents in running their own lives on a rundown housing estate until force has been used to stop gangs from intimidating ordinary people.

In early tribal societies conflicts of interest *were* settled through moral and social pressures. This historical reality is a huge resource for pursuing the argument that it is possible to find ways of bringing about order that dispense altogether with the use of the state. Max Weber's definition has implications that he himself did not see. When he read that Leon Trotsky had said that 'every state is founded on force', he commented 'That indeed is right' (Gerth and Wright Mills, 1991: 78). But in making this endorsement, Weber had not committed himself to Trotsky's Marxist analysis of politics. In the same way, we find Weber's definition immensely useful, even though we see implications in the definition, of which Weber himself would not have approved.

Moreover, it is not only tribal societies in the dim and distant past that were stateless. It is now nearly three decades since Hedley Bull (1977) noted the 'awkward facts' confronting a state-centric view of the world. These awkward facts embrace the following:

- the increasing importance of international law as a body of rules that has no wider monopoly of legitimate force to impose it;
- the **globalisation** of the economy that makes the notion of autonomous state sovereignty peculiarly archaic; and
- a growing number of issues – Bull mentioned the environment in particular – that can only be settled through acknowledging the common interests of contending parties.

This is why Bull characterised the international order as an 'anarchical society', and it is clear that developments of the kind noted above mean that statist solutions are

Influences and Impact:

The State

The state is often identified with civilisation, and it is easy to see why the state has such a profound impact upon our thought. Conventional religion depicts God as a sovereign overlord, and classical political thinkers such as Hobbes and Rousseau assumed that without a conception of God no state would be possible. It is also very tempting to translate contemporary concerns into a frozen notion of human nature as though how people behave in, for example, Britain today, represents the nature of humankind. Moreover, where people do resort to force to tackle their conflicts, a world without the state makes a bad situation even worse, and it would hardly be an advantage to do away with the state, if the alternative was rule by warlords or the Mafia. But it is ultimately an illusion to think that we can do away with force by resorting to the state. For what could be called a 'statist' mentality assumes that violent people are inexplicably evil. We cannot understand them; we can only crush them. The statist mentality never asks the question 'why?'. Why are people so brutalised that they resort to force? Of course, it is no help to merely invert the idea that people are evil so that we consider them to be naturally 'good' instead. Pacifists naively suppose that brutalised people or states will respond to moral pressures in a purely moral way, and anarchists fail to see that in conditions where force can be dispensed with we still need government to regulate social affairs. Firmness and rules are actually undermined by the use of force, since force encourages us to ignore complexities and not try and imagine what it is like to be in the shoes of another. The fact that the state remains hugely influential in our lives does not mean that we should not start thinking about ways and means of living without it.

becoming ever more dangerous as a mode of resolving conflicts. The increasing degree of interdependence that characterises both domestic and international society makes the resort to force (the chosen and distinctive instrument of the state) increasingly counter-productive. The fact that criminal individuals, like criminal states, are also the beneficiaries of a technology of violence (whose sophistication escalates all the time) means that if we want a secure future it is vital that we learn how to settle differences without the use of force, i.e. in a stateless manner.

Summary

The state is seen by some theorists as a modern institution that has, as its identifying features, a sharp separation of the public from the private; a capacity to exercise sovereignty throughout its domain and protect all who live in its territory; an ability to organise its offices along bureaucratic rather than patrimonial lines; and to extract tax revenues from its population.

The state can be defined in a way that sees its central attribute as the exercise of legitimate force; is based upon morality, or a mixture of the two. When it is defined in a way that stresses the importance of force, then it can be argued that modern states are crucially different from pre-modern states, but like all states, they claim to exercise a monopoly of legitimate force.

Three bodies of argument contend that politics is best identified without using the concept of the state. Behaviouralists argue that the state as a concept is too ambiguous and ideological to be useful, and the notion of a political system is preferable; linguistic analysts see the idea of the state as a practical institution rather than a coherent philosophical concept, while radicals argue that the notion of the state gets in the way of a pluralist and participatory politics.

The problem, however, is that the state does not simply disappear simply because it is not defined. The contradictory nature of the institution can only be exposed if we define it, and the definition of the state as an institution claiming a monopoly of legitimate force makes it possible to underline the state's problematic character.

The contradictory character of the state also undermines the notion of state sovereignty. Sovereignty can only be coherently defined as the capacity of individuals to govern their own lives.

Questions

1. Do you agree with the argument that the state is essentially a modern institution?
2. What is the best way of defining the state?
3. Is it possible to differentiate government from the state, and if so, how?
4. Do you see the notion of state sovereignty as irrelevant in the contemporary world?
5. Why do people physically harm one another?

References

Allen, J. (1990) 'Does Feminism Need a Theory of the State?' in S. Watson (ed.), *Playing the State* London: Verso, 21–37.

Ashley, R. (1988) 'Untying the Sovereign State: a Double Reading of the Anarchy Problematique', *Millennium* 17(2), 227–62.

Bentley, A. (1967) *The Process of Government* Cambridge, Mass.: Belknap, Harvard University Press.

Bull, H. (1977) *The Anarchical Society* Basingstoke: Macmillan.

Dahl, R. (1976) *Modern Political Analysis* 3rd edn, Englewood Cliffs, New Jersey: Prentice-Hall.

Dunleavy, P. and O'Leary, B. (1987) *Theories of the State* London and Basingstoke: Macmillan.

Easton, D. (1965) *A Framework for Political Analysis* Englewood Cliffs, New Jersey: Prentice-Hall.

Easton, D. (1971) *The Political System* 2nd edn New York: Alfred Knopf.

Easton, D. (1981) 'The Political System Besieged by the State' *Political Theory* 9, 203–25.

Easton, D. (1990) *An Analysis of Political Structure* New York and London: Routledge.

Gerth, H. and Wright Mills C. (1991) *From Max Weber* London: Routledge.

Gramsci, A. (1971) *Selections from the Prison Notebooks* London: Lawrence & Wishart.

Green, T.H. (1941) *The Principles of Political Obligation* London, New York and Toronto: Longmans, Green & Co.

Hamlin, A. and Pettit, P. (1989) 'The Normative Analysis of the State: Some Preliminaries' in A. Hamlin and P. Pettit (eds), *The Good Polity* Oxford: Basil Blackwell, 1–13.

Hegel, G. (1956) *The Philosophy of History* New York: Dover.

Hinsley, F.H. (1986) *Sovereignty* Cambridge: Cambridge University Press.

Hoffman, J. (1995) *Beyond the State* Cambridge: Polity Press.

Hoffman, J. (1996) 'Antonio Gramsci: *The Prison Notebooks*' in M. Forsyth and M. Keens-Soper (eds), *The Political Classics: Green to Dworkin* Oxford: Oxford University Press, 58–77.

Hoffman, J. (1998) *Sovereignty* Buckingham: Open University Press.

James, A. (1986) *Sovereign Statehood* London: Allen & Unwin.

Machiavelli, N. (1998) *The Prince* Oxford: Oxford University Press.

Mann, M. (1980) 'The Pre-industrial State' *Political Studies* 28, 297–304.

Marx K. and Engels, F. (1976) *Collected Works* Vol. 5 London: Lawrence & Wishart.

Pringle, R. and Watson, S. (1992) 'Women's Interests and the Post-Structural State' in M. Barrett and A. Phillips (eds), *Destabilizing Theory* Cambridge: Polity Press, 53–73.

Rosenberg, J. (1994) *The Empire of Civil Society* London: Verso.

Vincent, A. (1987) *Theories of the State* Oxford: Blackwell.

Weldon, T. (1953) *The Vocabulary of Politics* Harmondsworth: Penguin.

Further Reading

- Bhikhu Parekh's essay 'When Will the State Wither Away?' *Alternatives* 15, 247–62 is a thoughtful and accessible presentation on the state as a modern institution.

- John Hoffman's *Beyond the State* (referenced above) deals with the way in which different traditions have approached the state, and makes the case for the kind of conceptual distinctions needed to provide an effective critique.

- Alan James's *Sovereign Statehood* (referenced above) provides a clear defence of a traditional view of sovereignty with an attempt to sort out the confusions that the concept generates.

- David Easton's *The Political System* (referenced above) makes the classic case against the state and the need to conceptualise politics as a system rather than a set of institutions.

- Hedley Bull's *The Anarchical Society* (referenced above) seeks to argue that international society is a stateless order and yet there is order. An ingenious and extremely interesting text.

- Bernard Crick's *In Defence of Politics* Harmondsworth: Penguin, 1964 (and subsequent editions) offers a very interesting first chapter on the nature of political rule, and what he sees as distinctive about the political process.

- Adrian Leftwich's edited volume, *What is Politics?* Cambridge: Polity, 2004 (2nd edn) contains a very useful and thought-provoking Chapter 3 on the question of 'Politics and Force' by Peter Nicholson.

Weblinks

http://www.keele.ac.uk/depts/po/prs.htm
http://www.york.ac.uk/services/library/subjects/politint.htm

Chapter 2

Freedom

Introduction

Freedom is regarded by many as the pre-eminent political value, but what does it mean to be free? Do we have to justify freedom, or do it we take it as axiomatic that we should be free, and that it is *restrictions* on freedom which require justification? And what are those justifications? If we go into the street and survey people's attitudes to freedom, we might find that they favour the freedom to do things of which they approve, but are in favour of the state using its power to restrict freedom to do things that they dislike. Is there then a *principled* way to establish what we should be free to do? At the core of freedom is the idea of 'choice', but can we choose to do anything we want?

Chapter Map

In this chapter we will:

- Provide a working definition of freedom.

- Outline one of the most important contributions to the debate over freedom – the argument advanced by John Stuart Mill in his book *On Liberty*.

- Distinguish freedom of expression and freedom of action in Mill's argument.

- Use Mill's argument to provide a framework for a wider discussion of freedom and its limits.

- Illustrate arguments over freedom through the use of case studies, and, in particular, the proposed ban on smoking in enclosed public spaces.

Smoking in the Last Chance Saloon?

More and more cities, provinces and countries are adopting restrictions, and complete bans, on smoking in enclosed public places. Most attention has focused on bans in bars and restaurants. New York City and State, California State, the Republic of Ireland, New Zealand, Norway and Italy have already introduced such bans.

The policy adopted in Ireland has become the model for other countries. Technically the ban, which was introduced in March 2004, extends to all workplaces, and the protection of bar staff from the alleged effects of 'passive smoking' (environmental tobacco smoke – ETS) was advanced as one of the major reasons for its introduction. Owners of bars in which people are caught smoking are liable to be fined up to €3,000. Policing of bars is the responsibility of health inspectors. It is still possible to smoke outside a bar, and quite elaborate heated outdoor spaces have been created. A year after the ban it was estimated that there was a 94–97 per cent compliance rate from bars, and the ban commands a very high level of support among the Irish population, as judged by opinion poll research.

At the end of this chapter we will apply the arguments advanced through the course of the chapter to the smoking ban. But before tackling the rest of the chapter it would useful to consider your own reactions to the ban: how valid are the arguments listed above? Can you think of arguments against a smoking ban? Is it possible to develop a position midway between no significant regulation of smoking in enclosed public places and a complete ban? Alternatively, should the prohibition on smoking be extended to all public places, and even to private homes – in short, should the sale and use of tobacco be made illegal?

Freedom

The starting point for many, although not all, political theorists is what can be termed *the presumption in favour of freedom*. That is, we assume people ought to be free unless there are compelling reasons for restricting their freedom – much of the discussion of freedom focuses on the legitimate limits to freedom. In this chapter we use John Stuart Mill's defence of this presumption in his book *On Liberty*. But before considering Mill's argument we need a working definition of freedom, or **liberty**.*

Gerald MacCallum argues that 'freedom is . . . always *of* something (an agent or agents), *from* something, *to* do, not do, become, or not become something' (MacCallum, 1991: 102). Freedom is therefore a 'triadic' relationship – meaning, there are three parts to it: (a) the agent, or person, who is free (or 'unfree'); (b) the constraints, restrictions, interferences and barriers that make the agent free or unfree, and (c) what it is that the person is free to do, or not do. It is important that (c) means a person is free to do *or* not do something – that is, he has a *choice*: an inmate of a jail is not prevented from residing in that jail, but he has no choice whether or not he resides there. MacCallum's definition is useful, but it leaves open a couple of important issues. First, what is the source of (b)? Must it be another person (or persons) who constrains or restricts your action? Could the source of your unfreedom be yourself – that is, your own weaknesses and irrationality? Second, some things are trivial – is your freedom to watch inane daytime television as valuable as your freedom to study challenging poetry?

To cast some light on the first issue, a distinction is made between positive liberty and negative liberty. The distinction is credited to Sir Isaiah Berlin, who set it out in his famous essay 'Two Concepts of Liberty' (1991). Acknowledging that in the history of political thought there have been more than two concepts of freedom, Berlin maintains that these two have had the greatest influence, and the contrast between them throws into relief fundamental differences about the role of the state:

- *Negative liberty* is involved in the answer to the question: 'what is the area within which the subject – a person or group of persons – is or should be left to do or be what he is able to do or be, without interference by other persons?' (Berlin, 1991: 121–2)

- *Positive liberty* is involved in the answer to the question: 'what, or who, is the source of control or interference that can determine someone to do, or be, this rather than that?' (122).

So, negative liberty is about being left alone, whereas positive liberty is about being in control of one's life. For example, a person may be unfree to leave her home because she is under 'house arrest'; alternatively, she may be unfree to leave because she has a phobia that makes her fearful of leaving. In the first case, she is negatively unfree to leave, whereas in the second she is positively unfree. Of course, elements of both types

---

*Some writers draw a distinction between 'freedom' and 'liberty', arguing that the latter denotes political or legal freedom, whereas the former encompasses a broader range of activities and states. We do not make this distinction. For stylistic reasons, which include the possibility of using adjectival forms of the noun, we prefer freedom, but nonetheless we use freedom and liberty interchangeably.

of 'unfreedom' may be evident: she may be fearful about leaving her home because she suspects she is under surveillance and that she is at greater harm away from home. Perhaps she is slightly paranoid, but if that paranoia has been caused by actual past experience, then the source of the unfreedom, or 'control', is not straightforwardly internal or external. But even if we cannot determine the source of unfreedom we can still make an analytical distinction between such sources, and therefore also between positive and negative freedom. In passing, it should be noted that Berlin was very hostile to the concept of positive liberty. He thought it implied a belief in psychological sources of unfreedom concealed from the person who is deemed unfree – this belief forms the basis of a political theory in which people are 'forced to be free'. In the section on Harm to Self we suggest a way of understanding positive freedom that does not rely on a belief in hidden psychological drives.

In summary, we can say that freedom is a triadic relation that must involve choice. When analysing the nature of constraints – or 'unfreedom' – a valid distinction can be drawn between internal and external sources of constraint.

Mill's Defence of Freedom

Mill's essay *On Liberty* has been hugely influential in discussions of political freedom, especially in his native Britain. Although there is always a danger in applying the thought of a long-dead thinker to contemporary issues, nineteenth-century Britain is sufficiently close to the contemporary Western world for us to ask what Mill might have had to say on contemporary issues. Once the reader gets beyond the rather ponderous literary style, Mill's reflections – especially his concern with

Biography — John Stuart Mill (1806–73)

The son of James Mill, an important utilitarian philosopher, J. S. Mill was infamously the subject of a rigorously rationalist educational experiment by his father. He learnt Greek at the age of three but suffered a mental breakdown when he was 21.

For the rest of his life he sought to reconcile the rather austere elements of his father's utilitarianism to a more romantic individualism. This becomes clear in his essay *On Liberty*, which was published in 1859. In addition to important contributions to mainstream areas of philosophy, alongside *On Liberty* he wrote a number of other important political works, the most significant of which are *Considerations on Representative Government* (1861) and *The Subjection of Women* (1869). The latter essay, which owes a great deal to his wife Harriet Taylor, argued ahead of its time for the social and political emancipation of women.

Unusually for a political thinker he practised politics, being Liberal Member of Parliament for Westminster from 1865 to 1868. While an MP he made an unsuccessful attempt to extend the vote to women.

How to read:

Mill's *On Liberty*

On Liberty is a relatively short text – about 120 pages in length. There are many editions of the text, and most editions combine *On Liberty* with other essays by Mill. Despite the brevity of the text Mill can be convoluted and long-winded, although this reflects a certain Victorian style of writing. *On Liberty* is organised into five chapters. Chapter 1 is introductory, but important: among other things it sets out the harm principle. Chapter 2 is concerned with freedom of expression, and Chapter 3 with freedom of action – although this is not obvious from the title 'Of Individuality, as One of the Elements of Well-Being'. The core of the argument is in Chapters 1–3; however, Chapter 5 is important in explaining how the harm principle may be applied (unfortunately, in the process Mill contradicts himself). One final point: it is worth bearing in mind that more than many other philosophical texts Mill's essay is directed at a wide audience.

the tyranny of popular opinion – have a strikingly contemporary feel. Some of his arguments, such as his faith in human progress, appear very dated, but they are nonetheless provocative.

After some initial remarks about the danger of the majority tyrannising minorities, Mill articulates what has become known as the *liberty principle* (or *harm principle*):

> the sole end for which mankind are warranted, individually or collectively, in interfering with the liberty of action of any of their number, is self-protection. [. . .] The only purpose for which power can be rightfully exercised over any member of a civilized community, against his will, is to prevent harm to others. His own good, either physical or moral, is not a sufficient warrant (Mill, 1991: 14).

Mill goes on to clarify to whom the harm principle applies. Excluded are those who have not yet developed their intellectual and moral capacities, that is, children. But also excluded from the scope of the principle are those who live in societies that lack the cultural and institutional conditions for the exercise of freedom. Mill, as with most nineteenth-century thinkers, adopted an evolutionary view of **culture**.

Chapter 14:
Multiculturalism,
pp. 352–4

Underpinning the harm principle is a certain conception of what it means to live a properly human life, as distinct from a merely animal existence. To be human is to enjoy a sphere in which one is able to think, express ideas, and lead a lifestyle of one's own choosing. In developing his argument Mill introduces some important concepts:

- **Self-regarding and other-regarding actions** Some actions affect *directly* only the individual (self-regarding actions), whereas other actions have a direct effect on other people (other-regarding actions) (Mill: 16).
- **Direct and indirect effects** Mill acknowledges the adage that 'no man is an island', and that most actions have effects on others, however remote, or indirect, those effects may be (16). How we distinguish between direct and indirect effects is a problem to which we shall return.
- **Consent** You can permit another person to do something to you which in the absence of **consent** would be deemed direct harm and therefore prohibited. A good example is boxing – an activity that would, without consent, be physical assault (16).

Mill then sets out what he terms the 'appropriate region of human liberty'. It consists of the following:

- **The 'inward domain of consciousness'** This requires freedom of thought and feeling and an 'absolute freedom' of opinion on any subject. Mill concedes that expression of opinions may appear to extend beyond freedom of conscience because it affects other people, but he asserts that expression is 'almost of as much importance as the liberty of thought itself' and it rests on the 'same reasons' (16).
- **The 'liberty of tastes and pursuits'** We should be free to act on our beliefs, and pursue a 'plan of life' consistent with our individual character and desires, subject, of course, to the harm principle. Other people can think your lifestyle 'foolish, perverse, or wrong', but they should not interfere with it (17).
- **Freedom to associate with others** It follows from freedom of expression and action that people should be free to 'combine' with others. Obvious examples would be the formation of trade unions, professional associations, and political parties and movements, as well as the development of more personal relationships (17).

To tackle Mill's argument we need to distinguish freedom of thought and expression, discussed in Chapter 2 of *On Liberty*, and freedom of action, discussed in Chapter 3.

Freedom of Thought and Expression

Even if a person finds himself alone in expressing an opinion he should, according to Mill, be free to express it: 'if all mankind, minus one, were of one opinion, and only one person were of the contrary opinion, mankind would no more be justified in silencing that one person, than he, if he had the power, would be justified in silencing mankind' (Mill: 21). Mill has a neat defence of this claim:

- If the opinion is true then by suppressing it humanity is deprived of the truth and will not progress. (Mill observes that it has often been the case that today's heterodoxy is tomorrow's orthodoxy; an example might be Charles Darwin's theory of evolution by natural selection – in fact, today there is insufficient criticism of Darwin's theory (21).)
- If the opinion is false then humanity again loses, because if the opinion is false it will be shown to be so, but its expression is useful, for it forces us to restate the reasons for our beliefs. A competition of ideas is healthy (21).
- The truth is often 'eclectic' (52). This argument is frequently misunderstood. It can mean: (a) an opinion can be broken into a number of discrete claims, some of which are true and some false; (b) the conclusion of an argument might be correct and the premises sound, but the conclusion does not follow from the premises; (c) two conflicting arguments may require a third argument to resolve the conflict between them. What Mill did *not* mean by 'eclecticism' was that the truth is 'subjective'. Such a claim would undermine the fundamental basis of his defence of freedom of expression, which is that it is the means by which truth is advanced.

People who seek to suppress an opinion assume their own beliefs are infallible; they confuse *their* certainty with *absolute* certainty. Mill accepts that people must make decisions and act on them, and those decisions are based on beliefs. It would, for example, be irrational for you to jump off the edge of a cliff if that action were motivated by a belief that you could fly unaided; a rational person is guided by a belief in the law of gravity. However, Mill distinguishes between holding a belief to be certain, and not permitting others to refute it – people should be free to question the law of gravity, and this is consistent with the rest of us acting as if the law were true. (There is an issue about whether we should stop you acting on a false belief if that action has disastrous consequences for you; since this relates to freedom of action, we shall turn to it in the next section.)

Progress in knowledge and understanding, Mill argues, comes about not through experience alone, but also through discussion. This is interesting because it shows that Mill's defence of freedom of expression rests on the good consequences of permitting such freedom. This contrasts with an argument which asserts that individuals have rights 'to be left alone', and that freedom of expression is justified on the basis of those rights and not the social good generated by it.

Mill's defence of freedom of expression is paradoxical. While it is a good thing for people to express different and conflicting opinions, the basic justification is that truth is advanced in the competition of ideas. This assumes that there is a truth (or set of truths), and the pursuit of that truth sets an end for humankind. The implication is that as we progress false beliefs lose their power over us, and we increasingly come to hold the same true beliefs. What Mill fears is that as a result of this process the beneficial aspects of the expression of false beliefs will be lost: 'both teachers and learners go to sleep at their post, as soon as there is no enemy in the field' (48). This suggests a distinction between the prevalence of true beliefs, and how human beings hold those beliefs; it is essential that we understand the reasons for our beliefs, otherwise the belief becomes 'dead dogma'.

Finally, although there is a distinction between freedom of action and freedom of expression, the line between them is fuzzy: some forms of expression are very close to action. A person 'must not make himself a nuisance to other people' (55). And Mill goes on to argue that:

> an opinion that corn dealers* are starvers of the poor, or that private property is robbery, ought to be unmolested when simply circulated through the press, but may justly incur punishment when delivered orally to an excited mob assembled before the house of a corn dealer, or when handed about among the same mob in the form of a placard (55).

There is a close causal relationship here between speech and action.

Freedom of Action

In Chapter 3 of *On Liberty* Mill discusses freedom of action and lifestyle. While acknowledging that 'no one pretends that actions should be as free as opinions' (62)

---

*One of the major debates of the nineteenth century was over free trade versus protectionism, especially in foodstuffs; corn dealers controlled the price of corn and kept it high, relative to its free trade price, and so were deeply unpopular people. If you want a contemporary example, take the case of people who have served sentences for sexual offences against children and who have been released into the community: publicising their names and addresses may encourage vigilante groups to track them down and harm them.

Mill claims the same reasons which show an opinion should be free demonstrate that an individual should be free to put his opinions into practice, even if the action is foolish. The only constraint is that the agent should not harm others. Some doubts can be raised as to whether freedom of expression and freedom of action really do rest on the same arguments, but for the moment we will follow the course of Mill's argument.

In discussing freedom of action, Mill introduces a concept not used in the discussion of expression: *individuality*. He regards individuality as 'one of the principal ingredients of human happiness' (63), and so it is linked to the well-being of society. The development of individuality requires two things: freedom and a 'variety of situations' (64). Although children need to be guided by those who have had experience of life, adults must be free to develop their own lifestyle and values, and not be subject to *custom*. The word 'custom' can be defined as accumulated, shared and often 'taken-for-granted' experiences. Mill criticises custom:

- Experience may be too narrow, and wrongly interpreted.
- Other people's experiences may not be relevant to you, given *your* character and *your* experiences.
- The custom may be 'good', but to conform to it as custom 'does not educate or develop . . . any of the qualities which are the distinctive endowment of the human being' (65). People need to make choices, and following custom is an evasion of choice. Following custom is analogous to holding beliefs without understanding the reasons for those beliefs.

At the heart of the notion of individuality is *originality*. To be original is to bring something into the world; this need not be a creation out of nothing, and it is quite possible that other people have thought the same thoughts and performed the same actions. Nor indeed must an action be uninfluenced by others; what makes an action 'original' is that a person consciously sets himself against custom and thinks for himself. Originality is most likely to take a 'synthetic' form, that is, originality is demonstrated in the ability to produce something new through the synthesis of diverse experiences and reflections. It serves a social function, for it provides role models for those who, by character or inclination, may be more timid about thinking or acting in ways not supported by custom. Those who are 'original' are providing what Mill calls *experiments in living*, some of which may have bad, even disastrous, consequences, but taken together the existence of experiments is over time beneficial. The link between freedom of expression and freedom of action is clear: the original person is the 'one in a hundred' prepared to advance a heterodox belief, and the 'failed experiment' parallels the 'false belief'.

Mill rejects **paternalism** – that is, stopping people harming themselves. He does endorse what is sometimes called 'soft paternalism', but it is a matter of debate whether it really is paternalism: if a person starts to cross a footbridge, unaware that it is insecure and liable to collapse into the ravine below, then if we cannot communicate with him – perhaps we do not share a language – then we can intervene (Mill: 106–7). If, however, he knows the risk then we are *not* entitled to stop him. Paternalism is discussed further in the section on Criticisms and Development.

It should be stressed that we do not have to approve of other people's behaviour. If a person manifests a 'lowness or depravation of taste' we are, Mill argues, justified in making him a 'subject of distaste, or . . . even of contempt' (Mill: 85). What we are not justified in doing is interfering in his actions. There is a tension here between encouraging diversity of lifestyle as if it were an intrinsically good thing, but being free to disapprove of it. If diversity is to be *promoted* rather than merely *tolerated* then the state should not just protect people's freedom, but actually encourage a change in attitudes among the majority.

Criticisms and Developments

Mill's argument provides a useful framework for discussing the nature and limits of freedom. As we suggested at the beginning of this chapter many political theorists concerned with freedom presume freedom to be a good thing, and search for legitimate reasons for limiting it. Mill claims that only non-consensual harm to others can constitute a legitimate ground for limiting another person's freedom. But Mill may be wrong, and in the box below we present for consideration a number of additional 'freedom-limiting principles' alongside the non-consensual harm to others one.

Liberty-limiting principle:		Mill's view (YES: reason for restricting freedom; NO: not a reason)
Harm to others	Non-consensual	YES – only ground for restriction
	Consent	NO
Harm to self (paternalism)		NO (argument is closely tied to the consent-to-be-harmed argument)
Offensiveness		NO (but Mill is not consistent)
Harmless wrongdoing *or* badness (these two are not the same)		NO: harmless wrongdoing is a contradiction in terms.

Using these four, or arguably five, principles we can both criticise Mill and consider alternative perspectives on freedom.

Harm to Others

We start with some general comments about Mill's harm principle, ignoring for the moment the distinction between consensual and non-consensual harm to others. The first, and rather obvious, objection to the harm principle is: what, in fact, constitutes harm? Surely, no man or woman is an island – are there any truly self-regarding actions?

Mill concedes that no person is an 'entirely isolated being' (Mill: 88) and almost all actions have remote consequences. If by 'harm' we mean any 'bad' effect another person's action may have then few actions would be self-regarding and it would be difficult to use 'harm' as a criterion for restricting freedom at the same time as guaranteeing a significant sphere of freedom for the individual. Mill operates with a 'physicalist' rather than a 'psychological' definition of harm; if we were to expand the concept of harm beyond physical harm to the person (and his property) to include psychological harm then the private sphere in which a person would be free to act would be severely contracted.

Another kind of harm might be caused when a person sets a 'bad example': if Mill is going to appeal to the *good* consequences of 'experiments in living', he must surely accept that some experiments may also have *bad* consequences for other people. Part of Mill's response to this problem is to argue that you cannot have the benefits of freedom without also suffering the negative consequences. To try to determine what are good experiments in living and what are bad, and seek to restrict the latter is to prejudge what is good and bad, and it is precisely only in the competition of lifestyles that such a judgement can be made. The consequences of an action are always in the future, and so we cannot know those consequences *now* such that we can predict them.

The appeal to competing lifestyles is an important argument but it is quite different to a defence of freedom based on the possibility that many important actions are self-regarding and do not therefore 'harm' others. To save the harm principle Mill must clarify what can count as 'harm'. One option is to redefine harm as: having one's fundamental interests damaged such that one's life goes (significantly) less well than it would otherwise have gone. It could be added that in most circumstances the individual who is 'harmed' should judge what is, or is not, in her interests – this raises the issue of consent, which is discussed in the next section. Obviously, this needs to be elaborated, but the point is that the threshold for deeming an action 'harmful' is high; it cannot simply be an action which has negative effects on another person. This would rule out temporary discomfort caused by someone else's action: so, for example, if you feel a bit groggy after spending an evening in the bar breathing other people's smoke that cannot count as harm, but contracting cancer *is* harm. We might still want to attach some importance to temporary discomfort, but rather than call it harmful we call it offensive. If we do this then we need a different principle for judging something offensive – this principle is discussed in the section on Offensiveness.

Consent

Mill argues that people can consent to be harmed. Activities such as boxing or duelling, even though they carry the risk of considerable harm, and even death, must be free so long as the people concerned consented, and were capable of consent, where being 'capable' means being an adult. It might be objected that there is no necessary connection between harm and consent: if something is harmful to other people then we should be prevented from engaging in it.

pp. 42–43

But consent is important for Mill because it connects up with the third area in the 'appropriate region of human liberty': freedom of association. If the state were justified in interfering in consensual, albeit harmful, activities between consenting adults then the space in which people could associate would be severely restricted. A legal case in England from the early 1990s is interesting. In 1990 a number of men were charged with 'assault occasioning actual bodily harm' (*R.* v. *Brown and Others* (1993); the arrest was codenamed 'Operation Spanner'). The men had engaged in a rather protracted session of sadomasochistic sexual activity, which, foolishly, they had videotaped. Their defence – that they all consented – was dismissed by the court. Unsurprisingly, the parallel of boxing was used as part of the defence: if two men can beat each other up, then why can they not get sexual pleasure from inflicting pain on each other? The judge argued that consent was a ground for 'harm' but it had to be backed up by a justification of the activity itself, and the following were legitimate: surgery; a 'properly conducted game or sport'; tattooing and ear-piercing. On sport, Foster's *Crown Law* (1792) was cited: boxing and wrestling are 'manly diversions, they intend to give strength, skill and activity, and may fit people for defence, public as well as personal, in time of need'. The court deemed that consent was a necessary *but insufficient* ground for the action, and that the intrinsic qualities of the action could justify a restriction on the action. We return to this argument in the section on Harmless Wrongdoing.

Harm to Self

The issue of consent brings us to the question of harm to self: in effect, consenting to be harmed amounts to harming oneself and raises the issue of whether the state ought to protect people against themselves. For example, having an 'age of consent' for various activities amounts to a judgement that a person – or group of people, such as children – are incapable of giving consent, or, at least, *informed* consent. Laws that protect people against themselves are 'paternalistic', although, in everyday language advocates of paternalism avoid the term because of its pejorative overtones. The etymology of the word 'paternalism' suggests a parent–child relationship, and most people would accept that laws regarding children should be paternalistic – though in some cases children should be protected by the state against their parents – but it is more controversial when applied to adults and thus where it is the state that acts as the 'parent'.

A distinction is sometimes made between 'soft' and 'hard' paternalism: if someone does not understand that what he is doing is potentially harmful then a soft paternalist would argue that intervention is justified. A hard paternalist will say that even if a person knows what he is doing is harmful to himself intervention is justified. We have briefly discussed Mill's bridge example: you can stop a person crossing an unsafe bridge if you are sure he is unaware of the risks (soft paternalism), but you are not justified in stopping him if he is aware of the consequences. Of course, a soft paternalist must explain what is meant by 'understanding': does mental incapacity mean that some people cannot understand the implications of their actions? Mill addresses only indirectly the problem of adults who have been incapacitated by mental illness or have an inherited condition that renders them incapable of consent – he argues against extending the notion of 'child protection' to any adults (Mill: 89–90).

Mill suggests that if society wants the benefits of 'experiments in living' then it must also accept the risks. The difficulty is that there are some activities so patently harmful that there would be no loss to society if the agent were protected against himself. And even if this were not true, the loss to the individual concerned is so great that *his* good must warrant interference. The argument touched on in the section on Harm to Others earlier regarding not being able to predict the consequences of our actions applies only to novel actions – human experience tells us that if you jump off a cliff you will plunge to your death. We can debate the laws of gravity, and that is part of freedom of *expression*, but our *actions* should be governed by the subjective, experience-based certainty of what will happen if we jump.

It is, of course, possible to argue that many activities contain a good which cannot be separated from the risks involved. Boxing, for example, carries a significant danger of brain damage, but certainly in the past – in Mill's time – boxing gave pride and discipline to many working-class men. Nonetheless, if we are concerned with the capacity for freedom then 'harm to self' must *on occasion* be a ground for state interference: if you engage in action which ends your future capacity for action, such as consenting to be killed and eaten, then we cannot justify that action on grounds of human freedom, because the act itself extinguishes the capacity for freedom. This is where positive liberty is important. Adapting slightly Berlin's distinction we could argue that positive freedom entails a long-term capacity for choice, and for that reason it is conceptually possible for you to be the source of your own unfreedom: your actions *now* may harm your *future* self.

Offensiveness

The principles discussed so far have tended to be concerned with freedom of action; offensiveness relates as much to freedom of expression as to action, and so we begin with some problems with Mill's argument for freedom of expression. Mill assumes that expression, be it speaking, writing and publication, or visual media, always entails the communication of truth. The paradigm – or model – of communication for Mill is a propositional statement to which one assents or from

---

Exercise

Should the state intervene in the following situations (all people involved are consenting adults)?

(a) to require adults to wear seatbelts in cars;

(b) to prevent adults boxing;

(c) to prevent adults duelling;

(d) to prevent adults engaging in sadomasochistic sexual activities, where there is a danger of moderate physical harm;

(e) where a person has a painful, terminal illness, to prevent another person ending that life;

(f) to prevent an adult consenting to be killed in the context of a cannibalistic activity, where the person is fully aware of the consequences of consent.

Case (f) may seem extreme, but there was a recent case in Germany. The defendant in this case – Armin Meiwes – advertised on the internet for a man willing to be killed and eaten. Eventually he found a 'victim'. The prosecution accepted that from web traffic and other evidence the victim did 'consent' to be killed, and under German law they were required to seek a verdict of 'requested killing', which carries a lesser sentence than murder. Our concern is not with the interpretation of law, but with what the law should be: should a person be permitted to consent to be killed in this way?

which one can dissent: scientific 'truth claims', claims about, for example, the laws of gravity, are propositional statements. In effect, Mill views society as engaged in one gigantic university seminar. But there are plenty of examples where this is not the case. Think of abusive speech: the point here is not that all 'non-propositional' forms of expression are bad and should be banned, but that Mill provides an inadequate account of human expression. Above all, there seems to be no place in his theory for restricting freedom of expression on grounds that a certain expression might be offensive.

'A Ride on the Bus' – exercise below

Joel Feinberg's (1985) list of offensive situations should be sufficient to convince us that offensiveness can sometimes be a ground for restricting freedom. Although Mill does not directly address the problem of offensiveness, implicit in his argument is the view that to say 'I find x offensive' is equivalent to saying 'I do not agree with x', and he rejects disagreement as a ground for limiting a person's freedom. The alternative is to say that the action is not offensive but harmful – perhaps 'psychologically harmful'. This would, however, severely restrict the sphere in which a person is free to act. Mill does appeal to the notion of 'public decency' to forbid things that harm the agent and are done in public:

Exercise

'A Ride on the Bus'

Joel Feinberg in his book *The Moral Limits of the Criminal Law* (Vol. 2: *Offense to Others*) asks the reader to imagine taking a ride on a bus, and at various stages another passenger, or group of passengers gets on, and proceeds to do various things that while not harmful are offensive. He presents 31 'stories' in six groups (10–13), and we have reproduced (in abridged form) one from each group (no offence is intended by reproducing them here!). Ask yourself whether the agent(s) should be free to engage in the action.

1. **Affront to the senses:** a passenger turns on a radio to maximum volume; the sounds emitted are mostly screeches, whistles and static, but occasionally rock music blares through.

2. **Disgust and revulsion:** a group get on the bus, and sitting next to you spread a tablecloth over their knees and proceed to eat a picnic of live insects, fish heads and pickled sex organs of lamb, veal and pork, smothered in garlic and onions. Their table manners leave almost everything to be desired.

3. **Shock to religious sensibility:** a youth gets on wearing a T-shirt with a cartoon of Christ on the cross, underneath which are the words 'Hang in there, baby!'

4. **Shame and embarrassment:** a passenger masturbates in his seat.

5. **Annoyance and boredom:** the passenger next to you is a friendly and garrulous bloke, who insists on engaging you in conversation despite your polite but firm requests that you be allowed to read your newspaper. There is nowhere else on the bus to sit.

6. **Fear (resentment, humiliation, anger):** a passenger sits near you wearing a black armband with a large swastika on it.

There are many acts which, being directly injurious only to the agents themselves, ought not to be legally interdicted, but which, if done publicly, are a violation of good manners, and coming thus within the category of offences against others, may rightfully be prohibited. Of this kind are offences against decency; on which it is unnecessary to dwell . . . (Mill: 109).

It would, in fact, have been interesting to dwell a while on these activities, for Mill's argument is hardly consistent with the harm principle. Sex in public is not (normally) 'injurious' to the participants but most people, even if they themselves are not offended, would probably accept that it should be prohibited. The basic point is that Mill has no serious discussion of offensiveness.

Feinberg groups instances of offensiveness under six categories, but a simpler distinction would be that between immediate and mediated offence. *Immediate offence* is offence to the senses. Imagine the neighbours from hell: they party and play loud music all night; they have a rusting car in their front garden and pile up household refuse – which stinks – in the back garden. These things hit the senses – sight, sound, smell. Mediated offence is when a norm or value is violated: the swastika is only offensive if you associate it with Nazi Germany, and with the implication that the person wearing the armband sympathises with what happened in Nazi Germany (it is not offensive when, for example, it is found in decorations on buildings predating the 1930s – the swastika is an ancient South American symbol, and is also a Hindu symbol).

Cutting across the distinction between immediate and mediated offence is the question of intentionality: is an act offensive if it is unintended? It is quite possible that a person 'gives offence' without intending to do so – once it is realised that the 'offence' is unintended then it may cease to be offensive. Using these two pairs of distinctions there are four possible types of offensiveness, as shown in the next box.

(a) Intended immediate offence	**(b)** Intended mediated offence
(c) Unintended immediate offence	**(d)** Unintended mediated offence

If there are grounds for restricting freedom then it would not normally apply to (d). Some restriction – although it must be proportional – on immediate offence may be justified. Intended mediated offence is much more problematic. Take the case of Steve Gough, the so-called 'Naked Rambler'. Gough took seven months to walk naked – except for boots and a hat – from Land's End to John O'Groats, that is, from one end of Britain to the other. He was arrested 17 times and spent two brief terms in prison. He has a website on which he says he is engaged in a 'celebration of the human body and a campaign to enlighten the public, as well as the authorities that govern us, that the freedom to go naked in public is a basic human right' (www.nakedwalk.co.uk). Clearly, what he did was illegal, but the question is whether it should have been, and whether there ought to be a 'human right' to go naked in public. If what he did was offensive, then most likely it was mediated, rather than immediate, offence (it would be immediate offence if people found him physically repulsive).

The difficulty with mediated offence connects up with the last of the principles: harmless wrongdoing (and to the judgment in the Operation Spanner case). What offends us depends on our values, and in a pluralistic society people disagree about what is of value. The best approach may be to distinguish public and private, where 'public' need not be narrowly defined as 'behind closed doors' but is a space in which people might legitimately expect certain things to happen. For example, Germans are more tolerant of public nudity than the British and indeed have a whole movement based around it – *freie Körper Kultur* (FKK) – such that, weather permitting, there is widespread nakedness in German public parks. There is, therefore, a *legitimate expectation* that if you stroll through a German park you will come across naked people, but that tolerance would not be extended to a Gough-type character striding along the highways of that country. In this sense German parks, although public in an everyday sense, constitute a 'private space' in a philosophical sense.

Harmless Wrongdoing

This is the most difficult principle to grasp. In part, the difficulty lies in its formulation: if 'wrongness' is defined as 'that which is harmful' then harmless wrongdoing is a contradiction in terms. It may however be that a distinction is being made between, on the one hand, right/wrong, and, on the other, good/bad. In everyday speech, we use these pairs interchangeably, so right equals good, and wrong equals bad. But philosophers do make a distinction between (a) **rightness**, or that which is obligatory, and (b) **goodness**, or an end that we should pursue. For example, if we obey the law we are doing right – we are fulfilling our obligations – but 'doing right' tells us nothing about *why* we do right. We might obey the law from purely self-interested reasons, or we might obey it because we recognise that other people matter – they have interests just as we have interests. Goodness is a quality of character, whereas rightness is a quality of behaviour. For this reason, it would be better to use a different label to that of 'harmless wrongdoing'.

In Mill's lifetime a view was articulated – by James Fitzjames Stephen (Stephen, 1873) – that to permit an 'immoral' act is equivalent to allowing an act of treason to go unpunished: the good of **society** was at risk. This view was rearticulated in the 1960s by Patrick (Lord) Devlin (Devlin, 1965) in response to the recommendation of a commission (Wolfenden Commission, 1957) that laws on homosexuality should be liberalised. Devlin argued that there was a 'shared **morality**' and that permitting 'immoral acts' in private threatened that morality (Devlin: 13–14). There was a danger of social disintegration. At first sight, Devlin's argument appears simply to be the claim that no action is completely self-regarding, and, of course, we have discussed a revised Millian response, which is to suggest that fundamental interests must be at stake for an action to be deemed harmful. Devlin's argument is however a little more sophisticated: actions may not have discernible harmful effects, but cumulatively they erode social norms, and that erosion is *seriously* harmful. But this still seems to be concerned with harm. A number of objections have been raised to Devlin's argument (what has become termed the 'social cohesion thesis'): (a) He was wrong about homosexuality; (b) Is there really a shared morality? Don't people disagree about morality? (c) Even if there is a shared morality does permitting 'private immorality' undermine it?

What is worth reflecting on is whether there is something in Devlin's argument that cannot be captured in a debate dominated by the concept of harm. The problem with the concept of harm is that it always requires identifying harms to *particular* individuals or groups, whereas there may be a good which cannot be reduced to identifiable individuals or groups; this might be an image of society which guides people to behave in a certain way. We can call this a *free-floating good* because although it is the product of human experience it cannot be reduced to the interests of individuals, or even groups. It could be argued that no society will survive unless it pursues some goods and the protection and promotion of these goods provide the justification for restricting human freedom. (One could also argue that we have an obligation to future generations to reproduce these goods, that is, reproduce a particular kind of culture.) If certain things are objectively valuable then any rational mind, contrary to Mill's fallibility argument, will recognise them to be so. John Finnis, in his book *Natural Law and Natural Rights*, observes that almost all cultures, despite apparent differences between them, exhibit a commitment to certain goods. He cites anthropological research (although, unfortunately, fails to give any reference for that research), suggesting that almost all cultures value the following: human life and procreation; permanence in sexual relations; truth and its transmission; cooperation; obligation between individuals; justice between groups; friendship; property; play; respect for the dead (Finnis, 1980: 83–4).

Stephen, Devlin and Finnis would not reject the idea that people should have a sphere of freedom ('private sphere'), but would maintain that it is a function of the state to change human behaviour, and that law should reflect morality. This position is termed **legal moralism**. For example, Finnis has been a vocal critic of laws which treat homosexuals and heterosexuals equally, arguing that equal treatment implies that they are equally valid: a position he rejects, maintaining that homosexuality is contrary to natural law. There is a parallel between legal moralism and the judgment made in the Operation Spanner case. Recall that the judgment maintained that consent was a necessary *but not a sufficient* condition for permitting another person to harm you, for the activity in which you are engaged must have some intrinsic value. This suggests that the men involved in sadomasochism have to justify the practice of sadomasochism. Legal moralists would argue that such an activity cannot be justified: it is a sexual perversion – that is, a misdirection of the libido on to an inappropriate object.

pp. 47–48

The difficulty with legal moralism is that it assumes more than just a shared morality – it assumes a shared conception of what is *ultimately valuable*. Many defenders of freedom would agree that we need a shared morality – respecting other people, and not harming them without their consent, is a moral position. But such a morality leaves open many questions of what is truly valuable in life – individuals, it is argued, must find their own way to what is valuable. This does not mean that there are no objectively valuable ends, but simply that coercion, by definition, will not help us to get there: the state can stop people harming one another, but it cannot make people good.

Smoking Ban Reconsidered

We can now apply the framework discussed above to the case of the smoking ban. It should be stressed that this is a case study and that we could have selected many other examples – it is important that political theory raises *general* arguments applicable across *different* cases. In popular debate a common attitude to the smoking ban is: 'I'm not a smoker, so it doesn't bother me'. This is an inadequate basis for supporting the ban. Any ban must be supported by reasons that could be advanced by smokers and non-smokers alike – this is what we mean by a general argument.

To be fair to those engaged in popular debate, there is often an implicit recognition that reasons and principles are at stake that extend further than the smoking ban itself – when people get beyond the simple statement made above and actually engage in debate they use analogies. An opponent of a ban might say 'if you ban smoking, then why not ban the consumption of fatty foods'; a proponent of a ban might respond by pointing out that the analogy is false because there is no direct harm to others involved in the consumption of fatty foods. The point is that both proponent and opponent are attempting to apply general arguments to specific cases. Without necessarily realising it, they are engaging in political theory. So in the spirit of seeking general arguments that can be applied to the ban, let us apply the freedom-limiting principles discussed in Criticisms and Developments to the smoking ban (the last – harmless wrongdoing – is not really applicable to this case).

Harm to Others

We argued that Mill's harm principle needs to be revised so that harm is defined as serious harm, and suggested that the temporary discomfort of being in a smoky environment cannot constitute harm – although if you follow the popular discussion around the smoking ban the immediate discomfort from smoking is a common theme. If we do revise Mill's harm principle along the lines just suggested – that is, damage to a person's long-term interests – we still have a problem: your action in itself may not harm another person. If you go to a particular bar just once, and sit by the bar chain-smoking for a couple of hours, then your action will not kill the barman. Accepting for the purposes of the argument that passive smoking can kill, and that working long shifts in a bar puts a person in harm's way, then the barman will still contract cancer without your two-hour period of chain-smoking. The paradox is that if the barman comes into contact with thousands of people during his career *no single one of them* will be responsible for his death. This is Sorites Paradox: millions of grains of sand make a heap of sand, subtract a grain and you still have a pile, keep subtracting and you will end up without a pile, but no single grain makes the **difference** between a pile and no pile. So we have to make a second revision to the harm principle: your action (smoking in a bar) belongs to a set of actions (thousands of people smoking in that bar) which together cause harm.

Consent

This brings us to the second part of the harm to others principle: harm to others does not, for Mill, in itself constitute grounds for restricting freedom. Rather, it must be *non-consensual* harm to others that triggers a restriction. This is where debates about the effects of passive smoking slightly miss the point: we could agree that passive smoking is harmful, or, if we are not sure, we could adopt the 'precautionary principle' – we assume, until we have the evidence, that if smoking is harmful to the smoker, then sustained contact with cigarette smoke in an enclosed environment will be harmful to non-smokers. So let us just accept that passive smoking is harmful. That in itself does not justify a ban on smoking bars because non-smokers might consent to be harmed. That then shifts the debate to the meaning of consent: do low-paid bar staff consent? Maybe they have no meaningful alternative to working in a bar or club. If so, an alternative to a complete ban would be a licensing scheme.

A variant on the 'we-don't-consent' argument is that a group of friends, consisting of smokers and non-smokers, have no choice but to go to smoking bars and clubs. Of course, the reverse would also be true if there were only smoke-free bars. But there is a deeper point: should the state be responsible for individual relationships? Is it really the role of the state to 'enable' non-smokers to go to a bar with smoker friends? Should the state be responsible for your social life? A more weighty objection to the consent argument is that it assumes that by entering a bar a non-smoker *intends* to be among smokers, rather than entering a building in which he knows he will have to *tolerate* smokers. If you go into a boxing ring you intend to participate in an activity in which harm is intrinsic to the activity – you do not intend to get brain damage, but such damage is part-and-parcel of boxing. To make the equivalent case for consent to go into a smoking pub, you would have to say that smoking is an intrinsic part of pub life – it goes with the 'craich' as the Irish (no longer) say.

Harm to Self

Much of the argument in favour of banning smoking is not just to prevent harm to others, but is a public health measure intended to reduce the number of smokers. For some anti-smoking campaigners this seems to be the main objective of a ban. If it were not an objective then licensing rather than banning would be the obvious policy to adopt. Is the aim of reducing the amount of smoking justified? Some points in favour:

(a) It is a relatively soft form of paternalism – making the sale or use of tobacco illegal would be the hard measure.
(b) Smokers, it is claimed, want to give up – the ban will help them.
(c) Even if smokers do not want to give up it is in their interests to stop smoking.

The last argument is the core paternalist one. The state is saying to smokers – we are doing this for your own good. There are several arguments against paternalism, some of which we have discussed in relation to Mill's argument. First, paternalist actions by the state rest on the assumption that the state knows better than the individual what is in her interests. Sometimes there are good grounds for believing this to be so, but more often the choices individuals make are part of a complex that are more immediately accessible to the individual – for example, smoking may be a means of relieving tension, or, despite its health and financial costs, simply a pleasurable activity. Second, there is a 'slippery slope' objection: if the state decides that smoking is bad for the individual and for that reason it should be banned, then why not ban other unhealthy habits or dangerous activities? Paternalistic intervention erodes the sphere in which individuals make choices, whether or not those choices are 'good'. Third, and possibly the most philosophically significant, paternalism implies that agents cannot be persuaded that an activity is harmful – if the *coercive* power of the state is employed to *prevent* people behaving in certain ways then this implies that a society cannot be rational.

Offensiveness

Some people find smoking offensive – could this be a ground for banning it? Most likely it is the immediate 'offensiveness' of smoking that would create the basis for banning it. If you look at comments made by 'ordinary people' some of them describe smoking as a 'disgusting habit'. One advocate of a complete smoking ban, commenting on the inadequacy of having demarcated smoking areas, likened bars with segregated smoking areas to a swimming pool in which one lane is reserved for people to urinate in. Presumably this analogy was intended to convey the problems of restricting the harmful effects of smoking to one area of a bar, but perhaps it also reveals his disgust at smoking.

Summary

We have explored both freedom of expression and action, using Mill's harm principle as the starting point. That principle is not as 'simple' as Mill suggests, and to address the complexities of freedom we have discussed further liberty-limiting principles: harm to self, offensiveness, 'harmless wrongdoing'. It is for the reader to assess the validity of these different principles, but it is clear that a discussion of freedom must at least address the charge that the harm principle is inadequate as an explanation of the limits of freedom. Freedom is certainly regarded as a 'positive' word and this may reflect an underlying belief not just of political theorists, but also 'ordinary people', that although freedom must on occasion be limited we assume freedom to be a good thing – there is a 'presumption in favour of freedom'.

Questions

1. If the protection of a person's interests is so important should the state permit a person to harm him- or herself?
2. If the protection of a person's interests is so important should the state permit a person to consent to be harmed by somebody else?

3. Should the fact that someone finds an expression or action offensive be a reason for banning that expression or action?

4. Are some activities 'intrinsically bad' and therefore can they justifiably be banned?

References

Berlin, I. (1991) 'Two Concepts of Liberty' in D. Miller (ed.), *Liberty* Oxford: Oxford University Press.

Devlin, P. (1965) *The Enforcement of Morals* London: Oxford University Press.

Feinberg, J. (1985) *The Moral Limits of the Criminal Law*, Vol. 2: *Offense to Others* New York: Oxford University Press.

Finnis, J. (1980) *Natural Law and Natural Rights* Oxford: Clarendon Press.

MacCallum, G. (1991) 'Negative and Positive Freedom' in D. Miller (ed.), *Liberty* Oxford: Oxford University Press.

Mill, J.S. (1991) *On Liberty and Other Essays* (ed. John Gray) Oxford: Oxford University Press.

Further Reading

Apart from Mill's *On Liberty*, the best starting points for a further exploration of freedom are Tim Gray, *Freedom* (London: Macmillan, 1991), George Brenkert, *Political Freedom* (London: Routledge, 1991), and David Miller (ed.), *Liberty* (Oxford: Oxford University Press, 1991), which is a collection of important essays on freedom, and Alan Ryan (ed.), *The Idea of Freedom* (Oxford: Oxford University Press, 1979), again a collection of essays. Also useful, but arguing a line, is Richard Flathman, *The Philosophy and Politics of Freedom* (Chicago and London: University of Chicago Press, 1987). Matthew Kramer, *The Quality of Freedom* (Oxford: Oxford University Press, 2003), is far from introductory, but is interesting, especially as he stresses the measurability of freedom. Two books that explore 'autonomy', which is a concept cognate to freedom, are: Richard Lindley, *Autonomy* (Basingstoke: Macmillan, 1986) and Robert Young, *Personal Autonomy: Beyond Negative* and *Positive Liberty* (London: Croom Helm, 1985). Specifically on Mill, the following works are useful: John Gray, *Mill on Liberty: A Defence* (London: Routledge, 1996); Gerald Dworkin (ed.), *Mill's On Liberty: Critical Essays* (Lenham: Rowman & Littlefield, 1997); C. L. Ten, *Mill on Liberty* (Oxford: Clarendon Press, 1980); Nigel Warburton, *Freedom: An Introduction with Readings* (London and New York: Routledge, 2001). See also John Skorupski, *John Stuart Mill* (London: Routledge, 1989), and relevant essays in John Skorupski (ed.), *The Cambridge Companion to Mill* (Cambridge: Cambridge University Press, 1998).

Weblinks

- There are some interesting sites that attempt to 'measure' freedom in different countries. Obviously there are philosophical issues here, such as whether we can say one society is more free than another without making judgements about the value of different freedoms. The best-known site is http://www.freedomhouse.org/

- There are many libertarian sites. Although they define freedom in a controversial way their websites are interesting. You should take the test (the 'world's smallest political quiz') on this one: http://www.self-gov.org/

- There are a couple of good websites on John Stuart Mill: http://www.jsmill.com/ and http://www.utilitarianism.com/jsmill.htm

Chapter 3

Equality

Introduction

Equality is a fundamental political concept, but also a very complex one. While the core idea of equality is that people should be treated in the same way, there are many different principles of equality. To provide a coherent defence of equality requires putting the various principles in order of priority, and explaining what it is that is being equalised: is it income, or well-being, the capacity to acquire certain goods, or something else? Equality, or particular principles of equality, must then be reconciled with other political values, or principles, such as freedom and efficiency. For that reason, this chapter is primarily conceptual, in that it aims to set out a number of principles of equality, and explain the relationships between them. The discussion will necessarily refer back to Chapter 2 (Freedom), and forward to Chapter 4 (Justice).

Chapter Map

In this chapter we will:

- Provide, in summary form, a scheme setting out various principles of **equality**: formal equality, moral equality, equality before the law, equal liberty and equal access, material equality (**equality of opportunity**, equality of outcome and **affirmative action**).

- Discuss, in more detail, those principles.

- Consider the relationship between freedom and equality.

- Draw out the implications for theories of **justice** – these will be discussed in greater detail in Chapter 4.

What do People Deserve?

The chances are that anybody reading this book will either be on above-average income or be in the process of acquiring the skills that will generate such an income. Studies have shown that in Britain graduates earn, over a lifetime, 49 per cent more than people with only school-leaving qualifications (A levels and equivalent) and 209 per cent more than those without any qualifications (www. prospects.ac.uk). Precise percentages will vary, but studies from other European countries, and North America, reveal a similar picture. Do graduates *deserve* this advantage? If we go back a stage we could also ask whether those graduates deserved their university places. A common response to this question might be: it depends on what family advantages they had. Two students may have the same entry qualifications, but if one has a relatively disadvantaged family background, while the other is relatively advantaged, the former might be thought more deserving than the latter. The difference in attitude rests on a distinction between naturally derived and socially derived advantages: natural ability, such as intelligence, is widely considered a legitimate basis for distribution, and any inequality that results from the exercise of intelligence is justified, whereas benefiting from socially inherited advantages, such as an expensive schooling, is regarded as illegitimate. In addition, what a person does with his or her natural abilities is thought morally relevant: people deserve to keep what they have acquired through their own efforts. Of course, this belief in 'meritocracy' – IQ + effort – need not be absolute; most people would support an *unconditional* minimum set of resources.

Before moving on, ask yourself the following questions:

- Should university places be distributed simply on the basis of performance in public examinations, or should other factors, such as socio-economic background, be taken into account?
- How far should the state go in trying to create equality of opportunity?
- Should people with fewer natural abilities get extra state-funded educational resources?

Principles of Equality

The term 'equality' is widely used in political debate, and frequently misunderstood. On the political left, equality is a central value, with socialists and social democrats aiming to bring about if not an equal **society**, then a more equal society. On the political right, the attempt to create a more equal society is criticised as a drive to uniformity, or a squeezing out of individual initiative. However, closer reflection on the nature of equality reveals a number of things. First, there is no one concept of equality, but rather, as indicated in Figure 3.1, a range of different forms. Second, all the main ideological positions discussed in this book endorse at least one form of equality – formal equality – and most also endorse one or more 'substantive' conceptions of equality. Third, principles of equality are often elliptical, meaning that there is an implicit claim that must be made explicit if we are to assess whether the claim is valid. To explain, since human beings possess more than one attribute or good, it is possible that equality in the possession of one will lead to, or imply, inequality in another. For example, Anne may be able-bodied and John disabled. Each could be given equal amounts of resources, such as healthcare, and so with regard to healthcare they are treated equally, but John's needs are greater, so the equality of healthcare has unequal *effects*. If Anne and John were given resources commensurate with their needs, then they would be being treated equally in one sphere (needs) but unequally in another (resources). The recognition of this plurality of goods, and therefore spheres within which people can be treated equally or unequally, is essential to grasping the complexity of the debate around equality and inequality. What is being distributed – and, therefore, what we are equal or unequal in our possession of – is termed a 'metric'.

Ch 17: Difference, pp. 429–30

The most useful starting point for a discussion of equality is to set out a number of forms of equality, in the shape of a flow chart. It is simplified, but the 'flow' of the chart is intended to reflect progressive controversy over different concepts and principles of equality. The first concept – formal equality – is uncontroversial, for it

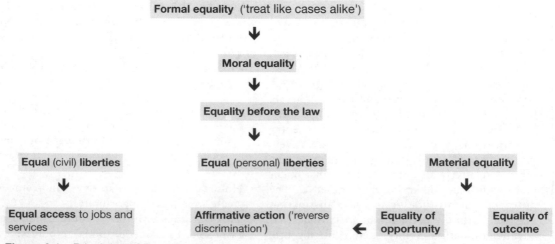

Figure 3.1   Principles of Equality

is tautological. Equality of outcome is, arguably, the most controversial. Although this claim is open to dispute, we would also argue that each form presupposes the previous one, so for example equality before the law assumes a belief in moral equality. The point is that you could plausibly stop at equality before the law and reject further principles of equality, but you cannot endorse the idea that people are equal before the law unless you also accept some idea of moral equality.

Each form is discussed in more detail in the course of the chapter, but an initial outline of each will help elucidate the connections between them.

- **Formal equality** To say we should treat like cases alike states nothing more than a tautological truth. If two people are alike in all respects then we would have no reason for discriminating between them; of course, no two people are alike, and the principle is indeed 'formal' – it does not tell us how to treat dissimilar people. Racists do not violate the principle of formal equality, because they argue that racial groups are not 'similar' and so need not, or should not, be treated in the same way.

- **Moral equality** The concept of moral equality is sometimes presented in negative form as a rejection of natural **hierarchy**, or natural inequality. In many societies it is taken for granted that people are, in important respects, deserving of equal consideration. Much discussion in political theory – especially in the dominant **liberal** stream of the discipline – is about the characterisation of moral equality, which, paradoxically, can take the form of *justifying inequality*: that is, if people are morally equal, how do we explain their unequal treatment in terms of the distribution of social goods, such as income. The very idea that such inequality must be justified assumes that people are morally equal – in a society where there is an overwhelming belief in natural inequality, such as, say, a **caste society**, it would simply not occur to those in a higher stratum that they must justify their advantaged position, or that those in a lower stratum should question their subordinate position.

Fascism in Germany, pp. 295–301

- **Equality before the law** That laws apply equally to those who are subject to them is widely accepted as a foundational belief of many, if not most, societies. It could be argued that this applied even in Hitler's Germany. After the 1935 Nuremburg Laws were passed Jews (as defined by the state) were denied many **rights**, but consistent with 'treating like cases alike' it could be argued that **legal equality** was respected insofar as all members of the class defined by the state as Jews were treated alike: all were equally subject to the laws, despite the laws themselves being discriminatory. However, we argue in the section on Legal Equality that equality before the law is a stronger idea, which implies that there must be compelling reasons for unequal treatment.

Contract-arianism, pp. 170–5

- **Equal liberty** A common assumption, especially on the right, is that equality and liberty (freedom) conflict. Certainly, if we were in Hobbes's state of nature, and enjoyed 'pure' liberty, that is, we were under no duties to refrain from behaving as we choose, then the exercise of liberty would reflect natural inequalities, including any bad luck that might befall us. But under a state, while our liberty is restricted, the possibility exists for a degree of protection (through 'rights'), such that a space is provided in which we are free to act without the danger of other people interfering in our actions. Once we move from pure liberty to protected liberty an issue of distribution – and, therefore, a trade-off between equality and liberty – arises. Although the state cannot distribute the *exercise of choice*, it can distribute *rights* to do certain things. Of course, even though liberty-protecting rights can be distributed this does not mean that equality and liberty never conflict (we discuss possible conflicts in the section on Equal Liberties).

- **Material equality** The most significant disputes in many societies are connected with the distribution of income, and other tangible material goods, such as education and healthcare. To understood this debate requires a discussion of **class**, because the capacity to acquire material goods is to some extent, and perhaps a very great extent, conditioned by structures that individuals do not control. From birth – and even before birth – a person is set on a course, at each stage of which she has some power to gain or lose material goods, but, arguably, the choices are restricted. Put simply, a person born into a wealthy family has more opportunities than someone with a poor background.

Civil Rights Movement pp. 476–7

- **Equal access** If a society places barriers in the way of certain groups acquiring material goods, such as jobs and services, as happened with regard to blacks in the Southern States of the United States until the 1960s, then equal access is denied. On the face of it, guaranteeing equal access may appear closely connected with material equality, but, in fact, it has more to do with equal civic and political rights, or, *liberty*: the liberty to compete for jobs, and buy goods.

- **Equality of opportunity** unlike equal access, *is* a principle of material equality, and although it commands rhetorical support across the political spectrum, in any reasonably strong version it has significant implications for the role of the state in individual and family life. If a society attempts to guarantee the equal opportunity to acquire, for example, a particular job, then it is going much further than simply removing legal obstacles to getting the job. Realising equal opportunity would require, among other things, substantial spending on education. Indeed, given the huge influence that the family has on a child's prospects, to achieve equal opportunity may entail considerable intervention in family life.

- **Equality of outcome** Critics of equality frequently argue that egalitarians – that is, those who regard equality as a central political principle – want to create a society in which everybody is treated equally irrespective of personal differences, or individual choice. This is a caricature, for it is possible to argue for equality of outcome as a prima facie principle, meaning that we should seek as far as possible to ensure an equal outcome consistent with other political principles. Equality of outcome may also function as a 'proxy' for equality of opportunity: if there are significantly unequal outcomes, then this indicates that there is not an adequate equality of opportunity. This last point leads us into a consideration of affirmative action.

- **Affirmative action** This term originated in the United States and is an umbrella term covering a range of policies intended to address the material deprivations suffered by (especially) black Americans, but also gender inequalities. Although it embraces a wider range of policies, it is often used as a synonym for 'reverse discrimination', or 'positive discrimination'. Examples of reverse discrimination include the operation of quotas for jobs, or a reduction in entry requirements

Exercise

Before discussing these forms of equality in more detail, it is useful to consider a range of attitudes to inequality. Below are listed a number of 'sources' of inequality – that is, character-istics, conditions, or events that may result in unequal treatment or unequal relationships. Looking at each in turn, and *considering the views of people you know*, would you say the weight of opinion is for or against each one as a legitimate ground for unequal treatment:

- **racial characteristics** (however 'race' is defined)

- **gender**

- **disability**

- **intelligence**

- **social class** into which a person is born

- **unpredictable bad luck,** such as being involved in an accident

- **predictable bad luck,** such as losing money as the result of a poor investment or career choice.

for college places. Reverse discrimination is best understood as operating somewhere between equality of opportunity and equality of outcome: the principle acts directly on outcomes, but is intended to guarantee equality of opportunity.

Moral Equality

Moral Autonomy and Moral Equality

That people are morally equal is a central belief – often implicit rather than explicit – of societies influenced by the Enlightenment (post-Enlightenment societies). Sometimes people talk of 'natural equality', but this has connotations of natural law – the belief that moral principles have a real existence, transcending time and place. Moral equality can, minimally, be understood as a negative: people should be treated equally because there is no reason to believe in natural inequality. In Chapter 2 it was suggested that in post-Enlightenment societies there was a presumption in favour of liberty, meaning that people should be free to act as they wish unless there was a good reason for limiting that freedom. Parallel to the presumption in favour of liberty, there is also a presumption in favour of equality – people should be treated equally unless there is a strong reason for treating them unequally. But the negative argument does not adequately capture the importance of moral equality: to be morally equal, that is, worthy of equal consideration, implies that you are a certain kind of being – a being to whom reasons, or justifi-cations, can be given. This reflects the roots of the concept of moral equality in the Enlightenment, which challenges authority, and assumes that the human mind is capable of understanding the world. Among the political implications of this philosophical position are, first, that the social world is not 'natural' – inequality must be justified and not dismissed as if it were simply the way of the world. Second, the Enlightenment stresses that human beings are *rational* – they are capable of advancing and understanding arguments, such that justifications for equality, or inequality, are always given to *individual* human beings.

It is a standard starting point of **liberalism** – but also of other ideologies such as **socialism, anarchism, feminism**, and **multiculturalism** – that coercively enforced institutions must be justified to those who are subject to them (although anarchists conclude that coercion cannot be justified); that is, subjects should in some sense consent to those institutions. Since it is unrealistic to think we can reach unanimity on how society should be organised, we must assume a moral standpoint distinct from the standpoints of 'real people'. The most famous recent elaboration of this idea can be found in the work of John Rawls. Rawls asks us to imagine choosing a set of political principles without knowing our identities – that is, we do not know our natural abilities, class, gender, religious and other beliefs, and so on. This denial of knowledge constitutes what Rawls calls the 'veil of ignorance': because the individual does not know his or her identity he or she must, as a matter of reason, put him- or herself in the shoes of each other person and people are necessarily equal. The idea of equality in Rawls's theory is highly abstract, and the use of the veil itself tells us little about how people should be treated. To generate more concrete principles of equality – that is, principles further down the flow chart – Rawls makes certain claims not implied by the veil of ignorance, and in that sense he goes beyond moral equality; nonetheless, the starting point for Rawls is a situation of moral equality.

pp. 240–3

Rawls, pp. 85–7

While Rawls draws strongly egalitarian conclusions from the idea of moral equality, other political theorists, while endorsing the idea of moral equality, derive rather different conclusions. Robert Nozick, in his book *Anarchy, State, and Utopia* (1974) argues that individuals have strong rights to self-ownership, and they enjoy these rights equally, and for that reason there are certain things we cannot do to people, including taxing their legitimate earnings, where **legitimacy** is established by certain principles of justice. We discuss Nozick's theory in more detail in Chapter 4, but the point is that a commitment to moral equality can lead in different directions in terms of whether or not we accept further principles of equality.

Moral Inequality: a Caste Society

We can better understand moral equality by comparing it to a social and political system in which people are assumed to be morally *unequal*. Although there is much debate among historians and anthropologists about its nature, a caste society would appear to be based on natural inequality. The most famous caste system is associated with Hindu society, especially India. Derived from the Portuguese word for lineage (*casta*), caste in Hinduism is based on four principal classes, Brahmans, Kshatriyas, Vaishyas, and Shudras, with the 'untouchables' outside the caste system, and so literally outcastes. From the standpoint of a discussion of moral equality and inequality, the caste system's key feature is that it fuses social position with moral responsibility. The caste into which a person is born is determined by his karmic influences, or behaviour in a previous life.

Each caste has a colour – white for Brahmans, red for Kshatriyas, yellow for Vaishyas, blue for Shudras – each of which may have racial overtones, but as likely has its origins in the association of each colour with a type of occupation, with the Brahman having the right to teach the sacred texts, the Kshatriyas responsible for security and justice, the Vaishyas concerned with trade and land cultivation, with the lowest caste, the Shudras, allocated the most physically demanding work. The outcastes may have developed as a class due to the prohibition on the castes dealing with the killing of animals and animal waste – traditionally, outcaste groups have worked as butchers and tanners, and refuse-collectors, hence the term 'untouchables'. Within the Varna caste system, there operates a *jati* sub-caste system. The Jati was a guild system, regulating employment within each caste – unlike caste, *jati* can be changed with relative ease.

The caste system could be understood to be a means by which evident inequality – in material possessions and social standing – is justified, but it is not justification *to each individual*; if you question your status as a Shudras, then you might be told that your actions in a previous life have determined that status, but there is nothing that you can do *in this life* which can change that status. In this sense, inequality is naturally determined, and caste stands opposed to the Enlightenment ideal of moral autonomy and equality. While caste is a fact of life in India it is explicitly rejected as the basis of citizenship, with the Indian Constitution outlawing caste, and government policies being geared to improving the position of *dalits* ('untouchables' or 'outcastes').

Today, caste discrimination is considered by many to be akin to racism, and India was criticised for refusing a discussion of it at the 2001 UN Conference on racism, held in Durban, South Africa. Caste is, however, an interesting phenomenon and it is worthwhile considering what is objectionable about it. The most obvious are its effects in terms of the treatment of people. One of the most extreme examples of its consequences was the hanging of two teenage lovers from different castes by villagers in 2001 in the province of Uttar Pradesh. But discrimination in employment and services is an everyday occurrence, even if caste is not legally institutionalised in the way that race was in Apartheid South Africa. Another objection – or perhaps observation – is that caste discrimination creates incongruous situations: in large cities, such as Mumbai (Bombay), people from different castes will work alongside one another, and a lower caste person may hold a much superior position. The incongruity of a more skilled and higher-paid person being regarded as inferior in some 'ultimate sense' should force people to consider the validity of caste stratification. Finally, caste, like **race**, is objectionable because the person assigned to a particular caste has no control over his membership of that caste; to believe in natural inequality based on caste (or race) implies a rejection of human autonomy.

With these objections in hand we can, however, ask whether forms of discrimination widely considered to be compatible with moral equality are really so. If caste and race are unacceptable because they are not within the power of individuals to change them, then surely the same can be said of intelligence, and yet intelligence is not only considered an acceptable basis for discrimination, but a laudable one. In the exercise you were asked to reflect on the attitudes of people you know to different grounds for inequality: racial characteristics; gender; disability; intelligence;

class origins; unpredictable bad luck; predictable bad luck. Your conclusions will depend to some extent on your society and **culture**. In many societies, racial discrimination is rejected as fundamentally incompatible with respect for human autonomy, and it may be thought unacceptable even to pose the question of whether race could be an acceptable ground for unequal treatment (for that reason, we asked you to reflect on other people's attitudes, rather than your own). Racism seems intuitively wrong, and by '**intuition**' we mean an immediate judgement, which does not entail or require reasons. Nonetheless, it is important to consider why race is unacceptable, because the same reasons may lead us, on reflection, to reject those bases for inequality widely accepted as legitimate, such as intelligence.

We suggested that caste was wrong because a person was incapable of changing his caste status, and so to construct a society around caste is to deny human autonomy, or human choice. For many political theorists 'choice' is a central concept in determining which inequalities are acceptable: if you end up in an unequal situation then that is acceptable so long as you are responsible for it. Using the idea of choice, or autonomy, sources of inequality can be grouped: (a) natural endowment – this includes your genetic make-up, and natural abilities, such as intelligence, or good looks, or robust health; (b) socially determined endowment – your class background insofar as this is beyond your control; (c) everyday 'brute' bad luck, such as being disabled as the result of an accident; (d) choice, including predictable bad luck. Ronald Dworkin, a leading US legal and political theorist, argues that choice must be a legitimate basis for inequality: distribution must be choice-sensitive, meaning that (a), (b) and (c) are not acceptable grounds for unequal treatment, while (d) is acceptable (Dworkin, 2000: 287–91). In arguing for this position, Dworkin is going much further than moral equality, but the main point is that his argument for those further principles of equality is based on a particular conception of moral autonomy and moral equality: we respect people by not discriminating against them as a result of characteristics beyond their control, but also by holding them responsible for the consequences of their choices. We return to this distinction later in the chapter.

Legal Equality

We need now to move from moral equality to more specific principles of equality, although the concept of moral equality must always be in the background. A starting point for building up a more substantial political theory would be to distinguish the 'core' legal–political institutions from broader socio-economic institutions. In most societies, but especially liberal–democratic ones, the core institutions of the state are divided into legislature, executive and judiciary. Put simply, the legislature creates laws, the executive administers powers created through law, and the judiciary interprets and enforces the law. But a social institution is any large-scale, rule-governed activity, and can include the economic organisation of society, such as the basic rules of property ownership, and various services provided by the state that extend beyond simply the creation and implementation of law. We will deal with the wider concept of a social institution later, but in this section we will concentrate on the narrower concept.

As indicated in Figure 3.1, we need to distinguish 'equality before the law' and 'equal civil liberties'. To be equal before the law is to be equally subject to the law, whereas to possess civil liberties is to be in a position to do certain things, such as vote or express an opinion, and obviously we are equal when we possess the same liberties. There is, however, a close relationship between equality before the law and equality of civil liberties, and a historical example will help to illustrate this point. On 15 September 1935 the German Parliament (Reichstag) adopted the so-called 'Nuremberg Laws' governing German citizenship, one of which defined German citizenship (citizenship law, or Reichsbürgergesetz). The law made a distinction between a subject of the state (Staatsangehöriger) and a citizen (Reichsbürger). Article 1 stated that 'a subject of the state is one who belongs to the protective union of the German Reich', while Article 2 stated that 'a citizen of the Reich may be only one who is of German or kindred blood, and who, through his behaviour, shows that he is both desirous and personally fit to serve loyally the German people and the Reich'. Only citizens were to enjoy full, and equal, political rights. The First Supplementary Decree (14 November 1935) classified subjects by 'blood', and denied citizenship to Jews, where Jewishness was defined by the state.

It could be argued that these citizenship laws are compatible with equality before the law, since all subjects are equally subject to the law, despite the fact that the laws are themselves discriminatory (and much the same argument could be applied to the laws of Apartheid South Africa). While on the face of it this argument appears valid, and seems to show how weak both the idea of moral equality and equality before the law are, there are grounds for arguing that Nazi Germany could not maintain that all subjects were equal before the law. US legal theorist Lon Fuller, writing in the early post-war period, observed that Nazi law was not really law at all because it violated certain requirements for any legal system. For Fuller, the essential function of law is to 'achieve **order** through subjecting people's conduct to the guidance of general rules by which they may themselves orient their behaviour' (Fuller 1965: 657). To fulfil this function law (or 'rules') must satisfy eight conditions:

1. The rules must be expressed in general terms
2. The rules must be publicly promulgated
3. The rules must be prospective in effect
4. The rules must be expressed in understandable terms
5. The rules must be consistent with one another
6. The rules must not require conduct beyond the powers of the affected parties
7. The rules must not be changed so frequently that the subject cannot rely on them
8. The rules must be administered in a manner consistent with their wording.

Fuller's argument is not uncontroversial, and many legal theorists will reject these rules, but it is plausible to maintain that a condition of a 'law' (so-called) being a law is that is not arbitrary. Since the first article of the penal code of Nazi Germany asserted that the will of the Führer was the source of all law, it was impossible for subjects to determine what was required of them. Once it is accepted that law cannot be arbitrary then certain conditions follow, including at least a minimal idea of equal basic civil liberties. Chief among the civil, or political, liberties are the right to vote and to hold office; significantly, both these rights were explicitly denied to 'non-citizens' in the Nuremberg Laws (Article 3, First Supplement).

There are other theories of law that do not rest on what Fuller terms an 'internal morality', and which presuppose neither moral equality nor equal liberties. Legal theorist John Austin characterised a 'law' as a general command issued by a 'sovereign' (or its agents). The 'sovereign' is that person, or group of people, who receives 'habitual obedience' from the great majority of the population of a particular territory. So whereas Fuller would argue that (most) Nazi laws were not really laws at all, Austin would have identified Hitler as the sovereign, who, insofar as he commands obedience, issues 'valid' law. This does not mean that his laws were moral: Austin made a sharp distinction between legality and morality. The relationship between morality and legality will be discussed in later chapters, and especially when we turn to the topic of human rights.

Equal Liberties

pp. 440–4

As suggested above, the state cannot directly distribute choice, but it can distribute the conditions for choice by granting individuals rights, or 'civil liberties'. In liberal democratic societies the most important rights, or liberties, are freedom of expression, association, movement, and rights to a private life, career choice, a fair trial, vote, and to hold office if qualified. A couple of points are worth noting. First, it is difficult to distribute liberty per se; rather, what is distributed are specific rights-protected liberties. Second, you can have freedom without that freedom being recognised by the state, for no state can exercise complete control. However, when we talk about the distribution of liberty, it is not so much the freedom itself which is being distributed, but rather the *protection* of that liberty – if Sam is guaranteed that he will not be thrown in jail for expressing views critical of the state, but Jane is not given that guarantee, then clearly Sam and Jane are not being treated equally. It is the 'guarantee' – the right to free expression – rather than the expression itself which is up for distribution. The separation between the 'guarantee' (protection of the capacity to choose; right to choose) and the action that is guaranteed does not hold for all liberties. In Figure 3.1 we distinguished between personal and civil liberties; among the latter are rights to participate in the political system. For example, voting – a 'participatory' rather than a 'private' or 'personal' right – is something which is clearly susceptible to *direct* distribution in a way that the freedom to marry whoever you wish (a 'private' right), or not get married, is not (you can, of course, still choose not to vote). Some people can be awarded extra votes than others, or whole groups, such as workers or women, can be denied the vote.

Do Freedom and Equality Conflict?

Freedom (or liberty) necessarily entails choice, and individuals must make choices for themselves. It would follow that the state cannot – and indeed should not – attempt to control individual choice. At best, it can affect opportunities to make choices through the distribution of rights. Does this mean that freedom and equality must necessarily conflict? In addressing this question we need to make a further distinction to the one already made between choice and the capacity, or opportunity, to make choices, so that we have a threefold distinction:

1. Choice, which must be under the control of the individual, and for which the individual can be held responsible.
2. Capacity, or opportunity for choice, which is not under the control of the individual, and for which the individual should not be held responsible.
3. Outcome of the choices of individuals, where outcomes are determined to a large degree by the interactive nature of choice.

Voting illustrates these points. You have a right to vote (2), which you may or may not exercise (1), but even if you exercise that right and vote for a party or a candidate, that choice may be less effective than another person's choice (3). It is less effective if your chosen party or candidate loses, but it might also be less effective in a more subtle way. Imagine that there is just one issue dimension, say the distribution of wealth, with the left supporting high tax and a high degree of redistribution of wealth, and the right supporting low taxes and a low degree of redistribution. These represent the two extremes and there are various positions in between. Voters are ranged along this axis from left to right. Consider the voter distributions shown in Figures 3.2 and 3.3.

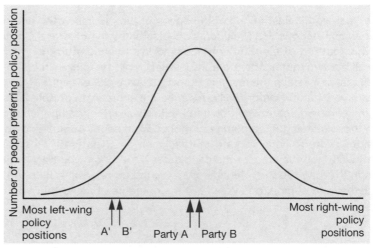

Figure 3.2 One-dimensional policy competition between two parties with voter preferences concentrated in the centre of the policy spectrum. From Laver 1997.

If there are just two parties then to maximise its vote a party has an incentive to adopt a policy position as close to the median voter as possible. This is the case even under Figure 3.3 where the median voter is in a tiny minority. The point is that where you locate yourself relative to other voters will determine how effective your vote is. Equality (or inequality) of outcome is therefore the result of an interaction between the choices of many individuals, and it is impossible to protect freedom of choice and at the same time guarantee equality of outcome.

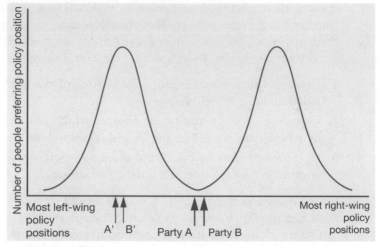

Figure 3.3 One-dimensional policy competition between two parties with voter preferences concentrated in the centre of the policy spectrum

Swing States

There are 'real-world' illustrations of the power of the median voter, one of which is the conduct of US Presidential elections. US Presidents are elected by the Electoral College and not directly by the people (this method of election is discussed in the case study at the beginning of Chapter 8). Because all but two states operate a 'winner takes all' system election campaigns focus on a small number of states in which the result is likely to be very close, and that therefore might 'swing' either way: even a very narrow victory will guarantee the entire slate of delegates. In the 2004 Presidential Election the campaign narrowed down to Pennsylvania, Florida and Ohio.

Within those states huge amounts of money were spent persuading small numbers of people to switch sides. Voters living in safe states, such as Utah (safe Republican) or New York (safe Democrat) were not pestered by the candidates – for those who hate politics this may have been a relief, but in the long run the interests of key swing groups will take priority over the great majority. There may be 'one person, one vote', but the outcome of using that vote varies greatly, depending on where you live.

The relationship of freedom to equality will be discussed in greater detail in Chapter 4, where the focus is on theories of justice – the aim here is simply to introduce the problem and encourage some reflection on it. At this stage it would be useful to consider two thought experiments (see Exercise opposite), the first of which is taken from the work of Robert Nozick, and the second from G. A. Cohen (the work of both theorists is discussed in greater detail in Chapter 4).

Let us consider, first, Nozick's example. If we measure equality by the number of marriage partners available then there is an unequal distribution: A and A' have the greatest number of options, and Z and Z' the fewest options. And if freedom is

Nozick: Marriage Partners

Imagine 26 men and 26 women, one for each letter of the alphabet. Each person wants to marry, and each of the 26 men has the same preference ordering of the women as the others, and likewise each of the 26 women has exactly the same preference ordering of the men. So if we name each person by a letter of the alphabet A, B, C, etc. for the men, and A', B', C', etc. for the women, each man prefers A' to B' and B' to C' and so on, down to the last preference Z'. Likewise, each of the women prefers A to B and B to C, etc., down to Z. That means that all the women want to marry A, and so A has plenty of choice! Likewise, with regard to the men A' has a full range of options. B and B' have one less option, but still a lot of choice, and so on, down to Z and Z' who have no choice but to marry one another (Nozick, 1974: 263–4). **Question:** are Z and Z' denied (a) freedom, and (b) equality?

Cohen: The Locked Room

There are ten of us in a locked room. There is one exit at which there is a huge and heavily locked door. At roughly equal distances from each of us there is a single heavy key (each of us is equally distant from the door). Whoever picks up the key (each is physically able to do so) and with very considerable effort opens the door can leave. But there is a sensor that will register when one person has left, and as soon as he or she leaves the door will slam shut and locked and nobody else will be able to leave – *forever* (Cohen, 1979: 22). Question: Are we free to leave?

understood as choice, then arguably Z and Z' have no freedom, because they have no choice but to marry each other. But, perhaps, the relevant liberty is determined by the relationship of each person to the *state*: in relation to the state Z and Z' have as many options as A and A'. It is the conjoint choices of individuals that creates an inequality of outcome. Nozick can legitimately maintain that Z and Z' are as free as A and A' because his starting point is the concept of a natural right (to self-ownership); that right will always be held equally regardless of how individuals exercise the right. Nozick's example shows rather more dramatically what we suggested earlier about the differential consequences of voting – each person has a vote, but the effects of exercising that vote vary.

We turn now to Cohen's locked room. If, prior to anyone leaving, a voice from outside asked each in turn 'are you free to leave?' then we would be forced to say 'yes'. If we – plural – were asked whether we were free, the question is more difficult. Collectively, we are not free to leave: *each* is free to leave but *we* are not free to leave. Once again, conditionality is at work, but Cohen draws a different conclusion to that of Nozick from this conditionality. Working with certain Marxist assumptions, Cohen argues that a collectivist political order – one in which there is a much more equal distribution of income – would, in effect, enable more people to leave the room. In 'real-world' terms, that means workers losing their subordinate class position. Unlike Nozick, Cohen is concerned with the choices people actually make, rather than their legal position vis-à-vis the state.

pp. 98–102

Material Equality

The example of inequality in the outcome of voting preferences illustrated problems of distributing political power, and certainly political power is a major good, but the most involved debates, both in everyday politics and in political theory, concern themselves with the distribution of material goods, such as income, or education, or healthcare. In liberal societies respect for equality before the law and equality of liberties is fairly well embedded in the political culture – while there is controversy over *particular* liberties, the majority of the population expresses support at least for the *principles*. The same cannot be said for principles of material equality. As was suggested in the section on Principles of Equality, while lip-service is paid to equality of opportunity, that term encompasses a great many possible principles of resource allocation, some of which entail radical state intervention in individuals' lives. More often than not, what is being advocated is equal access to jobs and services rather than equality of opportunity.

Equal Access

Equal access is sometimes referred to as 'formal equality of opportunity'. Equal access requires that positions which confer advantages on their holders should be open to all, and that the criteria for award of those positions is 'qualification(s)'. The qualifications required must be publicly acknowledged and intrinsically related to the position. The list of illegitimate grounds for denial of access to a position has gradually expanded, but in, for example, European Union countries, it would include: gender, race, ethnic or national origin, creed, disability, family circumstance, sexual orientation, political belief, and social or economic class. This list, which is not comprehensive, provides prima facie guidance on equal access.

It may be that certain of those characteristics are relevant to a job. For example, the priesthood in the Catholic Church is restricted to men, and normally unmarried, celibate, men. Employment in a women's refuge would normally be restricted to women. Legislation outlawing gender discrimination will contain clauses that permit what appears, at first glance, to be discrimination, but which may, in fact, be consistent with gender equality. We argued at the beginning of the chapter that there was a presumption in favour of equal treatment – people should be treated equally unless there were compelling grounds for unequal treatment. The nature of work in a women's refuge obviously provides compelling grounds, consistent with gender equality: since the client group in a refuge is seriously disadvantaged, women employed in the refuge are working towards a more gender-equal society. However, the restriction of the priesthood to men is more problematic and reveals the limits to equal access; this may not be a criticism, for we can say that because equality conflicts with other values, or principles, it necessarily has limits.

The 'compelling reason' for setting aside gender equality in the case of the priesthood is derived from the importance of the equal liberties (or freedoms), among which is freedom of **religion**. Since freedom of religion requires that adherence to a church is voluntary, the church could be said to constitute a private sphere in which consenting adults should be free to act, and that includes being free to discriminate. However this argument, if extended to other spheres of life, would corrode equal access: if churches can discriminate, then why not other employers? It is to block off the claim that firms, universities, shops, sports centres and so on are private spaces in which people should be free to discriminate, that anti-gender-discrimination legislation defines the public sphere widely. Churches are given a special exemption because of the interconnectedness of theological belief with employment: the very nature of the institution requires an all-male priesthood. This contrasts with, say, a restaurant where the customers may have a simple gut preference for eating with people of their 'own kind', and so seek to deny access to ethnic minorities. Nonetheless, there is a legitimate debate to be had over the correct limits between the public and private spheres: if you are renting out your house for a year while you go abroad, should you not be free to choose who occupies the house, where that choice might take the religion or **ethnicity** or marital status or sexual orientation of putative tenants into account? Other people may justifiably condemn your selection criteria, but taking liberty seriously may entail the recognition of a private sphere in which a person is free 'to do wrong'. On the other hand, it might be legitimate to prevent a landlord with a string of properties from applying discriminatory criteria in selecting potential tenants. We are not arguing for a particular line between public and private, but simply identifying a potential limit to the application of the equal access principle.

pp. 52–3

Equality of Opportunity

Equal opportunity is a much stronger principle of equality than equal access: as the name suggests, it requires that opportunities for acquiring favourable positions are equalised. This principle is attractive across the political spectrum because it seems to assume a **meritocracy**. The case study introduced at the beginning of this chapter was intended to test intuitive reactions to 'deserved' and 'undeserved' advantages. In Britain there is much popular debate about the social composition of the student bodies in the highest-rated universities. Students educated at fee-paying schools, or at state schools with relatively wealthy 'catchment areas', make up a disproportionately large part of the student intake of these universities. Even on the political right this situation is condemned: the brightest students, rather than the wealthiest students, should get, it is felt, the most desirable university places.

Although politicians disagree about the causes and the solutions to this situation, there is agreement that equal access alone does not ensure a meritocratic outcome. The difficulty is that an 18-year-old student has eighteen years of education and socialisation behind her – every day she has been presented with 'opportunities' that a peer may have been denied. Those opportunities will include the emotional support necessary to achieve self-confidence and a sense of self-worth, stimulating conversation that enables her to develop a range of linguistic skills, interesting foreign holidays and activities, the presence of books in the family home, the imposition of a degree of parental discipline sufficient to encourage self-discipline, family networks and contacts, a good diet, and the provision of an adequate workspace. This list could go on, and none of these items relate to formal educational provision. Even parents who do not send their children to fee-paying schools may pay for such things as ballet classes or piano lessons. In short, every day of her life for the previous eighteen years she has been given opportunities. To equalise such opportunities would require a very high degree of intervention in family life.

This description of a privileged child may overstate the requirement for an equalisation of opportunity. Perhaps it is not necessary that children have strictly equal opportunities, but rather that each child has a sufficient degree of opportunity to acquire advantageous positions. The idea is that there is a threshold level of opportunity below which a child should not fall. (Although it is not a serious objection to the threshold theory of equal opportunity, there would inevitably be dispute over the correct threshold.)

Another point about equality of opportunity is that the principle presupposes that inequality can be justified, so long as any inequalities are the result of desert. In the case study we distinguished social advantage, native ability (intelligence) and effort. It is a commonly held view that 'IQ + effort' is an appropriate ground for discrimination, and that equal opportunity policies should endeavour to eliminate social advantage as a cause of inequality. But Rawls argues that people no more deserve their native abilities, including their propensity to hard work, than they do those advantages gained from their family and social background (Rawls, 1972: 104). Other theorists, such as Ronald Dworkin and David Miller, argue that Rawls's rejection of desert is inconsistent with other important aspects of his theory, which stress the importance of choice and responsibility (Dworkin, 2000: 287–91; Miller, 1976: 131–55). Nonetheless Dworkin (especially) seeks to eliminate *natural ability* as a justification for inequality, while retaining responsibility for choices made. In this respect both Rawls's and Dworkin's arguments are significantly at variance with popular attitudes. This is an observation rather than a criticism – in Chapter 4 we discuss Rawls's argument in more detail.

Equality of Outcome

Equalisation of outcome seems, on the face of it, neither desirable nor coherent. It is not desirable because it would deny individual choice, and responsibility: if one person chooses a life of leisure and another person chooses a life of hard work why should the state seek to equalise the outcome of those choices? The outcome may not, in fact, be susceptible to equalisation. If income level is the 'metric' subject to distribution, then the outcome can be equalised *for that metric*; but 'welfare' (or 'well-being') is also a relevant metric, and the person living a life of leisure has presumably enjoyed greater well-being than the hard worker, such that the only way the two can enjoy an equal level of well-being is if they had not lived their respective lives of leisure and hard work. The point is that equality is always equality *of something*, and the attempt to equalise along one metric, say income, may result in inequality along another metric. Another difficulty with attempting to achieve equality of outcome is that some goods are 'positional'; for example, an expensive school is valued not simply because it seems to provide better facilities, smaller classes, and stronger discipline, but because it is perceived as socially superior, and it can only be superior if there is a limited supply of that type of school. Only a small number of schools can be like Eton in England, or Groton in the United States, such that if there was a substantial increase in public expenditure on schools not every school will be an Eton or a Groton.

pp. 89–91

Despite these objections, equality of outcome can play a role in political debate even if it cannot be made to work as a principle. Rawls justifies inequality by use of the difference principle, but that principle rests on recognising that any inequalities must be to the benefit of the worst off. This argument takes equality of outcome as the baseline against which alternative distributions are to be measured; in effect, Rawls maintains that moral equality generates equality of outcome, but may also generate inequality of outcome if the worst off consent to that inequality. Equality of outcome has, therefore, a special moral status in Rawls's theory. It should be noted that if Rawls recognised desert as a legitimate source of inequality this tight connection between moral equality and equality of outcome would not hold.

Rawls does not, in fact, defend equality of outcome as a substantive principle. Anne Phillips, however, does defend this principle of equality. Much of Phillips's work has been concerned with political representation, and especially the under-representation of women and ethnic minorities in political institutions, and she takes the case of women in parliament as an example of the need for a principle of equal outcome. The under-representation of women in the British Parliament cannot, she argues, be attributed to lack of ability, or the conscious choice not to enter politics, but must be a consequence of the failure of equal opportunity (Phillips, 2004: 8). Women are not denied equal access to parliamentary representation, and many political parties now have dedicated support for female candidates, which include women's officers, training days, support networks, and the requirement to have at least one woman on every short list for candidate selection in a particular constituency. But the only political party that has been successful in increasing female representation in the House of Commons (the elected chamber) has been the British Labour Party, and that success can be attributed to 'all-women' short lists imposed on local constituencies by the central party. The point being that all-women short lists guarantee an increase in the number of candidates in Labour-held or winnable seats – the policy acts on outcomes and not on opportunities. The inequality of outcome in the other political parties is an indication that, despite various efforts, equality of opportunity has failed.

pp. 327–39

Affirmative Action

Affirmative action policies involve an explicit departure from the normal 'equal access' and 'equal opportunity' criteria for awarding a person a favoured position. The normal criteria include: (a) the position is open to all, and (b) selection is by competence, which is measured by qualifications. There are various types of affirmative action policies:

- **Encouragement** The job is advertised in newspapers read by particular communities, such as ethnic minorities.

- **Tie-breaking** If two people are 'equally qualified' then you choose the person from the 'disadvantaged group'. This is the weakest form of affirmative action.
- **Handicapping** An example of this would be requiring higher entry points, or grades, for applicants to university from wealthy backgrounds.
- **Quota system** A certain percentage of jobs must be filled by a particular group – this is usually subject to a requirement of minimum competence.

All-women short lists are a version of the quota system and involve a setting aside of (a), and some critics would argue that it also entails setting aside (b). Affirmative action could, however, be defended on grounds that the evidence of qualification for a position cannot be taken as an accurate indication of a person's competence. To illustrate this point, let us imagine that entry to a good university normally requires 20 points in a school-leaving exam. Person A, from a poor background, scores 17 points, and person B, from a wealthy background, scores 21 points. However, evidence from the performance of previous cohorts of students suggests that '(economically) poor students' with lower entry points achieve a better final result on graduation than 'wealthy students' with higher entry points, and so person A is predicted to do better than B, and therefore 'objectively' is better qualified. Interestingly, this argument is meritocratic, and indeed is a 'technical', rather than a philosophical, objection to other principles of equality: existing evidence of competence is not reliable, so we have to broaden selection criteria to include prospective performance based not on the individual applicant's past behaviour but on the statistical behaviour of students from his 'background'. But distribution is still tied to the actions of individuals.

There are other ways of understanding affirmative action: it may be intended to provide role models; compensate a *group* for past injustices; increase the level of welfare of a disadvantaged group. Some defences are backward-looking, in that they seek to redress something that happened in the past; other defences, such as the one discussed above – prospective student performance – are forward-looking. A common, everyday objection to affirmative action is that it undermines respect and creates resentment: if a person achieves a position through 'positive discrimination' then others may not respect him, while the apparently better-qualified person passed over for the position will resent what seems an unfair selection procedure. This objection, whether or not valid, does identify an important aspect of equality (and inequality): there is an intersubjective dimension to human relationships, such that inequality can result in a lack of respect. Where that inequality seems unconnected to a person's actions – that is, when you end up in an unfavourable position regardless of what you have done – there is a feeling of *resentment* rather than simply disappointment. This suggests that equality should not be understood merely as a mathematical question of who gets what, but is intimately connected to other concepts, such as autonomy, responsibility, and well-being.

Summary

We have surveyed a number of principles of equality, and sought to put them into some kind of order. A coherent defence of equality requires a number of things: (a) clear distinctions between different kinds of equality; (b) recognition that any principle of equality must explain what is being equalised, because equality in one sphere (along one 'metric') can result in inequality in another; (c) a scheme for connecting different principles of equality together; (d) an explanation of how equality fits with other political principles, such as freedom and efficiency. One of the tasks of a theory of justice is to connect and order different political values and principles and so the discussion in the next chapter follows directly from this one.

Questions

1. Must freedom and equality conflict?
2. Are there any valid positional goods?
3. Should those of below-average aptitude get more resources than those of above-average aptitude?
4. Should the family be abolished in order to ensure equality of opportunity?

References

Cohen, G. (1979) 'Capitalism, Freedom, and the Proletariat' in A. Ryan (ed.), *The Idea of Freedom* Oxford: Oxford University Press.

Dworkin, R. (2000) *Sovereign Virtue: The Theory and Practice of Equality* London and Cambridge, Mass.: Harvard University Press.

Fuller, L. (1965) 'A Reply to Professors Cohen and Dworkin' *Villanova Law Review*, 655.

Laver, M. (1997) *Private Desires, Political Actions: An Invitation to the Politics of Rational Choice* London: Sage.

Miller, D. (1999) *Principles of Social Justice* Cambridge, Mass. Harvard University Press.

Nozick, R. (1974) *Anarchy, State, and Utopia* Oxford: Blackwell.

Phillips, A. (2004) 'Defending Equality of Outcome' *Journal of Political Philosophy*, 12/1.

Rawls, J. (1972) *A Theory of Justice* Oxford: Clarendon Press.

Further Reading

- J. Roland Pennock and John Chapman (eds), *Equality* (New York: Atherton Press, 1967), is a useful collection of essays. Single-authored general works include: Alex Callinicos, *Equality* (Cambridge: Polity Press, 2000); John Rees, *Equality* (New York and London: Praeger, 1971). A longer, and more advanced, work is Larry Temkin, *Inequality* (New York and Oxford: Oxford University Press, 1993). Other interesting single-authored works include Anne Phillips, *Which Equalities Matter?* (Oxford: Polity, 1999) and Matt Cavanagh, *Against Equality of Opportunity* (Oxford: Clarendon, 2002), who challenges traditional assumptions about the nature of meritocracy. Amartya Sen, *Inequality Reexamined* (Oxford: Clarendon, 1992) stresses the importance of the 'equality of what?' question (the importance of identifying 'metrics'). James Fishkin, *Justice, Equal Opportunity, and the Family* (New Haven and London: Yale University Press, 1983) explores the family as a problem for equality. The most important contributions to the equality debate are gathered together in a couple of edited collections:

Louis Pojman and Robert Westmoreland (eds), *Equality: Selected Readings* (New York and London: Oxford University Press, 1997) and in Matthew Clayton and Andrew Williams, *The Ideal of Equality* (Basingstoke: Palgrave, 2000).

Weblinks

A large number of 'equality' sites are maintained by pressure and interest groups, or formal government bodies dedicated to increasing equality. It is interesting to see how the concept is used by these organisations; do not, however, expect sophisticated philosophical discussions. The best sites are those maintained by universities, which provide further links:

- Equality Studies Centre at University College, Dublin (Ireland): http://www.ucd.ie/esc/

- Cardiff University: http://www.cardiff.ac.uk/learn/try/equality/

- Human Rights and Equality Centre, University of Ulster (Northern Ireland): http://www.ulst.ac.uk/hrec/hrec_otherlinks.phtml

Chapter 4

Justice

Introduction

Should people who are intelligent, or good-looking, or naturally charming, be allowed to keep whatever they gain from their exploitation of those natural attributes? Should people be free to pass on their material gains to whoever they choose? If it is a good thing for parents to care about their children, then why should they not be allowed to benefit them? These questions go to the heart of debates about distributive – or 'social' – justice. Distributive justice is concerned with the fair – or 'just' – distribution of resources. In the early modern period, the focus was on property rights as the moral basis for the distribution of resources, and justifications for the state – that is, individuals' obligations to obey the state – were often grounded in the role the state played in protecting those rights. In this chapter we concentrate on contemporary theories of justice, in which private property rights are often regarded as problematic – although one of the three theories discussed is a contemporary restatement and defence of strong private property rights.

Chapter Map

In this chapter we will:

- Discuss an important *liberal egalitarian* theory of justice – that of John Rawls.

- Contrast Rawls's theory with a *libertarian* alternative, advanced by Robert Nozick.

- Consider a major challenge to both theories – that of Gerald Cohen, who argues from a *Marxist* perspective.

- Apply these theories to real-world examples of distributive justice.

A Neet Solution?

Charles Murray, a US social theorist, has observed that Britain is a generation behind the United States in experiencing and addressing the consequences of the development of a social underclass, which he dubs the 'neets': 'not in education, employment or training' (*The Sunday Times*, 27 March 2005). Strongly correlated with single parenthood, Murray claims that attempts in the USA to solve the problem of the Neets through state intervention have failed. Pre-school socialisation programmes, 'enrichment programmes' for older children, guaranteed jobs for the unskilled, on-the-job training, schemes to prevent school drop-out have all produced a few 'heart-warming' success stories, but hard statistical data has demonstrated their failure. That the existence of this underclass is, for Americans, a 'dog that no longer barks' can be explained by tough penal policies and an aggressive reclamation of the cities. Streets have been cleared of beggars, schools are de facto socially segregated, graffiti has been cleared from walls, and, most importantly, the prison population has increased to 2 million (Britain would have to imprison 250,000 – compared to the present 80,000 – in order to match that). Murray predicts that by 2020, the slogan 'prison works' will be accepted across large parts of the political spectrum in Britain.

The implications of Murray's 'solution' to social inequality is that those born into the underclass cannot be saved. He accepts this is unfair; because life is a lottery, it is just bad luck to be born into the social underclass. For political theorists this is a crucial issue, and at the heart of the discussion of this chapter.

- Before reading the rest of the chapter, consider whether you agree with Murray's thesis and his solution to the 'problem'. His article can be found here: http://www.timesonline.co.uk/article/0,,2087-1543363_1,00.html

Theories of Just Distribution

Distributive justice is, as the name suggests, concerned with the just distribution of resources. Despite the mention of penal policy in the above case study, distributive justice must be distinguished from *retributive* justice, which is concerned with how a punishment fits a crime. What might be the basis for the distribution of wealth? Here are some possibilities:

- **Threat advantage** The amount a person earns is the result of that person's relative bargaining power.
- **Need** Everyone should have their needs satisfied – there should be a guaranteed minimum set of resources equivalent to that required to satisfy those needs.
- **Desert** If you work hard and as a consequence increase your earnings relative to others you deserve to keep those additional earnings.
- **Freedom** The pattern of distribution is the result of the choices people make – if you have a product that others *choose* to buy, in buying the product other people have *consented* to the income you gain from selling it, and therefore also to any resulting inequality.
- **Labour** The profit made from the sale of commodities should reflect the contribution that the producer (labourer) makes to the commodity.
- **Maximise utility** We should aim to maximise the overall level of utility in society; 'utility' may be defined as happiness or pleasure or welfare or preference satisfaction.
- **Equality** Resources should be distributed equally.
- **Priority to the worst off** The worst off should be as well off as possible.

Rather than run through all these options we will focus on the work of three thinkers – John Rawls, Robert Nozick and Gerald Cohen. In the course of the discussion comments will be made on all the above options.

How to read:

Rawls's *A Theory of Justice*

Students tend to find Rawls's *A Theory of Justice* a difficult read. Rawls has been criticised as a disorganised writer. However, the book does have a relatively clear structure. It is divided into three parts, nine chapters, and 87 sections. The first part sets out the theory in broad outline, with Chapter 1 a general introduction, Chapter 2 introducing the principles of justice, and Chapter 3 discussing the method by which those principles are derived. If you read nothing else, you should read the first four sections of the book (about twenty pages in total); beyond that the priority should be to read Part One. Part Two discusses the principles in more detail, and Part Three addresses issues relating to moral obligation, and the psychological aspects of adherence to principles of justice. Of the three parts, Rawls himself was least satisfied with the discussion of Part Three, and his later book – *Political Liberalism* (1993) – was, to a significant degree, a revision of it.

Biography   John Rawls (1921–2002)

A US academic, he spent most of his working life at Harvard University. Rawls is one of the most important political philosophers of the twentieth century, and his book *A Theory of Justice* (1971) is credited with stimulating a revival in the subject.

There are two 'biographical' points about Rawls directly relevant to our discussion. First, Rawls came from a relatively wealthy family, and had a powerful sense that wealth, or even 'natural assets' such as intelligence, cannot be the basis for a just distribution of resources, for we do not *deserve* our acquired and natural assets. It follows that the wealthy need to justify their wealth. Second, Rawls came from Baltimore (Maryland), which though not part of the Deep South was a Southern State. The sense of the *profound* immorality of slavery informs his work, and it is significant that his two 'heroes' were philosopher Immanuel Kant and President Abraham Lincoln, the former articulating the moral imperative to treat other human beings never merely as means but also as ends, and the latter leading the anti-slavery forces of the North in the American Civil War.

Rawls: an Egalitarian Liberal Theory of Justice

Rawls's book *A Theory of Justice* (published 1971) had a huge impact on political philosophy. In it he advances a method for making moral decisions about the distribution of resources – not just material resources, but also freedom and political power – and argues that the operation of that method would result in a particular conception of justice, one which is significantly 'redistributivist' (or egalitarian).

Contract-arionism, pp. 170–5

Rawls locates his work in the social contract tradition of Locke, Rousseau and Kant, and indeed he is credited with reviving this tradition, which had gone into abeyance after about 1800. The 'classical' idea of the contract was that it was the device by which power was legitimated: it is rational from the standpoint of the individual to hand over some (most, all) of the 'rights' he enjoys in the 'state of nature' to a coercive authority. Rawls differs from the classical theorists by taking it for granted that social cooperation under a state is normally a good thing, and so the focus of his theory is not the justification of the state but the distribution of the 'benefits' and 'burdens' of cooperation under a state. The benefits are material goods, personal freedom and political power. The burdens include not only any inequality which may arise, but the fact that principles will be coercively enforced – we are required to obey the state.

Before we set out Rawls's method for choosing 'principles of justice' and discuss what principles would be chosen, two very important points must be made:

1. A theory of justice applies to what Rawls calls the 'basic structure' of society. There is some ambiguity about this concept, but for the purposes of the present discussion we can say the basic structure consists of those institutions that

fundamentally affect a person's life chances. Included would be the structure of the economy – the rules of ownership and exchange – and the provision of services such as health and education, as well as constitutional rights that define how much freedom a person enjoys.

2. While Rawls has been influential on the left of politics, he is a philosopher rather than a politician. What is at issue is the basic structure of society, and not the detailed policy decisions that may be made *within* that basic structure. Furthermore, Rawls is not aiming to persuade merely a majority of people to endorse his theory – he is not fighting an election – but rather offering arguments that no reasonable person could reject: he is aiming for *unanimity*.

The Original Position

Rawls's theory has two parts: an explanation of how we decide what is just, and a discussion of what he believes we would decide is just. We start with the first part. Rawls employs what he terms the original position. The original position is a thought experiment – you are asking a 'what if' question: what if such-and-such were the case? It is not a 'place' – you only 'go into' the original position in a figurative sense. The most important feature of the original position is the veil of ignorance: you *do not* know your class and social position, natural assets and abilities, strength and intelligence, particular psychological characteristics, gender, to which generation you belong, who your family and friends are, and perhaps most controversially of all, your conception of the good – that is, your ideas about what makes life valuable or worth living, such as your religious and philosophical beliefs, but which are not necessarily shared by other people (Rawls, 1971: 12). You do know certain general things about your circumstances. You know you live in a society characterised by moderate scarcity: there are enough resources to satisfy basic needs and leave a significant surplus to be distributed, but that surplus is not sufficient to overcome conflict between people over its distribution. Rawls assumes that people want more rather than less of the benefits generated by cooperation. As well as knowing your society is marked by moderate scarcity you also have a general knowledge of psychology and economics.

Motivation in the Original Position

Rawls attributes to people in the original position a certain psychology, or set of motivations. It is important to stress that Rawls makes these assumptions *for the purposes of his theory*; he does not claim that 'real people' – that is, people who know their identities – have this psychology. In the original position the following holds:

- We *all* value certain things – what Rawls terms the (social) primary goods. The primary goods are rights, liberties, powers and opportunities, income and wealth, and the 'bases of self-respect'. The primary goods are valuable to many different ends, so if you choose a career trading in stocks and shares, or, alternatively, living in a self-sufficient community on a remote island you will value these things (Rawls, 1971: 93).

- You seek to *maximise* your share of the primary social goods (Rawls: 142).

- You are not a gambler. Rawls tries to avoid assuming a particular attitude to risk; nonetheless, the way the original position is set up would suggest that we would be 'risk averse' (Rawls, 2001: 106–7).
- You are not envious of other people (Rawls, 1971: 143).
- We are mutually disinterested: that is, we are not interested in one another's welfare. You do know, however, that once the veil has been lifted you will have family and friends who you do care about (Rawls: 144–5).
- We live in a 'closed society' – entered at birth and exited at death. Again, this point can easily be misunderstood. We do not know what principles of justice will be chosen – we have not got to that point yet – but it is highly likely that among the principles will be a right to emigrate. The reason Rawls assumes we live our whole lives in one society is that it makes the choice of principles very serious; John Locke argued that remaining in a society and using the state's resources – riding along the King's highway – constituted 'tacit consent' to the state. Rawls rejects that argument: for an individual to leave a society and seek asylum elsewhere (or migrate for economic reasons) is such a major step that 'deciding' not to seek asylum (or migrate) cannot be taken to constitute consent to the existing regime. This generates two motivational points: because the choice of principles is a serious one, we would (a) not gamble our interests (a point already made), and (b) we accept the chosen principles will be binding on us once the veil has been lifted – Rawls terms the acceptance of the principles the strains of commitment (Rawls: 145).

Locke,
pp. 175–7

It has probably struck you that there is something odd about the motivation of people in the original position. On the one hand, they are purely self-interested – they seek to maximise their individual shares of the primary goods. On the other hand, because they do not know their identities they are *forced* to be impartial, that is, each individual can only advance his or her interests by viewing the choice of principles from the standpoint of each individual. Expressed metaphorically, we have to put ourselves in each other's shoes.

Exercise

Imagine you do not know your age, gender, social class, what you look like, how intelligent you are, your beliefs (religious and philosophical views), who your family and friends are, and so on. The task is to get the best deal for yourself – the biggest income possible. Below is a table setting out a number of income distributions (A, B, C, D). These distributions represent average annual earnings for a whole lifetime (we use dollars in deference to Rawls, but you can choose any currency – it is the distribution that matters, not the absolute amounts). What you have to do is choose one. In making your choice, bear in mind the following:

- Because you don't know your identity you could end up in the top 10 per cent (decile) of earners, or the bottom 10 per cent, or anywhere in between.
- You care only about your own level of income – you are not envious of other people.
- You have got one shot – *whatever you choose is binding on you for the rest of your life.*
- Once you have chosen you will be told your identity.

Exercise

Table 4.1

Decile	Distribution A	Distribution B	Distribution C	Distribution D
Richest 10%	$210,000	$12,000	$158,000	$105,000
	$105,000	$12,000	$74,000	$61,000
	$61,000	$12,000	$53,000	$49,000
Everybody	$37,000	$12,000	$39,000	$35,000
in between	$29,000	$12,000	$31,000	$28,000
	$21,000	$12,000	$26,000	$25,000
	$16,000	$12,000	$22,000	$21,000
	$10,500	$12,000	$17,500	$18,000
	$5,000	$12,000	$13,000	$16,000
Poorest 10%	$1,000	$12,000	$4,000	$14,000
Average:	$49,550	$12,000	$43,750	$37,200

What would be Chosen in the Original Position?

Now we come to the second part of Rawls's theory: the choice of principles. Agents in the original position are completely free to choose whatever they wish, but Rawls does discuss some possible candidates (Rawls, 1971: 124). It should be noted that these are expressed in philosophical language – Rawls does not talk about choosing state socialism or a free market economy (we will say something about Rawls's attitude to socialism and capitalism at the end of the section):

1. Everyone serves my interests – I get what I want [first-person dictatorship].
2. Everyone acts fairly except me [free rider].
3. Everyone is allowed to advance his/her interests as s/he wishes [general egoism].
4. We maximise the aggregate level of goods [classical **utilitarianism**].
5. Option 4 but with a minimum level of goods for each individual.
6. We maximise the average (per capita) level of goods [average utilitarianism].
7. Option 6 but with a minimum level of goods for each individual.
8. Certain ways of life are to be privileged because they have greater intrinsic value [perfectionism].
9. We balance a list of prima facie valid principles, that is, we make an intuitive judgement about the correct trade-off between freedom and equality should they conflict [intuitionism].
10. The two principles of justice [democratic conception].

Ch 7:
Liberalism,
pp. 162–84

Rawls argues that we would choose option 10: the democratic conception. Options 1–3 are incoherent. Because you can only have one dictator we would never agree to dictatorship. Option 2 contradicts the strains of commitment, and 3 is unstable. Options 4–7 represent utilitarianism. Utilitarians hold that what we ought to do is maximise the overall *level* of well-being (or 'utility'). They are not concerned with the *distribution* of utility (although options 5 and 7 do give some weight to individuals – they create a 'floor' below which nobody should fall). Classical utilitarianism measures the level of welfare without reference to the number of utility-generating beings (we say 'beings' because non-human animals might generate utility), whereas average utilitarianism divides the level of welfare by the number of utility-generating beings. Compare the following two situations:

(a) 2,000 units of welfare divided by 500 beings;

(b) 1,000 units of welfare divided by 20 beings.

For a classical utilitarian (a) is superior to (b), whereas for an average utilitarian (b) is superior to (a): 50 units versus 4 units.

Perfectionists (option 8) hold that there are certain ways of life worthy of pursuit and the state should aim to bring these ways of life about ('perfect' means to complete, or bring to fruition). This argument does not have great significance for the distribution of income, but it certainly affects what amount of freedom we should have (it relates back to Chapter 2: John Finnis is one kind of perfectionist). Rawls argues that because we are denied knowledge of our particular conceptions of the good we would not opt for perfectionism; we would not, for example, choose to give a particular religion special status. Intuitionism (option 9) entails 'resolving' conflicts of values and interests on an ad hoc, case-by-case basis – we have no method for resolving them. The aim of Rawls's theory is to provide just such a method.

pp. 52–3

The Democratic Conception: the Two Principles of Justice

Rawls argues that agents in the original position would choose the democratic conception. He distinguishes between a special and a general conception, which are versions of the democratic conception. The general conception is: 'all social primary goods . . . are to be distributed equally unless an unequal distribution of any or all of these goods is to the advantage of the least favoured' (Rawls, 1971: 303). Rawls hopes that he can persuade the reader that the general conception would be endorsed even if the special conception, as one version of it, is rejected. The special conception consists of the two principles of justice. As Rawls's original presentation of the two principles was slightly confusing, we will use, in abbreviated form, his revised version from *Justice as Fairness: A Restatement* (Rawls, 2001: 42–3):

1. Equal liberty: each person is guaranteed a set of basic liberties.
2a. Equal opportunity: there must be equal access to jobs and services under fair equality of opportunity.
2b. Difference principle: inequalities are only justified if they benefit the least-advantaged members of society. (Also: just savings principle)

The first principle is a familiar one – each person has an equal right to free speech, association, conscience, thought, property, a fair trial, to vote, hold political office if qualified and so on. Principle 2a is also familiar – jobs and services should be open to all (equal access), but furthermore society should be so arranged that as far as possible people have an equal *opportunity* to get jobs and gain access to services.

2b – the difference principle – is the novel one, and it is the one we want to discuss. (The just savings principle relates to duties to future, unborn, not-yet-existing generations.)

Rawls maintains that there is a lexical priority of 1 over 2a and 2a over 2b. That means that you cannot sacrifice liberty for economic justice – you must satisfy fully the equal liberty principle before applying the difference principle (Rawls, 1971: 42–3). For example, the greatest source of unequal opportunity is the family – parents favouring their children – but Rawls argues that even though people in the original position are 'mutually disinterested' they do value personal freedom, which includes the freedom to form personal relationships, marry, have a family, and enjoy a 'private sphere' of life. They would, therefore, opt to protect this private sphere even if it resulted in unequal opportunity. Although Rawls's theory does not operate at the detailed level of public policy, he would probably have argued that, for example, outlawing private education contravenes the first principle of justice. On the other hand, he does support high inheritance tax, and that tax not only works directly against privilege but generates resources which can be used to fund an extensive state education system. Lexicality also entails that equal opportunity takes priority over the difference principle. Discrimination in access to jobs might improve the position of the worst off, but it would violate the equal opportunity principle.

Would we really Choose the Difference Principle?

If you consider the exercise on p. 87, we asked you to choose one of four distributions. Rawls argues that the rational strategy is to choose distribution D. The reasoning behind this is termed 'maximin': *maximum minimorum*, or the *maxi*misation of the *mini*mum position. Although Rawls avoids guessing individuals' attitudes to risk, only very risk-averse people would adopt maximin (D) over average utility (C).

It should be said that Rawls does have another argument for D over C, which does not follow from the exercise. The exercise presented a one-off 'time slice' of income, but in the original position we are not choosing a *particular* distribution but a *principle* of distribution, and the principles underlying C and D are quite different: C says 'maximise average expected utility' whereas D says 'maximise the position of the worst off'. There is a 'shifting sands' quality to C: it does not concern itself with any particular group in society, but is concerned only with the average income. It is possible that over time distributions could move quite dramatically and that compared to D the worst-off classes – not just the bottom 10 per cent – could become a lot worse off. D, on the other hand, always gives priority to the worst off.

Let us look at the other two distributions, and the reasoning that might lead to them. Maximax – maximise the maximum – is the reasoning leading to distribution A. This is a very risky strategy. One thing you might have noticed is that per capita income is higher in A than C, and thus one might think that the average utilitarian would opt for A over C. Note, however, we talk of *expected utility*. A maximiser wants to get the highest income possible – everybody, and not just a risk taker, wants to earn $210,000. However, each person knows that she has under distribution A only a 1/10 chance of earning that amount of money; she has a 1/10 chance that she will end up with $1,000 a year. The question is this: does her *desire* for $210,000 outweigh her *aversion* to earning only $1,000? Given certain facts about human psychology – the fact that the utility from an extra amount of income diminishes, the more income you have – she will reason that greater weight should be attached to the avoidance of lower incomes than the enjoyment of higher incomes. So finally we move to B. It is *relativities* that concern someone who opts for B. Rawls argues we are not envious, and therefore we are not concerned with what other people earn, so relativities are unimportant. It might, however, be argued that if one of the primary social goods is self-respect then any inequality will tend to undermine it: there is no easy answer to this, and it does seem that for 'real people' – as against people in the original position – self-worth is (to some extent) attached to income or social status. One possibility would be a trade-off between maximin and the avoidance of extreme inequality, but Rawls would argue that maximin is the best strategy if you were concerned about relativities.

Influences and Impact:

Rawls and Socialism

As suggested at the beginning of this section Rawls was a philosopher rather than a politician; nonetheless it is interesting to consider his relationship to socialism. You will have noted that the list of possible principles that might be chosen in the original position contained rather abstract philosophical positions, such as utilitarianism, perfectionism and intuitionism, and not more concrete economic systems, such as state socialism or free market capitalism. Rawls argued in *A Theory of Justice* that it was largely a technical judgement whether the two principles of justice would best be realised under a socialist or a capitalist system. However, most commentators interpreted Rawls as a 'welfare state capitalist' – the principles would best be realised in a society that combined the free market with a generous redistributive welfare state.

In his last book, *Justice as Fairness: A Restatement* (2001), Rawls indicated that the principles would be very difficult to realise under welfare state capitalism, because under capitalism there is a serious underlying inequality in the distribution of assets, such that transfers from rich to poor always take place *after* production, thus creating a tension between those who are taxed and those who benefit from taxation. Rawls argued for an alternative model, called a 'property-owning democracy' (Rawls: 135–40). In Britain that phrase was adopted by the right, under Prime Minister Margaret Thatcher, but Rawls derives it from economist J.E. Meade, whose theory was quite egalitarian. Meade maintained that inequality must be addressed 'at source', by ensuring that as many people as possible had 'productive assets', and that the state worked to prevent the transmission of privilege. In policy terms, what was required was considerable spending on education – directed particularly at those with less 'natural ability' – and very high inheritance tax.

Biography   Robert Nozick (1938–2002)

Like Rawls, Nozick taught most of his working life in the Philosophy Department at Harvard University. Born in Brooklyn, the son of Russian immigrants, he went on to study at the Universities of Columbia and Princeton.

In contrast to his colleague Rawls, his engagement with political philosophy was fairly short-lived – after the publication of *Anarchy, State, and Utopia* (1974) he concerned himself with other areas of philosophy, and he appeared to repudiate the claims he made in that book, although without engaging in a sustained self-critique. Nonetheless, despite his move away from political philosophy, the one book he did publish in that area has been enormously influential, and it is the work for which he is best remembered.

Nozick: a Libertarian Theory of Justice

Free Market Anarchists, pp. 243–5

Robert Nozick advanced an alternative to Rawls's egalitarian theory of justice; one that lays stress on the importance of private property rights. In his book *Anarchy, State, and Utopia* Nozick seeks to defend the notion of the state against philosophical anarchists, who argue the state can never be justified. But what he defends is a minimal state. A minimal state is a monopoly provider of security services. A more extensive state – one that intervenes in the economy and supplies welfare benefits – cannot be justified. 'Utopia' would be a world in which diverse lifestyles and communities would flourish under the protection of the minimal state.

Nozick's Starting Point: Private Property Rights

The very first line of *Anarchy, State, and Utopia* reads: 'individuals have rights, and there are things no person or group may do to them (without violating their rights)' (Nozick, 1974: ix). Jonathan Wolff argues that Nozick is a 'one-value' political philosopher (Wolff, 1991: 3–4). Other philosophers accept that there is more than one value; for example, they might maintain freedom is important, but so is equality, and since freedom and equality often conflict we need a method for 'resolving' that conflict. Rawls's *two* principles of justice express this idea. Wolff maintains that Nozick's 'one value' is **private property**, or, more precisely, the *right* to private property. When we use the term property in everyday speech we tend to think of real estate. Everyday usage is not wrong, but political philosophers have a wider conception of private property: it is the legally sanctioned (or morally legitimate) appropriation of things. A *right* is an advantage held against another person – if you have a right, then another person has a duty to do something (or *not* do something: that is, not interfere), so a right is a relationship between people. Bringing together the two concepts – private property and rights – we can say that a right to private property entails the exclusion of other people from the use of something. Nozick's 'entitlement theory' of justice is based on the inviolability of private property rights. There are three parts to the theory:

Part 1: **Just acquisition**

Part 2: **Just transfer**

Part 3: **Rectification**

Just Acquisition – Locke and Nozick

Biography, p. 176

The first question to ask is: how did anybody acquire the right to exclude other people from something? Nozick draws on the work of John Locke (1632–1704) and, specifically, his defence of private property, especially his argument for 'first acquisition'. We have to imagine a historical situation in which nobody owns anything, and then explain (justify) the parcelling up of that which has hitherto been held in common. The standard interpretation of Locke is that he was attempting to reconcile Christianity and capitalism at a time – the seventeenth century – when capitalism was beginning to replace feudalism as the dominant form of economic organisation. Locke began with three Christian premises:

1. God had entrusted the material world to human beings, who were its 'stewards' and thus had a duty to respect it.
2. The implication of 1. is that the world is owned in common by humanity.
3. God as creator had rights to what he created. As God's creatures human beings have a duty to God to preserve themselves.

Capitalism poses a challenge because it was wasteful of natural resources, which violates stewardship; capitalism implied private ownership and not common ownership, and it threatened to push large numbers of people into poverty and starvation, thus undermining their capacity to fulfil their duty to God to preserve themselves. For example, in seventeenth century England we begin to see the movement from smallholdings to large estates, with smallholders (serfs) forced to hire out their labour for a daily wage, thus becoming wage labourers. The creation of a class of rural wage labourers presaged the development of an urban working class with the industrialisation of the eighteenth and (especially) the nineteenth centuries. The risks of starvation were significantly greater for the wage labourers than for their earlier counterparts, the serfs.

Christian theology, Locke argued, did not strictly require common ownership, but rather the promotion of the common good, and capitalism, through its capacity to generate wealth, did indeed promote it (Locke, 1988: 291). Locke's starting point for a defence of capitalism is his account of how we go from common ownership to private ownership: if a person mixes his labour with something external to himself then he acquires rights in that thing. Mixing one's labour is sufficient to establish ownership so long as two 'provisos' are satisfied:

• **Sufficiency proviso** There must be 'enough and as good left for others' (Locke, 1988: 288).

• **Spoilage proviso** There must be no wasting away of the product (Locke: 290).

In practice these two provisos are easily met because of the development of wage labour and money (Locke: 293). Wage labour is premised upon the notion of having property rights in your own body – rights which you cannot alienate, that is, you cannot sell your body – but the product of the use (labour) of your body can be sold, such that your labour becomes a commodity which is hired out.

Wage labour is important for Locke because it enables the buyer of labour to say to the potential seller of labour (wage labourer) that you can acquire sufficient goods to preserve yourself if you sell your labour to me. If you do not, *you* (not me) are violating your duty to God to preserve yourself. Crucially – and of great significance for Marx – that labour does not create rights for the labourer in the product, since the labour which the labourer sells to the buyer is an extension of the buyer's body; Locke argued that 'the turfs my servant has cut are *my* turfs' (Locke: 289). Wage labour, therefore, satisfies the sufficiency proviso. Money deals with the spoilage proviso – a person's property can be held in this abstract form and thus will not 'spoil', unlike, say, crops, which rot, or animals, who die.

Nozick draws heavily on Locke's acquisition argument, but drops its theological basis. He begins with the assumption of 'self-ownership', that is, you own your body, and all that is associated with it – brain states, genetic make-up and so on, but this is no longer grounded in God's rights as creator. He then adopts Locke's mixed labour device, but he alters the provisos:

- **Sufficiency proviso** Locke was worried that there would come a point in the development of capitalism where some people really did not have enough to survive on, even with the possibility of wage labour. Nozick is not so concerned: so long as everyone is *better off* after appropriation then that appropriation is just (Nozick, 1974: 175–6).

- **Spoilage proviso** Nozick is not worried about 'spoilage', but he does insist that a person cannot acquire a monopoly control over certain goods, such as a water supply (Nozick: 180–1).

Exercise

Imagine a basketball match watched by 3,000 people, each of whom pay $20 to see Chamberlain play, and $8 of that $20 goes directly to Chamberlain (the $8 can be taken to be Chamberlain's marginal value: if he was not playing the organisers would have to sell the tickets at $12). Let us assume that each of the 3,000 spectators and Chamberlain earn $40,000. This is, of course, unrealistic, but it is intended to make a point. We can compare earnings – what Nozick calls 'holdings' – before and after the tickets were bought:

Table 4.2

	Spectators' holdings	Chamberlain's holdings
Before purchase	$40,000 × 3,000	$40,000
After purchase	$39,980 × 3,000	$64,000

Is there any reason why Chamberlain should not keep the $24,000 he has gained as a result of the ticket purchases?

Just Transfer

Just transfer is dependent upon just acquisition, for you cannot justly transfer what you have not justly acquired. Furthermore, acquisition is a very strong idea – it entails full control over the thing that is acquired, including the power to transfer it to another person. Nozick takes the example of Wilt Chamberlain (1936–99), considered by many to be the greatest basketball player of all time. Consider the exercise on page 94.

Nozick argues that so long as Chamberlain did not use threats or fraud to acquire each $8 then his additional earning is legitimately his by a simple transfer (Nozick, 1974: 161–3). The fact that such transfers will over time create significant inequalities – in the example we went from equality to inequality – is irrelevant, for what matters is that individuals have consented to the transfer. Those who object to such transfers want, in Nozick's words, 'to forbid capitalist acts between consenting adults' (Nozick: 163). To evaluate the force of Nozick's argument we need to compare his theory of justice with the alternatives.

Types of Theory

Nozick divides theories of justice up into two groups – end state and historical (Nozick, 1974: 153–5) – with a sub-division of the second into patterned and unpatterned theories (Nozick: 155–60):

End-state theories These theories are not concerned with what people *do*, but only with the *end result*. Utilitarian theories fall into this category – the aim is to maximise total, or alternatively, average utility. Who gets what under this arrangement is irrelevant: person A may get 25 units and person B 10, and the total is 35 (and average 17.5), but if A got 10 and B 25 the end result would be the same.

Historical theories What people have done (note the past tense) is relevant to the distribution of resources. For example, distribution according to desert, that is, hard work, is a historical principle (actually, 'historical' is a bad label – it would have been better, though less elegant, to talk of *person-regarding* theories, because it is not necessarily what a person has *done* that is relevant – need would be person regarding). Historical theories are further divided into:

- **Patterned** Any principle that involves the phrase 'to each according to _____' (fill in the blank: desert, need, labour and so on) is going to create a pattern (Nozick: 159–60). Nozick includes Rawls's theory as patterned: priority to the worst off (maximin) generates a pattern.

- **Unpatterned** Nozick calls his own theory unpatterned, because whatever distribution exists should be the result of choice. You could argue that this is patterned with the blank filled in as 'choice', but 'choice' is not really the same as desert or need – the latter two provide 'objective' criteria that can be used by a redistributive agency (the state) whereas you choose to do whatever you like.

Individuals may, under Nozick's utopian framework, aim to bring about an end-state or patterned distribution, but what may not happen is that the state *coerces* people into creating that end state or pattern. To appropriate some of Chamberlain's $24,000 is tantamount to forcing him to labour (Nozick: 172).

Influences and Impact:

Nozick and the 'New Right'

Although he was not the prime influence on the 'New Right', which emerged as a powerful political force in the 1980s – that role fell to philosopher Friedrich von Hayek (1899–1992) and economist Milton Friedman (born 1912) – Nozick did have a major impact within the academic community, and perhaps indirectly influenced politicians. Nozick provided powerful philosophical arguments for radically reducing the role of the state and 'setting people free'. Socialists, he argued, are obliged continually to interfere in our lives. Nozick was not, however, a *conservative* if by 'conservative' we mean a position which maintains that the state has a role to play in moulding human behaviour. Conservatives may offer qualified support for the free market, but they fear the consequences of too much freedom. Nozick, as a *libertarian*, argues that freedom is intrinsically good, and so he supported, for example, removing restrictions on recreational drug use and consensual sex.

Rectification

Nozick's comments on the third part of his theory are brief and underdeveloped. If something was acquired or transferred as the result of fraud or theft or force then some mechanism is required for rectifying the situation (Nozick, 1974: 152–3). All that Nozick offers in the way of a theory is the suggestion that counterfactual reasoning be applied: what would be the pattern of holdings if the unjust acquisition/transfer had not taken place? This raises the problem of increased value: if you steal a dollar and make a million dollars as a result, what should you pay back – the dollar or the million dollars? This is a live issue, for unlike Locke, who argued that the United States was 'unowned' prior to European colonisation (Locke, 1988: 299–301), Nozick argues that native Americans had rights to their land and these were violated and thus rectification is required. But Manhattan – whose only trace of native ownership is its name – has increased vastly in value since it was 'acquired' by Europeans: how do we rectify that injustice? Nozick provides no answer.

Cohen: a Marxist Perspective on Distributive Justice

Introducing
Marxism,
pp. 216–18

Marx's critique of private property has to be located in his theory of history: human beings have a drive to increase productivity, and this generates two struggles. The first is a struggle against nature, and the second a struggle between human beings. The two are related, for how we organise production will determine how effective we are at using nature to our advantage. Over time the particular structure of organisation – 'mode of production' – changes, but what characterises all modes is a class relationship in which one class exploits another. Exploitation is made possible by the unequal ownership of the two things that enable an increase in production: the means of production, and labour power. The former includes such things as factories and tools, while the latter consists of the skills of labour, both physical and mental. At the time at which Marx was writing – the mid-to-late nineteenth century – capitalism had emerged as the dominant mode of production. For Marx, the key features of capitalism are as follows.

- **Ownership** Under capitalism, in contrast to previous modes of production, every person owns his or her own labour power. However, a minority class – the capitalists, or bourgeoisie – own a monopoly of the means of production, with the consequence that the majority class – the working class, or proletariat – can survive only by selling their labour power to the capitalists.
- **Capital**, which can be defined as an 'expanding source of value', is unequally owned: one class (capitalists, or the bourgeoisie) are in a position to benefit from this expansion of value by virtue of their ownership of the means of production.
- **Exploitation** The true value of labour is not the price it commands in the market (the wage) but the amount of time that goes into the production of the commodity (labour value). The worker does not receive the full value of his product – the difference between the wage and labour value is the amount creamed off by the capitalist. This is what Marx means by exploitation.
- **Use value and exchange value** A distinction is drawn between the value we get from a commodity (use value) and its price (exchange value). Every commodity has a use value, but not everything that has a use value is a commodity. For example, air has a use value but it is not a commodity and hence does not have an exchange value. If pollution became very bad, and everybody had to carry a supply of clean air, and somebody started bottling and selling it, then it would acquire an exchange value in addition to its use value.
- **Markets** Interaction between individuals takes place through the laws of supply and demand. These laws fulfil two functions: (a) to provide information on how much of a particular product should be produced and at what price, and (b) to provide incentives to produce, and these incentives derive from self-interested motivations. Marx argues that the market is not in long-term equilibrium, and is subject to increasingly severe depressions. He further argues that capitalism assumes people are *by nature* selfish; this Marx rejects as an 'ontologisation' of historical experience – that is, turning something transitory into an ahistorical fact.

Marxists have tended not to engage in debate with liberals (or libertarians), rejecting as they do certain fundamental claims about the nature of human motivation and political epistemology. On human motivation, for example, Rawls maintains that the principles of justice apply to a society characterised by moderate scarcity in which people are in conflict over the distribution of those (moderately) scarce resources. A Marxist would maintain that when production levels reach a certain point – and capitalism is historically useful because it massively increases productivity – we will be in a position to say that there is no longer scarcity and the causes of social conflict will be removed. Regarding political *epistemology* – that is, how we *know* what is just – Marxists maintain that it is only in a post-scarcity situation that we will be able to determine the correct distribution of resources. For reasons too involved to explain here, Gerald Cohen is unusual amongst Marxists in his engagement with liberal (libertarian) thinkers such as Rawls and Nozick. What makes his argument interesting is that he attacks liberals on what they believe to be their strongest ground: freedom.

Biography	**Gerald Cohen (1941–)**

Born in Canada in 1941, Cohen's Russian-immigrant parents were members of the Communist Party, and up to his teens he attended a Jewish-Communist school.

In his book *If You're An Egalitarian, How Come You're So Rich* (2000), he explains how he gradually distanced himself from the economic determinism of the Communist Party, and without abandoning all Marxist insights saw morality as central to guiding human interaction. His first book, *Karl Marx's Theory of History: A Defence* (1978) was a relatively orthodox defence of Marx, although written in the non-Marxist idiom of what is called 'analytical philosophy'.

In the 1980s he further distanced himself from orthodox Marxism by engaging in a critique of Nozick. In the 1990s he turned his attention to Rawls. He is presently Professor of Social and Political Theory at Oxford University.

Cohen contra Nozick

Cohen does not deny that capitalism gives people freedom to buy and sell labour, but he argues that defenders of capitalism make the illegitimate claim that their society is comprehensively free: they falsely equate 'capitalism' with the 'free society'. Cohen maintains that liberals – both 'left-wing' (egalitarian) and 'right-wing' (libertarian) – are wrong. Capitalism does not guarantee the maximum amount of freedom possible. He argues that a moralised definition of freedom is used – the validity of private property rights is taken for granted, such that freedom comes to be defined in terms of private property, and any infringement of it is a reduction of freedom. Cohen provides an example to illustrate his point: Mr Morgan owns a yacht. You want to sail it for one day, returning it without any damage done to it. If you take it you will be violating Mr Morgan's rights, but which situation creates more *freedom*, Mr Morgan's exclusive use of the boat, or your one-day use combined with his 364-days-a-year use (Cohen, 1979: 11–12)?

Cohen argues that for *one day* Mr Morgan is prevented from using his yacht and is forced not to use it – his freedom has indeed been restricted. But Mr Morgan's private property rights prevent you from using the yacht for *365 days* in the year, and force you not to use it (Cohen: 12). Capitalism – the exercise of private property rights – is a complex system of freedom and unfreedom. One could, of course, maintain that the difference between Mr Morgan's use of the yacht and your use of the yacht is precisely that it is *his* yacht; but then we need to justify Mr Morgan's acquisition of the yacht – to say Mr Morgan ought to own the yacht because he does own the yacht is, of course, a circular argument.

A more restricted defence of capitalism is then discussed by Cohen: capitalists do not maintain that their preferred economic system promotes freedom in general, but merely economic freedom. So Mr Morgan's property rights do not restrict your economic freedom, and a capitalist society is better able than any alternative to maximise *economic* freedom (Cohen: 14). To grasp Cohen's response we need to refer back to the important distinction made earlier between use value and exchange value:

(a) If economic freedom is defined as the freedom to *use* goods and services then it restricts freedom whenever it grants it – Mr Morgan's freedom to use his yacht correlates directly to your unfreedom to use it.

(b) If economic freedom is the freedom to buy and sell – that is, exchange products – then this looks better for capitalists. But it is an extremely restricted definition of economic freedom.

Is there then an alternative to capitalism and – crucially – one that increases freedom? Cohen gives a 'homespun' example. Persons A and B are neighbours and each owns a set of household implements, such as a lawnmower, saws, paintbrushes and so on. Each owns what the other lacks. We now imagine a rule is imposed, whereby when A is not using something he owns, B has the right to use it, just so long as he returns it when A needs it. This 'communising rule' will, Cohen maintains, increase 'implement-using' freedom (Cohen, 1979: 16–17).

A capitalist response to this example would be that A and B could increase their implement-using freedom by entering a contract, either a kind of barter, or a money-based relationship. But Cohen's response to this move is to argue that in the example A and B are roughly equal and, therefore, capable of entering a freedom-enhancing contract, but if you generalise across society then that equality does not exist. In fact, there is another response to Cohen, which appeals to efficiency and *indirectly* to freedom: while Cohen's argument is in many ways sound – capitalism entails unfreedom as well as freedom – one has to look at the empirical consequences of different economic systems. Cohen's 'homespun' example does not help because it is a very simple situation in which there are no communication problems. One argument for capitalism is that it avoids an excessively powerful state; it might even be argued that liberalism is the unintended gift of capitalism. The history of socialism has been characterised by an attempt to acquire the advantages of coordination associated with the market, while avoiding the inequalities generated by it.

Cohen contra Rawls

We now turn to Cohen's response to Rawls. As we have seen Rawls does not defend unregulated capitalism, and advances a theory of justice that would entail a significant redistribution of income to the worst off. What then is wrong with Rawls? There are three main Marxist objections:

1. Rawls has an incoherent model of human psychology (motivation).
2. Rawls restricts the principles of justice to the basic structure of society, and that conceals exploitation.
3. Rawls rejects self-ownership as morally irrelevant to the distribution of resources. Curiously enough, on this point Cohen sides with the 'right-wing' libertarian Nozick against Rawls.

The first two objections are closely related to one another. If you recall, people in the original position are motivated to maximise their share of the primary goods, but from behind a 'veil of ignorance', meaning that although they are self-interested, they are forced by the way the original position is set up to be impartial. Rational people will, Rawls argues, select the two principles of justice, including the 'difference principle', which entails maximising the position of the worst off (maximin). The original position is intended to 'model' how real people *could* behave. The difficulty is that the theory itself pulls in two different directions: on the one hand Rawls assumes that we – that is, 'we' in the real world, and not in the original position – can develop a commitment to giving priority to the worst off in society, and the difference principle is the structural device by which this is achieved. But how much the worst off *actually receive* will depend on everyday human behaviour. Consider the exercise on p. 87: under maximin the richest 10 per cent get $105,000 and the poorest 10 per cent get $14,000. Imagine you are in the top 10 per cent. What motivations will you have in the 'real world', assuming you endorse Rawls's theory?

(a) You will be committed to giving priority to the worst off and so will regard redistributive income tax as legitimate.

(b) You will be motivated to maximise your income.

These two motivations do not necessarily conflict if we assume – as Rawls does – that inequality generates incentives to produce and thus help the worst off. But if you are really committed to helping the worst off do you not have a moral duty to:

(a) give *directly* – not just through tax – to the poor; and

(b) work to bring about a society in which the poorest earn more than $14,000?

Cohen borrows a slogan from the feminist movement: the 'personal is political' (Cohen, 2000: 122–3). How you behave in your personal life is a political issue. Rawls, along with most liberals, rejects this claim, arguing that the distinction between public and private is essential to a pluralistic society, and that not all aspects of morality should be enforced by the state: while it is right to require people to pay taxes to help the worst off, it is for individuals to decide what they do with their post-tax income. This may not resolve the tension that Cohen identifies between, crudely expressed, public generosity and private avarice, but the onus is on Cohen to explain the role of the state in 'encouraging' private generosity.

   This brings us to the second criticism, which relates to the basic structure argument. The rich fulfil their duties to the poor by accepting the legitimacy of taxation, and that taxation is used to fund certain institutions, such as the pre-university education system, money transfers (social security, pensions, etc.) and healthcare. Outside the scope of the original position is a 'private sphere' that includes the family. Rawls accepts that the family is a major source of inequality – the transmission from parent to child of privilege undermines equality of opportunity. But because liberty (the first principle of justice) takes priority over equality (the second principle) there has to be a legally protected private sphere. Not only is the private sphere a source of inequality, it also produces within itself inequality. Here Cohen joins forces with feminist critics of Rawls: families are based on a division of labour, and one loaded against women, but because the recipient of redistribution is the household, and not the individual, there is a class of people – mostly women – who are worse off than that class which Rawls identifies as the 'worst off'.

Cohen argues that what Rawls includes in the basic structure is arbitrary – Rawls cannot give clear criteria for what should or should not be included. He cannot say that the basic structure consists of those institutions which are coercively enforced, that is, we are forced to fund through taxation, because the basic structure is defined *before* we choose the principles of justice, whereas what is coercively enforced is a decision to be made in the original position (Cohen, 2000: 136–7). The basic Marxist point is this: Rawls assumes that human motivations are relatively constant – certainly, people can develop a moral consciousness, but they will remain self-interested. Motivations will always be a mix of self-interest and morality. Marxists reject this, and maintain that social structures determine how people behave.

We come, finally, to the third criticism. Marx argued that the workers do not get the full value of their labour. This argument assumes that there is something a person owns, which generates a moral right to other things: in effect, as a Marxist, Cohen, along with Nozick (who is not a Marxist!), endorses Locke's 'mixed labour' formula. What Cohen rejects is the idea that mixing your labour establishes merely 'first acquisition'. For Locke and Nozick, once the world is divided up into private property the mixed labour formula ceases to be of any use. Cohen argues that a worker *constantly* mixes his or her labour, such that there is a continuous claim on the product. Locke's argument that 'the turfs my servant has cut are *my* turfs' is rejected by Cohen; insofar as the servant (worker) does not get the full value of his labour he is exploited, and the resulting distribution is unjust. Rawls implicitly rejects the notion of self-ownership; that does not mean we do not have rights over our bodies, but rather we have no pre-social rights. The rights we have are the result of a choice made in the original position. This becomes clearer if we look at the concept of desert.

Desert is tied to effort: we get something if we do something. Rawls argues that because we are not responsible for our 'natural endowments' – strength, looks, intelligence, even good character – we cannot claim the product generated by those natural endowments. Under the difference principle one person may earn $210,000 and another $14,000, but not a dime of that $196,000 difference is *justified* by reference to desert. Of course, in *causal terms*, the difference may be attributed, at least in part, to native ability, but that does not *justify* the difference. Rawls goes as far as to say that natural endowments are a social resource to be used for the benefit of the worst off (Rawls, 1971: 179). It is strange that on desert Rawls is the radical, whereas Cohen sides with Nozick. It is true that Nozick does not believe that the rich are rich because they deserve to be rich – Wilt Chamberlain was rich because *other people chose to give him money* to play basketball – but the idea of self-ownership (private property rights) does imply a right to keep the fruit of your labour.

Whether you accept Cohen's argument against Rawls depends to some extent on whether you endorse Marx's labour theory of value. Many people would, however, follow Thomas Nagel in arguing that the value of a product is not the result of the amount of labour which went into it, but rather the other way round: the value of labour is the result of the contribution that labour makes to the product (Nagel, 1991: 99). Ask yourself this: if you have a firm making 'next generation' mobile telephones, which group of workers do you *least* want to lose: the canteen staff? Cleaners? Assembly line workers? Phone designers? Venture capitalists? It could be argued that the last two groups are the most important. The conclusion to be drawn is that if we want to justify an egalitarian distribution of wealth we need what Rawls attempts to offer, which is a moral justification that assumes that many of the poorest will get *more* than that to which their labour 'entitles' them.

Summary

Human beings need to decide how resources are to be distributed, and unless we endorse the anarchist position then the state, which is a coercive entity, will play a role in their distribution. Political theorists disagree about the extent of state involvement in the distribution of resources – Nozick argues for a minimal role, while Rawls – and, implicitly, Cohen – argue for a more extensive role. Underlying the three theories discussed are different conceptions of what it means to be an agent, and of human motivation. Rawls assumes that human beings have mixed motives: they are self-interested but also 'reasonable'. Nozick avoids a discussion of motivation by arguing for a strong conception of human agency – property rights are an extension of self-ownership: so long as we do not violate others' rights, what we do with our rights is for us to decide. Cohen endorses the emphasis on self-ownership, but uses it against Nozick's initial acquisition argument; he also rejects Rawls's motivational assumptions, arguing that we need to change our attitudes and become less acquisitive.

Questions

1. Do people *deserve* to keep the fruits of their labour?
2. If you are as well off as you could possibly be, can you have any grounds for objecting that other people are better off than you?
3. Is taxation 'forced labour'?
4. Should there be an unconditional minimum income for each person?
5. Should the state reward men and women for bringing up children, and doing housework?

References

Cohen, G.A. (1978) *Karl Marx's Theory of History: a Defence* Oxford: Clarendon Press.

Cohen, G.A. (1979) 'Capitalism, Freedom, and the Proletariat' in A. Ryan (ed.), *The Idea of Freedom* Oxford: Oxford University Press.

Cohen, G.A. (2000) *If You're An Egalitarian, How Come You're So Rich?* Cambridge, Mass.: Harvard University Press.

Nagel, T. (1991) *Equality and Partiality* New York: Oxford University Press.

Nozick, R. (1974) *Anarchy, State, and Utopia* New York: Basic Books

Locke, J. (1988) *Two Treatises of Government* (ed. Peter Laslett), Student edn, Cambridge: Cambridge University Press

Rawls, J. (1971) *A Theory of Justice* Oxford: Oxford University Press.

Rawls, J. (1993) *Political Liberalism* New York: Columbia University Press.

Rawls, J. (2001) *Justice as Fairness: A Restatement* Cambridge, Mass.: Harvard University Press.

Wolff, J. (1991) *Robert Nozick: Property, Justice and the Minimal State* Oxford: Polity Press.

Further Reading

The primary texts are Rawls (1971), Part One; Nozick (1974), Chapter 7; Cohen (1979); Cohen (2000). There are several good commentaries on Rawls, the first of which was Brian Barry, *The Liberal Theory of Justice* (Oxford: Clarendon, 1973); a collection of early essays on Rawls can be found in Norman Daniels (ed.), *Reading Rawls: Critical Studies on Rawls's A Theory of Justice* (Stanford, Calif.: Stanford University Press, 1989 (first published 1973)); slightly more recent works on Rawls are Chandran Kukathas and Philip Pettit, *Rawls: A Theory of Justice and its Critics* (Cambridge: Polity Press, 1990) and Thomas Pogge, *Realizing Rawls* (Ithica, NY: Cornell University Press, 1989). There are fewer works on Nozick. The best is Wolff (1991). Others – both collections of essays – are Jeffrey Paul (ed.), *Reading Nozick: Essays on Anarchy, State and Utopia* (Totowa NJ: Rowman & Littlefield, 1981) and David Schmidtz (ed.), *Robert Nozick* (Cambridge: Cambridge University Press, 2002).

Weblinks

- The following are useful websites on Rawls:
  http://www.epistemelinks.com/Main/Philosophers.aspx?PhilCode=Rawl
  http://plato.stanford.edu/entries/original-position/
  http://www.policylibrary.com/rawls/

- The following are useful websites on Nozick:
  http://www.epistemelinks.com/Main/Philosophers.aspx?PhilCode=Nozi
  http://dmoz.org/Society/Philosophy/Philosophers/N/Nozick,_Robert/

Chapter 5

Democracy

Introduction

It is very difficult to find anyone who disagrees with democracy these days. Politicians from the extreme left to the extreme right, insist that the politics that they support is democratic in character, so it is no wonder that the term is so confusing. Although fundamentalists may reject the notion of democracy, nobody else does, and whether the ruler is a military dictator, a nationalist demagogue or a liberal, the concept of democracy will be piously invoked in support of an argument.

So in asking what democracy is, we also have to address the question as to why it has become almost obligatory for politicians to claim adherence to the concept.

Chapter Map

- Democracy has been more and more widely acclaimed from almost all sections of the political spectrum; it has become increasingly confusing as a concept.

- Liberals traditionally opposed democracy, even if the universal assumptions of their theory led their opponents to argue that liberalism was democratic in character.

- Liberals only reluctantly converted to democracy in the nineteenth century, and then only on the assumption that extending the franchise would not undermine the rights of property.

- After World War II politics was seen as the business of a decision-making elite, and participation by the masses was discouraged.

- Democracy involves both direct participation and representation, and representation needs to be based on a sense that the representative can empathise with the problem of her constituents.

- There is a tension between democracy and the concept of the state, and this creates problems for Held's case for a 'cosmopolitan democracy'.

- The question of the state helps to account for the confusions about the polity in Ancient Greece, and among conservative critics of liberalism.

- A **relational** view of democracy enables us to tackle the 'tyranny thesis', and to defend the rational kernel of political correctness.

Inside the Voting Booth

Iraqi women stand in a queue at a polling station in Najaf, 30 January 2005.

You are standing in a voting booth, and you notice the people around you. One is a well-known business personality whose photograph you have seen in the local press. He is smartly dressed in an expensive suit, with shiny patent leather shoes. The other person who catches your eye is someone whom you have seen emptying your garbage. She has obviously taken time off work, and is wearing the protective clothing that the council gives to employees who do that particular job. After you have left the booth, and are wandering through the city centre, you notice a person begging. You remind him, after giving him some money, that there is a general election, and he snorts: 'You won't catch me voting: I am not on the voters' register anyway!'

Three different people attract your attention on voting day. A is a wealthy businessman, B is a council employee, and C is a beggar. In law all are equal, and they have equal political rights. Each has a right to cast a secret ballot, but is this sufficient for a system to be called democratic?

Consider the following: how important is it that A has a lot of wealth, B has relatively little, and C is a drug addict who has been disowned by his family and divorced from his wife, and has none? In law they are all equal citizens but, in practice, the amount of social power they have varies dramatically.

Should we take the view that A has worked hard and deserves his success, B has a job that lots of others could do, while C only has himself to blame? Are their differences proof of a free society or evidence that a society is yet to be fully democratic?

A and B want to see the prime minister about an issue that concerns them greatly. Who would you say the PM is likely to see? C has been told to put his life in order: how easy is it for him to become an effective citizen with good health, a reasonable job, and a home of his own?

Democracy and Confusion

The term democracy means rule of the people. But such a concept has created real problems for those who believe that political theory should be value-free in character. It is revealing that Dahl in the 1960s preferred to speak of 'polyarchies' rather than democracies, in the hope that the substitute term could appear more 'scientific' in character. For whether democracy in the past has been a good thing or a bad thing, it is difficult to say what democracy is without 'taking sides' in some ongoing debate.

As democracy has become more and more widely praised, it has become more and more difficult to pin it down. John Dunn has noted that 'all states today profess to be democracies because a democracy is what it is virtuous for a state to be' (1979: 11). A term can only be confusing if it is taken to mean contradictory things: majority rule or individual rights; limited government or popular sovereignty; private property as against social ownership. Consider the following: participation versus representation; the collective versus the individual; socialism versus capitalism. All have been defended as being essential to democracy!

It has been argued that the term should be abandoned, and Crick has taken the view that politics needs to be *defended* against democracy not because he is opposed (at least not under all circumstances) to the idea, but because he is in favour of clarity and precision against vagueness and ambiguity. Democracy, he comments, is perhaps 'the most promiscuous word in the world of public affairs' (1982: 56). Bernard Shaw once devoted an entire play – *The Apple Cart* – to the problem. The play tackled the ambiguities of democracy with such flair that it was banned by a nervous Weimar Republic in the 1920s; and in a witty preface Shaw complains that democracy seems to be everywhere and nowhere. It is a long word that we are expected to accept reverently without asking any questions. It seems quite impossible, Shaw protests, for politicians to make speeches about democracy, or for journalists to report them, without obscuring the concept 'in a cloud of humbug' (Hoffman, 1988: 132).

What makes democracy so confusing is that it is a concept subject to almost universal acclaim. But this was not always the position. In the seventeenth century, nobody who was anybody would have called themselves a democrat. As far as landowners, merchants, lawyers and clergymen were concerned – people of 'substance' – democracy was a term of abuse: a bad thing. Even in the nineteenth century, social liberals such as J.S. Mill felt it necessary to defend liberty *against* democracy. It is only after World War I that democracy becomes a respectable term. It is true that Hitler condemned democracy as the political counterpart to economic communism, but Mussolini, the Italian fascist, could declare in a speech in Berlin in 1936 that 'the greatest and most genuine democracies in the world today, are the German and the Italian' (Hoffman, 1988: 133).

The left have generally approved of democracy, but it is possible to find the Russian revolutionary, Trotsky, for example, declaring democracy to be irretrievably bourgeois and counter-revolutionary. A Communist Party secretary declared in Hamburg in 1926 that he would rather burn in 'the fire of **revolution** than perish in the dung-heap of democracy' (Hoffman, 1988: 133). But by the twentieth century attacks on the idea of democracy have become the exception rather than the rule, and with this growing acclaim, the concept has become increasingly confusing.

Crick complains that the term has become a bland synonym for 'All Things Bright and Beautiful', a hurrah word without any specific content (1982: 56). The glow of approval has made it an idea very difficult to pin down.

Democracy and Liberalism

Biography,
p. 176

Weldon, the linguistic analyst, has argued that 'democracy', 'capitalism' and 'liberalism' are all alternative names for the same thing (1953: 86). Yet this view has been challenged by a number of theorists. They note that historically liberals were not democrats, even if they were attacked as democrats by conservative critics of liberalism. John Locke, for example, took it for granted that those who could vote were men, merchants and landowners, and the question of universal suffrage (even for men only) is not even raised in his *Two Treatises of Government*. The fact that liberals declared that men were free and equal was taken by conservatives to denote support for democracy, but this was not true!

A hapless King Charles (1600–49) reproached English parliamentarians (who had taken him prisoner) for 'labouring to bring about democracy' (Dunn, 1979: 3). Yet it is clear that Oliver Cromwell (1599–1658) and his puritan gentry did not believe in democracy, and even the left wing of the movement – the Levellers – wished to exclude 'servants' and 'paupers' from the franchise. Cromwellians were alarmed that the egalitarian premises of liberal theory might extend the freedom to smaller property owners to rule (Hoffman, 1988: 154–5). It is true that de Tocqueville (1805–59), writing in the 1840s, could describe the United States of his day as a democracy, but in fact until the 1860s Americans themselves identified democracy at best with one element (the legislature) of the constitution – an element to be checked and balanced by others.

Madison, one of the founders of the US Constitution, had spoken in the *Federalist Papers* of democracies as 'incompatible with personal security or the rights of property', and John Jay, one of the authors of the famous *Papers*, declared that the 'people who own the country should govern it' (Hoffman, 1988: 135). De Tocqueville might describe Jefferson, author of the *Declaration of Independence* (1787) as 'the greatest democrat ever to spring from American democracy' (1966: 249), but in fact Jefferson was a liberal who took the view that voters should be male farmers who owned property. The US political scientist Hofstadter has commented on how modern US folklore has anachronistically assumed that liberalism and democracy are identical (Hoffman, 1988: 136), and it has missed the point which Crick makes, that there is 'tension as well as harmony' between the two bodies of thought.

Tension – because liberals did not intend the invocation of universal rights to apply to all adults – and *harmony* – because their critics from the right assumed that they did, and their critics from the left felt that if rights were universal in theory then they should be universal in practice. It is important not to assume that liberal theorists were necessarily democratic in orientation. Rousseau, the eighteenth-century French theorist, felt that democracy was unworkable. It assumed a perfectionism that human nature belied, and was a form of government ever liable to 'civil war and internecine strife' (1968: 113).

De Tocqueville's portrait of the United States is that of a society of radical liberalism, not of democracy: he himself notes the enslavement of blacks and the appropriation of the lands of native Americans. A government publication in the United States could describe democracy even in the 1920s as 'a government of the masses . . . Attitude towards property is communistic – negating property rights . . . Results in demagogism, license, agitation, discontent, anarchy' (Hoffman, 1988: 141). Thus spoke the voice of traditional liberalism!

Biography — Alexis de Tocqueville (1805–59)

Born into a royalist aristocratic family, his father having narrowly escaped execution from the radical French revolutionaries, the Jacobins. De Tocqueville entered government service in 1827 but found it impossible to support the new Orleanist monarchy established in the July Revolution of 1830 or to believe that the old Bourbon monarchy could be restored.

From the spring of 1831 until 1832 he visited the United States with his friend, Gustave de Beaumont, and together they published a book on the US penal system. His *Democracy in America* appeared in two parts – in 1835 and 1840. The book won him international acclaim and after the second part appeared he was elected to the *Académie française.* In the book he argued that democracy requires religion and individualistic customs, and he was struck by the high levels of local participation in the US polity.

In 1835 he visited Ireland, and noted the growing rift between Catholics and Protestants. In 1839 he was elected deputy in Normandy and remained a member of the Chamber until 1848. After the February Revolution of 1848 he was elected to the Constituent Assembly and served on the commission that drew up the republican constitution. He was elected to the new Legislative Assembly in 1849, became its vice-president and, for a few months, was minister for foreign affairs. He was bitterly opposed to Louis Napoleon's coup d'état that ended his political career.

In 1856 he published his unfinished masterpiece, *The Ancient Regime,* in which he characterised the French Revolution as the greatest property transaction in history. He also corresponded with J.S. Mill.

How to read:

de Tocqueville's *Democracy in America*

This is a massive work, usually published in two volumes. The author's preface and introduction in Volume 1 are worth a close read. If you are particularly interested in the political system of the United States, then the earlier chapters are important, but for the critique of democracy, read Chapters 7–9. Chapter 10 contains a breathtaking assessment of the position of blacks and native Americans. In Volume 2 Chapter 8 on equality deserves a careful read and, although the volume is full of fascinating topics such as 'How American Democracy has modified the English Language', Part II can be skim-read with the exception of Chapter 20, which is especially interesting. Part III can be skipped, but Part IV deserves attention and Chapter 6 sets out clearly de Tocqueville's reservations about democracy.

The Problem of Exclusion

Conservative critics could speak of democracy as turning 'natural' hierarchies upside down. In an historic passage, the ancient Greek theorist Plato complains that in a democracy, fathers and sons 'change places' and 'there is no distinction between citizen and alien and foreigner'. Slaves come to enjoy the same freedom as their owners, 'not to mention the complete equality and liberty in the relations between the sexes generally'. In the end, Plato adds with a flourish, even 'the domestic animals are infected with anarchy' (1955: 336).

It is true that during the fourth and fifth centuries BC an astonishing model of popular rule came to exist in ancient Athens. A popular assembly met some 40 times a year. All citizens were actually paid to attend. All had the right to be heard in debate before decisions were taken, and this assembly had supreme powers of war, peace, making treaties, creating public works etc. Judges, administrators and members of a 500-strong executive council were chosen, and since they only held office for one or two years this meant that a considerable portion of Athenian citizens had experience of government.

But despite the fact that some have referred to Athenian democracy as 'pure' and 'genuine', it was rooted in **slavery**, patriarchy and chauvinism. Slaves, women and resident aliens had no political rights so that, as has been said, the people in Athens were really 'an exceptionally large and diversified ruling class' (Hoffman, 1988: 145). Not only was Athenian society divided internally, but the payment for jury service, public office and the membership of the executive council, the expensive land settlement programme and the distribution of public funds would not have been possible without the Athenian empire. Democracy was an exclusive idea: the demos – the people with the right to participate in decision making were certainly not all the adults who lived in the society.

But surely all this changed when liberals became converted to the notion of democracy? It is true that after the French Revolution British liberals began to accept the case for universal suffrage, at least among men. But they did so very cautiously and reluctantly, with Macpherson arguing that liberals such as Jeremy Bentham (1748–1832) would have preferred to restrict the vote to those who owned their own houses, but this was no longer acceptable (Macpherson, 1977: 35). James Mill (1773–1836) asserts that all men should have the vote to protect their interests, and then argues that logically these interests could be secured if all women, all men under 40 and the poorest third of the male population over 40 were excluded from the vote. In Macpherson's view, James Mill and Bentham were less than wholehearted democrats (1977: 39).

The argument between the liberals and the liberals-turned-democrats was over whether the male poor would use their rights to strip the rich of their wealth, or whether they would leave decision making to the middle rank – whom James Mill described as the class in society which gives to science, art and legislation their most 'distinguished ornaments' and is the chief source of all that is 'refined and exalted in human nature'. Both sides of the argument agreed that the business of government is the business of the rich (Hoffman, 1988: 167).

The question of exclusion becomes more subtle as liberals become more enthusiastic about the idea of democracy. T.H. Green and Leonard Hobhouse, two

Biography — Jeremy Bentham (1748–1832)

A brilliant scholar, Bentham entered Queen's College, Oxford, at the age of 12 and was admitted to Lincoln's Inn at the age of 15. Financed by his father, he decided to dedicate his life to writing.

After reading the work of the radical liberal Joseph Priestley, Bentham ceased to be a Tory. In 1776 he wrote *A Fragment on Government*, published anonymously on the basis of his critique of Blackstone. In 1787 he produced a critique of Adam Smith's theory of usury. In 1789 *Introduction to the Principles of Morals and Legislation* was published, where Bentham argued famously that the proper objective of all conduct and legislation is 'the greatest happiness of the greatest number'. In Bentham's view, 'pain and pleasure are the sovereign masters governing man's conduct'. All acts are based on self-interest, it being the business of the law to ensure through painful sanctions that the individual subordinates his own happiness to that of the community. A plan for the reform of the French judicial system won him the honorary citizenship of France, but although he initially welcomed the French Revolution, he attacked the concept of natural right in his *Anarchical Fallacies*.

In 1798 Bentham wrote *Principles of International Law*, in which he argued that universal peace could only be obtained through European unity. He hoped that some form of European parliament would enforce the liberty of the press, free trade, the abandonment of all colonies and a reduction in the money being spent on armaments.

In 1809 he published *Catechism of Reformers,* where he attacked the law of libel as an instrument that could be used against radicals for 'hurting the feelings' of the ruling class. His work was praised and popularised by radical reformers and extracts of his work appeared in the campaigning *Black Dwarf.* When Burdett argued the case for universal suffrage in the House of Commons in 1818, he quoted the work of Bentham in his support.

In 1824 Bentham joined with James Mill to found the *Westminster Review*, the journal of the philosophical radicals.

His most detailed account of his ideas on political democracy appeared in his massive (and unfinished) *Constitutional Code*. Here he made the case for political reform on the grounds that this was the only way to secure the happiness of the majority. He also supported the abolition of the monarchy, the House of Lords and the established church. Women, as well as men, should be given the vote. Government officials should be selected by competitive examination. Politicians and government officials are, after all, Bentham argued, the 'servants, not the masters, of the public'.

Ch 13: Feminism, pp. 324–48

British social liberals, both supported the idea that women as well as men should have the vote, and by 1928 women were enfranchised. But Green could still take it for granted that men were the head of the family, and Hobhouse argued that women should stay at home and mind the children (Hoffman, 1988: 180). It could be argued that even when women had political and legal equality with men social equality eluded them, and their democratic rights were thereby impaired. This would be vigorously argued by feminists later. Socialists, for their part, continued to contend that even when workers have the vote they do not have the resources to

| Biography | **Leonard Trelawney Hobhouse (1864–1929)** |

Oxford educated, he was a temporary lecturer at the London School of Economics (LSE) in 1896–7 before becoming a journalist for the *Manchester Guardian* in 1897.

In 1904 he published *Democracy and Reaction* – a book that vigorously attacked imperialism and built upon the opposition he had expressed to the Boer War. He supported the social-reformist policy of the Liberal Party.

He returned to the LSE as a lecturer in 1904. In 1906–7 he became political editor of the short-lived *Tribune,* and in 1907 he was the first Professor of Sociology in a British university. He was pivotal in the establishment and foundation of sociology as an academic discipline and in the refinement of its methodology. All this time he maintained his output in the *Manchester Guardian* and played an active role in developing trade boards.

Strongly influenced by evolutionism, he published *Mind in Evolution* (1901)*, Morals in Evolution* (1906) and *Development and Purpose* (1913). His *Liberalism* in 1911 has rightly been described as the best twentieth-century statement of liberal ideals. While Hobhouse saw private property as necessary to the development of the individual personality, he regarded common property as a valuable expression of social life. The state had a paramount role to play in promoting social good, and guarding the moral and spiritual interests of its members. He was a major advocate of the social reforms of the Asquith government.

After World War I he became more pessimistic about freedom and was concerned that a powerful state could undermine the moral autonomy of individuals. In 1922 he published *The Elements of Social Justice.*

exercise their political rights as effectively as those who have wealth, social connections, the 'right' education etc.

What about international exclusions? Hobhouse argues that 'a democrat cannot be a democrat for his country alone'. Does democracy require support for political rights throughout the world? Hobhouse cannot make up his mind whether to support home rule for the Irish, and he argues that as far as the Crown colonies are concerned, a semi-despotic system is the best that can be devised (Hoffman, 1988: 181). The problem is still relevant. Is US endorsement of democracy compromised by the fact that the government supports regimes such as Kuwait and Saudi Arabia, which are not democratic?

The 'Tyranny of the Majority' Thesis

Both J.S. Mill and de Tocqueville raised the problem of democracy as a 'tyranny of the majority'. What is there to prevent a government representing the majority from crushing a minority? Crick endorses what has been called a 'paradox of freedom' – a situation in which an elected leader acts tyrannically towards particular individuals or groups. Crick gives the example of the German elections of 1933 that saw Hitler being appointed chancellor. A more recent example – which Barbara Goodwin raises (1997: 289) – is of the Islamic Salvation Front in

Ch 16:
Fundament-
alism,
pp. 392–413

Algeria winning an election, but being prevented from governing by the army, on the grounds that the intention of the Front was to install a non-democratic Islamic theocracy.

This resurrects the ancient Greek argument that democracy as the rule of the poor could take the form of a popular despotism. Crick cites the French revolutionary, Robespierre, who speaks of a democratic defence of terror, and Crick comments, in a rather startling passage, that the problem with (totalitarian) communists is that they do not merely pretend to be democratic: they 'are democratic' (1982: 60–1; 56).

This leads most commentators to say that democracy must be linked to liberalism so that the term liberal qualifies democracy. A democratic society must respect the rights of minorities as well as majorities. Otherwise, democracy can become dictatorial and oppress individuals by imposing majority tastes and preferences on society as a whole. Built into the US tradition is what one writer has described as a 'neurotic terror of the majority', and new liberals such as Hobhouse argued that checks should be placed upon the British House of Commons to restrain 'a large and headstrong majority' (Hoffman, 1988: 136; 181). Ian Paisley's conception of a 'Protestant state of the Protestant people' may appear democratic, but it certainly did not facilitate participation by the Catholic minority.

The Problem of Participation

Towards the end of World War II the concept of democracy was redefined, in order to bring it into line, so it was argued, with practical realities. Joseph Schumpeter, an Austrian economist and socialist, led the way, contending that the notion of democracy must be stripped of its moral qualities. There is nothing about democracy that makes it desirable. It may be that in authoritarian systems – Schumpeter gives the example of the religious settlement under the military dictatorship of Napoleon I – the wishes of the people are more fully realised than under a democracy (1947: 256).

In Schumpeter's view, democracy is simply a 'political method'. It is an arrangement for reaching political decisions: it is not an end in itself. Since all governments 'discriminate' against some section of the population (in no political system are children allowed to vote, for example), discrimination as such is not undemocratic. It all depends upon how you define the demos, the people. Schumpeter accepts that in contemporary liberal societies all adults should have the right to vote, but this does not mean that they will use this right or participate more directly in the political process. In fact, he argues that it is a good idea if the mass of the population do not participate, since the masses are too irrational, emotional, parochial and 'primitive' to make good decisions.

The typical citizen, he argues, yields to prejudice, impulse and what Schumpeter calls 'dark urges' (1947: 262). It is the politicians who raise the issues that determine people's lives, and who decide these issues. A democracy is more realistically defined as 'a political method' through which politicians are elected by means of a competitive vote. The people do not rule: their role is to elect those who do. Democracy is a system of elected and competing elites.

Biography	Joseph Alois Schumpeter (1883–1950)

Born in Austria to parents who owned a textile factory, Schumpeter was very familiar with business when he entered the University of Vienna to study economics and law.

He was a student of Friedrich von Wieser and Eugen von Böhm-Bawerk, and as early as 1908 Schumpeter published *Economic Doctrine and Method*. He was only 28 when he wrote his famous *Theory of Economic Development*. In this book he set out many of the ideas that featured in his later work, and he already displayed the broader concerns of the historian and the social scientist. In 1911 Schumpeter took a professorship in economics at the University of Graz, and he served as minister of finance in the Austrian government in 1919.

With the rise of Hitler, Schumpeter left Europe and the University of Bonn where he had been a professor from 1925 until 1932, and emigrated to the United States. In that same year he accepted a permanent position at Harvard, and remained there until his retirement in 1949. His *Business Cycles* appeared in 1939. In 1942 he produced *Capitalism, Socialism and Democracy,* in which

he argues that capitalism will decay not because of its failures, but because of its success. Capitalism would spawn, he believed, a large intellectual class that made its living by attacking the very bourgeois system of private property and freedom so necessary for the intellectual class's existence. Unlike Marx, Schumpeter did not relish the destruction of capitalism. 'If a doctor predicts that his patient will die', he wrote, 'this does not mean that he desires it.'

Capitalism is creatively destructive. The opening of new markets, new methods of production, new products and new types of organisation continually modify the structure of the system, and Schumpeter expressed a preference for monopoly and oligopoly over free competition. But entrepreneurial activity is undermined, not only by those who make it the target of intellectual wrath, but also by the growing bureaucracy and routinisation of large firms.

Schumpeter was president of the American Economic Association in 1948, and his *History of Economic Analysis* was published posthumously in 1954.

The 1950s saw a number of studies which argued that politics is a remote, alien and unrewarding activity best left to a relatively small number of professional activists. Elected leadership should be given a free hand, since 'where the rational citizen seems to abdicate, nevertheless angels seem to tread' (Macpherson, 1977: 92). The model of elitist democracy, as it has sometimes been called, argued the case for a democracy with low participation.

Solutions to the Problem of Low Participation

It could be argued, however, that low participation undermines democracy. How democratic are liberal political systems if, in the United States, for example, the president can be elected with hardly more than half the population exercising their vote? (Although in the 2004 presidential election the percentage of those voting rose to close on 60 per cent.) This means that whatever his majority, he is supported by a minority of the electorate.

In his *Life and Times of Liberal Democracy* Macpherson sets about constructing a participatory model, arguing that somehow participatory democrats have to break the vicious circle between an apathy which leads to inequality (as the poor and vulnerable lose out), and inequality that generates apathy (as the poor and vulnerable feel impotent and irrelevant). Macpherson's argument is an interesting one, because he takes the view that one needs to start with people as they are. Let us assume that the individual is simply a market-oriented consumer who does not feel motivated to vote, or if she votes, does so in order to further her own immediate interests. There are three issues that Macpherson feels work to break this vicious circle.

To consume comfortably and confidently, one needs a relatively decent environment. Going fishing assumes that there are fish to catch and they are safe to eat; swimming can only take place if the sea is not so polluted as to be positively dangerous. A concern about the environment leads the most politically apathetic consumer to contemplate joining an ecological organisation. That is the first loophole.

From a concern with the physical environment, the consumer moves on to the social environment. Inner urban decay, ill-planned housing estates, the ravages of property developers: all these and related issues compel people to become concerned with politics, while insecurity and boredom at the workplace make it inevitable that there will be involvement in trade union and professional association campaigns for job protection, better pensions etc.

One can add numerous other issues that are forcing people to take a greater concern in the political process. It is crucial not to define politics too narrowly since people participate in all kinds of different ways, and even the person who does not vote may join, say, Amnesty International or Greenpeace in Britain. There is an argument (which we will consider in a moment) for increasing the number of people who vote in parliamentary elections, but it is important to see that democracy requires participation at different levels, and in different ways. The large numbers of people who turned out to protest against the war with Iraq in London showed that a lack of concern with politics can be exaggerated, and the rise of what are usually called the New Social Movements – single issue organisations concerned with peace, the environment, rights of women, etc. – indicate that there is increasing participation, even if some of this participation seems unconventional in character.

There is a growing feeling that 'normal' political processes – in local government, in electing people to parliament – must change in the sense that these institutions need to become more accessible and intelligible to people on the street. In Britain, for example, there is growing interest in schemes to assist voting and voter registration; in reforming legislative chambers; making local government more exciting; introducing devolved and regional government; and other schemes to increase levels of interest and involvement in conventional political processes.

Even if voting is not the only form of democratic participation, it is important and there is, we think, a strong argument for compulsory voting in the United Kingdom. The argument that the citizen has a right not to vote ignores the fact that rights are indissolubly linked to responsibilities, and the act of non-voting harms the interests of society at large. It is true that some may feel that voting is a farce, but the defensible part of this objection – that the voter does not feel that existing parties offer real choice – can easily be met by allowing voters to put their cross in a box which states 'none of the above'. This would signal to politicians the extent to which people were voting negatively through protest.

It is true that the case for compulsory voting would not, taken simply on its own, create a more effective participation. It has to be accompanied by policies that address the inequalities underlying the problem of apathy. A lack of jobs, housing, adequate healthcare, physical and material security remain critical causes of despair and low self-esteem. There is plenty of evidence that mandatory voting raises participation levels and, as Faulks point out, when the Netherlands dropped compulsory voting in 1970, voting turn-out fell by 10 per cent (2001: 24). Italy, Belgium and Australia still compel their citizens to vote. Compulsory voting would encourage people to take an interest in political affairs – become more literate and confident – and it could reduce the time and resources parties use to try and capture the public interest in trivial and sensational ways.

While fines could be imposed upon defaulters, the real sanctions for non-compliance would be moral. Compulsory voting could play an invaluable role in altering our political culture in a socially responsible direction. Faulks quotes Lijphart, who comments that compulsory voting is an extension of universal suffrage (2001: 25). A simple and comprehensive system of voter registration in Britain would also assist people in taking responsibility for governing their own lives, and one can think of numerous devices to facilitate voting. The greater use of postal votes, the extension of time for voting, and a more proportional system would do much to overcome the cynicism that is often expressed at election times. Additionally, we would point to the use of referenda on important issues, and the employment of citizens' juries. In this latter case, a number of citizens, statistically representative of the wider population, discuss particular issues in an intense and deliberative way, and make recommendations based upon questions to relevant experts.

A number of writers have argued that the use of information technology could radically enhance the possibility for direct democracy since as a result of email, the internet, video conferencing, the digitisation of data, two-way computer and television links through cable technology, citizens could remain at home and shape policies rather than rely upon representatives to do so. Clearly such a technology has tremendous potential to empower citizens, and Faulks gives the example of how a citizens' action group used the communications network to raise $150,000 in Santa Monica, California, for the local homeless (1999: 157). Television shows in Britain such as *Pop Idol*, *Big Brother* and *Strictly Ballroom* already have vast numbers of viewers voting for their chosen 'star': does this indicate the potential for using TV as a medium for giving people greater choice on policies and personalities? Already TV programmes invite viewers to express their views on current controversies of the day.

Representational and Direct Democracy

Do we need to make a choice between representational democracy and direct democracy: between situations in which people elect representatives to govern them, or they directly take decisions themselves?

Rousseau, in a famous passage in *The Social Contract*, argues the case for direct involvement, passionately insisting that to be represented is to give up – to alienate – powers that individuals alone can rightfully exercise. Deputies are acceptable since they are merely the agents of the people. Representation, on the other hand, an odious modern idea, involves a form of slavery – a negation of 'will', one's capacity to exert influence (1968: 141). Rousseau's position is generally regarded as untenable. The very notion of representation as a re-presenting of the individual arises from the classical liberal view that citizens are individuals. This is an important and positive idea but, to be democratic, representatives can only act on behalf of those they represent if they understand their problems and way of life.

We do not, therefore, have to make a choice between representational or direct democracy. It is revealing that the argument associated with Edmund Burke (1729–97) – one of the great liberal conservatives – that representatives simply act in what they see (in their infinite wisdom) is the real interest of their constituents, inverts the Rousseauan view that representation is necessarily alienation. Those who have neither the time nor resources to make laws directly need to authorise others to do so on their behalf. Only through a combination of the direct and the indirect – hands-on participation *and* representation – can democratic autonomy be maximised. Of course, there are dangers that representatives will act in an elitist manner: but this is also true of what Rousseau called 'deputies'. Democracy requires accountability, so that people can get decisions made which help them to govern their own lives.

Representation, it should be said, involves empathy – the capacity to put yourself in the position of another – and while it is impossible to actually be another person, it is necessary to imagine what it is like to be another. Hence, as noted above, accountability is 'the other side' of representation: one without the other descends into either impracticality or elitism. The notion of empathy points to the need for a link between representatives and constituents. Unless representatives are in some sense a reflection of the population at large, it is difficult to see how empathy can take place. Women who have experienced oppression by men (or partners) at first hand are more likely to have insight into the problems women face than men who – however sympathetic they may be – may never have been the recipients of that particular form of discrimination. The same is true with members of ethnic and sexual minorities etc. To have experienced humiliation directly as a disabled person makes one far more sensitive to questions of disability. We need a form of representation that is sensitive to the particular identities and problems of those they represent.

Democracy requires participation, but it would be wrong to assume that this is only possible through direct involvement in political processes. Direct involvement needs to be linked to representation, and it is worth noting that in the ancient Greek polis – often held up as an example of direct democracy – the assembly elected an executive council.

The Argument So Far ...

- Democracy is a particularly confusing concept because nearly everyone claims to subscribe to it.
- In fact this is a relatively recent development. Liberals historically disagreed with democracy, but because liberal theory seemed to apply to everyone this makes it difficult to see who was being excluded. Conservatives accused liberals of wanting to be universally inclusive, just as Plato in ancient Greece accused democrats of wanting to abolish the distinction between citizen and slave.

Ideas and Perspectives:

The 'Mirror' Theory of Representation

It is sometimes argued that representation can only be fair if exact percentages of groups within the population at large are 'reflected' in the composition of representatives. If the population of a particular city (such as Leicester in England) contains, say, 40 per cent of people with black faces, then a mirror theory of representation demands that there should be 40 per cent of representatives who are black. The same is argued about poor people, gays etc. It is not difficult to see the problem with this notion. Ethnic minorities, as with people in general, are not all the same. Black people in Leicester are divided ethnically, regionally, along class and gender lines, etc. and it would be wrong to assume that one black person is the same as another. A black businessman may not identify with a black trade unionist. It does not follow, therefore, that black representatives will necessarily represent the interests of black constituents, any more than we can assume that women representatives will necessarily represent the interests of women. It is one thing to argue that representatives must have knowledge of (and experience of) the people they represent; quite another that they must represent them in precise numbers.

The mirror theory has a grain of truth in it: representatives should be sensitive to the problems of their constituents, and it helps if a predominantly black constituency, for example, has a black representative. But it has only a *grain* of truth: it is not the whole story. There are an infinity of other factors to consider – gender, class, sexual orientation etc. We need to distinguish between politically relevant differences and those 'differences' (such as wearing spectacles) that are not normally relevant.

- Liberals in the nineteenth century reluctantly accepted the need for universal suffrage, although continued to fear that democracy might express itself as a 'tyranny of the majority'. This fear helps to explain the post-war argument that a realistic view of democracy requires that the people only minimally participate.
- In fact, low participation is something that undermines democracy, and suggestions are offered as to how participation could be increased. But it is important in arguing for more participation that we see democracy as both representative and 'direct'.

Democracy and the State

The problem with much of the analysis of democracy is that it assumes that democracy is a form of the state. Yet it could well be argued that there is a contradiction between the idea of the 'rule of the people' and an institution claiming a monopoly of legitimate force for a particular territory.

This is not to deny that the more liberal the state the better, or that states that have the rule of law, regular elections and universal suffrage are preferable to states which do not. A liberal society has to be the basis for democracy: it is necessary, although not sufficient. Thus to the extent that, for example, Singapore does not allow its citizens to express themselves freely, it is undemocratic.

We want to argue that what makes a liberal society 'insufficient' is that it still needs a state, and the state, it could be suggested, is a repressively hierarchical institution that excludes outsiders and uses force to tackle conflicts of interest. Conservatives who complained that democracy is incompatible with the state are right. You cannot be said to govern your own life within the state. When the supreme ruler of the moon was told, as H.G. Wells recalls, that states existed on earth in which everybody rules, he immediately ordered that cooling sprays should be applied to his brows (Hoffman, 1995: 210).

Dahl, in fact, has argued that when individuals are forced to comply with laws, democracy is to that extent compromised (1989: 37). If you vote for a particular party through fear of what might happen to you if you do not, then such a system cannot be called democratic. Liberals have argued that a person cannot be said to act freely if they are threatened with force: yet the logic here points to a position that Dahl does not accept. If force is incompatible with self-rule, then it follows that the state cannot be reconciled with democracy. The use of force against a small number of people – something that no state can avoid – makes the idea of self-government problematic. This is why the notion of democracy as a form of the state is not self-evident, and it could be argued that this assumption weakens David Held's otherwise persuasive case for a 'cosmopolitan democracy'. Held acknowledges that the concept of democracy has changed its geographical and institutional focus over time. Like Dahl (1989: 194), he accepts that the notion of democracy was once confined to the city-state. It then expanded to embrace the nation-state, and it has now become a concept that stands or falls through an acknowledgement of its global character.

Since local, national, regional and global structures and processes all overlap, democracy must take a cosmopolitan form (Held, 1995: 21). Held argues (as, indeed, Dahl does) that people in states are radically affected by activities which occur outside their borders. Whether we think of the movement of interest rates, the profits that accrue to stocks and shares, the spread of AIDS, the movements of refugees and asylum seekers, or the damage to the environment, government is clearly stretching beyond the state.

What obstructs the notion of international democracy, Held argues, is the assumption that states are sovereign, and that international institutions detract from this sovereignty. The position of the United States under the Bush leadership (alarmingly reinforced rather than undermined by the reaction to the appalling events of 11 September 2001) is rooted in the archaic belief that institutions which look beyond the nation-state are a threat to, rather than a necessity for, democratic realities.

The post-war period has seen the development of what Held calls the UN Charter Model (1995: 86). However, although this has made inroads into the concept of state sovereignty (hence the US hostility to the United Nations), it coexists uneasily with what Held calls the 'the model of Westphalia' – the notion that states recognise no superior authority and tackle conflicts by force (1995: 78). A first step forward would involve enhancing the UN model by making a consensus vote in the General Assembly a source of international law, and providing a means of redress of human rights violations in an international court.

The Security Council would be more representative if the veto arrangement was modified, and the problem of double standards addressed – a problem that undermines the UN's prestige in the South (1995: 269). But welcome as these measures would be, they still represent, Held contends, a very thin and partial move towards an international democracy.

Held's full-blown model of cosmopolitan democracy would involve the formation of regional parliaments whose decisions become part of international law. There would be referenda cutting across nations and nation-states, and the establishment of an independent assembly of democratic nations (1995: 279). The logic of this argument implies the explicit erosion of state sovereignty and the use of international legal principles as a way of delimiting the scope and action of private and public organisations. These principles are egalitarian in character and would apply to all civic and political associations.

But how would they be enforced? It is here that Held's commitment to the state as a *permanent* actor on the international scene bedevils his argument. The idea of the state remains but it must, Held contends, be adapted to 'stretch across borders' (1995: 233). While he argues that the principle of 'non-coercive relations' should prevail in the settlement of disputes, the use of force as a weapon of last resort should be employed in the face of attacks to eradicate cosmopolitan law.

Held's assumption is that the existence of this force would be *permanent*. Yet these statist assumptions are in conflict with the aim of seconding this force, that is 'the demilitarisation and transcendence of the war system' (1995: 279). For this is only possible if institutions claiming a monopoly of legitimate force give way to what we have called governments, and the logic of government is, it has been argued above, profoundly different from that of the state. Held contends that we must overcome the **dualisms** between (for example) globalism and cultural diversity; global governance from above and the extension of grass roots organisations from below, constitutionalism and politics. These polarities make it impossible to embed utopia in what Held calls 'the existing pattern of political relations and processes' (1995: 286).

But as challenging as this model is, its incoherence is manifest in Held's continuing belief in the permanence of the state. In an analysis of democracy and autonomy, he argues that the demos must include all adults with the exception of those temporarily visiting a political community, and those who 'beyond a shadow of a doubt' are legitimately disqualified from participation 'due to severe mental incapacity and/or serious records of crime' (1995: 208). Temporary visitors would, it is true, be citizens of other communities. But excluding the mentally incapacitated from citizenship is far from self-evident, and while there may be a tactical argument for excluding serious criminals from voting (although the position on this is changing), the very existence of such a category of intransigent outsiders indicates how far we are from having a democracy.

Held argues that the nation-state would 'wither away' but by this he does *not* mean that the nation-state would disappear. What he suggests is that states would no longer be regarded as the 'sole centres of legitimate power' within their own borders, but would be 'relocated' to and articulated within an overarching global democratic law (1995: 233). Democracy would, it seems, be simultaneously statist, supra-statist and sub-statist, but although this is an attractive argument there remains a problem. States, after all, are institutions that claim a monopoly of legitimate force in 'their' particular territory. They are jealous of this asserted monopoly (which lies at the heart of the notion of state sovereignty) and, therefore, cannot coexist equally with other bodies that do not and cannot even claim to exercise a monopoly of legitimate force.

Held seeks to transform the world environment in the interests of self-government and **emancipation**, but he remains prisoner of the liberal view that the state is permanent. As far as Held is concerned, the state merely remains as one of many organisations. Yet the state is incompatible with democracy, and as it gives up its claim to a monopoly of legitimate force it ceases to be a state.

The Ancient Greek Polity and the Problem with Liberalism

The ancient Greek polity was, as noted above, exclusive, and Athenian democracy rested, among other things, upon imperialism. It is revealing that Rousseau, as an admirer of the ancient system, is uncertain as to how to respond to its reliance on slavery. On the one hand, he argues fiercely against slavery and takes great exception to Aristotle's comment that there are slaves 'by nature'. On the other hand, he concedes that without slavery democracy in ancient Greece would not have been possible (1968: 52; 142; Hoffman, 1988: 146).

The fact is that ancient Greek democrats took democracy to be a form of the state, although their concept of democracy was mystified by its apparent linkages with the old clan system of tribal times. When Kleisthenes overthrew the oligarchs and forged a new constitution at the end of fifth century BC, the external features of the old system were faithfully reproduced in the arrangements of the new. 'Restoring' the popular assembly, the festivals and the electoral system made it appear as though the people were simply recovering the ancient rights of their old tribal system.

The continuity was deceptive. The new units of the constitution, though tribal in form, were geographical in reality, so that in practice the new democratic constitution actually worked to accelerate the disintegration of the clan system. The development of commerce and industry helped to dissolve away the residues of the old kinship bonds, and introduce a system based on slavery. Morgan, a nineteenth-century US anthropologist, complained that a 'pure democracy' was marred by atrocious slavery (Hoffman, 1988: 147–8), but once we understand that this was a statist form of democracy, then the paradox of popular rule and slavery ceases to be a problem.

Conservatives failed to understand this when they feared that democracy would undermine 'natural' hierarchies. John Cotton, a seventeenth-century divine in New England, spoke of democracy as the meanest and most illogical form of government, since he asked: when the people govern, *over whom* do they rule? Many conservatives overlooked the statist character of classical liberalism. After all, the whole point of the classical liberal concept of the state of nature was to establish the impossibility of life without the state. It is true that classical liberals assumed that humans were 'naturally' free and equal, but they construed these qualities as market-based abstractions, so that inevitably as 'inconveniences' (as Locke politely terms them) set in, the state was required to maintain order.

Rousseau could speak of people leaving the state of nature in order to rush headlong into the chains of the state, but he takes it for granted that the legitimate rule, which forces people to be free, is of course a state.

When King Charles upbraided English liberals for labouring to bring in democracy, and told them that a subject and a sovereign 'are clear different things' (Dunn, 1979: 3), he need not have bothered. Liberals were clearly aware of this distinction. This is why de Tocqueville could describe the United States as a democracy – democracy could be many things, but de Tocqueville never imagined it doing away with the state. Dunn describes democracy as 'the *name* for what we cannot have' – people ruling their own state (1979: 27). But this is because he views the world from the standpoint of a liberal, and he takes it for granted that people cannot govern without an institution claiming a monopoly of legitimate force for a particular territory. One of the delegates of the South German People's Party declared at a conference in 1868 that 'democracy wants to become social democracy, if it honestly wants to become democracy' (Bauman, 1976: 43). It could be argued that the same thing should be said about democracy and the state. Only an institution that looks beyond the claim to exercise a monopoly of legitimate force can call itself a democracy!

Democracy and the Relational Argument

Once we challenge the idea that democracy can be a form of the state, then the argument that the will of the majority may favour arbitrary and repressive rule ceases to be persuasive.

For the point is that majorities cannot repress minorities unless their rule expresses itself in the form of the state. The examples that Crick gives are clearly statist in character, so that the problem is not really with majority rule: it is with the state. For how can we reconcile democracy with an institution claiming a monopoly of legitimate force?

The idea that democracy can express itself as a tyranny of the majority is not only empirically invalid, it is also logically problematic. For it assumes that individuals are completely separate from one another, so that it is possible for one section of the population (the majority) to be free while their opponents (the minority) are oppressed. But this argument is only defensible if we draw a sharp (and non-relational) line between the self and the other. If we embrace a relational approach, then the freedom of each individual depends upon the freedom of the other. As the Zimbabwean greeting puts it, I have slept well, if you have slept well: we may be separate people, but we are also related. It is impossible for a majority to oppress a minority, without oppressing itself.

Let me illustrate this logical point with an empirical example. Take the idea that was noted above of Ian Paisley's 'Protestant state for the Protestant people'. Up until 1972, it can be said that in Northern Ireland the Catholic minority were oppressed, and the Protestant majority ascendant. But how free was the majority? What happened if an individual Protestant wished to marry a Catholic, or became sympathetic to their point of view? What happened to Protestants who decided to revere the anti-colonial heritage of Protestants such as Wolfe Tone? How open

Biography   Carl Schmitt (1888–1985)

Born into a Catholic family in Westphalia.

Between 1919 and 1933 he pursued the career of academic jurist, moving from one chair to another. In 1933 he acquired the chair of public law at the University of Berlin. He acted as legal adviser to the national government when it defended itself against a case brought by Prussia in 1932.

From the early 1920s he had been a right-wing critic of the Versailles Peace Settlement and the League of Nations. He was also critical of the political structure of the Weimar Republic. In the 1920s and early 1930s he was closely associated with the Catholic Centre Party and in 1927 he published *The Concept of the Political*. A longer version appeared in 1932 and in 1933 certain alterations were entered into a further edition to make it acceptable to the Nazis. The book only appeared in English in 1976. In the book Schmitt argues that the friend/enemy distinction is a necessary feature of all political communities. Indeed, what defines the 'political' as opposed to other human activities is the intensity of feeling toward friends and enemies, or toward one's own 'kind' and those perceived as hostile outsiders.

From 1929 onwards, Schmidt contended that the president should exercise the emergency power granted him by Article 48 of the Weimar Constitution. He allied himself to General Schleicher. Schleicher resigned after his emergency proposals were rejected by Weimar President, Hindenburg. He was assassinated by the Nazis in 1934.

In 1931 and 1932 Schmitt urged Hindenburg to suppress the Nazi Party and to jail its leaders, and he sharply opposed those in the Centre Party who thought the Nazis could be tamed if they were forced to form a coalition government. The Weimar Constitution was overthrown by the Enabling Act of March 1933, and Schmitt joined the National Socialist Party in May of that year. He became director of the University Teachers' Group of the National Socialist League and endorsed the 'leadership principle' propagated by the Nazis. From 1934 he was subjected to attacks from Nazi ideologists and in 1936 he came under investigation from the SS. To ward off these attacks, he began to use racial and biological terminology and defend anti-Semitism, but as pressure continued to mount he retired from public life and devoted himself entirely to scholarly activities.

From September 1945 until May 1947 Schmitt was a prisoner of the US occupational forces in Germany. In the post-war period he continued to write, and despite hostile criticism a volume of his collected works appeared in 1958. His work continued to arouse interest and controversy and he favoured limiting the constitutional changes introduced through the amendment process. In this way he argued that the federal and democratic character of the Bonn constitution could never be altered.

In the 1990s (after Schmitt's death) his books became more influential and a stream of translations and analyses of his work appeared.

could loyalist-minded Protestants be about the partisan character of the police or the electoral malpractices designed to devalue Catholic votes? The point is that in a society in which there is a 'tyranny of the majority' no one is free and thus able to govern their own lives.

Chantal Mouffe, a radical post-structuralist theorist, has argued that democracy leads to the dictatorial rule of the popular will. It embodies the logic of what she calls identity or equivalence, whereas liberalism (which she prefers to democracy) respects difference, diversity and individual self-determination (1996: 25). But is this liberal polity a form of the state? On this crucial matter Mouffe is silent, and it is not surprising that her admiration for the pre-war conservative Carl Schmitt places her argument in still more difficulty. While she praises Schmitt for identifying politics with conflict, she is embarrassed by the avowedly statist way in which he interprets conflict (Hoffman, 1998: 60).

For Schmitt, the other is an enemy to be physically eliminated. While Mouffe identifies politics with conflict and difference, she is reluctant to see differences 'settled' in a statist manner through force. She seeks to distinguish between a social agent and the multiplicity of social positions that agents may precariously and temporarily adopt. The pluralism of multiple identities is 'constitutive of modern democracy' and 'precludes any dream of final reconciliation' (1996: 25). But if democracy is a form of the state then it will, indeed, rest upon an oppressive logic of equivalence that suppresses, rather than celebrates, difference.

The argument that democracy can be tyrannical makes the assumption that individuals and groups can be totally separated from each other. Democracy is conceived of as a Hobbesian Leviathan in majoritarian form (Hoffman, 1995: 202), by which is meant that democracy is analysed in terms of the kind of unrelated individuals that lie at the heart of Hobbes's argument for the state. Once we argue that the mechanisms of government must replace those of the state, then the notion of democracy becomes a way of resolving conflict in a way which acknowledges the identity of the parties to a dispute. It goes beyond the need for an institution claiming a monopoly of legitimate force – the state.

Summary

What makes democracy such a confusing concept is that it has been acclaimed from almost every part of the political spectrum – and is held to stand for contradictory ideals. Contrary to the notion of 'liberal democracy', it is important to remember that before the twentieth century liberals generally opposed democracy even though they were often accused by their conservative opponents of being democratic in character. Although liberalism presented its ideals in universal terms, there were all manner of exclusion clauses in practice. Liberals only reluctantly converted to democracy in the nineteenth century when they felt that extending the franchise would not undermine the rights of property.

The argument has been advanced even since World War II that democracy could mean a 'tyranny of the majority' and that democracy should be 'redefined' to involve a vote for competing elites to make decisions. In fact, increasing political participation is necessary for democracy and the argument for compulsory voting in elections should be taken seriously. It is misleading to argue that democracy involves either direct participation or representation. It involves both. Although representation does not require that those elected 'mirror' the precise proportions of the population, empathy between representative and elector is crucial.

If democracy is to involve self-government, there is a conflict between democracy, on the one hand, and the state, on the other. This is why Held's concept of a 'cosmopolitan democracy' can only be coherently sustained if the international community ceases to be composed of states. The question of the contradiction between democracy and the state has direct relevance for understanding the character and quality of the democracy in ancient Greece. Only

Ideas and Perspectives:

Democracy and Political Correctness

Political Correctness (PC) swept across US universities in the 1990s and occasioned much controversy. Although it has not made the same impact in British universities, it is often used in conservative discourse as a response to feminist and multiculturalist arguments. The law passed in the British parliament to outlaw fox-hunting – to take a recent example – has been condemned as PC by its opponents.

Political correctness is considered by its critics to be a negation of democracy. There is no doubt that what has given PC its unsavoury reputation is the problem of dogmatism. Feminist and multicultural arguments have been advanced on occasion in an anti-liberal manner that has enabled conservative-minded publicists and thinkers to identify emancipatory causes as being inherently illiberal in character. However, it could be argued that it is counter-productive (and indeed contradictory) to try and advance good causes through intolerance (and even worse harassment and the threat of violence). Emancipation should be liberating – to make it dreary and painful is to crush and distort it.

The cause of anti-racism or the cause of feminism, for example, is not advanced by pushing people into positions for which they are not qualified. The policy of affirmative action – promoting people because they are black or women or belong to a disadvantaged minority – is a risky one that only works at the margins and can easily backfire. The question is always: what is the best and quickest way of making our public and private institutions more representative of the population at large? Given the regrettable fact that elitism and prejudice have existed for so long that some even think they are 'natural' and 'normal', there are no quick and easy solutions – no short-cuts. Would that there were!

The insistence that the right kind of language is used is helpful in so far as it changes people's attitudes and behaviour. But what if it does not? What if people use the 'correct' language but still continue to behave in the old way? Democracy, alas, requires more than a change of language if it is to advance.

Democratic causes are those that empower people. If this is done in a way that commands wide support, we all benefit. Democracy can only advance if it tackles those who are hostile to democracy. PC needs defending both against those who advocate racism, sexism or homophobia, etc. and against those who ruin good causes by acting in an illiberal and unemancipatory manner. The best argument against those who promote good causes in an intemperate and divisive way is to tell them that they are not PC!

by analysing democracy in relation to the state can we develop a relational view that makes it possible to tackle the 'tyranny of the majority' argument effectively.

Questions

1. How democratic are 'liberal democracies'?
2. Is a society more democratic if more people participate in decision making?
3. Can a system be called democratic if it is illiberal in character?

4. Does democracy lead to the 'tyranny of the majority'?
5. Why is democracy such a confusing concept?

References

Bauman, Z. (1976) *Socialism as Utopia* London: George Allen & Unwin.

Crick, B. (1982) *In Defence of Politics* 2nd edn Harmondsworth: Penguin.

Dahl, R. (1989) *Democracy and its Critics* New Haven Conn.: Yale University Press.

Dunn, J. (1979) *Western Political Theory in the Face of the Future* London: Cambridge University Press.

Faulks, K. (1999) *Political Sociology* Edinburgh: Edinburgh University Press.

Faulks, K. (2001) 'Should Voting be Compulsory?' *Politics Review* 10(3), 24–5.

Goodwin, B. (1997) *Using Political Ideas* 4th edn Chichester, New York, Toronto: John Wiley & Sons.

Held, D. (1995) *Democracy and the Global Order* Cambridge: Polity Press.

Hoffman, J. (1988) *State, Power and Democracy* Brighton: Wheatsheaf Books.

Hoffman, J. (1995) *Beyond the State* Cambridge: Polity Press.

Macpherson, C. (1977) *The Life and Times of Liberal Democracy* London, Oxford and New York: Oxford University Press.

Mouffe, C. (1996) 'Radical Democracy or Liberal Democracy' in D. Trend (ed.), *Radical Democracy* New York and London: Routledge, 19–26.

Plato (1955) *The Republic* Harmondsworth: Penguin.

Rousseau, J.J. (1968) *The Social Contract* Harmondsworth: Penguin.

Schumpeter, J. (1947) *Capitalism, Socialism and Democracy* 2nd edn New York and London: Harper.

Tocqueville, A. de (1966) *Democracy in America* London and Glasgow: Fontana.

Weldon, T. (1953) *The Vocabulary of Politics* Harmondsworth: Penguin.

Further Reading

- Crick's Chapter 3, 'A Defence of Politics Against Democracy', in his *In Defence of Politics* (referenced above) is an absolute must for all interested in the question.

- C.B. Macpherson's *Life and Times of Liberal Democracy* (referenced above) contains a very useful assessment of different 'models'.

- Dahl's *Democracy and its Critics* (referenced above) is clear and comprehensive, and particularly memorable for its critique of majoritarian rule.

- John Dunn has a very thought-provoking chapter on democracy in his *Western Political Theory in the Face of the Future* (referenced above).

- M. Finley, *Democracy Ancient and Modern* London: Chatto and Windus, 1973 has an excellent description of ancient Greek democracy.

- David Held's *Democracy and the Global Order* (referenced above) is very useful for those particularly interested in reworking the concept in the light of international trends.

Weblinks

For the treatment of democracy in political theory, see:
http:// www.keele.ac.uk/depts/po/prs.htm or:
http://www.york.ac.uk/services/library/subjects/politint.htm

For those interested in the direct democracy debate, see:
http://www.homeusers.prestel.co.uk/rodmell/quest.htm

David Held's arguments can be seen at:
http://www.mpi-fg-koeln.mpg.de/pu/workpap/wp97-5/wp97-5.html

Chapter 6

Citizenship

Introduction

Is the term 'citizenship' legal, philosophical, political, social or economic? Or is it a combination of all these dimensions? Does this flexibility make the term so elastic that it is effectively unusable?

The literature on citizenship has burgeoned massively over the past decade, with a journal devoted to the concept; reports on the teaching of the idea to school students; ministerial pronouncements on the subject; and articles and books galore in scholarly and popular publications. There is even a ceremony that has been devised for new citizens! Although the classical concepts of citizenship go back to the ancient Greeks (as we shall see in a moment) and were reworked in classical liberalism, contemporary commentators have sought to develop a concept of citizenship that is much more inclusive than earlier views.

Chapter Map

- The limitations of the ancient Greek concept of citizenship, and the exclusiveness of the liberal view. The abstract character of the liberal view of citizenship, its universal claims to freedom and equality and the inequalities of class.

- Marshall's argument that citizenship, in its modern form, requires social as well as political and legal rights. The rise of the New Right in Britain and the United States and its challenge to the concept of citizenship in the welfare state.

- The barriers that women face to a meaningful citizenship. How and why these barriers prevent women from running their own lives and impoverish their citizenship.

- The case for a basic income as a way of enhancing citizenship.

- Global citizenship as a status that does not contradict citizenship as member of a state. Citizenship as an identity at local, regional and national levels as well. The development of citizenship in the European Union.

- The tension between the state and citizenship, the question of class and citizenship, the case for transforming the market, and the presentation of citizenship as a relational concept.

'Being British': Pride, Passports and Princes

Prince Charles attending citizenship ceremony at Brent Town Hall, 26 February 2004

In February 2004 19 immigrants received British passports in a ceremony in which they took an oath of allegiance to the Queen as head of state. The Prince of Wales handed out certificates, congratulating those receiving them. 'Being British', declared the Prince, 'is something of a blessing and a privilege for us all'. He hoped that the ceremony added something to the significance of acquiring British citizenship, and 'that it's reinforced your belief, if indeed any reinforcement is required, that you belong here and are very welcome'. He added that 'being a British citizen becomes a great source of pride and comfort for the rest of your life'. *Guardian* journalists in September 2003 found that when they questioned nine British citizens about key aspects of British life, the average score was just 37 per cent. Only a third of the sample could name the Home Secretary and knew what NHS Direct was, about 10 per cent knew what the national minimum wage was, and none knew what the basic rate of income tax was.

- Everyone agrees that British citizens should be able to speak English. But what other duties should someone fulfil in order to become a British citizen? Should they have a basic knowledge about British history, its political institutions and its society?

- Should would-be British citizens have to take an oath of allegiance to the Queen? What if they are republican minded, or feel as Jews, Catholics, Muslims, atheists, Hindus, Sikhs, etc. that the head of the state as an Anglican cannot be said to represent them?

- Should citizens have to vote in elections? Should they be expected to do community service at some stage? Should they receive as citizens a basic income from the government?

- Does citizenship require people to be involved in their locality and region? Should they also be concerned with developments in the European Union? Should they regard themselves as citizens of the world?

Citizenship and Liberalism

The notion of citizenship arises with ancient Greek thinkers (much of the argument here follows Hoffman, 2004). The citizen is traditionally defined as one who has the ability and chance to participate in government (by which is meant the state), but in Aristotle's aristocratic view, citizenship should not only exclude slaves, foreigners and women, but should be restricted to those who are relieved of menial tasks (1962: 111).

We must always bear this in mind when the argument is put for a 'revitalisation' and extension of the Aristotelian ideal of citizenship as the alternation of ruling and being ruled (Voet, 1998: 137). For the positive attributes of ancient Greek theory are undermined by the fact that they express themselves through gender, ethnic and (it should not be forgotten) imperial hierarchies, and we need to challenge the elitist notion of citizenship that the ancient Greeks took for granted.

Even when slavery was apparently rejected by a liberal view of humanity, the concept of citizenship has remained limited and exclusionary. It is revealing that Rousseau insists that the 'real meaning' of citizenship is only respected when the word is used selectively and exclusively (1968: 61). Citizens have property, are national (in their political orientation), and are public and male. Even the classical liberal opposition between citizenship and slavery is weakened by Rousseau's astonishing comment that in unfortunate situations (as in ancient Greece) 'the citizen can be perfectly free only if the slave is absolutely a slave' (1968: 143).

Ch 7:
Liberalism,
pp. 162–84

Classical liberalism injects a potential **universalism** into the concept of citizenship by arguing that all individuals are free and equal. Yet the universalism of this concept is undermined by support for **patriarchy**, elitism, colonialism – and as Yeatman has recently reminded us in the case of Locke – by an acceptance of outright slavery (Yeatman, 1994: 62; Hoffman, 1988: 162). Locke not only justifies slavery in his *Two Treatises* but he was a shareholder in a slave-owning company in Virginia. These rather startling facts coexist with the liberal notion of free and equal individuals.

Medieval thinkers, such as the ancient Greeks, have no universal concept of citizenship, because although medieval Christians, for example, had a notion of equality before the Fall, once humans are corrupted by sin ('the mother of servitude'), people divide into citizens and slaves, men and women, etc. in the time-honoured way.

Citizenship and Class

The recent literature on citizenship challenges the liberal concept of citizenship on the grounds that this concept leaves out many categories of people in society. The argument for a broader franchise was essentially an argument for broadening the concept of citizenship so that male workers could enjoy political rights.

Classical liberalism assumed that the individual had property, and as we shall see in the chapter on Socialism, some socialists such as Eduard Bernstein saw the notion of citizenship as something that workers could and should aspire to. Marx, on the other hand, appears to be bleakly negative towards the concept of citizenship, arguing that it seems to ignore the realities of a class-divided society. The rights of the citizen, he comments in an oft-cited passage, are simply the rights of the egoistic man (i.e. the property owner), of 'men separated from other men and the community' (Marx and Engels, 1975: 162). Marx's language is not only sexist, but he seems to be saying that citizenship is simply the right to exploit others through the ownership of private property. The possession of citizenship is seen as an anti-social activity.

But his argument is not quite as negative as it sounds. Marx comments that in the possessive individualist society, it is not 'man as *citoyen* but man as *bourgeois* who is considered to be the *essential* and *true* man' (Marx and Engels, 1975: 164). Marx's argument is that citizenship is abstract in so far as it implies an equality of an ideal kind, for this equality is contradicted by the concrete inequalities that exist in the real world. Even if the male worker can vote, how much power does he have over his life if his employer can have him summarily dismissed from this work?

It is important to stress that for Marx, the notion of abstraction does not imply unreality, in the sense that the abstract citizen does not exist. What makes the liberal notion of citizenship abstract is that it *conceals* beneath its benevolent-sounding principles the reality of class. While the *Communist Manifesto* sees the establishment of the 'modern representative State' (Marx and Engels, 1967: 82) as a crucial historical achievement, this state cannot be said to be representative of the community but acts on behalf of the capitalists. The celebrated description of communism as 'an association in which free development of each is the condition for the free development of all' (Marx and Engels, 1967: 105) could be taken, in our view, as a description of citizenship in a classless society.

Marx's concept of abstraction makes it possible to explain why Locke and the classical liberals of the seventeenth and eighteenth centuries could imagine that individuals existed in splendid isolation from one another in a state of nature, while continuing to trade as market partners. The market involves an exchange between individuals that conceals their differing social positions.

Marx's analysis can still be used as a critique of the liberal concept of the citizen, even though the notion of labour as the source of value is contentious. It is clear that how we evaluate goods depends upon the activities of numerous people – managers, workers, supervisors, consumers, entrepreneurs, etc. – and that it would be wrong to suggest that certain categories of people do not contribute to the labour process, and therefore, perhaps, should be 'second-class' citizens. This type of argument simply turns liberalism inside out: it discriminates against the haves in favour of the have-nots, whereas it could be argued that the point is to eliminate the distinction altogether.

Citizenship, Marshall and Social Rights

Liberalism establishes the formal freedom and equality of all members of society itself. Those who have no independent property cannot rest content with legal and political equality but must press on for social equality as well. The Chartists, although campaigners in the nineteenth century for political rights, were fond of saying that the vote is a knife and fork question: the demand for citizenship must

Biographies,
p. 41 and p. 111

be a demand for resources that make individuality not simply a condition to be protected, but a reality to be attained. J.S. Mill presents a developmental view of human nature when he argues that women and workers could become 'individuals'. T.H. Green and Hobhouse, as social liberals, argue the case for more security for workers.

Marshall (1893–1981), a British sociologist, wrote a much-cited essay on *Citizenship and Social Class* in 1950. He presents a classic argument that civil and political rights do not, on their own, create a meaningful citizenship. Social rights are also crucial. For Marshall, 'taming market forces was an essential precondition for a just society' (Marshall and Bottomore, 1992: vi). Marshall is concerned, despite the inadequacies of an argument that have been extensively commented upon, to try and give white male workers a human rather than a purely market identity. He cites with approval the nineteenth-century economist Alfred Marshall's notion of a 'gentleman' in contrast to a mere 'producing machine' (1992: 5) and he uses the terms civilisation and citizenship to denote people who are, he argues, 'full members of society' (1992: 6). As T.H. (not Alfred!) Marshall sees things, the right to property, as with the right of free speech, is undermined for the poor by a lack of social rights (1992: 21).

It is true that Marshall does not see himself as a critic of capitalism. His concern is to make a case for a basic human equality that is not inconsistent with the inequalities that distinguish the various economic levels in a capitalist society, and he even argues that citizenship has become the architect of legitimate social inequality (1992: 6–7). But the point is that he does perceive citizenship in tension with capitalism. In a famous passage he sees capitalism and citizenship at war, although (as Bottomore tartly comments), Marshall does not develop this argument (1992: 18; 56). It is important not to overlook the extent to which his new liberal reformism unwittingly challenges a class-divided society.

Ch 5:
Democracy,
pp. 104–26

As a social liberal, Marshall believes that a pragmatic compromise between capitalism and citizenship is possible, even though he can argue that the attitude of mind which inspired reforms such as legal aid grew out of a conception of equality that oversteps the narrow limits of a competitive market economy. Underlying the concept of social welfare is the conception of equal social worth and not merely equal natural rights (1992: 24). He notes – as part of his critique - early liberal arguments against universal male suffrage. The political rights of citizenship, unlike civil rights, are a potential danger to the capitalist system, although those cautiously extending them did not realise how great the danger was (1992: 25).

Citizenship has imposed modifications upon the capitalist class system on the grounds that the obligations of contract are brushed aside by an appeal to the rights of citizenship (1992: 40–2). In place of the incentive to personal gain is the incentive of public duty – an incentive that corresponds to social rights. Marshall believes that both incentives can be served – capitalism can be reconciled to citizenship since these paradoxes are inherent in our contemporary social system (1992: 43).

The preservation of economic inequalities has been made more difficult, Marshall concedes, by the expansion of the status of citizenship. To concede that individuals are citizens is to invite them to challenge the need for class divisions. The great strength of Marshall's argument is that he depicts the drive for social equality as a process that has been taking place for some 250 years (1992: 7). He opens up the prospect of the need to continue progress, given the fact that he later concedes that at the end of the 1970s the welfare state was in a precarious and battered condition (1992: 71).

It is certainly true that Marshall ignores the position of women and ethnic minorities, the sectarianism in Northern Ireland, and the peculiar conditions in the immediate post-war period that made a new liberal compromise seem plausible – to conservatives as well as to many social democrats. There were, as Bottomore has noted (1992: 58), exceptionally high rates of economic growth, and the deterrent example of the Communist Party states, the self-styled 'real socialism'. Marshall treats capitalism in terms of the income of the rich, rather than the property they own. But our point is that Marshall demonstrates that a concern with the social rights of the citizen challenges the class structure of a capitalist society.

Biography   Thomas Humphrey Marshall (1893–1981)

Marshall taught at the London School of Economics from 1925 until his retirement in 1956.

He was originally an economic historian. When he joined the LSE in 1925 it was as an assistant lecturer in social work. He moved to the sociology department in 1929, receiving a readership the following year.

Marshal played a key role in launching the *British Journal of Sociology* in 1949. He edited publications such as *Class Conflict and Social Stratification* and *The Population Problem* in 1938, and this activity played a crucial part in providing the foundations for social class and population studies at the LSE after the war.

He served in the Foreign Office during the war. In 1944 he was appointed Professor of Social Institutions and headed the social science department. From 1949–50 he served as the educational adviser to the British High Commission in Germany, and was appointed Martin White Professor of Sociology in 1954. From 1956–60 he was the director of the social sciences department of UNESCO.

Marshall perceived society as a social system of interrelated activities that allowed the individual free choice. He saw sociology as a discipline to be applied practically – hence his work in social policy and administration, planning, education and equality. He contributed to the development of social policy and administration through research stretching from social policy and the nature of citizenship to social welfare placed within the broader sociological context.

In 1950 he published *Citizenship and Social Class*, a key text in both British sociology and the study of citizenship. His *Social Policy in the Twentieth Century* (1965) provides a clear analysis of the development of welfare policy from 1890 and he argued for the compatibility of modified capitalist enterprise and collectivist social policies, postulating that a free economic market contributed to the enhancement and creation of welfare.

Marshall continued to write after his retirement. Other publications include *Class, Citizenship, and Social Development* (1964) and *The Right to Welfare* (1981).

Citizenship and the New Right

The expansion of social rights, it has been frequently noted, was checked in the mid-1970s, as the capitalist market economy became dominant over the welfare state (Marshall and Bottomore, 1992: 73). New Right or neo-liberal thought seeks to defend individualism and the market against what it sees as menacing inroads created by a post-war consensus around reform. The New Right project, which lasts until the 1990s, is indirectly related to the image of a citizen as a successful entrepreneur who benefits from 'free' market forces.

Ch 4: Justice, pp. 82–103

The argument is that the concept of society is a dangerous abstraction – there are only individuals – but although neo-liberals appear to return to the classical liberal position, gone is the assumption that humans are free and equal individuals. Free, yes, but equal, no. Individuals radically differ according to ability, effort and incentives and, therefore, it is a myth to imagine that they are in any sense equal. New Rightists argue that any attempt to implement distributive or social justice can only undermine the unfettered choices of the free market. 'Nothing', Hayek argues, 'is more damaging to the demand for equal treatment than to base it on so obviously untrue an assumption as that of the factual equality of all men' (1960: 86; see also Heater, 1999: 27). Equality before the law and material equality are seen to be in conflict, and Hayek is in the curious philosophical position of arguing for an 'ideal' or 'moral' equality while denying that any basis for this equality exists in reality.

Both Hayek and Nozick, despite their differences in many theoretical respects, agree that intervention in the market in the name of social justice is anathema. Both link citizenship to inequality. New Right thinkers, in trying to 'roll back the state', seek to confine it to its so-called negative activities – the protection of contracts. Not surprisingly, New Right policies under Thatcher in Britain radically increased the role of the state (in its traditional law and order functions), since weakening the trade unions, cutting welfare benefits and utilising high unemployment as a way of punishing the poor and the protesters, involved a radical concentration of state power. Both Thatcher and Hayek share an admiration for General Pinochet, who demonstrated in Chile that enhancing the power of the market may be bad for democracy!

Gray speaks of Hayek 'purifying' classical liberalism of its errors of abstract individualism and rationalism (Faulks, 1998: 61). It could be argued that the New Right supports the weaknesses of classical liberalism without its conceptual strengths. Faulks challenges the argument that the pressure against social rights takes the form of a reassertion of civil rights, since in practice, Faulks argues that civil rights without social rights are hollow and extremely partial. What is the point of allowing freedom of speech without the provision of education that develops linguistic capacity, or freedom under the law in a system which denies most of the population the resources to secure legal representation?

The notion of freedom as power or capacity is seen by Hayek as 'ominous' and dangerous (1960: 16-17). Hayek supports what he sees as purely negative freedom, but the truth is that negative without positive freedom is an impossible abstraction and a distinction that is alien to the classical liberal tradition. Classical liberal thinkers assumed that (certain) individuals had the capacity to act: what they needed was the right to do so. But Hayek divorces freedom from capacity, and contends that since to be free can involve freedom to be miserable, to be free may mean freedom to starve (1960: 18). No wonder traditional conservatives such as Ian Gilmour see these views as doctrinaire and utopian (1978: 117), and it is revealing that in *The Downing Street Years* Thatcher discusses socialism and 'High Toryism' in the same breath (Faulks, 1998: 79).

The New Right unwittingly demonstrates the indivisibility of rights. Hayek is far from enthusiastic about the exercise of political rights since the mass of the population might be tempted to use their political rights to secure the kind of capacities and power that the free market denies them. In practice, Hayek is an elitist and, as Faulks comments, his version of liberalism is difficult to distinguish from authoritarian **conservatism**. Conflict of a violent kind is simply increased by the creation of vast inequalities, and insofar as the modern United States approximates to the neo-liberal view of citizenship, it is not surprising that this is a society that marginalises its inner city areas and is afflicted by high rates of drug abuse and organised crime (Faulks, 1998: 71–2). A Hobbesian Leviathan state, aggravated by the hysteria that has followed the dreadful events of 11 September 2001, reveals the free market as a Hobbesian state of nature without the equality.

Thatcher argues, as Faulks has recalled, that many people fail in society because they are unworthy. 'With such a view, Thatcherism carried to its logical conclusion the abstract and elitist logic of the individualism in neo-liberal political theory' (1998: 86). She makes a distinction between *active* and *passive* citizens, and although the coexistence of the free market and strong state seems paradoxical, in fact, as Gilmour has commented, the establishment of a free market state is a 'dictatorial venture' that demands the submission of dissenting institutions and individuals (Faulks, 1998: 89; Gray, 1999: 26).

It would be wrong, however, to see the New Right in purely negative terms. Those who subscribed to New Right ideas sought to free 'individuals' from dependency upon others and often employed sophisticated theories to demonstrate their arguments. The New Right emphasised what is surely an essential ingredient

How to read:

Marshall's *Citizenship and Social Class*

This book usually comes with other essays. These essays are, of course, of interest, but for the purposes of this chapter they can be ignored. Concentrate on *Citizenship and Social Class*: it is a relatively short work. Skim read about half of section 1 until you reach the last couple of pages and then read carefully. Section 2 is important because here Marshall sets out what he considers to be the history of citizenship (at least in Britain) and he deals with the development of civil rights and the problem (as in the Poor Law) when they are divorced from social rights. Section 3 also deserves a careful read since it relates to the extension of political rights. Marshall clears the way for his most important argument noting (in the nineteenth century) the growing interest in the principles of equality and social justice. Section 4 is the most crucial part of his argument, entitled 'Social Rights in the Twentieth Century' and should be read (if necessary, re-read) with great care. Don't worry about the figures from the 1940s – concentrate on the wider points he is making. The 'conclusions' also deserve a read since it is a useful summing up of his argument as a whole.

in citizenship: the need to be independent and think critically for oneself. The challenge is to extend this notion to all inhabitants in society so that the skills of enterprise can be enjoyed widely.

Citizenship and the Case for a Basic Income

As long as social rights are seen as special entitlements for those who have 'failed' they will always be divisive, and reaffirm rather than undermine, class differences.

In her assessment of the welfare state, Pateman makes the case for a guaranteed income for everyone (Hoffman, 1995: 205), and the value of this proposal as a citizens' or basic income is that it would be universal. This proposal is also made by New Rightists who speak of the need for a 'negative income tax'. All would receive this income, regardless of employment status. As Faulks points out (2000: 120), it could decommodify social rights (i.e. take them away from the market), and break with the argument that those who lack capital must work for others. A guaranteed basic income would give people a real choice as to how and in what way they wanted to work, and empower citizens as a whole.

It would enable people to think much more about the 'quality of life' and the ecological consequences of material production. It would enhance a sense of community and individual autonomy, and underpin the social and communal character of wealth creation (Faulks, 2000: 120). It is not difficult to see how a basic income would also dramatically improve the position of women, whose precarious economic position makes them particularly dependent upon men or patriarchal-minded partners. It is true that were this idea taken in abstraction from other policies concerned with reducing inequality (as in the development of a democratic policy for ethnic minorities and movements towards genuinely universal education), then it could be divisive, tying women to domestic duties, and leaving the capitalist labour contract unreformed. But as Faulks comments, 'no one policy can address all possible inequalities' (2000: 120).

People seek to work outside the home for social reasons (and not simply economic ones), and a guaranteed income would give people time and resources to be more involved in community-enhancing activities such as lifelong learning, voluntary work and political participation. The argument that universal benefits undermine personal responsibility (Saunders, 1995: 92) seems to us precisely wrong since the assumption that people will only act sensibly if they are threatened with destitution and poverty reflects an elitist disregard for how people actually think.

But what of the cost? Surely a citizens' income is not economically feasible, given the argument that the rich will not tolerate paying higher levels of taxation? The idea of a guaranteed income appears to be a non-starter. There are a number of counter-arguments that should be put:

- A guaranteed income would markedly simplify the difficult and complex tax and benefit system: significant savings could be made here.
- People will pay for universal benefits if they are convinced of the need for them. The widespread support for, say, the British National Health Service as a

provider of universal benefits shows that increasing taxation is much more palatable if people are convinced that it is linked to changes which will really improve their lives. Adair Turner lists some of the collective goods – subsidised public transport, traffic-calming measures, noise abatement baffles and tree screens to make our motorways less intrusive – which he would prefer to (for example) a bigger and more stylish car. 'I would rather pay more tax to get those benefits than have the extra, personal income available to buy more market goods' (2002: 125).

- A guaranteed income is in the interests of all. A basic income would (along with many other egalitarian measures) help to reduce crime and the consumption of drugs, and make society as a whole a more secure and safer place. Would not the rich benefit from such a measure? Capitalism's beneficiaries, Adair Turner argues, should support investment in measures that promote social cohesion, out of their own self-interest (2002: 244). Gray argues that British public opinion wishes to see some goods – basic medical care, schooling, protection from crime – provided to all as a mark of citizenship (1999: 34). Is it not possible that given the right leadership and explanation, this could extend to the kind of economic security provided by a citizens' income?

Of course, it could be argued that a basic income will destroy incentives, just as it was said that a minimum wage would create unemployment, and in the nineteenth century it was contended that a ten-hour day would undermine the labour process. But a government committed to such a dramatic victory of 'the political economy of the working class' (in Marx's celebrated phrase) could find ways of presenting the case for a guaranteed income that would isolate diehard reactionaries.

It is important to stress that while a basic income would do much to increase the quality of citizenship, it would still leave open the question of including people from other countries in a global citizenship. Such an innovation would initially be limited to people of a particular community (Faulks, 2000: 123). It would only really succeed if it was part and parcel of policies that addressed the problem of inequalities between societies.

Citizenship and Women

Are women citizens in modern liberal states? Although women have been citizens in a formal sense in Britain, for example, since 1928 (when they received the vote), there are important senses in which women have yet to obtain real citizenship.

Women, even in developed liberal societies such as Britain, are significantly underrepresented in decision making, and this occurs because of structural and attitudinal factors. The exclusion of women from political processes has been justified by a liberal conception of a public/private divide.

Ch 13: Feminism, pp. 324–48

It is true that with Wollstonecraft's *Vindication of the Rights of Woman* (1792), the Enlightenment concepts of freedom and autonomy are extended to women. At the same time Wollstonecraft does not (explicitly at any rate) challenge the division of labour between the sexes or the argument for a male-only franchise. Women, she contends, if they are recognised as rational and autonomous beings, become better wives, mothers and domestic workers as a result – 'in a word, better citizens' (Bryson, 1992: 22–7). Here the term does not imply someone with voting rights, although it does suggest that the citizen is an individual whose activity is both public and private in character. Of course, when Wollstonecraft was writing most men could not vote, and there is some evidence to suggest that Wollstonecraft was in favour of female suffrage, but felt that it was not a demand worth raising at the time she wrote.

Bryson has noted that women find it more difficult to have their voices heard, their priorities acknowledged and their interests met (1994: 16). A recent report documents in detail the underrepresentation of women in all major sectors of decision making in Britain, from Parliament, the Civil Service, the judiciary, the legal profession, the police, local government, health, higher education, the media, public appointments and the corporate sector. For example, the United Kingdom is the fourth lowest in terms of the representation of women in the European Parliament at 24 per cent in 2000; it does better in a relative sense (in 1997) in terms of representation in national parliaments, where it has 18 compared to Denmark's 33 per cent. Only 4.3 per cent of life peers in the House of Lords were women in 2000, while in the most senior grades of the Civil Service 17.2 per cent were women in 1999. Of the High Court Judges in 1999 9 per cent were women, although this is three times as many as women who were Lord Justices! There were 6.4 per cent of chief constables who were women in 2000; ten years previously there were none (Ross, 2000).

It is true that the representation of women is complex, and it does not follow that women representatives automatically and necessarily represent the interests of women in general. But there is clearly something wrong, as Voet acknowledges, with political institutions that dramatically underrepresent women (1998: 106–8). Citizenship requires both the right and the capacity to participate in political decision making. The real difficulty of women's citizenship is 'the low level of female participation in social and political decision-making' (Voet, 1998: 124; 132).

The public/private divide, as formulated in liberal theory, prevents women from becoming meaningful citizens. It undermines the confidence of women; prejudices men (and some women) against them; puts pressures on leisure time; trivialises and demonises those women who enter public life; and through a host of discriminatory practices that range from the crudely explicit to the subtly implicit, prevent women from taking leadership roles. Women members of the British Parliament still complain that their dress or physical appearance is commented upon in the media, although it would be unthinkable to do the same for men.

It is true that the public/private divide as it operates as a barrier to citizenship is only implicit in liberal societies today. Whereas ancient (by which we mean slave-owning) societies and medieval societies explicitly divided the activities between men and women, under liberalism the public/private divide focuses on the relationship between individuals and the state.

Yuval-Davis (1997) has argued that we should abandon the public/private distinction altogether – a position Voet challenges (1998: 141). It is both possible and necessary to reconstruct the concept of the public and the private so that it ceases to be patriarchal in character. Liberal theory sees freedom, in Crick's words, as 'the privacy of private men from public action' (1982: 18). As Crick's comment (and his revealing use of language) suggests, this is a freedom that extends only to males, since (as MacKinnon puts it) 'men's realm of private freedom is women's realm of collective subordination' (1989: 168). Citizenship requires participation in public arenas. Domestic arrangements are crucial that allow women to be both childbearers (should they wish), and workers outside the home, representatives at local, national and international level, and leaders in bodies that are outside the domestic sphere. This is not to say that women (as with people in general) should not cherish privacy, but the public/private concept needs to be reconstructed (as we have suggested above) so that it empowers rather than degrades and diminishes women.

Women cannot be citizens unless they are treated as equal to men, and by equality we mean not merely sameness but an acknowledgement (indeed a celebration) of difference, not only between women and men but among women themselves.

The involvement of women in contemporary liberal societies as members of the armed and police forces is a necessary condition for women's citizenship because it helps to demystify the argument that only men can bear arms and fight for their country. Deeply embedded in traditionalist notions of citizenship is the idea that only those who go to war for their country can be citizens. It is worth noting, however, that armies in liberal societies will increasingly be used for peacekeeping and even development purposes, so that the notion of soldiers bearing arms is likely to become more and more redundant anyway. But being conscious of the link between patriarchy and war involves rather more than 'opening' up armies to women. It involves a recognition of the link between male domination and violence. Citizenship requires security – not simply in the sense of protection against violence – but in the sense of having the confidence, the capacity and the skills to participate in decision making. What Tickner calls a people-centred notion of security (1995: 192) identifies security as a concept that transcends state boundaries so that people feel at home in their locality, their nation and in the world at large.

It can be argued that the traditional caring role of many women brings an important dimension to citizenship itself. The notion that feminist conceptions of citizenship should be 'thick' (i.e. local and domestic) rather than 'thin' (i.e. public and universalist) rests upon a dichotomy which needs to be overcome. This is why the debate between 'liberals' and 'republicans' is, in our view, an unhelpful one for women (as it is for people in general). Both liberalism and republicanism presuppose that politics is a 'public' activity that rises above social life. Liberals argue for a negative view of the individual who is encouraged to leave public life to the politicians, while republicans stress the need to participate, but both premise their positions on a public/private divide that is patriarchal in essence.

Bubeck (1995: 6) instances Conservative proposals in Britain to extend the notion of good citizenship to participation in voluntary care, protection schemes or neighbourhood policing. These are useful ways of enriching citizen practices for both women and men. But what is problematic is a notion of political participation that ignores the social constraints which traditionally have favoured men and disadvantaged women. The fact that the obligation to care for children and the elderly has fallen upon women as a domestic duty does not make it non-political and private. Bubeck speaks of the existence of 'a general citizen's duty to care'

(1995: 29) and, as she puts it later, the performance of this care needs to be seen as part of what it means, or it implies, to be a member of a political community (1995: 31).

Care should be transformed from what Bubeck calls a 'handicap' of women to a general requirement for all (1992: 34). Providing care should be seen to be as much of an obligation as fighting in a war (1995: 35). But whereas fighting in a war implies a sharp and lethal **division** between friends and enemies, the provision of care seeks to heal such divisions. The notion of 'conscription' into service that could either exist alongside or be an alternative to the army is an attractive one. A caring service of some kind has an important role to play in developing a citizenship that combats patriarchy and recognises the position of women.

Ch 17:
Difference,
pp. 418–34

However, we cannot accept Pateman's argument that citizenship itself is a **patriarchal** category, although it is perfectly true that citizenship traditionally has been constructed in a masculinist image (Mouffe, 1992: 374). Men are different from women, and some women are different from others. Respecting difference is an important part of extending citizenship, so that Mouffe puts the matter in a misleading way when she argues that sexual difference is not a 'pertinent distinction' to a theory of citizenship (1992: 377). Biological differences remain 'relevant' to citizenship even if these should not be used as a justification for discrimination. Differences between men and women no more exclude the latter from citizenship than differences between men can justify exclusion. But it does not follow that these differences cease to be 'pertinent'. We should not, in other words, throw the baby out with the bathwater. One-sided points need to be incorporated – not simply cast aside. Differences between men and women remain relevant but they do not justify restricting citizenship – with all this implies – to either gender.

Global Citizenship

Is citizenship limited to the membership of a particular nation? Writers such as Aron (cited by Heater, 1999: 150) have declared that 'there are no such animals as "European citizens". There are only French, German or Italian citizens'. In this view, citizenship involves the membership of a national or domestic state.

Cosmopolitans argue, however, that the assertion of rights and responsibilities at the global level in no way contradicts loyalties at a regional, national and local level. People, in whatever area of government they are involved, must be respected and empowered, whether they are neighbours in the same block, people of their own nation and region, or members of the other countries in distant parts of the world. One of the most positive features of globalisation is that people meet others of different ethnic and cultural origin and outlook, not only when they travel abroad, but even at the local level. The media (at its best) presents people suffering and developing in other parts of the world as though they were neighbours, so that it becomes increasingly possible to imagine what it is like to be the other. Modern conditions have contributed much to realise Kant's argument that 'a violation of rights in *one* part of the world is felt *everywhere*' (cited by Heater, 1999: 140).

Lister links the notion of 'global citizenship' with a 'multi-layered conception' of citizenship itself (1997: 196), with states acknowledging the importance of human rights and international law. Each layer, if it is democratically constructed, strengthens the other. Global citizenship – a respect for others, a concern for their well-being and a belief that the security of each person depends upon the security of everyone else – does not operate in contradiction with regional, national and local identities. People can see themselves as Glaswegian, Scottish, British and European. Why do they have to make a choice? As Lister puts it, either/or choices lead us into a theoretical and political cul-de-sac (1997: 197). Heater argues that the 'singular concept' of citizenship has burst its bounds (1999: 117) and it is true that dual citizenship (which already exists in some states) represents a much more relaxed view of the question so that a person can exercise state-centred citizenship rights in more than one country. Heater presses the case for a fluid and flexible notion of citizenship, stating that membership of a voluntary association in civil society can qualify a person for citizenship, so that we can legitimately speak of a person as the citizen of a church, a trade union, a club, an environmental group etc. (1999: 121). Heater insists that civil society offers a useful and even superior option to traditional state membership (1999: 121).

It goes without saying that the notion of a world or global citizen cannot prescribe rights and responsibilities with the precision that citizenships set out in written (or indeed unwritten) constitutions can and do. Nor, as Heater shows at some length, is the notion of a world citizen a new one. He gives examples of cosmopolitanism in ancient Greek thought, and quotes the words of the ancient Roman, Marcus Aurelius, that 'where-ever a man lives, he lives as a citizen of the World-City' (1999: 139).

The celebrated Kantian argument for world government is for a loose confederation of states. Heater is sympathetic to the notion of a global citizen, writing that 'a fully-fledged modern world state' might well require 'a transfer of civil allegiance from the state to the universal polity' (1999: 151). He argues that 'political citizenship, so intimately reliant on the possession of the means of force by the state, must remain absorbed in the state as the necessary catalyst for its vitality' (1999: 152). The ideal of cosmopolitan citizenship is the condition in which all human beings have equal recognition as co-legislators within a 'global kingdom of ends' (Linklater, 1999: 56). Soysal even insists that the identity of personhood stressed in human rights discourse takes us beyond both citizenship and the state. Her point is national and citizenship identities are, in her view, unthinkable without the state (1994: 165).

The Argument So Far . . .

- Citizenship has traditionally been seen as membership of the state.
- This has linked citizenship to *exclusion*, whether of slaves, women or the propertyless.
- The problem of exclusion has been addressed by developing a concept of citizenship that embraces not merely political and legal, but social rights as well. The latter have proved controversial and the New Right has argued that the welfare state creates a 'dependency' that undermines the autonomy of the citizen. The idea of giving all citizens a basic income as of right could, it has been argued, enhance citizenship.

Biography

Immanuel Kant (1724–1804)

Born in Königsberg, the capital of East Prussia, the child of poor but devout followers of Lutheran Pietism. Kant's promise was recognised by the Pietist minister Franz Albert Schultz, and he received a free education at the Pietist gymnasium. At 16, Kant entered the University of Königsberg, where he studied mathematics, physics, philosophy, theology and classical Latin literature.

Kant left university in 1746, and his first work was published three years later – *Thoughts on the True Estimation of Living Forces*. Kant then worked as a tutor, serving in households near Königsberg for the next eight years. When he returned to the university in 1755, however, he had several works ready for publication. The first of these was *Universal Natural History and Theory of the Heavens*, a much more successful scientific work than his first. Kant also published two Latin works, which earned him the right to offer lectures at the university as a *Privatdozent* paid directly by his students. The following year Kant published a work on natural philosophy that made him eligible for a salaried professorship, although he was not to receive one until 1770. In these years, Kant also published four essays on earthquakes and winds.

Kant began lecturing in the autumn of 1755. His topics included logic, metaphysics, ethics and physics, and he subsequently added physical geography, anthropology, pedagogy, natural right and even the theory of fortifications. Except for one small essay on optimism (1759), he did not publish again until 1762, when a further four publications earned Kant widespread recognition in Germany. During this period, Kant was deeply struck by the work of Jean-Jacques Rousseau, and he was also acquainted with the philosophy of David Hume.

Kant was appointed Professor of Logic and Metaphysics in Königsberg in 1770. Beginning in 1781, with the first edition of the *Critique of Pure Reason*, Kant unleashed a steady torrent of books. From a politics point of view, the most significant of these include his two essays, 'Idea for a Universal History from a Cosmopolitan Point of View' and 'What is Enlightenment?' in 1784 and *The Groundwork of the Metaphysics of Morals*. In 1793 he wrote the political essay 'On the Common Saying: "That may be right in theory but does not work in practice"', and *Towards Perpetual Peace* appeared in 1795.

Kant retired from lecturing in 1797, at the age of 73, and devoted his remaining years to a work that was to be entitled 'The Transition from the Metaphysical First Principles of Natural Science to Physics', but which was far from complete when Kant ceased working on it in 1803. After a lifetime of hypochondria without any serious illness, Kant gradually lost his eyesight and strength and died in 1804.

- Even in liberal societies where women have acquired political rights, it is arguable that they have been confronted with a number of barriers preventing them from exercising their rights.
- Cosmopolitans argue that citizenship should extend to the world as a whole, so that people are not merely citizens of a particular country, but citizens of the globe.

Citizenship within the European Union

The European Union (EU) is concerned about equalisation and redistributive social policies. Richard Bellamy and Alex Warleigh's edited *Citizenship and Governance in the European Union* (2001) sees the EU and its concept of citizenship as a paradox and a puzzle. Is the Union seeking to establish a new kind of political entity or is it simply another (and larger) version of a state? The EU, this volume argues, has two aspects: one is the market, the other is democracy. Neo-liberals may think of the two as synonymous, but that view is not shared by the contributors to this volume who point out that citizenship is a political issue that necessarily transcends a market identity.

The argument advanced is that while the current rights of the EU citizen may at present seem somewhat limited, we should be concerned with unanticipated outcomes. Under the provisions of the Maastricht Treaty European citizens have the right to stand and vote in local and European parliamentary elections even if they are not nationals in the states where they reside; they can petition the newly created Ombudsman as well as the European Parliament, and they are entitled to diplomatic protection in third states where one's 'own' state is not represented (2001: 23).

To be sure, the EU was initially conceived as a transnational capitalist society, an economic union that was a free trade area. It could, however, be argued that people such as Jean Monnet had explicitly political objectives right from the start. There is a logic to the EU that extends beyond the purely economic. It may well have been (for example) the *intention* of EU founders to confine sexual equality to the notion of a level playing field constituted by the cost of factors of production, but economic rights require a political and social context to be meaningful. It is the *potential* of EU citizenship that is important. It is this that links a rather passive, state-centred notion to a much more 'active, democratic citizenship' (Bellamy and Warleigh eds, 2001: 117), a move from a politics of identity – which implies a rather repressive homogeneity – to a politics of affinity that recognises and respects difference.

Citizenship is a 'surprisingly elusive concept' (Bellamy and Warleigh eds, 2001: 143), and the concept is an excellent example of an idea that compels us to think the unthinkable. Indeed, the very notion of citizenship was introduced as an attempt to overcome the 'democratic deficit' – to combat the view that the EU is an alien body and that only nation-states really matter. Undoubtedly there is a 'dualism' at the heart of concept of EU citizenship. On the one hand, the term is tied to states and markets. On the other hand, the European Court of Justice has interpreted the question of freedom of movement in broad social terms, as a quasi-constitutional entitlement, and not simply as a direct economic imperative. Thus, to take an example, the right to freedom of movement is linked to the right not to be discriminated against by comparison with host-state nationals (Bellamy and Warleigh eds, 2001: 96).

Bellamy and Warleigh (and those who contribute to their volume) acknowledge that current rights of EU citizens are limited, but their point is that once the notion of citizenship is established the anomaly of confining political rights to those who

Biography   Jean Monnet (1888–1979)

Born in Cognac, France, Monnet started his professional life as a salesman in his family's cognac business.

During World War I he worked in London in the field of economic cooperation among the Allies and in 1920 was appointed Deputy Secretary-General of the newly established League of Nations. He left the League in 1923 to return to his family business. For the next 15 years he was active in international finance before returning, this time in Washington, to planning economic cooperation between the United Kingdom, France and the United States. It was Monnet who, as France was in retreat before the German advance of June 1940, persuaded Winston Churchill to forward to the French prime minister a draft declaration proclaiming an 'indissoluble union' between France and the United Kingdom.

After the war he was put in charge of the *Commissariat du Plan* responsible for the economic recovery of France. In 1950 he suggested to Robert Schuman, the French foreign minister, the idea of pooling French and German coal and steel production. This led to the establishment of the European Coal and Steel Community (ECSC) with Monnet as the first President of the High Authority (the forerunner of the European Commission).

However, his other great plan of this period, the European Defence Community, came to nothing, and in November 1954 he resigned from the High Authority to devote himself to freelance campaigning on behalf of European unification. He famously commented that national sovereignty was a barrier to peace in Europe, and that 'prosperity and vital social progress will remain elusive until the nations of Europe form a federation'. He was in constant conflict with de Gaulle during the 1960s.

are already citizens of member states becomes plain. Already, limited rights – such as the right to petition the parliament and refer matters to the Ombudsman – are bestowed on individuals even if they are not members of one of the constituent nation-states, and are therefore not 'citizens'. In Heater's view, the EU is a sophisticated example of a new kind of citizenship: but 'at the moment, to be honest, it is a mere shadow of that potential' (1999: 129).

The European Ombudsman was introduced in 1992 as a result of Spanish enthusiasm for EU citizenship and Danish concern for administrative efficiency. The Ombudsman can deal with a wide range of issues including matters relating to the environment and human rights. Questions of administrative transparency and the use of age limits in employment have been vigorously pursued, and the Ombudsman should not be seen as a 'stand-alone' institution, but one that coexists with courts, tribunals, parliaments and other intermediaries at European, national, regional and local levels.

It is clearly wrong to think that greater rights for European citizens will happen automatically. Those who favour this development will need to struggle for it, arguing that a European identity does not exist in competition with other identities. On the contrary, European institutions have the potential to add to and reinforce national and sub-national governance, although conflict and dialogue exist between these levels.

This requires a movement both upwards and downwards – involving more and more people at every level. The crucial question facing the EU at the moment seems to us to be the status of residents who are currently excluded from EU citizenship.

Here, as the Bellamy and Warleigh volume argues, a statist 'nationality' model currently prevails, with ethnic migrants being seen as vulnerable 'subjects' rather than as active and entitled members of the EU. Yet, as is pointed out, Article 25, for example, of the draft Charter of Fundamental Rights does allow residents who are non-citizens to vote and stand for EU elections (Bellamy and Warleigh eds, 2001: 198).

Enlargement of the EU poses another set of challenges. The accession of a state such as Turkey can only broaden the cultural horizons of Europeans, and the problem with Turkey's admission arises around the question of human rights, not because the country is predominantly Muslim in its culture. European citizenship, it could be argued, demonstrates that a citizenship beyond the state is a real possibility.

Does the State Undermine Citizenship?

Citizenship has generally been conceived as membership of the state. Lister comments that 'at its lowest common denominator' we are talking about the relationship 'between individuals and the state' (1997: 3). Voet likewise takes it for granted that citizenship is tied to the state (1998: 9). Oomen argues that the term is meaningless unless it is anchored to the state, so that notions of 'global' or 'world' citizenship cannot be authentic until we have a world or global state. Thus European Union citizenship, he insists, will only become a possibility when the union becomes a multinational federal state (1997: 224). Although Carter is critical of those who reject cosmopolitanism, she takes it for granted that global citizenship requires a global state (2001: 168). Marcus Aurelius is cited by Heater as saying that we are all members of a 'common State' and presenting the 'Universe' as if 'it were a State' (1999: 135).

Yet the case for assuming that being a citizen is only possible if one is a member of a state is contestable. There is, for example, considerable unease among feminist scholars about presenting citizenship as membership of the state. Virginia Held argues that the notion that the state has a monopoly on the legitimate use of force is incompatible with a feminist view as to how society should be organised (1993: 221). Jones sees the nation-state 'as an out-moded political form' (1990: 789) and speaks of the need for a women-friendly polity.

But the question of the state needs to be addressed explicitly. It is not enough to speak, as David Held does, of limiting drastically the influence of the state and market (1993: 224). There has to be a plausible way of looking beyond both institutions, so that an emancipated society becomes possible. It could be argued that the state is actually a barrier to the notion of citizenship, defined here as a set of entitlements which include *everyone*.

Rowan Williams, the Archbishop of Canterbury, delivered a Dimbleby lecture on 19 December 2002, in which he argues – and this was the aspect of his lecture headlined in *The Times* (27 December 2002) – that 'we are witnessing the end of the nation state' (2002: 1). He takes the view that we need to do some hard thinking about what these changes mean for being a citizen. These changes are, he argues, 'irreversible' (2002: 2). Williams's contention is that the nation-state is in decline and is giving way to something he calls the 'market state'. Although he is critical of the latter, he shies away from the argument that the state itself – in all its forms – is the problem.

The notion of citizenship needs to be separated from the state. As we pointed out in Chapter 1, the state is an institution that claims a monopoly of legitimate force for a particular territory: it is a contradictory institution which claims a monopoly it does not and cannot have. This is true both of its claim to have a monopoly of force and a monopoly of legitimacy. This critique of the state challenges the standard view of citizenship as denoting membership of a state. For how can one be a citizen when laws are passed and functionaries exist to manage an institution that is underpinned by, and claims to exercise a monopoly of legitimate force? Even when force is authorised, it still prevents the recipient of this force from exercising rights and duties that are crucial to citizenship, and it means that those against whom such force is not directly exercised live in its shadow. They know that the laws they obey can be 'enforced', so that the absence of fear which is central to citizenship cannot be proven to exist in a society that centres around the state.

It is the role of the state to impose solutions by force when faced with divisions and conflicts of interest that cannot be tackled through arbitration and negotiation. A person who is not free is not a citizen. It may be objected that the state does not simply use force, but claims – in the celebrated definition that is central to our analysis – a monopoly of *legitimate* force. But this is not a convincing argument since legitimacy implies limits, whereas force cannot be limited (however hard authorities might try). Legitimate force is thus a contradiction in terms, and the state, therefore, is an institution that seeks to achieve the impossible. Williams argues that the state can no longer protect citizens, given the existence of intercontinental missile technology (2002: 2), but the state's mechanism for protecting 'its' subjects has always been contradictory and paradoxical.

The Problem of Class

Williams argues that the 'market state' is 'here to stay' (2002: 5), but the nation-state itself has been a 'market state' as long as capitalism and the market have been around. For these systems create divisions of interests that make the interventions of the state necessary.

Hence an inclusive citizenship has to chart a path beyond both the state and capitalism. Class divisions are, however, more complex than classical Marxism has assumed, even though inequality is crucial to the existence of the state since the challenge to the monopoly of the state comes from those who either have too much or too little. Because interests radically conflict, force is necessary to try and sort them out. This is the link between class and the state, and both act as barriers to an inclusive citizenship. Although Marx argues that people are not simply 'individuals' but members of a class, workers also have a gender and national identity, etc., and this materially affects how they relate to others. It is not that the class identity is unimportant: it is merely that it fuses with other identities since these other identities are also a crucial part of the process that organises individuals into a **class**. If blacks or Catholic Irish in Northern Ireland or northerners in Britain are more likely to be unemployed, their negatively perceived social identity is an integral part of their class status.

It could be argued that membership of a class is a barrier to citizenship. Working-class people often feel that they should not stand for parliament or take part in politics since they lack the confidence, linguistic skills and education to make decisions. Upper-class people may take it for granted that they and their offspring are 'natural' rulers, and in this way display an insensitivity and little understanding of the less well off. Whether class expresses itself in gender or national terms, regional or sexual terms, etc., a society that does not recognise difference in a positive way is a society with a restricted citizenship. By difference, we do not mean division. Divisions prevent people from 'changing places' and having common interests. Common interests make it possible to resolve conflicts in a way that relies upon arbitration, negotiation and compromise, and avoids violence. But how is it possible to overcome class division and capitalism? Marx argues that every historically developed social form is 'in fluid movement' – it has a transient nature (1970: 20). In the third volume of *Capital*, Marx refers to capitalism as a 'self-dissolving contradiction' (1966: 437) in which each step forward is also a step beyond.

The struggle by women to achieve respect and autonomy, the demands by blacks that they should be treated as people and not as a despised racial category, and the insistence by gays that they should be recognised as a legitimate group in society, etc. is as much a blow against the 'free market' as traditional trade union demands for a fairer share of profits. For each time a challenge is successful, the concrete human identities of supposedly abstract individuals is affirmed, and with this challenge the propensity of the market to deal with real people as abstractions is overcome.

Marx, as is argued in Chapter 9 on socialism, is torn between a view of revolution simply as change, and a notion, derived from the 'model' of the French Revolution, of revolution as a dramatic single event. Reforms have a revolutionary significance, and underpin the character of capitalism as 'a self-dissolving contradiction'. Yet it is both central to the dialectical logic of Marx's analysis and to some of his explicit statements, that capitalism can be gradually transformed so that, increasingly, a society develops in which freedom and individuality become more and more meaningful.

Citizenship can only develop at the expense of capitalism. Bryan Turner argues that while capitalism promotes early notions of citizenship, it also generates massive inequalities that prevent the achievement of citizenship. He sees a conflict between the redistributive character of citizenship rights and the profit motive of the free market (1986: 38; 24). It is true that he assumes that citizenship should be defined as membership of a state, and he takes a rather abstract view of class which means, as noted above, that he juxtaposes class to gender, ethnicity, etc. in a somewhat mechanistic fashion. Nevertheless, he regards the welfare state as a site of struggle, and he stresses over and over again the contradictory character of capitalism and its fraught relationship with citizenship.

Citizenship, he says, develops as a series of circles or waves (1986: 93). It is radical and socially disruptive, moving through a number of expanding processes, so that social membership becomes increasingly universalistic and open-ended.

Citizenship exists (as he puts it pithily) despite rather than because of capitalist growth (1986: 135; 141). The point is that the argument that citizenship requires a transformation of capitalism can be posed without having to make the case for a dramatic one-off revolution.

A number of 'issues papers' put out by the British Department for International Development point to the fact that the private sector can and must change. Indeed, the argument implies that to speak of capitalist companies simply as 'private' is itself problematic: the largest of these companies can – and need to – be pressurised further along a public road so that they operate according to social and ethical criteria. The reputation and image of companies with prominent interests abroad are tarnished by adverse publicity around issues such as the pollution of the environment, the use of child labour, and the support for regimes that have poor human rights records. Companies should join organisations such as the Ethical Training Initiative (DFID, 2002: 6). It is revealing that some companies speak of a corporate citizenship which shows awareness that production and sales are social processes with political implications. The link between profit and support for ethically acceptable social practices demonstrates that capitalism can be transformed by a whole series of 'victories for the political economy of the working class' – an ongoing process which, arguably, is still in its relatively early stages.

There are no short cuts to the transformation of capitalism. Where the market cannot provide universal service 'autonomously', as it were, it needs to be regulated – and it is through regulation that capitalism is transformed. Adair Turner establishes this interventionist logic when he argues that where market liberalisation (i.e. making people conform to capitalist norms) conflicts with desirable social objectives, 'we should not be afraid to make exceptions' (2002: 174). If citizens desire an efficient and integrated transport service, then this is an objective that must be governmentally provided if the market cannot deliver. Perhaps the exceptions are rather more prolific than Adair Turner – an advocate of socially responsible capitalism – imagines, but it is only through demonstrating that the market cannot deliver that it is possible to transcend the market. Adair Turner is right to argue that the demand for a cleaner environment, safer workplaces, safe food, and the right to be treated with respect in the workplace whatever one's personal characteristics, are just as much 'consumer demands' as the desire for more washing machines, internet usage or more restaurant meals (2002: 187).

Where the market cannot meet these kind of consumer demands, regulation is necessary. The need for public interventions is, Turner argues, increasing as well as changing. This intervention is more explicit in the provision of services that deliver equality of citizenship (2002: 238). Who can disagree with Turner's proposition that we cannot intervene too strongly against inequality in the labour market (2002: 240)? Indeed, for Turner, the key message of 11 September 2001 is the primacy of politics – the need to offset the insecurities and inequalities that capitalism undoubtedly creates (2002: 383). Here, in a nutshell, is the case for transformation.

Transcending the market means that the objectives of the market – freedom of choice, efficiency in delivery – can only be met through regulation and controls. It is not a question of suppressing or rejecting the market but seeking to realise its objectives through invoking standards 'foreign to commodity production'. Adair

Exercise

Imagine that there are five people in a room. One is a well-to-do male financier, the second a female academic, the third a female cleaner, the fourth a male Albanian asylum seeker, and the fifth an unemployed Somalian woman who is an 'illegal' refugee.

The first obviously regards himself as a citizen: he not only votes but dines frequently with cabinet ministers and the permanent secretaries of the Civil Service. The second has useful contacts with the legislature where she is researching into the question of women MPs. The third only occasionally votes but has a passport and travels to Spain for her holidays. The fourth is currently in receipt of modest benefits while his application for asylum is being looked into, while the fifth lives in constant fear that her status will be uncovered and she will be deported.

They are all human beings:

- In what sense can they all be regarded as citizens?

- What kind of programmes can be introduced to help persons four and five?

- What kind of policies will 'encourage' the first person to use his influence to help others?

- Can the second person do more to help? Is the third person really a citizen if she ignores the plight of the less fortunate?

Turner argues that demands for public intervention are going to rise as our markets become freer (2002: 191). Freedom of the market can only be justified when it meets human need: this is the radical difference between suppressing the market and going beyond it.

We are arguing that because markets abstract from differences, at some point they will need to be transcended – but only at the point at which it is clear that they cannot deliver the objectives that a society of citizens requires. Turner takes the view that the market economy has the potential to 'serve the full range of human aspirations' (2002: 290), but he himself acknowledges market failures (as he calls them) in transport policies where there is a bias in favour of mobility and combating environmental degradation (2002: 300). It is these failures that make the case for transformation.

Citizenship as a Relational Concept

Why can't some be citizens while others are subject to force? This argument can only be met if we adopt a 'relational' approach that means that we can only know who we are when we know the position of others. When these others are deprived of their freedom we have no freedom either. Although force particularly harms those who are targeted, the perpetrators of force also lose their autonomy, so that unless everyone is a citizen, then no one is a citizen.

It could be argued that the 'market state', as Williams describes it (2002: 7), promotes an **atomistic** attitude by which we mean an attitude that denies that individuals must be seen in relationship to one another. For example, the critique

Ideas and Perspectives:

Citizenship as a Momentum Concept

Momentum concepts are those that are infinitely progressive and egalitarian: they have no stopping point and cannot be 'realised'. **Static concepts**, by way of contrast, are repressively hierarchical and divisive. The latter must be discarded whereas the former have an historical dynamic that means they must be built upon and continuously transcended. The state, patriarchy and violence are examples of static concepts; freedom, autonomy, individuality, citizenship and **emancipation** are examples of momentum concepts. De Tocqueville famously formulated democracy as a momentum concept – a concept that has no stopping point. However, his account is marred by static features, such as a traditional notion of God and a fatalist view of 'destiny'. Momentum concepts, as we formulate them, seek to avoid this inconsistency by being infinite in their egalitarian scope. It is crucial to avoid the kind of scepticism and relativism that makes it impossible to identify progress at all.

Citizenship is a momentum concept in three ways:

1. The struggle for citizenship can be developed even by those who seek only limited steps forward and are oblivious of a more wide-ranging agenda.
2. Citizenship involves a process of change that is both revolutionary and evolutionary – it is important we do not privilege one over the other.
3. Citizenship is an ongoing struggle with no stopping point.

It is not that the ends of an inclusive **citizenship** are not important: it is rather that achieving one element of inclusion (for example the enfranchisement of women) enables us to move to the next – (for example the unfair allocation of tasks in the home). People do need to have the right to vote, speak freely and stand for election: but they also need to think about those whose conduct makes it necessary to put them in prison. This is why the case for an inclusive **citizenship** makes it essential that we look beyond the state.

of patriarchy can be called relational because it argues that men cannot be free while women are subordinated. It is true that in a patriarchal society men enjoy privileges which make them 'victors', but patriarchy oppresses *everyone* (albeit in different ways). Men have begun to realise that patriarchy not only strips them of involvement in childrearing, but subjects them in particular to the violence of war. The idea that our 'right' to exploit or be violent has to be curbed is a problematic use of the term right, since ultimately being exploitative or violent not only harms others, but it also ultimately harms the perpetrator himself. No one, it could be argued, can have a right to harm themselves.

A dramatically unequal world is a world in which large numbers of people will move out of poorer countries in search of a 'better' life. It is in the interest of the 'haves' that they pay attention and work to rectify the deprivations of the 'have nots'. This is what is meant by a relational view of citizenship. Unless everyone is a citizen, then no one is a citizen. It could be argued that if we want to work towards a more inclusive view of citizenship we need to isolate those who are staunchly opposed to extending citizenship whether on misogynist (i.e. anti-female), racist, nationalist grounds or because they are so privileged that they cannot identify with others. The well-being of each depends upon the well-being of all.

Ch 17:
Difference,
pp. 418–34

It is important that we evaluate all differences positively. Although it is likely that the struggle for an inclusive citizenship will be pursued by those who are the victims rather than the beneficiaries of the market and state, people with education and status have a vital part to play in the struggle for emancipation. They may be less subject to prejudice based upon ignorance. In the same way 'outsiders' are more likely to see the need to integrate with the host community in a way that enables people to contribute to (rather than passively accept) dominant norms. The need for self-government affects *everyone* for even the well-to-do are vulnerable to problems in the social and natural environment.

Summary

Ancient Greek notions of citizenship are linked to notions of slavery and imperialism, and liberalism historically has regarded citizenship in an exclusive way. The liberal view of citizenship suffers from being *abstract,* which means that while in theory it offers freedom and equality to all, beneath the abstractions is to be found inequality.

Marshall argues that citizens require social rights as well as political and legal ones, since the latter are seriously weakened if access to material resources is denied. The New Right in Britain and the United States rejected as 'socialistic' the argument for social rights, preferring to define citizenship in marketing rather than in welfare terms. Women are subject to informal pressures in liberal democracies that prevent them from exercising an effective citizenship. It could be argued that individuals would become more independent and involved as citizens if they were in receipt of what has justifiably been called a 'citizens' income'.

Cosmopolitans take the view that it would be wrong to juxtapose involvement at local, regional and national levels with a concern with the world. The European Union has pioneered a concept of citizenship that, although undeveloped, offers a tantalising glimpse of what is possible in the future.

Despite the tendency to define citizenship as membership of the state, it could be argued that the state is actually a barrier to citizenship. As an institution claiming a monopoly of legitimate force, its interventions undermine rather than enhance citizenship. Like the state, the existence of class divisions restricts meaningful citizenship. This point can be underlined when we develop the idea of citizenship as a relational and momentum concept.

Questions

1. Is the notion of global citizenship simply a dream?
2. Is the use of force a barrier to citizenship?
3. Should we extend citizenship to children and animals?

4. Is the liberal view of citizenship satisfactory?
5. Is the view of Marshall as a pioneer of the modern concept of citizenship justified?
6. Does a relational view of citizenship help to assess citizenship in relation to *either* class *or* the state?

References

Aristotle (1962), *The Politics* Harmondsworth: Penguin.

Bellamy, R. and Warleigh, A. (eds) (2001) *Citizenship and Governance in the European Union* London and New York: Continuum.

Bryson, V. (1992) *Feminism and Political Theory* Basingstoke: Macmillan.

Bryson, V. (1994) *Women in British Politics* Huddersfield: Pamphlets in History and Politics, University of Huddersfield.

Bubeck, D. (1995) *A Feminist Approach to Citizenship* Florence: European University Institute.

Carter, A. (2001) *The Political Theory of Global Citizenship* London and New York: Routledge.

Crick, B. (1982) *In Defence of Politics* 2nd edn Harmondsworth: Penguin.

DFID (Department for International Development) (2002) *Issues Paper 3* Kingston upon Thames: DFID Development Policy Forums.

Faulks, K. (1998) *Citizenship in Modern Britain* Edinburgh: Edinburgh University Press.

Faulks, K. (2000) *Citizenship* London and New York: Routledge.

Gilmour, I. (1978) *Inside Right* London, Melbourne and New York: Quartet Books.

Gray, J. (1999) *False Dawn* London: Granta Books.

Hayek, F. (1960) *The Constitution of Liberty* London and Henley: Routledge & Kegan Paul.

Heater, D. (1999) *What is Citizenship?* Cambridge: Polity Press.

Held, D. (1995) *Democracy and the Global Order* Cambridge: Polity Press.

Held, V. (1993) *Feminist Morality* Chicago, Ill. and London: University of Chicago Press.

Hoffman, J. (1988) *State, Power and Democracy* Brighton: Wheatsheaf Books.

Hoffman, J. (1995) *Beyond the State* Cambridge: Polity Press.

Hoffman, J. (2004) *Citizenship Beyond the State* London: Sage.

Jones, K. (1990) 'Citizenship in a Women-Friendly Polity' *Signs* 15(4), 781–812.

Linklater, A. (1999) 'Cosmopolitan Citizenship' in K. Hutchings and R. Dannreuther (eds), *Cosmopolitan Citizenship* Basingstoke: Macmillan, 35–59.

Lister, R. (1997) *Citizenship: Feminist Perspectives* Basingstoke: Macmillan.

MacKinnon, C. (1989) *Toward a Feminist Theory of the State* Cambridge, Mass: Harvard University Press.

Marshall, T.H. (1950) *Citizenship and Social Class and Other Essays* Cambridge: Cambridge University Press.

Marshall, T. and Bottomore, T. (1992) *Citizenship and Social Class* London: Pluto Press.

Marx, K. (1966) *Capital* Vol. 3 Moscow: Progress Publishers.

Marx, K. (1970) *Capital* Vol. 1 London: Lawrence & Wishart.

Marx, K. and Engels, F. (1967) *The Communist Manifesto* Harmondsworth: Penguin.

Marx, K. and Engels, F. (1975) *Collected Works* Vol. 3 London: Lawrence & Wishart.

Mouffe, C. (1992) 'Feminism, Citizenship and Radical Democratic Politics' in J. Butler and J. Scott (eds), *Feminists Theorize the Political* New York and London: Routledge, 369–84.

Oomen, T. (1997) *Citizenship, Nationality and Ethnicity* Cambridge: Polity Press.

Ross, K. (2000) *Woman at the Top* London: Hansard Society.

Rousseau, J. J. (1968) *The Social Contract* Harmondsworth: Penguin.

Saunders, P. (1995) *Capitalism: A Social Audit* Buckingham: Open University Press.

Soysal, Y. (1994) *The Limits of Citizenship* Chicago, Ill. and London: University of Chicago Press.

Thatcher, M. *The Downing Street Years* London: HarperCollins.

Tickner, J. (1995) 'Re-visioning Security' in K. Booth and S. Smith (eds), *International Relations Theory Today* Cambridge: Polity Press, 175–97.

Turner, A. (2002) *Just Capital* London: Pan Books.

Turner, B. (1986) *Citizenship and Capitalism* London: Allen & Unwin.

Voet, R. (1998) *Feminism and Citizenship* London, Thousand Oaks, Calif., New Delhi: Sage.

Williams, R. (2002) 'Full text of Dimbleby lecture delivered by the Archbishop of Canterbury', http://www.Guardian.co.uk/religion, 1–9.

Yeatman, A. (1994) *Postmodern Revisionings of the Political* London: Routledge.

Yuval-Davis, N. (1997) 'Women, Citizenship and Difference' *Feminist Review* 57, 4–27.

Further Reading

- Faulks's book (2000, referenced above) is a very useful overview.

- Lister (referenced above) surveys the feminist and citizenship literature with commendable thoroughness.

- *Cosmopolitan Citizenship* (referenced above) is a collection of essays that is worth reading for those concerned about the idea of a global citizen.

- A very interesting critique of the Crick Report on Citizenship Education and much else besides can be found in Osler, A. and Starkey, H. 'Citizenship Education and National Identities in France and England: inclusive or exclusive?' *Oxford Review of Education* 27(2), 288–305.

- Bryan Turner's *Citizenship and Capitalism* (referenced above) provides a very useful view of the strengths and weaknesses of the Marxist analysis of citizenship.

- Heater's work on citizenship (1999 – referenced above) is very comprehensive.

Weblinks

For a very useful overview: http://www.citizen21.org.uk/citizenship/index.html

For material explicitly on being a British citizen:
http://www.historylearningsite.co.uk/citizenship.htm

For material on European citizenship, see:
http://www.whsmith.co.uk/whs/go.asp?breakcontext=y&pagedef=/yso/about.htm

Part 2 Classical Ideologies

What is Ideology?

The term 'ideology' has acquired a fairly unsavoury meaning. Politicians regularly condemn policies they disagree with as 'ideological', meaning that such policies are dogmatic, prejudiced and blinkered. Ideologies are seen as closed systems, beliefs that are intolerant and exclusive, so that socialists, conservatives, liberals and anarchists are often anxious to deny the ideological character of their thought.

We are sceptical about this narrow use of the term ideology. An ideology is a system of ideas, organised around either an attempt to win state power or to maintain it. To call a set of beliefs ideological is merely to argue that ideas are organised for a particular statist purpose: they form the basis of a political movement (focused around the state) whether this is a movement we approve or not. The term is generally used to denote a belief system: in our view, it is more than this. Ideologies are belief systems focused around the state. 'Moderate' movements are as ideological as extremist ones although some movements may embrace many ideologies, and in the case of nationalism, for example, ideologies that contradict one another. Tony Blair spoke of the 1997 election as the last election in Britain based on ideology, although he certainly identified New Labour as embracing a set of ideas.

The 'negative' connotation of the term can only be preserved by linking ideologies to the state; a post-ideological world is a world without the state.

Origins and Development of the Term

The reality of ideology goes back to the birth of the state, so that it is impossible to agree with Habermas's argument that 'there are no pre-bourgeois ideologies' (McLellan, 1995: 2). We would see no problem in describing Aristotle's theory or St Thomas Aquinas's position as ideological since these were ideas that impacted upon society and moved people into action in relation to the state. However, the term itself was coined in the aftermath of the French Revolution by Antoine Destutt de Tracey, who used the idea positively to denote a science of ideas. The term denoted ideas that were progressive, rational, based upon sensation and free from metaphysical and overtly religious content. De Tracey was placed in charge of the *Institut de France* and regarded the spreading of ideology as the spreading of the ideas of the French and European Enlightenment.

However, the term soon became pejorative as Napoleon denounced ideology as an idea that was radical, sinister, doctrinaire and abstract – a 'cloudy metaphysics' that ignores history and reality (McLellan, 1995: 5). This seems to have been the view that Marx and Engels put forward in *The German Ideology* (1845, first published 1976), but they inject into the term two new connotations. First, ideologies are seen as infused with idealism – ideas held by individuals are substituted for reality: the belief that people drown because they subscribe to the notion that gravity exists is supremely ideological, as it blithely ignores the harsh facts of material reality. But second, ideologies appear to be ideas that mask material interests. Bourgeois 'ideologies' may support the proposition that it is natural for people to exchange products and for the thrifty to accumulate wealth, but these beliefs merely reflect the interests of the capitalist class. Unmasking such an ideology requires placing such ideas in their historical and social context.

Does that mean that Marxism itself cannot be ideological? Lenin and his Bolshevik supporters used the term ideology positively, so that Marxism was described as a scientific ideology that reflected the class interests of the proletariat. Because the proletariat was the class whose historical mission is to lead the struggle to convert capitalism into communism, its outlook (as interpreted by Marxists) is deemed scientific *and* ideological. Leninist Marxists would have no problem in describing their views as both ideological and true. Having nothing to fear from history and reality, the outlook of the proletariat is free from the 'cloudy metaphysics' that characterises the thought of classes that are in decline.

Is it possible to reconcile the views of Marx and Lenin on this matter? It could be argued that when Marx and Engels speak negatively of ideology they are referring to idealist ideology. There is an analogy here with their use of the term 'philosophy'. Marx refers dismissively to philosophers, not because he rejects philosophy, but because he challenges those who substituted philosophy for a study of historical realities. In other words, the term 'ideology' is used negatively when it refers to idealists such as the Young Hegelians but Marx and Engels's own theories are themselves ideological in the sense that they seek to transform society and the state through a political movement.

In the post-war world, many academic political theorists argued that ideology was 'dead' – by which they meant that ideas such as Marxism which sought to transform society from top to bottom were now archaic and dated. But this was itself the product of a political consensus as Partridge (1967) pointed out at the time, and it was a view held not only by academics but by politicians as well. The argument was that all sensible people agreed on the foundations of society – liberal, welfare state capitalism – so that disagreements were over details and not the overall direction of society. Bernard Crick wrote a lively book, *In Defence of Politics,* in which he argues that politics is a flexible, adaptive and conciliatory activity. As such, it needs defending, he argues, against ideology. Ideological thinking is totalitarian in character: it reduces activity to a 'set of fixed goals'. It is rigid and extremist, and should be rejected by conservatives, liberals and socialists who believe in debate, toleration and the resolution of conflict through negotiation (Crick, 1982: 55). But Crick also identifies politics with the state and, in our view, this makes his own definition of politics ideological.

Isms as Ideologies

Liberals often argue that their values are too coherent and rational to be called 'ideological'. Here is a belief system (liberals contend) that has a plausible view of human nature, links this with a wide view of freedom and has become the dominant set of values in modern democratic societies: how can such views be called ideological? Certainly **liberalism** is a very successful ideology, and that has rendered acute the problem of the variety of liberalisms that confront the student of politics. This problem afflicts all ideologies, it is true, but liberalism seems particularly heterogeneous and divided. Old liberalism expresses the belief in a free market, limited state and an individual free from external interference. New liberalism, on the other hand, champions an interventionist state, a socialised and regulated market and social policies that are concerned with redistributing wealth and supporting collectivist institutions such as trade unions and cooperatives. Indeed, in the United States, old liberalism is confusingly called '**conservatism**' and new liberalism identified as a form of socialism. The 'L' word is highly pejorative, and it is a brave politician in the United States who calls herself a 'liberal'.

Nevertheless, two points can be made about liberalism that bear upon the question of ideology. The first is that all forms of liberalism have a belief in the priority of the individual even though old and new liberals differ significantly in how they interpret the freedom of this individual. Second, and perhaps more importantly, what makes liberalism an ideology is that it is a movement focused on the state. All liberals feel that the state is necessary to the well-being of society even though they differ in the kind of state they would support, and they may champion different movements to achieve their political ends. The fact that liberalism is a movement that has rationality, toleration and universality as its key virtues does not make it less ideological than movements that challenge these values. Liberalism is a belief system concerned with building a particular kind of society through a particular kind of state – that is enough to make it ideological.

For the same reason, conservatism is an ideology, although some conservatives strenuously deny this. Ideologies, they argue, ignore realities and existing institutions, and seek to impose abstract values upon historical facts. Ideologies seek to perfect the world whereas the truth is that humans are imperfect, and it cannot be said that people are rational beings who seek to govern their own lives. But the fact that conservatives may even disapprove of explicit political ideas on the grounds that it is an ill-governed country that resorts to political theory does not make their 'ism' non-ideological. Ideals might be identified as abstractions imposed upon a complex reality, and tradition exalted as a source of wisdom and stability. However, this does not make conservatism less of an ideology than say liberalism or socialism. The point about ideologies is they differ – not only from other ideologies – but internally as well. The relationship of the New Right and Thatcher's ideas and policies to conservatism (to take a British example) is quite complicated: there is a break from traditional conservatism in some areas that is sharp enough to allow her critics to accuse her of liberalism or, a peculiarly British term, Whiggism, i.e. seventeenth- and eighteenth-century liberalism. But conservatives see the state as essential even though they are more inclined (than old liberals) to view it as a 'natural' institution that is necessary to keep 'fallen' men and women in order. This makes conservatism ideological. It is true that where conservatism denotes an attitude, as in the argument, for example, that Stalinist communists are conservative in the sense that they idealise the past, it is not ideologically specific, but this is not a politically informed use of the term.

But what of socialism? Social democrats have long regarded themselves as pragmatic and flexible and regarded their opponents – whether on the left or the right – as being rigid and 'ideological'. Giddens has written a work entitled *Beyond Left and Right* (1994) in which he seeks to defend a non-ideological politics, and the New Labour hostility to ideology is linked to a belief in a 'third way' that tries to avoid the choice between traditional socialism and traditional capitalism. But whatever social democracy is (and it is a divided movement), it is certainly ideological in the sense that its policies and beliefs focus on the state. However, what are we to say of Marxism? This is a strand within socialism that explicitly rejects what it calls 'utopias' – beliefs that do not arise from the historical movement going on before our eyes – and sees its objective as the attainment of a society that is both classless and stateless in character. Marxism raises an important point about ideologies. Although it seeks to usher in a stateless society, it is ideological for two reasons. First, because it seeks to organise its supporters around a set of ideas that are concerned with the seizure of state power, and second, because although its long-term objective is the disappearance of the state, it could be argued that it makes assumptions which ensure that it will fail to achieve this end. It is therefore a statist doctrine, and that makes it as ideological as any other political movement.

Ch 9: Socialism, pp. 208–32

The one exception to this argument appears to be anarchism. After all, anarchists argue that political movements as they conventionally operate concentrate power in unaccountable leaderships, and seek either to control an old state or build a new one. Anarchism seeks to do neither. Surely, therefore, it is not an ideology. Here we must sharpen up a distinction that is implicit in our earlier analysis. Just as conservatives (or socialists and liberals) may *think* that they are not being ideological, but are, so is this true of anarchists as well. In practice, anarchists have to organise, and if they were ever successful they would, we think, have to establish a state in the short term, and what we will call government in the long term – contrary to their own principles. A state tackles conflicts of interest through force; government, as we will define it, addresses conflicts through social pressures of a negotiating and arbitrational kind. Both ideas are rejected by anarchists, but it is impossible to envisage a society without conflicts of interest, and therefore it is impossible to envisage any society without a government to resolve these. Whether ideology will dissolve with the dissolution of the state is a matter we will tackle later, but it is clear that anarchism in practice would have to organise in relation to the state, and that makes it (in the particular view of ideology we have adopted here) ideological.

Ch 10: Anarchism, pp. 238–61

But what about **nationalism**? Nationalism has the opposite problem to anarchism. Nationalists are clearly ideological because they seek to organise 'their' people to win or to maintain the power of the state, but they attach themselves to different ideologies in doing so. Nationalists may be conservative or socialist, liberal and (in practice) anarchist, so that to call someone a nationalist is to leave open which particular social, economic and state policies they advocate.

Nationalism, in our view, is ideological in a general sense: all nationalists use beliefs to galvanise their followers into action around a state. But the particular values that they adopt differ significantly, and invariably one finds one nationalism in collision with another. The African National Congress sees South Africa as a country that is mostly inhabited by blacks but in which there is a significant white minority: the old National Party (now dissolved) saw South Africa as a white country and sought through apartheid to give black Africans homelands in separate states. Both are or were nationalist: but their nationalism had a very different political content.

All political movements that seek to run the state are ideological in character, since we define ideologies as belief systems that focus on the state. Even movements that claim to reject ideology are ideological nevertheless, if this is what they do.

Mannheim's Paradox: Are We Stuck?

Karl Mannheim wrote a classic book in 1929 entitled *Ideology and Utopia*, in which he raised an intriguing problem. Can we talk about ideology without being ideological ourselves? After all, if ideologies arise because of a person's social context, then is not the critique of ideology also situationally influenced, so that the critic of ideology is himself ideological? Mannheim was conscious that the term 'ideology' was often regarded as a pejorative one, so that he sometimes substituted the word 'perspective' when he talked about the way in which a person's social position influences the ideas they adopt (McLellan, 1995: 39).

Mannheim's argument raises very sharply the question as to whether we should define ideologies negatively or positively. If, as is common, we identify ideologies as negative bodies of thought, then we identify them as dogmas, authoritarian thought constructs that distort the real world, threats to the open-minded and tolerant approach that is crucial to democracy. But the negative definition seems naive, because it implies of course that while our opponents are ideological, we are not. The dogma expelled through the front door comes slithering in through the back, since the implication of a negative view of ideology might be that while ideologists distort reality, we have the truth. This seems not only naive, but also uncritical and absolutist.

On the other hand, a purely positive or non-judgemental view of ideology raises problems of its own. Supposing we insist that all ideas and movements are equally ideological, how do we avoid what philosophers call the problem of relativism? This is the idea that all ideas are of equal merit. There are a number of dictums – 'beauty lies in the eye of the beholder', 'one man's meat is another man's poison', etc. – which suggest that it is impossible to declare that one's own views are right and another's wrong. If all belief systems are ideological, does this imply that all are equally valid? After all, which of us can jump out of our skin, our time and place, and escape the social conditions that cause us to think one way rather than another? A relativist view of ideology has at least two problematic consequences.

The first is that it prevents us from 'taking sides'. Supposing we are confronted by a Nazi storm trooper dragging a Jewish child to be gassed in a concentration camp. Each has their own set of values. A purely positive view of ideology might lead us to the position in which we note the ideology of the Nazi and the (rather different) ideology of his victim, and lamely conclude that each are valid for their respective holders. Mannheim sought to resist this argument by contending that his theory was one of 'relationism' and not relativism, and a relational position seeks to prefer a view that is more comprehensive and shows 'the greatest fruitfulness in dealing with empirical materials' (McLellan, 1995: 40). But are not 'comprehensiveness' and 'fruitfulness' other words for the truth? The question still remains: what enables some observers to find a true ideology, while others have ideologies that are false?

Mannheim's solution to the paradox was to focus on the particular social position of intellectuals, arguing that they constitute a relatively classless stratum that is 'not too firmly situated in the social order' (McLellan, 1995: 42). It is true that intellectuals do have positions that may allow for greater flexibility and a capacity to empathise with the views of others. Reading widely and travelling to other countries 'broadens the mind', but does it follow from this that intellectuals can cease to be ideological? John Gray cites the words of a Nazi intellectual who speaks of the need to exterminate gypsies and Jews, enthusing that 'we have embarked upon something – something grandiose and gigantic beyond imagination' (2002: 93). Expansive ideas need not be progressive. It could be argued that intellectuals are particularly prone to impractical ideas which are especially ideological in the sense that they take seriously values and schemes that 'ordinary' people would reject. The attempt to transcend ideology by being a supposedly classless intellectual has been unkindly likened to Baron Munchausen in the German fairy story trying to get out of a bog by pulling on his own pigtail. It cannot be done!

We need a view of ideology that is both positive and negative. On the one hand, ideology is problematic and distorting, but it is inescapable in our current world. On the other hand, the notion of ideology as a belief system focused on the state does, we will argue, combine both the negative and the positive. While it is impossible not to be ideological in state-centred societies, in the struggle to move beyond the state itself we also move beyond ideas and values that are ideological in character.

Facts, Values and the State

We have argued in the introduction to our book on political concepts that it is impossible to separate facts and values, since all statements imply that a relationship exists, and relationships suggest that values exist within facts. Thus, behaviouralists – a school of empiricial theorists who claim to be scientific and value free – argue that when people do not vote, this enables experts to make decisions for society. The link between apathy and democracy is deemed 'functional', but this contention necessarily implies that apathy is a good thing. When apparently value-free linguistic philosophers define the word democracy in parliamentary terms, they are taking a stand on the debate between representative and participatory democracy that is certainly evaluative or normative in character. One meaning of the term ideology is thought that is normative, but this, we would suggest, is unsatisfactory for at least two reasons. First, it naively assumes that ideas can be non-evaluative or purely factual in character. And second, it fails to see that ideology can be transcended, not by avoiding morality in politics, but by moving beyond the state.

But why should the state be linked to ideology? In our view, the state is best defined as an institution claiming a monopoly of legitimate force – a claim that is contradictory and implausible. In claiming a monopoly of legitimacy, supporters have to denigrate those who challenge this monopoly, presenting their own values as an exclusive system. Inevitably, a statist focus distorts realities. This problem is exacerbated by the fact that the state not only claims a monopoly of legitimacy, but a monopoly of force, and the use of force to tackle conflicts of interest acts to polarise society into friends and enemies, those who are respectable and those (an inexplicably violent minority) who are beyond the pale. This gives ideas an absolutist twist that is characteristic of ideologies, and explains why ideologies are problematic in character. This is unavoidable where the objective of a movement is to win (or retain) state power. The Movement for Democratic Freedom seeks to unite conservatives, liberals and socialists against the tyrannical rule of Robert Mugabe and his ZANU (PF) party, and it cannot avoid an ideological character. In the same way, gay rights activists who organise to protect their interests and call upon the state to implement appropriate policies are acting ideologically.

But movements are not purely ideological, where they seek not only to transform the state but to move beyond it altogether. Take feminists, for example. Feminists do not normally believe that punishing aggressive men through the courts will solve the problem of male domination, although they may support it as a short-term expedient. In the longer term, they would argue that we need to change our culture so that force is seen as an unacceptable way of tackling conflicts of interest, and that we must resolve conflicts in what we have called a governmental way – i.e. through negotiation and arbitration and not through force. This longer-term aim is non-ideological because it rests upon trying to understand why violence arises and how we can move beyond it. It involves a politics beyond the state, and in seeking to face reality in all its complexities it is moving beyond ideology as well. The notion of 'monopoly' and the use of 'force' that are inevitable when the state is involved limit the realism of ideas and make them ideological.

References

Crick, B. (1982) *In Defence of Politics* 2nd edn Harmondsworth: Penguin.
Giddens, A. (1994) *Beyond Left and Right* Cambridge: Polity Press.
Gray, J. (2002) *Straw Dogs* London: Granta.
McLellan, D. (1995) *Ideology* 2nd edn Buckingham: Open University Press.
Mannheim, K. (1936) *Ideology and Utopia* London: Routledge & Kegan Paul.
Marx, K. and Engels, F. (1976) *Collected Works* Vol. 6 London: Lawrence & Wishart.
Partridge, P. (1967) 'Politics, Philosophy and Ideology' in A. Quinton (ed.), *Political Philosophy* Oxford: Oxford University Press, 32–52.

Chapter 7

Liberalism

Introduction

Liberalism has emerged as the world's dominant ideology, and much of the political debate of 'liberal democratic' societies takes place within liberalism. Because of its dominance liberalism can be a difficult ideology to pin down, and there are several quite distinct streams of thought within it. Liberals take individual freedom – or liberty – as a fundamental value, and although an individual's freedom can be limited – because it clashes with the freedom of others or with other values – what defines liberalism is the *presumption* that freedom is a good thing, meaning that limitations on freedom must be justified. A less obvious aspect of liberalism is its emphasis on equality, and again the presumption is that people are equal. Although this appears to generate a major contradiction at the heart of liberalism – after all, the exercise of freedom will often lead to inequality – the two can be reconciled if we assume people are *naturally* equal. Natural, or 'moral', equality may be compatible with material, or social, inequality. To say people are naturally equal amounts to the claim that political institutions must be justified to each individual, and each individual counts equally.

Chapter Map

In this chapter we will:

- Explore the historical roots of liberalism.

- Identify the fundamental philosophical core of liberal thought.

- Recognise the distinct streams of liberal thought, and the tensions between them.

- Analyse political practice in liberal democracies and apply the insights gained to that practice.

Prostitution Laws in Sweden

In 1998 the Swedish Parliament passed the Prohibition of the Purchase of Sexual Services Act. The Act does what its title suggests: it prohibits the sale of sexual services. Most countries have legal controls on prostitution, which often include banning brothels, pimping, kerb-crawling and advertising. The Swedish Act tightened up on these aspects, but it achieved international attention because it went much further than other European countries: it made it illegal to purchase, or attempt to purchase 'casual sexual services'. The prohibition applied not only to street prostitution, brothels and massage parlours, but also escort services or 'any other circumstances' in which sexual services are sold. Obviously existing laws covered many of these cases, but the new law was a 'catch-all', and in that sense quite radical. One important point was that the buyer rather than the seller was criminalised.

It may seem odd to begin a chapter on liberalism with a discussion of prostitution laws in Sweden, but the reasons employed to justify the law reveal much about the nature of liberalism and, importantly, the tensions within it. And it is these reasons that are our focus. In a fact sheet produced by the Swedish government a number of arguments are advanced for this law and we outline these at the end of the chapter.

- List arguments for and against the criminalisation of the purchase of sexual services.
- Do you think the Swedish government was right to enact such a law?

The Meaning of Liberalism

Liberalism has emerged as the world's dominant **ideology**. Europe provides a good example of the spread of liberal-democratic values and institutions: the 1970s saw the transition from right-wing, military regimes in Greece, Spain and Portugal, and in 1989–91 the process of democratisation spread to Eastern Europe in the dramatic overthrow of state socialism from the Baltic states to Romania. While the depth of commitment at elite and popular levels to liberal-democratic values in the 'emergent democracies' of Eastern Europe is a matter of much debate among political scientists, all these states subscribe to a liberal ideology. The accession in 2004 of nine Eastern European states, plus Malta, to the European Union, bringing the total from the original 6 in the 1950s to 25 today, is indicative of this commitment.

The very dominance of liberalism can make it a difficult ideology to grasp. In the history of political thought quite different bodies of thought are identified as 'liberal'. And in popular political discourse confusion can be caused when the term is applied to particular parties, movements or strands of thought *within* a liberal democracy. For example, many political parties have the word 'liberal' in their name; in Canada the Liberal Party is towards the left of the political spectrum, while in Australia the Liberal Party is to the right. In many European countries liberalism is associated with a strong commitment to the free market, whereas in the United States the term denotes a belief in central – that is, federal – state intervention in society and the economy, and so to be 'liberal' is to be on the left. Clarification is sometimes provided by a qualifying adjective: *economic* liberalism or *social* liberalism. Occasionally the term *classical* liberalism is employed to denote support for free trade and the free market.

Some distinctions will help to cut through the confusions of popular usage:

- **Justification** Political institutions can be described as 'liberal', but so can the method by which they are justified. Hobbes's defence of the state is a good example of this distinction. The institutions he defends appear highly illiberal but his method of justifying those institutions – **contractarianism** – is liberal. State authority is justified because we, as rational individuals, would calculate that it is in our interests to submit to it. Most of our attention in this chapter will be on the justification of institutions.

- **Constitution and policy** Turning to institutions, we can distinguish between the constitution and policy (or law making). The constitution determines the procedure by which laws are passed, while to a large extent leaving open the content of those laws. Although there may be debate about the constitution, most people are implicitly 'liberal' on the essentials of the constitution: the division of powers and the basic rights of individuals. They may not, however, support parties that describe themselves as liberal. The struggle between political parties normally operates *within* the constitution, rather than being a battle over the constitution. In short, at the constitutional level most of us are liberals, but at the policy level this may not be the case.

- **Attitudes** There is a distinction between how political theorists have defended – justified – liberal principles and institutions, and popular attitudes to those institutions. Understanding such attitudes is primarily the focus of empirical political science, using quantitative methods such as surveys. Although we do not discuss it here, the work of political scientists provides a useful perspective on liberalism – if people find it difficult to endorse liberal values then it should force liberals to reconsider how they defend liberal institutions.

Moral Equality, pp. 65–68

Keeping these distinctions in mind, we can now attempt a rough definition of liberalism. As the etymology of the word implies, liberals emphasise liberty (freedom). As we will argue, a less obvious aspect of liberal thought is its emphasis on equality – not necessarily material equality, but a basic moral equality. A more precise definition of liberalism carries the risk of excluding from the liberal tradition important strands of thought. The best approach then is to look at a number of liberalisms. Although there may be more, four important ones can be identified: liberalism as **toleration** (or modus vivendi liberalism), contractarianism, rights-based liberalism (and, relatedly, **libertarianism**) and utilitarianism. If we look at ideas in their social context we will find these strands coexist. Much of the debate *within* liberalism is generated by the tensions between these different forms of liberalism, such that separating them out and clarifying each one is essential to understanding the values that underlie liberal democratic society.

Liberalism as Toleration

The Reformation and Wars of Religion

Many historians of political thought locate the origins of liberal discourse in the struggle for religious toleration generated by the Reformation and subsequent Wars of Religion. Although the term 'Wars of Religion' is sometimes reserved for a series of civil wars fought in France between 1562 and 1598, the term can be used more widely to include the struggle of the Protestant Netherlands (United Provinces) to free themselves from Catholic Spain, and the Thirty Years War (1618–48) in Germany. That the motivations of the protagonists was not necessarily theological in character does not detract from the fact that these wars produced a *philosophical discourse* in which toleration of difference became a central concern. It is this discourse, rather than the details of the wars, that concerns us.

Reformation box, p. 166

To understand the development of the concept of toleration we need a basic understanding of the theological core of the Reformation. The causes of the Reformation are many and varied, and as suggested a moment ago it is possible to explain it in social and economic, rather than theological, terms. However, we will take seriously the Reformation as a theological dispute. It is important to recognise that what is termed the Reformation had a number of distinct streams.

The two theological issues central to the Reformation were how doctrine is established and how human beings achieve salvation. Let us consider doctrine. Christianity is a bibliocentric religion – its teachings, or doctrine, are determined

The Reformation

We can identify two broad Reformation movements, which scholars term the Magisterial (or mainstream) Reformation, and the Radical Reformation (McGrath, 1988: 5–12):

- **Magisterial** (or Mainstream) **Reformation**: associated with Martin Luther (1483–1546), Huldrych Zwingli (1484–1531) and John Calvin (1509–64). There were some significant theological disputes between Lutherans and Calvinists, but they were agreed on many theological points and were committed to a strong church–state relationship.
- **Radical Reformation**: contained many different sects – and tended to be highly fractious. Radical reformers were 'theological individualists' – they rejected any role for a state-sponsored church.

Note: the term 'Protestant' as a synonym for the Reformation movement is misleading. Strictly speaking it denotes a particular protest at Speyer (1529) against the refusal of the Holy Roman Emperor to tolerate the religious conscience of a number of German princes and city-states.

There was also within the Church of Rome what came to be termed the **Counter-Reformation** – although many scholars reject that label on the grounds that it implies reaction to the 'Protestant' Reformation, and instead call it the **Catholic Reformation**. This reform movement can be traced back to the Council of Trent (1545–63).

by a body of scripture. However, there has always been a debate over the correct interpretation of scripture and, relatedly, whether the Bible is a sufficient source of truth – the Catholic Church (Church of Rome) maintained not only that the priesthood played a special part in interpreting scripture, but that the Church, because it was founded by Christ, had the authority to augment Christian doctrine. Considering this question from the standpoint of the various movements outlined in the box above (and including the Catholic position) we can identify three opposing positions on the question of doctrine:

1. **Catholic – tradition 1 plus 2** Doctrine is determined by scripture as interpreted by the Church (tradition 1) and developed by the Church's leaders (tradition 2).
2. **Magisterial reformers – tradition 1** Human beings still require a body – the church – which provides authoritative interpretation (tradition 1), but Christianity should rid itself of post-Biblical accretions, so no tradition 2. In addition, the Bible should be translated into vernacular languages so that believers – or at least the literate among them – can read it.
3. **Radical reformers – tradition 0** When you read the Bible you have direct experience of the word of God, unmediated by any tradition (McGrath: 144).

The second major theological issue was the nature of salvation. The common medieval view was that God had established a covenant with humanity, whereby he was obliged to justify – that is, allow into a relationship with himself, or 'save' – anybody who satisfied a minimum standard, which was defined as recognising one's sin. In practical terms it meant remaining 'in communion' with the church. Luther challenged this, arguing that human beings were so damaged by sin that there was nothing they could do by their own – or the church's – efforts to save themselves. Rather, God freely gives – gratis, by grace – to those who have *faith* in him the means of salvation. The Catholic view came to be known, somewhat misleadingly, as salvation by works, in contrast to the Reformed position of salvation by faith alone.

Taken together these two theological disputes generated significantly different views of the role of the church. For the mainstream reformers the church's task is to teach doctrine rather than create it, and it has no direct role in human salvation – the church cannot guarantee salvation. As the label suggests, the radical reformers went further: it was for individuals to determine correct doctrine. We can summarise the three positions on the nature of the church:

1. **Catholic position** The church was a visible, historical institution, grounded in the authority of Christ through his Apostles.

2. **Magisterial position** The visible church is constituted by the preaching of the word of God – legitimacy is grounded in theological, not historical, continuity. The church will contain both the saved and the unsaved.

3. **Radical position** The true Church was in heaven and no institution on earth can claim the right to be the community of Christ.

These two theological disputes, and the consequent re-evaluation of the role of the church, had important immediate and long-term political implications. The immediate impact was on the relationship of the secular and spiritual powers. In the longer term the theological ideas generated by Reformed Christianity, and also, importantly, by Reformed Catholicism, gave rise to secular equivalents. For example, the theological individualism of Protestantism was 'translated' into a secular, philosophical individualism, which stressed individual responsibility. As we shall see, some theorists attribute the rise of national consciousness to the translation of the Bible into the vernacular languages of Europe. We shall focus here on the immediate political impact of the Reformation.

pp. 269–70

Simplifying a great deal: political power in medieval Europe was characterised by a dual structure. On the one side there was the spiritual authority of the pontiff, and on the other his secular equivalent, the Holy Roman Emperor. The latter was relatively weak, and most secular power resided in the national and city-state powers. Nonetheless, the loyalties of individual citizens were split between pontiff and the national (or local) secular powers. Throughout the fourteenth century there were continual pressures on the Church to reform itself, and this was expressed as a demand for a general council (a council of lay people) to discuss reform. Although the Church of Rome was relatively tolerant of doctrinal difference – it only became 'authoritarian' after the Reformation – there was a refusal to call a council. Had such a council been called it is a matter of conjecture whether the schism between Rome and the various streams of the Reformation would have taken place; but the fact is that a council was not called, and an *institutional* break became inevitable.

The religious intolerance that eventually hardened into war cannot be attributed to the Church of Rome's attempt to suppress dissent. Rather, the institutional break created a legitimation crisis for the secular authorities. In states where the prince (or elector) had embraced Lutheranism or Calvinism, the continuing allegiance of some of their citizens to Rome was a threat to the prince's authority. Conversely, where the prince had remained loyal to Rome but some of his subjects had embraced Reformed religion there was a loss of spiritual authority – an authority that had underwritten secular authority in the pre-Reformation period.

Reformation and Wars of Religion

1517: The first indication of the Reformation comes with Luther objecting to what he regarded as the Church's corrupt and theologically unsound practices

1525: The rise of Anabaptism – an important radical Reformation movement

1529: Diet of Speyer ends toleration of Lutheranism in Catholic districts – 6 princes and 14 cities 'protest', giving rise to the term Protestantism

1545-63: Council of Trent – beginnings of the Catholic (Counter-) Reformation

1555: Treaty of Augsburg

1568: Revolt of the (Protestant) United Provinces (Netherlands) – beginning of the 'Eighty Years War'

1572: St Bartholomew's Day Massacre of French Protestants (Huguenots) in Paris

1598: Edict of Nantes granted toleration of Protestants in France

1618: Beginning of the Thirty Years War

1648: Peace of Westphalia – regarded as the settlement of the major wars of religion

1640–9: English Civil War

In addition, the medieval division of spiritual and secular power had resulted in a dual structure of law, with much domestic law – for example, marriage – the responsibility of church courts rather than secular courts. In Reformed states, the legitimacy of that domestic law was now in question.

The first Europe-wide attempt to address, rather than simply suppress, this conflict of loyalties was the Treaty of Augsburg (1555), which produced the formula: *cujus regio, eius religio* – roughly translated as 'the ruler determines the religion'. Two points can be made about this formula. First, it tolerated rulers and not individual citizens. Second, it was a mere modus vivendi – that is, a way of living together, but without any underlying respect for the other person's beliefs or way of life. It was a recognition of the reality of power: neither could destroy the other, and it was in neither's interest for there to be continual war, so they 'agreed to disagree'. However, once the balance of power shifted, the newly dominant side had no reason not to suppress the other. Not surprisingly, the Augsburg settlement proved unstable, and it took a century more of conflict before the so-called Peace of Westphalia (1648) created a new, and relatively stable, European order. The Peace of Westphalia is the name given to a series of treaties that ended the last of the great wars of religion – the Thirty Years War (1618–48). It reaffirmed the formula of *cujus regio, eius religio*, but made some concession to toleration of individuals by respecting the beliefs of those resident in a particular territory prior to 1618. In addition, there was an implication that private belief and public practice should be separated – there were to be 'no windows into men's souls', to use Elizabeth I of England's expression. So long as there was outward conformity, there could be inner dissent.

Toleration

The settlement of the Wars of Religion is credited with making toleration a central concept of political life, and in the process generating a body of political reflection and writing that can be described as 'liberal'. The term 'toleration' has, to twenty-first-century ears, a slightly negative connotation. It suggests grudging acceptance rather than respect. However, toleration remains an important concept for liberals and it is important to be clear about its structure.

Toleration appears to require approving and disapproving of something at the same time. For example, person A:

- believes that the salvation is mediated by the Church (of Rome), so that outside the Church there can be no salvation;
- accepts that person B has the right to express her religious (or other) beliefs – person B is justified in not seeking salvation through the Church (of Rome).

The apparent tension between 1 and 2 is resolved if we recognise they refer to different actions: 2 is not direct approval of person B's choices, because that would contradict 1. The 'approval' in 2 might be of B's capacity to make a choice (we say 'might' because other reasons are possible). Nonetheless, there is still a tension between 1 and 2; what is required is a 'bridge' between them.

One bridge might be the acceptance of the sheer fact of religious difference. This is the Augsburg modus vivendi argument applied to toleration of individuals: terrible torture and other deprivations will not force (some) people to abandon their religious beliefs and practices, so it is both useless and politically destabilising to oppress them. Toleration grows out of recognition of this reality. But this is not really a justification for toleration – it does not provide reasons for toleration. To go beyond a modus vivendi person A would have to find something in his own religious beliefs that enables him to accept B's dissent from those beliefs. In the history of the development of religious toleration in the sixteenth and seventeenth centuries a range of such arguments were advanced. They included the following:

- *Latitudinarianism*: the belief in a minimal set of Christian doctrines, and the acceptance of dissent beyond that minimum.
- *Catholicism* (in the generic sense): the importance of Christian unity over uniformity.
- *Christian choice*: God gives us a choice, and so we are not entitled to deny people choice.

The list is far from exhaustive. What is striking, however, is that there is assumed an underlying commitment to Christianity, however Christianity might be understood. Insofar as there was toleration in the sixteenth and seventeenth centuries it tended to be limited to Catholicism and the two major branches of the magisterial Reformation – Lutheranism and Calvinism. It was rarely extended to radical Reformers, Jews and atheists. Only in the Netherlands and Poland did toleration go further. The explanation for this wider toleration in those two countries is complex, but in the Dutch case it is clearly connected to the early rise of capitalism, while in the Polish case it may have had its roots in a delicate religious balance.

In the eighteenth and nineteenth centuries the 'circle of toleration' is extended to include previously untolerated groups, and the justification of toleration shifts from religious to secular grounds. Here are a few secular arguments:

- *Scepticism*: it is impossible to prove the existence of God.
- *Progress*: humanity progresses if there is a competition of ideas (see John Stuart Mill's argument).
- *Autonomy*: how we should behave can be determined rationally through the exercise of human reason.

pp. 43–4

Some contemporary theorists argue that these secular arguments are themselves intolerant and incompatible with a pluralistic society: scepticism is a rejection of religious belief, and autonomy, while not a rejection, cannot be endorsed by someone who believes revelation or natural law is the source for guidance on moral conduct. For this reason there has been a 'rediscovery' of modus vivendi toleration, and this is reflected to some extent in the multiculturalism debate. This rediscovery is also a reaction to the development of liberal thought in the following three centuries. In the rest of this chapter we consider that development, by focusing on three strands of theory: contractarianism, rights-based liberalism and utilitarianism.

pp. 362–3

Contractarianism

Thomas Hobbes's *Leviathan* (1651) was published against the background of the English Civil War, which was, in part, a manifestation of the wider religious struggles in Europe. *Leviathan* is one of the great books of political theory, and arguably the first significant work of modern political thought. The conclusion Hobbes draws – that it is rational to submit to a powerful sovereign – may not appear liberal, but the way he reaches that conclusion draws on ideas which have become a major part of liberal reflection on the state. The method he uses for justifying obligation to the state is contractarian: we are to imagine a situation in which there is no state – the state of nature – and ask ourselves whether it is better we remain in the state of nature or agree to submit to a sovereign (or state).

It is important to understand the historical context of Hobbes's work. To a large degree Hobbes is concerned to provide an argument against rebellion. In mid-seventeenth-century England it was radical reformers – sects such as the Levellers and the Diggers – who were among the most likely rebels. A large part of *Leviathan* is concerned with blocking off theological arguments for rebellion. There is a tendency for contemporary readers to ignore this part of the book, regarding it as anachronistic, and concentrate on the apparently more 'secular' parts. But given that it is still the case that political order is challenged not just by competing interests, but also competing moral conceptions (some of which have a theological basis), the concerns which motivated the work cannot be dismissed as entirely irrelevant to the contemporary world.

Hobbes was the first of the classic contract theorists – later important contractarians are Locke, Rousseau and Kant. The contract tradition went into decline around the end of the eighteenth century. John Rawls is credited with reviving it in

| Biography | **Thomas Hobbes (1588–1679)** |

Hobbes was born in 1588 in Malmesbury, Wiltshire. Allegedly his birth was brought on early as his mother heard of the approaching Spanish Armada – Hobbes was later to say 'fear and I were born twins'. His father was the local vicar, but after involvement in a brawl outside his own church fled to London, leaving his son to be brought up by a wealthy uncle.

Hobbes was educated at the local grammar school and at Oxford University. After graduation (1608) he became tutor to William Cavendish (later the 2nd Earl of Devonshire). A European tour with Cavendish (1610) reignited Hobbes's interest in scholarship; with relatively light duties to the Cavendish family Hobbes had time to read and write. William became the 2nd Earl in 1626, but died just two years later, and Hobbes lost a friend and employer.

For the next three years he was tutor to Sir Gervase Clinton, during which time he published a translation of Thucydides (1629). In the early 1630s Hobbes worked on the physical doctrine of motion; while not obviously political, his model of 'matter in motion' became a central premise of his later political theory. By the end of that decade England was experiencing considerable turbulence, culminating in the Civil War of 1642–9. It is, however, notable that his first important political work – *De corpore politico* (*The Elements of Law*), although published in 1646, was written ten years earlier, and was not overly influenced by the political events of the time.

Hobbes, whose sympathies were with the soon-to-be-defeated Royalists, spent much of the late 1640s in, or near, Paris, working on his greatest work, *Leviathan* (full title: *Leviathan, or the Matter, Form and Power of a Commonwealth, Ecclesiastical and Civil*), which was published in 1651. The book had an impact: the secularism of the book alienated Royalists and Hobbes was forced to seek the protection of Oliver Cromwell's revolutionary government.

During the 1650s Hobbes was engaged in a controversy with Bishop John Bramhall over the possibility of free will and with John Wallis, Professor of Geometry, over the nature of mathematics.

After the restoration of the monarchy (1660), Hobbes was in favour with the new king, who awarded him a relatively generous pension and protected him from new laws intended to root out atheism. Nonetheless, out of fear of arrest Hobbes burnt many of his papers, and avoided writing on moral and political questions, preferring to translate the *Iliad* and *Odyssey*. He died in 1679, at the age of 92.

the second half of the twentieth century. There are important differences between these thinkers, but there is a common, three-part structure to a contract theory:

1. a description of a situation in which there is no state;
2. an outline of the procedure for either submitting to a state or agreeing to a certain set of coercively enforced political principles – this is the 'contract';
3. a description of what is chosen – the state, or political institutions.

Since our concern is with contractarianism rather than the details of specific political theories, we will employ a modern treatment to explain the contract. In the following exercise a situation is described in which you have a choice. The important feature of this exercise is that the outcome is partly determined by your choice, and partly determined by the other 'player'.

The Prisoner's Dilemma

Two people are arrested for a crime they may or may not have committed – their guilt or innocence is irrelevant. Each is invited to confess to the crime. The sentence each receives will depend, in part, on what the other does. As Table 7.1 shows, if both confess, each gets five years in prison; if they both remain silent, each gets a year; if the first prisoner confesses while the other remains silent, then the former goes free and the latter gets ten years; if the second confesses and the first remains silent, the former goes free while the latter receives ten years (the first number of each pair refers to the first prisoner's sentence, and the second number to the second prisoner's sentence).

Table 7.1

		Second prisoner Remains silent	Confesses
First prisoner	Remains silent	1, 1	10, 0
	Confesses	0, 10	5, 5

If you were the first prisoner, what would you do: confess or remain silent?

The Prisoner's Dilemma is used to 'model' all three stages of the contract set out above. If we assume that the prisoners are purely self-interested then each will attempt to achieve her first preference. The preference-ordering of each can be tabulated as follows:

Table 7.2

	1st Preference	2nd Preference	3rd Preference	4th Preference
First prisoner	0, 10	1, 1	5, 5	10, 0
Second prisoner	10, 0	1, 1	5, 5	0, 10

It is not rational to remain silent while the other prisoner confesses, so the likely outcome is that each will confess, with the consequence that each will satisfy only her third preference. What, of course, makes the 'game' interesting is that each could do better by agreeing to remain silent. The Prisoner's Dilemma is a non-zero sum game: a gain for one prisoner does not result in an equivalent loss for the other. The explanation of how, through cooperation, each prisoner might move from her third to her second preference is a contemporary rendition of the reasoning behind Hobbes's argument. The third preference represents the non-cooperation that characterises the state of nature, the agreement to remain silent is equivalent to the contract itself, and the satisfaction of the second preference equates to life under a state. Translated into political terms, the state provides 'public goods', the most important of which is security. (A public good is one the enjoyment of which cannot be restricted to those who have directly paid for it – it has 'spill-over effects'.)

Some commentators argue that the rational strategy for each prisoner is to forgo her first preference in order to achieve her second preference. This is incorrect: for each prisoner, achieving her first preference should remain her goal. What she wants is an agreement with the other prisoner that each will remain silent, but then to break the agreement in the hope that the other prisoner will honour it. Individual rationality dictates that she will aim to free-ride on the other's compliance; that is, gain the benefits of cooperation, which is the avoidance of five years in prison, without paying the cost of cooperation, which is one year in prison. Of course, as rational actors, each prisoner understands the motivations of the other, and so a 'voluntary' agreement is ineffective. What we need is a third-party enforcer of the agreement. The enforcer imposes sanctions on free-riders, such that there is an incentive to comply. In political terms, the enforcer is the state, an entity, that, in the words of Max Weber, successfully commands a monopoly on the use of coercion in a particular territory.

There are three difficulties with the Hobbesian solution to the Prisoner's Dilemma:

1. The existence of an enforcer, or state, does not fundamentally alter the motivations of those subject to it: each still seeks to satisfy her own interests. This engenders a fundamental instability in the political order: we are always looking over our shoulder at other people, convinced that given the opportunity they will break the law. Such lawbreaking might, for example, take the form of evading payment of taxes necessary to maintain a police force.

2. The second objection to Hobbes can be broadened out into a critique of the aims of classical contract theory – as distinct from the aims of the contemporary contractarianism of Rawls. Hobbes, Locke, Rousseau and Kant were occupied above all with the question of an individual's obligation to obey the state and its laws. A law by its nature commands obedience, but what is termed 'political obligation' is concerned with the existence of moral reasons for obeying the law: by asking whether a person has a political obligation we put into question the legitimacy of law. From the preceding discussion it is not difficult to see how a contractarian might argue for political obligation. We are all better off under a state than in a state of nature and therefore we are under an obligation to obey the state. But what if the benefits of cooperation are unequally distributed? Consider another version of the Prisoner's Dilemma:

Table 7.3

		Second prisoner Remains silent	Confesses
First prisoner	Remains silent	4, 1	10, 0
	Confesses	0, 10	6, 5

The preference ordering of each prisoner is identical to the first version. The difference lies in the respective pay-offs from cooperation relative to non-cooperation: the first prisoner gains two years of freedom whereas the second prisoner gains four years. It might therefore be *rational* for each prisoner to submit to an enforced agreement, but it is not necessarily fair. Given the unfairness of the situation it is hard to argue that those who are disadvantaged relative to others have a *moral* obligation to obey the state. And this brings us to the third objection to Hobbes.

3. In both versions there was a unique solution to the dilemma – but what if instead of one set of pay-offs there were multiple sets? Let us imagine that the agreement is not about simply obeying or not obeying the state, but is concerned with the creation of a certain kind of state. We have to decide on the economic and political structure of society: should power be concentrated or dispersed? Should there be strong private property rights or, alternatively, collective ownership of economic resources? How much freedom should individuals have? Do we want an extensive welfare state or should individuals be required to buy health cover and education? Whatever is chosen, we are all better off under some kind of state than no state, but there is not a unique solution. The principles or institutions we choose will benefit people in different ways: if 'a' represents the state of nature, and 'b . . . z' a range of alternative political systems, then you might be better off under any of 'b . . . z' than under 'a', but your preferred system will not be shared by all other citizens. For twentieth-century contractarians the aim of the contract is to create a certain set of political institutions – or principles of justice – rather than simply contract into the state. For example, Rawls accepts the logic of the solution to the Prisoner's Dilemma, but that is merely the starting point for a theory of justice: it has to be both rational *and reasonable* to submit to the state.

The fundamental problem with Hobbes's argument is that he reduces the legitimacy of the state to self-interest. His starting point is a materialist conception of human nature: human beings are 'bodies in motion', continually desiring things, and never fully satisfied (Hobbes, 1991: 118–20). Because there is scarcity of desired objects, humans are brought into conflict with one another. Their greatest fear is death, and that fear is the key to understanding why the state of nature is a 'war of all against all' (Hobbes: 185–6). Although Hobbes outlines the 'laws of nature' that he claims exist in the state of nature, these are best interpreted as akin to scientific, rather than moral, laws. For example, we are required to seek peace, unless war is necessary for self-defence, but this can be understood as a prudential instruction rather than a moral requirement (Hobbes: 190).

A twentieth-century theorist, John Plamenatz, criticised Hobbes on grounds that if his description of the state of nature were accurate, then people would be too nasty to stick to any agreement, and if they stick to the agreement then the state of nature cannot be as Hobbes describes it (Plamenatz: 193–7). One of the insights of game theory, of which the Prisoner's Dilemma is an example, is to provide a solution to this apparent paradox: what we seek is an agreement, equivalent to the prisoners' agreement to remain silent, but what we fear is that other people will 'defect' from the agreement. It follows from this that Prisoner's Dilemma-type situations are 'assurance games'. In short, people are not nasty but fearful. Furthermore, the real challenge is not agreeing to create a state, but *maintaining* the state. Consequently the 'game' that models the problem is not a one-off Prisoner's Dilemma, but a repeated Prisoner's Dilemma. Using a real-world example: should you honour business contracts? If you acquire a reputation for breaking such contracts then people will not do business with you, so it pays to be trustworthy. Strictly speaking, this is not a Prisoner's Dilemma, for the incentive structure is changed; nonetheless, it supports Hobbes's argument without relaxing the derivation of political authority from self-interest.

Even if the need for a good reputation solves the first problem, it leaves unresolved the second and third problems. The second might simply be dismissed by Hobbes – after all, he makes no claim to the fairness of the state. All that is required is that each individual can ask himself or herself: am I better off under this state than in a state of nature? If the answer is 'yes' – and it almost certainly will be – then it is rational to submit to the state. The third problem is trickier. We said the context to Hobbes's political thought was the challenge to state authority generated by religious dissent. Given Hobbes's model of human nature, there seems no place for religious motivations. But if the Kingdom of God is not of this world, then contrary to what Hobbes claims, physical death is *not* the thing to be most feared. The worst thing is separation from God. Hobbes was certainly aware of the force of theologically grounded motivation, and argued that there should be a single state religion, with outward conformity, but no attempt to coerce a person's inner thoughts. What he did not reckon with was the challenge to the stability of the state – the agreement to submit – arising not from a clash of interests, but from differing moral judgements. When we contract into the state we do not simply give up our natural liberty to pursue our interests, we also give up the right to determine what is morally correct.

Hobbes and Liberalism

The claim that Hobbes is a liberal rests on a number of characteristics of his thought:

(a) It implicitly entails a rejection of natural authority – the authority of the sovereign derives from a contract and not from inheritance or divine right.

(b) People are equal in the state of nature because, with stealth, the weakest can kill the strongest. Admittedly this is a claim about individuals' physical powers – and a questionable one at that – rather than a claim for moral equality.

(c) Later contract theorists fundamentally revised the nature of the contract, but the basic method remains, so Hobbes's argument has proved remarkably productive of liberal thought.

In the next section we turn to two other contract theorists – Locke and Kant – but we argue that their thought is sufficiently different to Hobbes's to warrant attributing a distinct stream of liberal argument to them.

Rights-based Liberalism

Locke

Most courses in the history of political thought yoke together Thomas Hobbes and John Locke, and compare and contrast their contract theories. A simplistic comparison would describe Locke's state of nature as a rather less unpleasant place to be than the Hobbesian equivalent, and that this affects their attitude to the contract, and to the rights individuals should enjoy under the state. For example, Locke thinks we have a right to rebel against the state, whereas Hobbes rejects such a right. But these superficial differences conceal more significant ones, such

Biography — John Locke (1632–1704)

Born in 1632, and raised in a Puritan family, Locke was educated at Oxford University, graduating in 1656; he later earned a bachelor of medicine (1674).

In 1666 he met Anthony Ashley Cooper (1st Earl of Shaftesbury), who had come to Oxford to seek treatment for a liver infection, and Locke became Shaftesbury's physician, adviser and friend, moving into Shaftesbury's home in London in 1667, where he continued his medical training under the supervision of Thomas Sydenham. When Shaftesbury's condition worsened Locke oversaw the operation that removed the cyst. As Shaftesbury's power as Lord Chancellor grew, so did Locke's influence; however, in 1675 Shaftesbury fell from favour and Locke left England for France, where he continued his scholarly activities.

Shaftesbury's political fortunes underwent a brief revival in 1679, and Locke returned to England. However, under suspicion of involvement in the 1683 Rye House Plot – a plot to kill the king and ensure a Protestant succession – Locke fled to the Netherlands, where he remained until after the 'Glorious Revolution' and the accession of the Protestant William and Mary to the throne (1689). His major works were published between 1689 and his death in 1704: *A Letter Concerning Toleration* (1689), which argued for a 'broad' Anglican church; *An Essay Concerning Human Understanding*, and his most important political work, *Two Treatises of Civil Government*, both published in 1690.

that it is possible to say that Locke was not simply the next in line in the contract tradition, but articulated a distinct stream of liberal thought, one which emphasised moral rights. That tradition has had a huge impact not only on political thought in Locke's native England, but also, and perhaps especially, in the United States.

As we saw, Hobbes maintained that people were free and equal in the state of nature, and that there existed 'natural laws'. On the face of it, Locke offers a similar description of the state of nature, but his understanding of freedom, equality and natural law is quite different to that of Hobbes:

- Hobbes's liberty is simply the absence of restraint, whereas Locke's liberty takes the form of actionable rights.
- Hobbes understood equality in naturalistic rather than moral terms. For Locke, we are equal because no person has a natural right to subordinate another.
- Unlike Hobbes's laws of nature, Locke's laws have a theological basis – we have a natural duty to preserve ourselves, a duty owed to God, who created us.

For Locke, moral rights precede the contract to create a state, and the role of the state is to settle disputes over the interpretation of those rights, and ensure that violations of the rights are punished. The most important among the rights are rights to private property, which are grounded in rights in one's own body. Self-ownership is, however, derivative of God's right, as creator, in his creatures (Locke's theory of private property was discussed in relation to a contemporary

pp. 93–4

reworking of it by Robert Nozick). Economic and social life is possible in the state of nature. People can enter contracts – that is, exercise their powers – and individuals have the right to enforce them. Furthermore, at an early stage in the economic development of society individuals are materially satisfied – they do not compete for scarce resources. Only later, with a rise in population, does the problem of scarcity arise (Locke 1988: 297–8).

What makes the state of nature 'inconvenient' is the absence of a body that can *authoritatively* determine when rights have been violated and *effectively* enforce a remedy (Locke: 329–30). Hobbes was obsessed with effectiveness, but because there was no pre-contractual law in Hobbes's state of nature there was nothing to adjudicate. Because individuals in Locke's state of nature have the capacity to recognise the moral law, and the state is created as a judge and an enforcer, it follows that should the state fail in these tasks individuals are justified in rebelling against it.

Locke and Liberalism

There is much that is anachronistic in Locke. In particular, his claim that native Americans could not possess property because they could not recognise natural law, and thus the United States was 'unowned' (Locke: 293), is an embarrassment to contemporary defenders of Locke. Also, the Christian basis of his thought is problematic in modern, pluralistic societies, although his appeal to natural law does provide a route to a secularised notion of human rights. However, overall, the key contributions that Locke made to the liberal tradition are:

Human Rights Conventions, pp. 440–4

(a) The idea that there are what Robert Nozick calls 'side constraints', which limit what the state, or society in general, can do to human beings (Nozick 1974: ix).

(b) Natural (or moral) rights provide a standpoint from which we can judge the state. Unlike Hobbes, obligation to obey the state is not for Locke an 'all or nothing' matter. Although we give up a certain degree of moral judgement when we contract into the state, we do not 'hand over' all our autonomy.

(c) There is much more discussion of the institutions of liberal democracy in Locke than in Hobbes, and that discussion has been hugely influential. Locke is identified as a key influence on the formation of the American Constitution.

Kant

Biography, p. 142

From a different intellectual tradition Kant defends the idea of 'side constraints', and thus moral rights. More difficult to understand than Locke, but arguably a much more sophisticated philosopher. His moral theory is a standard part of the moral philosophy syllabus, whereas his political theory is less commonly found in a course on the history of political thought. However, one very powerful reason for studying Kant is that in the twentieth century there has been a huge revival of interest among political philosophers in his work, and he has been an important influence on such major thinkers as John Rawls and Jürgen Habermas.

We will briefly outline Kant's moral theory, and then explain how it underwrites his political theory. In *Groundwork of the Metaphysics of Morals* (Kant 1996: 37–108) Kant outlines a method for determining how we should behave – the categorical imperative. He offers a number of formulations, the differences intended to capture different aspects of moral relationships. Simplifying a great deal, what is morally right is what would be chosen if we were to view a situation from the standpoint of autonomy, unaffected by emotional, and other, attachments. If we abstract from those attachments then we will necessarily see the world from a universal standpoint; moral reasoning entails *universalising* a 'maxim' (a maxim is a claim that we intend to form the basis of a moral law). If we cannot universalise that maxim then it cannot become a moral law.

Kant provides a simple example: a shopkeeper knows he can get away with over-charging a customer, but feels moved to inform the customer that she has been over-charged. So the 'maxim' is: 'I should always be honest' (Kant 1996: 53). This maxim can form the basis of a moral law only if it can be universalised, meaning that anybody in the shopkeeper's situation can make the same judgement, and the shopkeeper in a different situation can apply that maxim. Universalisation entails abstraction from people and situations. Perhaps the customer is a friend, and friendship moves the shopkeeper to be honest, or alternatively, the customer is a child, and the shopkeeper feels bad about cheating a child, or maybe the shopkeeper 'just knows' it is wrong to over-charge. These cannot justify the maxim because they depend on the particular identities of the agents, or on particular emotions.

The categorical imperative is not a tool for making everyday judgements. This becomes clear when Kant, in one of the formulations, maintains that one should will that your maxim becomes a 'universal law of *nature*' (Kant: 73). This indicates that the task is not to make case-by-case judgements, but think 'holistically': we imagine a *society* governed by universal laws. Such a society Kant describes as a 'Kingdom of Ends', for if we universalise we must necessarily treat other human beings as ends and not means (Kant: 80). In contrast to Locke, these laws are not given to us by God, or through our senses, but are 'constructed' by human beings exercising powers of reason. Through construction of moral laws we lift ourselves above our animal natures and prove our autonomy. There is a crucial political point here: we can be coerced into *conforming* with what morality requires, but we cannot be coerced into acting *for the right reasons*. The shopkeeper can be motivated to be 'honest' by threat of punishment, but he would not be acting morally because he is not being moved by reason.

Some contemporary political theorists draw an anarchist conclusion from Kant's argument. Robert Paul Wolff argues that we can never reconcile moral autonomy and political authority. But, in fact, in his political writings Kant does defend the state. He even maintains that a civilised state is possible among a 'nation of devils . . . just so long as they get the constitution right' (Kant: 335). To understand the relationship between morality and politics we need to distinguish internal freedom and external freedom. The former – which can also be called autonomy – entails the ability to be motivated to act morally by the force of reason alone. The latter is the idea that the freedom of one person must coexist with the freedom of all others. This is expressed as a system of rights, coercively enforced by the state.

The state serves the end of morality by helping to realise the 'Kingdom of Ends'. The difficulty with this argument is that human agents must will the creation of that 'Kingdom', whereas in a political community – under the state – we are coerced into behaving in accordance with other people's rights. Attempting to resolve the conflict between autonomy and coercion has been central to the liberal project. One way of resolving it would be to posit two standpoints that a citizen can adopt: the standpoint of moral autonomy and the standpoint of a subject of law. As an autonomous agent you will the creation of a political community in which each person's rights are respected, but you also know enough about human nature to recognise that rights will have to be protected through coercion, such that you are at the same time willing the creation of a *coercive* political community. This would, of course, create a divide within human psychology between moral autonomy and political subjectivity.

Kant and Liberalism

The rights-based tradition of liberalism has sometimes been characterised as entailing the priority of the right over the good. These terms are attributed to Kant, but the precise definition was given by moral philosopher David Ross. He defined the right as 'that which is obligatory' and the good as 'that which is worth pursuing' (Ross, 1930: 3). There are many different forms of goodness: aesthetic evaluation, friendship, the pursuit of truth are but a few. Kant's political theory can be categorised as 'right based' because the purpose of the state is not to realise goodness but to ensure that people respect each other's rights. The 'right' – note the singular – is the name Kant gives to the coexistence of individual rights. A political consequence of the priority of the right over the good is that the state's functions are limited.

pp. 200–1

If the state is only justified insofar as it protects individual rights it cannot have purposes of its own which are independent of that function. Michael Oakeshott, whose work draws on liberal and conservative thought, makes a useful distinction between the state, or political community, as an *enterprise association* and as a *civil association*. In an enterprise association people have a shared project, and the state acts as an agent to realise that project. Such a project might be theological in character, but it could also be secular. For example, the attempt to create an 'equal society', where equality is an end in itself, would constitute an enterprise. Oakeshott argues that a political community is a civil association of individuals with disparate aims, and the state works to permit the continuation of that association: the association has no ends of its own.

Utilitarianism

Utilitarians hold that political institutions function to increase the overall level of welfare – or utility – of a society. At first sight this appears fundamentally opposed to rights-based liberalism, and indeed to contractarianism: utility maximisation implies that there is a thing called 'society' which has aims over and above those of individuals, or that the aims and interests of individuals are subsumed in 'society'. While there are tensions between utilitarianism and rights-based liberalism, and much of the debate within the liberal tradition is between these positions, there are shared historical roots, such that they are both clearly part of the liberal tradition. Furthermore, in the twentieth century revisions to utilitarian theory have had the consequence of closing the gap to some degree between utilitarianism and rights-based liberalism.

The claim that utilitarianism entails the maximisation of utility requires elaboration: what is utility? How do we maximise it? What does utilitarianism actually require of individuals? Different utilitarian thinkers have defined utility in different ways: Jeremy Bentham defined it as happiness, John Stuart Mill as pleasure, G.E. Moore as certain ideal states of mind. All of these definitions conceptualise utility as something 'mentalistic' – a feeling or state of mind. This raises an epistemological question: how do we know someone is happy, or feeling pleasure, or has the right state of mind? Contemporary utilitarians avoid the epistemological question by defining utility as preference satisfaction. This has the advantage that there are available real-world systems for ordering preferences: voting and markets. When we cast a vote or buy a pair of shoes we are expressing a preference.

To maximise utility we have to be able to measure it, and two options are available: either we add up instances of utility (cardinal measurement), or else we rank instances of utility (ordinal measurement). The definition of utility affects how we go about measuring it: mentalistic definitions lend themselves to cardinal measurement, while preference satisfaction fits best with ordinal measurement. In fact, it was the difficulty of measuring pleasure or happiness that led to a shift to defining utility as preference satisfaction.

We now come to the third – and most obviously political – question: if we are utilitarians, how should we behave? There are some standard criticisms of utilitarianism:

- What makes people happy, gives them pleasure, or what they prefer is completely open: if torturing another person gives you pleasure, then it must be counted into the 'maximand' (that which is to be maximised).
- We cannot respect the law if breaking it will increase utility.
- Utilitarians cannot respect individual rights – J.S. Mill's attempt to establish a 'sphere of non-interference' (rights) on the basis of 'human interests in the widest sense' (utility) is incoherent.
- One person could be made to suffer excruciating pain in order to give a million people each a minuscule amount of pleasure. A less extravagant criticism is that utilitarians cannot be concerned about the distribution of welfare, but merely its overall level.
- You are as much responsible for what you allow to happen as what you do in a more direct sense of doing. For example, given the choice between (a) killing 1 person and 'allowing' 19 to live, or (b) 'standing by' while all 20 are killed, utilitarianism requires you to kill that 1 person (Williams, 1973: 98–99).

pp. 41–6

These criticisms are dismissed by utilitarians as unrealistic. The way to avoid them, it is claimed, is to distinguish between direct and indirect utilitarianism. Direct utilitarianism – or 'act utilitarianism' – requires that you seek to maximise utility on every occasion. Indirect utilitarianism, which includes 'rule utilitarianism' and 'institutional utilitarianism', separates action and justification: what we should do is follow rules, such as respecting individual rights, and the consequence of doing so is that utility will be maximised. Institutional utilitarianism is compatible with contractarianism: in the contract situation we agree to a set of institutions, the operation of which will maximise utility.

Utilitarianism and Liberalism

There is no doubt that since the early nineteenth century, when Bentham advanced his – incoherent – requirement to seek the greatest happiness of the greatest number (incoherent, because you cannot simultaneously *maximise* two numbers), utilitarianism has developed in sophistication. However, our concern is with the relationship of utilitarianism to the other members of the 'liberal family'. What makes utilitarianism part of the family?

(a) As do Hobbes, Locke (despite his Christianity) and Kant, utilitarians reject 'natural authority'. Although it is possible to give utilitarianism a Christian cast, there is no doubt that it developed out of a secular, 'natural–scientific', world view. The calculability of pleasure or happiness fits neatly with the rise of science and the rejection of the idea that there are forces beyond human consciousness.

(b) Utilitarians still hold to the liberal 'presumption in favour of freedom' and the 'presumption of natural equality'. People are free to express their preferences, and coercion is only justified in order to bring about the greatest good. And people are equally 'generators' of utility – John Stuart Mill attributed this formula to the earlier utilitarian thinker Jereny Bentham: 'each to count for one and nobody for more than one' (Mill 1991: 198–9).

(c) In concrete political terms, utilitarians have invariably been progressive or radical in their attitudes to social problems. In many ways they represent the 'left-wing' liberal alternative to the libertarianism of Locke and Kant, although you need not be a utilitarian to be on the left of the political spectrum.

(d) Most important of all, utilitarianism grew in parallel with the development of democracy. The high point of utilitarian thought was the nineteenth century, although it continued to be the dominant philosophical method for justifying political principles until the 1960s when there was a revival in contractarianism. The decline of contract thinking around 1800 went hand in hand with scepticism about using the contract – actual or hypothetical – to explain political obligation in a *mass* society. Utilitarianism seemed to provide a much more convincing method of justification in democratic societies: the calculation of utility dovetails with the counting of votes, although it was only in the twentieth century, with the development of preference satisfaction as the definition of utility, that a more direct link between utilitarianism and democracy was established.

Conclusion: the Swedish Case Study

We began this chapter with a discussion of anti-prostitution laws in Sweden, and especially the prohibition on the purchase of sexual services. A number of arguments have been advanced by the Swedish government for that prohibition:

1. Prostitution is 'harmful not only to the individual prostituted woman or child, but also to society at large'.

2. Combating prostitution is central to Sweden's goal of achieving equality between men and women, at the national level as well as internationally. Prostitution is a gender-specific phenomenon: most prostitutes are female, and most buyers are male.

3. Women who suffer additional oppression, such as racism, are overrepresented in the global prostitution industry. In societies where the status of women has improved, prostitution has fallen.

4. The fact that an exchange relationship operates – sex for money – does not justify the relationship, because there is an immense imbalance in the power relation of buyer to seller.

5. It is important to 'motivate persons in prostitution to attempt to exit without risking punishment' (note: the seller of sexual services is not prosecuted).

6. Because it is assumed that men who buy sex are acting from a natural, male drive, their 'underlying motives have seldom been studied or even questioned'.

7. By adopting these measures Sweden has 'given notice to the world' that it regards prostitution as a serious form of oppression of women.

8. Since the Act came into force there has been a 'dramatic drop' in the number of women in street prostitution, and the number of men who buy sexual services has also fallen.

9. Public support for the law is 'widespread and growing': an opinion poll in 1999 revealed 76 per cent supported the law, and 15 per cent opposed it. In 2001 the figure in favour was 81 per cent, with 14 per cent against. (http://www.sweden. gov.se/content/1/c6/03/16/13/110ab985.pdf)

The first point to make is that critics of the law would argue for a distinction between public and private: it is possible to disapprove of prostitution but believe that consenting adults should have the right to make choices. This is a development of the argument for toleration, but here extended far beyond religious toleration. It may appear that the Swedish state has simply rejected toleration but, in fact, the language used to justify the law is an implicit acknowledgement that the limitation on the purchaser's freedom requires justification: 'in any other context, [prostitution] would be categorized as sexual abuse and rape' and 'the fact that these acts are committed in exchange for payment does not in any way diminish or mitigate the immense physical and mental damage inflicted on [prostitutes'] bodies and minds'. The power imbalance between prostitute and client is so great that the former cannot be deemed to be a consenting adult. Obviously one can disagree with this assessment, but the debate over the harm caused by prostitution, and whether prostitutes can really **consent**, is fought out on liberal terms.

Several of the arguments set out in the Swedish government's defence of the Sexual Services Act make reference to the good *consequences* of banning the sale of sexual services. It is often commented that Sweden has a particularly strong idea of the 'common good', and this has sometimes resulted in laws which seem to impinge on individual freedom. There are a number of reasons for this, one being the dominance of the centre-left Social Democrats in post-war Sweden. The general point is that utilitarian – or consequentialist – reasoning is clearly in evidence in the justification for the anti-prostitution law. The harm caused by prostitution is harm to 'society at large'; the law is part of a package aimed to promote gender equality;

the operation of the law has resulted in a dramatic drop in prostitution. In addition, the high level of public support is taken as a justification for the law. Obviously, in a democracy you have to win support for laws, but quite often legislatures will pass laws that are unpopular, or decline to pass laws which would be popular. As we have argued in previous chapters liberalism and democracy should not be run together, for individual freedom can conflict with democracy, which in a mass society often takes the form of preference aggregation.

Finally, several arguments make reference to 'motivations': prostitutes should be 'motivated' to exit their way of life and male motives should be 'questioned'. In addition, Sweden had 'given notice to the world' that it regarded prostitution as a form of oppression, with the implication that it sought to change attitudes in other countries. The Swedish state is using its coercive power to motivate people and change attitudes, and thus to bring about a 'good' state of affairs. For a rights-based, Kantian, liberal this is an illegitimate extension of state power, and indeed a contradiction in terms, for you cannot coerce people into acting for the right reasons. It is important to distinguish the motivation argument from the harm argument. A defender of rights-based liberalism might accept that prostitutes cannot consent, and so buying their services is a form of harm and should be illegal. But 'motivating' people – that is, changing their attitudes – even if it were successful, would be incompatible with moral autonomy.

Summary

At the heart of liberalism is the belief that people are naturally free and equal. That does not mean that there are no limitations on freedom, or that people must be equal, or treated equally, in all respects. Rather, we are presumed to be free and equal, and departures from freedom and equality require justification. Viewed historically, liberalism developed out of the settlement of the Wars of Religion, with the emphasis on toleration of religious difference. Such toleration was gradually extended beyond the sphere of religion to other aspects of belief and lifestyle. Several strands of liberalism emerged after the seventeenth century, and we identified three: contractarianism, rights-based liberalism (and libertarianism) and utilitarianism. Although there are significant philosophical differences between them, they are all clearly part of the 'liberal family'. Much of the left–right debate in contemporary politics operates around different interpretations of liberalism. For example, both Rawls and Nozick can be described as 'liberal', but they come to quite different conclusions about the role of the state.

Questions

1. Is 'toleration' a coherent concept?
2. Can the justification for the state be reduced to 'mutual advantage' – that is, the combined effects of the pursuit of self-interest?

3. Can you believe in moral rights if you do not believe in God?
4. Can there be a utilitarian theory of rights?

References

Hobbes, T. (1991) *Leviathan* (ed. C.B. Macpherson) London: Penguin.

Kant, I. (1996) *Practical Philosophy* (ed. M. Gregor) Cambridge: Cambridge University Press.

Locke, J. (1988) *Two Treatises of Government*, ed. Peter Laslett, Cambridge: Cambridge University Press.

McGrath, A. (1988) *Reformation Thought: An Introduction* Oxford: Blackwell.

Mill, J.S. (1991) *On Liberty and Other Essays* (ed. J. Gray) Oxford: Oxford University Press.

Plamenatz, J. (1992) *Man and Society: Political and Social Theories from Machiavelli to Marx*. Vol. 1, *From the Middle Ages to Locke* London: Longman.

Ross, W. (1930) *The Right and the Good* Oxford: Oxford University Press.

Williams B. and Smart, J.J.C. (1973) *Utilitarianism: For and Against* Cambridge: Cambridge University Press.

Further Reading

There are a couple of good, short, introductions dealing with liberalism as a whole: John Gray, *Liberalism* (Buckingham: Open University Press, 1995), and David Manning, *Liberalism* (London: Dent, 1976). Of the major thinkers discussed in this chapter, the Oxford University Press 'Past Masters' series provides very short, useful, overviews, written by major scholars in the field, with guidance on further reading: Richard Tuck, *Hobbes* (Oxford: OUP, 1989); John Dunn, *Locke* (Oxford: OUP, 1984); Roger Scruton, *Kant* (Oxford: OUP, 1982); John Dinwiddy, *Bentham* (Oxford: OUP, 1989). More generally on the social contract tradition (which does encompass Locke and Kant), the following are helpful: Michael Lessnoff, *Social Contract* (London: Macmillan, 1986); Jean Hampton, *Hobbes and the Social Contract Tradition* (Cambridge: CUP, 1986); Patrick Riley, *Will and Political Legitimacy: a Critical Exposition of Social Contract Theory in Hobbes, Locke, Rousseau, Kant, and Hegel* (Cambridge Mass: Harvard University Press, 1982). On utilitarianism see: Geoffrey Scarre, *Utilitarianism* (London: Routledge, 1996); Anthony Quinton, *Utilitarian Ethics* (London: Duckworth, 1989); and for a very readable debate between a utilitarian and a critic of utilitarianism see Williams (1973).

Weblinks

- General site on liberalism: www.en.wikipedia.org/wiki/Liberalism

- Some sites devoted to classical and economic liberalism ('right-wing' liberalism):
  www.free-market.net/directorybytopic/liberalism/
  www.en.wikipedia.org/wiki/classical_liberalism
  www.libertyguide.com

- A site devoted to social liberalism (although more of a 'campaigning' site):
  www.korpios.org/resurgent/tenets.htm

Chapter 8

Conservatism

Introduction

Conservatism is an elusive ideology. Although there are conservative streams of thought in parties and movements calling themselves 'conservative', the main ideology of these movements is a combination of liberalism and nationalism, with the former particularly dominant. There are far fewer 'small c' than 'big c' conservatives. But despite its marginalisation, conservatism is a distinct ideology, and conservative thinkers present arguments of continuing relevance. Above all, conservatives challenge the idea that society can be planned in a rational way without regard to tradition and historical experience. This core idea leads them to support national institutions, but not radical nationalism; individual liberty against state power, but not the natural rights that many liberals defend; spontaneous order, but not anarchism; community, but not socialist collectivism.

Chapter Map

In this chapter we will:

- Outline the main elements of conservatism.

- Discuss the work of four key conservative thinkers: David Hume, Edmund Burke, Michael Oakeshott and Leo Strauss.

- Draw out the practical implications of conservative thought.

- Distinguish conservatism from the other traditional ideologies.

Reform or Revolution?

George W. Bush takes the Oath of Office on Capitol Hill in Washington, 20 January 2005

The election of George W. Bush in 2000 was controversial. A protracted dispute in Florida was finally settled by a 5–4 vote in the Supreme Court in favour of suspending further recounts and certifying Bush's victory in Florida over Al Gore, thus giving Bush the state and, with it, the Presidency. Another aspect of the election which became the focus of attention, but not of legal dispute, was the fact that even after winning Florida Bush won fewer popular votes than Gore: 50.5 million (47.9%) to Gore's 51 million (48.4%). On paper, the 2004 election was more decisive, with Bush securing his re-election with 62 million votes (50.7%) to John Kerry's 59 million (48.2%). But had Kerry won the state of Ohio he, not Bush, would have taken the Presidency. Both the controversy in Florida and the fact (2000) and distinct possibility (2004) of 'minority' winners is due to the electoral college system. In all but two states, the candidate who takes most votes wins the entire slate of delegates: Bush's 537-vote victory (out of 6 million votes cast) in Florida gave him the entire 25-person Floridian delegation, and a national 271–266 (with one abstention) victory in the electoral college. After the 2000 election there was a clamour for a change in the way the President is elected, but defenders of the system argued that it was tried-and-tested – in essence, Americans should judge the system not by its apparent unfairness, but by its success over the last two centuries.

- Do you find this 'conservative' defence of the Electoral College convincing?

A useful web-based defence of the electoral college is provided by William Kimberling of the US Federal Election Commission: http://www.fec.gov/pdf/eleccoll.pdf

Conservatism: An Elusive Ideology?

Anybody with a basic knowledge of party politics, but coming to political theory for the first time, may assume that 'conservatism' is simply the ideology of political parties calling themselves 'conservative', such as the Conservative Party in Britain, or the Conservatives in Canada (or one of its predecessor parties, the Progressive Conservatives). However, an analysis of the aims and policies of these parties would suggest that their ideological make-up is hybrid and changeable. Take the British Conservative Party, which was during the twentieth century the most electorally successful 'conservative' party in the world; its ideology shifted to such an extent that under Margaret Thatcher (British Prime Minister, 1979–90) it would be best described as 'national liberal'. The Thatcher government was economically liberal: it extended the use of market mechanisms in the domestic sphere, and pursued a pro-free trade policy in the international sphere, through, for example, the Single European Act (1986). But it was 'national' in that emphasis was placed on the restoration of national pride after what was perceived to be a policy of 'managed decline' in the period 1945–79. Although parties carrying the name 'liberal' tend to have a stronger social dimension, maintaining that welfare provision is necessary to enable people to live autonomous lives, social liberalism and economic liberalism are members of the same ideological family. They are not conservative.

If the Thatcher government was not really conservative, then what is conservatism? Etymology can mislead, but it is useful to start with the word 'conservative'. The idea of 'conservation' or 'preservation' suggests that conservatives stand opposed to progress. This is why the name of one of the predecessor parties to the Canadian Conservative Party – the Progressive Conservatives – seems like an oxymoron. In fact, as with compound names of many political parties, it was the result of a merger of two parties, rather than the 'progressive' being an adjectival qualification of 'conservative'. Nonetheless, even if it had been a deliberate ideological label, it is not an oxymoron: conservatives can be progressive. What is distinctive about conservatism is its attitude to progress – progress must be careful, tentative, respectful of past practices, pragmatic, and go with the grain of human nature. If conservatism has an enemy, it is 'rationalism' – an approach to political problems derived from the application of abstract concepts. Quite often conservative thinkers appear to reject abstract thought altogether, with the consequence that it is difficult to talk of a conservative political *theory*. However, it is still possible to identify features of conservative thought that are distinct and allow us to describe conservatism as a distinct ideology.

Basic Elements of Conservatism

As with all ideologies there are significant differences between different thinkers and streams of thought, but there are also some common elements, or themes, in conservatism. In this list of features we begin with the most 'philosophical' elements and gradually move to the more concrete, political ones:

1. **Rejection of 'rationalism'** Conservatives often use the metaphor of a ship at sea to explain their objections to what they call 'rationalism' (it should be noted

that rationalism is a pejorative term and those identified as rationalists by conservatives would not use this label to describe themselves). You are at sea, and your ship develops a fault, which if not dealt with will result in the ship sinking. The 'ship' is the state, or the set of political institutions that make up the state, while the 'sea' is society or culture in the widest sense. The fault is analogous to those stresses and strains that political institutions frequently face, such as the crisis Americans faced after the 2000 Presidential Election. Rationalism would entail 'analysing' – or breaking down – the ship into its components in the hope of understanding the source of the fault and so rectifying it. The conservatives' point is not hard to discern: we cannot deconstruct the ship while at sea, but we must do something about the fault or we will drown.

2. **Experience matters** Continuing with the metaphor of the ship, our response to the fault must be based on past experience and, if necessary, a cautious process of trial and error. The 'conservatism' of conservatives rests not on an irrational veneration of the past but on a recognition of the limited nature of human reason, and for this reason conservatives can be progressive, and embrace change. What they fear are radical experiments: human beings cannot adequately predict the full consequences of their actions, and while some experiments may make the world a better place we cannot be sure that they will.

3. **Human nature** While there are some marked differences within conservative thought concerning human behaviour, capabilities and motivation, there is broad agreement that human beings are limited in their capacity to comprehend the society in which they live. This does not mean that humans are stupid, but rather that no individual mind can understand the complexity of social relations, and there is no 'super mind' which is capable of doing so. Here the conservative critique of socialism is most apparent: socialist planning presupposes a mind capable of making complex economic decisions. Socialism is doomed to failure because, first, it is inefficient, and, second (and perhaps more worryingly), it requires a concentration of power in the hands of the state. Conservatives tend to support the free market on the grounds that the distribution of goods depends on the decisions made by millions of individuals without the necessity for central control. This brings them close to the libertarian stream of liberalism but, importantly, conservative support for markets is not based on the individualist premise of moral rights to private property, but on a claim about the limits of human capabilities.

pp. 92–6; Rights Based Liberalism, pp. 175–9

4. **Rejection of 'visionary politics'** Conservative thinker Edmund Burke famously observed that 'at the end of every vista, you see nothing but the gallows' (Burke, 1975: 344). He had in mind the visionary politics of the French Revolution (1789). Visionaries do not recognise the pluralism of everyday life – the fact that individuals have conflicting needs, desires and values. A vision implies a common project for society which overrides that pluralism. A later thinker, Michael Oakeshott, makes a distinction between society as a 'civic association' and an 'enterprise association': an enterprise implies a common purpose, whereas a civic association rests on certain rules of conduct that allow individuals to live together.

5. **Respect for institutions** An institution is a rule-governed activity. Conservatives maintain that institutions evolve, rather than being created at a determinate point in history. This may seem to misdescribe the history of many

national institutions; for example, the United States and modern France had 'founding moments', and the process of decolonisation in the period after 1945 resulted in the creation of many new states. However, conservatives argue, first, that the instability of many newly created states is evidence of the importance of evolution, and, second, where institutions appear to be successful it is because they have adapted over time. The US political system is a good example – contemporary US institutions are radically different to those created by the founding fathers. The fact that many Americans do not recognise this fact, and hold that their institutions are continuous, actually reinforces the conservatives' argument: a belief in continuity, alongside adaptation, is a 'necessary fiction'. Institutions suppress the asocial tendencies of human nature, and they provide a focus for allegiance.

6. **Suspicion of authority** This feature of conservatism may seem to contradict the last one; however, to say that conservatives are suspicious of authority does not entail its rejection. What conservatives are wary of is the accumulation of state power, which for reasons discussed above is incompatible with a recognition of the limits of individuals to grasp complex social relations. Although politicians calling themselves 'conservatives' are not shy about using state power to suppress movements they consider to be a threat to social order, more reflective conservatives will argue that institutions are not abstract entities, but have to be run by human beings, who are always in danger either of abusing their position or, even if well meaning, of putting into practice policies which have unintended bad consequences. From this position conservatives can make some interesting alliances – while rejecting statements of universal human rights detached from a social or legal system, they nonetheless stress 'our ancient liberties' and will join forces with civil liberties groups against, for example, measures intended to combat terrorism.

These points are intended to provide an overview of conservatism. To get a better idea of conservative thought, and to understand its strengths and its weaknesses, it is best to consider the work of particular thinkers. We focus on four: David Hume (1711–76), Edmund Burke (1729–97), Michael Oakeshott (1901–90), and Leo Strauss (1899–1973). Of the four Leo Strauss's work least manifests the above elements of thought. However, he is an important influence on what is called **'neo-conservatism'** – a term much used in current political debates in the United States – and the discussion of Strauss will allow us to assess the degree to which neo-conservatism is really conservative.

David Hume

Eighteenth-century Scottish philosopher David Hume is often described as the first conservative political theorist; certainly he is the first major thinker to offer a

Exercise

How valid is the metaphor of the ship to explain the nature of progress? Can you think of social and political problems that require *radical* solutions?

Civil Liberties and Counter-terrorism Legislation

The challenge that terrorism poses to civil liberties provides an interesting example of how conservatives and liberals can join forces on a public policy issue but from subtly different perspectives. In the wake of the attack on the World Trade Center on 11 September 2001, many Western countries have introduced new counter-terrorism laws; in Britain, most controversially, this entailed internment of non-nationals on the authority of the Home Secretary (Interior Minister). That judgement was subject to a judicial review, but in secret, without all the evidence being available to an internee's lawyer, and internment being ultimately decided by the 'balance of probabilities' that the person is a threat rather than the belief that it is 'beyond reasonable doubt' that he or she is a threat. The highest legal authority (the Law Lords) determined that the law was unfair because it applied only to non-nationals, and was a 'disproportionate' response to the threat; in response the government offered 'control orders', such as restrictions on movement, instead of incarceration, and extended this to nationals as well as non-nationals. Liberals – in the wide, non-party, sense of that term – argued that the anti-terrorist laws in both original and revised versions were a violation of human rights, where rights are entitlements individuals have irrespective of their nationality. Conservatives – again, in the wide sense of the term – also attacked the legislation, but focused much more on the *erosion* of 'ancient liberties', such as habeas corpus – liberties achieved over centuries and contained in documents, such as Magna Carta (1215) and the Bill of Rights (1688).

philosophical defence of conservatism. For that reason it is necessary to explain how Hume derives his political theory from his epistemology (what we can know) and practical philosophy (how we should behave, or what motivates us to act in certain ways).

Although their relevance to politics may not, at first sight, be obvious, it is necessary to set out a number of Hume's philosophical claims:

1. Human understanding must be drawn from experience. All the materials of thinking – perceptions – are derived either from sensations or from reflection. Although 'reflection' will generate complex ideas, which we do not directly experience, all such ideas are combinations of simple sensations. If philosophers use a term, such as 'cause' or 'freedom', then we can test whether it has any meaning by breaking the idea down to its simple sensations, or 'impressions'.

2. Simple impressions must be connected together, or 'associated'. At any moment there is a great deal going on in a person's mind, but we cannot reason if the contents of one's mind are arbitrary: we need to connect, or associate, ideas. There are three principles of association: resemblance, contiguity and causation. The last is problematic because it takes us beyond experience: Johnny throws a brick through the window and so 'causes' the window to break, but all we *see* are Johnny and his body movements, the trajectory of the brick, and the breaking window.

3. We attribute causes to events on the basis of experience, and more specifically, habit. For example, we grasp the 'causal properties' of gravity by observing falling objects. Beliefs are built on habits, but a belief is itself a sensation and not something external to experience. Although every occurrence is a simple, or unique, sensation, the observation of repetition creates an 'internal impression', or reflection.

In summary, we can say that what Hume rejects is the idea that 'reason' transcends, or goes beyond, what can be observed. To grasp the political significance

| Biography | David Hume (1711–76) |

Born into a relatively wealthy Scottish Borders family, Hume was educated by his widowed mother until, at the age of 11, he went to Edinburgh University. After leaving the university he was encouraged to pursue a career in law, but increasingly his interest turned to philosophy. As a consequence he engaged in private study, during which time he composed his three-volume *Treatise of Human Nature*, which was published in anonymous instalments (1739, 1740). That work is now regarded as a canonical text, but the lack of interest in it among his contemporaries led Hume to complain that it fell 'stillborn from the press'. The *Treatise* ranges over the central problems of philosophy, many of which have relevance to his political thought.

However, of more direct significance for politics was the two-volume *Essays, Moral and Political* (1741, 1742). In 1744–5 he was forced to withdraw as a candidate for the Professorship in Moral Philosophy at Edinburgh University in the face of opposition from the church, who claimed – probably correctly – that Hume was an atheist.

Concerned that the *Treatise* had failed to attract attention because of its style rather than its content Hume published a single-volume 'popular' version entitled *Enquiry Concerning Human Understanding* (1748). It was based largely on Volume 1 of the *Treatise* but included direct attacks on religious belief; a rendition of volume 3 was published as an *Enquiry Concerning the Principles of Morals* (1751), and is regarded as important in the development of utilitarianism.

Rejected by Glasgow University for a chair in philosophy, Hume used his position as librarian of the Advocate's Library in Edinburgh to pursue his interest in history; while there he wrote most of his six-volume *History of England* (1754–62).

Aged 50, in 1761, Hume was invited by the Earl of Hertford to accompany him as his secretary to Paris, where he received a warm reception. It was through French thinkers that Hume's thought percolated throughout Europe – French being the language of the educated. Returning to Edinburgh he spent his last years revising his works and eating, drinking and playing backgammon with friends.

of this rejection we need to consider Hume's moral philosophy. Morality is concerned with action, but not simply action, for a person's motives or 'reasons for action' are important in assessing whether an act is right or wrong, good or bad. In keeping with his emphasis on experience as the basis of knowledge, and applying it to action, Hume argues that any assessment of a person's actions, and that person's own assessment of what she should do, cannot be based on something which transcends experience. Indeed, reasoning about what should be done is itself severely limited: one can at best assess the most effective means to a given end, but the end itself is beyond assessment. If Jane wants to murder John, then reason can be used to determine the most effective means – shooting, poisoning, strangulation and so on – but it cannot be employed to assess the end itself, that is, whether Jane ought to kill John. Hume is not arguing that murder is acceptable, but rather that what stops Jane murdering John is *sentiment*: to twenty-first-century ears this word has slightly saccharine overtones, but in the eighteenth century it was an important philosophical concept. A sentiment is a pre-rational feeling towards somebody or something. Against Hobbes's theory, Hume does not believe that human beings are motivated purely by self-interest, but rather their sentiments are limited: they are concerned with their own interests, or those very close to them, such as family, but they are capable of 'sympathy', and so are moved to act in ways beneficial to other people.

Human beings' motives are mixed: although they are self-interested they are capable of limited sacrifices of their own self-interest for the benefit of others. And it is important that such 'beneficence' is based on a simple sympathy rather than being concealed self-interest. In Hobbes's political theory, although each person was better off under a – any – state than under no state, the absence of genuine moral sentiments made people distrustful of one another, and rendered society unstable. As does Hobbes, Hume argues that we are all better off under a state, especially a state that guarantees the protection of private property, but for Hume the very success of such mutual advantage depends on a suspension of self-interest. This observation leads to Hume's famous rejection of the social contract and, by extension, his rejection of the liberal tradition.

Contractar-
ionism,
pp. 170–5

The social contract is a fiction: no political society was ever created by a contract. More important than Hume's historical observation is his discussion of the implications for political legitimacy of holding the view that society was the result of a contract. Political authority, or legitimacy, arises from the habit of obedience to a power that initially is recognised as neither legitimate nor illegitimate, but as simply 'given' – in legal language, such power would be termed de facto, as distinct from de jure (Hume 1963: 462). The implication of Hobbes's argument was that any monopolistic political power was preferable to none at all, such that this distinction is invalid: whatever gets us out of the state of nature is 'legitimate'. Hume, in part, endorses Hobbes's argument for state over anarchy, but because Hume ties legitimacy to sentiment, and sentiment only develops gradually, the state acquires legitimacy after the fact of its existence (Hume: 538). And, crucially, the degree to which it is legitimate depends on how effective it is in protecting individuals' interests and engendering moral sentiments conducive to social order. While Hume rejects revolution as a leap into the unknown, the implication of his argument is that repressive, authoritarian states will have limited success in building their legitimacy.

Justice is a virtue operating in any society in which strangers come into contact with one another. The rules of justice are the product of 'artifice' and 'contrivance', and are intended to protect private property. Crucially, the rules evolve over time as people become habituated to them. We recognise that they serve our interests, but our allegiance to them cannot be reduced to self-interest, for we respect them even when it might be in our interest to break them. There develops an 'intercourse of sentiments' – a 'conversation' between citizens out of which emerges a limited benevolence detached from narrow self-interest (Hume, 1978: 602). Many critics suspect that moral sentiments, or sympathy, are still egoistic, for what human beings care about is that they will be held in esteem by others, and, therefore, doing the right thing is pleasurable. Hume himself seems to suggest this: 'every quality of the mind, which is *useful* or *agreeable* to the *person himself* or to *others*, communicates a pleasure to the spectator, engages his esteem, and is admitted under the honourable denomination of virtue or merit' (Hume: 277). However, pleasure is compatible with sociability in a way that self-interest is not.

Biography **Edmund Burke (1729–97)**

Born in Dublin to a Protestant father and Catholic mother, Burke was educated at a Quaker boarding school and Trinity College, Dublin (Dublin University).

Abandoning a legal career in favour of writing, in 1756 Burke published *Vindication of Natural Society* as well as his main contribution to aesthetics: *Philosophical Inquiry into the Origin of our Ideas of the Sublime and Beautiful*. In 1765 he entered the British Parliament; once there he made significant contributions to the debate over the Crown's powers, arguing for greater parliamentary control of royal patronage and spending. He was later to be instrumental in reforming the 'civil list'; the money paid by parliament to the Crown. On colonial matters, Burke was progressive, arguing for recognition of indigenous cultures. Britain's taxation policies in the American colonies provoked a violent reaction, and Burke argued for more pragmatism.

His respect for India, and its Hindu society, led him to propose the East India Bill (1783), intended to control the activities of the East India Company. When that failed he sought the impeachment of the Governor-General of Bengal, Warren Hastings; the post of Governor was intended to act as a control on the East India Company, but Hastings had worked 16 years for the Company. There followed a seven-year trial (1788–95), which became a public spectacle as Burke argued his case against Hastings, and ultimately British policy in India. The culmination of the trial was Hastings' acquittal. However, it was not colonialism that was Burke's most famous target, but the 1789 Revolution in France, and it is his book, *Reflections on the Revolution in France* (1790), which is regarded as the classic statement of conservative thought. As Burke seems to have predicted the so-called Reign of Terror (1793–4), he became, unwittingly, the spokesman for counter-revolutionaries across Europe.

Edmund Burke

If Hume was the first great conservative thinker, then Burke must be the most famous. In part this is due to the fact that in the canon of *general* philosophers Hume is up there with Plato and Kant as one of the 'greats' but, because his contributions were primarily to the core areas of philosophy, Hume's political reflections are regarded as subsidiary. Burke, on the other hand, is not among the great general philosophers, and is regarded primarily as a political thinker (he did, nonetheless, make a notable contribution to aesthetics). Indeed, Burke was not only a political thinker, but that rarity among political philosophers – a politician.

As with Hume, the philosophical starting point for Burke's conservatism is his rejection of 'abstractions', such as the natural rights proclaimed by the French Revolutionaries in 1789. Abstractions become embodied in theories, and theories become dogma, and a dogmatic approach will not permit criticism. The political consequence of abstract thought, Burke argues, is terror. Against abstraction, theory and dogma, Burke defends habit, taste and prejudice. The concept of prejudice is the single most important concept in Burke's conservative political theory. Today, 'prejudice' is a pejorative term, so it is important to understand how Burke uses it. A prejudice is a 'pre-judgement', or a judgement made without

How to read:

Burke's *Reflections on the Revolution in France*

The full title of this work is *From Reflections on the Revolution in France, and on the Proceedings in Certain Societies in London relative to that Event: in a Letter intended to have been sent to a Gentleman in Paris.* The 'gentleman' in question was Charles-Jean-François Depont, a friend of Burke who sought his views on the 1789 Revolution in France. Once Burke had begun writing he realised that the topic required a literary form more extensive than a private letter, and, in fact, the real addressee of the 'letter' was an English radical, Richard Price, who compared the French Revolution favourably with the English Glorious Revolution of 1688. Although the work is relatively brief, there are no section breaks to help the reader. However, it can be divided into two parts. The first part, which takes up about two-thirds of the work, argues that the French enthusiasm for liberty has blinded them to the recognition that it is but one value, and indeed, crucially, only possible when balanced by other values, such as order. The second part focuses on equality, and maintains that the distribution of power between the three branches of state – executive, judiciary, and legislature – had weakened political authority to the point where a military takeover was highly likely.

recourse to theoretical abstractions; in contemporary philosophical language we might use the term 'intuition' rather than prejudice. For Burke, the wisdom of other people, including previous generations, is a resource that must be respected if we are to avoid disastrous social consequences. The main thrust of Burke's *Reflections on the Revolution in France* is to contrast a society – France – which has abandoned prejudice in favour of 'theory', with a society – Britain – which has remained close to its traditions, to which it is prejudiced. Burke, claiming to speak on behalf of his fellow countrymen, observes:

> that we have made no discoveries, and we think that no discoveries are to be made, in morality; not many in the great principles of government, nor in the ideas of liberty, which were understood long before we were born, altogether as well as they will be after the grave has heaped its mould upon our presumption, and the silent tomb shall have imposed its law on our pert loquacity (Burke 1969: 84).

If Burke's view seems to us excessively deferential, it is worth considering a contemporary example of Burkean prejudice. Unless you have appropriate medical training, when you go into the operating theatre as a patient you permit people to do things to you that you do not fully understand, and to this extent you defer to the judgement of other people. But perhaps this example is a poor illustration of Burkean prejudice, because surgery is a technical skill, whereas we assume that any rational person can make a judgement, based on reason, regarding the organisation of society. Surgery is a specialism, politics is not. In the following section we discuss a more sophisticated version of this argument: Oakeshott's distinction between technical and practical knowledge.

To mid-twentieth-century conservatives, faced with what they termed 'totalitarian societies', Burke seemed ahead of his time, with the terror he predicted would follow the French Revolution being repeated in a more organised form in Stalin's Soviet Union and Hitler's Germany. However, it should be noted that Burke opposed the extension of democracy which would take place in the nineteenth century, and although there are, as John Stuart Mill observed, dangers in majoritarian democracy, the combination of civil liberties and participatory political structures – what later political scientists would term the 'civic culture' (Almond and Verba: 5–10) – has served as a bulwark against political authoritarianism. And, of course, while post-1789 French history has been complex, the Revolution did lay the groundwork for a strong liberal–democratic system.

Burke, as does Hume, rejects the liberal idea of a contract. Indeed, unlike Hume, he does not attempt to explain duty in any terms. To attempt an explanation of duty is futile, and liable to have deleterious political consequences. Furthermore, unlike liberals, Burke does not make a sharp distinction between state and society: the 'state' is the political organisation of society, and for that reason it emerges from society. Although Burke himself does not pursue this line, a consequence of this argument is that the state has, for many conservatives, a role in shaping human behaviour, even in what liberals term the 'private' sphere. The legal moralism of James Fitzjames Stephen and Patrick Devlin has its roots in a Burkean view of the relationship between state and society. The irreducibility of duty to something else, and this organic state–society relationship give Burke's politics a religious cast. Although Burke was highly ecumenical in his religious beliefs – he admired Hinduism, and defended Irish Catholics – he does value religious belief and organisation, arguing that they are central to a prosperous, stable society.

pp. 52–3

Burke's conservatism is often misunderstood. He is sometimes assumed to be a straightforward reactionary. Yet his interventions on policy towards the American colonies, India and Ireland, would suggest he was, in the context of his time, a progressive. In addition, he argued strongly for parliamentary control over the Crown. And, finally, he was not opposed to all revolutions, maintaining that the Glorious Revolution of 1688 in England was an historic achievement (although he denied the Glorious Revolution was, in fact, a revolution at all, but rather it was a reassertion and restoration of 'ancient liberties'). He also defended the American Revolution. While Burke is sometimes wrongly painted as a reactionary, there is another danger, and that is using Burke's arguments out of their historical context. Burke's famous 'Speech to the Electors of Bristol' has been quoted in subsequent centuries by elected representatives who vote in ways contrary to the wishes of their electors (as measured by such things as opinion polls). On his election as the representative for the English city of Bristol Burke addressed his 5,000 electors:

Biography p. 194

> Parliament is not a congress of ambassadors from different and hostile interests; which interests each must maintain, as an agent and advocate, against other agents and advocates; but parliament is a deliberative assembly of one nation, with one interest, that of the whole; where, not local purposes, not local prejudices, ought to guide, but the general good, resulting from the general reason of the whole. You choose a member indeed; but when you have chosen him, he is not member of Bristol, but he is a member of parliament. If the local constituents should have an interest, or should form an hasty opinion, evidently opposite to the real good of the rest of the community, the member for that place ought to be as far, as any other, from any endeavour to give it effect (Burke 1975: 158).

Burke's argument needs to be handled with care; he believes that parliament as an *institution* is what matters. Individuals do not have natural rights, the use of which transfers the individuals' authority on to the institution, but rather the institution has shaped individuals' rights, such as the right to vote. And this also explains why Burke was prepared to submit himself to the electors of Bristol and yet at the same time ignore their wishes if they conflicted with the collective judgement of parliament (in fact, faced with defeat at the subsequent election, in 1780, Burke decided against submitting himself once again to the electors of Bristol). When Burke is quoted today it is without adequate understanding of his conservatism; while a (philosophical, ideological) liberal may defend the idea that constituents' wishes on occasion be set aside, the reasons for doing so, and the mode in which it is done will be quite different to that of a (philosophical, ideological) conservative. For a liberal the strongest grounds for a representative to reject the majority preference of her constituents would be to defend minority rights; but, equally, a liberal would maintain that the representative should explain, or justify, her position to her constituents.

Michael Oakeshott

Hume and Burke were, in approximate terms, contemporaries, writing as they were in the eighteenth century. We now, however, jump a century to consider the work of Michael Oakeshott. For Anglophone political theorists, Oakeshott is generally regarded as the key conservative thinker of the twentieth century. However, his philosophical position underwent a significant shift in the 40 years between his first major work, *Experience and its Modes* (published in 1933), and his last major work, *On Human Conduct* (1975). Our focus will be on one highly influential essay 'Rationalism in Politics' (1947), with a few comments on the latter book.

The 'rationalism' to which Oakeshott refers characterises Western culture as a whole, and not simply one particular ideology or party. Oakeshott's critique is not, therefore, directed solely at socialism, but at modern 'conservatives' who, in fact, are liberal rationalists. A rationalist 'stands (he always stands) for independence of mind on all occasions, for thought free from obligation to any authority save the authority of reason' (Oakeshott 1962: 1). Oakeshott goes on to provide a detailed list of attributes of the rationalist in a florid style of writing that will attract some to Oakeshott's thought, but irritate those with a more analytical cast of mind. But then it is the analytical approach that, for Oakeshott, characterises rationalism.

The rationalist rejects (Burkean) prejudice, custom and habit, and believes in the 'open mind, the mind free from prejudice and its relic, habit' (Oakeshott: 3). The rationalist holds that it is possible to reason about political institutions, and the fact that something exists, and has existed for a long time, is no ground for respecting or retaining it. This lack of respect for the 'familiar' engenders a political attitude of radical change rather than gradual reform. Conservatives, who respect the familiar, will seek to 'patch up' existing institutions. The rationalist disrespect for institutions extends to the world of ideas; instead of a careful engagement with the complex intellectual traditions that have shaped Western societies, a rationalist engages in a simplification – an 'abridgement' – of those traditions in the form of an 'ideology' (Oakeshott: 7). The rationalist in politics is, in essence, an 'engineer', obsessed with the correct technique for solving the problem he perceives to be immediately at hand. Politics is a series of crises to be 'solved'. Because he rejects appeal to tradition, and

Biography | **Michael Oakeshott (1901–90)**

Born in Kent (England), Oakeshott was the second of three sons of Joseph Oakeshott, a civil servant and Fabian (Fabianism being a branch of, or movement within, English socialism).

He was educated at a progressive co-educational school (St George's, Harpenden), and at Cambridge University, graduating in history in 1923. He spent time at the German universities of Marburg and Tübingen.

Elected (appointed) a fellow of a Cambridge college in 1925, Oakeshott published his first major work, *Experience and its Modes*, in 1933. After serving in the British Army during World War II, Oakeshott returned to Cambridge in 1945, subsequently moving to Oxford as a fellow (1949–51), before taking up the chair (chief professorship) in political science at the LSE. He was there from 1951 to his retirement in 1969.

While at the LSE he published *Rationalism in Politics and Other Essays* (1962), as well as *The Voice of Poetry in the Conversation of Mankind* (1959). After his retirement he wrote *Hobbes on Civil Association* (1975) (he had previously written a book on Hobbes – *Hobbes's Leviathan* – in 1946), *On Human Conduct* (1975), and *On History* (1983). Many other essays and lectures have been published since Oakeshott's death in 1990. Described by one commentator, Noel Malcolm, as 'fey, almost Bohemian', with a 'complicated' love life, Oakeshott shunned the role of 'public intellectual', and turned down the offer of a knighthood.

tradition is specific to a particular culture, the rationalist assumes that there are universal solutions to problems, and that political institutions cannot be peculiar to this or that culture. Under the umbrella term of 'rationalism' Oakeshott places what appear to be diverse political positions, theories, projects and ideologies: the early nineteenth-century utopian socialism of Robert Owen; the League of Nations and the United Nations; all statements of universal human rights; the right to national or racial self-determination; the Christian ecumenical movement; a meritocratic Civil Service. He even goes on to list 'votes for women' as a rationalist project (Oakeshott: 6–7). We have not reproduced the entire list – it is long – but it is worth noting that it is so heterogeneous, and its items almost arbitrary, that one cannot help wondering whether Oakeshott himself is guilty of 'abridging' traditions of thought by subsuming diverse phenomena under the pejorative label of 'rationalism'. Aware of this charge, later on in the essay he maintains that rationalism, like an architectural style, 'emerges almost imperceptibly', and that it is a mistake to attempt to locate its origin (Oakeshott: 13).

In Part Two of his essay Oakeshott's argument becomes more interesting as he advances a theory of knowledge. Oakeshott distinguishes two kinds of knowledge: technical and practical (Oakeshott: 7–8). Technical knowledge is formulated into rules that are deliberately learnt, remembered, and put into practice. Whether or not such knowledge has *in fact* been formulated, its chief characteristic is that it *could* be. An example of technical knowledge is driving a car, the rules of which are, in many countries, set out in books, such as, in Britain, the *Highway Code*. Another example is cooking, where the rules can be found in cookery books. Practical knowledge, on the other hand, is acquired only in use; it is not reflective, and cannot be formulated as rules. Most activities involve the use of both types of knowledge, so a good cook will draw on both technical and practical knowledge. If you want to be a cook technical knowledge will be insufficient, for what you need is practice. The acquisition of practical knowledge requires an apprenticeship, but the key feature of an apprenticeship is not subordination to a 'master', but continuous contact with the object of the practice: it is the food that is important, not the master chef. This argument gives Oakeshott's observations a libertarian, even an anarchist, cast.

Rationalists reject practical knowledge, and recognise only technical knowledge. Because the latter can be contained between the covers of a book it seems to guarantee certainty, whereas practical knowledge is diffuse. An ideology, which is a form of technical knowledge, can be expressed in a set of propositions, whereas a tradition of thought – which is a kind of practical knowledge – cannot be. The list of features of conservatism provided in the first section of this chapter might be an example of 'rationalism', as it appears to reduce conservatism to a set of propositions, or elements (we would, however, argue that these elements were open, and fluid, and were only intended to orient the thinker, rather than provide an exhaustive description). The certainty that the rationalist attributes to technical knowledge is, Oakeshott claims, an illusion, for technical knowledge is simply a reorganisation of existing knowledge, and only makes sense in the context of such pre-technical knowledge (Oakeshott: 12–13).

At the time of writing – 1947 – Britain, as with most other Western European democracies, was in the process of creating a relatively comprehensive welfare state, and developing more state interventionist economic policies, such as the nationalisation of key industries. The essay 'Rationalism in Politics' can be seen as part of a broader intellectual intervention. It is notable that a number of works that could be interpreted as critical of the extension of state planning, and state power, were published at this time, including Friedrich von Hayek's *Road to Serfdom* (1944) and Karl Popper's *The Open Society and its Enemies* (1945). But both of these works were clearly in the liberal (or libertarian) 'rationalist' tradition. Oakeshott observes that Hayek's book, although critical of state planning, exemplifies rationalism, for it develops one rationalist doctrine – free market libertarianism – in order to counter another – namely, state socialism (Oakeshott 1962: 21–2). What this shows is that one can only participate in contemporary – that is, 1940s – politics by advancing a doctrine. This argument is leant retrospective force by the fact that Hayek became one of the major influences on the free market, or neo-liberal, reaction to the welfare state in both Britain, under Margaret Thatcher, and in the United States, under President Ronald Reagan. As we suggested at the beginning of this chapter, the Thatcher Government (1979–90) was not really conservative, and despite the Republicans' use of the term 'conservative' the Reagan Administration (1981–9) was likewise not, in Oakeshott's terms, conservative, but 'rationalist'.

Oakeshott is quite rude about politicians:

> . . . book in hand (because, though a technique can be learned by rote, they have not always learned their lesson well), the politicians of Europe pore over the simmering banquet they are preparing for the future; but, like jumped-up kitchen-porters deputizing for an absent cook, their knowledge does not extend beyond the written word which they read mechanically – it generates ideas in their heads but no tastes in their mouths (Oakeshott 1962: 22).

Rationalism is the politics of the 'inexperienced'. Oakeshott uses the term 'experience' in a philosophical sense, meaning contact with tradition – certainly, politicians who have held office are experienced in the everyday sense of the word, but it is experience in problem solving rather than the recognition of the importance of tradition. Oakeshott argues that the history of Europe from the fifteenth century onwards has suffered from the incursion of three types of political inexperience: the new ruler, the new ruling class and the new political society. If a person does not belong to a family with a tradition of ruling then he requires a 'book' – a 'crib' – to tell him what to do. Machiavelli provided an early example, with *The Prince*. Later 'books' include Locke's *Second Treatise of Civil Government*, but in the history of rationalism nothing compares with the work of Marx and Engels, who wrote for a class 'less politically educated . . . than any other that has ever come to have the illusion of exercising political power' (Oakeshott 1962: 26). This is a crude caricature of Marx and Engels, and indeed of their readership, although it does contain an element of truth: the recitation of doctrine can relieve people of the effort of thought.

Interesting in the light of Burke's support for American independence is Oakeshott's critique of the US political tradition. The newly independent United States had the advantage of a tradition of European thought to draw upon, but unfortunately the 'intellectual gifts' of Europe largely consisted of rationalist ideas. This, combined with the mentality of a 'pioneer people' creating political society from scratch, has given rise to a highly rationalist political system with, unsurprisingly, a powerful emphasis on legal documents, such as the Constitution. Somewhat ambivalently, Oakeshott suggests that this gave the United States an advantage; he does not develop this thought, but he might mean that the United States was eminently suited to the increasing rationalisation of domestic and world politics, and was 'on track' to become a superpower.

Oakeshott's critique is radical; indeed it is difficult from a reading of 'Rationalism in Politics' to see what political order would reconcile technical and practical knowledge. The attack on the 'new class' of politicians is so comprehensive as to imply that even Burke was insufficiently conservative. Oakeshott's argument would suggest a rejection of democracy. Since any return to a non-rationalist political project would itself be rationalist – for that non-rationalist order would have to be set out in a programme – Oakeshott's argument appears purely negative. And its negativity creates a contradiction: is not rationalism itself a tradition? This is a standard problem with conservative thought: if what matters is what exists, and if what exists is an apparently rationalist political order, then on what grounds can a conservative criticise it? The restoration of the 'old order' is not, and cannot be, a conservative project. Oakeshott's distinction between technical and practical knowledge, and the idea of an increasing predominance of the former over the latter, are interesting ideas, but they are not necessarily conservative ones.

In his book *On Human Conduct* Oakeshott presents a more 'positive' conception of politics. In that book he makes an important distinction between a civil association and an enterprise association. An enterprise association exists for, and justifies its existence in terms of, a particular end, or relatively coherent set of ends (Oakeshott 1975: 108–18). These ends may be 'abstract', such as the maximisation of utility, or more concrete, such as the desire to maintain a particular cultural community. The enterprise association may not have a fully comprehensive set of aims – it might grant that individuals pursue different projects – but it will have some common aims. The commonly expressed desire to 'make the world a better place' would imply an enterprise attitude, even if people disagree over the best means of achieving it. A civil association, on the other hand, is a situation of mutual freedom under the rule of law. It is more than a Hobbesian state, for it implies mutual respect, and as such is a moral conception, but it is less than an enterprise. The best way to think about a civil association is as a set of rules that command respect not simply because they serve each person's self-interest, but because they allow human beings to choose how to live their lives. Although Oakeshott appears reactionary with regard to democratic politics, his argument in *On Human Conduct* comes close to being a liberal one.

Leo Strauss and American Neo-conservatism

Am émigré from Nazi Germany to the United States, Strauss is regarded as an important influence on what is called neo-conservatism. Given the prominence of neo-conservative ideas in contemporary US political debate this makes Strauss a controversial figure and, as his ideas have become popularised, also a misunderstood one.

To understand Strauss's conservatism it is necessary to start with his approach to the history of ideas and the interpretation of texts. As we will see Strauss's conservatism is very different to that of Hume, Burke and Oakeshott, and it reflects the culture of both his adopted home of the United States and the history of his country of origin, Germany. After a brief discussion of Strauss's work we consider its influence on contemporary neo-conservative thought in the United States.

Strauss sought to revive both the reading of texts in the history of political thought and the natural right tradition. The relationship between *reading* and *natural right* may not, at first sight, be obvious, and even less their relationship to *conservatism*. But the three are closely entwined. Natural right stands opposed to cultural relativism. Modern thought, according to Strauss, is characterised by a rejection of objective validity in favour of relativism (Strauss 1953: 9). The starting point for a defence of natural right is the claim that radical historicism – that is, the view that morality is the product of immediate historical circumstances – must hold at least one thing as given by nature, and that is experience. There are many definitions of nature, but Strauss identifies two relevant ones: nature as the beginning of all things and nature as the character of something. For human beings, recognition of the first must depend on authority. For example, in Judaism and Christianity, the book of Genesis provides an account of humankind's origins. A refusal to accept the authority of the Bible undermines the force of that account, and leads to disagreement about human origins. Recognition of the second – nature as the character of something – depends upon human experience. Hume exemplifies this approach: there must be a sensation in order to have confidence that a thing exists. Since moral ideas – right and wrong – cannot be observed, modern political thinkers deny their existence.

Natural right teaching, which can be traced back to the ancient Greeks, holds that the good life is that which perfects human nature – we become what, by nature, we

Biography | Leo Strauss (1899–1973)

Born in Kirchhain, Hessen (Germany), Strauss became a Zionist at the age of 17, and although his political and religious thought evolved his Judaism remained an important source of political and philosophical ideas throughout his life. He was educated at various German universities: Marburg, Freiburg and Hamburg.

In 1934, as a consequence of Hitler's rise to power, he moved to England, and between 1935 and 1937 held an academic position at Cambridge University. Moving to the United States in 1937, Strauss became research fellow in History at Columbia University (New York), and then lectured in political science at the New School for Social Research (1938–48). He became a US citizen in 1944. From 1949 to 1968 he was Professor at Chicago University.

Among political theorists, Strauss is regarded primarily as a historian of political thought. His peculiar method of reading historical texts has given rise to the label 'Straussian'. But among a wider audience in the United States he is seen as one of the 'fathers' of neo-conservatism. In fact, this situation has come about largely because of the influence of his protégé Alan Bloom (1930–92), whose book *The Closing of the American Mind* (1987), caused a significant impact. Strauss's best-known works are *Persecution and the Art of Writing* (1952, 2nd edn 1973), *Natural Right and History* (1953), *Thoughts on Machiavelli* (1958), and *Socrates and Aristophanes* (1966).

should be ('nature' is here used in the second sense of 'character', rather than the first sense of 'origin'). The logic of natural right is that those possessing the greatest wisdom should rule, and their power should be in proportion to their possession of the virtue of wisdom (Strauss 1953: 102). This is incompatible with the modern – that is, post-Hobbesian – emphasis on consent: the rulers rule by the consent of the ruled and not by appeal to the rulers' superior wisdom. Strauss argues that under modern conditions the conflict can be reconciled by the rulers drawing up a code – or constitution – to which the people consent, and to which they can pledge allegiance. It is not difficult to see where this argument is heading: the recognition of the United States Constitution as the expression of natural right. And that Constitution should not be interpreted simply as a framework through which conflicts are settled, but must be understood as embodying religious virtue. Commitment to a 'politics of virtue' requires the resistance of tyranny, and this has practical implications for foreign policy, which we discuss briefly at the end of this section.

Strauss links his defence of natural right with a particular interpretation of the history of political thought. Drawing on Judaic ideas, Strauss argues that when we read pre-modern – and some modern – political texts we must 'read between the lines' (Strauss 1941: 490). Writing has two levels: a popular or edifying teaching directed to a contemporary audience (the exoteric), and a 'hidden' or secret teaching that is only revealed on careful reading (the esoteric). The great political thinkers had a storehouse of literary devices that allowed them to obscure the meanings of their texts. The reason why they had to do this is made clear in the title of Strauss's *Persecution and the Art of Writing*. Thought is the enemy of tyranny, but it can only fight tyranny in its own way, and on its own terms, and that is in a literary way. Esoteric writing survives tyranny and transmits its message between political thinkers, and to their intelligent readers, across the centuries. Quite clearly, a cultural relativist will reject this claim, and argue that the only audience capable of being moved by a writer is the contemporary, or near-contemporary, one.

Strauss died in 1973, but if you enter cyberspace and do a web search using the keywords 'Leo Strauss' you will encounter a heated debate over his influence. Like much internet debate, the subtleties of thought tend to be lost. However, it is interesting to explore the connections between Strauss and neo-conservatism. Although the term 'neo-conservative' – or 'neo-con' – is more often used as a pejorative term by its opponents than by those identified as neo-conservative it still has validity. The prefix neo- is intended to identify the movement as a distinct stream within US conservatism. It indicates that adherents are new to conservatism, but also that traditional conservatism is the subject of critique, and must be infused with new policy positions.

Many, but not all, leading neo-conservatives began their political life supporting what, in US terms, is the left: state intervention in the economy, policies to overcome poverty and the civil rights movement. In demographic terms neo-conservatives are drawn disproportionately from the Jewish and the Catholic communities of mainland European origin. This is significant because traditional conservatism was perceived as dominated by the so-called WASPs (white Anglo-Saxon Protestants) and hostile to the waves of immigrants who came to the United States in the late nineteenth and early twentieth centuries. Those waves of immigrants were subjected to 'assimilationist' policies (the 'great melting pot') and neo-conservatives place great value on the idea of a common US culture against what they see as the separatist multiculturalist policies in operation since the 1960s. While many neo-conservatives strongly believe that the civil rights movement was justified in its aims, they oppose affirmative action policies. Furthermore, neo-conservatives are much more prepared to support state spending if it will enable people to become responsible citizens, but this is combined with an emphasis on rewarding hard work through reductions in taxation. This twin-track approach is manifested in several key domestic policies of the Bush administration: the 'No Child Left Behind Act', which involves increased intervention by the centre (federal government) in the education system in order to improve educational standards among deprived groups; large tax cuts for the well off; and, partial privatisation of the state pension system. There is a Straussian influence here: objective 'natural right' presupposes common standards and a common culture on which is based a political community that promotes virtue. The discrimination against black (and other) Americans is morally wrong, but so is what neo-conservatives believe to be the separatism inherent in multiculturalism. Individual initiative should be rewarded because it reflects a 'perfectionist' ideal: that is, we realise, or perfect, our nature through virtuous acts.

It is, however, in foreign policy that the influence of neo-conservatives is most keenly felt. As suggested above, Strauss argued that tyranny should be resisted, and that resistance must sometimes be in the face of widespread opposition. International institutions such as the United Nations simply reflect cultural relativism, such that a vote in the UN General Assembly or by the Security Council signifies nothing more than the balancing of interests, or cultural differences. A just nation must find the justification for its actions out of a reflection on natural right, and not through the support of international organisations, although it should attempt to persuade other nations to join it in a 'coalition of the willing'. What drove many thinkers and political activists from the Democratic Party to the Republicans was the perceived weakness of the left in confronting the Soviet Union in the 1970s – whereas the left sought containment of the USSR, the neo-conservatives argued for a 'roll-back' of Soviet power. In policy terms, the left supported Strategic Arms Limitation Treaties (SALT), whereas the neo-conservatives argued for an aggressive arms war so as to force the Soviet Union to spend beyond its means. Significantly, this critique of perceived weakness extended to traditional conservatives such as President Richard Nixon (US President, 1969–74) who initiated the SALT talks and also famously engaged with (Communist) China. At the beginning of the twenty-first century neo-conservatives see fundamentalist Islam as the main source of tyranny and liken the refusal of many European countries to engage with this perceived threat as a political manifestation of a deeper cultural relativism.

Summary

The neo-conservatism inspired by Strauss seems a long way removed from the conservatism of Hume, Burke and Oakeshott. Given the historical distance from present events of Hume and Burke it is difficult, and perhaps intellectually suspect, to speculate on how they would respond to events in the twenty-first century, but certainly Oakeshott, who is not so distanced, would have rejected the foreign policy adventures of neo-conservatives. However, Oakeshott's work was aimed at a deeper level than policy, or even institutional design, for he saw rationalism in all spheres of social life, and in all political movements. Apart from a common emphasis on the interpenetration of state and society, and consequently the recognition that politics is concerned with the development of virtue and not simply the resolution of conflicting interests, there is little that holds the four thinkers together (and Oakeshott, in his later work, rejects the idea that politics should promote virtue). The contemporary relevance of traditional conservatism is seen less as an active ideology – party political conservatives are not really conservatives – but as an important source of ideas critical of the dominant liberal ideology. The core of conservatism is its critique of rationalism.

Questions

1. If conservatives are sceptical about reason how can they criticise society?
2. What are the arguments for, and against, the monarchy, as it operates in the United Kingdom, the Netherlands, Spain and other countries? To what extent are arguments for the monarchy 'conservative'?

3. Under what circumstances should people attempt to overturn the existing political system?

4. 'Those who do not remember the past are condemned to repeat it' (George Santayana). Do you agree?

References

Almond, G. and Verba, S. (1963) *The Civic Culture: Political Attitudes and Democracy in Five Nations* Princeton, NJ: Princeton University Press.

Burke, E. (1975) *On Government, Politics and Society* (ed. B.W. Hill) London: Fontana/The Harvester Press.

Hume, D. (1963) *Essays, Moral, Political and Literary* Oxford: Oxford University Press.

Hume, D. (1978) *A Treatise of Human Nature* (ed. L.A. Selby-Bigge) Oxford: Clarendon Press.

Kimberling, W. 'The Electoral College' – http://www.fec.gov/pdf/eleccoll.pdf

Oakeshott, M. (1962) *Rationalism in Politics and Other Essays* London: Methuen.

Oakeshott, M. (1975) *On Human Conduct* Oxford: Clarendon Press.

Strauss, L. (1941) *Persecution and The Art of Writing Social Research*, 8, 1:4.

Strauss, L. (1953) *Natural Right and History* Chicago, Ill.: University of Chicago Press.

Further Reading

General introductions to conservative thought and practice include: Noel O'Sullivan, *Conservatism* (London: Dent, 1976); Ted Honderich, *Conservatism* (London: Penguin, 1991); Roger Scruton, *The Meaning of Conservatism* (Basingstoke: Palgrave, 2001). Both Scruton and Honderich are quite polemical – Scruton from a 'right-wing' perspective sympathetic to conservatism, Honderich from a hostile 'left-wing' perspective. John Kekes, *A Case for Conservatism* (Ithaca, NY and London: Cornell University Press, 1998), is not an introduction but is interesting if you want a more involved defence of conservatism. There are various anthologies of conservative thought, the most useful being Roger Scruton (ed.), *Conservative Texts: An Anthology* (Basingstoke: Macmillan, 1991), and Jerry Muller (ed.), *Conservatism: An Anthology of Social and Political Thought from David Hume to the Present* (Princeton, NJ: Princeton University Press, 1997). In these books you will find extracts from the most important conservative thinkers, including the four discussed in this chapter. Scruton has also edited a series of essays on conservative thinkers, although, as with the anthologies, the definition of 'conservative' is stretched quite wide: Roger Scruton (ed.), *Conservative Thinkers: Essays from the Salisbury Review* (London: Claridge, 1988). Finally, a discussion of Strauss's influence on US conservatism can be found in Shadia Drury, *Leo Strauss and the American Right* (Basingstoke: Macmillan, 1997).

Weblinks

Web searches using the key words 'conservative', 'conservatism' and even 'conservative thought' tend to throw up party political sites, or highly polemical sites. It is worth taking a look at these simply to get a flavour of how the term is used, and possibly abused, in cyberspace. However, for sites of greater relevance to this chapter we would recommend those dedicated to the conservative thinkers:

- David Hume: http://www.humesociety.org/; http://plato.stanford.edu/entries/hume/

- Edmund Burke: http://www.kirkcenter.org/burke/ebsa.html; http://plato.stanford.edu/entries/burke/

- Michael Oakeshott: http://www.michael-oakeshott-association.org/

- Leo Strauss: http://www.frontpagemag.com/Articles/ReadArticle.asp?ID=1233; http://www.straussian.net/

- Also useful is Roger Scruton's website: http://www.rogerscruton.com/ (as you will see from the Further Reading section Scruton is a prominent contemporary British conservative thinker).

Chapter 9

Socialism

Introduction

Is socialism dead? This provocative point was argued by many conservatives, and the former British Prime Minister, Mrs Thatcher, in particular, after the collapse of the Communist Party states.

The difficulty in deciding whether socialism is dead is that socialism, as feminism, is bedevilled by the problem of variety. Socialism comes in many different shapes and forms. The recent Iraq War saw the British government, which would consider itself socialist, waging armed struggle along with the United States against a regime that would also call itself socialist. Do the diverse kinds of socialism have anything in common?

Can **socialism** be defined? Is it an impossible dream? Do more 'realistic' forms of socialism sacrifice their very socialism when they become more pragmatic? These are all questions we shall try to answer.

Chapter Map

- The problem of variety and a working definition of socialism.

- The problem of utopia as one to which socialism is peculiarly prone. Three nineteenth-century socialists, regarded by Marxists as utopian, but who consider their own work scientific and realistic.

- Marxism as one of the variants of socialism: Marxism is a theory that tends to authoritarianism in practice.

- The distinct character of democratic socialism or social democracy and the impact made upon British labour by the 'revisionist' theory of Eduard Bernstein.

- The link between class and agency, freedom and determinism.

- The argument that socialists do not have to choose between being utopian or being realistic.

Tanks in the Streets of Prague

Soviet tanks line Atlstaedter-Ring Street in Prague early on 28 August 1968

You are studying in Prague in 1968. In the spring there is much excitement because the leader of the Communist Party argues that Czech socialism is crying out for reform. Although you feel that the changes proposed are rather modest, you see them as steps in the right direction. With the Action Programme, passed in 1968, a much freer electoral system is proposed. There is no question, however, of opposition parties being permitted.

However, you are understandably alarmed by the claims by the USSR in September that West Germany is planning to invade Czechoslovakia, and you are concerned that some communists regard the new proposals as dangerously 'revisionist'. In August of the same year, tanks roll into Prague from other countries in the Warsaw Pact (of which Czechoslovakia is a member), led by the USSR. Following the invasion Dubcek and the new president, Svoboda, are taken to Moscow and after 'free comradely discussion' they announce that Czechoslovakia will be abandoning its reform programme.

The claim is made that Dubcek intended to take his country out of the Warsaw Pact and reintroduce a capitalist society. Half a million members of the Czech Communist Party are expelled, and large numbers of writers, scientists and artists lose their jobs. It is estimated that only 2 per cent of the population supports the invasion.

Confronted with a collision of this kind:

- Would you see one side as socialist and the other side as not?
- Or would you feel that two different kinds of socialism had come into opposition?

Are the members of the Warsaw Pact who invade Czechoslovakia:

- Betraying their commitment to socialism?
- Or is this the kind of action that flows from their commitment to Marxist principles?

Is Dubcek being naive to consider himself as a communist at all? Would the notion of change that he is proposing undermine not only Soviet control over Eastern Europe but lead to the development of market forces that would necessarily destroy socialism itself and lead to the introduction of capitalism?

The Problem of Variety

Tony Wright calls his book *Socialisms* (1996) in order to emphasise the plurality of approaches and doctrines that make up the socialist movement. The term is certainly elastic and covers a wide range of contradictory movements.

Some socialists are religious, other doggedly atheistic in character. Some advocate revolution, others reform. Nor are the alignments simple. Authoritarian socialisms may be atheistic (as in the communist tradition) but they need not be (think of Saddam Hussein's regime, which claimed adherence to some kind of Islamic tradition). Some socialists such as Tony Benn may be radical and admire the role of parliament, other socialists may stress the importance of parliament as a bulwark against **radicalism**. Still others invert this view and see parliamentary democracy as an obstacle to socialist advance.

The distinction between Marxism and social democracy is the major fault line among socialisms. We will use the term social democracy interchangeably with democratic socialism. The history of socialist thought is thick with accusations of betrayal. Lenin believed that social democrats were traitors to socialism because they supported World War I and opposed the Russian Revolution; socialists influenced by libertarian or anarchist ideas felt that Lenin and the Bolsheviks had betrayed the Soviet experiment by crushing the rebellion of Bolshevik sailors that took place in Kronstadt in 1921; Trotsky and his supporters felt that Stalin had reneged on the revolutionary traditions of Lenin by seeking to build socialism in one country; Mao and many Chinese communists believed that the Russians had surrendered to capitalism and the market after 1956.

see Case Study, p. 209

These differences have deeply divided socialists. The British Labour Party repeatedly refused the request for affiliation from the Communist Party of Great Britain (CPGB) on the grounds that the latter supported dictatorship and not democracy, while communists have been deeply divided among themselves. This could come to armed conflict – as between the Soviet Union and the People's Republic of China in the 1960s – or the intervention of Vietnam into Cambodia or Kampuchea in 1978. The Warsaw Pact's interventions into Hungary in 1956 or Czechoslovakia in 1968 were intended to snuff out reform communists, and Western communists influenced by social democratic and liberal ideas called themselves 'Eurocommunists' so as to distance themselves from the Soviet system.

Social Democracy/Democratic Socialism	Marxism/Scientific Socialism
Moderate classes	Eliminate classes
Utilise the state	Go beyond the state
Parliament	Workers' Councils
Ethically desirable	Historically inevitable
Nation as a whole	Workers and their allies

Defining Socialism

It is interesting that Bernard Crick in his book *In Defence of Politics,* which originally appeared in 1963, saw conservatives, social democrats and liberals as exponents of politics – which Crick defined as an activity that seeks to conciliate and compromise. He contrasted them with nationalists, communists and extremists of various kinds. Nevertheless, despite their differences, we shall locate the common features of *all* socialists in terms of the following:

(a) **an optimistic view of human nature** – a view that human nature is either changeable or does not constitute a barrier to social regulation or ownership. The notion that humans are too selfish to cooperate and have common interests contradicts socialist doctrine.

(b) **a stress on cooperation** – all socialists hold that people can and should work together so that the market and capitalism need at the very least some adjustment in order to facilitate cooperation. Competition may be seen as an aid to, or wholly incompatible with, cooperation, but the latter is the guiding principle.

(c) **a positive view of freedom** – a notion that the question of freedom must be examined in a social context and therefore in the context of resources of a material kind. The right to read and write, for example, requires the provision of schooling if such a right is to be meaningful.

(d) **support for equality** – socialists define equality in dramatically different ways, but all, it seems to us, must subscribe to equality in some form or other. This, Crick argues, is 'the basic value in any imaginable or feasible socialist society' (1987: 88).

These characteristics explain why socialism, though a broad church, is not infinitely elastic. Dr Verwoerd, the architect of apartheid, was sometimes accused by his free market critics of being a socialist, and the Nazi Party described itself as a 'national socialist' organisation. We want to argue that although socialism stretches from Pol Pot to Tony Blair it cannot incorporate those who specifically and deliberately reject the notion of equality.

There is a further characteristic of socialism that is more contentious.

The Problem of Utopia

All socialists are vulnerable to the charge of utopianism – of trying to realise a society that is contrary to human experience and historical development. Socialists disagree as to whether utopianism is a good thing or a bad thing. In his famous book on the subject, More in *Utopia* created the notion of a good society (eutopia) that is nowhere (utopia = no place) (Geoghegan, 1987:1). Karl Mannheim (an inter-war German sociologist) in *Ideology and Utopia* (1936) defined utopia as an idea that was 'situation transcending' or 'incongruent with reality': it 'breaks the bonds of the existing order' (1960: 173).

While some socialists have seen utopia as a good thing, liberals and conservatives regard the notion of utopia as negative – an irresponsible idealism that rides roughshod over the hard facts of reality that can at worst lead to nightmarish regimes of a highly oppressive and totalitarian kind. Heywood argues that all socialists are utopians since they develop 'better visions of a better society in which human beings can achieve genuine emancipation and fulfilment as members of a community' (1992: 96). He even extends this to Marxism where he describes communism as 'a utopian vision of a future society envisaged and described by Marx and Engels'. On the other hand, he acknowledges that the issue is controversial, since he also notes that Marx and Engels supported 'scientific socialism' and rejected what they called the 'utopian socialism' (1992: 115; 127).

Geoghegan declares himself 'in praise of utopianism' despite the fact that utopianism is characterised as a defence of an activity that is 'unrealistic', 'irrational', 'naive', 'self-indulgent', 'unscientific', 'escapist' and 'elitist'. He premises his praise on support for an 'ought' that is in opposition to an 'is' (1987: 1–2). But does this mean that socialism can never be realised? It is not clear from Geoghegan's argument whether socialist utopianism is an 'ought' permanently at war with an 'is', or whether the problem lies with the critics of utopianism who are guilty of a 'sad dualism': unreality, error and subjectivity on the one side; realism, truth and objectivity on the other (1987: 22). Can **socialism** overcome this dualism – so that it is both realist and utopian at the same time?

Bauman argues that we should view utopias positively – as a necessary condition of historical change (1976: 13). But is it possible for a utopia to avoid the charge that it is inherently unrealistic? Bauman insists that a utopia 'sets the stage for a genuinely realistic politics'. It extends the meaning of realism to encompass the full range of possible options (1976: 13). Utopias make conscious the major divisions of interest within society: the future is portrayed as a set of competing projects (1976: 15). Bauman draws a distinction between perfection as a stable and immutable state, and perfectibility that paves the way for utopia (1976: 19).

But it is still unclear whether we can ever have a society that is socialist. Bauman appears to argue that socialism is the counter-culture of capitalist society (1976: 36), and it cannot be empirical reality, a society in its own right.

Oscar Wilde commented:

> A map of the world which does not include Utopia is not worth glancing at, for it leaves out the one country at which Humanity is always landing. And when Humanity lands there, it looks out and, seeing a better country, sets sail. Progress is the realisation of Utopias.
>
> *('The Soul of Man Under Socialism', Complete Works of Oscar Wilde, p. 1184, Glasgow: HarperCollins, 1996).*

Science and the 'Utopian Socialists'

Three socialists were singled out by Engels as being utopian:

- Henri Saint-Simon (1760–1825)
- Charles Fourier (1772–1837)
- Robert Owen (1771–1858)

In fact, each of them considered their own work to be scientific and practical.

Biography — Claude-Henri de Rouvroy Saint-Simon (1760–1825)

The son of a minor noble, Saint-Simon was born in Paris. Privately educated, he served in the French Army during the American War of Independence. Afterwards he travelled to Mexico and Spain trying in vain to persuade the Viceroy of Mexico to finance a canal linking the Atlantic and Pacific through Lake Nicaragua.

A supporter of the French Revolution in 1789, he immediately renounced his title. He made a fortune buying and selling the houses abandoned by exiled or executed noblemen. He was imprisoned during the Terror but was released after spending nine months in captivity. He became convinced that a programme of social reorganisation was needed and moved from liberalism to a doctrine containing socialist elements.

His first book on political theory, *Letters of a Genevan to his Contemporaries,* was published in 1802. This was followed by his *Work of Science in the 19th Century* (1807), *Memoir on the Science of Man* (1813), *On the Reorganisation of European Society* (1814) and *The New Christianity* (1825). In this final work he argued that a new religion led by the most able thinkers in society (scientists and artists) would express dominant beliefs for a new industrial order.

Saint-Simon argued that Europe was in 'critical disequilibrium' and would soon undergo reconstruction. He argued strongly for a planned economy. He suggested a framework of three chambers: one body made up of engineers and artists to propose plans, a second of scientists responsible for assessing the plans, and a third group of industrialists whose task would be that of implementing the schemes according to the interests of the whole community.

After his death in 1825 Saint-Simon's ideas were developed by a group of loyal followers such as Olindes Rodriguez, Armand Bazard and Barthelemy-Prosper Enfantin. In 1830 the group published *An Explanation of the Doctrine of Saint-Simon*. They interpreted Saint-Simon as a socialist and argued for the redistribution of wealth for the benefit of society. Saint-Simon's theories also influenced figures such as Alexander Herzen, Thomas Carlyle and J.S. Mill.

Saint-Simon took the view that the French Revolution had neglected class structure in the name of human rights. He included industrialists and bankers in the 'producing' class, believing that workers and capitalists have a unity of interests, sustained by what Saint-Simon believed would be a spread of wealth and ownership across society as a whole.

Is it right to call this argument 'utopian'? Saint-Simon believed that the old order had unwittingly produced the basis for a new order, and indeed he sounds like a Marxist steeped in Hegelian dialectics when he argues that 'everything is relative – that is the only absolute' (Geoghegan, 1987: 11). His celebrated argument that the state gives way to administration (so central to Marxist theory), was based upon a belief that the modern credit and banking system had already demonstrated its attachment to scientific principles, and that these could exert a discipline that would make the state redundant. Why did Engels call this system 'utopian' when it

Charles Fourier (1772–1837)

Born in Besancon. The son of a cloth merchant, he was educated at the local Jesuit college. During the French Revolution he witnessed the hoarding of the merchants, and lost his patrimony. After serving in the French Army he worked as a clerk in Lyon.

In 1808 he published his first book, *The Social Destiny of Man*, where he criticised the immorality of the business world, arguing that 'truth and commerce are as incompatible as Jesus and Satan'. In the book Fourier advocated a new socialist system of cooperation, urging that 'phalansteries' should be established. These would be scientifically planned to offer a maximum of both cooperation and self-fulfilment to their members. Fourier suggested that these communes should contain about 1,600 people and should attempt to be compatible with each member's 'natural talents, passions, and inclinations'.

One of Fourier's supporters, Victor Considerant, established a newspaper in order to promote the cause. Others attempted to establish their own phalanstery. This included one at Rambouillet in France that was under-capitalised and eventually went bankrupt (1834–6). Another, more successful attempt, was made by George Ripley at Brook Farm in Massachusetts (1841–6).

Although no long-term phalansteries were established, Fourier's ideas influenced a generation of socialists, anarchists, feminists, pacifists, internationalists and others questioning the morality of the capitalist system. Marx and Engels used Fourier's ideas to develop their theory of alienation.

Fourier also published *The New World of Communal Activity* (1829) and *The False Division of Labour* (1835). However, his attempts to find a rich benefactor to fund a phalanstery ended in failure.

so manifestly stresses the importance of science and historical necessity? Saint-Simon clearly does not fit into Engels's view that modern socialism is based upon the class antagonism between capitalist and wage worker (Marx and Engels, 1968: 399). But it does seem unfair to ascribe to Saint-Simon (as Engels does to the utopians in general) the view that socialism is not an 'inevitable event' but a happy accident, when Saint-Simon had laid so much emphasis on science and historical development.

Fourier, on the other hand, did consider the worker and capitalists to have conflicting interests. He was particularly concerned at the way in which the industrial revolution has stripped work of its pleasure. His solution was to establish 'phalanteres' – cooperative communities of some 1,600 people working in areas of around 5,000 acres in the countryside or small towns. Fourier was adamant that his was not a utopian socialism. He described utopias as 'dreams', schemes without an effective method that have 'led people to the very opposite of the state of well being they promised them' (Geoghegan, 1987: 17). He believed that his socialism was based on a scientific project for reconstruction. Indeed, so precise a science was socialism that Fourier took the view that civilised society has 144 evils; humans have 12 basic passions; they do 12 different jobs, and need nine meals to sustain them.

Biography   Robert Owen (1771–1858)

The son of a saddler and ironmonger from Newtown in Wales, Owen did well at his local school, and at the age of 10 he was sent to work in a large drapers in Stamford, Lincolnshire. In 1787 Owen found employment at a large wholesale and retail drapery business in Manchester.

With the financial support of several businessmen from Manchester, Owen purchased Dale's four textile factories in New Lanark. However, he was not only concerned with making money, but interested in creating a new type of community at New Lanark. Owen believed that a person's character is formed by the effects of their environment. He was a strong opponent of physical punishment in schools and factories and immediately banned its use in New Lanark.

One of the first decisions taken when he became owner of New Lanark was to order the building of a school, and he stopped employing children under 10 and reduced child labour to ten hours a day. The young children went to the nursery and infant schools that Owen had built. Older children had to attend his secondary school for part of the day.

In 1813 he wrote *The Formation of Character* and the following year *A New View of Society*, where he argued that religion, marriage and private property were barriers to progress. In 1815 Owen sent detailed proposals to Parliament about his ideas on factory reform, and appeared before Peel and his Commons committee in April 1816.

Owen toured the country making speeches on his experiments at New Lanark. He was, he argued, creating a 'new moral world, a world from which the bitterness of divisive sectarian religion would be banished'. Disappointed with the response he received in Britain, Owen decided in 1825 to establish a new community in the United States based on his socialist ideas. He purchased an area of Indiana for £30,000 and called the community he established there New Harmony.

By 1827 Owen had sold his New Lanark textile mills and while his family moved to New Harmony he stayed in England supporting organisations attempting to obtain factory reform, adult suffrage and the development of successful trade unions. In *The New Moral World*, published in 1834, he presented socialism in the manner of an inspirational gospel.

Owen also played an important role in establishing the Grand National Consolidated Trade Union in 1834 and the Association of All Classes and All Nations in 1835. Owen also attempted to form a new community at East Tytherly in Hampshire. However, like New Harmony in the United States, this experiment came to an end as a result of disputes between members of the community. Although disillusioned with the failure of these communities and most of his political campaigns, Robert Owen continued to work for his 'new moral order' until his death.

As for Robert Owen: he saw himself as a practical, hard-headed person of business, and he owned cotton mills in New Lanark in Scotland. He was struck as to how under rational socialist management they could still be profitable, and he decided to advocate village cooperatives between 300 and 2,000 people working land between 600 and 1,800 acres. It is true that his schemes were dogged by failure. The community that he established at New Harmony in the United States collapsed after three years in 1827, and his labour bazaars at which goods were to be exchanged according to the amount of labour embodied in them did not survive the economic crisis of 1834. His national trade union was called a 'grand national moral union for the productive classes', but his dictatorial leadership demonstrated the problem with his theory of character. Character was, as Geoghegan points out, externally determined, so that only an exceptional person (such as Owen!) could initiate reform for a relatively passive population (1987: 14).

He had, however, a lasting effect on the British labour movement as a practical reformer, and the consumer cooperatives that he advocated – the Co-op stores – still exist on almost every high street in British cities today. Although Owen's notion of science stems from an uncritical reading of the Enlightenment, he certainly regarded himself as a person of scientific, secular and empirical values. Indeed, a youthful Engels was to describe Owen's views as 'the most practical and fully worked out' of all the socialists (Geoghegan, 1987: 23).

Introducing Marxism

The belief that socialism should be scientific and not utopian is highly contentious. There is a terminological point that we need to tackle right away. In the *Communist Manifesto* of 1848, Engels was to explain that the term 'communism' was preferred because it was seen as a working-class movement from below. Socialism, he argued, was a respectable movement initiated from above (1967: 62). Later Marxists called themselves socialists and social democrats. It was only after 1917 when Lenin and the Bolsheviks wanted to distance themselves from other socialists (who had supported World War I and opposed the Russian Revolution) that the term 'communist' was resurrected.

Berki has argued that Marx transformed socialism from underdog to a 'fully grown part of the modern landscape' (1974: 56). Both Marx and Engels prized scholarship and learning highly. Marx was a philosopher, who devoted most of his life to studying political economy, and in 1863 published *Das Kapital*, or *Capital*, a work that Engels was to describe as the bible of the working class. Engels, for his part, read and wrote widely about natural science, anthropology, history, politics and economics, and both regarded science, not as the pursuit of facts rather than values, but simply as coherent and systematic thought.

Why did Engels in particular see Saint-Simon, Fourier and Owen as utopians? In the *Communist Manifesto* Marx and Engels praised the 'utopians' for producing 'the most valuable materials for the enlightenment of the working class'. Measures such as the abolition of the distinction between town and country; the disappearance of the family; the wages system; the private ownership of industry; the dying out of the state; and a positive relationship between the individual and society were suggested by the 'utopians' and became part of Marx and Engels's own arguments. Nevertheless, the label is contentious, for Marx and Engels clearly regarded the 'utopians' as painting 'fantastic pictures of a future society', a fantasy that reflected the historically undeveloped state of the working class itself (1967: 116).

Why then was Marxism seen as scientific? Marxism, Marx and Engels argued, is a scientific socialism, because it is:

- **a theory of class conflict** It holds that in class-divided societies there are incompatible social interests that lead to exploitation. This is why class is both an economic and a political reality, since between the classes there is war. In contrast, the utopians seek change through general principles of 'reason' and 'justice'.

- **a theory of revolution** Such is the incompatibility of class interests that change can only come through revolution. Although the *Communist Manifesto* describes revolution in violent terms, Marx's later position was that revolutions can be peaceful, even constitutional, but they will be violent if necessary. Because classes are political as well as economic entities, they seek to control the state in their own interest, so that the state has a class character. Utopians, by contrast, seek peaceful and sometimes piecemeal change, appealing to all classes in society for support, and invariably seeing the state as part of the solution rather than part of the problem.

- **a theory of history** All societies are basically moulded by the conflict between the forces of production (which embrace science and technology) and the relations of production (the system of ownership). These two elements form a basis upon which arises a 'superstructure' that incorporates political institutions, educational systems, culture and ideas. In class-divided societies the conflict between the forces and relations of production creates the need for revolution, so that under capitalism the social character of the forces of production come into sharp and increasing conflict with the private relations of production. That is why revolution is inevitable. After this revolution, class divisions disappear, and with the disappearance of these divisions the need for a state itself 'withers'.

- **a theory of society** Central to this theory of history is a theory of society which argues that people enter into relations of production 'independent of their will'. This means that although human activity is a conscious activity, the consequences of this activity are never the same as those intended. Capitalism is seen as a system that unwittingly creates the working class, educates them through factory production, goads them into struggle and ultimately drives them to revolution. By way of contrast, 'utopians' do not see capitalism as a contradictory system, a system that is self-destructive. They do not accept the particular role of the workers in providing leadership to a political movement for social emancipation, nor do they accept the need for a communist or socialist party to provide leadership for revolution. Socialism, as far as they see it, is merely 'desirable' and not inevitable.

Karl Marx

Born in Trier, Germany and, as a child, became a Protestant. After schooling in Trier (1830–5), Marx entered Bonn University to study law. At university he spent much of his time socialising and running up large debts. His father insisted that he moved to the more sedate Berlin University.

Here he came under the influence of one of his lecturers, Bruno Bauer, whose atheism and radical political opinions got him into trouble with the authorities. Bauer introduced Marx to the writings of Hegel, who had been the professor of philosophy at Berlin until his death in 1831.

In 1838 Marx decided to become a university lecturer. After completing his doctoral thesis at the University of Jena, Marx hoped that his mentor, Bruno Bauer, would help find him a teaching post. However, in 1842 Bauer was dismissed as a result of his outspoken atheism and was unable to help.

Marx moved to Cologne, where the liberal opposition movement was fairly strong. *The Rhenish Gazette* published Marx's defence of the freedom of the press. In 1842 Marx was appointed editor of the newspaper, but in 1843 the newspaper was banned by the Prussian authorities.

Warned that he might be arrested, Marx moved to Paris, where he became the editor of *Franco-German Yearbook*. Mixing with members of the working class for the first time, he now described himself as a communist. In 1844 Marx wrote *Economic and Philosophic Manuscripts*, where he developed his ideas on the concept of alienation. While in Paris he became a close friend of Engels, and they decided to work together. In 1845 Marx was deported from France and went to Brussels, where he wrote *The German Ideology*, a work not published in his lifetime.

In 1847 Marx attended a meeting of the Communist League's Central Committee in London, and this was the organisation that commissioned the *Communist Manifesto*. Marx moved to Cologne, where he founded the *New Rhenish Gazette*, which published reports of revolutionary activity all over Europe. The revolutions were defeated, the *New Rhenish Gazette* closed down, and Marx settled in Britain. With only the money that Engels could raise, the Marx family lived in extreme poverty.

Between 1852 and 1862 Marx wrote for the *New York Daily Tribune*, and in 1859 he published *A Contribution to the Critique of Political Economy*. In 1867 the first volume of *Das Kapital* appeared. Marx began work on the second volume of *Das Kapital*, but died in 1883. Volumes 2 and 3 appeared after his death, as did the *Theories of Surplus Value*.

The Authoritarian Consequences of 'Scientific Socialism'

In our view, there are a number of problems with the theory (and not merely the practice) of 'scientific socialism'. We would list them as follows:

(a) the argument of inevitability – the major problem;

(b) the theory of class war;

Born in Barmen, Germany, the eldest son of a successful industrialist. Engels was sent to Britain to manage the factory in Manchester, and in 1844 he published his *Condition of the Working Classes in England*.

In the same year he began contributing to the *Franco-German Yearbook,* edited by Marx. During a six-week spell in Britain Engels introduced Marx to several of the Chartist leaders – radicals who were campaigning for universal suffrage.

Engels took part in developing a strategy of action for the Communist League, and after the revolutions of 1848 broke out helped form an organisation called the Rhineland Democrats. After the defeat of the revolutions he moved with Marx to London, and in the 1850s published *The Peasant War in Germany* and *Revolution and Counter-Revolution in Germany.* He retired in 1869 and, involved with the German Social Democratic Party, he wrote a fierce critique of a German socialist – *Anti-Dühring*. His *Socialism: Utopian and Scientific* appeared in English in 1892, a popularising work that was widely read, and in 1894 he applied his materialist method to anthropology in the *Origin of the Family, Private Property and the State*. In 1888 he wrote *Ludwig Feuerbach and the End of German Classical Philosophy* and his *Dialectics of Nature* was published posthumously in 1927.

After Marx's death Engels devoted the rest of his life to editing and translating Marx's writings.

(c) a rejection of 'moralism';

(d) the question of leadership – a relatively minor problem.

It will be argued that together these problems explain why Communist Party (CP) states following the theory of 'scientific socialism' have proved vulnerable to popular (even proletarian) protest. We have seen how attempts to make Communist Party states more democratic were resisted by the Soviet leadership in 1968 and today only North Korea, Cuba, China and Vietnam remain as CP states. Former CPs changed their names – usually to include democracy in their title – and they invariably describe themselves as socialist rather than communist. What relationship exists between the hapless fate of these states and the theory of scientific socialism? It is worth giving this question some thought.

The Inevitability Argument

In Part I of the *Communist Manifesto* the victory of the proletariat is described as 'inevitable', as in the famous comment that 'what the bourgeoisie . . . produces, above all, is its own grave-diggers. Its fall and the victory of the proletariat are equally inevitable' (1967: 94). This has become a central theme of Marxism in general, and Engels was to argue that revolutions are 'the necessary outcome of circumstances, quite independent of the will or guide of particular parties' (Hoffman, 1995: 135). Marxism is 'scientific' because it arises from the real movement of history that compels people to do things whether they like it or not.

Revolution is (in some sense of the term) a 'natural' process, driven by the antagonistic conflict between the forces and relations of production at the heart of society. It is therefore unavoidable. There are a number of problems with the 'inevitability argument'.

What happens when revolutions are 'bourgeois' in character?

In the *Communist Manifesto* Marx and Engels declare that 'Communists everywhere support every revolutionary movement against the existing order of things' (1967: 120). Contrary to the 'utopians', who support socialism rather than capitalism, Marxists will support a 'bourgeois revolution' in countries where liberal constitutionalism has yet to prevail: in Germany, as the *Communist Manifesto* points out, communists will fight with the bourgeoisie where the latter are acting in a revolutionary way. This notion is of the utmost importance for it explains the attraction of Marxism in colonial countries or autocratic regimes of a feudal or semi-feudal kind. But what has a liberal revolution to do with communism?

One of the most contentious aspects of the *Communist Manifesto* derives from the argument that once the old absolutist regime has fallen, 'the fight against the bourgeoisie itself may immediately begin'. The argument here focuses on Germany in 1848. Given the much more advanced conditions of European civilisation and 'a much more developed proletariat', 'the bourgeois revolution in Germany will be but the prelude to an immediately following proletarian revolution' (1967: 120). This sentence was seen by the Bolsheviks as giving the October revolution its classical Marxist credentials, since Russia of 1917 was deemed analogous to Germany of 1848, because of the combination of material backwardness and heightened political consciousness. The destruction of Tsarism – the bourgeois revolution – could then be 'the prelude to an immediately following proletarian revolution'.

Hunt has argued at some length that this formulation – which occurs nowhere else in Marx's writing – was put in to appease the members of the Communist League who commissioned the *Manifesto*. They did not like the idea of a bourgeois revolution anyway, but a bourgeois revolution immediately followed by a proletarian one was enough to sugar the pill. Hunt's argument is that this notion of permanent revolution – that a bourgeois revolution becomes relatively quickly a proletarian one – does not square with classical Marxism and the emphasis placed elsewhere in the *Communist Manifesto* on the gradual, step-by-step, education of the proletariat preparing them for revolution and power (Hunt, 1975: 180; 246). Whatever tactical considerations played their part in this fateful formulation, the argument is never actually repudiated by Marx and Engels, although they did later speak of the *Communist Manifesto* as a 'historical document which we have no longer any right to alter' (1967: 54). Whether or not we find Hunt's argument convincing, the point is that the notion that one revolution can immediately follow another has had significant historical consequences, and has come to be seen as part and parcel of Marxist theory.

The implication is that relatively undeveloped countries can become socialist or communist without the lengthy period of preparation which capitalism unwittingly and normally allows the proletariat. Since this period is precisely the one in which workers become familiar with liberal ideas and institutions, it is not difficult to see that the omission or dramatic compression of such a period can only increase the need for the authoritarian leadership of a 'vanguard' party, and authoritarian political institutions themselves. Is it surprising then that the USSR, and later the People's Republic of China, followed a development in which the liberal tradition was suppressed, rather than made the basis for further political advance?

What happens when revolutions are 'pre-mature'?

Ch 10: Anarchism, pp. 238–61

Engels told the German socialist Weydemeyer that 'we shall find ourselves compelled to make communist experiments and leaps which no-one knows better than ourselves to be untimely' (Hoffman, 1995: 135). But if revolution is deemed inevitable, then Marxists will 'find themselves' compelled to support 'experiments' and 'leaps' that are not only untimely, but can only be sustained by authoritarian institutions. A good example of this problem can be seen in relation to Marx and Engels's attitude towards the Paris Commune. Because of the heroism of the Communards, Marx extolled the virtues of the Commune. This he did in a book called *The Civil War in France*, which outlined a radical polity that became the basis of Lenin's blueprint in *The State and Revolution* written in 1918.

The Paris Commune

The Paris Commune was created in 1871 after France was defeated by Prussia in the Franco-Prussian war. The French government tried to send in troops to prevent the Parisian National Guard's cannon from falling into the hands of the population. The soldiers refused to fire on the jeering crowd and turned their weapons on their officers.

In the free elections called by the Parisian National Guard the citizens of Paris elected a council made up of a majority of Jacobins and Republicans and a minority of socialists (mostly Blanquists – explicitly authoritarian socialists – and followers of the anarchist Proudhon). This council proclaimed Paris autonomous and desired to recreate France as a confederation of communes (i.e. communities). Within the Commune, the elected council members were paid an average wage. In addition, they had to report back to the people who had elected them and were subject to recall by electors if they did not carry out their mandates.

The Paris Commune began the process of creating a new society, one organised from the bottom up. By May, 43 workplaces were cooperatively run and the Louvre Museum became a munitions factory run by a workers council. A meeting of the Mechanics Union and the Association of Metal Workers argued that 'equality must not be an empty word' in the Commune. The Commune declared that the political unity of society was based on 'the voluntary association of all local initiatives, the free and spontaneous concourse of all individual energies for the common aim, the well-being, the liberty and the security of all'.

On 21 May government troops entered the city, and this was followed by seven days of bitter street fighting. Squads of soldiers and armed members of the 'bourgeoisie' roamed the streets, killing and maiming at will. Over 25,000 people were killed in the street fighting, many murdered after they had surrendered, and their bodies dumped in mass graves.

The Commune had lasted for 72 days, and Marx, as President of the International Working Men's Association – the First International – expressed solidarity and support for the action. Yet ten years later Marx declared that the Commune was the rising of a city under exceptional conditions; that its majority was by no means socialist, nor could it be, and that with a 'modicum of common sense' a compromise with the French government at Versailles could have been reached (1975b: 318).

Biography   Rosa Luxemburg (1871–1919)

Born in Zamosc, in the Polish area of Russia. She became interested in politics while still at school and emigrated to Zurich in 1889 where she studied law and political economy.

While in Switzerland she met other socialist revolutionaries from Russia living in exile, and in 1893 helped to form the Social Democratic Party of Poland. As it was an illegal organisation, she went to Paris to edit the party's newspaper, *Sprawa Robotnicza* (Workers' Cause). She criticised the 'revisionism' of Bernstein in her first major work, *Social Reform or Revolution* (1899).

She settled in Berlin, where she joined the Social Democratic Party, and in 1905 she became editor of the SPD newspaper, *Vorwarts* (Forward). During the 1905 Revolution she returned to Warsaw and the following year published *The Mass Strike, the Political Party, and the Trade Unions*. She argued that a general strike had the power to radicalise the workers and bring about a socialist revolution.

Her book on economic imperialism, *The Accumulation of Capital*, was published in 1913. Although she continued to advocate the need for a violent overthrow of capitalism, she took the side of the Mensheviks in their struggle with the Bolsheviks. She opposed Germany's participation in World War I, and was involved in establishing an underground political organisation called *Spartakusbund* (Spartacus League).

In 1916 she wrote the highly influential pamphlet, *The Crisis in the German Social Democracy*, and in the same year she was arrested and imprisoned, following a demonstration in Berlin. It was here that she criticised the dictatorial methods used by the Bolsheviks.

She was released in 1918 and was a founding member of the German Communist Party (KPD). In 1919 Luxemburg helped organise the Spartakist Rising in Berlin. The army was called in, the rebellion was crushed, and Luxemburg (along with Liebkneckt) was executed without trial.

Yet the Commune was in reality influenced by Blanquism (a rather elitist and coercive **egalitarianism** named after the French socialist Blanqui, 1805–81) and anarchist trends, and reflected what has been called 'an unsophisticated anti-bureaucratism' (Hoffman, 1995: 137) – an anti-bureaucratism that enshrined anti-liberal political practices. Despite his private reservations, Marx felt obliged publicly to support an 'experiment' that could only have succeeded if power had been concentrated in an unambiguously authoritarian manner.

Rosa Luxemburg, the Bolshevik Revolution and Stalinism

Marx's 'support' for the Paris Commune is not an isolated example. The Polish Marxist, Rosa Luxemburg, was to defend the Bolshevik revolution in the same way and for the same reasons that Marx and Engels had praised the Paris Commune. The Bolsheviks, she argued, have acted with immense heroism: the revolution was an act of proletarian courage, and she supported it. On the other hand, she was alarmed by the authoritarianism of Lenin and Trotsky and she was particularly critical when the

Biography   Vladimir Ilich Lenin (1870–1924)

Born Ulyanov in Simbirsk, Russia, he was educated at the local Gymnasium. In 1887 Lenin's brother was executed for his part in the plot to kill Tsar Alexander III, and while at university Lenin became involved in politics. Expelled from Kazan University, he studied law in Petrograd (today known as St Petersburg). In 1895 he formed the Union of Struggle for the Emancipation of the Working Class. In 1896 Lenin was arrested and sentenced to three years internal exile, where he wrote *The Development of Capitalism in Russia*, *The Tasks of Russian Social Democrats*, as well as articles for various socialist journals.

Released in 1900, Lenin moved to Geneva and became involved with *Iskra*, the official paper of the Social Democratic Labour Party. In 1902 Lenin published *What is to be Done?* in which he argued for a party of professional revolutionaries dedicated to the overthrow of Tsarism. His long-time friend, Jues Martov, disagreed, believing that it was better to have a large party of activists. Martov won the vote 28–23 but Lenin was unwilling to accept the result and formed a faction known as the Bolsheviks. Those who remained loyal to Martov became known as Mensheviks.

Lenin returned to Russia during the 1905 Revolution but after its failure he called on Bolsheviks to participate in the elections for the Russian parliament or Duma (a legislature with limited powers). In 1913 Lenin moved to Galicia in Austria, but was arrested the following year as a Russian spy. After a brief imprisonment he was allowed to move to Switzerland, where he branded World War I as an imperialist conflict and wrote *Imperialism: The Highest Stage of Capitalism*. Russia's incompetent and corrupt system could not supply the necessary equipment to enable the army to fight a modern war. Food was in short supply and in February 1917 a large crowd marched through the streets of Petrograd breaking shop windows and shouting anti-war slogans.

Attempts to close down the Russian parliament led that body to nominate a Provisional Government, and in March 1917 the Tsar abdicated. Lenin, now desperate to return to Russia, travelled to Petrograd. In his *April Theses* he argued the case for a socialist revolution and Kerensky, head of the Provisional Government, gave orders for Lenin's arrest. Lenin escaped to Finland, where he completed his *State and Revolution*, a pamphlet that made the case for soviet (or council) rule in Russia. Lenin returned to Petrograd but remained in hiding. The Bolsheviks set up their headquarters in the Smolny Institute. When Kerensky moved to crush the Bolsheviks the Winter Palace was stormed and the Cabinet ministers arrested.

In October 1917 Lenin was elected chairman of the Soviet Council of People's Commissars. Land was distributed to peasants. Banks were nationalised and workers' control of factory production introduced. The Assembly elected to draw up a new constitution was closed down, other political parties were banned, and in 1918, with German troops moving towards Petrograd, Lenin ordered Trotsky to sign the Brest–Litovsk Treaty that resulted in the surrender of the Ukraine, Finland, the Baltic provinces, the Caucasus and Poland. This decision increased opposition to the Bolshevik government and a civil war followed. This came to an end in 1918, and the following year there was an uprising against the Bolsheviks at Kronstadt. Lenin now introduced the New Economic Policy that allowed some market trading and denationalisation.

After being shot by a member of the Socialist Revolutionaries Lenin's health declined, and in April 1922 Stalin occupied the new post of general secretary. An operation left Lenin paralysed, three days after dictating a 'will and testament', in which he called for the removal of Stalin from the post of general secretary. Lenin was so rude about all the members of the party leadership that the testament was suppressed and Stalin was confirmed in post. Lenin had a third stroke and died in 1924.

How to read:

The Communist Manifesto

This is a relatively short work and can be found in many editions. It is crucial to use an edition that contains all the prefaces since these are an invaluable aid to understanding the *Manifesto* and placing it in historical context. Both the prefaces to the later German edition (1872) and the Russian edition (1883) were written by Marx and Engels and contain fascinating comments that throw light on the character of the state and Marxism as a theory of history. The later prefaces should certainly be skim read. Part 1 of the *Manifesto* itself should be read carefully and it contains many passages that have been quoted many times. Part 2 is important since here Marx talks about the nature of communists and their character as a 'party'. Part 2 ends with a ten-point programme that throws important light on the relationship in Marxist theory between revolution and reform. Part 3 is somewhat dated and needs only to be skim read, but Part 4 is crucial since it contains the historically important reference to Germany and what is (in fact) the theory of permanent revolution.

two leaders dispersed the Constituent Assembly in 1918, when it was returned with a socialist, but not a Bolshevik majority. She thought that the revolution was bound to fail. In fact, the Russian Revolution succeeded by crushing its opponents, and Luxemburg, who was assassinated by German soldiers in 1919, never lived to see how a virtue was made of necessity first by Lenin and then by Stalin.

A whole generation of communists in liberal countries were prepared to support Stalin and Stalinism on the grounds that such rule was 'inevitable'. This position also created a grave dilemma for Stalin's critics such as Trotsky who supported the Russian Revolution and had shown his own illiberal tendencies. Crick expresses quite a common view when he says that 'it would have made little difference had Trotsky, not Stalin succeeded Lenin' (1987: 62). Engels was to argue (in response to the anarchists) that 'revolution is the most authoritarian thing there is' (Tucker, ed., 1978: 733). A theory that regards such an event as 'inevitable' will produce despotic political practices.

The Concept of Class War and the Problem of Morality

Let us look at the other factors that arguably demonstrate a link between Marxism as a scientific socialism and the authoritarianism which created the popular upheavals in 1989. Marxism embraces a polarising concept of class war, and this can only reinforce its authoritarian consequences. Such a concept has excluded or marginalised a whole series of struggles – for women's equality, gay rights, religious toleration, ecological sensitivity, etc. – that are clearly central to the goal of emancipation, but which don't fit in with the notion that the proletariat, and only the proletariat, has a leading role to play. A disdain for moral argument encourages the view that rights do not matter since we must choose between proletarian morality and bourgeois morality.

Leadership is a problem for all political movements that seek to change society in the interests of the poor and the relatively inarticulate, since people from relatively comfortable backgrounds will tend to monopolise leadership skills. But this problem is aggravated by a belief that utopian ideals are mere fantasies. A 'scientific' attitude ought to be tolerant and empirical, but in Marxism the notion of leaders spearheading revolutionary processes that are deemed inevitable and historically necessary must give a further twist to an authoritarian version of socialism whose state and political institutions are illiberal, and – despite Marxist theory on this point – refuse to 'wither away'.

The Dilemma of Democratic Socialism

Up until 1914 (as noted above), the term 'social democrat' was widely adopted. It was used both by the Bolsheviks and the British Labour Party. In 1914 a great schism occurred. Some socialists supported World War I, and this divide was deepened when the Bolshevik revolution took place in 1917. Although socialists generally welcomed the fall of Tsarism in February 1917 many, including those who considered themselves Marxists, saw the seizure of power by Lenin in October 1917 as the act of mad man, a *coup d'état* rather than a genuine revolution, a premature act that ignored the 'unripe' conditions in Russia.

From then on, the concept of a social democrat became a term of differentiation, with the emphasis on *democracy*. Socialists who opposed the Russian Revolution and subsequent Leninist and Stalinist rule invariably called themselves democratic socialists – a term we shall use interchangeably with social democrat. Socialism, it was argued, is concerned with reforms, not revolution: it must develop through parliamentary democracy, not through workers councils or soviets. It must express itself through electoral victory, not a seizure of power: nor should socialists tie themselves to the leadership of the working class. Socialism involves the whole nation – not simply a part of it – and socialism must be realistic, attained through piecemeal reforms and in a manner that works with, and respects, the liberal tradition. As the French socialist Jean Jaures put it, 'the great majority of the nation can be won over to our side by propaganda and lawful action and led to socialism' (Berki, 1974: 91–2).

Social democracy sees itself as everything that Marxism is not: democratic, reformist, realistic, open-minded and concerned with the moral case for socialism. What is its dilemma? It is so anti-utopian that it is vulnerable to the charge that it is no different in essence from liberalism and even more flexible versions of conservatism. Is it a movement in its own right? Berki makes the point that just as in Aristotle aristocracy can turn into its degenerate form, oligarchy, so social democracy can turn into its degenerate form, which is electoralism (1974: 104), i.e. a concern to win elections without worrying about principles at all.

In other words, social democracy suffers from a serious identity problem. It is so pragmatic and flexible, so concerned with avoiding divisiveness and outraging, as Durbin puts it, 'the conservative sections of all classes' (Berki, 1974: 103), that it becomes a form of conservatism itself (or liberalism), and cannot be called socialism at all. Socialism, we have argued, is vulnerable to the charge of utopianism: but a forthright rebuttal of utopianism of any kind may mean that the transformative element in socialism is lost, and socialism 'degenerates'.

Eduard Bernstein and the German Socialists

Eduard Bernstein is a significant figure to examine, for his critique of classical Marxism formed the theory and practice of what came to be called social democracy. He influenced a tradition that was resistant to theory. In his work, social democracy is not only contrasted explicitly and in detail to Marxism, but its own premises are lucidly displayed. Indeed, the book that has the English title *Evolutionary Socialism* was actually called (if one translates the German directly) *The Premises of Socialism and the Task of Social Democracy*.

Bernstein joined the German Socialists in 1872. When the warring groups united the party went from electoral success to electoral success. In 1876 it won 9 per cent of the votes cast (Gay, 1962: 38–9). Bismarck, the German chancellor, used the attempt to assassinate the Emperor (not, it should be said, by socialists) to harass the party. Bernstein, who was in Switzerland at the time, became converted to Marxism.

Despite the problems caused by Bismarck's anti-socialist law (which only lapsed in 1890), the party polled 12 per cent of the vote in the elections of 1881 (Gay, 1962: 52). In 1884 the party sent 24 members to the Reichstag – the German parliament. Under renewed pressure from Bismarck Bernstein was forced to leave Switzerland, and went to London. In 1890 the party secured nearly 20 per cent of the vote in the national elections and increased its number of MPs to 35. By 1903 the SPD had 81 seats in parliament (Gay, 1962: 230).

Bernstein, Revisionism and the British Tradition

Engels, who died in 1895, had already expressed his concern for Bernstein's enthusiasm for the Fabians – British socialists who explicitly rejected Marxism and named themselves after the Roman emperor Fabius, famed for his step-by-step approach to fighting war. Engels was to accuse the Fabians (whose society was established in London in 1874) of 'hushing up the class struggle' (Gay, 1962: 106). Bernstein was impressed by the tolerance and liberalism he found in London, so much so that Karl Kautsky, then the great champion of Marxist orthodoxy, was to declare Bernstein 'a representative of English socialism' (Gay, 1962: 80).

In 1899 Bernstein wrote his *Evolutionary Socialism* – described as the 'bible of revisionism'. Bernstein had been asked by Engels to be one of the executors of the Marxist papers, and Bernstein was reluctant to accept that he had – in the theological jargon which Marxists embrace – 'revised' Marxism. He argued that his critique was a way of further developing Marxism: he was not destroying Marxism since, as he put it, 'It is Marx who carries the point against Marx' (1961: 27). But what he argued was certainly explosive, and a different kind of socialism emerged in his critique.

Bernstein's Argument

Bernstein views are as follows:

• Small and medium-sized enterprises were proving themselves viable. Hence members of the possessing classes were increasing, not diminishing (Bernstein,

1961: xxv). Society was not becoming more simplified (as the *Manifesto* declared) but more graduated and differentiated (1961: 49). Moreover, the constantly rising national product was distributed, albeit unequally, over all segments of the population, so that the position of the worker was improving (1961: 207). In agriculture, the small and medium landholding was increasing, and the large and very large decreasing (1961: 71).

- Bernstein followed the Fabians by arguing that the theory of value or surplus value in Marxist theory was unnecessary. Depressions are becoming milder. Modern banking and the internationalisation of trade create adjustment and flexibility in capitalism – not breakdown.

- He saw Marx's emphasis on dialectics (the world consists of opposing forces) as a snare, uncritically taken over from Hegel. Why not assume that cooperation is just as important as struggle? Socialism must be based on the facts, and it is a fact that there is compromise and cooperation between the classes.

- Ethical factors, in Bernstein's view, create much greater space for independent activity than was seen to be the case in classical Marxism (1961: 15). The notion of inevitability – a fusion of what is and what ought to be – must be decisively rejected. 'No ism is a science' (Gay, 1962: 158). Socialism is about what is ethically desirable: science is about what is.

- Democracy, for Bernstein, is 'an absence of class government' – it avoids both the tyranny of the majority and the tyranny of the minority. Democracy is the high school of compromise and moderation (1961: 142–4). The notion of the 'dictatorship of the proletariat' has become redundant. Socialism seeks to make the proletarian into a citizen 'and to thus make citizenship universal' (1961: 146).

- Socialism, declared Bernstein, is 'the legitimate heir' to liberalism 'as a great historical movement' (1961: 149). There is no really liberal thought that does not also belong to socialism. Industrial courts and trades councils involve democratic self-government (1961: 152). Socialism is 'organising liberalism' and requires the constant increase of municipal freedom (1961: 159). He was devoted to liberal parliamentarism (1961: 299) and, if this parliamentarism becomes excessive, the antidote is local self-government.

- The SPD must fight for all those reforms that increase the power of the workers and give the state a more democratic form (Gay, 1962: 225). Bernstein described the SPD as a 'democratic-Socialist reform party'. Hence the trade unions, far from being schools for socialism (in Marx's revolutionary sense), were concerned with practical and non-revolutionary improvements. Trade unions are, declared Bernstein, 'indispensable organs of democracy' (1961: 139–40).

- He linked the practicality of trade unions with the empirical orientation of the cooperative movement (1961: 204). The class struggle continues, but it is taking ever-milder forms. Cooperatives, particularly consumer co-ops, encourage democratic and egalitarian forms of management.

Bernstein exemplifies the dilemma of democratic socialism. How can the social democratic party navigate between what Gay called the Scylla of impotence and the Charybdis of betrayal of its cause (1962: 302)? How can it be 'realistic' and yet remain socialist?

The British Labour Party and the Fabians

The British Labour Party has never been a party of theory. Although its members (and some of its leaders!) may not even have heard of Bernstein, it is Bernsteinism that provides the underpinning for its practice.

We have already mentioned the importance of the Fabians. The Fabian Society became a kind of think tank for the Labour Party. The Fabians were influenced by the same kind of theories that so appealed to Bernstein – empiricism, a philosophy which argues that our knowledge comes through the observation of 'facts' – and a belief in piecemeal reform through parliamentary democracy. Socialism was not a philosophy for life, but a highly focused doctrine that concerns itself with the organisation of industry and the distribution of wealth. Examine Fabian pamphlets today and what do you find? Specific proposals on organising the Civil Service, the health service, tax reforms, social security benefits, European Monetary Union, and the like. Beatrice Webb (1858–1943), who played a key role in the Fabian Society and in the formation of the Labour Party, took the view that the whole nation was sliding into social democracy.

The Labour Party, Constitutionalism and the Trade Unions

The Labour Representative Committee in 1900 was formed by trade unions. These unions felt that they needed a political voice and would cooperate with any party engaged in promoting legislation 'in the direct interest of labour' (Miliband, 1973, 19). The Liberal Party did not oppose the two Labour candidates who won their seats in 1900.

After the formation of the Labour Party in 1906, a Trades Dispute Act was passed that strengthened the right of unions to strike, while the Trade Union Act of 1913 allowed the trade unions to affiliate to the Labour Party. Ramsey MacDonald, the Party leader, made it clear that political weapons are to be found in the ballot box and the Act of Parliament – not in collective bargaining (Miliband, 1973: 35).

The party itself received a constitution in 1918 and the famous Clause IV that spoke of common ownership of the means of production was (rather cynically) inserted by the Webbs to give the party some kind of ideological distance from the Conservatives and the Liberals. Sidney Webb would, Tony Blair commented in 1995, be astonished to find that the clause was still in existence some 70 years later (1995: 12). It was not intended, Blair argued, to be taken seriously.

The 1922 programme made it clear that Labour stood for neither Bolshevism nor Communism, but 'common sense and justice' (Miliband, 1973: 94). It is true that it suited the Liberals and Conservatives to present, in Churchill's words, Labour as 'the party of revolution' (Miliband, 1973: 99), but in fact Labour's politics were always of a liberal and constitutional nature. It is revealing that during the crisis of 1936, when MacDonald was expelled from the Labour Party for entering into a national government with the Conservatives, the Tory leader, Sir Herbert Samuel, argued that it would be in the general interest if unpalatable social measures to deal with the economic crisis could be imposed by a Labour government (Miliband, 1973: 176). In the 1930s the Labour leadership was opposed to the Popular Front government in Spain, and contributed significantly to the appeasement of the extreme right.

Ch 10: Anarchism, pp. 238–61

Biography	**Eduard Bernstein (1850–1932)**

Born in Berlin. The son of Jewish parents, his father was a railroad engineer. Bernstein worked as a bank clerk and in 1872 he joined the Social Democrat Party (SDP). In the 1877 General Election in Germany the SDP won 12 seats. This worried Bismarck, and in 1878 he introduced an anti-socialist law that banned party meetings and publications.

After the passing of the anti-socialist law Bernstein emigrated to Switzerland, where he became editor of the underground socialist journal *Der Sozialdemokrat*. After being expelled from Switzerland he moved to England where he worked closely with Engels and members of the Fabian Society.

While living in London Bernstein gradually became convinced that the best way to obtain socialism in an industrialised country was through trade union activity and parliamentary politics. He published a series of articles where he argued that the predictions made by Marx about the development of capitalism had not come true. He pointed out that the real wages of workers had risen and the polarisation between an oppressed proletariat and oppressive capitalist class had not materialised. Nor had capital become concentrated in fewer hands.

Bernstein's revisionist views appeared in his extremely influential book *Evolutionary Socialism* (1899). His analysis of modern capitalism undermined the claims that Marxism was a science and upset revolutionaries such as Lenin and Trotsky. In 1901 Bernstein returned to Germany. This brought him into conflict with the left wing of the SDP, which rejected his 'revisionist' views as to how socialism could be achieved. Socialists such as Bebel, Kautsky, Liebkneckt and Luxemburg still believed that a Marxist revolution was possible.

Bernstein was elected to the Reichstag (1902–6 and 1912–18) where he led the right wing of the SDP. However, he sided with the left wing over Germany's participation in World War I and in 1915 voted against war credits.

In April 1917 Bernstein worked with Kautsky and Hilferding to form the Independent Socialist Party. After the war he joined the leadership of the SDP in condemning the attempted seizure of power by the communists. In the government formed by Ebert, Bernstein served as secretary of state for economy and finance.

Elected to the Reichstag in 1920 Bernstein opposed the rise of the extreme right and made several powerful speeches against Hitler and the Nazis.

Although the right-wing publicist Evelyn Waugh saw the country under occupation after the Labour electoral victory of 1945, in fact Morrison made it clear that the socialisation of industry would only work 'on the merits of their specific cases. That is how the British mind works. It does not work in a vacuum or in abstract theories' (Miliband, 1973: 279). There is a clear link between Sidney Webb's statement to the Labour conference of 1923 that the founder of British socialism was not Karl Marx but Robert Owen – the doctrine underlying the Party is not that of class war but human brotherhood – and Harold Wilson's comment at the 1966 conference that no answers are to be found in Highgate cemetery (i.e. where Marx is buried) (Miliband, 1973: 98; 361).

Blair's Socialism

The position of Tony Blair follows this tradition of pragmatism, moralism and constitutionalism. Indeed Blair makes it clear that the elimination of the old Clause IV was to facilitate a return to Labour's ethical roots (Wright, 1996: x). We must retain, he argues, the values and principles underlying democratic socialism but apply them entirely afresh to the modern world (1992: 3).

The values of democratic socialism are 'social justice, the equal worth of each citizen, equality of opportunity, community'. Socialism is, if you will, social-ism (Blair, 1994: 4). In the 50th anniversary lecture of the 1945 Labour victory, Blair describes socialism as 'the political heir of radical liberalism' (1995: 8). He sees the New Liberals as social democrats, and he defines socialism as a form of politics through which to fight poverty, prejudice and unemployment, and to create the conditions in which to build one nation – tolerant, fair, enterprising and inclusive. Socialists have to be both moralists and empiricists. They need, on the one hand, to be concerned with values, but at the same time they must address themselves to a world as it is and not as we would like it to be (1995: 12–13).

International Social Democrats

These notions have been internationally endorsed. The German SPD has sternly repudiated communism, and in its Bad Godesburg Resolution of 1959 – described by Berki as 'one of the boldest, most impressive "liberal" party manifestoes ever written' – it argues for competition where possible, planning 'as far as it is necessary'. It follows what the Swedish social democrats have called a 'matter-of-fact conception of man' (Berki, 1974: 98–9).

These comments capture the dilemma. Berki suggests that in a way social democracy can be characterised as 'utopian socialism minus utopian expectations', since it does not believe that ideals such as justice, goodwill, brotherliness and compassion could be 'unreservedly realized' (1974: 101). Is social democracy so pragmatic and flexible that it cannot be called socialism at all?

Can Marxism be Rescued?

The idea of communism as a 'scientific socialism' does, indeed, lead to authoritarianism. But this is not because communism aims to create a classless and stateless society. Rather it is because Marxist theory embraces elements that make it impossible for the state to 'wither away'.

Of the problems that need to be tackled if Marxism is to made credible, the first is discussed below.

The Notion of Revolution

The concept of revolution as a dramatic element focused around a seizure of power is problematic. Marx uses the term revolution in different ways. He and Engels speak in the *Communist Manifesto* of the constant 'revolutionizing of production' under capitalism (1967: 83) and in that sense, revolutions are occurring all the time. But revolution is also used to denote a transformation of state and class power – an event in which the character of society as a whole changes.

It is true that Marx was to argue that such an event did not have to be violent, and he even puts the view in 1882 that if in Britain 'the unavoidable evolution' turns into a revolution, that would not only be the fault of the ruling classes but also of the working class. Every peaceful concession has been wrung out through pressure, and the workers must wield their power and use their liberties, 'both of which they possess legally'. That suggests that each step forward is a kind of revolution in its own right, and that the notion of revolution as a dramatic event which inevitably changes the character of society is redundant (Hoffman, 1975: 211).

But this is not typical of Marx's view. The notion of revolution as a dramatic event linked to a seizure of power was, it seems to us, inherited uncritically from the French Revolution of 1789. It creates a polarisation that makes the assertion of common interests and consensus more, not less, difficult. Engels is right: revolutions are authoritarian events, and they create a new state that clearly distinguishes between revolution and counter-revolution, and this leads to the kind of insecurity and division that generates despotism rather than democracy.

The Inevitability Problem and the Liberal Tradition

Clearly the notion of revolution as inevitable creates the problem of supporting revolutions that generate authoritarian states, and the consequent abuse of human rights. A scathing attitude towards morality can only aggravate the problem. But it does not follow from this that all elements of Marxism are authoritarian in orientation. Here the attitude towards liberalism is crucial. Not only did Marx begin his political career as a liberal steeped in the ideals of the European Enlightenment, but when he becomes a communist, he seeks to go beyond rather than reject liberal values.

The distinction between 'transcending' and 'rejecting' liberalism is crucial to our argument. To transcend liberalism is to build upon its values and institutions: it is to develop a theory and practice that extends freedom and equality more consistently and comprehensively than liberalism is able to do. Socialism as a **'post-liberalism'** seeks to turn liberal values into concrete realities so that those excluded by classical liberalism – the workers, the poor, women, dependants – become free and equal, as part of an historical process that has no grand culminating moment or climax. Socialism as a 'pre-liberalism', on the other hand, negates liberal values by introducing a system that imposes despotic controls upon the population at large (whatever its claim to speak in the name of the workers), and it is well described in the *Communist Manifesto* as a reactionary socialism because it hurls 'traditional anathemas' against liberalism and representative government (1967: 111).

The problem with Marxism is that it is an amalgam of pre- and post-liberalism. It is post-liberal insofar as it stresses the need to build upon, rather than reject, capitalist achievements. But while (conventionally defined) revolutions make sense in situations in which legal rights to change society are blocked, in societies that have, or are attempting to build, liberal institutions, revolutions lead to elitism, despotism and a contempt for democracy. The notion of class war does not place enough emphasis on the need to create and consolidate common interests, to campaign in a way that isolates those who oppose progress.

Again there is a tension here in Marx's writings between his view that a classless society will eliminate alienation for all, and his argument that the bourgeoisie are the 'enemy' who must be overthrown. This leads to the privileging of the proletariat as the agent of revolution, and hostility to all who are not proletarians.

The Question of Class and Agency

Socialists are right when they see class as something that is negative; freedom for all, as Marxism argues, is only possible in a classless society. Class privileges come at the expense of others. In liberal societies class encourages an abstract approach to be taken to equality and power so that formal equality coexists with the most horrendous inequalities of power and material resources. Class is thus divisive, and it generates the kind of antagonisms that require force (and therefore the state) to tackle them.

For this reason Marx is right to argue that if we want to dispense with the need for an institution claiming a monopoly of legitimate force we must dispense with classes. In a well-known comment, Marx argues that in class-divided societies social relations are not 'relations between individual and individual, but between worker and capitalist, between farmer and landlord, etc. Wipe out these relations and you annihilate all society' (Marx and Engels, 1975a: 77). But this comment is not concrete enough. For workers also have a gender and national identity, etc., and this materially affects how they relate to others. It is not that the class identity is unimportant: it is rather that it fuses with other identities since these other identities are also a crucial part of the process that creates class. Brown argues that class has become invisible and inarticulate, rarely theorised or developed in the multicul-turalist mantra, 'race, class, gender, sexuality' (1995: 61). The point is that we do not need to present these other identities as though they are separate from class.

In our view, class is only *seen* in 'other' forms. Thus we are told (*Independent*, 8 May 2003) that whereas 4.5 per cent of white British men (aged 16–74) are unemployed, this figures rises to 9.1 per cent for men of Pakistani origin, 10.2 per cent of Bangladeshis and 10.4 per cent of Afro-Caribbean men. There are not simply two sets of figures here (black and Asian men *and* unemployment): rather it is that unemployment is integral to the discrimination from which black and Asian men suffer. Class only becomes visible through the position of women, gays, ethnic minorities etc. The diversity of form in which classes express themselves is of the utmost importance, and it is the reason why no particular group should be privileged over any other in the struggle to achieve a classless and stateless society.

Socialists must, in other words, seek to mobilise all those who are excluded by contemporary institutions. This goes well beyond the concept of a 'proletariat', although those who are poor and have to subject themselves to the 'despotic' rules of employers are an obvious constituency in the struggle to govern one's own life. It is impossible to be free and equal if one is subject to aggressive pressures from employers and managers. Democratising the workplace to allow greater security, transparency and participation is critical, and all those who suffer from these problems are natural constituents in the struggle for socialism.

The Problem of Determinism and Free Will

Bauman has argued that utopianism is compatible with everything but determinism (1976: 37), and in his hostility to utopianism Marx sometimes gives the impression that he does not believe in free will. When he speaks of his theory of history as one in which people enter into relations 'independent of their will', does this mean that people have no will? What it means, it seems to us, is that what people intend (i.e. humans are beings with purpose and thus will) is never quite the same as what actually happens.

Take the following assertion of Marx's. The capitalist and landlord are 'the personifications of economic categories, embodiments of particular class interests and class relations' so that his or her standpoint can 'less than any other' make the individual 'responsible for relations whose creature he socially remains, however much he may subjectively raise himself above them' (1970: 10). This comment seems to suggest that our will cannot transform circumstances, and therefore we cannot create new relations. Yet Marx's third thesis on Feuerbach had already stated (against mechanical materialism which saw people as passive and lacking in agency) that the changing of circumstances and human activity coincide as 'revolutionary practice' (again – an identification of revolution with ongoing change, not a dramatic one-off event). This, it seems to us, is the answer to the problem of determinism and inevitability. If we assume that determinism negates free will and that we need to make a choice between them, then clearly determinism is a problem for socialism. For how can we change society if we do not have the will to do so? But what if we go beyond such a 'dualism' and argue merely that determinism means that free will always occurs in the context of relations? Why is this concept of determinism a problem?

Circumstances determine our capacities. Our capacity to change circumstances involves recognising these circumstances and making sure that we correctly appraise their reality. To successfully strengthen the struggle for socialism we need to attend to movements within our existing society which demonstrate that we can regulate our lives in ways which increase our capacity to get the results we want – whether it is in terms of transport policy, cleaning up the environment, giving people greater security and control in the workplace.

Whether these reforms or 'revolutionising activities' are effective depends upon how carefully we have assessed the circumstances that determine the context and the event. This kind of determinism does not undermine free will: on the contrary, it makes it possible to harness free will in a sensible and rational manner. If Marx is suggesting that there was a 'dualism' between free will and determinism, he would simply be turning classical liberalism inside out and not going beyond it. Classical liberalism argues for a notion of freedom independent of circumstances and relationships, and socialists might find it tempting (since they are critical of liberalism) to take the view that since circumstances determine the way people are, therefore people have no freedom or will-power. But if this was the position of socialists such as Robert Owen (Hoffman, 1975: 139), arguably it was not the position of Marx's 'new' materialism, even though he and Engels sometimes gave the impression that it was.

But the point is that we cannot exclude the wealthy and the 'beneficiaries' of the market and state from the struggle for socialism even though it would be foolish and naive to assume that the 'haves' will be enthusiastic proponents for a socialist future! Nevertheless, it has to be said that those who drive cars (however rich they are) are still vulnerable to the health problems associated with pollution. They suffer the nervous disorders linked to congestion and frustration on the roads. Inequalities and lack of social control, whether within or between societies, make everyone insecure, and result in a futile and wasteful use of resources. Wealthy people who try to 'buy' peaceful neighbourhoods are seeking to escape from problems that will inevitably affect them too.

Take another issue. It is becoming increasingly clear to 'establishments' in advanced industrial countries that if nothing is done about the divisions within the international community then liberal traditions will be eroded, as refugees move around the globe. We will *all* suffer as a consequence. The British government has just announced measures to place terrorist suspects under 'house arrest'. Although the victims of crime in, say, contemporary South Africa are predominantly the poor who live in the shanty towns, this scourge does not simply affect those who are on the margins of society. Everyone can be the victim of crime. Socialism – making people conscious that they are living in society and that everything they do affects (and may harm) others – is, it could be argued, in everyone's interests. There is an interesting parallel here with measures taken to combat cholera in nineteenth-century British cities. The disease was no respecter of class or wealth: it was in everyone's interests that it was eradicated. What is the point of having wealth and power if your health is devastated?

Marxists might argue that, with divisiveness in the world growing through a kind of globalisation which increases inequality, the notion of a proletariat must be viewed internationally rather than simply nationally. But the danger still remains that such a perspective will take a narrow view of class and underplay the problem of cementing common interests across the globe.

Socialism and Inevitability

Marx sometimes makes it seem that socialism will arrive come what may. He speaks of 'the natural laws of capitalist production' 'working with iron necessity towards inevitable results', and in a famous passage he likens the birth of socialism to pregnancy (1970: 10). The development of socialism is as inevitable as the birth of a child. This argument is, however, only defensible as a *conditional* inevitability – not an absolute certainty independent of circumstances. In the *Communist Manifesto* Marx and Engels comment that class struggle might end 'in a revolutionary constitution of society at large' or 'the common ruin of the contending classes' (1967: 79). Not only is it impossible to establish a timescale for socialism, but its inevitability is conditional upon, for example, humanity avoiding a nuclear conflagration that wipes out humans, or the destruction of the environment which makes production impossible. Nor can it be said that liberal societies might not turn to the right before they turn to the left.

What a conditional inevitability merely states is that if humanity survives then sooner or later it will have to regulate its affairs in a socially conscious manner, and that, broadly speaking, is socialism. Only in this qualified and conditional sense can it be said that socialism is inevitable. Marxism can be rescued if it makes it clear that 'inevitability' is conditional, drops a notion of revolution as a concentrated political event and, with it, a polarised and narrow notion of class. Whether it would still be Marxism is a moot point.

The Problem of Utopianism

We have argued that a credible socialism must draw upon social democratic *and* Marxist ideas. The problem with 'pure' social democrats as well as 'pure' Marxists is that they can be said to either embrace a (liberal) empiricist framework or they simply turn such a framework inside out.

Bernstein is a case in point. On the one hand, he saw himself as a positivist who stuck rigorously to the facts. On the other hand, since he was living in a society that was clearly not socialist, socialism is, he tells us, a piece of the beyond – something which ought to be, but is not (Gay, 1962: 158; 163). Abstract 'realism' coexists with abstract utopianism. The role of ethics is not integrated into a concern with the facts, and Marck has pointed out that such a theory can pay too much attention to 'short-run developments', ruling out in a dogmatic fashion dramatic and unanticipated actions, 'apparently contradicted by the happenings of the day' (Gay, 1962: 162).

Bernstein's position on economic concentration bears this out. As Gay comments, after 1924 German industry centralised and cartelised as never before (1962: 172). The trends he analysed in 1899 were not irreversible. In the same way Bernstein assumed that a new middle class would be democratic and pro-socialist. Yet anyone who knows anything about German history after World War I, comments Gay, 'will recognize the fallacious assumptions of Bernstein's theory'. Inflation and the world depression traumatised large groups within the German middle classes: they saw descent into the proletariat as a horrendous possibility (1962: 215). Bernstein's analysis put into the context of Germany between the wars turned out to be wishful thinking. Whether government through a representative parliament can work depends upon the social structure and political institutions of a country – it allows no dogmatic answer (Gay, 1962: 236).

Once we see that reality is in movement, then we can fuse utopia and realism. Utopia derives from the transformation of existing realities: but this utopia is not to be located outside existing realities, it is part of them. In arguing that socialism must be a 'utopian realism', we avoid the dualism between facts and values, utopia and reality, a dualism that bedevils so many exponents of socialism, whether of the right or the left. Bernstein's argument that socialists should always avoid violence is right under some circumstances. But it could hardly apply when the Hitler leadership in Germany destroyed parliamentary institutions and embraced fascism.

As will be argued in Chapter 10 (Anarchism), we need a state as long as humanity cannot resolve its conflicts of interest in a peaceful manner. For Bernstein, because the state exists, it is here to stay. The 'so-called coercive associations, the state and the communities, will retain their great tasks in any future I can see' (Gay, 1962: 246). But to identify the state with community, and regard its mechanisms for settling difference as only apparently 'coercive', shows how far 'pure' social democracy is still steeped in the abstract aspects of the liberal tradition.

Gay is surely right when he comments that Bernstein's optimism was not well founded: it took short-run prosperity and converted it into a law of capitalist development (1962: 299). If, as A.J. Taylor has said, Marx was a dogmatic optimist (1967: 47), so was Bernstein. Socialism requires a conditional concept of inevitability and a 'dialectical' determinism – one that takes full account of human agency – so that it is neither 'optimistic' nor 'pessimistic' but a utopian realism.

Summary

Socialism is certainly a 'broad church', but underlying its numerous forms is a concern with cooperation and equality, a belief that human nature can change and that freedom requires an adequate provision of resources. Socialism is peculiarly prone to the problem of utopianism because it seeks to establish a society that differs from the world of the present.

The work of Saint-Simon, Fourier and Robert Owen demonstrates that socialists who were labelled 'utopian' by their Marxist critics did not regard themselves in this light. Marxism is a variant of socialism that leads to authoritarianism insofar as it emphasises an unconditional inevitability, has a particular notion of revolution, and is apparently disdainful of moral judgement. Social democracy or democratic socialism rejects utopianism but runs the risk of a dogmatic adherence to a doctrine of 'realism' that can be at variance with the facts.

Marxism can only be rescued from the problem of authoritarianism if it rejects the notion of revolution as a single political event, and adopts a broader view of class and a conditional notion of inevitability. The problem of utopia in socialism needs to be meaningfully addressed by constructing socialism as a 'utopian realism' so that neither half of this construct is stressed at the expense of the other.

Questions

1. Are Marxist organisations necessarily authoritarian?
2. Can the notion of revolution play a part within a democratic socialism?
3. Is socialism inevitable?
4. Is parliament a barrier to, or a precondition for, a viable socialism?
5. Is socialism necessarily utopian?

References

Bauman, Z. (1976) *Socialism as Utopia* London: George Allen & Unwin.
Bernstein, E. (1961) *Evolutionary Socialism* New York: Schocken.
Blair, T. (1992) 'Pride without Prejudice', *Fabian Review* 104(3), 3.
Blair, T. (1994) *Socialism* Fabian Pamphlet 565, London.
Blair, T. (1995) *Let Us Face the Future* Fabian Pamphlet 571, London.
Brown, W. (1995) *States of Injury* Princeton, NJ: Princeton University Press.
Crick, B. (1982) *In Defence of Politics* 2nd edn Harmondsworth: Penguin.
Crick, B. (1987) *Socialism* Buckingham: Open University Press.
Gay, P. (1962) *The Dilemma of Democratic Socialism* New York: Collier.
Geoghegan, V. (1987) *Utopianism and Marxism* London and New York: Methuen.

Heywood, A. (1992) *Political Ideologies* Basingstoke: Macmillan.

Hoffman, J. (1975) *Marxism and the Theory of Praxis* New York: International Publishers.

Hoffman, J. (1991) *Has Marxism a Future?* Discussion Papers in Politics: University of Leicester.

Hoffman, J. (1995) *Beyond the State* Cambridge: Polity Press.

Hunt, R. (1975) *The Political Ideas of Marx and Engels*, Vol. 1, Basingstoke: Macmillan.

Independent, 8 May 2003: 'Britain Today: A Nation Still Failing its Ethnic Minorities'.

Mannheim, K. (1960) *Ideology and Utopia* London: Routledge & Kegan Paul.

Marx, K. and Engels, F. (1967) *The Communist Manifesto* Harmondsworth: Penguin.

Marx, K. and Engels, F. (1968) *Selected Works* London: Lawrence & Wishart.

Marx, K. and Engels, F. (1975a) *Collected Works* Vol. 4 London: Lawrence & Wishart.

Marx, K. and Engels, F. (1975b) *Selected Correspondence* Moscow: Progress.

Miliband, R. (1973) *Parliamentary Socialism* 2nd edn London: Merlin.

Tucker, R. (ed.) (1978) *The Marx-Engels Reader* 2nd edn New York and London: W.W. Norton.

Wright, T. (1996) *Socialisms* London and New York: Routledge.

Further Reading

- Wright's *Socialisms* (referenced above) is a most valuable summary of different positions.

- Crick's *Socialism* (referenced above) is very useful, with a chapter excerpting texts on British socialism.

- Miliband's *Parliamentary Socialism* (referenced above) is a classic critique on Labourism.

- Geohegan's *Utopianism and Marxism* (referenced above) is a useful defence of the utopian tradition.

- Gavin Kitching's *Rethinking Socialism* London and New York: Methuen, 1983 offers a very challenging attempt to rework socialism during the Thatcher period.

- The David McLellan edition of *Marxism: The Essential Writings* Oxford: Oxford University Press, 1988 includes valuable excerpts from various Marxist traditions and a piece on Eduard Bernstein.

Weblinks

Very useful on the history of socialism and the various personalities that predominate: http://www.spartacus.schoolnet.co.uk

Allows one to look at original texts on different aspects of socialism: http://www.inter-change-search.net/directory/Society/Politics/Socialism/

Easy to get information of the different 'varieties' of socialism: http://www.the-wood.org/socialism/

Material on Marxism: http://www.marxist.org.uk/htm_docs/princip2.htm

Full text of the *Communist Manifesto*: http://www.socialistparty.org.uk/manifesto/m2frame.htm?manifesto.html

Chapter 10

Anarchism

Introduction

Much is made in the press about the frequent anti-capitalist protests happening in various cities throughout the world, and it is argued that anarchists are behind these demonstrations. The word 'anarchist' is often used as a term of abuse, and is sometimes misused – but what exactly does it mean? What does it stand for, and why have some argued that anarchism has enjoyed a resurgence in recent years? On the face of it, it seems an absurdly self-defeating philosophy, so why does it remain influential? Who does it attract and why?

To answer these questions, in this chapter we will try to establish what anarchism is, and how different varieties of anarchism advocate different strands of argument.

Chapter Map

In this chapter we will explore:

- The overlap with other ideologies while grasping the distinctive character of anarchism.

- Philosophical anarchism and free market anarchism, while noting their difficulties.

- The views of anti-capitalist anarchists such as Proudhon, Bakunin and Kropotkin.

- An actual experience of anarchism, during the Spanish Civil War.

- The problem of violence, and what role it plays in the new social movements.

- The problem organisation poses for anarchism.

- The difficulties that arise when the distinctions between the state and government and force and constraint are ignored.

Death in Genoa

Riot police storm past a dead protester who has been shot and killed by carabiniere, 20 July 2001

On a sunny Italian morning a group of young politics students landed in Genoa to protest against the G8 summit. Before travelling they had been leafleted by anarchist groups and emailed regarding the details of the demonstrations, where they should stay and where preliminary meetings were being held locally. They met their rendezvous outside the airport and hitched a lift to the Carlini Stadium. Inside the stadium they first noticed a group the Italian Ya Basta group, also called *tutti bianci* ('all white').

There is a definite uneasy atmosphere in the stadium – the Ya Basta group want only to stage an act of civil disobedience such as a peaceful march and protest – whereas the anarchists are aiming to dismantle the 'Red Zone' fence that separates delegates from protestors. Although they tell the group that they support the demonstrations against capitalism in principle, they also remind everyone of their own specific demands they want made, maintaining that a revolution against capital must be linked to a revolution against the state and government.

Once the details have been amicably agreed upon, they march to the fence. Almost immediately the protestors are drenched by the Italian police with water cannons. When the increasingly angry crowd try to pull down the fence the police use tear gas against them. Violent confrontations break out between the police and certain groups of protestors. Rumours (later confirmed) start that a protestor has been killed by the police.

Imagine you are a member of an anarchist committee whose job it is to contact the 250 people planning on travelling from Britain to Genoa, placing information on the internet, consulting on leaflets, arranging accommodation etc. How does this level of organisation compare to your initial conception of what it is to be an anarchist?

At the G8 summit, force was answered with force. Imagine you were the Genoan Police Chief responsible for ensuring public order. How would you have tried to counter and control the anarchists?

The Relationship with Socialism

In her *Using Political Ideas* (1997) Barbara Goodwin has a separate chapter on anarchism and argues that the anarchist is 'not merely a socialist who happens to dislike the state'. She concedes, however, that there is much overlap and that many anarchists have analysed capitalism in a way that resembles that of socialists (1997: 122).

R.N. Berki, however, in his influential book *Socialism,* treats anarchism as a current within socialism and notes, for example, that it was Proudhon (a key anarchist as we shall see later in this chapter) who first called his doctrine 'scientific socialism' (1974: 12), and that Proudhon's significance for socialism is enormous (1974: 84). Berki makes many acute observations about anarchism in the context of his chapter on the evolution of socialism. In a section on socialist thought at the turn of the century he describes Michael Bakunin as a precursor to both Russian socialism and anarcho-syndicalism, about which more will be said later (1974: 83–8).

Andrew Vincent, as does Goodwin, has a separate chapter on anarchism, and makes the point that the doctrine overlaps with both liberalism and socialism (1995: 114). But whatever the overlap between some kinds of anarchism and socialism, there is also an anarchism that is explicitly non-socialist, and in some of its forms even anti-socialist. It will be useful to say something about these first, since they are dramatically different from 'socialist' forms of anarchism.

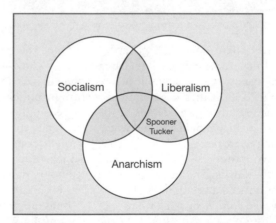

Figure 10.1

Philosophical Anarchists

We will take the view that, although anarchism is a very old theory, it only emerged in systematic form in the eighteenth century as part of the Enlightenment. We will begin with what is widely agreed to be the first comprehensive account of anarchist principles, William Godwin's classic *Enquiry Concerning Political Justice* (1793).

Godwin was really a liberal, even though he abandoned the classical liberal view of natural rights and a state of nature. He argues that humans are social beings, are moulded by their environment and are imbued with a capacity to reason. True happiness, as far as Godwin was concerned, lies with the development of individuality. All individuals have a right to private judgement. Everything understood by organisation is 'in some degree evil' and he argued that communal institutions, even theatre and musical performances, could be seen as an invasion of our individuality. Society should be regarded as a 'luxury', rather than a 'necessity' and can never be more than the sum of its parts (Vincent, 1995: 125). Compulsory restraint violates a privately determined pursuit of happiness, and it is said that Godwin ends where Hobbes begins. While Godwin sees the state as vicious, evil and tyrannical, the premises of his theory are militantly individualistic. If this atomistic and abstract view of the individual leads to radical insecurity and arbitrariness in Hobbes, in Godwin it generates the 'unspeakably beautiful vision of a world' in which individuals freely exercise their private judgement (Hoffman, 1995: 114).

Godwin was opposed to property, the market and acquisitiveness in general, but he was no socialist. His opposition to the state extends to social relationships, and all individuals retain a sphere of private judgement that shuts society out. He may have hoped that small face-to-face communities would replace the state (with temporary coordinating bodies being transitionally necessary to resolve disputes and repel invaders), but he has been rightly called a 'philosophical anarchist' since his main preoccupation is with principles rather than practice.

Max Stirner is often bracketed with Godwin as a philosophical anarchist, but unlike Godwin Stirner does not see individuals as benevolent and rational. He enthusiastically embraces the argument that consciousness (which is always 'alienated') is the source of our oppression. In Stirner's case, concepts such as humanism, communism and liberalism are inherently oppressive because they are necessarily imposed upon the sovereign individual. The state of nature adhered to by classical liberals was essentially social in character, but individuals constitute the highest reality, and Stirner exhorts them to desert their natural condition. People have no rights of any kind. As a conscious egoist, the individual, in Stirner's view, is beyond good and evil and the oppressiveness of the state is no different in essence from the oppressiveness of all social relationships, indeed of ideologies. All subject the ego to some 'generality or other' (Hoffman, 1995: 115).

Stirner sees the natural world as a war of all against all, but unlike Hobbes who posits a powerful state to tackle this problem, Stirner advocates the formation of an association of sovereign individuals – a union of conscious egoists – who would spontaneously and voluntarily come together out of mutual interest. All 'teleological' categories – goals, purposes and ends – are oppressive even if they are imposed by individuals upon themselves. This means that even a system of direct democracy is unacceptable. His union of egoists would enable individuals to accomplish more than they could on their own, and though Stirner's world is one without rights and morality, the union would create security and put an end to poverty. Marx and Engels in their lengthy critique of Stirner's *The Ego and His Own* point out that Stirner employs a concept of the unique individual that in practice morally obliges other individuals, so that he is in the hapless position of attacking authority from moral premises which are not supposed to exist (Hoffman, 1995: 115).

In a more recent exposition of philosophical anarchism, Wolff argues that all adults are responsible beings who have a capacity for choice and a potential for autonomy that they lose if they obey the dictates of another. A person's primary obligation is to be autonomous. However, unlike Stirner and Godwin, Wolff

Biography   **William Godwin (1756–1836)**

The son of a poor Presbyterian minister, Godwin was influenced by Dissenters and became a Presbyterian minister himself in 1768. He did not make a success of this and decided to earn his living from writing.

Although this was precarious, he got his publisher to finance him and he produced his major work, *An Enquiry Concerning Political Justice*. This was first published in 1793 and substantially revised for a second (1795) and third edition (1797). In 1794 he wrote his most successful novel, *Caleb Williams,* and three years later he married Mary Wollstonecraft who died in childbirth some five months after their marriage. His *Memoirs* lost him public support and,

although he continued to write, he lived his final 30 years in debt and relative obscurity.

His anarchism was based on a belief that individuals were rational and social beings whose autonomy was necessarily corrupted by government. A representative assembly was only permissible as a transitional expedient.

The capacity of individuals to judge is sacrosanct and, as perfectible beings, they can only progress through knowledge, truth and understanding. Many commentators find his anarchism implausible and concentrate on his utilitarianism, which they see as making an important contribution to the history of political thought.

accepts the case for a direct democracy, and he argues that people are bound by the decisions they have taken. The advantage of such a system is that the authority to which each citizen submits 'is not of himself simply, but that of the entire community taken collectively'. Not only does this sound rather authoritarian, but Wolff argues that each person encounters 'his better self in the form of the state, for its dictates are simply the laws which he has, after due deliberation willed to be

Biography   **Max Stirner (1806–56)**

Born Johann Kaspar Schmidt at Bayreuth in Bavaria, he was of poor parents. He studied at the University of Berlin from 1826–8 where he attended the lectures of Hegel.

He returned to Berlin in 1832 and managed to get a teacher's certificate, but the Prussian government refused to appoint him to a full-time post. He married in 1837 but his wife died in childbirth a few months later. He acquired a post at a girls' school and was able to associate with Young Hegelians such as the Bauer brothers.

He wrote an article, 'The False Principle of our Education' for Karl Marx's *Rheinische Zeitung* (Rhineland Gazette) in 1842, and in 1845 published his principal work, *The Ego and His Own*.

Influenced by Hegelianism, he saw history as culminating in his sovereign individual, which is unique and creates everything. Because he argued that sovereign individuals must emancipate themselves from society, he was dubbed 'Saint Max' by Marx and Engels in the ferocious critique they wrote of him (and other left Hegelians) in *The German Ideology*.

He married a member of the Young Hegelian circle, and although he had adopted the *nom de plume* Max Stirner so as not to alarm the head of the school where he taught, he lost his job. He spent the rest of his life in poverty.

To earn a living, he translated the work of English economists. His wife left him, and in 1852, four years before his death, he wrote a *History of Reaction*.

enacted' (cited by Dahl, 1989: 348). As an anarchist, he treats direct democracy as a form of the state!

All philosophical anarchists have the problem of moving from the individual to some kind of collective organisation that, on the one hand, is deemed necessary to realise anarchism, but which, on the other, contradicts anarchist principles. We will see if the free market anarchists are better able to tackle this problem.

Free Market Anarchists

Nineteenth-century Americans such as Spooner and Tucker argued for an anarchism that was an extension of liberalism: if individuals are free and equal, why should they accept the compulsion of the state? Locke's **state of nature** was seen as a world in which individuals are not subject to external discipline: why shouldn't things stay that way? But whereas nineteenth-century free market anarchists were concerned about the structural inequalities that the market might generate – and they took the view that everyone should be an entrepreneur – more recent free market anarchists have accepted capitalism, arguing that exploitation and coercion are simply the product of the state. Substantial inequalities are inevitable in a free society.

Free market anarchists such as Murray Rothbard take the view that state welfare is as pernicious as state warfare. Any attempt to regulate production prevents consumers from purchasing commodities that *they* wish to buy, while goods that everybody wants, such as sanitation, roads, street lighting, are best provided by private enterprise. Disadvantaged groups, for example the elderly, the unemployed and the disabled, should be catered for by charity since state provision is invariably wasteful and open to abuse (Hoffman, 1995: 117).

It is not only the 'positive' functions of the state that ought to be 'privatised'. As far as modern-day free market anarchists are concerned, the market should take over the state's 'negative' role as well. Rothbard contends that people could insure themselves against bodily assault in the same way that they currently insure their possessions against theft. Aggrieved parties could then seek compensation and redress for injury through private tribunals, with the free market ensuring that arbitrators or judges with the best record in settling disputes would be hired.

But how would these judgements be enforced? Recalitrants who refused to abide by tribunal decisions would be subject to boycott and ostracism, and in more serious cases guards and police could be hired to defend injured parties and enforce judgments. People who refused to comply with judgments could be placed in private prisons, and aggrieved individuals might decide (with the help of friends and relatives) to retaliate in person. Rothbard describes the state as 'the great legalized and socially legitimated channel of all manner of social crime', and getting rid of the state would strengthen the 'good' in human nature and discourage the bad (Hoffman, 1995: 118). But humans remain possessive individualists by nature, and it is this assumption that leads the libertarian thinker, Robert Nozick, in his classic work *Anarchy, State, and Utopia* (1974) to make the case for the minimal state.

Nozick's argument is interesting because he seeks to construct his non-anarchist case on individualist anarchist principles. He argues that individuals have natural rights, and their goods and bodies are protected by private protective associations. However, unlike Rothbard and the free market anarchists, he accepts that through competition one of the protective associations will emerge as dominant, and when it protects all who live in its domain, whether they pay privately or not, it then becomes a 'minimal state'.

Some form of government seems to be essential if the problem of 'externalities' or 'spillovers', as they are called, are to be dealt with. Negative externalities arise when, for example, a factory pollutes the environment and the cost that results is much less to the individual than to society at large. Some kind of collective association is needed to bring the offending individual to book, and make him change his ways. But the principle of the minimal state is also necessary to tackle positive externalities as in a situation in which some, but not all, households in a neighbourhood pay for the protection of a policing agency. However, the presence of a policing agency may have a deterrent effect from which *all* households benefit, and premium payers, indignant at the fact that they are paying for services from which 'free riders' benefit, withdraw from the scheme, which then collapses.

But how does Nozick justify the services of a minimal state that applies to all? Who funds such a service? Nozick argues that a minimal state emerges in a way that violates no one's rights in the process. But how is the dominant protection agency that becomes the minimal state to exist without violating the rights of its competitors? Nozick's argument is that these competitive agencies are compensated because the minimal state provides protective services free of charge. But what happens if the agencies do not accept the monopolistic role of the minimal state? People are being compensated whether they like it or not, so that it is difficult to see how the minimal state avoids compulsion.

Biography — Murray N. Rothbard (1926–95)

Educated in New York City, and in 1945 studied at Columbia University. His doctoral thesis (1956) was on Welfare Economics and from then on there followed a steady stream of publications.

In 1965 (to 1968) he edited *Left and Right*, and published a biography on the Austrian free marketeer, Ludwig von Mises. He was particularly interested in the problem of economic depression, and in 1970 he wrote a book exposing what he called 'The Hoover Myth'. He produced a Libertarian Manifesto, entitled *For a New Liberty,* which was published in 1973. He also wrote on the US colonies in the seventeenth century (1975) and the first half of the eighteenth century (1976), and complained of Nozick's 'Immaculate Conception of the State'. He edited the *Journal of Libertarian Studies* through to 1995, and published a major work in 1982, *The Ethics of Liberty.* He was made a Distinguished

Professor of Economics at the University of Nevada, Las Vegas, describing Karl Marx in 1990 as a religious eschatologist.

In all, he wrote 25 books and thousands of articles and Volumes One and Two of his history of economic thought appeared just after his death.

He was devoutly anti-socialist as well as being anti-statist, and in 1993 he declared that 'in an age of galloping statism, the classical liberal, the advocate of the free market, has an obligation to carry the struggle to all levels of society'.

He had been bitterly opposed to Roosevelt's New Deal. He identified with the Confederates, the anti-federalists, and objected to taxation. Indeed he argued that the taxing power defines the state in the same way that theft defines a robber. The only civil rights are property rights. He died in New York in 1995.

Exercise

You are walking down the street when someone attacks you. Since you are living in a stateless society of an anarchist kind there are no public order offences, since everything has been privatised. There is, however, a tribunal to which you can turn in order to sue the person who assaulted you, for compensation, and this you are determined to do.

A number of problems face you:

- The person who attacked you obviously does not regard you as a fellow human being who deserves respect.

- Will he attend the tribunal hearings and pay up if the ruling goes against him?

- What kind of pressures can be brought to bear upon this person to ensure that he cooperates? The tribunal has officials and you know where this person lives, but they have no powers to compel the person to attend.

- The individual does have friends and family. Can they be relied upon to pressurise him to attend?

Moreover, once this compulsion has been justified, this is a principle capable of infinite extension. After all, if the provision of protection is deemed too 'risky' for competing agencies, why could not one argue, say, that the provision of low-cost housing or accessible medical services are too 'risky' to be left to private agencies? The New Liberals of the late nineteenth century showed just how painlessly the notion of 'protection' can be broadened. Will people feel 'secure' if they are destitute and have no job? Are contracts really respected if the rich invade the security of the poor? Once you have the state, a consistent free market anarchist could argue, how do you stop it from expanding?

Pressures to conform can only really be successful when everyone is, broadly speaking, in the same boat and can change places. There has to be a sense of common interest – freedom *and equality* – and if we begin with an order in which possessive individualism has divided society, how do we move to a condition of equality without regulation and compulsion, and even – horror of horrors – a role for government? Indeed, Marshall argues that 'anarcho-capitalists' should not be called anarchists at all (1993: 565).

Anti-capitalist Anarchists: Proudhon, Bakunin and Kropotkin

Proudhon was certainly a socialist, although he objected to communism on the grounds that it subordinates the individual to the collectivity (Marshall, 1993: 238). It is the unequal distribution of property that creates disorder, but the answer, as he saw it, was 'mutualism' – a system that avoided the vices of both private property and collective ownership, and was based upon exchange and credit. Exchange would occur through associations that calculated the necessary labour time involved in a product. People could start businesses by borrowing from a mutual credit bank, and this economic reorganisation would make the state redundant. In Proudhon's view, parliamentary democracy is futile and counter-productive – 'Universal suffrage is counter revolution' is one of his many celebrated dictums (Marshall, 1993: 244).

Proudhon aroused the wrath of Marx, who wrote his *Poverty of Philosophy* against Proudhon's *Philosophy of Poverty*. Marx objected to Proudhon's opposition to political involvement and trade unionism, and regarded his principles of justice and equality as woefully unhistorical. Proudhon's rejection of liberal principles of government meant that he regarded all forms of the state as anathema. He was also strongly nationalistic, patriarchal, and for a period supported the autocratic Emperor Napoleon III who suspended parliamentary politics. Proudhon popularised the view that anarchy stood for order – despite the frequent use of the word as a synonym for chaos – and he is widely regarded as the father of anarchism.

Influenced by Proudhon but strongly collectivist in orientation was the Russian anarchist Bakunin. Bakunin declares with an anti-Hobbesian fervour that 'man is born into society, just as ant is born into an ant-hill and bee into its hive' (Marshall, 1993: 291). The analogy with nature is important for Bakunin, since he takes the view that sociability and the desire to revolt is *instinctive*. It is both universal, and stronger among some rather than others. Bakunin took the view that the instinct for revolt was particularly strong among the Latins and the Slavs, and particularly weak among Germanic peoples. He saw revolution as a violent process, and what Marshall calls his 'apocalyptic fantasies' (1993: 306) manifest themselves in his belief that to create is to destroy. This slogan reappears during the May events – the student rebellion – in 1968 in Paris, and Berki notes that Bakunin's ideas became very fashionable in the 1970s in Western libertarian socialist circles (1975: 84).

Bakunin clashed with Marx in the First International and he was expelled in 1872. Nevertheless, although he and the 'authoritarian' Marx disagreed over strategy, he greatly admired Marx's critique of capital, and he was opposed not simply to the repressive hierarchy of the state but to the inequalities and exploitation identified with capitalism. He was, however, passionately opposed to Marx's notion of the workers becoming a ruling class and having to control a transitional state. The workers' state, he insisted, would be nothing but a barracks; a regime where working men and women are regimented. We will have 'despotic rule over the toiling masses by a new, numerically small aristocracy of genuine or sham scientists. The people . . . will be wholly regimented into one common herd of governed people. Emancipation indeed!' (Maximoff, ed., 1953: 287). Not only was Bakunin sceptical about the 'authority' of science, but he regarded religion and the notion of God as inherently statist and authoritarian.

Yet Bakunin argued the case for a secret association in which a revolutionary general staff would serve as intermediaries 'between the revolutionary idea and the instincts of the people', and this presumably accounts for his temporary attraction to the notorious Nechaev, a nihilist, terrorist and a man of no scruples. Against one's will, declared Bakunin, one is obliged to use 'force, cunning and deception' (Marshall, 1993: 282–4). Bakunin was hugely influential. Not only did he make an enormous impact upon French labour, Italian revolutionaries and, as we shall see, the socialist movement in Spain, but his anti-capitalism attracted support among those who espoused what was called anarcho-syndicalism.

Bertrand Russell has referred to syndicalism as 'the anarchism of the market place' (Berki, 1975: 87) and it focuses on the role of industrial workers who are to organise themselves into revolutionary syndicates, making 'war on the bosses' and not bothering with politics (Marshall, 1993: 441). The general strike is seen as the best weapon for ushering in the new order. Syndicates should take on social functions as the germ of the stateless, socialist society. But not all anarchists agreed with syndicalism. Emma Goldman feared that syndicalism trampled upon the rights of the individual by accepting a principle of majority rule, while the Italian Malatesta saw syndicalism simply as one of many means to achieve anarchist ends (Marshall, 1993: 444).

The contrast between Kropotkin and Bakunin is striking indeed. Although they were both Russian and both influenced by Marx's critique of capitalism, Kropotkin had great respect for science and was an accomplished geographer. Kropotkin espoused the ideal of a federal and decentralised society with the land and factories owned by the producers. He was sympathetic to syndicalism and argued that the great gains in the past had been made by the force of popular revolution, not through 'an evolution created by an elite' (Marshall, 1993: 317).

Anarchism must proceed with the method of the natural scientists. Mutual aid was far more important to the evolution of the species than mutual struggle. The species that cooperates the most is most likely to survive. Humans are by nature social and moral, and the greatest individual development comes through practising the 'highest communist sociability'. The socialist notion of a 'people's state' – here Kropotkin agreed with Bakunin – is 'as great a danger to liberty as any form of autocracy' (Marshall, 1993: 321–6). Whereas Bukunin saw distribution as linked to the performance of work, Kropotkin also stressed need: production and distribution are integrated in communal enterprises so as to meet the physical and cultural needs of all (Vincent, 1995: 133).

He was offered a cabinet position (which he turned down) in the Provisional Government of Kerensky after the overthrow of Tsarism in 1917, and was bitterly critical both of the Bolshevik Revolution (he sent letters to Lenin in vain) and the tactics adopted after the Revolution. Kropotkin called himself a communist anarchist; Bakunin preferred to see himself as a collectivist, while Proudhon regarded himself as a mutualist; but all were critical of capitalism, and all saw anarchism as a solution to the kind of inequality generated by a capitalist society.

How to read:

Bakunin's *God and the State*

This is a relatively short work and therefore the whole book should be read. Of course, the arguments are presented in a fairly jumbled fashion, since Bakunin moves from philosophy to theology to politics in a very unsystematic way. It is important to suspend criticisms in the face of Bakunin's very strong language in order to try and grasp, as sympathetically as possible, what he is arguing. It is true that Bakunin dismisses religion and idealism as inexplicable stupidity, but it is important (however tempting) not to adopt the same dogmatic tone against Bakunin. The link between religion and the state has been acknowledged by many political thinkers, even if they see something positive where Bakunin sees only the negative. The challenge is to think of condemning slavery and oppression in ways that are more effective than Bakunin's celebrated polemic. His analysis of science, its strengths and weaknesses, raises important points that need an answer. Read the book critically but sympathetically!

Biography — Pierre-Joseph Proudhon (1809–65)

Born in Besançon near the Swiss border from a peasant background. He went to the best school in the town but when his father became a bankrupt he was forced to drop out of school, and in 1827 he became a printer's apprentice.

Proudhon developed an extensive knowledge of Christian doctrine but this had the effect of making him an atheist who identified God with tyranny and property. In 1838 he won a scholarship to the Academy of Besançon. After winning a prize for an essay for the *Sunday Observance,* he wrote his *What is Property?* in which he espoused anarchy as 'the true form of government' and developed his famous paradox, 'Property is Theft'. His target was large-scale property and collectivism, and although he was prosecuted for his *Warning to Property Owners* that followed in 1842, he was acquitted on the grounds that the book was too complicated for ordinary people to understand!

He became interested in dialectial philosophy, went to Paris in 1844–5 where he clashed with Marx – whom he described as 'the tapeworm of socialism' – and published his two-volume *System of Economic Contradictions* in 1846. He described communists as 'fanatics of state power'. He issued a manifesto in 1848, having being elected as a deputy to parliament.

After Napoleon's *coup,* he was sent to prison for three years. Here he wrote *Confessions of a Revolutionary,* but his greatest work on ethics, *Justice in the Revolution and Church* (1858), brought him another three-year sentence. He fled to Belgium, where he wrote about war and art, and after his return he urged abstention in the presidential elections of 1863. Although he became increasingly conservative, espousing nationalism, patriarchy and anti-Semitism, he retained great influence over French workers, and his followers were the largest group to support the Paris Commune six years after his death.

Biography — Michael Bakunin (1814–76)

Born north-west of Moscow, Bakunin was the son of a retired diplomat who had liberal sympathies. At 15, he was sent to the Artillery School at St Petersburg. He was posted to a brigade in Poland but resigned from the army in 1836 in order to teach philosophy in Moscow.

Influenced by Fichte and Hegel, Bakunin went to Berlin in 1840 and joined the Young Hegelians. He travelled to Zürich where Weitling, a German communist, made a deep impact upon him. In Paris, he met Marx in 1844 but preferred Proudhon. Expelled from Paris under Russian pressure – he advocated the independence of Poland from Russia – he took part in the French Revolution of 1848 and wrote a fiery *Appeal to Slavs* in Prague in the same year. He participated in the insurrection in Dresden in 1849. Captured by Prussian troops, he was eventually deported to Russia and spent eight years in prison. When Alexander II became Tsar in 1855 Bakunin was banished to Siberia, where he married and remained until 1861.

When he moved to Italy, he began to advocate social rather than national revolution, and developed his theory of anarchism. He established a secret revolutionary brotherhood, hierarchical and centralised, while calling for the destruction of the state and for the organisation of society by free association and federation. He joined the First International but in 1869 clashed with Marx, who accused him of trying to set up an International within the International. He worked for a short time with Nechaev, a Russian nihilist, and in so doing damaged the reputation of anarchism. He hoped that the defeat of Napoleon in the Franco-Prussian war of 1870 would lead to a French uprising, and he was involved in the short-lived insurrection in Lyon.

Bakunin was enthusiastic about the Paris Commune of 1872 and wrote his first and last book, *The Knouto-German Empire and the Social Revolution* between 1870 and 1872.

| Biography | **Peter Kropotkin (1842–1921)** |

Born into an aristocratic family. His father was an officer in the imperial army, and Kropotkin attended the most select military academy in Russia. He then became a military administrator in Eastern Siberia, concluding in his close observations of the natural world that cooperation is the most important factor in evolution.

It was in Siberia that Kropotkin became an anarchist. He returned to St Petersburg in 1867 and enthusiastically welcomed the Paris Commune in 1871. His views were confirmed by Marx's handling of the dispute with Bakunin in the First International. For two years he worked closely with a populist group called the Chaikovsky circle, publishing a manifesto in 1873 entitled *Must We Occupy Ourselves with the Ideal of a Future System?* He was imprisoned for three years but escaped and wrote a number of pamphlets and helped set up the journal *Le Révolté.*

In 1882 he was sentenced to five years' imprisonment by the French authorities, but was released in 1886 following an international outcry. The following year he wrote *In Russian and French Prisons,* having settled in London. He was active in anarchist politics and had a high reputation as a scientist. He opposed indiscriminate violence but was not a pacifist. In 1892 he published *The Conquest of Bread* in Paris, and seven years later his *Memoirs of a Revolutionist.*

Kropotkin supported Britain and France during World War I. He returned to Russia after the revolution, and although he was opposed to the 'dictatorial tendencies' of the Bolsheviks he argued against foreign intervention. When he died he was offered a state funeral, but his family refused.

The Argument So Far . . .

Godwin believed that individuals should be allowed to express freely private judgements.

Stirner thought that individuals were sovereign and form a voluntary and spontaneous union of like-minded beings.

Rothbard was a free marketeer who took the view that the market could replace the state.

Nozick argued that a state was needed, but a minimal state that would protect property and enforce contracts.

The following were not only against the state, but against capitalism as well:

Proudhon believed in 'mutualism' – a scheme that allowed individuals to exchange goods and secure credit without the need for political involvement or trade unions.

Bakunin argued that humans should work together collectively and they had a natural instinct for revolt and solidarity.

Kropotkin believed that a communist society was possible through mutual cooperation and revolution.

Republican Spain and the Anarchist Experience

The Spanish Republic has become a valuable historical laboratory for trying to understand anarchism because this is the only example in the twentieth century in which anarchism succeeded in constructing a new society, at least in particular regions and for a few years. As Thomas comments, 'the Spanish Anarchists are the only Anarchists in European history to have made any mark upon events' (1965: 279).

The liberal tradition was weak in Spain. During the nineteenth century the Church and the army had intervened to prevent or paralyse a liberal constitution and this had strengthened the widespread scepticism towards conventional political processes. Anarchist strength centred in Barcelona in the north where it was reinforced by separatist sentiments among the Catalans (and took the form of anarcho-syndicalism), and it was also strong among the impoverished peasantry in the south. When a Spanish Communist Party was formed in 1921 the anarchists were four times more numerous than the socialists. In Spain the mass of workers and peasants had followed Bakunin when he broke with Marx. The Confedacion National del Trajbajo (CNT) had over a million members at the time of World War I, and in 1933 the anarchist weekly *Tierra y Libertad* declared grandly:

> Workers! Do not vote! The vote is a negation of your personality . . . All the politicians are enemies . . . we need neither state nor government . . . Do not be concerned whether the Right or the Left emerge triumphant from this farce . . . Parliament . . . is a filthy house of prostitution . . . Destroy the ballots! Destroy the ballot boxes . . . hack off the heads of the ballot supervisors as well as of the candidates . . . (Thomas, 1965: 95)

One could well argue that revolutions do not have to be violent but this was not how Spanish anarchists saw the issue. The communists had, following the Seventh Comintern Congress, thrown their weight behind the idea of a Popular Front (an alliance of liberal and left-wing forces), and in 1936 the left won a substantial electoral victory on a programme of radical reform. Franco, with the army mostly loyal to him, led a rebellion. The socialists (and communists) were strong in Madrid but the anarchists retained control of Barcelona where all large industries passed to the CNT, and expropriation was considered the rule. Large numbers of people belonging to the old order were killed, and churches were destroyed. In some places money was replaced by coupons, while in Andalusia in the south, where the anarchists were also strong, each town acted on its own responsibility. By 1937 some 3 million people were living in rural collectives.

The anarchists adopted military methods of organisation, and Miller cites Borkenau's comment that in one of the villages of Aragon the agrarian revolution was almost the automatic consequence of executions (1974: 106–7). In September 1936 the anarchists entered the Catalan government calling it the Revolutionary Defence Council so as to avoid giving the impression 'to their already alarmed extremist followers' that they had joined a real government (Thomas, 1965: 367). Marshall argues that in so doing they had started down the slippery slide to parliamentary participation and this meant sacrificing the social revolution to the war against Franco (1993: 461).

As the crisis continued, the anarchists entered the government in Madrid, with the anarchist Garcia Oliver becoming Minister of Justice and the CNT recognising the republican state as 'an instrument of struggle' (Thomas, 1965: 404). The defence of this action by the CNT's daily paper is regarded by Marshall as 'an unparalleled bout of dissimulation' (1993: 465). Oliver, 'for all his devotion to Bakunin', proceeded to establish a new code of state laws and defended the need for iron discipline in the popular army (Thomas, 1965: 470; Marshall, 1993: 465). In late April 1937 a civil war between the anarchists and the communist-backed government broke out in

Orwell comments that:

I had come to Spain with some notion of writing newspaper articles, but I had joined the militia almost immediately because at that time and in that atmosphere it seemed the only conceivable thing to do. The Anarchists were still in virtual control of Catalonia and the revolution was in full swing . . . it was the first time that I had ever been in a town where the working class was in the saddle. Practically every building of any size had been seized by the workers and was draped with red flags or the black and red flag of the Anarchists; every wall was scrawled with the hammer and sickle and with initials of the revolutionary parties; almost every church had been gutted and its images burnt . . . Every shop and café had an inscription saying it had been collectivised . . . Waiters and shop-walkers looked you in the face and treated you as an equal. Servile and ceremonial forms of speech had temporarily disappeared . . . There were no private motor cars, they had all been commandeered . . . And it was the aspect of the crowds that was the queerest thing of all. In outward appearance it was a town in which the wealthy classes had practically ceased to exist. (Orwell, 2001: 32)

Barcelona, and some 500 were killed. Anarchist influence ebbed away, and although the CNT continued to collaborate with the government they no longer took even nominal responsibility for its actions (Thomas, 1965: 558).

On 18 March 1938 the CNT signed an agreement with the socialist Union General Trabajadores (UGT) to subject industry to central economic planning – collectivisation everywhere was giving way to state control (Thomas, 1965: 671). In Madrid, the anarchists backed attacks on the communists, putting the blame for the perilous military position on the Popular Front government (Thomas, 1965: 750). By the end of March, Franco's victory was secured.

Influences and Impact:

Spanish Civil War

What does the civil war reveal about anarchism as an ideology? Leaving aside its fierce opposition to Marxism that had already been evident in the nineteenth century, the civil war points to a paradox at the heart of anarchism. In order to be effective, the militias had to adopt more conventional methods of organisation and the anarchists had to agree to enter into governments, trying in the Catalan instance to disguise the character of this institution. This points to a wider predicament. Anarchism is only likely to flourish in deeply divided conditions. A revolutionary situation inevitably throws up counter-revolutionary forces so that anarchists are likely to find themselves in positions of power in civil war-type situations. Dramatic changes are called for, but how is it possible to carry these through without organisation and a state? It takes a state to get rid of a state – that in essence seems to be the lesson of the events in Spain.

This argument conflicts with Marshall's view that the defeat of the anarchist movement in Spain arose from the failure to carry through the social revolution. The latter was sacrificed for the war effort, and if this and the seizure of power by the communists had not taken place the outcome would have been very different. The failure, he suggests, was not a failure of anarchist theory and tactics (1993: 467).

The Problem of Violence

The question of violence is linked to the question of transition – how gradual is the movement towards a stateless society to be? Can a dramatic transformation of society take place bit by bit?

Godwin believed that it would take considerable time before society became sufficiently enlightened to adopt anarchist institutions, and Marshall has suggested that different types of anarchist organisation could be taken to secure progression towards the anarchist goal. Thus Proudhon's mutualism (involving the regulation of different private producers) could give way to Bakunin's collectivism (where people are rewarded according to their work), which in turn might yield to the more egalitarian idea of Kropotkin's communism where each is rewarded according to their need (Hoffman, 1995: 124).

It is true that many anarchists have seen that violence involves an intolerable conflict between ends and means. The Russian anarchist and novelist, Leo Tolstoy (1828–1910) rejected all forms of violence, whether revolutionary or statist: is there any difference, he asked, between killing a revolutionary and killing a policeman? 'The difference is between cat-shit and dog-shit . . . I don't like the smell of either' (cited in Marshall, 1993: 377). Gandhi, influenced by Tolstoy, also espoused a militant pacifism. But Carter argues that there are elements within anarchism that are peculiarly receptive to violence. The belief that many anarchists held, that a golden age might be realised through one apocalyptic outburst, an all-embracing revolution, can only encourage what Bakunin called the 'poetry of destruction' (Carter, 1978: 337).

Paris Commune
box, p. 221

Part of this 'utopianism' is the shunning of political organisation in its conventional form, for it might be argued – as we saw with the anarchists in Spain – that it is worse to cast a ballot than fire a bullet. If constitutional procedures are identified with 'statist' liberalism, then the alternative may have to be despotism and violence. It is revealing that Robert Michels turned from anarchism to authoritarianism, arguing that because the German Social Democratic Party was too hierarchical, all organisation is oligarchical in character. One sympathetic commentator has argued ruefully that 'a streak of pathological violence' runs through anarchism (Hoffman, 1995: 126). We see how after the crushing of the Paris Commune in 1871 many anarchists resorted to a 'propaganda by deed' – dramatic action designed to shake the masses out of their passivity – and these propagandist deeds often degenerated into acts of terror. The agonised slogan of radical black youth in the South African townships in the 1980s – 'liberation before education' – echoes comments by Italian followers of Garibaldi and Proudhon in the 1870s. A belief that everything is right that is not 'legal' can easily lead to violence even if it is justified as a way of avenging wrongs against the people, inspiring fear in the enemy and highlighting the evil practices of the state (Miller, 1974: 98–9).

Marshall quotes a passage from the CNT constitution printed on the membership card which states that 'the adversary does not discuss: he acts' (1993: 457), and even Kropotkin, whose personal life is often described in saint-like terms, displays what Marshall calls 'an uncomfortable mixture of quietism and aggressive elements'. Indeed, at one point in his life, Kropotkin supports the arguments of the anarcho-syndicalist Sorel that violence is the revolutionary whirlwind that energises 'sluggish hearts' (Hoffman, 1995: 126).

The problem of abolishing the state and authority seems to us to lead inevitably to the resort to violence; the perpetuation of the state in a new form, and a legacy of division and mistrust. But how are people to free themselves when they are oppressed? Oppression arises when a person is deprived of material and social resources and lacks esteem. But how is this emancipation to be secured without organisation? Marshall argues that anarchists only reject authoritarian organisation, but it could be argued that all organisation requires some form of hierarchy and leadership – the very political qualities that anarchists reject (Hoffman, 1995: 124).

Miller cites the sad reflections of Emma Goldman as she compares the weaknesses of Russian anarchists when set against the organisational strengths of the Bolsheviks. The work of the anarchists, she remarks, 'would have been of infinitely greater value had they been better organized' (Miller, 1974: 97–8). But she fails to ask herself whether these weaknesses were a product of anarchist theory itself. What are anarchists to do if the masses fail to rise in revolt? Two responses are possible. Either anarchists simply wait (as Godwin seems to argue) until the spirit of rational enlightenment takes root in the minds of the masses, or (as in Bakunin's case) the people need a helping hand. He advocates, as we have seen, an 'invisible dictatorship' that seems flagrantly to contradict anarchist ideals.

Certainly it is difficult to see how anarchists can combine revolutionary effectiveness without resort to force, given the fact that politics in terms of organisation, representation, leadership and compromise are ruled out in terms of the theory adopted. This is a problem not only for left-wing anarchists, but it also afflicts anarcho-capitalists who see the market as a source of freedom, but have the problem (among others) of tackling those who have vested interests in perpetuating concentrations of state power. Rothbard notes that anarchists have to contemplate 'the extremely difficult course of a revolution against a power with all the guns in its hands' (Hoffman, 1995: 124).

Despite Marshall's argument that the civil war in Spain demonstrated the strengths and not the weaknesses of anarchist theory, it is difficult not to see that event pointing to the fact that anarchists in practice can only operate in contradiction to their own theory. Those who see anarchism as having a built-in propensity to violence, whatever the pacifist claims of some of its adherents, are right. The theory cannot be understood without seeing a contradiction between ends and means.

Anarchism and the New Social Movements

Anarchism continues to be influential, with adherents such as Herbert Read stressing the relevance of anarchism to the struggle for peace, secularism, a respect for art and the democratising of education. Comfort argues the case for sexual freedom, while Paul Goodman before his death in 1972 influenced many who took part in the counter-culture movements of the 1960s and 1970s. The relevance of anarchism to green movements and a concern about the deterioration of the urban and rural environment has been memorably stressed in the work of Murray Bookchin. Nature, he argues, is a 'complex of life', charged with ethical meaning. Nature is essentially creative, directive, mutualistic and fecund (Marshall, 1993: 605–6). This confirms the sociability and decency of humans. Without anarchism, there will be ecological disaster.

Bookchin's work is particularly important, because many of his positions have been adopted in the new social movements by people who may be unfamiliar with anarchism and would not regard themselves as anarchists. The new social movements concern themselves with a wide array of causes – animal rights and ecology; peace and women's rights; road building and private transport; to name just some. New social movements are characterised, in our view, by a general anti-authoritarianism which sees conventional politics as stifling and treacherous; by a concern with breaking down barriers between the personal and political, and adopting a style of campaigning that unites ends and means and links enjoyment to efficiency. All this suggests that particular anarchist ideas have made a huge impact, even if anarchism considered as a comprehensive philosophy and systematic movement has not.

Green parties, such as that in Germany, have enjoyed some electoral success, and have built into their procedures a libertarian distrust of authoritarianism, and what are regarded as the dangers inherent in conventional political organisation. But at the same time they have not ignored parliament or the state, and they have treated anarchism less as a dogma and more as a set of values, some of which are more relevant and valid than others.

The philosophy of direct action – that laws and private property are not sacrosanct – stems from an anarchist suspicion of the state. When people in Britain refused to pay their poll tax in the 1980s or occupied military and nuclear bases they were acting according to anarchist values – understood in the sense of particular attitudes that may be appropriate for particular situations. Writing to your MP is all very well – but much more immediate action may be called for. A commitment to social justice; a belief in the worthiness of human nature; adherence to equality; a dislike of repressive hierarchy; a concern with the destruction of the environment; anxiety about poverty in the so-called Third World – these and many other movements are inspired by parts of anarchism, though not by anarchist philosophy as a whole.

Classical anarchism is seen as being in the same boat as classical Marxism: rigid, dogmatic, old-fashioned, weak on issues of women, children's rights and the environment – too concerned with ideological rectitude and theoretical 'rigour'. Anarchists often link their dislike for large organisations to a belief that the market is corrupting and capitalism unfair. Turner argues that the natural supporters of anarchist values are those who are excluded from consumerist society and who see politicians as an elite and incapable of engineering real change. He speaks of anarchism having a more receptive and permanent home among an underclass that might include 'disaffected youth, the long term unemployed and inner-city dwellers in perpetual poverty' (1993: 32). Anarchism and anarchist values are clearly the price society pays for a conventional politics that fails to ameliorate inequality and ecological damage.

The Problem of Organisation and Relationships

It has been said that anarchism 'owes more to conventional liberalism than some of its adherents are willing to admit' (Hoffman, 1995: 113). It is not only philosophical and free market anarchists who embody the problems of the liberal tradition, so too do the anti-capitalist anarchists. The problem is that even when liberalism is militantly opposed liberal values are turned inside out – they are inverted, but never meaningfully transcended, or moved beyond.

Marshall captures the problem in a graphic way when he criticises Bookchin and Kropotkin for committing the naturalistic fallacy of deriving an 'is' from an 'ought'. 'There is', he argues, 'no logical connection to make us move from fact to value' (1993: 620). But this is a misuse of the notion of a 'naturalistic fallacy'. The 'naturalistic fallacy' should, it seems to us, refer to an erroneous belief in the timelessness of nature and of human links with nature. It is however quite another thing to argue that we cannot move from facts to value. This is a positivist (or empiricist) dictum that arises because thinkers cannot see that facts themselves embody relationships. Indeed, it is the relational nature of facts that gives them their evaluative or normative content. Thus, the fact that there are many women lawyers but few women judges tells us something about the **relationship** between men and women in our society, and therefore it would be erroneous to assume that such a fact has no ethical implications.

Biography   Murray Bookchin (1921–)

Born in New York, Bookchin entered the communist youth movement in the 1930s. Deeply involved in organising activities around the Spanish civil war (he was too young to participate directly), he drifted away from the communists because of their role in Spain and the occurrence of the Moscow trials. After the Stalin–Hitler pact of September 1939, he was formally expelled from the Young Communist League for 'Trotskyist–anarchist deviations'.

After returning from service in the US Army during World War II, Bookchin participated in the great General Motors strike of 1946, but he began to question traditional Marxist ideas about the 'hegemonic' role of the industrial proletariat. In the late 1940s and early 1950s Bookchin wrote agitational literature that opposed not only nuclear weapons but also the peaceful uses of the atom because of radioactive fallout. In 1956 he demanded US intervention on behalf of the uprising in Hungary against the Soviet Union.

He started publishing articles on ecological issues, and in his *Our Synthetic Environment* he calls for a decentralised society and the use of alternative energy sources as part of an ecological solution. *Ecology and Revolutionary Thought* (1964) argues for a political marriage of anarchism and ecology, while *Towards a*

Liberatory Technology (1965) asserts that alternative technologies could provide people with the free time necessary to engage in civic self-management and a democratic body politic. These articles laid the groundwork for the body of ideas that Bookchin called social ecology.

At the same time, in the 1960s, Bookchin was deeply involved in both the counter-culture and New Left and worked to fuse the two movements. Bookchin's essays from the 1960s have been anthologised in *Post-scarcity Anarchism*. In the late 1960s he taught at the Alternative University in New York, and later at City University of New York. In 1974 he co-founded the Institute for Social Ecology and became its director; in the same year he began teaching at Ramapo College of New Jersey, where he eventually became a full professor and retired in 1981 with emeritus status.

Bookchin has also written extensively on urban issues, and his 'libertarian municipalism' is a politics based upon the recovery or creation of direct-democratic popular assemblies on municipal, neighbourhood and town levels. He has continued to publish, and is currently working on a three-volume history of popular movements in the classical revolutions, called *The Third Revolution*.

This argument suggests that Marshall, an enthusiastic anarchist, is still committed to a liberal methodology, and to a liberal opposition to understanding individuals in terms of the relationships that identify them. We see this position in anarchist attitudes to organisation. Marshall may insist that he does not reject organisation per se, but only authoritarian organisation. The fact remains, however, that he accepts a philosophical standpoint which makes it impossible to see organisation as deriving from the relational character of humans. Even anarchists such as Kropotkin and Bookchin fail to go along with the full implications of seeing humans as relational beings. By arguing that anarchism is based upon 'a mechanistic explanation of all phenomena' (Marshall, 1993: 318), Kropotkin accepts a static view of humanity – to which (as does Bakunin) he ascribes an 'instinct' for sociability. His notion of the natural sciences is positivist and he appears to argue that because humans have evolved from nature they are simply the same as other natural beings. The specificity of human relationships is not understood.

While Bookchin does stress that humans have a 'second nature' – different from but linked to their biology and their 'first nature' – it is revealing that he calls his blending of anarchism and ecology an 'ecotopia'. He proclaims that 'our Science is Utopia' without seeing that (traditionally defined) utopias 'on their own' are static and ahistorical, and postulate some kind of final end of history (Marshall, 1993: 621). This emphasises the ideal at the expense of the facts and ignores the dynamic and fluid nature of the real world. This abstract approach makes it impossible to account for relationships and the need for organisation – not simply to achieve a 'utopia' – but as an ongoing expression of human relationships.

The Problem of Hierarchy

Anarchists in general use the term 'hierarchy' in a negative way. But hierarchy itself is part and parcel of human relationships.

Turner notes the work of A.S. Neil, who believed that education was possible without any hierarchy. Neil was the founder of the 'free school' movement, whose designs for education modelled at his Summerhill school conformed to anarchist prescriptions. There were to be no compulsory lessons; no authority of teachers over pupils; an emphasis upon self-development rather than 'instruction'; no testing of knowledge against prescribed targets, and no need to attend anything (1993: 31).

p. 6

But while Summerhill school may have avoided authoritarianism, did it really avoid hierarchy as such? It is certainly true that the use of force in relationships is counter-productive and is incompatible with the nature of relationships themselves. Hence *repressive* hierarchy is inherently undesirable. But it does not follow from this that hierarchy in itself is wrong or oppressive. On the contrary, it exists in all relationships. The term 'authority' can be taken to assume persuasion and consent, but an authoritative relationship is one based on hierarchy. Surely when you go to a doctor you accept her 'authority', not because you are unwilling to question her advice, but because *in this situation* there is a hierarchy born of the fact that the doctor has a specialist knowledge of health that you lack. This is not a static hierarchy – you may become more knowledgeable yourself – nor is it a comprehensive hierarchy. If you are a motor mechanic the doctor may well come to you for help, and the hierarchy is reversed.

But, in our view, it is impossible to conceive of a relationship without hierarchy. Each party is different, and it is this difference that creates the hierarchical character of relationships. There is clearly a hierarchical relationship between parents and children. This does not mean that they are not equal, for equality, in our view, means sameness *and* difference. The hierarchy is fluid and interpenetrating: sometimes the parent teaches the child; on other occasions the parent learns from him. It is difficult not to conclude that anarchist opposition to hierarchy arises from what is essentially a liberal view that equality can only mean sameness, and that freedom is a spontaneity born of the complete absence of restraint – an abstraction that derives from the classical liberal view of individuals who 'originate' in a 'natural' world without constraint or relationship.

The Question of Self-determination and Constraint

Anarchists argue for self-determination and this is a valid objective to aim at. But it is misleading to imagine that self-determination, as with autonomy or emancipation (to take just two related concepts), is a condition that we 'finally' reach, for like the notion of 'perfection', emancipation would turn into a nightmare if it ever 'arrived'. For what would happen to those deemed unemancipated? They would inevitably be 'forced to be free'.

What makes emancipatory concepts absolute as well as relative is the fact that our relationships with other humans, as with our relationships with the wider world of nature, are continually changing. We are absolute in the sense that all humans are the same – they must relate to nature and to one another in order to survive. But we are also relative to one another. The way we relate depends upon the world we find ourselves in, and the world we construct, and this makes us different.

Not only are humans both absolute and relative in their rights, but we are agents whose freedom derives from the recognition and transformation of necessity. This is why we are both free and constrained at the same time, for this world of necessity constrains us. Marx and Mill use the term 'coercion' to embrace morality and circumstances, but we favour a narrower view of coercion: coercion involves the threat of credible force. The kind of pressures that arise from being in society is better conceived of as a constraint and these constraints arise out of relationships, and are part and parcel of the price we pay as social beings, who can only become conscious of our individuality through relationships with others.

It is crucial to make the distinction that anarchism fails to make, between force and constraint. Force disrupts relationships, because one party loses their subjectivity and becomes a mere 'thing'. Constraint on the other hand, while sometimes unpleasant, is unavoidable and a condition for freedom. It is not possible to be free without recognising and transforming the constraints that act upon us, and even the most spontaneous act can only succeed if it acknowledges and works to change a world of constraint. When Bakunin took part in the uprising in the French city of Lyon and proclaimed 'that the administrative and governmental machinery of the state' have been abolished (Marshall, 1993: 286), he learnt that it takes more than

Ideas and Perspectives:

Utopianism and Realism

Anarchists are right to see the state as problematic. But to look beyond the state, the state has to be presented in a way that is realistic. Why should we assume that if an idea is realistic it cannot also be utopian? Utopianism and realism need to be creatively combined, but this is only possible if one makes distinctions of a kind that break with the liberal tradition.

Of course, it is wrong to force a person to act against her will. But it does not follow from this that force can simply be abolished. The use of force as a way of addressing conflicts of interest can only be dispensed with when people have sufficient in common that they can 'change places'. An opposition to force under all circumstances constitutes utopianism without realism, for we need to work to create the conditions under which force becomes redundant.

Moreover, realism requires us to face the fact that relationships constrain as well as empower. This constraint becomes severe when used deliberately as a punishment, and although we would accept that the less of these kind of constraints the better, it is unrealistic to imagine that people can relate to one another and to the wider world of nature without some kind of constraint being employed and involved. Hence the attempt to eliminate force as a way of tackling conflicts is strengthened by the distinction between constraint and force. Society is inconceivable without constraint and hierarchy, and anarchists weaken their arguments against the state by refusing to accept this.

words to overthrow a despotic state and, unsurprisingly, the rising was speedily crushed. The point is that alliances must be formed; existing institutions utilised; the people must be prepared and feel that such an action is justified, and the forces of the opponent must be marginalised and neutralised – all the things which require organisation and the acknowledgement of constraints are crucial if a political action is to meet with hope of success.

Anarchism and the Distinction between State and Government

The distinction between force and constraint translates into the opposition between state and government, and by condemning both anarchists again leave themselves open to the charge that they are being utopian without at the same time being realistic.

Ch 1: The State, pp. 14–31

The distinction between state and government is a crucial one. Anarchists tend to regard the two as synonyms. Godwin finds that government is opposed to society. It is static and oppressive – 'the only perennial causes of the vices of mankind' – and looks towards its 'true euthanasia' (Marshall, 1993: 206–7). Kropotkin makes a distinction between state and government, but considers both equally oppressive and that both should be abolished. Representative government is no more than rule by the capitalists (Marshall, 1993: 325). It is not difficult to see that this negative view of government, as well as the state, is linked to a failure to distinguish between force and constraint.

Godwin saw public opinion as oppressive and as irresistible as whips and chains. Orwell is cited sympathetically as an anarchist who found Tolstoy's pacifism potentially coercive, while Gandhi's doctrine of non-violence has coercive overtones that Marshall sees as bullying and constituting a 'totalitarian danger' (Marshall, 1993: 650). It is one thing to warn (as J.S. Mill did) that public opinion can be intolerant and needlessly intrusive. But it is quite another to suggest that moral pressures are a kind of 'coercion' and as unacceptable as brute force. If the constraints imposed by Mill's natural penalties and the use of moral pressures are deemed authoritarian, then constitutionalism and the rule of law have to be rejected, even when these institutions operate in a purely governmental, as opposed to an oppressively statist, way (Hoffman, 1995: 127).

Government, it could be argued, is inherent in organisation and relationships. It involves the use of constraint in order to resolve conflicts that arise from the fact that each of us is different from the other. For this reason conflict is inevitable and so is government, but just as a sharp distinction needs to be drawn between constraint and force, so a distinction needs to be made between state and government. To link the state and government as twin enemies of freedom is to ignore the fact that stateless societies have governments, and that even in state-centred societies the role of government is positive and empowering. With the rise of new liberal and socialist administrations significant programmes of social reform have been introduced; the power of the trade unions has been strengthened; the health and security of the most vulnerable sections of society has been improved; and a modest redistribution of income and resources has been introduced. But these reforms are vulnerable and can be reversed, and force employed in an increasingly divisive way by the state. Indeed one radical theorist has protested that were the state to disappear overnight, 'there would be an orgy of unlimited repression and exploitation by capitalism', but this comment rests upon a confusion of state and government. It is crucial to see that many of the activities undertaken in the name of the state are not necessarily and intrinsically statist in character (Hoffman, 1995: 123).

Anarchist attacks on the 'welfare state' as bureaucratic and oppressive can only be legitimately described as *anti-statist* if they are able to show that the provision of welfare and security undermines self-development and is thus part and parcel of the state's exercise of force. If this cannot be shown, then the provision of welfare and security – to the extent that it is genuinely developmental – is governmental rather than statist in character. The existence of 'interference' and constraint is not in itself evidence of oppression since such attributes are inherent in all organisations and in relationships.

Ch 1: The State, pp. 14–31

Carter is right to argue that administration in itself does not require the use of violence (1978: 324), although, of course, administrators may act in a high-handed and undemocratic fashion and thus contribute to the alienation which causes the use of force, both by the opponents of the state and by the state itself. Nevertheless, we need to keep government and the state conceptually separate, since it is wrong and counter-productive to identify government with oppression, simply because it involves pressures and sanctions of a constraining kind. Without a distinction between state and government, it is impossible to move beyond the state.

Summary

Anarchism is often analysed as part of socialism, but anarchism is so distinctive that it deserves treatment in its own right. Philosophical anarchists are concerned with the autonomy of the individual as a theoretical problem, while free market anarchists argue the case for replacing the state with an unfettered market.

Anti-capitalist anarchists are critical of Marxism either because, as does Proudhon, they dislike collectivist solutions to the problem of inequality, or because, in the case of anarchists such as Bakunin and Kropotkin, they are unconvinced by the need for a dictatorship of the proletariat in the transformation of capitalism into communism. The Spanish civil war constitutes a veritably historical laboratory in understanding anarchism since anarchists were extremely influential during this period and their clashes with other sections of the left, and the tactics they adopted, are extremely instructive.

Anarchism is unable to handle the problem of violence, but it has played a significant role in the formation of new social movements. Anarchism runs into particular difficulty in its treatment of the problem of hierarchy and organisation. It is weakened through its failure to distinguish between state and government, and force and constraint.

Questions

1. Should those who seek to replace the market with the state be called 'anarchists'?
2. Discuss the proposition that the new social movements, such as the movement for peace, **environmentalism** and women's rights, embrace part of anarchism rather than anarchism as a whole.
3. What do anarchists understand by 'hierarchy' and does it interfere with the demands of political organisation?
4. What do you see as the lessons of the Spanish civil war?
5. Is the notion of a stateless society a mere anarchist fantasy?

References

Berki, R.N. (1975) *Socialism* London: Everyman.

Carter, A. (1978) 'Anarchism and Violence' in J. Pennock and J. Chapman (eds), *Anarchism* New York: New York University Press, 320–40.

Dahl, R. (1989) *Democracy and its Critics* New Haven, Conn. and London: Yale University Press.

Goodwin, B. (1997) *Using Political Ideas* 4th edn Chichester and New York *et al.*: John Wiley and Sons.

Hoffman, J. (1995) *Beyond the State* Cambridge: Polity Press.

Marshall, P. (1993) *Demanding the Impossible* London: Fontana.

Maximoff, G. (ed.) (1953) *The Political Philosophy of Bakunin* New York: Free Press.

Miller, D. (1974) *Anarchism* London: Dent.

Nozick, R. (1974) *Anarchy, State, and Utopia* New York: Basic Books.

Orwell, G. (2001) *Orwell in Spain* (ed. P. Davison) Harmondsworth: Penguin.

Thomas, H. (1965) *The Spanish Civil War* Harmondsworth: Penguin.

Turner, R. (1993) 'Anarchism: What is it?' *Politics Review* 3(1), 28–32.

Vincent, A. (1995) *Modern Political Ideologies* Oxford: Blackwell.

Further Reading

- Marshall *Demanding the Impossible* (referenced above) is a detailed and highly readable account of anarchist doctrines and personalities.

- Turner's short piece on 'Anarchism: What is it?' (referenced above) is very clear and comprehensive and raises the question as to why anarchists still continue to make an impact.

- Orwell's *Homage to Catalonia* (within *Orwell in Spain*, referenced above) provides a vivid account of the way in which the anarchists operated in Spain, and the difficulties under which they worked.

- Carter's piece on 'Anarchism and Violence' (referenced above) is both thoughtful and rigorous, and raises important theoretical problems within anarchism.

- Chapter 3 in Dahl's *Democracy and its Critics* (referenced above) contains an amusing and instructive dialogue between characters he calls 'Demo' and 'Anarch' that is both critical and fair.

- Shatz's edition of *The Essential Works of Anarchism* London, New York and Toronto: Bantam Books, 1971, contains extracts from classical and more recent anarchists so that you can read the arguments 'in the original'.

- A useful exposition of anarcho-capitalism can be found in Stone, C. (1978) 'Some Reflections on Arbitrating our Way to Anarchy' in J. Pennock and J. Chapman (eds), *Anarchism* New York: New York University Press.

Weblinks

This is very comprehensive. A1 & 2 are particularly valuable, as is A4 and some of A5: http://www.anarchistfaq.org

Used selectively, something of value here: http://www.anarchism.ws/

For anyone who wants a more detailed analysis of anarchism in Spain: http://www.struggle.ws/spaindx.html

Chapter 11

Nationalism

Introduction

Nationalism has been a powerful force in modern history. It arouses strong feelings – for some, nationalism is tantamount to racism, but for others nationalist sentiment creates solidarity and stability, which are preconditions for freedom. These two perspectives are informed by history: in its most extreme form nationalism was at the root of the genocidal policies of Nazi Germany, and yet it has also been the basis of liberation movements in such regions as Eastern Europe, Africa and Asia. The challenge for political theorists is to explain how the 'nation' can be a source of value and an object of allegiance. And this is indeed a challenge: most liberals (and many anarchists) hold that the *individual human being* is the ultimate source of value, and the individual has claims against collective entities, such as the nation; many socialists are collectivists, but for them it is *class*, or *humanity* as a whole, that is the proper object of concern.

Chapter Map

In this chapter we will:

- Outline the debate around the origins of the 'nation' and of **'nationalism'**.

- Discuss the relationship between nationhood and nationalism.

- Consider the ethical implications of nationalism by reference to the distinction between **civic nationalism** and ethnic nationalism.

- Analyse the role of nationalism in the work of two liberal thinkers (Mill and Herder), and in the work of Marx and Engels.

Mountains, Muesli, Cuckoo Clocks and Yodellers

Switzerland has an unusual citizenship law. It is based on three principles: (1) triple citizenship level; (2) *jus sanguinis*, or determination of citizenship through the family line, as distinct from *jus soli*, or determination of citizenship through place of birth; (3) prevention of statelessness. With regard to the first principle, every Swiss is a citizen of her commune of origin, her canton of origin, and of the Confederation. Children born to Swiss parents living abroad will lose their citizenship by the age of 22 unless they indicate to the authorities they wish to retain it, although 'reinstatement' is a possibility, especially in order to prevent statelessness.

The most controversial aspect of Swiss citizenship law is the rejection of *jus soli*: it is possible to be a third-generation resident and still be denied citizenship. Naturalisation requires approval by a local citizenship committee; individual applications may be put to a local referendum in which voting information includes pictures of the applicants. One native-born 'foreigner', 23-year-old Fatma Karademir, whose parents are Turkish, applied for citizenship through her local village citizenship committee, but was rejected and told she had to live another ten years in Switzerland before the committee could really judge her suitability for citizenship. She complains that longevity in the country counts for less than the answers she gives to the committee: 'They'll ask me if I can imagine marrying a Swiss boy . . . or if I like Swiss music, or who I'll support if Switzerland play Turkey at football – really stupid questions' ('Long Road to Swiss Citizenship', BBC website, 20 September 2004). In 2004 a proposal to ease the naturalisation process was defeated by 57 per cent to 43 per cent in a national referendum; a separate proposal to grant the right to citizenship to grandchildren of immigrants was defeated by 52 per cent to 48 per cent.

• Do you think the Swiss law is valid?

Nations and Nationalism

In the period from around 1850 to the start of World War I in 1914 there was a marked rise in popular nationalist consciousness across Europe, with the unification of Italy in 1861 and Germany in 1871, and the so-called 'scramble for Africa' pitting the European nations against one another on that continent, while a precarious balance of power was maintained within Europe. After its defeat in World War I the Austro-Hungarian Empire fragmented into 'new' nations such as Czechoslovakia and Hungary. There was much discussion of the right to national self-determination. But in the period after World War II there was less theoretical interest in nationalism, with ideological debate centred on the struggle between liberal capitalism and state socialism; this was despite the fact that it was a period of significant **nation** building in Africa and Asia in the wake of decolonisation. Since the dramatic events in Eastern Europe in 1989 there has been an extraordinary resurgence of interest in nationalism; in large part this has been due to the recognition that powerful nationalist sentiments survived 40 years of state socialism in Eastern Europe. So while nationalism is a 'traditional ideology' it is very much one the study of which is in the ascendant.

Definitions

In previous chapters we have cautioned against overreliance on dictionary definitions of concepts in political theory. While it can be useful to trace the etymology of words, everyday usage is too diverse and conflicting to provide guidance on the correct employment of concepts, the meanings of which are bound up with particular theories. The word 'nation' is a good example of the dangers of dictionary definitions. Dictionaries trace the word 'nation' to the Latin *natio*, and the Latin term was certainly used in the medieval period. For example, there is a debate about whether Scotland was really a nation before the Act of Union with England in 1707; one of the documents used in favour of the claim that Scotland was a nation is the Declaration of Arbroath (1320), which was written in Latin and uses the term *natio*. The difficulty with this argument is that *natio* can be translated as 'place of birth' – note the English word 'natal' – and the 37 signatories when they make reference to themselves as a 'nation' may not necessarily have possessed the modern consciousness of nationhood (Davidson, 2000: 48–9). The point is that words do not, in themselves, settle arguments over the nature of nationalism. Meanings are embedded in theories, and we will discuss different theories in the course of this chapter. However, it is useful to set out a variety of *competing* definitions of 'nation' and of 'nationalism', and try to identify commonalities and divergences. We start with 'nation':

- **Otto Bauer** The totality of people who are united by a common fate so that they possess a common (national) character. The common fate is . . . primarily a common history; the common national character involves almost necessarily a uniformity of language (Bauer in Davis, 1967: 150)
- **Max Weber** A nation is a community of sentiment that could adequately manifest itself in a state of its own: hence a nation is a community which

normally tends to produce a state of its own (Weber in Hutchinson and Smith, 1994: 25).

- **Anthony Smith** [A nation is] a named human population that shares myths and memories, a mass public culture, a designated homeland, economic unity and equal rights and duties for all members (Smith, 1991: 43)

- **Benedict Anderson** [A nation] is an imagined political community – and imagined as both inherently limited and sovereign . . . all communities larger than primordial villages of face-to-face contact (and perhaps even these) are imagined. Communities are to be distinguished, not by their falsity/genuineness, but by the style in which they are imagined (Anderson, 1991: 6).

- **James Kellas** A nation is a group of people who feel themselves to be a community bound together by ties of history, culture and common ancestry. Nations have 'objective' characteristics that may include a territory, a language, a religion or common descent (though not all of these are always present), and 'subjective' characteristics, essentially a people's awareness of their nationality and affection for it (Kellas, 1998: 3).

All five definitions begin with the idea of a 'collective': 'totality of people', 'community of sentiment', 'named human population', 'imagined political community', 'group of people ... community'. But disagreement exists on how this collective is held together. Bauer maintains the nation possesses a 'common character' or 'common fate', which necessarily entails a shared language. Weber argues that sentiment – or fellow feeling – holds the collective together, but that it also has a political project, namely the drive to create a state. Smith is more pluralistic in his understanding of what makes the collective cohere: myths, memories, mass public culture, homeland, economic unity, rights and duties. The last basis is, however, distinctly political: the nation has a legal dimension. Anderson maintains that we 'imagine' the nation: because we will never meet more than a tiny fraction of our fellow citizens the national community is imaginary, constructed above all through the medium of literature. Finally, Kellas draws attention to the objective *and* subjective dimensions of nationhood – nations require 'objective materials' such as territory or language, but there must also be a corresponding consciousness of belonging to a nation. It may be that, for example, Switzerland's multilingual character increases the necessity of a populist mechanism for citizenship, even if the Swiss are open to the charge of racism. An important issue is raised by these competing definitions: what are the origins of the nation? If, as Bauer implies, there is an ethnic basis to nationhood, then, to use a cliché, does not the nation have its roots in the 'mists of time'? If, however, the nation is a distinctly political project, and political structures change over time, then nationhood would appear to be a relatively recent phenomenon. We pursue this issue in more detail in the following section. What then of 'nationalism'? Again, we have competing understandings of nationalism:

- **Ernest Gellner** It is a theory of political legitimacy, which requires that ethnic boundaries should not cut across political ones, and in particular, that ethnic boundaries within a given state . . . should not separate the power holders from the rest (Gellner, 1983: 1).

- **Elie Kedourie** Nationalism is a doctrine invented in Europe at the beginning of the nineteenth century. It pretends to supply the criterion for the determination of the unit of population proper to enjoy a government exclusively of its own, for the legitimate exercise of power in the state and for the right organisation of a society of states. Briefly, the doctrine holds that humanity is naturally divided into nations, that nations are known by certain characteristics which can be ascertained, and that the only legitimate type of government is national self-government (Kedourie, 1993: 9).

- **Montserrat Guibernau** By nationalism I mean the sentiment of belonging to a community whose members identify with a set of symbols, beliefs and ways of life and have the will to decide upon their common political destiny (Guibernau, 1996: 47).

Whereas the term 'nation' refers to some kind of entity, 'nationalism' would appear to be a body of doctrine, theory or beliefs about the nation, its historical significance and moral importance. Common sense would suggest that nations precede nationalism: there must exist this entity we call a 'nation' in order to develop attitudes or beliefs towards it. This view is, however, challenged by 'modernists', who maintain that nations are the product of nationalism. Against them, 'perennialists' argue that nations do exist before the development of nationalism: the former are pre-modern, while the latter is modern.

Modernism versus Perennialism

Most of the discussion of nationalism has been between political scientists rather than political theorists. While it is acknowledged that nationalist sentiment has been a powerful political force, political theorists, who tend to operate with *universalist* concepts such as human nature, freedom, equality and justice, have found it difficult to explain nationalism, which is, essentially, *particularist* – that is, it assumes that national boundaries are morally significant. At best, nationalism has been incorporated into other ideologies, such as liberalism or socialism, as a subsidiary, or derivative concern. For example, liberals or socialists may argue that all human beings are equally worthy of moral concern, but the world is a better place if it is organised into nations – world government would be inefficient, or dangerous, because it would concentrate rather than disperse power. Given this relative neglect of nationalism within the history of political thought the best approach is to consider the political science debate and see whether it has implications for the ethical issues that are at the heart of political theory.

Within political science attention has focused on explaining the origins of *nations* and, distinct from nations, *nationalism*. As suggested above, two positions can be identified on the question of the origin of the nation: modernist and perennialist. For modernists, the nation is a modern creation, dependent on certain features of **modernity**, such as the unification of territory and the rise of a popular consciousness of belonging to this entity called a 'nation'. Nationalism – the ideology of nationhood – precedes the creation of nations. Perennialists accept that *nationalism* is modern, and that the nation itself has undergone significant changes in the modern period, but that the nation is continuous with an older community, which may have an ethnic, linguistic or cultural basis: nationhood can be 'forgotten' but it can also be 'recovered'. Anthony Smith provides a useful summary of the differences between modernism and **perennialism** (Smith, 1998: 22–3), as shown below.

Perennialism	Modernism
1. **Cultural community:** the nation is a politicised ethno-cultural community – a community of common ancestry that stakes a claim to political recognition on that basis.	**Political community:** the nation is a territorialised political community – a civic community of legally equal citizens in a particular territory.
2. **Immemorial:** the history of the nation stretches back centuries, or even millennia.	**Modern:** the nation is recent and novel – a product of modern conditions.
3. **Rooted:** the nation is 'rooted' in place and time and embedded in a historic homeland.	**Created:** the nation is consciously and deliberately 'built' by its members, or segments of its membership.
4. **Organic:** the nation is a popular or demotic community – a community of 'the people' and mirroring their needs.	**Mechanical:** the nation is consciously constructed by elites who seek to influence the emotions of the masses to achieve their goals.
5. **Qualities:** belonging to a nation means possessing certain qualities – membership is a state of 'being'.	**Resources:** belonging to a nation means possessing certain resources – membership is a capacity for 'doing'.
6. **Seamless:** nations are seamless wholes, with a single character.	**Divided:** nations are typically riven and divided into a number of (regional, class, gender, religious, etc.) social groups.
7. **Ancestry based:** the underlying principles of the nation are of ancestral ties and authentic culture.	**Communications based:** the principles of national solidarity are to be found in social communication and citizenship.

The terms modernism and perennialism are broad categories encompassing a number of different theories, and to make sense of the two positions we need to say more about these particular theories.

Modernist Theories

Ch 9: Socialism, pp. 216–27

Although there are many non-Marxist modernist theories of nationhood, it is the writings of Marx and Engels that have been the most influential in the formation of the modernist perspective on nationalism. Recall that for Marx and Engels class is the central concept in history – history is, at base, class conflict. Nation, unlike class, does not have an objective existence; whereas your class is determined by your objective position in the relations of production, independently of whether or not you recognise yourself as belonging to that class, membership of a nation is, in large part, determined by consciousness of membership of it. In the case of class, we move from an objective reality to a subjective consciousness of that reality; in the case of nations we move from subjective consciousness to objective reality. A few qualifications are, however, required to this distinction between class and nation:

- There must be a significantly large group for national consciousness to develop – individuals cannot, at will, create nations.
- An individual may be recognised as a member of a nation without recognising herself as a member; for example, her language or religion or family origin may mark her out as a member of a particular nation, even if she does not recognise herself as a member.
- There must be some 'objective materials' in order to construct a national consciousness.

The construction of the nation can be likened to the selection of ingredients for a meal: there is a choice to be made, such that the ingredients are akin to fragments of nationhood, which are then put together to make a single thing. Examples of such 'fragments' might include a particular language, or a dialect raised to a linguistic standard; a constructed history, with significant dates, myths, stories and interpretations; a common ancestry based on phenotypical similarity (how people look); a territory; religion; political institutions. The inclusion of the last item may seem odd: surely, having political institutions presupposes the existence of a nation, rather than being an ingredient in the construction of nationhood? We consider the distinction between 'state' and 'nation' in a later section, but the point to make here is that for modernists the existence of 'national' political institutions does not necessarily indicate the existence of national *consciousness*: such institutions could be 'elite', and thus not the object of a *popular* consciousness.

For Marx and Engels the growth of a national consciousness, and thus a nation, is bound up with the development of capitalism, which requires determinate legal institutions, a bounded territorial market, a shared means of communication, flexible labour markets and so relatedly a certain level of education, a single unit of currency, trade agreements and so international recognition of independent nation-states. On top of these economic requirements there is a need to legitimate the state, and this necessitates the development of a psychological identification with the nation. To generate that legitimacy may require drawing on pre-modern bases of group identification, such as ethnic symbolism. Neil Davidson, in his book *The Origins of Scottish Nationhood* (2000), arguing from a particular Marxist perspective, claims that Scotland only became a nation after the union with England in 1707, and the process involved the 'Celtification' of Scotland: prior to the defeat of the Jacobite Highlands in 1745, Scottish nationhood had been unable to develop precisely because there had existed a deep division of Highland and Lowland marked by geography, language, religion, and the absence of a single market. After the defeat of the Highlands, its symbols – tartanry, bagpipes, the kilt, Celtic myths – were disseminated throughout Scotland, such that they came to symbolise what it meant to be Scottish, and be the means by which a group of people identified one another as Scottish. Pre-modern symbols were pressed into service to create *for the first time* a Scottish nation (Davidson: 139).

We will consider the more normative aspects of Marx and Engels's views of nationalism in the section on Socialism and Nationalism, but at this stage we are concerned to identify the basic elements of the Marxist and non-Marxist modernist view of nationalism. Modernists talk in general terms about the relationship between modernity (capitalism, industrialism) and nationhood, but more detailed theories are required if we are to explain the differences between nations and, in particular, why some nations appear to have a stronger 'ethnic' character than others. Space prevents more than a selection of the most influential theories:

- **Tom Nairn** explains nationalism in terms of the uneven development of capitalism: marginalised 'elites' on the periphery of industrialised regions mobilise the masses so as to create 'a militant, inter-class community . . . strongly (if mythically) aware of its own separate identity vis-à-vis the outside forces of domination' (Nairn, 1977: 340). The wealthy centre has no need for such romantic, **ethnic nationalism** because it derives pride and confidence from its economic achievements. Such an analysis could be used to explain 'regional' nationalisms in Europe, but also nationalisms in the 'developing world', where the 'core' is the developed world.

- **Michael Hechter** offers a 'rational choice' analysis of nationalism (Hechter, 1998: 271). For Hechter, nations are no different to other groups, and individuals join groups in order to gain benefits. Nations are 'solidarity groups' that apply sanctions to prevent individuals gaining the benefits of membership while evading the costs. Because secession from the group carries a very high cost, it will only succeed if enough people want to secede, and the benefits of secession outweigh any costs imposed on those who attempt to secede. It follows that existing nations must provide inducements as well as impose sanctions if they wish to avoid secession. Rational choice theory cannot, however, explain the *passion* with which many people identify with the nation.

- **Eric Hobsbawm** and **Benedict Anderson** offer rather different explanations of nationalism, but are both part of a tradition of theorising the nation as involving 'invented traditions' (Hobsbawm) or being an 'imagined community' (Anderson). For Hobsbawm, the memory of having belonged to a political community is extended by an elite to the masses, and in the process 'traditions' are 'invented' that give rise to a consciousness of the nation as 'ancient' (Hobsbawm, 1983: 13–14). Anderson argues the nation is 'imagined' because its members will never meet; in the absence of meeting, each member imagines the nation as limited, bounded and sovereign. Print communities, facilitated by capitalism, permitted the development of a linguistic standard, and a literary imagination (Anderson, 1991: 6).

The Reformation, pp. 165–8

Anderson's argument draws attention to an important dimension of nationalism: language. It is commonplace to trace the development of the system of nation-states back to the Treaty of Westphalia (1648), which was the final 'settlement' of the Wars of Religion that had raged in Europe in the previous 100 or more years, and which had been caused in part by the schism with Christianity between the Reformers ('Protestants') and the Church of Rome ('Catholics'). Most modernists would claim that 1648 is too early a date from which to mark the beginning of the nation-state; many would, however, acknowledge the importance of Protestantism in the development of nationalism. As was argued in Chapter 7, a significant aspect of Protestantism was the translation of the Bible into the vernacular languages of Europe. In many cases these translations set a *national standard* for the languages concerned, and led to a process of linguistic unification within a particular territory.

Perennialist Theories

Hans Kohn, writing in 1944, distinguished two forms of nationalism: organic and voluntarist, with voluntarism corresponding to modernism. Organic nationalism assumes that the world consists of 'natural' nations, and has always done so, and that nations are the primary actors in history. Each nation is an 'organic whole', with a distinct character (Kohn, 1944: 3–24). Many such nations have, however, lost their 'self-consciousness' as nations, along with their political independence, and so nationalism is a 'restoration project' rather than a 'construction project': the creation of Hungary and Czechoslovakia in the wake of the collapse of the Austro-Hungarian empire after its defeat in World War I exemplifies the restoration project.

While the normative task of nationalists is to restore both consciousness and independence, the theoretical challenge for such perennialist nationalism is twofold: explaining the basis of such *natural* nations, and accounting for the loss of consciousness. There are a variety of accounts of such nations:

- **Pierre van den Berghe** argues that a nation is an extended kinship group. Human sociality is based on three principles: kin selection, reciprocity and coercion. Nations originate from tribes, or 'super-families', defined by territory; he does not claim that there is necessarily a genetic *identity* – migration and conquest rule that out – but what holds the group together are powerful sentiments of kinship, which give rise to a drive for genetic reproduction within the group. Human beings need markers for discriminating 'our kin', and these include language, dress and other cultural traits (van den Berghe, 1978: 403–4).

- **Clifford Geertz**, in his study of post-colonial nations in Africa and Asia, argues that such nations are caught between the 'modern' demand for economic success and a 'primordial' desire to belong, based on 'assumed blood ties' (Geertz, 1993: 259–60). Given that the boundaries of these nations encompass a plurality of 'assumed blood tied groups' they tend to instability, as groups struggle with one another for control of the state.

- **Joshua Fishman**, in his analysis of ethnicity and language in Eastern Europe, argues that nationalism can be understood only 'from the inside' – that is, by considering how the participants themselves view it. Ethnicity is the basis of nationhood, but it is not primarily a matter of biology, rather ethnic identification is achieved through a process of 'authentification', meaning that nations change, but the change has to be compatible with how the citizens of that nation see themselves (Fishman, 1980: 84–5). In essence, nationalism answers a deep psychological need for belonging.

Few perennialist theorists claim that nations equate to biological groups, although that belief certainly has been at the basis of racist theories of nationhood. But what then distinguishes perennialism from modernism? After all, many modernists accept that people value the nation because it appears to correspond to an ethnic group, and that the process of nation building entails drawing on that ethnic loyalty. What distinguishes perennialism from modernism is a belief that the 'building blocks' of the modern nation are pre-existing communities grounded in kinship relations; the smallest such community is the family.

Nationalism: the Ethical Debate

Implications of the Modernist–Perennialist Debate

While we need to be careful about drawing conclusions for political theory from what are descriptive theories, it is not difficult to see how competing modernist and perennialist explanations of nationalism *may* carry moral-political implications. Using Smith's table, set out in the box on p. 267, we can turn each of his points into a moral-political question:

1. **Who belongs to the nation?** What does a person have to do, or what qualities must he possess, in order to be the citizen of a particular nation-state?
2. **What is the purpose of the nation?** If the nation is 'recent' and 'novel' then there is an implication that it was created, or came about, to fulfil specifically modern functions, and if it fails then it should be dissolved or in some way reconstituted. If, however, the nation is 'ancient', then it may be that continuity and survival are what matter – simply existing is what matters.
3. **What is the relationship of the nation to 'land' or 'soil', as against the struggle for resources?** Politics is, in large part, a struggle over resources, including territory, but if 'land' has historical resonance, then territory is not simply an interchangeable resource. Although the most striking example of the struggle over symbolically charged territory is that between Israel and Palestine, it might also be argued that there is a struggle over resources, such as access to water, and that an overemphasis on the symbolic elements of the Israel–Palestine conflict obscures the more 'mundane' aspects of that conflict.
4. **What role does the nation play in engendering loyalty to the state?** To what extent is a person's *individual* identity bound up with membership of a particular nation? If, as modernists argue, the nation is constructed by elites, then national loyalty would seem to be shallow. If, however, nations are not created but develop 'organically' from more basic kinship groups, then loyalty to the state, as the political expression of the nation, is 'deep'.
5. **Is the nation an end-in-itself – that is, intrinsically valuable?** If a person's identity is bound up with the nation, and human beings are 'ends in themselves', then it follows that nations must be intrinsically valuable. But modernists would argue that nations are simply means for acquiring and securing resources.
6. **Does loyalty to nation 'trump' all other loyalties?** For a modernist, the nation is one loyalty among others, but for a perennialist it is a seamless whole. The most extreme perennialist position maintains that the nation is an 'organic' whole, such that the value of its parts is derivative from their relationship to the whole.

7. **What is the basis of national solidarity – why care about fellow nationals, as against other people?** This question raises issues of international justice – in a world of nations, what obligations does one nation have to another? Indeed, should international obligations hold between *nations*, or between *individual human beings*?

We have expressed the ethical issues raised by the perennialism-modernism debate in somewhat abstract terms, but answers to these questions carry implications for more concrete matters of political organisation and public policy. These include the following:

- the treatment of minorities within a national territory;
- the possible conflict between the rights of the individual and the rights of the nation;
- immigration policy;
- the relationship between nation-states, including conflict over resources;
- the tension between respecting the sovereignty of a nation-state and militarily intervening on humanitarian grounds in the affairs of that state.

The debate within political theory tends to focus on the conflict between the rights of individuals and sub-national groups as against the rights of nation, and on the conflict between nation-states within the international system of states. And corresponding closely, but not completely, to the distinction between perennialism and modernism is a distinction between civic (or civil) nationalism and ethnic nationalism.

State versus Nation

pp. 16–20

Before considering civic and ethnic nationalism it is important to highlight a conceptual distinction implicit in the preceding discussion: we have used the terms 'nation', 'state' and 'nation-state' interchangeably. We discussed the concept of the state in Chapter 1, and argued that it was a complex and allusive concept, but was associated with the organisation of power, or coercion, and those who exercised such power make an implicit or explicit claim to legitimacy in exercising it. Whether or not those subject to such power accept it as legitimate, we can at least say that the state is bound up with the concept of legality. Certainly, in international law, the state is an 'artificial person', bearing rights and duties. If we were to define a nation as a state we would encounter two problems: first, we would be unable to account for the phenomenon of nationalist consciousness, because not all groups who make claims to nationhood possess the attributes of statehood. Possible examples of stateless nations include Palestine, Scotland, Kurdistan, Tibet, Kosovo and Quebec. Second, by identifying nations with states, we encounter an ethical problem, namely, that many nationalist conflicts are about a claim to statehood on the basis of the existence of nationhood. Such a claim depends on a conceptual distinction between state and nation. That said, there is a close relationship between the concepts of nation and state: even if we reject Weber's definition of the nation as 'a community which tends to produce a state of its own', most nationalists do express a demand for political independence – they want to turn their 'nation' into a 'nation-state'.

Civic Nationalism and Ethnic Nationalism

Michael Ignatieff defines a civic nation as 'a community of equal, rights-bearing citizens, united in patriotic attachment to a shared set of political practices and values' (Ignatieff: 7). For a civic nationalist 'belonging' to a nation entails a rational choice rather than an inheritance. In contrast, an ethnic nationalist maintains 'that an individual's deepest attachments are inherited, not chosen' (Ignatieff: 7). The distinction between the two forms of nationalism has been attributed to Hans Kohn, who, in his discussion of nationalism in the nineteenth century, defined 'Western' nations, such as France, Britain and the United States as civic, and 'Eastern' nations, such as Germany and Russia, as ethnic. Indeed, our discussion of Swiss citizenship law at the beginning of this chapter appears to lend plausibility to this categorisation, with the principle of *jus sanguinis* suggesting ethnic criteria for citizenship, while *jus soli* implies a civic conception. But this is an oversimplification.

Drawing on the discussion of citizenship laws (p. 274) consider, for example, those of Germany. Germany was unified relatively late, and it is argued that national consciousness preceded the formal creation of Germany as a political entity, albeit Prussia had existed as a significant power since the late seventeenth century and, in addition, there emerged a federation of German states and principalities after Napoleon Bonaparte's defeat in 1815. Despite this gradual unification of Germany, only in 1871 was there achieved an approximate correspondence of national and political boundaries, such that Germany was, prior to 1871, in effect a stateless nation. We have to say 'approximate' because the cultural boundaries of Germany, defined above all by the German language, did not correspond to the political boundaries even of post-1871 Germany. The consequence was that the newly unified Germany had serious difficulty in defining citizenship, and it was only in 1913 that the citizenship law was codified. The self-understanding of the German nation as primarily a cultural entity, which had been given political identity as a state, fundamentally affected that law. On the face of it, German nationalism would appear, therefore, to be 'ethnic' rather than 'civic', and the overtly racist laws passed during the Nazi years appears retrospectively to reinforce this perception of German nationalism. Much of the discussion in the German and international media in the late 1990s of the German citizenship law reforms focused on what appeared to be archaic 'blood-line' notions of citizenship. However, it is quite possible to interpret the 1913 German citizenship law as a response to modern conditions: a developing nation with indeterminate boundaries requires criteria for citizenship, and some idea of culture or ethnicity seemed the most appropriate. In modernist terms, the available ingredients of nationhood meant that Germany had to rely on 'ethnic' criteria in order to create a *modern* nation. This is not to say that there is no connection between the 1913 law and the citizenship laws promulgated by the Nazis in the 1930s, but simply that the use of apparently ethnic criteria does not preclude the possibility that Germany was – Nazi years apart – basically a civic nation. Conversely, those nations described by Kohn as 'civic' are not free of ethnic criteria for citizenship.

As with Germany, the development of British and US citizenship laws were a response to their specific geographic and historic conditions. As Samuel Huntington argues, the United States can be considered a settler society rather than

Citizenship Law: Germany, Britain and the United States

We started this chapter with a discussion of Swiss citizenship law. It is useful to compare Swiss law with those of Germany, Britain and the United States, and then reflect below on what these laws say about each of the countries.

Germany

The traditional basis for acquiring German citizenship was through descent (*jus sanguinis*), meaning that you had to prove that one or more parents was German, with the possibility of restoration of citizenship to those stripped of it by the Nazi regime, or to their descendants. A law passed in 1953 extended the concept of membership of the nation (*Volkszugehörigkeit*) to all ethnic Germans in Eastern Bloc countries. Thus the law was highly inclusive of anyone who could prove German descent. On the other hand, until the year 2000 millions of 'guest workers' were denied the right to citizenship because the law did not recognise the principle of acquisition of citizenship by place of birth (*jus soli*), except under certain circumstances and at the discretion of the state. The new law, which came into effect on 1 January 2000, allowed the children of non-German parents to acquire, by right, citizenship if one parent has had a minimum legal residence in Germany of eight years and has held an unlimited residence permit for at least three years. Under most circumstances, the child who acquires citizenship in this way must, before the age of 23, revoke any other nationality – in principle, Germany does not tolerate multiple citizenship. In addition, new citizens must demonstrate competence in the German language, and swear allegiance to the principles of the constitution.

Britain

In theory, loyalty to the British monarch, as expressed through the holding of a British passport, has been the primary determinant of 'nationality'; however, there are different categories of passport, not all of which grant *citizenship*. In the period from 1948 to 1981 Britain moved closer to other European countries in adopting a citizenship law, partly based on *jus sanguinis* and partly on *jus soli*. Compared to many countries, the proof of integration required as part of the naturalisation process is light: basic competence in English (or Welsh, or Scots Gaelic), being of 'good character', and swearing (or affirming) that you will 'be faithful and bear true allegiance to Her Majesty Queen Elizabeth the Second her Heirs and Successors according to Law'. Citizenship ceremonies were introduced in 2004, and since then new citizens have also been required to pledge loyalty to the country's rights, freedoms and democratic values. Multiple citizenship is permitted.

United States

The United States sees itself as, historically, a 'country of immigration'. For that reason, the principle of *jus sanguinis* might be thought weak; however, as in most countries, a family connection does provide a person with a privileged access to citizenship. That said, historically, naturalisation has been an extremely important route to citizenship; perhaps unsurprisingly, the symbolic dimensions are very important. In addition to legal residency requirements, an applicant must be of 'good moral character', and there is a long list of criminal offences that preclude a person from citizenship. He must show attachment to the principles of the Constitution, be competent in the English language, demonstrate knowledge of US history and government (a pass of 6 out of 10 questions from a battery of 100 is required). Finally, the applicant must swear an oath of allegiance – this takes rather longer than the seven-second British oath.

The Debate over German (Re-)unification

The fall of the Berlin Wall in 1989 and the 1990 (re-)unification of East and West Germany generated an interesting debate between three German intellectuals: philosopher Jürgen Habermas, cultural critic Karl-Heinz Bohrer and novelist Günter Grass. Each presented a distinct position on the nature of the German nation, and more broadly on the role of nationalism in political life. Grass argued against unification mainly on the grounds that 'there can be no demand for a new version of a unified nation that in the course of barely 75 years, although under several managements, filled the history books, ours and theirs, with suffering, rubble, defeat, millions of dead, and the burden of crimes that can never be undone' (Grass in James and Stone, 1992: 57–8). The division must remain as a tangible symbol of those crimes. Bohrer, on the other hand, argues that the crimes to which Grass refers have their roots, in part, in the parochialism of the 'police states' which constituted the pre-1871 Germany; what Germany needs is a sense of nationhood. He accepts that the Holocaust is the 'great, unavoidable fact of our modern history', but a cultural regeneration of Germany – nationalism rather than parochialism – is the best guarantor of liberal democracy. Habermas, while accepting the legitimacy of unification – and it is unification rather than reunification, for the 'two Germanys' in no way correspond to the Germany of 1937 – argues for a form of civic nationalism, based on what he calls 'constitutional patriotism'. His argument revolves around a complex debate concerning the legal nature of the 1990 unification: in effect, it extended the West German 'constitution' (1949 *Grundgesetz* – Basic Law) to East Germany, rather than creating a new constitution (*Verfassung* – this word was not used in 1949 because it was always assumed that the division of East and West would be temporary). Had there been a new constitution, endorsed by a referendum, the German people would quite literally have 'constituted' themselves rather than seeing the unified nation as the product of 'pre-political imponderables like linguistic community, culture, or history' (Habermas in James and Stone, 1992: 97).

Note: This debate is reproduced in Harold James and Marla Stone (eds), *When the Wall Came Down: Reactions to German Unification*.

an immigrant society, and those original settlers defined themselves as British and Protestant; while post-Independence America sought to distance its political institutions from any particular Christian denomination, a belief in God was implicit in being American, and the structures of the Protestant world-view were deeply embedded in the nation. The large numbers of non-Protestants who migrated to the United States in the period between the civil war (1861–5) and World War I were 'assimilated' into the existing value system (Huntington, 2004: 95–8). In the case of Britain, the very loose citizenship laws that operated until 1981 were a response to the specific historical conditions of British nation building and transformation; in particular, the need to cement the relationship between England and Scotland, which was achieved to a significant degree through the building of an empire. The point is that 'being British' relied on ethnic criteria just as much as 'being German' did; what made British identity appear more 'civic' was that loyalty to the nation was expressed through loyalty to a constitutional monarchy, rather than to the 'British people'.

Nationalism and Exclusivity

There is some validity in the distinction between civic nationalism as based on allegiance to political institutions and ethnic nationalism as entailing a belief in unity through blood or culture. But the distinction is overstated. In the post-World War II period the – justifiable – concern with Nazism resulted in a strong focus on the racist aspects of nationalism to the detriment of a concern with the conflict between nations over resources. All nations are, by definition, exclusive: each must determine its membership. A civic nation may do so, first, by accepting the existing population of a territory, irrespective of its ethnic and cultural identity, and, then, by granting citizenship to those who can demonstrate allegiance to the nation. But to demonstrate allegiance you have to live in the country, and immigration controls prevent people entering the country. It is possible to have a 'colour-blind' immigration policy, but then some other criteria are required. One possibility is entry on the basis of skill, but the result of such a policy is to poach the most able members of poorer countries. Every nation must answer the question 'who belongs?', and there is no answer to that question that does not generate some form of political conflict.

Liberalism and Nationalism: Mill and Herder

Liberalism versus Nationalism

pp. 164–5

At first sight liberalism and nationalism appear odd bed-fellows: for nationalists the most significant moral entity is the nation, whereas for liberals the most significant is the individual human being. Where there is a conflict between the claims of the individual and those of the nation, liberals and nationalists will diverge over which should take precedence. Furthermore, the priority given to the individual by liberals normally rests on features all human beings share, such that the logic of liberal individualism is moral *universalism* (individualism might also lead to egoism, but we will ignore that possibility here). In contrast, nationalists are *particularists*: although some nationalists will argue that there is a universal need to belong to a nation, nationalism entails regarding one's own nation as 'special'. The difference between liberalism and nationalism can be expressed in the following way:

Entity	Moral Attitude or Response
Humanity	Universalism
Nation	Particularism
Individual	Universalism (or Egoism)

The difficulty with this apparent rejection of nationalism is that historically liberalism and nationalism have often been combined into a single political programme: the struggle for national self-determination has been expressed in the language of freedom, self-government and accountability. The question is whether the apparent affinity of liberalism and nationalism is simply a historical accident, or whether there is a deeper philosophical compatibility that is not captured by an oversimplistic derivation of universalism from individualism.

Jean-Jacques Rousseau can be taken as the first significant liberal thinker to make an explicit case for nationalism. His defence of nationalism was based on the importance of a 'people' possessing a general will, the recognition of which supposedly guarantees individual freedom; the general will is not reducible to the wills of individuals, or to a simple aggregation of wills. Rousseau's theory is highly abstract, and seems unconnected to the political realities of his time, but it has been influential in the development of a popular nationalism based on democratic self-government. What provides the link between liberalism and nationalism in Rousseau's theory is the idea of democracy, such that a better understanding of the relationship between the individual and the nation is:

Nation ◄—► Sovereign People (democracy) ◄—► Individual

However, there are still difficulties involved in reconciling nationalism and liberalism. First, as we have argued, democracy and liberalism, while closely related, can conflict: democracy does imply that each person's interests should be given equal consideration, but to make decisions we have to rely on a voting system, such that some people's preferences will almost inevitably be overridden. To protect individual freedom, we need rights that cannot be removed by the majority. The threat from majorities exists whether or not there is strong nationalist sentiment, but it is deepened by the existence of such sentiment. Second, even if we can guarantee the rights of individuals within a democracy, a world divided into nation-states raises issues of international justice: there are strong and wealthy nations, and there are weak and poor nations. If individuals matter then they matter irrespective of their nationality.

While the nation *may* be a threat to liberty and to international justice, there are grounds for holding that a world of nation-states is more likely to guarantee liberty and justice than some other form of political organisation. Two quite different lines of argument suggest themselves; both are liberal but, in fact, correspond respectively to civic and ethnic forms of nationalism. The first – civic – argument is that the world is more stable and efficient if organised around nation-states, where each nation respects the territorial integrity of the others. This argument attaches *instrumental* value to the nation: that is, the nation serves the purposes of individuals. The second – ethnic – argument maintains that individuals need culture as a means of self-expression, and the nation-state is the embodiment of culture. Such an argument assumes that nations have *intrinsic* value – valuing individual lives means respecting an individual's culture, the political expression of which is the nation-state. In terms of the history of political thought, John Stuart Mill was an important exponent of the first position, while Johann Gottfried von Herder defended the second.

John Stuart Mill

Biography, p. 41

In his book *Considerations on Representative Government* (published 1859) Mill argues that 'free institutions are next to impossible in a country madeup of different nationalities' (Mill, 1991: 428). A 'nation' Mill defines as a portion of humankind united 'among themselves' by common sympathies, which make them cooperate with each other more willingly than with those of other nations. These common sympathies may be based on 'race and descent', language, religion, shared memory and political antecedents. Mill states that the last of these is the most important, and yet his brief discussion of nationalism actually focuses much more on the need for a shared language than the existence of historic political institutions. Without a shared language a 'united public opinion' cannot exist; if, say, two major languages coexist, then public life is vertically divided, with each group reading different newspapers, books and pamphlets, and each looking to its own political class, which speaks to them in their own language.

The danger with a 'multi-national' – meaning, a multilingual – state is that the army, as the security wing of the state, is held together by obedience to its officers, and not by a shared sympathy. Although Mill does not argue for a popular militia, he does imply that the army, and other security forces, must have popular legitimacy. Faced with popular discontent, an army made up of one particular ethnic-linguistic group will just as soon 'mow down' the members of another group, as they will 'foreigners' (Mill: 429). In a multi-national state the objective of the government will be the maintenance of stability, and that will entail balancing competing linguistic groups, such that instead of developing fellow feeling differences will become institutionalised. Mill concedes that there are successful multi-national states, the best example being Switzerland, and he also accepts that geographical 'intermingling' can be such that some states must be multi-national. But he considers it preferable that 'peripheral' minorities be absorbed by larger nations: a Breton is better to share 'the advantages of French protection, and the dignity and prestige of French power, than to sulk on his own rocks, the half-savage relic of past times' (Mill: 431). Similarly, Wales and the Scottish Highlands are better absorbed into Britain. Today, these remarks seem anachronistic: the emphasis now is on respecting differences within the nation-state, and ensuring that 'threatened' languages such as Breton, Welsh and Scots Gaelic survive – note, for example, that the British naturalisation process requires competence in English *or* Welsh *or* Gaelic. However, the anti-ethnic basis of Mill's argument is significant: the 'admixture' and 'blending' of nationalities is to the benefit of humanity, because it softens the extremes between people (Mill: 432). In essence, Mill's nationalism is 'assimilationist' – nations are culturally hybrid, but the political project must be to create fellow feeling, because this guarantees the development and reinforcement of individual freedom.

Johann Gottfried von Herder

Herder is a major point of reference within the tradition that takes the nation to be a pre-modern ethnic community. For this reason it might be thought that he cannot also be a liberal. Yet, in fact, Herder has been influential among those liberals who see human beings as necessarily cultural beings. At the heart of culture is language, and Herder anticipates one of the dominant themes of twentieth-century philosophy in arguing that human self-consciousness is dependent on language: the very capacity to think presupposes language. Furthermore, language is necessarily collective, and while it is possible to identify universal features, languages are particular; a language is not simply a means by which we name things, but in writing, reading and speaking a particular language, such as English or German, we locate ourselves and others in a particular world

| Biography | **Johann Gottfried von Herder (1744–1803)** |

Herder was a major influence on the formation of German nationalism; his reflections on the importance of culture inspired the Grimm Brothers (Jacob and Wilhelm) in their collection of Germanic folk stories.

Herder was born in Mohrungen in Prussia (it is now in Poland, and in Polish is called Morag). He studied at the University of Königsberg. In 1764 he went to Riga as a preacher and teacher; in his 1770 essay 'On the Origins of Language' he wrote that no man lives for himself alone, he is 'knit into the whole texture' of society. That essay received some critical notice, and it brought him into contact with the great German writer Johann Wolfgang von Goethe (1749–1832), and many intellectual historians locate the beginnings of the Sturm und Drang (Romantic) movement to their meeting.

In 1771 Herder became pastor at Bückeburg, moving in 1776 to Weimar, where Goethe was resident. He published *Stimmen der Völker in ihren Liedern* (*Voices of the People in their Songs*) (1773), which was used later by poets and composers under the title *Des knaben Wunderhorn* (*The Boy's Magic Horn*).

of emotion and sentiment. (For a modern application of Herder's reflections, see Breuilly, 1993: 55–9)

Herder is attempting to reconcile Enlightenment and Romanticist views of human nature. Under the influence of the former, Herder argues that to be free, autonomous agents we need language, but under the influence of the latter, he maintains that language summons up an emotional world. Herder also attempts to reconcile progress and tradition: the transmission of culture from one generation to another involves both the preservation of culture, or tradition, and the confrontation of the old with the new. This has implications for his understanding of nationalism: since newness is part of tradition, and can come from outside a culture as a 'foreign influence' nations should not be chauvinistic. However, while Herder distances himself from extreme nationalism, he also maintains that cultures cannot be manufactured out of nothing, and that each culture – or nation – has a distinct character which should be preserved.

While language is one of the most fundamental capacities of human beings, the roots of political organisation lie in the family, and this is what gives rise to his organic view of the nation: the nation is not an organism in the sense that there is a hierarchy of parts, as the metaphor of the human body would imply, but rather the nation develops from its most basic unit of organisation. And Herder draws an egalitarian and non-authoritarian conclusion from this: elites cannot create nations, and they must not impose their wills on individuals, but rather individuals must be free to develop themselves. Like the growth of an oak tree from an acorn, national development must come from 'within'. The difficulty with Herder's argument is that the family inevitably has paternalistic, if not patriarchal, overtones, and derivation of the nation from the family is problematic, for citizenship involves relationships with people you have never met and will never meet. Ethnic nationalism embodies all the limitedness of the family without preserving its positive features as a small-scale, 'face-to-face' community, based, at its best, on ties of affection.

Socialism and Nationalism: Marx and Engels

Introducing
Marxism,
pp. 216–22

Marx and Engels make various comments on nationalism in the *Communist Manifesto*: responding to the charge that communists want to abolish the nation-state Marx and Engels argue that the workers have no nation of their own, and that national divisions have become increasingly irrelevant as capitalism has developed – the capitalists have created a single world bound together by free trade. Marx and Engels were 'collectivists', but the historically significant 'collective' was the working class, as the most advanced, and first 'truly revolutionary', class. Although they avoid using the language of morality, believing that moral beliefs are the product of existing (capitalist) society, and the task is to create a new society, it is possible to discern a moral message in their work: the task is to create a classless society in which human beings recognise their common humanity. In his early work, Marx called this 'species consciousness'. So the historical task is to develop (proletarian) class consciousness, and the ultimate moral aim is to overcome human alienation. This appears to leave little room for nationalism.

Marx and Engels do, however, argue that during the revolutionary phase the workers must 'make themselves into a nation': 'since the proletariat must first of all acquire supremacy, must rise to be *the* national class, must constitute itself the nation, it is, so far, itself national, though not in the bourgeois sense of the word' (Marx and Engels, 1967: 23). During what they call the 'dictatorship of the proletariat' it is necessary to take hold of the state and use it both to defeat counter-revolutionaries and to transform the relations of production. But this a temporary phase, and just as the aim is for the state 'to lose its political character', that is, its coercive character, so it is necessary that the nation lose what might be termed its 'particular' character – in the latter phases of the process the national revolutions will become international. Because Marx and Engels said very little about what a classless society – or world – would look like, it is unclear what place nationalist consciousness would have in such a society, or world. Cultural differences would not necessarily disappear, but they could not determine the distribution of resources. Nonetheless, even if the future of nationalism is unclear, nationalist consciousness does play a role in the revolutionary period, and broadly speaking Marx and Engels argued that if nationalist movements serve the class struggle, then they should be supported. More specifically, they maintained:

1. Nations must have a certain *minimum size* and large and powerful ones were to be encouraged – what Engels called the 'miserable remnants of former nations' should dissolve. A distinction is drawn between historic and non-historic nations, where 'history' is understood as actions and movements possessing class significance. The 'miserable remnants', examples of which include the Basques, Bretons and Gaels, have no historic significance. They argue that after a workers' revolution there will always be the danger of counter-revolution, led by 'conservative' elements in society, and that these 'rotting remnants' would be among them. Interestingly, Mill also maintains that these peoples are better absorbed into larger nations.

2. National self-determination was to be encouraged if it helped revolution. In the main Marx and Engels believed that national struggles should only be encouraged in the big nations of central and west Europe: France, Britain and

Germany. Struggles on the 'edge of Europe' were not generally supported. Which means, for example, that they did not in 1848 support the Irish struggle against the British – they later changed their views, and the reasons for the shift in their position are briefly discussed below.

3. They opposed Russia, which they saw as the primary source of reaction in Europe, and so tactically supported the Habsburg (Austro-Hungarian) Empire – which meant opposing nationalist movements among, for example, the Czechs, Slovaks and Serbs (Mill supported these struggles). Basically, their attitude to the nationalisms of their time was determined by the role that they played in the historic class struggle.

4. Ireland: from an orthodox Marxist perspective Ireland in the nineteenth century appears backward – Engels describes it as the agricultural appendage of Britain, or more specifically England. It had not developed capitalism (except in a small north-eastern corner of the country) – which was a precondition of a workers' revolution. What is more, the Catholic Church was a source of 'false consciousness'. But Marx and Engels gradually shifted to the view that the liberation of Ireland was a condition for revolution in Britain: Britain (or England) was the nation most likely to experience revolution, but the Irish constituted a source of competition to British workers, which worsened the conditions of the latter, but without fuelling revolution, because British workers saw their struggle against Irish labour as nationalist (and religious) in character. Paradoxically, through granting Ireland independence British and Irish workers would develop class solidarity, and recognise that the bourgeoisie was their true enemy.

Conclusion: Banal Nationalism

Michael Billig argues that the central thesis of his book *Banal Nationalism* is that 'there is a continual "flagging", or reminding of nationhood' (Billig, 1995: 8). Political leaders in France, the United States, or Britain do not define themselves as 'nationalist' – nationalism is a term applied to those on the 'fringe', whether fighting for independence from a larger nation or seeking to radicalise the consciousness of a nation through, for example, racism. But those leaders *are* nationalist, for they daily remind their citizens of the importance of nationhood through 'banal' – that is ordinary, everyday – acts. Political and cultural discourse is suffused with nationalist rhetoric: the word 'national' appears in official titles of state bodies, along with visual symbols; newspapers have 'national' and 'international' news; the promotion of tourism rests on a few identifiable 'signifiers'. Sport itself is organised around the nation-state. The 'cricket test' ('Tebbit test') is a prime example of consciously elevating the banal to the status of a supposedly essential criterion for allegiance to the nation-state. As Billig says, 'the metonymic image of banal nationalism is not a flag which is being consciously waved with fervent passion; it is the flag hanging unnoticed on the public building' (Billig, 1995: 8). A metonymic image is one that locates a person in relation to something else, in this instance a collective entity – the nation.

While Billig's argument can be criticised it is a useful way of concluding our discussion on nationalism. Billig argues that nationalism is a powerful force, but most of the time we do not realise its force; only at times of crisis does it 'erupt'. Political theorists, operating with universalist concepts, find nationalism a difficult phenomenon to understand, let alone use as a justification; they cannot, however, ignore it. The question is whether we should be so concerned about nationalism – does it matter which team a person supports so long as he or she obeys the law? After all, millions of people do not support any cricket, football or rugby team, professing themselves utterly bored with sport. The most compelling argument for taking nationalism seriously is, as Mill observed, that it does provide connections between people that, at a time of crisis, may be essential for the maintenance of liberal-democratic institutions. Those ties may be sporting, or linguistic, or based on an appreciation of cities and landscape, and it is possible that we do not need to share all of them – we can be bored by sport – but we need some of them. The danger is that those who quite justifiably do not share such ties will suffer when there are crises – in the 1930s Italian restaurants were the only decent places to eat out in for most people in Britain; when Italy declared war on Britain in 1940 suddenly Italian restaurants were burned out, possibly by the same people who had frequented them. To address this 'dark side' of nationalism requires a theory of culture and multiculturalism, and that is a topic for a later chapter.

Ch 14:
Multiculturalism,
pp. 350–68

Summary

For political theorists nationalist sentiment is problematic because it seems to resist universalist concepts. While it is possible to talk about universal rights to national self-determination and assert that all nations are equal, both the reality of international politics and, perhaps more importantly, the concept of nation undermines that claim. Even the softest, most 'civic', nationalist will be forced to concede that his nation is special, for how else can he explain the value of nationhood? Of course, if we say, as liberals do, that the individual is the ultimate source of value and focus of concern, a similar objection can be raised: your individual life is especially valuable to *you*. However, because the nation-state entails a massive concentration of power the ethical particularism within nationalism is of special concern. On the other hand, a world of nation-states may offer the best way to realise values such as freedom, justice and equality, and a history of nationalism that focused on the extremism of Nazi Germany or the virulent nationalisms of some contemporary states – thinking here of the Balkans in the 1990s – may fail to do justice to nationalism as a liberationist ideology.

Questions

1. Is the 'nation' a product of 'modernity'?
2. Is a multilingual nation inherently unstable?
3. Are nationalism and socialism compatible?

4. What are the arguments in favour of the abolition of nations and the creation of a world government?
5. A Scottish nationalist, bemoaning the lack of majority support among Scots for independence, labelled Scots '90-minute nationalists'. Is it possible to be a strong supporter of a national football team but reject political nationalism?

References

Anderson, B. (1991) *Imagined Communities: Reflections on the Origin and Spread of Nationalism* London: Verso.

Berge van den, P. (1978) 'Race and Ethnicity: a Sociobiological Perspective, *Ethnic and Racial Studies*, Vol. 1.

Billig, M. (1995) *Banal Nationalism* London: Sage.

Breuilly, J. (1993) *Nationalism and the State* Manchester: Manchester University Press.

Davidson, N. (2000) *The Origins of Scottish Nationhood* London: Pluto Press.

Davis, H. (1967) *Nationalism and Socialism: Marxist and Labor Theories of Nationalism to 1917* New York: Monthly Review Press.

Fishman, J. (1980) 'Social Theory and Ethnography: Language and Ethnicity in Eastern Europe' in P. Sugar (ed.) *Ethnic Conflict and Diversity in Eastern Europe* Santa Barbara, CA: ABC-Clio.

Geertz, C. (1993) *The Interpretation of Cultures: Selected Essays* London: Fontana.

Gellner, E. (1983) *Nations and Nationalism* Oxford: Basil Blackwell.

Guibernau, M. (1996) *Nationalisms: The Nation-State and Nationalism in the Twentieth Century* Cambridge: Polity Press.

Hechter, M. (1998) 'Rational Choice Theory and The Study of Ethnic and Race Relations' in J. Rex and D. Mason (eds) *Theories of Ethnic and Race Relations* Cambridge: Cambridge University Press.

Hobsbawm, E. and Ranger, T. (1983) *The Invention of Tradition* Cambridge: Cambridge University Press.

Huntington, S. (2004) *Who Are We?: America's Great Debate* London: Free Press.

Hutchinson, J. and Smith, A. (1994) (eds) *Nationalism* Oxford: Oxford University Press.

Ignatieff, M. (1993) *Blood and Belonging: Journeys into the New Nationalism* London: BBC Books and Chatto & Windus.

James, H. and Stone, M. (eds) (1992) *When the Wall Came Down: Reactions to German Unification* New York and London: Routledge.

Kedourie, E. (1993) *Nationalism* Oxford and Cambridge, Mass.: Blackwell.

Kellas, J. (1998) *The Politics of Nationalism and Ethnicity* Basingstoke: Macmillan.

Kohn, H. (1944) *The Idea of Nationalism: A Study on its Origins and Background* London: Macmillan.

Marx, K. and Engels, F. (1967) *The Communist Manifesto* introduction and notes by A.J.P. Taylor, London: Penguin.

Mill, J.S. (1991) *On Liberty and Other Essays* (ed John Gray) Oxford: Oxford University Press.

Nairn, T. (1977) *The Break-Up of Britain: Crisis and Neo-nationalism* London: NLB.

Smith, A. (1991) *National Identity* London: Penguin.

Smith, A. (1998) *Nationalism and Modernism: A Critical Survey of Recent Theories of Nations and Nationalism* London: Routledge.

Further Reading

There are several good introductions to the study of nationalism. From the above bibliography Kellas (1998), Smith (1991) and Smith (1998) are useful overviews (also by Anthony Smith: *Nationalism: Theory, Ideology, History*, Cambridge: Polity Press, 2001). Other books in the bibliography very much argue a line – the most influential are Anderson (1991), Gellner (1983), Hobsbawm (1992), and Kedourie (1993). General – and brief – introductions not listed in the bibliography include: Kenneth Minogue, *Nationalism* (London: Batsford, 1967) and Fred Haliday and Umut Özkirimli, *Theories of Nationalism: A Critical Introduction* (Basingstoke: Palgrave Macmillan, 2000). For a useful collection of essays: Umut Özkirimli, *Nationalism and its Future* (Basingstoke: Palgrave Macmillan, 2003). Books focusing on the ethical aspects of nationalism include Yael Tamir, *Liberal Nationalism* (Princeton, NJ: Princeton University Press, 1995); David Miller, *On Nationality* (Oxford: Clarendon Press, 1995); Andrew Vincent, *Nationalism and Particularity* (Cambridge and New York: Cambridge University Press, 2002); Margaret Moore (ed.), *National Self-Determination and Secession* (Oxford: Oxford University Press, 1998).

Weblinks

An article with an extensive bibliography:
http://plato.stanford.edu/entries/nationalism/

A very extensive list of (largely academic) links:
http://www.nationalismproject.org/

Another extensive list of links, although more of a mix of 'popular' and academic:
http://www.socresonline.org.uk/2/1/natlinks.html

A more history-oriented site:
http://www.fordham.edu/halsall/mod/modsbook17.html

Chapter 12

Fascism

Introduction

The word 'fascist' is often used as a word of abuse. Fascists are seen as people who act in authoritarian ways and seek to impose their views and values on others. But fascism is more complicated than this. First because fascism needs to be more precisely defined, and second, the question arises as to whether it is a movement of the past, or can it be said that fascist movements still exist today? Everyone has heard of Hitler (1889–1945) but Hitler called his party the National Socialist German Workers Party: can he still be called a fascist? Not many movements have come to power since 1945 that can unambiguously be called fascist – but can we describe movements in these terms when they do not necessarily declare themselves in favour of Hitler or the founder of Italian fascism, Mussolini?

This chapter will explore these issues, and those listed below, in order to tackle the questions: what is fascism; is it an ideology at all; and can a grasp of it help us in understanding certain political movements in today's world?

Chapter Map

- A definition of **fascism** is offered – a task that is clearly crucial if the question of whether it is a general movement or simply an Italian movement of the inter-war period is to be tackled.

- The development of fascism in Italy: this was the particular movement that gave the general movement its name.

- The relationship of Nazism to fascism – it will be argued that Hitler's National Socialism was an extreme form of fascism.

- The relationship of fascism to capitalism and class. This not only throws light on the

relationship between fascism and socialism but is important if we are to explain the rise of fascism.

- The view taken by fascists towards liberal ideas and the European Enlightenment in order to gauge the depth of the rejection of 'reason', liberty and equality.

- The fascist view of the state.

- Fascism today, the form that it takes, and the conditions under which it is likely to become increasingly influential.

'Never Again': Contemporary Forms of Fascism

Gypsy woman suffering from typhus at Bergen Belsen concentration camp waiting with other gypsies for medical treatment, Germany, April 1945

Ÿou are conscious of considerable media coverage given to the 60th anniversary of the destruction of the Nazi concentration camp at Auschwitz and of the existence of Holocaust Day, a day that commemorates the murder by the Nazis of millions of European Jews, the killing of travellers (gypsies) and of political opponents.

Interviews with victims bring tears to your eyes, and former concentration camp attendants explain why they were able to kill inmates. You are horrified at the information you receive – the starvation, brutality, the killing and the sophisticated methods used for nefarious purposes – and you can only agree with the general theme of 'never again'. At the same time you have read about the **genocide** of the Tutsis in Rwanda in Africa, and the grisly ethnic cleansing in former Yugoslavia where whole communities were wiped out, women raped and men placed in concentration camps. The media is full of the following: Jewish cemeteries have been desecrated, black people killed by gangs and even by the police, Muslims are 'blamed' for terrorist atrocities such as the destruction of the Twin Towers in 2001 because these actions were committed in the name of Islam, and extreme right-wing movements such as the British National Party or the Freedom Party in Austria are campaigning to have immigrants expelled from the countries in which they have settled. At the same time you read about left-wing regimes denounced as fascist when they violate the human rights of political opponents. Inevitably a number of questions suggest themselves.

- Are we witnessing the re-emergence of fascism in our modern world?
- When does a racist become a fascist? Are the two synonymous and if not, how do we differentiate between them?
- Can we call people who support nationalism, fascists?
- Is opposition to immigration fascist in character?

Defining Fascism

Ch 9: Socialism,
pp. 208–37

Fascism is sometimes used as a word of abuse – against movements or individuals who are intolerant or authoritarian. Fascism is certainly intolerant and authoritarian, but it is more than this. It is a movement that seeks to establish a dictatorship of the 'right' (i.e. an ultra-conservative position that rejects liberalism and anything associated with the 'left'). It targets communists, socialists, trade unionists and liberals through banning their parties and their members, so that these groups cannot exercise their political, legal or social rights. It is anti-liberal, regarding liberal values as a form of 'decadence', and sees them as opening the floodgates to socialist, communist and egalitarian movements.

Defining fascism raises a problem. Fascism as a movement extols action and practice over ideas and theory. It uses ideas with considerable opportunism, mixing socialist ideas, avant-garde positions, anti-capitalist rhetoric, ecological argument and pseudo-scientific ideas to do with 'race' and ethnicity in a veritable pot-pourri. Is it an ideology at all? Trevor Roper described fascist ideology as 'an ill-sorted hodge-podge of ideas', and Laski has argued that any attempt to find a 'philosophy of fascism' is a waste of time (Griffin, 1995: 1; 276). Kitchen contends that the 'extraordinary collection of half-baked and cranky ideas certainly did not form a coherent whole' (1976: 28). We shall argue however, that while fascism is peculiarly 'flexible' as an ideology, there are particular features that characterise it, so that a general view of fascism can be created. Vincent argues that fascism 'often occupies a middle ground somewhere between rational political ideology on the one hand and opportunist adventurism on the other' (1995: 142).

Battle of
Capareto box,
p. 289

The term derives from the 'fasces' – the bundle of rods carried by the consuls of ancient Rome and the word 'fascio' was used in Italy in the 1890s to indicate a political group or band, usually of revolutionary socialists (Heywood, 1992: 171). National defence groups organised after the Italian defeat at Caparetto in 1917, also called themselves 'fasci' (Vincent, 1995: 141).

Fascism is, however, essentially a twentieth-century movement although it draws upon prejudices and stereotypes that are rooted in tradition. Italian fascism saw itself as resurrecting the glories of the Roman Empire and Rocco, an Italian fascist, saw Machiavelli as a founding father of fascist theory. Nazism (which we will argue is an extreme form of fascism) was seen by its ideologues as rooted in the history of the Nordic peoples, and the movement embodied anti-Semitic views that go back to the Middle Ages in which Jews, for example, were blamed for the death of Christ, compelled to be moneylenders, confined to ghettos and acquired a reputation for crooked commerce.

Fascism and Communism

Ch 11:
Nationalism,
pp. 262–84

Fascism appeals particularly to those who have some property but not very much, and are fearful that they might be plunged by market forces into the ranks of the working class. We would, however, agree with Griffin that there is nothing 'in principle' that precludes an employed or unemployed member of the working class,

Battle of Caparetto

This battle involved some 600,000 Italian casualties and was the worst disaster in the history of the Italian armed forces. Ernest Hemingway based his *A Farewell to Arms* (1929) on the war between Austria and Italy between 1915 and 1917, reading military histories and first-hand reports to flesh out the background. His novel centres around an American, Frederic, who speaks Italian, and fights for the Italians. He lived, we are told, 'in Udine' and saw that things were going 'very badly' (1985: 10).

Frederic tells the priest (whom he befriends): They (the Italian army) were 'beaten to start with. They were beaten when they [the military authorities] took them from their farms and put them in the army. That is why the peasant has wisdom, because he is defeated from the start. Put him in power and see how wise he is' (1985: 157).

In October 1917 Italy was occupied by Germany. Germany reached Udine on 28 October 1917 and the Italians lost about 600,000 men in a week. This is the lowest point in the war and Frederic deserts.

an aristocrat, city dweller or peasant, or a graduate 'from being susceptible to fascist myth' (1995: 7). Fascism is particularly hostile to communism, since it is opposed to the cosmopolitan contentions of Marxist theory, and its belief in a classless and stateless society. It is a movement that dislikes universal identities of any kind, although of course fascists may call for unity with kindred spirits in other countries. Nevertheless, it is intensely nationalistic, and takes the view that the people must be saved from enemies whose way of life is alien and threatening. Differences are deemed divisive and menacing, and war extolled as a way of demonstrating virtue and strength. The idea that people are divided by class is rejected in favour of the unity of the nation or people, so that industry is to be organised in a way that expresses the common interest between business and labour. In practice, this did not happen, and Kitchen argues that the social strata which provided the mass basis for fascism did not actually gain from its policies (1976: 65).

Fascism and Religion

Fascists vary in their attitude towards the Church (extreme fascists may see religious organisations as a threat to the state) but they regard religion in a loose sense as being a useful way of instilling order and loyalty. Certainly they use a religious style of language in invoking the need for sacrifice, redemption and spiritual virtue and attacking materialism, consumerism and hedonism as decadent and unworthy. Although women can be fascists as well as men, fascism is a supremely patriarchal creed, by which we mean that women are seen as domestic creatures whose role in life is to service men, to have children, to be good mothers and wives, and to keep out of politics.

Fascism and Liberalism

Fascism is hostile to the liberal tradition, and its dislike of the notion of 'reason' makes it difficult to pin down (as we have commented above) as an ideology. It stresses 'action' as opposed to words and yet propaganda and rationalisation are crucial to the movement. It regards the individual as subordinate to the collectivity in general, and the state in particular. Liberal freedoms are seen merely as entitlements that allow the enemies of the 'nation' or the 'people' to capture power. Fascist regimes are highly authoritarian, and use the state as the weapon of the dominant party to protect the nation, advance its interests and destroy its enemies. They are strongly opposed to the idea of democracy (although fascists may use democratic rhetoric to justify their rule or use parliamentary institutions to win access to power), and regard the notion of self-government (the idea that people can control their lives in a rational way and without force) as a dangerous myth. As a movement based upon repressive hierarchy, fascism argues that all institutions should be controlled by 'reliable' leaders, and the 'leadership principle' comes to a climax with the supreme leader, seen as the embodiment of the nation and the people. Fascist leaders may be civilians, but they are closely identified with the army and police, since these institutions are crucial to rooting out opponents. Fascist movements extend beyond the state, but the violence of these movements is condoned and encouraged by the state and, given tight control over the media, this violence is then justified in the light of fascist values.

Fascism and Conservatism

Fascists see themselves as revolutionary in that they are concerned to 'rejuvenate' a tired and decadent society, and some fascists speak of creating a 'new man' in a new society. They are, therefore, anti-conservative as well as anti-liberal, although, as we shall see, they may form tactical alliances with other sections of the right where they can establish momentary common ground. Many regimes, loosely called fascist, are in fact conservative and reactionary systems – Franco's Spain, Petain's 'Vichy' France (a regime that collaborated with the Nazis who occupied the country), Japan under Tojo etc. They may have fascist elements within them, but they are not really anti-conservative in character.

Fascism in Italy

Commentators generally agree that there was no fascism before World War I and that it began in 1922–3 with the emergence of the Italian fascist party. The fascist movement was in power in Italy for 18 years (1925–43). Benito Mussolini, the leader of the Italian fascists, had campaigned for Italy's entry into World War I. The parliamentary Fascio of National Defence was formed in 1917 and drew heavily upon veterans from the war to make up its extra-parliamentary forces. The movement took off when the left organised factory occupations in Milan during the 'red years' of 1919–20, and in November 1920 a fascist party was formed. In October 1922 Mussolini persuaded the king, Victor Emmanuel III, by means of a threatened putsch (dramatised by the march on Rome) to allow him to become prime minister of a coalition government.

The 'action squads', veteran soldiers from an elite battalion, were in theory absorbed into the Voluntary Militia of National Security, but in June 1924 dissatisfied elements killed the socialist deputy, Matteotti, who was a major parliamentary critic of Mussolini. Mussolini then suppressed all the other parliamentary parties and created a regime made up purely of fascists. Until 1929 Mussolini was concerned to consolidate the new system, and in the next decade he embarked upon the conquest of Abyssinia and formed an alliance with Hitler's Germany. Although Italy joined World War II on Hitler's side, in July 1943 Mussolini was ousted by the king and disaffected fascist leaders and Italy sued for peace with the anti-German allies. Mussolini was 'rescued' by German troops and in a small town near Lake Garda an Italian Social Republic was proclaimed that lasted from 1943 to 1945.

Nationalism and War

Mussolini had argued strongly for intervention in World War I, and war was treated by the fascists in Italy as a force for rejuvenation and life. War enabled the nation to constitute itself as a vital, living force, hence Maronetti (1876–1944), leader of the Futurist movement, spoke of the need for a nationalism that was 'ultra-violent, anti-traditionist and anti-clericalist', a nationalism based on 'the inexhaustible vitality of Italian blood' (Griffin, 1995: 26). World War I was crucial to win the battle for civilisation and freedom. Maronetti believed that this war would enrich Italy with 'men of action', while in 1914 Mussolini broke with the 'cowards' who opposed the war, and declared in 1917 that those who fought in the trenches were the 'aristocracy of tomorrow', 'the aristocracy in action' (Griffin, 1995: 26–8). The regime's slogans were 'believe, obey, fight'.

The war was regarded by Roberto Farinacci (1892–1945) as the creator of a new Italian nation, and in Mussolini's view World War I brought about a 'profound psychological transformation' among the peasants in the countryside, with veterans becoming leaders in the rural areas. In Hemingway's *Farewell to Arms* Frederic says to the priest that the Italian army 'were beaten to start with' when they took the peasants from their farms 'and put them in the army. That is why the peasant has wisdom, because he is defeated from the start. Put him in power, and see how wise he is' (1985: 157). Clearly, Mussolini would not have agreed with Hemingway!

Physical exercise was to develop skills, according to the Italian leader, 'which may be necessary in a future war'. War was linked to nationalism. The nation, Mussolini declared shortly before the march on Rome, is a myth to which all must be subordinated, and Costamagna (1881–1965) insisted that from a cultural point of view only the individual nation constitutes a *universum*, a concrete universal. The Italian nation, argued the National Association in 1920, embraces people of the future as well as the present, in a venture that is both domestic as well as international in character: the nation either perishes or dominates. War has, said Luigi Federzoni (1878–1967) of the same Association, 'regenerating properties' that 'have taken effect miraculously and mysteriously in the soul of the Italian people'. War is 'the sole hygiene of the world' (Griffin, 1995: 38; 41–2; 44–5; 71, 85).

Corporativism, Violence and the State

There is a strong economic imperative for fascism. D'Annunzio, a fervent nationalist and military leader who had occupied the Adriatic port of Fiume in September 1919, argued for a corporate structure that embraced employees and employers, public and private, within a state that expressed the common will of the people. Mussolini organised the whole country into 22 corporations. Lyttelton argues that these were held up as fascism's 'most imposing creation': in fact they served no serious function except as a front for groups of leading industrialists to control raw material allocations and investment decisions (Lyttelton, 1979: 97).

The trade unions were seen as contributing loyal employees within this structure – strikes and lockouts were banned – and syndicalists such as Sergio Panunzio (1886–1944) saw in revolutionary trade unionism or syndicalism a force that would transcend its adolescent phrase by building up the state. A new national class was to be created – the essence of a civilisation that is neither bourgeois nor proletarian. Mussolini spoke of 'conscious class collaboration', and although the regime attacked both liberalism and socialism, the tiny Italian Social Republic declared that it aimed to abolish the whole internal capitalist system (Griffin, 1995: 47; 49; 64; 87). In practice employers were regulated by the Italian state, but anti-capitalism was more rhetoric than reality.

Ch 20:
Terrorism,
pp. 486–507

Maronetti spoke of 'violence, rehabilitated as a decisive argument', and when links were forged with Hitler's Germany Mussolini declared that both fascists and Nazis believe in violence 'as the dynamo of their history'. The work of the French anarcho-syndicalist, Sorel, was hugely influential because Sorel had extolled both the importance of myth and the need for violence (Griffin, 1995: 36; 45; 79).

Not surprisingly, the state was given a pivotal role, a spiritual and moral entity that, Mussolini declared, is the conscience of the nation. The state is the foundation of fascism: the state organises the nation and is concerned with the growth of empire. Giovanni Gentile (1875–1944) was the key intellectual of the regime and, drawing upon a version of Hegelian idealism, he pronounced the fascist state to be an 'ethical state': it is the state of 'man himself'. The leader is revered with a capital 'L'. Mussolini ridiculed the 'demo-liberal' civilisation, while praising Hitler for creating 'a unitary, authoritarian, totalitarian state, i.e. a fascist one', although he acknowledges that Hitler operated in a different historical context. Oneness is asserted with a vengeance: in Mussolini's words, the 'order of the day is a single, categorical word which is imperative for all' (Griffin, 1995: 63; 70; 72–3; 79; 82).

Reason is rejected: as an anonymous fascist put it, 'blood is stronger than syllogisms'. (A syllogism is a logical statement in which a conclusion is drawn from two propositions, e.g. all dogs are animals, all animals have four legs, and therefore, all dogs have four legs. A false syllogism!) Mussolini was likened to a Messiah who evangelised millions and, despite the anti-clericalism of some fascist supporters, a pact with the Vatican was signed. Irrationalism and mysticism expressed itself in racism. It is a myth to think that racism was only developed by the Italian fascists at the insistence of the Nazis. The invasion of Ethiopia was presented as the salvation of the Italian race, and even before the alliance with Hitler Mussolini had spoken of the danger that the (so-called) 'coloured races' posed to the 'white race' with their fertility and rate of multiplication. Miccari (1898–1989), one of the key fascist intellectuals, warned against the kind of modernity that is a racket manipulated by 'Jewish bankers, war-profiteers, pederasts, brothel keepers', and Volpe (1876–1971), official historian of fascism, argued that the voice of anti-Semitism was not entirely new in Italy (Griffin, 1995: 60; 80). It is true that a much more systematic racism developed as a result of Nazi pressure (many Jews had actually been recruited to the party and were now expelled), but we can certainly say that fascism built upon a racist culture that is integral to fascism.

Intellectual Roots

Although fascist intellectuals drew upon Machiavelli, Nietzsche and Hegel, there was an important tradition of elitism in Italian political thought that was more recent and more influential.

Mosca (1858–1941) had taught constitutional law at the University of Palermo between 1858 and 1888, and at the Universities of Rome and Turin. In 1884 he published *Theory of Governments and Parliamentary Government*, but is best known for his *The Ruling Class*, which appeared in 1896. All societies, he argued, are governed by minorities whether these are military, hereditary, priestly or based on merit or wealth. He accepted that ownership of property could be a factor in accounting for elite rule, but he rejected the Marxist account that sought to privilege this particular factor. The ruling class or elite owes its superiority to organisational factors, he argued, and its skills alter according to circumstance. What he called the 'political formula' or the ideological mechanisms of rule varied, but whatever the form, all states are necessarily elitist in character, whether their legitimating myth is the divine right of kings, popular sovereignty or the dictatorship of the proletariat.

Democracy, in his view, is simply a more subtle form of manipulation, and the parties offered inducements for people to vote for them. The 'political class' need to be distinguished from other sections of the elite, such as industrialists, but in 1923 Mosca introduced in his work the argument that elites could compete through rival political parties. People of lower socio-economic origin can be recruited in order to renew elites. Unlike other elitists he was, however, fiercely critical of Mussolini, and his theory is best described as conservative rather than fascist.

Rather more hawkish was Pareto (1848–1923). Pareto had taken the chair in political economy at the University of Lausanne in 1894, publishing his *Cours d'économie politique* (1896, 1897). In 1900 he declared himself an anti-democrat, arguing that the political movements in Italy and France were simply seeking to replace one elite by another. While he approved of Marx's emphasis upon struggle, he rejected completely the notion that a classless society was possible. In 1906 Pareto published his *Manual of Political Economy*, where he presented pure economics in mathematical form.

As far as he was concerned, human action is mostly non-logical in character, and stems from non-rational sentiments and impulses: what Pareto called underlying 'residues'. In his most important political and sociological work, the *Mind and Society* that he wrote in 1916, he distinguishes between Class I residues, inventive, imaginative capacities, and Class II residues, conservative, persistent tendencies.

All government is government by an elite who use a combination of coercion and consent. Class I residues predominate when 'foxes' are in control – manipulative politicians who create consent – and Class II residues when violence is necessary. Each of these residues has its strengths and weaknesses, and the 'circulation of

Born in Forli, Italy. His father was a democrat and a socialist, and Mussolini was expelled from the first school he attended. He went to Switzerland in 1902 in order to evade military service, but returned two years later to become first a journalist with and then the editor of the socialist paper *Avanti*. Initially a socialist and an opponent of war, he resigned from the party, becoming a strong nationalist and supporter of the war. He fought in the war but was wounded and returned to Milan to edit the right-wing *Il Popolo d'Italia*.

He was angered by the fact that the Peace Treaty failed to support Italy's demands, and he helped to found the Fascist Party. After the march on Rome he was appointed prime minister by the king, and headed a coalition of fascists and nationalists until the murder of Matteotti in 1924. Left-wing parties were then suppressed and Italy became a one-party state in 1929. After seeking to reorganise the economy, he sent the army into Ethiopia in 1935. Some 400,000 troops fought in this campaign: the capital was captured, poison gas was used and the Emperor of Ethiopia fled to Britain.

League of Nations' sanctions were ineffectual (and opposed by Britain and France), and Mussolini formed a pact with Hitler in 1936. He supported Franco's 'nationalists' and sent troops to support him during the Spanish civil war (1936–9). In 1939 Albania was invaded, and in 1940 war (with Nazi Germany) was declared on Britain and France.

Fighting broke out in North Africa but attempts to invade Greece ended in failure, and Tobruk in Libya was seized by the British in 1941. Italy was now becoming increasingly dependent on Nazi Germany, and Britain and the United States decided to invade Sicily. Although German troops cut off the mainland, the fascist state got the king to dismiss Mussolini, but in 1943 he was freed by German commandos and he set up a fascist regime in northern Italy.

Rome was captured by the allies in 1944, the German resistance disintegrated, and in 1945 Mussolini was captured and shot by partisans while trying to escape to Switzerland.

elites' can be explained as 'lions' – those who rule through brute force – replacing 'foxes'. He saw in Mussolini a politician with a lion-like character who had displaced wily politicians.

But perhaps most important of all in analysing the intellectual roots of fascism was the work of Michels (1876–1936), a disillusioned German socialist who gained an academic position in Turin, and was greatly influenced by syndicalism. In 1911 he published *Political Parties*. Here he argues that all societies and all organisations are subject to 'an iron law of oligarchy' (i.e. a small group controlling the masses). Struck by what he saw as the contrast between the official statements of the German Social Democratic Party and the timidity of its political practice, he argued that oligarchy is present even in parties apparently committed to the norms of democracy. The fact that leaders are in practice autonomous from their followers derives from the constraints of organisation. Although he wrote a good deal about psychology, Michels argued that oligarchical tendencies are based upon organisational rather than psychological factors. The complexity of organisations can only be grasped by professional leaders who have communication skills, and who understand the rules of elections and other external pressures. This leadership is made all the more entrenched by what Michels regarded as the incompetence and emotional vulnerability of their mass membership.

In 1914 Michels wrote a study of Italian imperialism and published widely on politics and sociology. In 1930 he wrote the entry on 'Authority' for the *Encyclopaedia of the Social Sciences*. He admired fascism and argued that, as with Bolshevism, it was a reflection of the general tendency to oligarchy. Michels also wrote a good deal on nationalism, with his later writings becoming increasingly anti-democratic in tone (Beetham, 1977).

Fascism in Germany

Ideas and Perspectives, p. 302

Nazism is, in our view, a form of fascism. Despite historical and cultural differences, both Hitler and Mussolini saw striking similarities in each other's regimes, and the Nazis were greatly influenced by Mussolini's theory and tactics. It is true that Hitler's movement was more extreme than that of Mussolini's. Its racism was more aggressive, its hatred of democracy more intensive, and its expansionism more grandiose. But, as will become clear from the analysis of its features, it was a form of fascism, and there is no need to take the position that the differences between Hitler and Mussolini's regimes outweighed their similarities.

A Brief History

The collapse of the German war effort saw the creation of a republic: an uprising of the left had been smashed by a socialist government that cooperated with the army and the employers. As Griffin has shown in detail, there were German fascists whose version of nationalism, idealisation of war, anti-liberalism and anti-Semitism was at variance with the Nazi view (1995: 104–15). Hitler had made contact with the German Workers' Party (DAP or Deutsche Arbeiterpartei), a fanatical nationalist grouping. Since the clauses of the Versailles Treaty limited the Reichswehr (the German army) to 100,000, Hitler was demobilised in 1920. He became leader of the DAP, which was then renamed the National Socialist German Workers' Party (NSDAP). A putsch was attempted in 1923, and Hitler was given a short prison sentence by a sympathetic court. Nazis have been regarded as isolated fanatics until 1930: yet in 1933 the movement had seized power. In 1928 the NSDAP won only 2.6 per cent of the popular vote. The Versailles Treaty that ended World War I had punitive effects on Germany: all colonies were lost, while it is calculated that the reparations bill equalled 1.5 times the total GNP of Germany in 1929. Although the economy had improved in the 1920s, the depression had catastrophic effects. Investment and industry collapsed, and unemployment was officially estimated at some 30 per cent: the real figure was nearer half.

The SPD (Social Democratic Party of Germany) had headed a coalition government until 1930: when this fell apart the president ruled by decree for three years, real wages were halved, and Hitler had meanwhile stressed the need for a party capable of winning elections and conducting effective mass propaganda. In the elections in 1930 the Nazis came second to the SDP, and two years later they received 37 per cent of the vote. Large employers began to support the Nazis and, although many thought Hitler 'tactless' and his economic policies 'utopian', his militant anti-Bolshevism appealed to them, and they backed him for chancellor. He was appointed to the position in 1933, and the Nazis received 3 posts in an 11-strong cabinet. Goebbels vowed that 1933 would strike the French revolutionary year of 1789 out of history.

By July 1934 Germany had become a one-party state, and the Nazis embarked on their task of building a 'Third Reich' and New European Order. War broke out in 1939 and the defeat of the Nazis was secured in 1945.

Anti-capitalism

Although virulently anti-Marxist, the Nazi movement was in the 1920s strongly anti-capitalist as well. The first programme of the party spoke of the need to share profits, nationalise the trusts, increase pensions and provide free education. Hitler referred to the need to make the working people national, while Strasser (1892–1934), killed in the purges of 1934, attacked capitalism and argued for the emancipation of the worker through 'participation in profits, property and management'. Gründel saw the creation of a new type of human being as constituting the end of the property-owning bourgeois (Griffin, 1995: 117; 123; 128), while Goebbels had said in 1928 that 'no honest thinking person today would want to deny the justification of the workers' movements'. Indeed he had complained in 1926 that Hitler wanted to 'compensate the aristocrats' and not 'disturb private property. Horrendous! . . . we are Socialists. We don't want to have been so in vain!' There is evidence to suggest that those who supported the Nazis were less likely to be unemployed, but rather threatened with unemployment, i.e. the middle and lower middle classes rather than the industrial workers.

The body particularly concerned with advancing Nazi interests among trade unionists (the NSBO) became an increasing embarrassment to the Nazi leadership. The 'Night of the Long Knives' that saw the liquidation of the leadership of the SA (stormtroopers) was justified by Hitler on the grounds that a second revolution had to be avoided at all cost. Socialism continued in the party's title, but it was mere rhetoric. The Nazi economic programme was presented as a form of 'soldierly socialism', but the real target was Marxism and democracy. Marxism, it was said, 'always follows capitalism as its shadow'. Steding (1903–38) spoke contemptuously of 'the purely mercenary capitalism of the stock exchange' (Griffin, 1995: 141; 152). These policies often involved taking away certain freedoms from employers. For example, the introduction of some labour-saving machinery was banned and government permission had to be obtained before reducing their labour force. The government also tended to give work contracts to those companies that relied on manual labour rather than machines.

Anti-Semitic
Propaganda,
p. 298

The German economy remained capitalistic, although with extensive state control. The attack on the Jews was clearly linked to the virulent opposition to Marxism and internationalism, and although Germany had a potent anti-Semitic tradition to draw upon, it has been argued that before 1933 the Nazis placed relatively little emphasis upon anti-Semitism.

Hitler had attacked Jews in *Mein Kampf*, but he had toned down his anti-Semitism while gaining power since he was anxious not to alienate Jewish business leaders. Henry Ford had been compelled to stop publishing anti-Semitic attacks in the United States after the Jewish community organised a boycott of Ford cars in the late 1920s. In the same way Lord Rothermere, owner of the *Daily Mail*, had been forced 'to toe the line' when Jewish businessmen had withdrawn advertising from the newspaper. Hitler began to leave out anti-Semitic comments from his speeches during elections, and during the 1933 general election Jewish businessmen even contributed money to his party.

However, after 1933 Jews were increasingly excluded from mainstream life, and the Nuremburg laws of 1935 stripped Jews of their citizenship and made intermarriage illegal. During Crystal Night over 7,500 Jewish shops were destroyed and 400 synagogues burnt down; 91 Jews were killed and an estimated 20,000 sent to camps. The only people who were punished for the crimes committed on Crystal Night were members of the SA who had raped Jewish women (since they had broken the Nuremberg Laws in so doing). The numbers of Jews wishing to leave the country increased dramatically, and it has been calculated that between 1933 and 1939 approximately half the Jewish population of Germany (250,000) left the country. This included several Jewish scientists (such as Albert Einstein) who were to play an important role in the fight against fascism during the war. Speer recalls that the Ministry of Education was not inclined to support nuclear research on the grounds that nuclear physics was seen as the product of the Jewish mind (1970: 228).

By the beginning of 1942 over 500,000 Jews in Poland and Russia had been killed by the SS, and at the Wannsee Conference in 1942 a final solution was proposed that led to the systematic termination of Jewry. It has been estimated that between 1942 and 1945 around 18 million were sent to extermination camps. Of these, it has been suggested that between 5 and 11 million were killed.

Statism, Women and Colonialism

The Nazis extolled the principle of oneness. The party was Germany, with a single will, faith, flag and leader. Although the Nazis opposed organised religion, a concordat was signed with the pope (the Catholic Church could continue if it did not 'interfere' in politics) and Himmler (1900–45), head of the SS, told the SS that they must believe in God. The religion of the Jews is godless.

Goebbels spoke of 'forging the German nation into a single people'. Benn, who ceased to support the Nazis after the purges of 1934, had declared that Nazi rule manifested itself in the 'total state' – an institution that asserts the complete identity of power and spirit, individuality and the collective. 'It is monist, anti-dialectic, enduring, and authoritarian'. The strong state, argued Schmidt, transcends diversity: every atom of its existence is ruled and permeated by the principle of leadership (Griffin, 1995: 134–5; 138–9; 147).

Women in Nazi Germany, p. 301

The Nazis, of course, espoused an explicit and militant patriarchy. Paula Siber, acting head of the German Association of Women, argued that 'to be a woman means to be a mother'. The woman belongs wherever care is required and she manages 75 per cent of the nation's income by running the home. Hitler disliked women who were interested in politics. By introducing measures that would encourage women to leave the labour market, the level of unemployment could be further lowered. Women in certain professions such as medicine and the Civil Service were dismissed, while other married women were paid a lump sum of 1,000 marks to stay at home.

Anti-Semitic Propaganda

It is worth noting that before 1933 Streicher's virulently anti-Semitic *Der Stürmer* was opposed by some Nazis, and it was only after taking office that its circulation reached half a million. As is argued in the Comenius History Project, a survey of NSDAP members and their reason for joining found that 60 per cent of respondents made no reference at all to anti-Semitism, while 4 per cent openly expressed disapproval of it.

An analysis of Nazi posters in the period from 1928 to 1932 is shown in Table 12.1.

Table 12.1 Enemy groups targeted by NSDAP posters, 1928–32

	Total no. of posters	Percentage
The 'system'	15	12.1
'November-parties'	25	20.1
SPD/Marxism	39	31.5
Centre Party/allies	10	8.1
KPD	6	4.8
Jews	6	4.8
Miscellaneous	23	18.6

The subjects chosen for front-page headlines in the official daily, the *Volkische Beobachter*, between the crucial July 1932 election and Hitler's installation in power, confirm the picture. Between 1932 and 1933 anti-Semitism only featured in just over 3 per cent of the cases: the paper was much more concerned with the 'threat' of Bolshevism, Marxism and the trade unions, and the economic problems facing people. (http://www.stevenson.ac.uk/comenius/articles/totalitarianism/uk_dg/naz_1h.htm)

Biography   **Adolf Hitler (1889–1945)**

Born in the Austrian town of Braunau on 20 April 1889. His parents had come from poor peasant families.

He was deeply religious as a child and contemplated going into the Church. Instead of joining the Civil Service as his father hoped, he became an artist, volunteering for the German army on the outbreak of World War I, and decorated with the Iron Cross for bravery and boldness. After the war he was stationed in Munich, Bavaria, and was bitterly opposed to the decision to declare Bavaria a socialist republic. The republic was overthrown in May 1919, and Hitler was identified as an enthusiastic supporter of the military. It was the Jews and Marxists, he argued, who had undermined the war effort.

He became a leading figure in the German Workers' Party (a nationalist and anti-Semitic organisation that the army had feared might foment communist revolution). He established a reputation as an orator, and in 1920 the National Socialist German Workers' Party was created, and a year later he became leader. After being sent to prison for being involved in violence towards a rival politician he established his own private army – the SA. The members were invariably veterans from the war. The attempt to overthrow the government in Bavaria failed dismally, and Hitler received (an extremely lenient) five-year prison sentence. The prison authorities allowed him to have his autobiography ghost written. *Mein Kampf*, a passionate diatribe against Jews, socialism and liberalism, made the case for empire: Hitler was released after serving a year of his prison sentence.

His *Road to Resurgence* was written in 1927 in order to assure industrialists that he supported private enterprise and was opposed to any social and economic reconstruction of Germany. Unemployment soared during the Depression, and by 1930 the Nazi Party was the second largest party. Two years later it was the largest party in the parliament. In 1933 Hitler was appointed chancellor: in the elections of 1933, despite his persecution of communists and socialists, the Nazis only received 43 per cent of the vote, and with the support of the Catholic Centre Party an Enabling Act was passed giving Hitler dictatorial powers. By the end of 1933 150,000 people were in concentration camps. The inmates included beggars, prostitutes and anyone incapable of working.

Ernst Roehm, as head of the 4.5 million strong SA, was feared particularly by the army. After his murder and the purges, the SS became dominant. In October 1933 Hitler withdrew from the League of Nations; the army trebled in size and military conscription was introduced. The Rhineland was reoccupied, and in 1938 Austria was united with Germany. Hitler marched his troops into the German-speaking part of Czechoslovakia, the Sudetenland, and in 1939 the army was ordered into Poland. With the declaration of war Norway, the Netherlands, Belgium and France were occupied.

Britain was bombed, and in 1941 the invasion of the USSR began. German advances were halted, and the German army suffered massive losses. Hitler's health deteriorated, but attempts to assassinate him were unsuccessful. Soviet troops took Berlin in May 1945, and he committed suicide.

Biography   **Ernst Roehm (1887–1934)**

Born in Munich, he joined the army in 1906 and became a major during World War I.

Roehm became active in right-wing politics after the war, recruiting Hitler to spy on the German Workers' Party. When assured that it was not communist, he joined this party and helped to fund it with army resources.

He took part in the putsch in Munich, and although found guilty of treason he was released and dismissed from the army, becoming a military instructor in Bolivia. In 1931 he returned to Germany, where Hitler placed him in charge of the SA. He increased its numbers, and by 1934 it had a membership of 4.5 million. The army and Hitler's own minister of war became concerned about SA influence, particularly as Roehm argued, as a member of the National Defence Council, that the SA should be responsible for war and was more important than the army itself.

A dossier was assembled on Roehm and the SA, and evidence was created to suggest that Roehm had been paid by the French to overthrow Hitler. Hitler was unmoved by these arguments since Roehm and the SA had played a crucial role in tackling his political opponents and helping him to state power.

On the other hand, Roehm had upset not only the army but industrialists. The latter were unhappy with Roehm's argument that the economy needed to be organised on socialist lines and that a real revolution had yet to take place. The SA leaders were ordered to attend a meeting in Wiesse, and on 29 June 1934 Hitler, accompanied by the SS, personally arrested Roehm. Although many of the SA leaders were shot, Hitler sought to pardon Roehm, but was persuaded by Goering and Himmler that Roehm had to die. When he refused to commit suicide he was shot by the SS.

The purge of the SA was justified by Hitler on the grounds that their leaders were guilty of treason. Eleven years later Goebbels described Roehm as 'a homosexual and an anarchist' and incapable of reforming the army.

Hitler argued that the slogan 'emancipation of women' had been invented by Jewish intellectuals. The woman's world is her husband, her family, her children and her home. The distinction between the two worlds was natural and necessary. 'The woman', he declared, 'has her own battlefield. With every child that she brings into the world, she fights her battle for the nation'.

A mystical belief in the state went hand in hand with a contempt for democracy and a belief in colonialism. The pursuit of colonies was defended as a source of raw materials and as an activity that was vital for Germany's living space. It was not, Ritter argued in 1937, 'an expression of imperialism' but a 'vital natural necessity' (Griffin, 1995: 137; 145).

> By rejecting the authority of the individual and replacing it by the numbers of some momentary mob, the parliamentary principle of majority rule sins against the basic aristocratic principle of Nature . . .
>
> The receptivity of the great masses is very limited, their intelligence small, but their power of forgetting is enormous. In consequence of these faults, all effective propaganda must be limited to a very few points and must harp on these in slogans . . .

Adolf Hitler, *Mein Kampf* (1925) London: Radius Books/Hutchinson, p. 24, p. 165

Women in Nazi Germany

Women were seen as inferior beings who must procreate for the good of the nation. They were to give up work in order to fulfil this biological purpose. During the election campaign of 1932 Hitler promised to take 800,000 women out of employment within four years. In August 1933 a law was passed that enabled married couples to obtain loans to set up homes and start families, which meant that single men and childless couples were taxed more heavily. Married women doctors and civil servants were dismissed in 1934 and from June 1936 women could no longer act as judges or public prosecutors. Women were ineligible for jury service since Hitler believed that they were unable to 'think logically or reason objectively, since they are ruled only by emotion'.

However, during the war it proved necessary to allow women to work in artillery factories and on farms. Medals were provided for women who had large families. The number of women in universities fell significantly. Girls were educated into becoming mothers – women were not to smoke or diet in case this affected their health as mothers.

In 1934 the *Ten Commandments* for the choice of a spouse were propagated:

1. Remember that you are a German.
2. If you are genetically healthy you should not remain unmarried.
3. Keep your body pure.
4. You should keep your mind and spirit pure.
5. As a German choose only a spouse of the same or Nordic blood.
6. In choosing a spouse ask about his ancestors.
7. Health is also a precondition for physical beauty.
8. Marry only for love.
9. Don't look for a playmate but for a companion for marriage.
10. You should want to have as many children as possible.

This was a common rhyme for women:

Take hold of kettle, broom and pan,
Then you'll surely get a man!
Shop and office leave alone,
Your true life work lies at home.

Information from http://www.historylearningsite.co.uk/Women_Nazi_Germany.htm
http://www.germanculture.com.ua/library/weekly/aa080601b.htm
http://www.spartacus.schoolnet.co.uk/GERwomen.htm

Fascism and Capitalism

There can be little doubt that fascists were anti-capitalist in their rhetoric. Radek, one of the communist leaders, was to describe fascism as the 'socialism of the petty bourgeois masses' (Kitchen, 1976: 2). Ramos (1905–36), a Spanish fascist, blamed the bourgeoisie and its 'agents, advocates and front men' for fragmentation, impotence, exhaustion and egoism. Rivera argued that fascism was neither capitalist nor communist: he advocated a national syndicalism that would pass surplus value, as he called it, 'to the producer as a member of his trade union'. La Rochelle, a French fascist, spoke of 'annihilating' liberalism and capitalism. A

Ideas and Perspectives:

Nazism and Fascism

A fiercely debated question relates to the relationship between Nazism and Italian fascism. Is there a general fascism of which Nazism is an example, or is Nazism so unique and particular that it cannot be categorised in this way? As Griffin has pointed out (1995: 93), a number of scholars have argued that Nazism is *sui generis*, unique to the history of Germany.

Allardyce, a US scholar, took the view that a generic fascism does not exist (Griffin, 1995: 302):

Similarities	Differences
Impact of World War I	Attitude to organised religion
Hatred of liberalism and Marxism	Degree of anti-Semitism
Rejection of parliamentary democracy	Global aspirations
Belief in leadership principle	Use of socialism to describe party
Commitment to colonialism	
Admiration for the state	

Not only do we have the profound influence exercised over Hitler and the Nazis by the success of Mussolini in Italy, but the conditions that contributed to the rise of fascism in Italy exercised their influence in Germany as well. The list above shows that Kershaw is right to argue that the similarities between Nazism and other brands of fascism are 'profound' (cited by Griffin, 1995: 93).

Nazism is better understood by seeing it as a variant of fascism – of course with its own particular features. The idea that racism was a German import into Mussolini's Italy is untrue, even though German fascism was much more extreme (and competent) than its Italian counterpart, and the genocidal policies towards the Jews were not part of the anti-Semitism of Italian fascism. Nevertheless, the case for considering Nazism as a form of fascism is overwhelming, and bears upon the important question of other forms of fascism that arose, not only in the inter-war years, but in the post-war period. Griffin's collection of documents is noteworthy for its inclusion of non-Nazi forms of German fascism. Spanish fascists such as Primo De Rivera denied that they were imitating Hitler and Mussolini: he argued that 'by reproducing the achievements of the Italians or the Germans we will become more Spanish than we have ever been' (Griffin, 1995: 188).

Latvian fascist made it clear that 'we acknowledge private enterprise and private property' but are opposed to anarchy (Griffin, 1995: 186; 189; 203; 218).

Biography, p. 333

Zetkin influenced the Comintern in its argument that fascism 'by its origin and exponents' 'includes revolutionary tendencies which might turn against capitalism and its state' but in fact it is counter-revolutionary, supporting capitalism in a situation in which the old, allegedly non-political apparatus of the bourgeois state 'no longer guarantees the bourgeoisie adequate security' (Griffin, 1995: 261). The argument echoes Marx's comment in *The Eighteenth Brumaire of Louis Bonaparte* that when the parliamentary system seems to aid the socialists, then 'the bourgeoisie confesses that its own interest requires its deliverance from the peril of its own self-government' (Marx, 1973: 190). The merits of this argument are that it indicates the dangers which an explicitly illiberal regime poses to the bourgeoisie, and that in 'normal times' a liberal parliamentary system would be much more congenial to a 'bourgeois' regime than an explicitly authoritarian one. It is only when there is the fear that a parliamentary system might help the enemies of capital to power in a situation of crisis and revolutionary threat that 'deliverance' is sought. Miliband stresses that capitalists had to pay a high political price for a system that advantaged them: they had no real control over a dictatorship which arguably served their interests (1973: 85).

Miliband argues that the 'anti-bourgeois resonances' (1973: 80) are important, if only to enable fascist movements to acquire a mass following, nor need we deny that supporters of these movements believed that an anti-capitalist revolution was under way. It is not only Jewish capitalists we will hang, but all capitalists! declares a poster in the museum at the Dachau concentration camp. But Miliband cites Mussolini in 1934 defending private property, and notes that big business under Hitler was given a key role in managing the economy. There was a dramatic increase in the power of capital over labour and an increase in profits. Miliband concedes that business under fascism had to submit to a greater degree of intervention and control than they would have liked, and put up with policies they found disagreeable. Kitchen points out that industrialists disliked particular aspects of Nazi policy (the use of foreign slaves rather than women in the factories, for example, or the economic inefficiency involved in the mass murder of Jews), but he argues that, in broad terms, the industrialists were satisfied with Nazi policy (1976: 59).

As for fascism's supposedly revolutionary character: Miliband contends that the state not only does not significantly change in the composition of its personnel (except to purge it of 'traitors', liberals, etc.), but in Nazi Germany, for example, there were fewer people in the state from working-class origin than before (1973: 82–4). This is why it is not satisfactory to describe fascism as 'a party of revolutionaries' (Linz, 1979: 18), since fascism sought not to transform society and the state but to prevent it from being transformed. It is thus counter-revolutionary rather than revolutionary in character. It is impossible to agree with Eugen Weber that fascism is not a counter-revolution but merely a rival revolution (to communism) (Weber, 1979: 509).

The orthodox communist position – enshrined in the theses of the Comintern or Third International – was that fascism represented 'the most reactionary, most chauvinist, and most imperialist elements of finance capital' (Griffin, 1995: 262). It was only in the mid-1930s that communists dropped the notorious argument that social democrats were 'social fascists' and the enemy of the working class. 'Finance capital', in the orthodox definition cited above, refers to Lenin's argument in *Imperialism* that bank capital has merged with industrial capital, but it seems less contentious to accept Miliband's point that fascism represented industrialists as well as bankers in a situation in which threat of left 'extremism' made right 'extremism' a necessary, if far from ideal, choice. The Coles argued that fascism is state-controlled capitalism 'operated in the interests of the broad mass of property owners'. Horkheimer, a key figure in the neo-Marxist Frankfurt School, declared that 'whoever is not prepared to talk about capitalism should also remain silent about fascism' (Griffin, 1995: 267; 272).

Psycho-analysts argued that fascism is rooted in the human character – it is a form of personality structure, an authoritarian character. But this does not mean, as Adorno acknowledged, that such a structure can only be modified by psychological

How to read:

Kitchen's *Fascism*

Kitchen's short book starts with an introduction that should be read carefully. His next two chapters – dealing with orthodox communist theories and psychological theories of fascism – contain useful information and can be skim read. The same is true of the following two chapters – dealing with the theory of totalitarianism and Ernst Nolte's theory of fascism. Both are powerful critiques but skim reading should enable the reader to get the gist of the argument.

Chapters 5 and 6 deserve closer attention. Kitchen's examination of the links between fascism and industry and fascism and the middle classes are exceptionally compelling, and merit a close reading. The chapter on Bonapartism is useful but again can be skim read, while the conclusion contains a valuable summary of his argument, and deserves a careful look.

means (Griffin, 1995: 289), and it could well be argued that we still need to refer to capitalism and crisis to understand why fascism arises in certain societies and at certain historical periods, and not at others. Reich, who was expelled from the German Communist Party in the 1930s for his dissident views, had argued that fascism is the result of thousands of years of warping in the human structure: a number of later studies contended that fascism was an attempt to compensate for mothering and family life (Kitchen, 1976: 13; 23).

Fascism, Liberalism and the Enlightenment

'1789 [the year of the French Revolution, and the inauguration of the era of Liberty, Equality and Fraternity] is abolished' (Heywood, 1992: 174). This was how the Nazis proclaimed their victory in 1933. Although fascists specifically targeted Marxism, they saw it as an ideology that built upon, and was thus rooted in, the assumptions of liberalism and the Enlightenment. Dunn quotes the words of Hitler: 'National Socialism is what Marxism could have been had it freed itself from the absurd, artificial link with the democratic system' (1979: 21).

The State of Nature, Equality and the Individual

Fascists not only deny that humans have ever lived outside of society, but they interpret 'nature' in a repressively hierarchical manner. Although the idea that humans are self-contained atoms who are naturally separate and unrelated to one another constitutes a mystification of social reality, fascism attacked abstract individualism because of its universal and egalitarian claims. It dramatically threw the baby out with the bathwater.

Classical liberalism sees individuals as naturally free and equal. Fascism takes the view that nature is a force that embodies violence, instinct and superiority: hence it rejects the whole notion of equality, even as a formal attribute. Individuals are created by the community, and the community is interpreted in statist terms. It is true that Nazi ideologists gave a specifically racial and *völkisch* (peoples') dimension to the notion of community so that the community constituted a kind of soul. But all fascists see the community as 'natural', animated by some kind of life force – it is an emotional organism, not a rational construct – and it assigns superiority to the few and inferiority to the many.

The notion of humanity was attacked for two reasons: first because it ignored what was deemed to be racial superiority – of Aryans over Jews, whites over blacks, etc. – and second because it implied that the mass of humans mattered. The progress and culture of humanity, declared Hitler, 'are not a product of the majority, but rest exclusively on the genius and energy of the personality' (Vincent, 1995: 157). The individual denotes not the ordinary and everyday human being, but the leader, the genius, the person who must be obeyed.

Nationalism

Liberalism has an ambivalent position towards nationalism because it has an ambivalent position towards the state. In the state of nature individuals are deemed cosmopolitan – they are outside both nation and state – but as they become conscious of the 'inconveniences' of such a position they not only form a state but acquire a national identity. Liberal nationalism, as does the liberal state, seeks to reconcile universal freedom and equality with the 'necessary evil' of particular institutions that divide the world. Liberal nationalists argue that all nations are equal, and the liberal state seeks to provide security for the free citizen. Just as fascism sees the community as somehow prior to the individual (an inversion of the liberal abstraction), so it sees the nation as the embodiment of superiority and domination.

Nationalism necessarily takes an explicitly xenophobic form, based on hatred. Hatred of foreigners, aliens, the weak, the vulnerable, the disabled, the needy, the female, and a characterisation of 'lesser' peoples and nations in terms of these 'despised' categories. Mussolini challenged those who saw Machiavelli as the founder of fascism, on the grounds that Machiavelli was insufficiently contemptuous of the masses – the herd, as Mussolini liked to call them – who gratefully accepted inequality and discipline (Vincent, 1995: 156).

Rationality

Liberalism and the Enlightenment see all individuals as rational, and thus capable of governing themselves. Fascism regards 'reason' as inherently abstract, and extols action as a force based upon instinct and feeling. You should 'think with your blood', and de Rivera of the Spanish Falange (a fascist movement that Franco tolerated and used) declared that the movement is not a way of thinking but 'a way of being' (Vincent, 1955: 155). It is the soul, not the mind, emotion and instinct, not reason and logic that ultimately count. Again fascism challenges, in a spirit of negative inversion, the abstractions of the Enlightenment. Reason is rejected – not made historical and concrete. Fascism dismisses not merely the weaknesses of liberalism (its chronic tendency to abstraction), but its conceptual strengths (its argument for the individual, universality, reason and self-government).

Colin Jordan, who founded the White Defence League in 1958 and the National Socialist Movement in 1962, declared himself in revolt against liberalism, singling out for particular mention its 'cash nexus', 'its excessive individualism', 'its view of man as a folkless, interchangeable unit of world population', its 'sickly humanitarianism' and its 'fraudulent contention' that the wishes of the masses are 'the all-important criteria' (Griffin, 1995: 325–6).

Fascism, Stalinism and the State

Fascism identifies the individual and the community with the state. Fascism inverts the classical liberal thesis, that humans dwell in a stateless order of nature, by arguing that humans derive their very nature and being from membership of the state. Although the Nazis liked to speak of the community in racial terms, they too held that the repressive hierarchies of the state are central to human identity.

Hence the explicit and dramatic statism of the fascist analysis. By arguing that humans are statist in essence, fascists reject the idea that freedom and force stand as mutually exclusive entities. On the contrary, force becomes something that ennobles and distinguishes humans and, since the exercise of force implies the existence of a repressive hierarchy, fascism rejects the notion of equality. The individual is a person who stands out from the mass, so that the leadership principle is woven into social analysis. Leaders are outstanding individuals who dictate to and mould the formless and ignorant masses.

It follows from this avowedly statist doctrine that the nation has enemies both from without and within who threaten its purity and cohesion. War and violent conflict are the only viable responses so that the crushing of the other is the way to affirm the self. Xenophobia and racism are built into the statism of fascist premises, and so is male chauvinism. The superior individual must be a 'he' since the notion of the female is identified with passivity and cowardice.

It is important not to see the state as itself a fascist institution, since states can be liberal and anti-authoritarian in character in which, through devices such as the rule of law and parliamentary representation, state force is regulated and limited. On the other hand, it is also important to see the continuities as well as the discontinuities between fascism and the state. The use of force polarises, and can only be justified against those who are deemed 'enemies' of society. The nationalism that reaches its extreme form in fascism is inherent in the state, and it could be argued that there is a real tension between the state as an institution claiming a monopoly of legitimate force and the notion of democracy as self-government.

Stalinism

Can one describe Stalinism – authoritarian communism – as a form of fascism? There are of course similarities. The concept of dictatorship is central to Stalinism and a particularly vicious and exclusionary form of class struggle is used to justify purges, mock trials and authoritarian practices in general. But there are also significant dissimilarities, so that however tempting, it is, in our view, erroneous to see left and right authoritarianism, Stalinism and fascism as interchangeable.

Stalin's Purges

Stalin was admired by Hitler, and the latter told Speer that if Germany won World War II Stalin would remain in charge of Russia (Speer, 1970: 306). The famine in the early 1930s that followed collectivisation killed between 6 and 7 million people. The purges that began in the mid-1930s were directed against dissidents within the party and in society at large, and took millions of lives. About 35,000 military officers were shot or imprisoned. Robert Conquest has estimated that by 1938 there were 7 million victims in the labour camps, where the survival rate could drop to some 2 or 3 per cent. The purges have been summarised as follows:

Arrests, 1937–8 – about 7 million

Executions – about 1 million

Died in camps – about 2 million

In prison, late 1938 – about 1 million

In camps, late 1938 – about 8 million

By the time Stalin died (in 1953), the camps' population had increased to some 12 million.

Source: www.gendercide.org

In other words, the argument that became widespread during the cold war, identifying communism and fascism as forms of *totalitarianism*, is superficial and misleading. Mommsen makes the point that this theory glosses over the structural features peculiar to the fascist party. The theory of democratic centralism may have operated to strengthen the leadership of Communist Parties but it was a theory of

Exercise

You are having a cup of coffee in a crowded coffee shop in your Students' Union when four young men sit at your table and begin talking. Because you are on your own you cannot but hear their conversation. 'There are too many blacks around here', says A. 'I agree, they should all be sent back to their place of origin', comments B. 'But some of them were born here', interjects C. 'That's irrelevant', says D. 'Whether they were born here or not, they are not part of our race, and they just don't fit in'. 'Indeed', declares A, 'I have noticed that the lecturers make a fuss of them, as though they are more important than us whites'. 'Yeah', says B, 'what do you expect when most of the lecturers are communists and Jews? I think that the university should only employ decent-minded Christians – people with sensible views'. C protests: 'That would be undemocratic'. 'So what', says D. 'Our democracy is a farce anyway – we need strong rule by someone we can look up to. This notion of majority rule is an idiotic liberal idea anyway'. 'In fact', comments A, 'there are blacks in my street and tonight a group of us are going to show them what we think of them with something hard and large through their windows'.

- A, B and D are clearly right-wing extremists. They are racists.

- Which would you say is a fascist?

- Although you find their views deeply upsetting, would you call the police?

organisation alien to fascism (Mommsen, 1979: 153). Moreover, fascist and communist ideology are poles apart. Stalinism seeks to build a world that is ultimately stateless and classless in character – it draws upon a Marxist heritage to argue that under communism people, all people, will be able to govern their own affairs.

This is not deny the authoritarianism that existed (and still exists) in Communist Party states, but it could be argued that the 'cult of the personality', the denial of democracy, the male chauvinism, etc. in these societies stand in contradiction to the theories of communism. In fascism, on the other hand, these features are not in contradiction with the doctrine: they are explicitly enshrined in the theories and movements. This argument may not seem of much comfort to the inmate of a 'gulag' who is worked to death in inhuman conditions, but it points to a qualitative difference between the statism of fascism and statism of Stalinism. Moreover, as Kitchen points out, communism sought to radically change the means of production, whereas fascist regimes did not, and this throws further doubt on the proposition that similarities between fascism and communism outweigh the differences (1976: 31).

Fascism Today

One of the objections that Kitchen makes to the German thinker, Ernst Nolte's, theory of fascism, is the view that fascism belongs only to the past. It does not exist today. This is not only a complacent view of fascism, it confuses a movement with its historical manifestations (Kitchen, 1976: 40–1). It is true that fascism arose in the inter-war period, and that one of the problems of identifying post-war fascism is that the revulsion of most of the world against Nazism in particular has meant that contemporary fascism generally avoids too close an identity with the 'models' of the past. Fascists in Europe have had the problem in the post-war period of getting to grips with the defeat of Mussolini and Hitler in World War II. There have been a variety of responses.

The Unrepentant Apologists

Some have taken the view that Hitler and Mussolini were correct in their policies although they were defeated by the Allied forces. Jordan, who founded the White Defence League in 1958 and the National Socialist Movement in 1962, took the view that fascism (even in its extreme Hitlerian form) is as relevant as ever, and the West European Federation set up in 1963 espoused explicitly Nazi doctrine. The New European Order established in Switzerland supported similar views (Griffin, 1995: 326–8).

The Holocaust Deniers

Some fascists try to undercut the argument of their critics by denying that the Nazis had in fact brought about the Holocaust. The leader of the Belgian fascist movement during World War II, Degrelle, argued to the Pope in 1979 that

Auschwitz could not have exterminated large numbers of Jews, travellers, etc. and that anyway, the terror bombing of the Allies and the gulags of Stalin put into perspective any human rights abuses the Nazis might have caused. The term 'final solution' did not mean extermination – this is another of the deniers' contentions – and that during the war other nations had concentration camps too (Griffin, 1995: 330–7). Irving, an historian who has built his reputation on 'reassessing' the Holocaust, admits the terrible atrocities of the camps, but argues that these took place against the instructions of Hitler, who merely wanted to have Jews transported to Madagascar, an island off the African coast (Griffin, 1995: 330–7). To deny the existence of the Holocaust is a criminal offence in Germany, although it could be argued that obnoxious contentions such as these should be exposed through argument rather than crushed by law.

The Critical Fascists

Mosley, the leader of the British Union of Fascists, before World War II, argued that Hitler had overreached himself – tried to achieve too much – and this was the reason for his downfall. The concentration camps and the sacrifice of the youth tarnished an otherwise noble ideal. Mussolini had badly miscalculated when he entered the war, but the harshness of his *squadristi* can be excused by 'the incredible savagery and brutality of the reds'. Chesterton, the first chair of the National Front, admits that fascism failed disastrously, and the 'excesses' of Hitler, in particular, discredited the cause (Griffin, 1995: 323–4).

Some, such as Ernest Niekisch (1889–1967) argued that the fascist revolution had been hijacked by demagogues (i.e. leaders who appeal to prejudices for support) such as Hitler, who was a travesty of the spiritual elite really required (Griffin, 1995: 319).

Eurofascism

The European Social Movement, founded in 1951, sought to unite Europe against 'communism', with Evola, an Italian fascist, arguing that such a Europe must be an empire. Mosley, on the other hand, spoke of the need for Europe to become a 'nation', with a pan-European government using Africa as a resource base (Griffin, 1995: 333–5). A number of those associated with what can be called a 'New Right' (not to be confused with the neo-liberalism of free marketeers) speak of the need to regenerate Europe so that it stands apart from communism and capitalism that in its liberal form, eradicates identity and imposes a vulgar and soulless 'rule of quantity' upon life (Griffin, 1995: 351).

Nationalist Salvation

Some fascists have turned to nationalism, arguing that a national revolution is necessary as a 'cleansing fire of purification'. Ultra-nationalists have utilised punk rock, heavy metal music and football hooliganism (Griffin, 1995: 360, 363). However, parties such as the British National Front claim to stand for democracy, and accuse their opponents of not being supporters of 'genuine democracy'.

South African Apartheid

There is no doubt that the South African National Party and its policies of apartheid were widely admired by the extreme right elsewhere, including explicit fascists. A Mosley supporter, Webster spoke of the South African nationalists as following 'the same path as Hitler did, but they will not be as hasty as he was' (Bunting, 1969: 71). During World War II, the National Party (NP) communicated with Nazis over their campaign to withdraw South Africa's support from the Allies. The NP had cordial links with the Ossewabrandwag (the Ox-wagon Sentinel), which also had connections with the Nazis and whose paramilitary wing sought to overthrow the government. Vorster, a future prime minister, declared in 1942 that his Christian nationalism 'was an ally of national socialism' (Bunting, 1969: 98).

When Germany and Italy were defeated, the National Party began to distance itself from anti-English and anti-Semitic policies, and concentrated on developing the doctrine of apartheid. All those serving sentences for wartime offences were released after the Nationalist electoral victory in 1948. The stripping of Africans and (so-called) coloureds of their political rights, the outlawing of sexual relations between the 'races', the Suppression of Communism Act (which banned the party and imposed house arrest on opponents of the regime), the reservation of skilled jobs for whites, the control imposed on the trade unions – all these and many more acts had been envisaged by the National Party during the war period (Bunting, 1969: 110).

Bunting's detailed account of what he calls the Nuremberg Laws of grand apartheid and the title of his book, *The Rise of the South African Reich*, raises the question whether apartheid South Africa can be considered a fascist regime. The regime certainly resorted to terror against its opponents, and was brutal, explicitly racist and authoritarian. On the other hand, it was a parliamentary system for whites, and allowed limited liberalism in its treatment of the press, judiciary and opposition parties, provided they were relatively conservative in character. It comes close to being a fascist regime, and certainly Griffin is right to regard Afrikaner nationalist organisations such as the Afrikaner–Weerstandsbeweging (the Afrikaner Resistance Movement), which developed in the post-apartheid period, as fascist in practice (Griffin, 1995: 376).

Nevertheless we would say that, although apartheid was extremely right wing, it was not technically fascist, despite its pre-war and wartime roots.

Nationalism is presented as a doctrine for the equality of nations. The National Front (NF) sees itself 'as a radical party seeking deep and fundamental changes in British society. Unlike many other radical parties, particularly those of the past, we do not seek to impose our views on the population'. The implication is that such a party distances itself from the explicit authoritarianism of interwar fascism (see http://www.nfne.co.uk/nfsop.html).

In 1982 John Tyndall formed the British National Party (BNP), and although he speaks of the 'degenerative forces' poisoning national life linked to liberalism and internationalism, the party speaks of wishing to extend democracy (go to http://www.bnp.org.uk/mission.htm), and objects to the idea that it is fascist or

Sir Oswald Mosley (1896–1980)

Educated at Winchester and Sandhurst, Mosley fought in World War I. In 1918 he was elected to Parliament as a Conservative MP for Harrow, but broke with the Conservatives and won a seat as an independent in 1922.

Two years later he joined the Labour Party and in 1927 he was elected to the party's National Executive Committee. He was appointed by the Labour leader to the post of Chancellor of the Duchy of Lancaster when Labour won the election in 1929. In 1930 Mosley proposed a programme that he believed would help deal with the growing unemployment in Britain. Using ideas derived from the economist John Maynard Keynes, Mosley proposed that the state should stimulate foreign trade, direct industrial policy and use public funds to promote industrial expansion. When these proposals were rejected he resigned his post.

In 1931 he founded the New Party, but despite his influential supporters the party failed to secure a seat in the election of 1931. The following year he met Mussolini and, impressed by the Italian regime and its leader, he dissolved the New Party and set up the British Union of Fascists (BUF) in its stead.

The BUF was strongly anti-communist and argued for a programme of economic revival based on government spending and protectionism. By 1934 Mosley was organising marches through Jewish districts in London. The 1936 Public Order Act outlawed the wearing of political uniforms, and private armies were also made illegal. Threatening and abusive words were made a criminal offence, and the Home Secretary had the powers to ban marches. This seriously affected the activities of the BUF.

In October 1936 Diana Mitford secretly married Mosley in Nazi propaganda minister Joseph Goebbels's drawing room in Berlin, with Hitler one of the guests at the ceremony. Mosley's party lost further support with the outbreak of World War II and in 1940 Mosley was arrested and, along with other prominent members of his organisation, sent to prison. The British Union of Fascists was dissolved and its publications banned.

Mosley and his wife were treated extremely leniently in prison, and in 1943 he was released, despite protests, with Mosley's own sister-in-law describing the release as 'a slap in the face of anti-fascists': 'a direct betrayal of those who have died for the cause of anti-fascism'.

After the war Mosley ran a publishing house for right-wing authors, and in 1947 he formed the Union Movement, which argued for an integrated Europe and an end to Commonwealth immigration.

In 1949 Mosley went to live in France, close to the Duke of Windsor who had been forced to abdicate as king some 13 years earlier. He published *The European Situation* in 1950, arguing that the union of Europe needed to be accompanied by a national government able to act rapidly and decisively and be subject to parliamentary control. In 1958 he wrote *Europe: Faith and Plan*. Mosley stood for parliament in 1959 (for Kensington North) and in 1966 (for Shoreditch and Finsbury). He was unsuccessful on both occasions.

312 Part 2 Classical Ideologies

authoritarian. It is difficult to avoid the conclusion that parties such as the BNP and the NF are parties of the extreme right rather than fascist in the way we have defined the term. On the other hand the BNP, for example, has links with and invites speakers from explicitly fascist groups, so that the 'democratic' appearances of such organisations should not be taken at face value. La Oeuvre France, founded in 1968, describes itself as 'a strictly nationalist movement' and treats the accusation of 'fascism' and nazism' as slurs against French people 'of good stock' (Griffin, 1995: 371–2). Of course ultra-nationalist movements will be sensitive to the idea that they are the derivatives of other movements, and hence are likely to resist the label of fascism on that score as well.

However, groups on the far right that have sprung up in former Communist Party states, such as Romania, may espouse more explicitly fascist positions. The New Right movement, founded in 1993 in Romania, speaks of the need for an 'ethnocratic' state that it explicitly contrasts to a democratic state. The National Democratic Party of Germany, eclipsed in the late 1980s by the Republican Party and the German People's Union, espouses Germany as a *völkish* national entity, but calls for social justice and equality within Germany's borders. The Italian Social Movement which won 12.7 per cent of the vote with the National Alliance (in March 1994), seeks to reconstruct the Italian state and regards Mussolini as the greatest statesman of the twentieth century (Griffin, 1995: 379; 382; 387).

Summary

Although fascism is a chaotic and opportunist movement, it can and should be defined. There are a number of characteristics – anti-liberalism, ultra-nationalism, the extolling of violence, militant statism, mass support, etc. – that distinguish this twentieth-century movement from other movements.

Fascism arose first in Italy. The development of fascism in Italy needs to be explained, since this was the particular movement that gave the general movement its name. Contrary to widely held views, Mussolini's regime was racist, although it is true that systematic anti-Semitism only developed after the alliance with Hitler.

Nazism is seen as a form of fascism, and not simply as a historically unique movement. It is an extreme kind of fascism, emphasising the racial character of nationalism in a more aggressive and systematic manner. Its anti-capitalism was ultimately rhetorical, as the liquidation of the leaders of the Nazi 'left' in 1934 demonstrates. Although fascism acquired mass support through espousing a rhetorical anti-capitalism, once in power fascist movements consolidated their links with big business. It is true that fascist leaders directed businesses and implemented policies that were not always to the satisfaction of the business community, but it is also true that backing from large capitalist corporations was crucial for fascism's success.

Fascism rejects liberalism and the Enlightenment. Ideas of reason, equality, emancipation are contemptuously dismissed in a specifically negative manner. Although there are problems with the ideas of liberalism and the Enlightenment, fascism unceremoniously throws the baby out with the bathwater. Fascists see the state itself as central to human identity and vital to the idea of community. The violence that the state both exercises and seeks to regulate is extolled by fascists, and although the liberal state is significantly different from the fascist one there are similarities as well as differences in all forms of the state. Similarly, all left-wing authoritarianism is also statist in character; it is not correct to describe Stalinism, say, as a form of fascism. There are similarities, but these are outweighed by their differences.

Fascist movements exist today, but there are a number of problems in identifying them. Fascism was discredited by the defeat of Nazi Germany and fascist Italy in World War II, and of course by the atrocities committed by the Nazis in the concentration camps. Post-war movements of the extreme right often deny that they are fascist in character – they may even claim to espouse democracy, although these claims should be approached with caution. The other problem with identifying post-war fascism is that extreme nationalist movements (which are not German or Italian) feel that to express allegiance to fascism would compromise their own claims to 'authenticity' and national uniqueness.

Questions

1. Can fascism be defined and, if so, how?
2. Is fascism a purely Italian phenomenon?
3. Why does fascism reject liberalism and the Enlightenment?
4. 'Stalinism is a form of fascism.' Discuss.
5. Comment on the argument that fascism is a movement of the inter-war period.

References

Beetham, D. (1977) 'From Socialism to Fascism: The Relation between Theory and Practice in the Work of Robert Michels', *Political Studies* 25, 3–24, 161–81.

Bunting, B. (1969) *The Rise of the South African Reich* Harmondsworth: Penguin.

Dunn, J. (1979) *Western Theory in the Face of the Future* Cambridge: Cambridge University Press.

Griffin, R. (1995) *Fascism* Oxford and New York: Oxford University Press.

Hemingway, E. (1985) *A Farewell to Arms* London: Heinemann Educational.

Heywood, A. (1992) *Political Ideologies* Basingstoke: Palgrave.

Kitchen, M. (1976) *Fascism* Basingstoke: Macmillan.

Linz, J. (1979) 'Some Notes towards a Comparative Study of Fascism in Sociological Historical Perspective' in W. Laqueur (ed.), *Fascism: A Reader's Guide* Harmondsworth: Penguin, 13–78.

Lyttelton, A. (1979) 'Italian Fascism' in W. Laqueur (ed.), *Fascism: A Reader's Guide* Harmondsworth: Penguin, 81–114.

Marx, K. (1973) 'The Eighteenth Brumaire of Louis Napoleon' in D. Fernbach (ed.), *Surveys from Exile* Harmondsworth and London: Penguin and New Left Review, 143–249.

Miliband, R. (1973) *The State in Capitalist Society* London: Quartet.

Mommsen, H. (1979) 'National Socialism: Continuity and Change' in W. Laqueur (ed.), *Fascism: A Reader's Guide* Harmondsworth: Penguin, 151–92.

Speer, A. (1970) *Inside the Third Reich* London: Weidenfeld & Nicolson.

Vincent, A. (1995) *Modern Political Ideologies* 2nd edn Oxford: Blackwell.

Weber, E. (1979) 'Revolution? Counter-Revolution? What Revolution' in W. Laqueur (ed.), *Fascism: A Reader's Guide* Harmondsworth: Penguin, 488–531.

Further Reading

- Griffin's reader on fascism (referenced above) is an invaluable source of material with acute introductions and prefaces.

- Kitchen's *Fascism* (referenced above) is comprehensive and readable, short and incisive.

- Fromm's *Fear of Freedom* (London: Routledge & Kegan Paul, 1942) is a classic interpretation of fascism that draws upon psychoanalysis for its explanation.

- For detailed analyses of fascism in the inter-war period see *The Fascism Reader*, ed. A. Kallis, London and New York: Routledge, 2003.

- Albert Speer *Inside the Third Reich* (referenced above) is a fascinating read.

Weblinks

For information about the Holocaust: http://www.thinkequal.com

For useful sites on fascism: http://dictionary.reference.com/search?q=fascism

For further information and bibliography: http://en.wikipedia.org/wiki/Fascism

What is a New Social Movement?

We have argued that an ideology is a belief system focused around the state. The 'classical ideologies' discussed in Part 2 took the legitimacy of the state to be a central concern, and this is true even of anarchist theories: although most anarchists reject the claim to legitimacy made on behalf of the state one of their main objectives is to challenge the state, and in this sense anarchists are 'state focused'. Despite talk of 'globalisation' and the 'hollowing out of the state', the state remains important in political theory, and the new ideologies discussed in this part of the book do not dismiss it. They do, however, challenge the *sharp* distinction between domestic and international politics. For example, multiculturalists argue that cultures do not equate to nations, and therefore allegiance to the state does not, as the British politician Norman Tebbit claimed, require that British Asians support the English cricket team against Pakistan. Similarly, an important feature of feminism is the linking together of women's experience across the world. While a traditional ideology, such as socialism (or Marxism, as one variant of socialism), stressed that the workers 'know no nation', and therefore class solidarity should transcend the state, the focus of socialist (communist) political action was capture of the state. Feminists, on the other hand, while prepared to work through state structures to achieve legal change, identify power relations at both sub-state and supra-state levels: women can be oppressed through family structures as well as by global forces. Ecologism represents an even more radical challenge to the significance of the state as the central focus of political thought. Ecologists – as distinct from environmentalists – see 'nature' as an interconnected whole, protection of which requires both small-scale organisation and global action. Small-scale, quasi-anarchistic communities are required as a means of avoiding environmentally damaging transportation of goods, while global agreements are necessary to tackle problems that by their nature do not respect state boundaries. Fundamentalism may also represent a challenge to the state: Islamic fundamentalism regards the state as a corruption of Islam (US fundamentalism and Zionism do, however, appear highly nationalistic, although some variants of Zionism conceive of the Jewish State as a religious, rather than a secular, entity, and thus as quite different to the traditional state).

But the challenge to the distinction between national and international politics is not the only significant divider between classical and new ideologies. In trying to understand what is 'new' about the new ideologies three differences – or 'discontinuities' – can be identified. The first we have already identified – the challenge to the significance of the state. The second may appear trite: the 'new ideologies' are recent in origin. This point can, however, be expressed in a more sophisticated way: the new ideologies have emerged as a response to fundamental changes in the social and economic structures of advanced industrial societies. The third difference relates to the intellectual relationship of the new ideologies to the traditional ones: the former engage *critically* with the latter.

Social and Economic Change

Ch 13:
Feminism,
pp. 324–48

The four ideologies that we discuss in Part 3 emerged after World War II. While they have intellectual roots predating the war, and indeed the roots go back centuries – think of Mary Wollstonecraft – *consciousness* of each as a *relatively unified system of thought* has only developed in the last 40 or so years. While it is crude to date an ideology simply from its first usage in public debate, the employment of these labels – these -isms – in everyday debate is of some significance and, roughly speaking, the terms 'feminism' and 'ecologism' (environmentalism, Green thought) became current in the 1960s, multiculturalism in the 1970s, and fundamentalism (which had been employed in debates within US Protestantism in the 1920s) began to achieve wider application in the 1970s and 1980s. Without reducing these new ideologies to social and economic changes we suggest that they are, in part, the product of certain new socio-economic structures.

We have seen in Parts 1 and 2 that the traditional ideologies themselves changed in response to the massive social and economic change of the nineteenth century: John Stuart Mill's defence of representative democracy is a response to the rise of 'mass society', as is his concern with the 'tyranny of the majority'. Mill's political world is very different to that of, say, John Locke. Similarly, Mill's near-contemporary Karl Marx contrasts his own socialism with that of earlier 'utopian' socialists. And conservatism, the ideology that above all others claims to be 'historical' – in the sense of responding to the world as it is, rather than providing a model of an alternative world – has undergone considerable adaptation from the eighteenth-century thinkers Hume and Burke to twentieth-century thinker Oakeshott. Given the extent of social 'rationalisation' which Oakeshott so bemoans, his thought has an elegiac quality when compared with that of earlier conservative thinkers. Fascism is, of course, a response to specific social and economic conditions, most especially a perceived mismatch between the development of state and economic structures. By entitling the first two parts of this book 'Classical Ideas' and 'Classical Ideologies' we are not suggesting that they are 'dead': they are continually developing as ideologies, and indeed some thinkers have argued that we are all liberals now (Fukuyama, 1992). Rather than seeing the contrast between classical and new ideologies as a distinction between 'dead' and 'living' we understand new ideologies as distinct systems of thought that have emerged out of, and in response to, changing social and economic structures, and those changes have also affected the classical ideologies.

Ch 8:
Conservatism,
pp. 186–206

What then are these changes? One way of addressing this question is to consider what might be termed the 'crisis of Marxism'. The development of this 'crisis' can be understood in terms of historical events, of which the final and most spectacular was the overthrow of state socialism in Eastern Europe in 1989 followed by its collapse in the Soviet Union in 1991. In the period dubbed 'the short twentieth century' (Hobsbawm, 1995) – 1914–91 – there have been a series of key events that arguably presaged the final collapse of the socialist project: the Molotov-Ribbentrop Pact between the USSR and Nazi Germany in 1939, the Soviet invasions of Hungary (1956) and Czechoslovakia (1968), and the imposition of martial law in Poland in the early 1980s. But in parallel to these concrete political events there has been a deeper intellectual crisis. The central problem for Marxists has been the failure of the working class to develop a truly 'revolutionary consciousness'. Far from rising up as one, the working class (or classes?) splintered. In, for example, Weimar Germany (1919–33) there was a major split between the communists and the social democrats, as well as between left and right, with a significant section of the working class attracted to the far right Nazi Party (or NASDP). And, as critics of Marx point out, those countries such as Russia that underwent proletarian revolutions were not the ones 'marked down' for it because they lacked sufficient industrial development. The fragmentation of Marxism into different streams of thought (McLellan, 1979) was a response to the crisis, but so was the adoption of Marxist categories of thought by (essentially) non-Marxist theorists. These theorists use the language of collective agency, oppression and liberation, but they are no longer applied to the working class, and the strategy of liberation is much more 'particularistic' – whereas the root idea of Marxism was that the transition to a classless society ultimately resulted in the liberation of humankind, and not simply one oppressed socio-economic class; new social movements, be they feminist, multiculturalist or ecological, do not *necessarily* make such a claim. We say 'not necessarily' because there is still a hint that women's liberation is good for men, or that human beings are part of 'nature', and so 'ecological justice' is also 'human justice'. Fundamentalism – or, at least, Islamic fundamentalism – can also be understood as a response to the crisis of Marxism: many parts of the Arab-Islamic world embraced Marxist ideology in the 1960s as a form of development, or 'catch-up', ideology. The failure of state-led socialism opened a space for another ostensibly egalitarian ideology – Islamic fundamentalism.

We have suggested that the four new ideologies are, in part, a response to the failure of Marxism, but conversely at least two of them – feminism and ecologism – have emerged due to rising levels of economic well-being (of course the survival of capitalism, against Marx's predictions, is part of the explanation of the crisis of Marxism). This may seem a strange claim, given that both are concerned with oppression. However, that feminism and ecologism emerged in the 1960s is significant. If we consider gender relations, even prior to the 1960s there were social changes taking place that fundamentally affected the balance of power between men and women: the wartime mobilisation of women to work in factories and on the land is generally regarded as significant in breaking down the distinction between the 'private' (home) and the 'public' (work and the civic sphere). The development of household appliances and a general improvement in living conditions reduced to some extent the pressure on women as the chief source of 'domestic labour'. By the

1960s the speed of change had picked up, with Western industrialised countries experiencing significant economic and social changes: a shift from manufacturing ('blue-collar') jobs to service ('white-collar') jobs; greater availability of contraception, especially the 'pill' (oral contraception); increasing educational opportunities, and the narrowing of the gap between men and women in educational attainment. Certainly feminism does champion oppressed women, but the leadership of women's organisations, as well as academic feminist theorists, are drawn disproportionately from relatively privileged social groups. This is not in any way to denigrate feminism – our concern here is simply to identify the reasons why feminism emerged as a fully fledged ideology when it did.

Turning now to ecologism, the link between rising prosperity and ecological consciousness may seem much more tenuous. However, political scientist Ronald Inglehart identified the emergence in the 1970s of a generation born during, or just after World War II – sometimes called the generation of '68 (with '68 a reference to the student disturbances of 1968) – that espoused 'post-materialist values': questioning of authority, liberal attitudes to human relationships, rejection of job security, importance of 'self-realisation' and individuality (Inglehart, 1977). The preceding generation, which had directly experienced the inter-war depression, World War II and the hardships of the immediate post-war period, were much more inclined to hold 'materialist values'. The word 'materialist' should not be read as 'selfish' – the war generation simply wanted an end to the deprivations of the war, and so were strongly committed to job security and rising prosperity. The post-war generation might be thought more selfish because they took for granted the opportunities provided by the welfare state and economic growth policies. Nonetheless, the post-war generation did, according to Inglehart, display a distinct set of values, and it is not difficult to see how these values might lead that generation to reject traditional political ideologies and movements in favour of an ecological consciousness.

The socio-economic conditions that gave rise to the development of multiculturalism are slightly different, but are still connected to rising levels of prosperity among certain key groups. The post-war period was characterised by increasing levels of economic migration from south Asia and the Mediterranean fringe to the countries of central and northern Europe. For example, the so-called 'economic miracle' (*Wirtschaftswunder*) in West Germany was made possible by 'guest labour' from (especially) Turkey. And large numbers of south Asians came to Britain in search of work. These groups – disproportionately made up of men – tended to seek protection in their own communities, especially as tensions rose in the late 1950s. However, by the 1960s there emerged organisations that campaigned against discrimination. It is, however, significant that 'race' rather than 'culture' was the central concept, with the emphasis on overcoming 'skin prejudice'; this was paralleled on a much larger scale in the United States, with the emergence of a powerful Civil Rights Movement (although, of course, the African-American community had a quite different history to European immigrant communities). It is only in the 1970s and 1980s that there emerges a shift from the language of race, and the idea of a *multiracial* society, to culture, and the notion of a *multicultural* society. Certainly, some of the advocates of multiculturalism were first-generation immigrants, but many were the children of first-generation immigrants who argued that the recognition of pluralism required an analysis of society centred on culture rather than race. Again, as with feminism, while the aim was to overcome disadvantage, the political and intellectual leadership of this movement was relatively advantaged.

Critique of Classical Ideologies

We have already suggested that the new ideologies emerged, in part, as a response to the failure of Marxism. And we have also argued that rising prosperity changed the expectations and outlook of certain groups – women, the post-war generation and 'ethnic' (cultural) minorities. The combination of a recognition of the crisis of Marxism and the underlying socio-economic conditions which have given rise to these new ideologies means that there is a need to reconsider liberalism. With the collapse of state socialism it may be argued that liberalism lacks any competitor. This is the claim Francis Fukuyama made in his 1992 book *The End of History*; his thesis is contentious but were we, for the sake of argument, to accept that liberalism is the last (effective) ideology, it is still possible to see three of the new 'ideologies' – feminism, multiculturalism and ecologism – as critical responses to the liberal tradition (fundamentalism stands opposed to liberalism, but there are few societies that can be described as *effectively* organised around fundamentalist ideas). These three ideologies are engaged in a *critique* of liberalism. It is important to use that word carefully: to engage in a critique of liberalism does not entail rejecting it but, rather, drawing out its truth. In particular, the central ideas of freedom and equality are taken up from the liberal tradition and turned against it. It might also be argued that the new ideologies employ the 'fragments' of competing classical ideologies – socialism, anarchism, and even conservatism and nationalism – and seek to revitalise them through integration into a new kind of liberal ideology. How this is achieved will become clearer in our discussion of the particular ideologies, but it is useful to identify a couple of examples of critical engagement with the classical ideologies.

First, feminists and multiculturalism in particular have sought to challenge the liberal claims to freedom and equality. The dual claim to freedom and equality is subjected to an analysis of how *informal* power relations operate in society, and how formal legal and political relations, despite the appearance of impartiality, actually serve to reinforce informal inequalities. Of course, this line of attack is not new: Marxists have argued that material inequality restricts the effectiveness of the economic freedoms guaranteed by the liberal–capitalist state. But Marx still operated with a universalist model of liberation, whereby the abolition of capitalist relations of production would ensure equal treatment. The model of a classless society – which, admittedly Marx did not outline in any detail – did not adequately account for 'difference', that is, the apparently paradoxical idea that equal treatment of men and women, or of cultural groups, requires recognition of the differences between them. Ecologists are even more radical in their adoption of the ideals of freedom and equality, in that they extend the 'moral community' to include non-human animals and even plant life.

Second, drawing on socialism (in particular, Marxism), the new ideologies take up the idea of collective oppression and collective action. Just as Marx argued that there was a revolutionary process of 'consciousness raising' whereby workers achieve, first of all, workplace consciousness, and then trade union consciousness, followed by national, and international, class consciousness, so feminists, multiculturalists, ecologists and fundamentalists argue for a process whereby the oppressed – women, cultural minorities, non-humans, co-religionists – come to recognise their oppression and, crucially, the causes of that oppression. Obviously the ideologies – and different streams within each ideology – will define the causes of oppression in their own way. Our linking together of these four ideologies is not intended to suggest mutual sympathy between them: many feminists regard multiculturalism as, in the words, of Susan Okin, 'bad for women' (Okin *et al.*, 1999), and fundamentalists of all hues consider multiculturalism to be the political expression of the moral and cultural relativism that they are fighting. The affinities between the four ideologies relate to the historical conditions under which they have emerged, and the style in which they engage with the classical ideologies.

References

Fukuyama, F. (1992) *The End of History and the Last Man* London: Penguin.

Hobsbawm, E. (1995) *Age of Extremes: The Short Twentieth Century, 1914–1991* London: Abacus.

Inglehart, R. (1977) *The Silent Revolution: Changing Values and Political Styles among Western Publics* Princeton, NJ: Princeton University Press.

McLellan, D. (1979) *Marxism after Marx: An Introduction* London: Macmillan.

Okin, S. *et al.* (1999) *Is Multiculturalism Bad for Women?* Princeton, NJ: Princeton University Press.

Chapter 13

Feminism

Introduction

Feminism is an ideology that has always been highly controversial. It asks such questions as: do women have too much or too little power? It is not only controversial as far as traditional defenders of the status quo are concerned. Some women feel that they are in favour of equality with men, but do not like the idea of feminism. It has been said that we live in a 'post-feminist' age and some contend that the main goals of feminism have been realised, so that it is quite unnecessary for feminists to continue their argument against male domination.

Feminism, however, is also controversial in the sense that different feminists mean different things by the term. There are different varieties that seem to have little in common. Just as writers have spoken of 'socialisms', so feminism has also been presented in the plural in order to indicate the diversity involved. In this chapter we shall follow the example of many writers in trying to explain these different feminisms, and also try to suggest a way of extracting some kind of unity out of this formidable diversity.

Chapter Map

In this chapter we are going to explore:

- The immense variety of different kinds of feminism.

- Liberal feminism; its strengths and weaknesses.

- Radical feminism and its claim to be a 'true feminism'.

- The meaning of socialist feminism and its limitations.

- Black feminism.

- 'Philosophical feminisms' and postmodern feminism in particular.

Women's Work?

A huge amount of attention has been devoted in the media to the changing roles of women. An example of this can be found in a 2003 cover story of the *Observer* magazine, in which women who had become corporate executives were questioned as to how they perceived both *their* position, and those of women in general, in society.

- Sunita Gloster is head of an advertising agency and argues that more and more women are facing reality head-on. 'Success', she says, 'used to be defined by a traditional male standard – rising up the corporate ladder, with rewards of money and status. Now women define success by a more feminine standard: satisfaction, fulfilment, making a difference – and that can come in many forms'.

- Sahar Hashemi, who co-founded a chain of companies and who runs her own consultancy, insists that women want equality with, and not superiority over, men, and that they should celebrate being women, 'not try to disguise it'. 'It's about being women in our own right and doing things on our own terms.'

- Patricia Hewitt, as a member of the British cabinet, argues that things are getting better but too many women who work outside the home feel that it is impossible to have children. 'An unofficial "parent bar" is operating, and I think that's the biggest issue for working women.'

- Caroline Plumb, who developed a graduate recruitment and research agency, notes that women need to be stronger on self-promotion, declaring that 'success for me is about having an interesting life, and being exposed to a wide range of experiences and people'.

- Ronnie Cook, a New Yorker running her own design consultancy in the United Kingdom, compares the 'warrior spirit' of American women with the more laid-back approach she finds in London.

- Dr Laura Tyson, Dean of the London Business School, finds that 'women are talented team players, and the need in business now is for individuals who can lead and inspire through influence rather than by dictating. Women are more consensual, and the old power hierarchies are crumbling'.

- Helen Fernandes, the first ever female surgeon at Addenbrooke's Hospital, Cambridge, argues that 'medicine has changed and the old sexism is dying out, but perception and archetypes still put women off'.

Do the testimonies above suggest to you that women should pursue careers outside the home? How possible do you think it is to combine outside work and parental responsibilities?

Make a list of men you know, and see whether you agree with the point that younger men are more egalitarian than older men.

Now make a list of women you know, and ask yourself whether they seek:

- equality with men;
- superiority over men;
- a position of subordination to men.

Liberal Feminism

Liberal feminism would appear to be the earliest form of feminism. Feminism has a particular relationship to liberalism, and it has been said that all feminism is 'liberal at root' (Eisenstein, 1981: 4). We are assuming here not only that earlier treatments of women were anti-feminist in character, but that the ancient Greek philosopher, Plato, does not count as a feminist although his views on women were remarkably atypical at the time.

Plato argues in *The Republic* that women can be among the elite who rule philosophically in his ideal state. Whereas Aristotle had contended that 'the relation of male to female is naturally that of superior to inferior, of the ruling to the ruled' (Coole, 1988: 44–5), Plato adopted (at least in *The Republic)* a gender-free view of political capacities. On the other hand, what makes his feminist credentials suspect is his explicit elitism. Only a tiny number of women would have been 'eligible' to become rulers, and those that did, would (it is said) have to act just like men.

The position of women in medieval theory is depicted in explicitly hierarchical terms, with women being seen as more sinful than men, inferior to them, and not equipped to take part in political processes. Aquinas follows Aristotle in arguing that a wife 'is something belonging to her husband', although she is more distinct from him than a son from his father or a slave from his master (1953: 103). Had not the Bible made the inferiority of women clear?

Mary Wollstonecraft

What is remarkable about the liberal tradition is that it challenges the notion that repressive hierarchies are natural. It thus opens the way for the feminist argument that if all are free and equal individuals, why can women not be equal to men? It is true that Mary Astell had contended, as early as 1694, that women should be educated instead of being nursed in the vices for which they are then upbraided (Brody, 1992: 28). But Mary Wollstonecraft is rightly regarded as the first major feminist, and in her famous *Vindication of the Rights of Women* (first published in 1792), she argues for women's economic independence and legal equality. At the time she wrote, a married woman could not own property in her own right, enter into any legal contract or have any claim over the rights of her children. History, philosophy and classical languages were considered too rigorous for women to learn; botany and biology were proscribed from their educational curriculum, and physical exercise thought unsuitable.

Wollstonecraft directs her argument to middle-class women – women in what she calls the 'natural state'. The middle-class woman is the woman who is neither dissipated by inherited wealth nor brutalised by poverty. Wollstonecraft had taken from Richard Price the Enlightenment principle that all people are rational. The problem lay with the environment. Physical frailty derives from a cloistered upbringing, and this was thought to impact negatively upon intellectual ability. She tackles in particular Rousseau's traditionalist view that women are inferior, seeing this as a betrayal of the liberal assumptions of his political theory. What Rousseau thought charming, Wollstonecraft considered immoral and dangerous. It is inconsistent to value independence and autonomy in men but not in women, particularly as **patriarchy**, or male domination, degrades men as well – 'the blind lead the blind' (1992: 104).

Women, Wollstonecraft argues, are placed on a pedestal but within a prison (Brody, 1992: 50–1). Women ought to be represented in government and have a 'civil existence in the State' (Wollstonecraft, 1992: 265; 267). They should not be excluded from civil and political employments (1992: 291). The enlightened woman must be an 'active citizen' 'intent to manage her family, educate her children and assist her neighbours' (1992: 259). Friendship rather than gentleness, docility and a spaniel-like affection 'should prevail between the sexes'. The emancipation of women is, in Wollstonecraft's view, part and parcel of the case against autocracy and arbitrariness in general: why contest the divine right of kings if one continues to subscribe to the divine right of husbands (1992: 118; 119)?

Wollstonecraft's position has a number of shortcomings that we will deal with later, but it is generally acknowledged that she tended to juxtapose reason to feeling, identifying feelings with animal appetites that men exploited. Moreover, she saw perfection as a realisable ideal, a position undoubtedly influenced by the intensely religious character of her argument. But Wollstonecraft's position was complex – and she has been seen by some writers as 'ambivalent, contradictory and paradoxical' – reformer and revolutionary, rationalist and woman of feeling (Brody, 1992: 67, 70).

John Stuart Mill

John Stuart Mill (influenced by his partner Harriet Taylor) wrote *The Subjection of Women* in 1869. In it he argues that women should enjoy equal rights with men – including the right to vote. Women, he contended, were still slaves in many respects, and to argue that they are inferior by 'nature' is to presume knowledge of nature: until equality has been established, how do we know what woman's nature is? It cannot be said that women are housewives and mothers by nature, although Mill does say – and this position is controversial among feminists today– that they are 'most suitable for this role', and he feels that female suffrage can only assist women in supervising domestic expenditure (Bryson, 1992: 55–63; Coole, 1988: 144). Mill, it is suggested, contributed to liberal feminism by extending his liberal principles to the position of women (Shanley and Pateman, 1991: 6), and, as did Wollstonecraft, he argued that the family must become a school for learning the values of freedom and independence.

Liberal Feminism in Britain and the United States

Throughout the nineteenth century liberal feminism had developed often as an extension of other emancipatory movements. In the United States, figures such as Elizabeth Cady Stanton (1815–1902) and her lifelong friend, Susan Anthony (1820–1906) raised the issue of women's freedom and equality as a result of experience in anti-slavery movements. Both edited a feminist journal in the 1860s

Exercise

You meet a woman who describes herself as a feminist. 'All women should be equal and be free to choose their own lifestyle', she argues.

You feel uneasy. You note the following factors in your mind:

- Her mother is an MP and her father a headmaster.

- The woman concerned went to a very good school and has had a university education.

- She has a job outside the home that is well paid.

- She has young children and can afford to put them all day in a nursery.

- Because her and her partner are both employed and are on good salaries, they employ someone to clean their house twice a week.

How important are these 'other' factors? The feminist you have met argues that *all* women should be equal to men, but how many other women are in her relatively privileged position?

called *The Revolution*. A National Women's Suffrage Association was set up after the civil war and women's suffrage was attained in the United States as a result of the 19th Amendment to the Constitution in 1920. In Britain, Mill's classic work had been preceded by the campaign against the Contagious Diseases Act (1864) that gave the police draconian powers to arrest prostitutes and those considered prostitutes, and when limited suffrage for women was achieved after World War I the struggle for its further extension was consolidated in the National Union of Societies for Equal Citizenship.

British liberal feminism appeared to have its greatest triumph when all women became eligible to vote in 1928 in Britain. In other countries this was attained later – in France after World War II, while in Switzerland women only received the vote in 1970. In Britain the Sex Discrimination Act and the Equal Opportunities Commission were established in the late 1960s.

Liberal feminism identifies itself, in the words of Winifred Holtby, 'with the motto Equality First' (Humm, 1992: 43) and it extended its concerns with the publication of Betty Friedan's *The Feminine Mystique* (1963), which argued that middle-class American women suffered from depression and alienation as a result of giving up a career outside the home. They were incarcerated in a 'comfortable concentration camp' – Friedan's dramatic name for the home. She was instrumental in setting up the National Organization of Women in 1966 that not only campaigned for equal rights (including 'reproductive rights' – a right to abortion and birth control), but also assisted American women in re-entering the labour market, and supported the establishment of childcare facilities in workplaces.

Problems with Liberal Feminism

Liberal feminism has been criticised on a number of grounds.

Radical Feminist Critique

Radical feminists protest that liberal feminism is too superficial in its approach. All feminisms agree with the extension of liberal principles to women in terms of the vote and civil liberties, but radicals argue that the notion of equality is too abstract to be serviceable. The point about women is that they are different from men, and to argue for equality implies that they aspire to be like men. But why?

Men not only oppress women but they are responsible for war, violence, hierarchy and the exploitation of nature and their fellows. Is this the model to which women should aspire? Radicals argue that it is not equality that women should want, but liberation – and freedom for women means being separate and apart from men. It means celebrating their difference from men and their own distinctive sexuality. Liberal feminists not only regard sexuality as irrational and emotional, but they uncritically accept that feelings should be transcended and they adopt a notion of reason that reflects male experience. Feminism is not an extension of another ideology. It is concerned with the interests of women, and a new set of words needs to be developed to reflect the separateness of women. Some radicals, such as Mary Daly, adopt a different style of writing, so as to make it clear that feminism represents as total a break as possible with male-constructed society. Politics is not simply about the law and state, as liberals think. It is about human activity in general and the celebrated slogan – 'the personal is political' – captures the radical feminist argument that inter-personal relations are as 'political' as voting in elections. Radicals encourage women to meet separately – to voice their problems without men – and to take personal experience much more seriously than the liberal tradition allows.

Radicals see themselves as sexual revolutionaries, and thus very different from liberal feminists who work within the system. We shall see later that radicals have very different views from liberals on questions such as prostitution and pornography.

Socialist Feminist Critique

The socialist critique of liberal feminism argues that liberal feminists ignore or marginalise the position of working-class women and the problems they have with exploitation and poor conditions in the workplace. The question of gender needs to be linked to the question of class – and legal and political equality, though important, does not address the differential in real power that exists in capitalist society.

Marxist feminists in particular want to challenge the view of the state as a benevolent reformer, and to argue that the state is an expression of class domination. The freedom of women has to be linked to the emancipation of the working class in general, with a much greater concentration on the social and the economic dimensions of gender discrimination. Why should the right to join the armed forces and the police be a positive development if the police are used to oppress people at home and the army to oppress peoples abroad? Liberal feminism neglects the question of production and reproduction that lies at the heart of human activity.

Other Critiques

The black feminist critique particularly takes issue with the tendency of liberal feminists to treat women in abstract fashion, and to assume that women are not only middle class, but white as well. Many of the objections that liberal feminists raise to the hypocritical politeness of men hardly apply to women who are subject to racist abuse and treated in a derogatory fashion because they are black.

The feminisms looked at so far can be called 'ideological' feminisms, and they overlap with what can be labelled 'philosophical feminisms': feminist empiricism, standpoint feminism and postmodern feminism.

Feminist empiricists take the view that feminism should be treated as an objective science that concentrates on the *facts* relating to discrimination. Feminist empiricists feel that it is unnecessary and counterproductive to hitch feminism to an ideological position, and that the norms of liberalism involve a value commitment which narrows the appeal of feminist analysis.

Standpoint feminists take the view that the position of women gives rise to a different outlook, so that liberal feminists are wrong to argue simply for equality with men, and to concern themselves only with legal and political rights.

As for postmodern feminists, they consider the tradition of the Enlightenment and liberalism to be hopelessly abstract. Not only is liberalism oblivious to the importance of difference – both between women and men and within women themselves – but the notion of freedom and autonomy as universal values reflects a prejudice that is part of the modern as opposed to the postmodern tradition.

Biography | **Mary Wollstonecraft (1759–97)**

Born in Spitalfields, London. In 1784 she became friends with Richard Price, a minister at the local Dissenting Chapel. At Price's home she met the publisher, Joseph Johnson, who commissioned her to write *Thoughts on the Education of Girls*. In 1788 she helped Johnson found the *Analytical Review*.

Edmund Burke's *Reflections on the Revolution in France* was written in response to a radical sermon by Richard Price. Wollstonecraft's *A Vindication of the Rights of Man* not only supported Price but also criticised the slave trade, the game laws and way that the poor were treated.

In 1790 she published *A Vindication of the Rights of Women,* and as a result was described as a 'hyena in petticoats'. In 1793 Burke led the attack on The London Corresponding Society and the Unitarian Society (both of which Wollstonecraft supported), describing them as 'loathsome insects that might, if they were allowed, grow into giant spiders as large as oxen', while King George III issued a proclamation against seditious writings and meetings.

In June 1793 Wollstonecraft decided to move to France with the American writer Gilbert Imlay. After her relationship with Imlay came to an end she returned to London. She married William Godwin in March 1797 and soon afterwards Mary (the author of *Frankenstein*), was born. The baby was healthy but as a result of blood poisoning Wollstonecraft died on 10 September 1797.

How to read:

Wollstonecraft's *A Vindication of the Rights of Women*

Her 'Introduction' and 'Dedication' contain useful summaries of her overall position and should be read carefully. Chapters 1–2 are important and it is vital that you pay particular attention to the critique of Jean-Jacques Rousseau. The section on Gregory can be skim read, but Chapter 3 continues the critique on Rousseau and deserves careful attention. The poetry cited in Chapter 4 can be skim read. Chapter 5 returns to Rousseau and Gregory – and you can remind yourself about Wollstonecraft's response to these two authors (though references to Rousseau are more important than those to Gregory). Chapters 6 and 7 stress the importance of education and deserve a careful read. Chapter 12 is devoted to education. Chapters 8 and 9 are also important, and if you are concerned about the impact of the family on women read Chapter 11 carefully. The final chapter, though interesting, can be skim read.

Socialist Feminism

Socialist feminism arose out of the belief that feminism is not simply a legal and political question – though socialists (by which we mean socialist feminists) do support the case for the legal and political emancipation of women. Socialists take the view that women's emancipation is also – and primarily – a *social* question so that the movement for women's freedom needs to be linked with the struggle to transform capitalism itself.

Early socialists such as the Frenchman Charles Fourier saw the liberation of women as integral to redefining the labour process so that it becomes pleasurable and fulfilling, and he saw, as Marx did, the position of women as symptomatic of the level of civilisation of a given society. Marx tended to see women as the victims of market forces, and he argues in an early text that the prostitution of women is only a specific expression of the general prostitution of the labourer (Marx and Engels, 1975: 295). In the *Communist Manifesto*, for example, Marx takes the view that women under capitalism are mere instruments of production. But Marx showed little interest in the position of women and regarded the relation of men and women as 'natural' rather than moulded by class relationships.

Engels's Contribution

Engels was much more interested in women, and in his celebrated work, *The Origin of the Family, Private Property and the State*, published in 1894, he argues that in early tribal societies men, women and children lived together as part of larger households in which production was for use rather than exchange. Decision making involved both men and women and, because paternity or the position of a particular man as father could not be established in group marriage, collective property descended through women (i.e. matrilineally). 'The world-historical defeat of female sex', as Engels graphically describes it, occurs when men begin to domesticate animals and breed herds. Women seek monogamous relations in marriage (one wife–one husband) and the family is privatised. In the later bourgeois family, the woman's formal right to consent to marriage is neutralised by her lack of economic independence, and in the working-class family, the husband represents the bourgeois and the wife the proletarian – what nineteenth-century socialists liked to call the 'slave of a slave'.

In Engels's view, male domination would only disappear with the socialisation of production. With women involved in paid employment outside the home, housework itself would become a public and collectivised activity (Sacks, 1974: 207).

Bebel and Later Socialists

August Bebel of the German Social Democratic Party wrote a much more influential book than that of Engels – *Woman Under Socialism* (1878) – which followed the argument that women could only be emancipated through a proletarian revolution that resulted in their economic independence and the collectivisation of housework and childcare. However, unlike Engels, he was also conscious of the problems that were peculiar to women. Capitalist employment resulted in women being paid less than men, and women suffered from the problem of having to do all or most of the housework. Bebel also noted that economic subordination was linked to non-economic forms of oppression, such as double standards of sexual morality and inconvenient forms of dress (Bryson, 1992: 121).

Clara Zetkin, a German socialist who was to be a founder member of the German Communist Party, argued that class must take primacy over gender interests. She refused to cooperate with other women in campaigns for improved education, employment prospects and legal status, on the grounds that proletarian and 'bourgeois' women had nothing in common. Lenin was to declare at the time of the Russian Revolution that 'the proletariat cannot have complete liberty until it has won complete liberty for women' (Rowbotham, 1972: 163) but this did not prevent him from extracting a pledge from Zetkin that personal matters would not be raised in political discussions (Bryson, 1992: 125). It is true that the new Soviet government was the first in history to write women's emancipation into the law (in 1918), but the right to abortion was removed in 1936 and the family, which radical Bolsheviks had sought to 'abolish', was idealised under Stalin as a crucial part of the disciplinary mechanism of the state.

Alexandra Kollontai was commissar or minister of social welfare in the first Bolshevik government and she sought to encourage women to set up, with state help, nurseries, laundries and educational campaigns. But she fell from power in 1921 and the Women's Department that she headed was abolished in 1929. She is also interesting because she argued for a new kind of relationship between men and women – one that would be less exclusive and not monogamous (Bryson, 1992: 137–40).

Women in the Communist Party States

In terms of more recent developments in Communist Party states, the regime in Romania was particularly oppressive, with Ceauşescu stating in 1986, some 20 years after an anti-abortion law had been passed, that those 'who refuse to have children are deserters, escaping the law of natural continuity' (Funk and Mueller, 1993: 46). In the German Democratic Republic (East Germany) abortion was legal and used as the main means of birth control, while 90 per cent of women of working age were in paid employment, and 87 per cent had completed vocational training (Funk and Mueller, 1993: 139). Despite the authoritarian character of these Communist Party states, the position of women in post-communist societies has worsened as reproductive rights have been scaled down (although in Poland the attempt to pass an anti-abortion law was blocked in 1991). Women have left the workforce, are much less represented in legislatures and have suffered as state nurseries have been closed; the gender gap in pay has widened, and pornography and prostitution have dramatically increased (Hoffman, 2001: 141).

The Domestic Labour Debate

Of course many socialists disagreed vehemently with the Communist Party states, even while they maintained a loyalty to Marxism. The domestic labour debate that took place in the pages of the British journal, *New Left Review*, sought to examine the position of women in the home and their relationship to the capitalist economy. Some argued that domestic labour produces value in the same way that other labour does, and therefore women who work at home should be paid. Despite controversy on this point there was general agreement that the family is linked to capitalism, and that domestic labour, and who does it, is an important issue for feminists to tackle (Bryson, 1992: 241).

Even socialists who disagree with Marxism have accepted the need to ensure that women in the workforce are paid equally and should be able to combine domestic

---

Biography   Clara Zetkin (1857–1933)

As Clara Eissner she studied at Leipzig Teacher's College for Women and became a socialist and feminist.

In 1881 Zetkin joined the Socialist Democratic Party, and married Ossip Zetkin, a Russian revolutionary living in exile. The couple had two children before Ossip died of tuberculosis in January 1889.

In 1891 Zetkin became editor of the party's journal, *Die Gleichheid* (Equality). A strong campaigner for women's suffrage, she was appointed secretary of the International Socialist Women in 1910.

In December 1914 she joined with Liebknecht and Luxemburg in an underground organisation called *Spartakusbund* (Spartakus League). She supported the Russian Revolution and joined the Independent Socialist Party in 1917. In January 1919 she took part in the Spartakist uprising in Berlin. The rebellion was crushed, and a year later she helped to form the German Communist Party (KPD).

Zetkin was elected to the Reichstag (the German parliament) in 1920 and served on the Central Committee of the KPD. She was also appointed to the executive committee of Comintern, which meant she spent long periods in the Soviet Union. In 1932 Zetkin was once again elected to the Reichstag. Here she took the opportunity to make a long speech in which she denounced the policies of Hitler and the Nazi Party. Clara Zetkin died on 20 June 1933.

and professional duties. Women and men may receive the same pay for the same job, but where there are occupations in which women predominate (such as nursing and primary school teaching), workers in these occupations receive relatively low pay. Women in Britain earn about 75 per cent of men's pay – whereas the average over Europe is 79 per cent (http://news.bbc.co.uk/1/hi/business/1962036.stm). Socialist feminists feel that the market and free enterprise do impact upon women's lives, and that improving pay, employment prospects and conditions of work are crucial questions for feminism to consider.

Problems with Socialist Feminism

Liberal Feminist Critique

Liberal feminists, such as Betty Friedan and Naomi Wolf (who wrote *Fire with Fire* in 1993), feel that socialist feminists are divisive in not accepting that some women might go into, and make a success of, business. Their dynamism and entrepreneurial flair should be both rewarded and acknowledged, and to regard feminism as a class question is unhelpful and narrowing. All women will benefit from a free system of production, based on the market and capitalism.

Women are individuals who should be entitled to exercise choice, and the tendency by socialist feminists to see work outside the home as crucial for emancipation is not borne out by the many women who choose to stay at home and live fulfilled and happy lives. Liberal feminists are not opposed to reforms that facilitate working outside the home, but they are opposed to an ideological position which seems to privilege this.

Liberal feminists would (as would many other feminists) point to the authoritarian character of Communist Party states as evidence, not only of the generally problematic character of socialism, but of the negative way in which it impacts upon women's lives.

Radical Feminist Critique

Radicals are sceptical that the problems facing women are simply to do with capitalism. It is true that some socialist feminists have argued that there is a dual system which oppresses women – capitalism *and* patriarchy. Capitalism may reward men as 'breadwinners', thereby creating a division of labour that disadvantages women, and writers such as Ann Ferguson see patriarchy as semi-autonomous – sexual oppression exists alongside class oppression and is not 'reducible' to it (Bryson, 1992: 243–5). But radicals feel that this argument merely serves to deepen the theoretical crisis faced by socialist feminists, since there is no reason to believe that pornography, prostitution and male chauvinist attitudes are specifically linked to a particular mode of production.

Indeed, many radical feminists developed their position as a result of experience in socialist movements where they were expected to take menial and 'feminine' roles by socialist men. Attempts to introduce the concept of **patriarchy** alongside the analysis of capitalism fail to get to grips with the fact that the former is wholly independent of the latter, and that when Marx treats the relations between men and women as natural this is symptomatic of an inadequate methodology which cannot be rectified by simply tacking a critique of sexism on to Marxism or socialism. Catherine Mackinnon, in a much-quoted comment, argues that 'sexuality is to feminism, what work is to marxism' (Humm, 1992: 117). The logics of the two are quite different, and any attempt to 'synthesise' Marxism and feminism, or feminism with socialism more generally, is bound to fail.

Black Feminist and the Philosophical Feminist Critique

Black feminists believe that socialist emphasis upon class is as abstract as liberal emphasis upon the individual. Socialist feminism does not take the question of ethnicity seriously: it suffers from the problem of abstract universalism, which means that it unthinkingly privileges a particular group or culture.

Feminist empiricists see in socialism the problem of ideological bias, and although some standpoint feminists such as Nancy Hartsock are sympathetic to Marxism, standpoint feminism in general is unhappy with any privileging of class. After all, women experience oppression as women, and Gilligan argues in *In a Different Voice* (1992) that because women are socialised differently from men they grow up with quite different notions of morality and relationships. This occurs in both working-class and 'bourgeois' homes.

As for postmodern feminists, socialism has what they call an emancipatory 'metanarrative' – particularly strident in Marxism – that stems from the Enlightenment and expresses an absolutist prejudice. The belief in progress, equality and autonomy, though different from the views of liberal feminists, still reflects a belief in a 'philosophy of history' that is ultimately arbitrary and implausible.

Radical Feminism

Radical feminism, as indicated from its critiques of other positions, takes the view that feminism ought to deal with the position of women, independently of other ideological commitments. As MacKinnon argues, 'feminism is the first theory to emerge from those whose interests it affirms' (Humm, 1992: 119).

Radical feminists argue that women are oppressed because women are women, and men are men. Male domination permeates all aspects of society – from sport to literature, dress to philosophy, entertainment to sexual mores. As Mary Daly argues, 'we live in a profoundly anti-female society, a misogynistic "civilization" in which men collectively victimize women, attacking us as personifications of their own paranoid fears' (Humm, 1992: 168).

Ch 1: The State, pp. 14–37

This ubiquity of 'maleness' extends to the state itself. Weber's view of the state as an institution that claims a monopoly of legitimate force is too limited, in MacKinnon's view, since this monopoly 'describes the power of men over women in the home, in the bedroom, on the job, in the street, through social life' (1989: 169). **Patriarchy** is a comprehensive system of male power and it arises from men.

Oppression, as the *Manifesto of the New York Redstockings* in 1969 declared, is total, 'affecting every facet of our lives' (Bryson, 1992: 183–4).

Moreover, the radicals argue that women's oppression is the oldest and most basic form of oppression, and whether it arises from socialists who expect women to make tea while men develop political strategy, or it is expressed through black men such as Stokely Carmichael, who see women as having only bodies and not minds, the same point holds: all men oppress women, and all receive psychological, sexual and material benefits from so doing. Germaine Greer argues that her proposition in *The Female Eunuch* (1971) still holds 30 years later – men hate women at least some of the time. Indeed she reckons that in the year 2000 'more men hate more women more bitterly than in 1970' (1999: 14). Greer gives as good as she believes that women get, and argues that 'to be male is to be a kind of idiot savant, full of queer obsessions about fetishistic activities and fantasy goals' – a freak of nature, fragile, fantastic, bizarre (1999: 327).

Why does the antagonism between men and women arise? Brownmiller appears to suggest that the root is biological, and she speaks of the 'anatomical fact that the male sex organ has been misused as a weapon of terror' (Humm, 1992: 73), but radical feminists are aware of the dangers of a naturalist argument that reduces male domination to biology. Although MacKinnon speaks highly of Robert Dahl and endorses his view of politics as a system of power, authority and control, she almost certainly would not endorse his once-expressed view that women's subordination arises from the superior physical strength of males (Hoffman, 2001: 97). The relation of man and women is a social product, she argues, and a 'naturalist' view fails to see these relationships as historical and transitory (MacKinnon, 1989: 56). Nevertheless, radical feminists reject Marxist accounts that male domination arose historically from class divisions, and they argue that patriarchy has always been around. Although radicals disagree as to how and when patriarchy came about, they all agree that it exists and it has done so in every known society (Bryson, 1992: 188).

What can be done about it? Radical feminists developed in the late 1960s the idea of an all-women's 'consciousness-raising' group. Indeed, MacKinnon describes 'consciousness raising' as the 'feminist method' (Humm, 1992: 119) – a coming together by women to describe problems collectively so that the existence of oppression can be confirmed. The solution can only be separatism, for the consequence of the fact that the personal is political (and by political is meant the exercise of repressive power) is that men and women should live their lives as separately as possible. As Greer puts it rather wittily, 'both could do without each other if it were not for the pesky business of sexual reproduction' (1999: 68).

One radical actually famously argued that the basis of women's oppression lies with child bearing, as well as child rearing, and the conception of love (Bryson, 1992: 204, 201). Others are doubtful that this 'pesky business' can be so easily avoided. But sexuality is seen as an expression of power so that the distinction between rape and sexual activity is not a meaningful one, and the reason why radical feminists are so passionately opposed to pornography and prostitution is that they see these institutions as fundamentally linked to a demeaning view and treatment of women. Whether men intend to oppress women is beside the point: **patriarchy** is a structural system of male oppression that operates, whether men are conscious of oppressing women or not.

Radical feminists have sometimes advocated lesbianism as a solution to the problem of oppressive encounters with men. Feminists in general would accept that lesbianism is a legitimate lifestyle choice, but radicals often go further and argue that it is a necessary way of preventing male domination. Rich advocates a broader notion of lesbianism so that it does not have to embrace genital activity, but denotes a rejection of a compulsory heterosexuality imposed to prevent women from being individuals in their own right (Humm, 1992: 176–7). Because **patriarchy** is seen as a comprehensive system of male domination, even the most intimate of relationships becomes a matter for political scrutiny.

MacKinnon sees the whole notion of the public/private divide as oppressive and nothing more than a dangerous myth. The public is the private, just as the personal is political. Women's interest lies in overthrowing the distinction itself (1989: 120–1). Radical feminism is revolutionary. It is averse to differentiating one kind of patriarchy from another, and it is opposed to the kind of reforms that do not tackle the problem at its root. Radical feminists tend to identify pornography with sexual violence, and they regard prostitution as an act of force (Hoffman, 2001: 193).

Women, in the view of radical feminists, do not want equality with men. They want liberation, and liberation is only possible if patriarchy is overthrown.

Problems with Radical Feminism

Liberal Feminist Critique

Liberal feminists disagree with radical feminists on a range of grounds. The first is that they see the idea that there is a war between the sexes as unfruitful. Men can be sympathetic to feminism (as J.S. Mill famously was), and it is wrong to assume that men cannot become adherents to the feminist cause. The notion of separatism is pessimistic and self-defeating.

Nor are liberal feminists persuaded by the arguments for patriarchy. The notion that male domination enters into the very fibre of relationships ignores the importance of privacy and choice. Women are, or can be, agents, and the notion that the personal is political is a totalitarian credo that does not allow individuals to decide matters for themselves.

Some liberal feminists argue that prostitutes are sex workers who choose a profession that others dislike, and the legalisation of prostitution would enable women who wish to pursue careers in this area to do so without hindrance and condemnation. Liberal feminists see the campaigns against pornography as oppressive and authoritarian. Not only do such campaigners find themselves working with extremely conservative pressure groups, but the attempt to ban pornography leads to censorship – the prevention of people acting in unconventional ways that, liberal feminists insist, do not harm others.

Their attitude, in the eyes of liberal feminists, towards the state and legal reform is generally negative, and radical feminists suffer from an absolutist outlook which prevents them from seeing that gradual change, based upon rational discussion, is far more effective than utopian fantasies.

Socialist Feminist Critique

Socialist feminists have no difficulty in extending the notion of politics at least to workplaces and the family. But they see the idea of sisterhood as dangerously abstract. Socialist feminists want to stress that women belong to different classes and their interests vary according to their class position. Socialist feminists are not necessarily opposed to the notion of patriarchy, but they insist that it is much more complex than the radicals imagine.

In the first place, it is a system that arises historically, and even if Engels's account is not wholly plausible he is correct to assume that patriarchy has not always existed, and that it is connected with private property and the state. Second, socialist feminists want to distinguish between different kinds of patriarchy. There is an important distinction to be made between the kind of explicit patriarchy that exists in medieval and slave-owning societies, and a liberal patriarchy in which male domination coexists with liberal notions of consent and freedom. In fact, it is the gulf between theory and practice that makes the socialist critique possible, for women in developed liberal societies enjoy formal rights that contrast with their lack of real power. This kind of analysis is only possible if patriarchy itself is placed in a very specific historical context.

Socialist feminists, as do liberal feminists, see no problem in forming alliances with men, since men can be in favour of emancipation just as privileged women can be opposed to it. It is true that men benefit from patriarchy, but the socialist emphasis upon *relationships* means that men have their own lives limited and warped as a result of patriarchal prejudices which regard women, for example, as the natural guardians of children.

Even though socialist feminists would not accept extreme left-wing strictures against feminism as being inherently 'bourgeois' and a distraction from class struggle, they tend to see the concern of radical feminists with lifestyle and sexuality as the product of a middle-class outlook that ignores the problems faced by women workers.

Black Feminist and the Philosophical Feminist Critique

Black feminists are sceptical about a supra-ethnic notion of sisterhood. All women are not the same, and the notion that they are fundamentally oppressed by men could only be advanced by those who have never suffered from racist stereotyping. Women themselves can be racists and oppress black women (as well as black men), and the experiences of subject women under slavery and colonialism demonstrate very different patterns of family and economic life to those assumed by radical feminists.

Rape is a case in point. The view of a black man as a potential rapist has been a formidable racist stereotype (particularly in the southern states of the United States) and black women who report assaults to racist-minded police have a very different experience from white women who have been raped. Audre Lorde puts the matter in a nutshell in her open letter to Mary Daly when she comments: 'The oppression of women knows no ethnic nor racial boundaries, true, but that does not mean that it is identical within those differences' (Humm, 1992: 139). A feminism that ignores ethnic or 'racial' differences is a feminism which unthinkingly privileges one group over others.

Feminist empiricists reject the notion that science and objectivity are somehow male activities. It is true that patriarchal prejudices can claim scientific warranty, but this is poor science. Science is not to blame for male domination but is a powerful weapon for exposing and combating it. Facts that point to discrimination and inequality are crucial to the arsenal of feminist argument, and make it much more difficult for unsympathetic men to dismiss feminism as a 'man-hating', irrational doctrine.

Standpoint feminists are, it seems to us, more likely to be influenced by radical feminists, and they can only distance themselves from radical feminism where they defend an argument that a woman's standpoint depends upon the particular social experience she has.

Postmodern feminists hold to the fact that power is exercised at every level in society, and it would seem, therefore, that they should be sympathetic to the radical feminist argument that male domination extends to apparently private as well as public institutions. In reality, however, postmodern feminists are particularly hostile to radical feminism since, as we shall see, they regard the whole notion of a 'woman' as problematically universalist in character. Radical feminism, in their eyes, suffers from deep-rooted binary divides – between men and women, reason and emotion, etc. – which leads these feminists to invert patriarchal arguments by accepting that there is a fundamental sexual divide. Instead of demonising women, they demonise men, but the same absolutist logic is at work.

Ideas and Perspectives:

The Pornography Debate

Andrea Dworkin and Catherine MacKinnon, two radical feminists in the United States, campaigned against pornography on the grounds that it harmed the interests of women everywhere.

They secured the passing of the 'MacKinnon-Dworkin' ordinances in Minneapolis and Indianapolis in 1983 and 1984. These would have made it possible for women who considered that they had been harmed to sue producers, distributors and retailers of pornography. The first ordinance was vetoed by the mayor and the second overruled by the federal courts.

These attempts were seen as a model for use elsewhere. Campaigners have sought to achieve restrictions on pornography in Britain, and in 1986 Clare Short sought to introduce the 'Page Three Bill' that would have banned 'naked or partially naked women in provocative pages in newspapers' and fined offending publishers. The attempt failed. The Campaign Against Pornography was launched in the House of Commons in 1988. These campaigns have been challenged by other feminists who argue that pornography is a symptom rather than a cause of women's oppression; a legal attack on pornography, they argue, allies feminists with right-wing fundamentalists who are opposed to any portrayal of explicit sexual material through art and the media. The US liberal feminist Nadine Strossen sees both obscenity laws and feminist proposals to restrict pornography by law as violations of free speech (Bryson, 1999: 174–7).

Germaine Greer (1939–)

Well-known radical feminist who was born in Australia and educated at the universities of Melbourne, Sydney and Cambridge. A rigorous Catholic education helped her on her way to renouncing the Church and embracing sexual liberationism.

The Female Eunuch (1970) created an enormous stir, and in *The Obstacle Race* (1979) she discusses the social and financial difficulties faced by women painters. Her book *Daddy We Hardly Knew You* (1989) is a family memoir, while her more recent *Whole Woman* (1999) (which her contemporary Camille Paglia called 'seriously unbalanced' in the *New York Times*) shows that her views in many respects have not changed.

She is seen by many feminists as outdated and an anachronism who relies upon media coverage to keep her brand of 1960s and 1970s feminism alive. In her latest work, *Boy*, she includes an attempted defence of under-age sex tourism guaranteed to raise as many moral hackles as her contention that female circumcision is no different in principle from an operation for breast cancer.

She is currently professor of English and comparative literature at the University of Warwick, and appears frequently in media programmes on both literature and sexuality. A respected academic, she has written about art, literature, abortion and infertility, and the menopause. Her appearances on cultural chat shows lead to feisty confrontations. Angela Carter described her as 'a clever fool'. Margaret Cook called her 'paranoid' and 'a bit obsessive' and Edwina Currie called her 'a great big hard-boiled prat'. In 1989 she resigned from teaching at Newnham, Cambridge when a male-to-female transsexual was appointed Fellow at her women-only college.

Black Feminism

Black feminists are acutely aware of the question of difference. Indeed, the very existence of a 'black feminism' is a protest against the idea that women are all the same. Beneath the supposedly universal notion is to be found women who are often white, university-educated and of middle-class background.

Black feminists argue that there is sufficient in common in Britain between Afro-Caribbean women, African women and Asian women to assert a common identity. Of course each of these categories is itself extremely diverse, but black women are considered to have a common experience. In the case of Britain, they are all 'outsiders', regarded as 'invisible' by the dominant culture, and judged to be 'ethnic' and abnormal, as though the majority community is itself without an ethnic identity and embodies normality.

Black feminism is a protest against marginalisation and the belief in monolithic identities. It rejects the idea that black women have to choose whether they want to be humiliated as women by patriarchal black movements or disregarded as blacks by a feminist movement that really speaks for white women. When the Nation of Islam marched in the United States in 2002, many black women found it very painful to decide between their dislike of patriarchy (which the Nation of Islam explicitly represented) and their concern about racism.

It is true that many white women turned to feminism as a result of their experience in anti-slavery and civil rights movements, but they failed to see that oppression is never simply universal – it always takes differential and particular forms. The notion that there is an *analogy* between women and blacks (Gayle Rubin wrote an essay in 1970 entitled *Woman as Nigger*) assumes that somehow black women do not exist!

The specific existence of black feminism contributes significantly to feminist theory as a whole by stressing the importance of a concrete approach that takes account of people's real-life situations and differences. By noting that some women are black in societies where whiteness is seen as the 'norm', one is more likely to observe that women may also be poor, disabled, illiterate etc. Black feminism alerts us to the dangers of privileging one identity over others.

The assumption that the family is problematic for women is invariably made without taking account of the particular features of the black family that, in the United States for example, is often headed by women who have also to work outside the home. Barrett and McIntosh have conceded that their own study of the family ignored the very different structures which exist in the families of Afro-Caribbean and Asian people in Britain (Bryson, 1992: 254). As for rape and sexuality, quite different assumptions are made of black women, and in Whelehan's view, black women suffer from poorer mental health than their white counterparts (Whelehan, 1995: 117).

Black feminists have argued that it is not just a question of disadvantages accumulating alongside one another – as independent entities – so that a black woman may suffer from gender, ethnic and class attributes. It is a question of developing a theory of oppression in which these 'multiple oppressions' reinforce one another, and lie at the root of stereotyping. Indeed, it is remarkable how similar class, 'racial' and gender stereotyping are. This warns us against absolutising one kind of oppression, and opens the way to multiple alliances – of some women with some men for specific purposes. As the African-American writer bell hooks has argued, black feminism stresses the value of solidarity – which unites similarity and difference – over the oppressively homogenous notion of sisterhood (Bryson, 1999: 35).

Whelehan has noted that during the 1970s it was commonly felt by radical feminists that analysis of 'related' issues needed to be shelved, so that full attention could be given to the question of women. As she comments, this kind of argument ignores the fact that women can also suffer oppression as a result of their class, racial, gender and sexual orientation (1995: 111). Not only does black feminism provide a challenge to a theory of domination, it poses a challenge to political theory as a whole. It invites a reconceptualisation of the notion of power and freedom, since those who are the subjects of black feminism have no, in Bryson's words, 'institutionalised inferiors' (1999: 34). Given the fact that there are relatively few black feminist academics, black feminism also poses the challenge of mobilising the considerable knowledge which the community has but has not produced in what Whelehan calls 'high theoretical' form (1995: 120).

Problems with Black Feminism

Liberal, Socialist and Radical Feminist Critiques

Liberal feminists are concerned about what they see as the divisiveness of black feminism as a distinct variety of feminist argument. Black feminists are rightly opposed to racism but the answer to exclusion and marginalisation is to expand the notion of the individual so as to incorporate groups such as blacks whose experience of repression has been very different.

Lynne Segal speaks for many socialist feminists who express concern at the fragmentation that has taken place within the women's movement, and she notes in particular the problem of the growth of 'Black feminist perspectives' (Whelehan, 1995: 121). What about the real class differences that exist within black communities – will they not be ignored if a feminism is created which highlights blackness as the defining criterion?

Radical feminists are concerned that the opposition to male domination is diffused by a concern with difference. Although MacKinnon does not address herself to black feminism as such, she is suspicious of the argument about difference. Inequality comes first, she insists; difference comes after: difference, she says, is the velvet glove on the iron fist of domination (MacKinnon, 1989: 219). In other words, difference can distract us from the force and repression inherent in patriarchy, and distinguishing between black and white women, can – radical feminists argue – play into the hands of men who are anxious to downgrade the plight of all women.

The Critique of Philosophical Feminisms

Feminist empiricists believe that anything that 'ideologises' feminism is a mistake. The statistic that 80 per cent of the mortality rate of illegal abortions came from women of colour (slightly broader than 'black' women) in the years preceding its decriminalisation in the United States (Whelehan, 1995: 117) is a revealing fact, and the danger is that it will not be as widely known as it deserves to be if it is presented by a feminism perceived to be 'separatist' and 'extremist'. Standpoint feminists would acknowledge that different experiences are important and need to be taken into account, but this should not be juxtaposed to the common experiences that all women have, and which mould their particular outlook.

Although postmodern feminists are sympathetic to the point about difference, they argue that 'blackness' represents another form of **'essentialism'**, i.e. the belief in an abstract 'essence'. Some black women might not only reveal class differences, as the socialists warn: what about hierarchies in the communities that lead black Americans to be suspicious of Asian-Americans? Differences such as these are simply swept under the proverbial carpet if blackness becomes the criterion for a particular kind of feminism. Whatever black feminists may say in theory, in practice the notion of a black feminism inevitably privileges 'blackness' over other differences, while the idea that 'race' must be explored in relation to gender and class ignores the other differences – of sexual orientation, region, religion, etc. – which problematise the very existence of the notion of woman.

Philosophical Feminisms

Feminist Empiricism

Feminist empiricists take the view that sexist and 'andocentric' (or male chauvinist) biases can be eliminated from scholarship and statements if there is a strict adherence to existing norms of scientific inquiry. If projects are rigorously designed, hypotheses properly tested and data soundly interpreted, then sexist prejudices can be dealt with alongside all other prejudices – as thoroughly unscientific in character (Hoffman, 2001: 55).

The more female researchers there are in the profession, the better, since women are likely to be more sensitive to sexist prejudices than men. However, the question is not one of female science, but of sound science. The fact is that women are dramatically under-represented in the decision-making structures of the United Nations or in legislative bodies or in the world of business – indeed in the 'public' world in general, except perhaps in certain new social movements such as the peace movement and in certain professions. These facts can only be established through sound statistical techniques, and they establish the existence of discrimination in ways that cannot be ignored.

Feminist empiricism ensures that feminism has come of age, entering into mainstream argument and debate.

Standpoint Feminism

Standpoint feminism arose initially as a feminist version of the Marxist argument that the proletariat had a superior view of society because it was the victim rather than the beneficiary of the market. Standpoint theorists argue that because women have been excluded from power – whether within societies or in international organisations – they see the world differently from men.

Standpoint theorists differ in explaining *why* women have an alternative outlook. Do women have a more respectful attitude towards nature than men, because they menstruate and can give birth to children, or is it because they are socialised differently, so that nature seems more precious to them than it does to many men? Peace activists may similarly differ in accounting for the fact that women in general are more likely to oppose war than men.

Ch 1: The State,
pp. 14–37

But whatever the emphasis placed upon nature or nurture, standpoint feminists generally believe that women are different to men. One of the reasons why standpoint feminists see women as more practically minded than men is because they often have to undertake activity of a rather menial kind. Bryson refers to Marilyn French's novel *The Women's Room* (quoted by Hartsock) in which a woman has the job of washing a toilet and the floor and walls around it: an activity, says French, that brings women 'in touch with necessity' and this is why they 'are saner than men' (Bryson, 1999: 23). Indeed Hartsock seeks to redefine power as a capacity and not as domination, arguing that women's experience stresses connection and relationship rather than individuality and competition (Hartsock, 1983: 253).

Postmodern Feminism

Some make a distinction between postmodern feminism and feminist postmodernism. The distinction, it seems to us, is not a helpful one and we use the two terms indistinguishably. Those who say they are postmodern feminists but not feminist postmodernists sometimes define postmodern feminism as '**postmodernism** with a standpoint bent' (Hoffman, 2001: 63), and we would suggest that the question of a 'standpoint bent' is best understood by looking at the section preceding this one.

Ch 1: The State,
pp. 14–37

Postmodernists seek to overcome the dualistic character of traditional theory. We should refuse to accept that we are either critical (and want to overturn everything) or conservative (and want to keep things as they are). We need to be both subjective or objective, valuing the individual *and* society. In this way we avoid making the kind of choices that postmodernists call 'binary' and absolutist. This leads postmodernists to stress the importance of difference and plurality, and this is why postmodern feminists or feminist postmodernists argue that the notion of feminism as the emancipation of women is doubly problematic. First because emancipation sounds as though at some privileged point in time women will finally be free and autonomous, and second because the very term 'woman' implies that what unites women is more important than what divides them.

This, postmodernists argue, violates the logic of both/and, since it privileges sameness over difference. Indeed Kate Nash argues that because postmodernism (we use the term interchangeably with poststructuralism) commits us to arguing that woman 'is not a fixed category with specific characteristics', we have to be committed to the concept of woman as a 'fiction' in order to be a feminist at all (Hoffman, 2001: 78).

Problems with the Philosophical Feminisms

Liberal Feminist Critique

Liberal feminists are sympathetic to feminist empiricism. Indeed, one writer has described feminist empiricism as the 'philosophical underpinning of liberal feminism' (Hoffman, 2001: 56), and naturally liberal feminists are attracted to the stress on rationality, science and evidence. On the other hand, liberal feminists argue that questions of freedom and autonomy, the rule of law and individual rights involve values, and feminist empiricists seem to be committed to a notion of science that excludes values, basing their hypotheses and findings simply on facts.

Standpoint feminists suffer from the same one-sidedness that afflicts radical feminism. By probing woman's experience in general, it does not respect the division between the public and the private, and by arguing for the superiority of the female standpoint it makes alliances with well-meaning men more difficult. Both factors make standpoint feminists liable to embrace an authoritarian style of politics.

As for postmodern feminism, liberal feminists feel that its aversion to absolutes and modernism leads to scepticism and renders problematic the whole concern with women's rights.

Socialist, Radical and Black Feminist Critiques

Socialist feminism challenges the feminist empiricist notion of science as value free and not itself ideological. An emphasis upon relationships leads to the view that facts do not speak for themselves but imply evaluation, and therefore it is naive to imagine that a purely scientific (rather than explicitly ideological) presentation of feminism will be more persuasive.

As for standpoint feminism, socialists argue that an emphasis upon women's experience needs to take more specific account of the impact of class and capitalism, while postmodern feminism leads to a kind of academic conservatism that makes emancipatory politics impossible.

Radical feminists feel that the emphasis upon science is male oriented and feminist empiricists underestimate the extent to which male mores have penetrated the academy. Radicals are more sympathetic to standpoint feminism, particularly where the difference and even superiority of women is emphasised, while postmodernist feminism is seen as a betrayal of women's interests and a rejection of the need for feminism at all.

To black feminists, feminist empiricism seems elitist and very 'white' since most black women find it difficult to obtain academic positions. As for standpoint feminism, it speaks (as does radical feminism) of women in abstract terms, and therefore unthinkingly adopts the position of white women. Postmodern feminism is seen as indulgent and sceptical, and for all its emphasis upon difference, ignores the problems that black women face, and which make the notion of emancipation a meaningful ideal. Deconstructing modernity seems a rather hollow enterprise when women who are black have yet to obtain 'modernist' goals of equality and autonomy.

Ideas and Perspectives:

Feminism and Diversity

It could be argued that the emphasis upon different strands of feminism is itself counter-productive. If **feminism** is defined broadly as the emancipation of women, then it becomes possible to see each of the different feminisms making a positive contribution to the development of feminism overall, while betraying a certain one-sidedness that needs to be discarded. One work has spoken of the need to recover 'feminisms from the intolerance of other feminisms' (Zalewski, 2000: 142) and it seems to us that we do not need to choose between one feminism and many feminisms. Feminism can only be constructed as a viable and dynamic theory through multiple feminisms.

Thus liberal feminism stresses the importance of people as free and equal individuals but, as Steans argues, 'liberal feminism is not merely feminism added onto liberalism' (1998: 17), while socialist feminists rightly emphasise the importance of class and capitalism as social institutions that negatively impact upon women. Despite its weaknesses, radical feminism argues for a notion of patriarchy that extends into all areas of life and it invites attention to relationships as the location of conflict.

Black feminists warn us eloquently against the dangers of ethnocentrism. Women can be black as well as white, and analyses say of the family and sexuality that might apply to white women will not necessarily apply to black women. As for the philosophical feminisms, feminist empiricists stress the importance of a sophisticated presentation of the facts, while standpoint feminists are concerned with the way in which women's experience impacts upon their behaviour and outlook. Postmodernist feminism helpfully warns against static and ahistorical views of women that ignore the differences between them.

There is no need to juxtapose separate feminisms from the development of a feminism that is sensitive to difference, sees the need for alliances with men, acknowledges the problems from which all women suffer (albeit in different ways), and seeks to make feminism as convincing and well researched as possible.

Exercise

The Problem of Prostitution and Pornography

To many people (who would not necessarily call themselves feminists at all) prostitution is scandalous and unacceptable. Surely it is right that soliciting and brothels are illegal even if prostitution as such is not. Prostitution is an affront to freedom, marriage and the dignity of women. To others, this is a moralistic position that ignores the reasons why women become prostitutes. Prostitute women need help and recognising them as sex workers who should work in safer conditions (and pay tax!), would be a just and humane way of tackling the issue.

Draw up a list of arguments for and against the decriminalisation of prostitution and say why *your* solution to the question would meet the interests of both prostitutes in particular and women in general.

Pornography also arouses strong feelings. Is it merely a portrait of sexuality to which the prudish and puritanical object, or does pornography harm the interests of women and should it be 'cleansed' from society?

How would you define pornography? Of course it can hurt people (think of the exploitation in which children may be involved), but does it have to? Based on your definition of pornography, consider the pros and cons of banning pornography.

Summary

Liberal feminism seeks to give women the same political and legal rights that men enjoy so that women can be regarded as rational and autonomous individuals. Liberal feminists are accused by their critics of disregarding the negative impact that capitalism and the market make upon women's lives, of ignoring male oppression in the so-called private sphere, and of embracing an ideology that is abstract and absolutist in tone.

Socialist feminism argues that questions of gender must be considered alongside questions of class. Marxist feminism particularly emphasises the problem posed by capitalism to the interests of women. Liberal critics contend that women can legitimately display their equality through becoming executives in business, and argue that it is wrong to assume that all women should work outside the home. Other feminists feel that socialists ignore the general problems faced by women in all societies, while postmodernists feel that the socialist 'metanarrative' is as abstract as the liberal one.

Radical feminists pride themselves on concentrating exclusively on women's problems, and insist that male oppression manifests itself in inter-personal relations as well as in more conventionally political arenas. They are accused by their critics of an authoritarian disregard for the individual and a prejudice against men. The differences between women, whether 'racial' or class based, must be taken into account, and it is wrong to assume that a scientific view expresses masculinist values.

Black feminists take the view that ethnic 'outsiders' must be explicitly considered, and generalised views of women are unacceptable. Their critics feel that black feminists focus one-sidedly upon what is one form of oppression among many, and that they are guilty of 'essentialising' blackness.

The philosophical feminisms stress either the importance of rigorous scientific methods (the feminist empiricists), the need to understand the distinctive character of a woman's outlook (the standpoint feminists), or the importance of plurality and difference (the postmodern feminists). Their critics feel that empiricism is vulnerable to the argument that facts themselves imply values, that a woman's standpoint varies dramatically according to circumstance, and that an excessive emphasis upon difference casts doubt upon the whole feminist project.

These divisions can be resolved by a notion of feminism that seeks to incorporate the strengths of each of the feminisms and exclude their weaknesses.

Questions

1. Is feminism still relevant in today's world?
2. Which theory of feminism – the liberal, the socialist, the radical or the black – do you find the most persuasive?
3. Can men become feminists or is feminism an ideology that only relates to women?
4. Do the biological differences between men and women have any social significance?
5. Are some women more likely to favour emancipation than others?

References

Aquinas, St T. (1953) *The Political Ideas of St Thomas Aquinas* (ed. D. Bigongiari) New York: Hafner.

Bebel, A. (1904) *Women under Socialism* New York: Labor Press.

Brody, M. (1992) 'Introduction' in M. Wollstonecraft, *A Vindication of the Rights of Women* London: Penguin, 1–73.

Bryson, V. (1992) *Feminist Political Theory* Basingstoke: Macmillan.

Bryson, V. (1999) *Feminist Debates* Basingstoke: Macmillan.

Coole, D. (1988) *Women in Political Theory* Hemel Hempstead: Harvester-Wheatsheaf.

Eisenstein, Z. (1981) *The Radical Future of Liberal Feminism* London: Longman.

Engels, F. (1972) *The Origin of The Family, Private Property and the State* London: Lawrence & Wishart.

French, M. (1978) *The Women's Room* New York: Jove.

Friedan, B. (1963) *The Feminine Mystique* Harmondsworth: Penguin.

Funk N. and Mueller, M. (eds) (1993) *Gender Politics and Post-Communism* New York and London: Routledge.

Gilligan, C. (1992) *In a Different Voice* London: Harvard University.

Greer, G. (1970) *The Female Eunuch* London: Paladin.

Greer, G. (1999) *The Whole Woman* London: Doubleday.

Hartsock, N. (1983) *Money, Sex and Power* New York and London: Longman.

Hoffman, J. (2001) *Gender and Sovereignty* Basingstoke: Palgrave.

Humm, M. (ed.) (1992) *Feminisms* New York and London: Harvester-Wheatsheaf.

MacKinnon, C. (1979) *Toward a Feminist Theory of the State* Cambridge, Mass.: Harvard University Press.

Marx, K. and Engels, F. (1975) *Collected Works* Vol. 3 London: Lawrence & Wishart.

Mill, J.S. (1869) *The Subjection of Women* Cambridge Mass. and London: MIT Press.

Plato (1953) *The Republic* Harmondsworth: Penguin.

Rowbotham, S. (1972) *Women, Resistance and Revolution* London: Allen Lane/Penguin.

Rubin, G. (1970) 'Woman as Nigger' in L. Tanner (ed.) *Voices from Women's Liberation* New York: Mentor.

Sacks, K. (1974) 'Engels revisited: women, the organization of production and private property' in M. Rosaldo and L. Lamphere (eds), *Women, Culture and Society* Stanford, Calif.: Stanford University Press, 207–22.

Shanley, M. and Pateman, C. (1991) 'Introduction' in M. Shanley and C. Pateman (eds), *Feminist Interpretations and Political Theory* Cambridge: Polity Press, 1–10.

Steans, J. (1998) *Gender and International Relations* Cambridge: Polity Press.

Whelehan, I. (1995) *Modern Feminist Thought* Edinburgh: Edinburgh University Press.

Wolf, N. (1993) *Fire with Fire* London: Chatto and Windus.

Wollstonecraft, M. (1992) *A Vindication of the Rights of Women* London: Penguin.

Zalewski, M. (2000) *Feminism after Postmodernism* London and New York: Routledge.

Further Reading

- Bryson's *Feminist Debates* (referenced above) is particularly useful. It is comprehensive and accessibly written. Chapters 1 and 2 contain a valuable introduction to the feminist 'landscape'.

- Nicholson's *Feminism/Postmodernism* London and New York: Routledge, 1990 contains a series of essays (Nicholson is the editor) written at a time when postmodernism was beginning to make an impact. Yeatman and Hartsock's essays are especially useful.

- Greer's *The Whole Woman* (referenced above) is lively and gives the reader a very good flavour of feminism as it emerged in the 1960s and 1970s.

- Engels's *The Origin of the Family, Private Property and the State* London: Lawrence & Wishart, 1968 has been much commented upon, but is worth reading in the original.

- Shanley and Pateman's *Feminist Interpretations and Political Theory* (referenced above) contains critiques on a wide range of classical political thinkers and more recent theorists. Accessible and full of insights.

- Funk and Mueller's *Gender Politics and Post-Communism* (referenced above) has articles on the position of women after the collapse of the Communist Party states. Some very useful material here.

Weblinks

Have a look at: http://news.bbc.co.uk/1/hi/business/1962036.stm Up-to-date material on women's pay in relation to men.

For a survey of different feminisms, see: http://www-lib.usc.edu/~retter/lst2.html

Chapter 14

Multiculturalism

Introduction

Beliefs and values, language and family traditions, dress and diet, are central to an individual's sense of identity. Most people would say that these things should be respected, and liberal democracy has developed into an ideology that places great stress on respecting diversity of belief and lifestyle. A fully human existence entails the freedom to live according to your cultural traditions. But what if a particular cultural tradition is hostile to liberalism? What if, for example, it holds that girls should be educated to fulfil a subservient role, limited strictly to the private sphere of the family? What if it advocates discrimination, or even violence, against adherents of other religions, or homosexuals, or different ethnic groups? These are questions raised by multiculturalism, an ideology that has emerged since the 1960s, but which – arguably – has roots in the religious struggles of the sixteenth and seventeenth centuries.

Chapter Map

In this chapter we will:

- Disentangle various concepts that often get run together in debates over multiculturalism; in particular, we will distinguish between culture, race, ethnicity and religion.

- Consider the historical development of multiculturalism and, in particular, its relationship to the older ideology of liberalism.

- Set out a number of theories – what we term 'models' – of multiculturalism, and thereby show the diversity of thinking within multiculturalism.

- Apply these theoretical perspectives to 'real-life' case studies.

Religious Dress Ban: Equality or Oppression?

Muslim girls demonstrate in Marseille against a ban on wearing Islamic headscarves in French public schools, 14 Jan 2004

In February 2004 the French National Assembly voted 494–36 in favour of banning 'conspicuous' religious symbols in schools. The ban came into effect in September 2004, at the beginning of the new school year. France has a long tradition of *laicitie* (secularity), which is intended to draw a strict line between the state and religion; some advocates of the ban argue that it is necessary to protect the French state – of which the public education system is a part – from the 'threat' of Islamic fundamentalism. Others offer a more subtle defence: the ban ensures that Muslim girls and young women receive equal treatment as French citizens. By preventing those women wearing a veil (*hijab*), or other Muslim dress, they are being protected from their families who are intent on denying them equality in educational provision. Against the charge that the ban discriminates against Muslims it is stressed that the law applies also to Jewish skullcaps, large Christian crosses and Sikh turbans.

This case draws attention to questions of identity and equality: does treating people equally mean treating them in the same way? Most French people – 70 per cent of whom supported the ban – are either committed or nominal Christians, or have no religious beliefs and adherence; for them there is no injunction to wear a particular form of dress. For Muslims, on the other hand, there are requirements, although there are different interpretations of those requirements among Muslims. Apart from conspicuous crosses, the new law does not have any impact on Christians and non-believers, whereas clearly it does affect Muslims. On the other hand, it could be argued that Islam treats men and women unequally, and this is manifested in gender-differentiated dress codes; the French parliament is, therefore, striking a blow for gender equality.

• What do you think: was the French parliament justified in passing this law?

What is Multiculturalism?

The term 'multiculturalism' has gained wide currency in both academic and popular debate, and its employment is not restricted to political theory or political science: there are multicultural perspectives not only in other social sciences, but also in the humanities, and even in the natural sciences. For this reason it is important to demarcate the debate in political theory, and this requires making some distinctions:

(a) **Multiculturalism as an attitude** Although it is more usual to describe a person as 'cosmopolitan' than 'multicultural', the two can be taken as synonyms, which define either a positive and open attitude to different cultures or, at least, respect for people, where such respect means recognising their rights to make choices about how they live their lives.

(b) **Multiculturalism as a tool of public policy** If you conduct an online search of university library holdings using the word 'multiculturalism' most items will be concerned with education policy, followed by other areas of public policy such as health and social services. Multicultural education policy is concerned with school organisation and curriculum; health and social policy focuses particularly on social inclusion and identifying the special needs of particular cultural groups.

(c) **Multiculturalism as an aspect of institutional design** Whereas policy questions assume the existence of a particular set of political institutions, the question here is what kind of institutions we should have. Examples of institutional design that make explicit the concern with cultural diversity include the power-sharing Assembly and Executive created in Northern Ireland as a result of the 1998 Belfast Agreement, and the constitutional arrangements for Bosnia-Herzegovina which resulted from the 1995 Dayton Peace Accords.

(d) **Multiculturalism and moral justification** Institutions are important, but political theory is not concerned merely with what political institutions should exist, but with how they are justified. It is possible for institutions to be respected for bad reasons, so 'justificatory multiculturalism' is concerned with reasons that all reasonable people can accept. What constitutes 'reasonableness' is, of course, central to the debate.

Culture, Race, Ethnicity and Religion

Culture

A difficulty that runs through the multiculturalism debate is the failure to explain what is meant by culture. Will Kymlicka, for example, in the opening lines of his book *Multicultural Citizenship*, makes the following claim:

> Most countries are culturally diverse. According to recent estimates, the world's 184 independent states contain over 600 living language groups, and 5,000 ethnic groups. In very few countries can the citizens be said to share the same language, or belong to the same ethnonational group (Kymlicka, 1995: 1).

In a few short sentences it is implied that 'culture' equates to a language group, an ethnic group and an ethnonational group. Kymlicka goes on to define the kind of culture with which he is concerned as an 'intergenerational community, more or less institutionally complete, occupying a given state territory, sharing a distinct language and history' (Kymlicka: 18) and further suggests that a culture provides 'meaningful ways of life across the full range of human activities' (Kymlicka: 76). The problem is that there is a proliferation of concepts with which culture is equated but this simply shifts the strain of definition on to these other, equally problematic, concepts. Other political theorists, such as Tully (1995), do make explicit their reliance on a particular theory of culture – in Tully's case Clifford Geertz's semiotic theory – but they fail to discuss fully the implications of such commitments. And in popular discussion 'culture' is frequently run together with race, ethnicity and religion; while there are important connections between these concepts they are not synonyms. The structure of a religion is quite different to the structure of, say, a linguistic community, and each generates distinct political claims. (Race and ethnicity, and religion, are discussed later in this section.)

If we want to find a serious discussion of culture we have to turn to anthropologists, for whom arguably 'culture' is the central, defining concept of their discipline. Edward Tylor's definition of culture as 'that complex whole which includes knowledge, belief, art, morals, law, custom, and any other capabilities and habits acquired by man as a member of society' (Tylor, 1871: 1), while very broad, does capture the notion of culture as something artificial, in contrast to 'nature' that is a 'given'. We can characterise the anthropologists' discussion of culture as an attempt to answer the question: given a shared biological nature and largely similar physical needs, why is there such cultural diversity? From Tylor onwards responses have fallen into two categories: universalist and relativist. These categories contain, of course, a huge variety of different theories. In the universalist camp we find those Marxists who argue that 'forms of consciousness' (culture) are to be explained by underlying material forces, and cultural change is derivative of changes in the relations of production. For such Marxists culture is a secondary phenomenon, and not the true 'subject of history'. But a universalist can hold culture to be basic, maintaining that cultural diversity is explained by different rates of evolution. Nineteenth-century anthropologists, Tylor included, viewed what they termed 'primitive cultures' as of the same type as earlier European cultural forms. This has clear imperialist overtones, and it is no coincidence that anthropology developed on the back of colonisation. Evolutionism could, however, take a liberal form, if one maintained, as John Stuart Mill did, that human beings have innate rational capacities that can only be realised under particular cultural conditions (Mill, 1991: 231). These Marxist, 'imperialist', and liberal theories are all evolutionary, but universalism need not be evolutionist. One might argue that there are underlying non-cultural needs that are satisfied by diverse cultural forms; such a *functionalist* view explains culture in terms of something non-cultural without a commitment to the evolutionary superiority of one culture over another (Malinowksi, 1965: 67–74).

In its early phase anthropology was dominated by universalist theories, but by the late nineteenth and early twentieth centuries it came under sustained attack by relativists, such as Franz Boas (Boas, 1940: 290–4), and his students Ruth Benedict (Benedict, 1935: 1–14) and Alfred Kroeber (Kroeber, 1952: 118–35).

Benedict, in her book, *Patterns of Culture*, quotes Ramon, chief of the Californian Digger Indians, who laments that with colonisation American Indian culture had died and, taking Ramon's analogy of a cup, Benedict maintains that his culture could not be preserved by 'tinkering with an addition here, lopping off something there', rather, 'the modelling had been fundamental, it was somehow all of a piece' (Benedict, 1935: 16). A culture, Benedict suggests, is as an integrated pattern of intelligent, albeit sometimes unconscious, behaviour. It involves an apparently arbitrary selection of ways of being that are reinforced over time; the correlative of such selection is the implicit rejection of other ways of being. There are no underlying non-cultural needs, drives or capacities, nor is a particular culture, following Hegel, an instantiation of a process of cultural change. Pattern theory implies that there can be no cultural *diversity* within a society, for culture is integral, and it is perhaps not surprising that those political theorists, such as Tully (1995), who make explicit their anthropological commitments, appeal to an alternative and more recent form of cultural relativism, that advanced by, among others, Geertz (1993). Culture for Geertz is a complex of signs, whose meaning is dependent upon perspective, not in the sense that an 'outsider' cannot understand the signs, but rather that such understanding – *interpretation* – must make reference to the context of the participants. For Geertz one does not 'have' a culture in the sense that culture is predicated upon a subject, but rather culture is a shorthand for a 'multiplicity of complex conceptual structures, many of them superimposed upon or knotted into one another, which are at once strange, irregular, and inexplicit' (Geertz, 1993: 10).

Race and Ethnicity

Race and ethnicity are concerned with somatic, or phenotypical, differences between people: that is, how other people look or sound, or any other way in which they are *perceived* to be different. There is a considerable sociological literature on race and ethnicity, but very little intellectual exchange between sociologists of race and political theorists of multiculturalism. The terms race and ethnicity are used interchangeably. Ethnicity denotes a group of people bound by 'blood-ties', and has its etymological roots in the Greek word for 'nation' – *ethnos* (although some Biblical commentators translate it as Gentile). Although most sociologists reject the notion that racial differences have a biological basis – there is greater genetic variation *within* groups perceived to be the same than *between* such groups – they accept that the discourse of race affects human attitudes and behaviour. Because it has social effects, race is 'real'.

Until relatively recently, race (or ethnicity) rather than culture was the dominant concept in debates about citizenship and immigration. This is reflected in law. British legislation intended to outlaw discrimination were titled Race Relations Acts – of which there were three: 1965, 1968, 1976. The 1976 Act, which superseded the previous ones, defined a 'racial group' as 'a group of persons defined by reference to colour, race, nationality or ethnic or national origins' (Macdonald, 1977: 49). There is no mention of culture, or indeed religion. A complex relationship exists between anti-racist politics and multiculturalism. Since a person can be defined as 'different' by a range of characteristics, including language (and accent), bodily characteristics, dress, religion and diet, where the salience of each varies from one situation to another, legislation designed to protect that person cannot easily slot discrimination into a single category, such as racial, or religious, or cultural, or ethnic. In this sense race and culture are inextricably linked. However, race is relatively fixed as against culture – even if we reject race as a biological category, a person's race is *perceived* as fixed. Culture, because it is concerned with beliefs and lifestyle, possesses a greater fluidity. The danger which some anti-racists see in multiculturalism is that, in the name of respecting difference and fighting discrimination, multiculturalists deny people autonomy – they assume that cultural traits are fundamental to that person's identity.

Religion

Liberalism as
Toleration,
pp. 165–70

Much debate about cultural diversity is really about the relationship of religion and politics – that is, of the consequences of the existence of conflicting belief systems, including secular ones, within a political territory. As such, multiculturalism has its roots in debates going back to the sixteenth century: the appearance in the same political territory of rival, mutually exclusive, authoritative and comprehensive belief systems caused a political crisis, which was 'settled' with the development of conceptions of religious toleration. The extent to which contemporary debates over, for example, the role of Islam in Western societies, are a continuation of these older debates is something we shall discuss in the last section of this chapter. Here we make a few general remarks about religion and multiculturalism.

The first point to make is that religion is a highly complex phenomenon. Eric Sharpe identifies four 'modes' of religion, that is, ways in which human beings are religious:

1. the *existential* mode, in which the focus is on faith;
2. the *intellectual* mode, which gives priority to beliefs, in the sense of those statements to which a person gives conscious assent;
3. the *institutional* mode, at the centre of which are authoritative organisations that maintain and transmit doctrines;
4. the *ethical* mode, which stresses the behavioural relationships between members of a religious community, and those outside it (Sharpe, 1983: 91–107).

What differentiates different religions and sects is the centrality of one mode relative to another. For example, many Protestant Christians place personal experience (mode 1) at the centre of their religion, and their interpretation of scripture (mode 2), allegiance to the Church (mode 3), and personal behaviour (mode 4) are determined by their religious experience. There are other traditions within Protestantism which make scriptural interpretation (mode 2) central, and the other modes derivative. Catholicism stresses Church teaching and authority (mode 3). Some work in comparative religion contrasts Christianity as a religion of orthodoxy, with Islam, along with Judaism, as a religion of orthopraxy. There is, for example, no equivalent in Islam to the Nicene Creed; while the first of the Five Pillars of Islam – *Shahada* – is a declaration of faith, the remaining four pillars stress correct practice. This simple distinction is open to challenge, but insofar as it holds, the central mode for Muslims is 4.

Exercise

If you were to leave the society in which you were brought up and live in another, what aspects of behaviour, belief and lifestyle would you give up first, and which would you give up last, or not give up at all? How you approach this exercise may depend on a number of factors:

- the age at which you emigrate;

- the circumstances of your emigration – it may be relatively 'free', or forced on you by persecution, or economic circumstances;

- the differences between the community from which you emigrate and the community of immigration;

- your gender may be relevant.

You may, in fact, have experienced migration. In that case, you can draw on your experience.

Each of these modes can contain considerable diversity. For example, most religions stress the importance of experience, but that experience can be focused on a divinity, expressed through doctrines, and possibly mediated through religious institutions, such as a priesthood, or a very diffuse and 'free' mysticism. Many great religions have mystical traditions, and those who express their faith through a mystical existential mode may have more in common with one another than with those who are nominally their co-religionists. Again, the three great monotheistic religions – Judaism, Christianity and Islam – place emphasis on scripture, but there are divergent approaches *within* each of these religions. Some claim there is a literal and accessible truth to scripture; others claim that truth is only recoverable by reconstructing the context in which scripture was formed; yet others maintain that truth is relative, or that there are plural sources of truth. In passing, it should be said that the extent to which a religion is 'literate' – that is, stresses reading scripture – as against 'audio-visual' is undoubtedly a reflection of the level of development of society: popular religion in a largely illiterate society will likely be audio-visual, although alongside it there may exist an 'elite' literate religion.

When considering the relationship of religion and politics in contemporary society it is important to keep in mind the dominant mode of a particular religion or sect, as well as the particular content of its beliefs or practices. As we have argued, the development of liberalism depended both on toleration of religious difference and the recognition of a distinction between public and private. One of the central questions for multiculturalists is whether that distinction reflects a particular mode of religion, and therefore a specific religion, or whether liberalism has a broader reach.

Multiculturalism, Liberalism and Modernity

Liberalism and multiculturalism stand in a close but complex relationship to one another. Liberals accept that we live in a pluralistic society – there is no single good way to live your life, or if there is, there is no means of persuading others that you have found it – and diversity of culture is one expression of that pluralism. But the compatibility of liberalism and multiculturalism turns upon the conceptualisation of pluralism. If by 'pluralism' we mean an irreconcilable difference over the good, then allegiance to the state might simply be understood as a willingness not to impose upon others our conception of the good, and the justification for such 'toleration' of 'difference' is nothing more than social peace. If, however, we see pluralism as a natural outcome of the exercise of human freedom then the justification for tolerance of other conceptions of the good is grounded in something that is itself a good, namely, personal autonomy. Once personal autonomy takes on the status of a political value, the question arises as to whether the political order depends upon the existence and sustenance of particular cultural forms to the exclusion of others.

Biography, p. 358

Multiculturalists argue that 'traditional' liberalism fails to recognise the role that culture plays in the self-worth of individuals. Charles Taylor, who is both a liberal and a multiculturalist, argues that the sense of who we are is constructed in the eyes of others, so that to fail to be recognised by others is to be denied the basis of one's identity: 'non-recognition or misrecognition can inflict harm, can be a form of oppression, imprisoning someone in a false, distorted, and reduced mode of being' (Taylor, 1994: 25). The politics of recognition is a modern concept, developing out of the collapse of hierarchies in the eighteenth century. Hierarchies were the basis of honour, and honour was linked to distinction, and hence inequality; against honour we have dignity, which Taylor takes to be the basis of a liberal–democratic society. At the same time as we shift from honour to dignity, we also experience individualisation: morality is no longer to be understood in terms of mores but is a matter of individual conscience, either in the form of a moral sense or, following Kant, the capacity of an individual to will the moral law. However, after Kant we get what Taylor terms a 'displacement of the moral accent': the inner voice is no longer primarily concerned to tell us what to do – to connect us to an objective moral order – but has become an end in itself. It is the terminus of identity. We have to be true to our 'inner voice' if we are to be 'full human beings'. The conjunction of inwardness and authenticity – following that inner voice – creates a danger that we lose sight of the fact that one's identity is only possible through other people's recognition of us. Somehow we need to reconcile the inwardness of authenticity with the 'outwardness' of recognition. In the days of 'honour' the two were unproblematic because 'general recognition was built into the socially derived identity by virtue of the very fact that it was based on social categories that everyone took for granted' (Taylor: 34). Inwardly derived, as distinct from externally imposed, identity does not enjoy this automatic recognition, but must win it, and that process may fail, such that 'what has come about with the modern age is not the need for recognition but the conditions in which the attempt to be recognized can fail' (Taylor: 35). Recognition is recognition of *difference*, but this is combined with a traditional liberal emphasis on equality:

> The politics of difference often redefines non-discrimination as requiring that we make these distinctions the basis of differential treatment. So members of aboriginal bands will get certain rights and powers not enjoyed by other Canadians . . . and certain minorities will get the right to exclude others in order to preserve their cultural integrity, and so on (Taylor: 39–40).

The conflict between 'traditional' liberalism and identity politics would be less severe were it not for the fact that 'the demand for equal recognition extends beyond an acknowledgement of the equal value of all humans potentially, and comes to include the equal value of what they have made of this potential in fact' (Taylor: 42–3).

What is interesting about this presentation of multiculturalism is that 'culture' is conceptualised not as an imposition or constraint, but as something we *identify with*, and in the process it becomes our *identity*. Despite Taylor's criticisms of traditional liberalism, his historical reconstruction of the development of multiculturalism as one strain of the politics of recognition – another is feminism – owes a huge amount to a liberal conception of the human subject. Culture is not, for Taylor, something set apart from human beings, but rather it is through culture that we acquire the recognition of other people, and so self-respect. Although there are different models of multiculturalism – we discuss some in the next section – they share what may be called a 'post-liberal' emphasis: that is, they have absorbed liberal conceptions, but at the same time engage in a critique of them. A consequence is that multiculturalism *as an academic debate* cannot be understood as a return to early liberal debates about religious toleration, debates rooted in a quite different conception of human nature. And it is striking that, with the exception of Rawls's contribution, religion is not in the foreground of these models of multiculturalism. The difficulty is that the *popular debate* – in, for example, the media – does tend to focus on religion, and especially the relationship of Islam to liberal–democratic values. We will make some observations on this disjunction between the academic and popular debates in the last section.

Models of Multiculturalism

In this section we survey five 'models' of multiculturalism. One of the aims of this presentation is to show that although the field of multiculturalism is diverse, there are common concerns with human identity, rationality, freedom and equality.

Biographies

Charles Taylor (1931–). A leading Canadian political theorist. He has written an important book on Hegel, and made significant contributions to contemporary political philosophy.

Jeremy Waldron (1953–). A New Zealander, he has taught legal and political philosophy in Britain and the United States.

Will Kymlicka (1962–). Another Canadian academic, he has written extensively on multiculturalism. His first book, *Liberalism, Community and Culture*, was a defence of Rawls against communitarian critics, such as Sandel.

James Tully (1946–). Also a Canadian academic – the interest among Canadians in multiculturalism

reflects, in part, the culturally fragmented nature of their country. Tully's background is in the history of political thought. His reflections on multiculturalism were first given in lectures at Cambridge University in the mid-1990s.

John Rawls – see p. 85.

Edward Said (1935–2003). Born into a wealthy Arab-Christian family in Jerusalem during the British Mandate, as a teenager he was sent to school in the United States, and went on to spend most of his life in that country, becoming Professor of Comparative Literature at Columbia University (New York).

Jeremy Waldron: Hybridity

Waldron takes as his starting point the controversy surrounding Salman Rushdic's novel *The Satanic Verses*. That novel, published in 1988, offended many Muslims, and resulted in a *fatwa* being proclaimed the following year against the author by the Ayatollah Khomeini. Waldron quotes from an essay in which Rushdie describes *The Satanic Verses* as a 'migrant's-eye view of the world'. It is, Rushdie says, written from the experiences of 'uprooting, disjuncture and metamorphosis'. He goes on to say that 'the Satanic Verses celebrates hybridity, impurity, intermingling, the transformation that comes of new and unexpected combinations of human beings, cultures, ideas, politics, movies, songs' (Rushdie, cited in Waldron, 1995: 93). Rushdie argues that 'mongrelization' is the way that 'newness enters the world'.

The concept of hybridity is at the heart of Waldron's understanding of multiculturalism, which, he argues, must be 'cosmopolitan'. Understood in this way, multiculturalism represents a challenge to both liberalism and **communitarianism**. Against liberalism it implies a less 'rigid' conception of what it means to live an autonomous life: 'if there is liberal autonomy in Rushdie's vision, it is a choice running rampant, and pluralism internalized from relations *between* individuals to the chaotic coexistence of projects, pursuits, ideas, images, and snatches of culture *within* an individual' (Waldron, 1995: 94).

Communitarians, on the other hand, fail to define 'community': is it a neighbourhood or the whole world? For the purposes of his argument Waldron defines community as an 'ethnic community' – 'a particular people sharing a heritage of custom, ritual, and way of life that is in some real or imagined sense immemorial' (Waldron: 96). Although we may need culture in a wide sense, we do not need to exist in a single culture, such as an ethnic community. Indeed, he goes further and argues that the only authentic response to modernity is the recognition of cultural hybridity: 'from a cosmopolitan point of view, immersion in the tradition of a particular community in the modern world is like living in Disneyland and thinking that one's surroundings epitomize what it is for a culture really to exist' (Wadron: 101).

Waldron does recognise the counter-charge to cosmopolitanism: that living with fragments of culture generates incoherence. As Benedict argued, the meaning of a particular item of culture depends on the whole, for a culture is all of a piece. Waldron argues, however, that real communities are disparate and overlap and are nothing like the aboriginal hunting bands or the 'misty dawn in a Germanic village' (Waldron: 102). Respecting culture does not entail valuing an entire culture, as if a culture were a self-contained thing, but rather 'meaningful options' come from a variety of cultural sources, and 'cultural erosion' is the key to cultural evaluation: the failure of a culture to survive indicates that one culture – or cultural trait – is better than another. Waldron's argument can be read either as a critique of multiculturalism or a particular model of multiculturalism. It is a critique if by multiculturalism is meant a deliberate policy of maintaining, either through financial support or the restriction of individual freedom, a particular culture, where culture is understood as an organic whole. It is a model of multiculturalism insofar as it presents a model of political society in which cultural diversity is valued.

Will Kymlicka: Right to Cultural Membership

Theories of Just
Distribution,
pp. 85–91

In his first book, *Liberalism, Community, and Culture*, Kymlicka argued that Rawls's theory of justice could, with a few revisions, accommodate the value of community. In subsequent work he has sought to defend cultural diversity within a Rawlsian framework: he argues that as individuals we have (moral) rights to cultural membership. He argues that culture provides a 'context of choice'. This is problematic, for it is unclear whether culture is instrumentally or intrinsically valuable: does value reside in what we choose or in the fact that we have chosen it? If the ends we choose are of instrumental value then it would not much matter with which culture you identified, although the more compatible with liberal values the better.

Although Kymlicka makes clear that it is the ends we choose which matter, rather than our capacity to choose, the idea of culture as a context of choice does suggest that oppressive and illiberal cultures are less valuable than those which permit freedom, and so human autonomy – the capacity to choose – must have some intrinsic value. Kymlicka avoids addressing this tension within his theory and instead appeals to empirical examples to show that culture need not be oppressive. He cites Quebec as a culture that has 'liberalised':

> Before the Quiet Revolution [1960–6], the Québécois generally shared a rural, Catholic, conservative, and patriarchal conception of the good. Today, after a period of liberalization, most people have abandoned this traditional way of life, and Québécois society now exhibits all the diversity that any modern society contains . . . to be a Québécois today, therefore, simply means being a participant in the francophone society of Quebec (Kymlicka, 1995: 87).

In the absence of an adequate theorisation of culture it is not clear whether the example of Quebec can help us to see whether 'cultural membership' enhances or diminishes freedom. After all, the struggle within Quebec is fundamentally over language, and although the freedom of one linguistic community is threatened by the other, the capacity to use language, whether it is French or English, is fundamental to human autonomy. Other dimensions of culture, such as religion, may not contain the same freedom-enhancing potential. Quebec shows that a culture *can* be liberal, but it does not establish that a culture is *necessarily* liberal.

Kymlicka argues that individuals should have rights to cultural membership. Rights are central to a liberal polity, and for the purposes of this discussion we can define a right as an advantage held against another (or others). Kymlicka distinguishes between three different types of right: self-government rights, polyethnic rights, and special representation rights. Self-government rights usually entail the devolution of power to a political unit 'substantially controlled by the members of an ethnic minority' (Kymlicka: 30). Examples of polyethnic rights would be state funding of 'cultural institutions' and exemptions from certain policies, such as those relating to the slaughter of animals (Kymlicka: 31). Special representation rights are intended to ensure the 'fair' representation of minority groups (Kymlicka: 32). Each of these types of rights, but especially the first two, can take the form of an 'internal restriction' or an 'external protection' (Kymlicka: 35–44). Kymlicka maintains that empirical evidence shows most campaigns for cultural recognition take the form of a demand for external protections from wider society, rather than restricting the freedom of the members of that culture, and so are compatible with liberalism (Kymlicka: 38–40). The basic problem is that rights are a specific cultural form, and the effects of rights on a culture depend on how one conceptualises culture. If cultures are integral patterns (Benedict; Kroeber) then rights may well upset those patterns. If, on the other hand, we conceive culture(s) as overlapping semiotic relationships (Geertz) then we have a different problem: rights imply a uniform legal system and yet a semiotic theory of culture suggests that interpretation may be relativistic.

James Tully: Constitutional Diversity

Tully's work has the virtue of making explicit its anthropological and philosophical presuppositions: from anthropology he defends the semiotic theory of Geertz against what he calls the 'stages' – that is, evolutionary – theory of nineteenth-century 'imperialists', and from philosophy he draws on Ludwig Wittgenstein's later language theory.

Constitutional uniformity (or modern constitutionalism) is the object of Tully's attack, and modern political thinkers are (largely) its proponents. Modern constitutionalism stresses sovereignty, regularity and uniformity, and this contrasts with the implied rejection of sovereignty and the irregularity and pluralism of 'ancient constitutionalism'. Although there are notable exceptions, Tully maintains that the process of colonisation entailed the confrontation of these two forms of constitutionalism, and contemporary cultural conflicts in, for example, the Americas have their roots in the imposition of an alien constitutional form on Native Americans (Tully, 1995: 34). This imperial legacy is still with us, not simply in political practice, but also in political theory. Writers such as Rawls, Kymlicka and Habermas, while arguing for cultural diversity, do so in the language of modern constitutionalism (Tully: 44).

Drawing on Geertz and Wittgenstein, Tully contrasts two models of intercultural communication (he prefers the term 'interculturalism' to multiculturalism). The first requires shared terms of reference – so, for example, we might disagree about what rights people have, but we implicitly assume that rights have certain features (Tully: 85). The second is based on 'family resemblances' between cultures: we find common ground not through an implicitly agreed, shared language, but by a piecemeal case-by-case agreement, based on affinities between our different cultural traditions (Tully: 120). This suggests that constitutional formation cannot be understood from an abstract standpoint, such as Rawls's original position. And Europeans have resources within their own culture(s) to engage in such case-by-case communication; English Common Law is an example of an ancient constitution, and Tully considers it significant that there were examples of interaction between Europeans and Native Americans based on recognition of the *affinities* between their legal systems.

Tully's argument, while interesting and provocative, has a number of weaknesses. First, there is a tension between his espousal of a semiotic theory of culture, which stresses looseness of cultural boundaries, and his talk of 12,000 'diverse cultures, governments and environmental practices' struggling for recognition (Tully: 3) (he provides no source for that figure) and '15,000 cultures who demand recognition' (Tully: 8) (again, no source). To count something you have to identify it, and identification implies 'hard boundaries'. Second, he says very little about how cultural conflicts can be mediated in the contemporary world, despite the underlying purpose of his work being to show the relevance of ancient constitutionalism. It is not clear what institutional forms would express cultural diversity, especially for geographically dispersed minorities. Third, and most important, he fails to address the charge that protection of culture can have detrimental consequences for individual freedom. He does maintain that culture is the basis of self-respect, such that to be denied recognition is a serious thing, but he offers only metaphorical observations to support the claim that interculturalism is not a threat to individual freedom (Tully: 189).

John Rawls: Overlapping Consensus

We have encountered Rawls's work in previous chapters. The focus there was on his first book, *A Theory of Justice*. In a later book, *Political Liberalism* (first published 1993), Rawls engages in a critique of the earlier work, arguing that it did not fully account for the 'fact of reasonable pluralism'. The idea that principles of justice are generated from a moral standpoint occupied by autonomous moral agents is a form of comprehensive liberalism, and as such is controversial. Reasonable people can deny that people are autonomous, or that political values derive from such autonomy. As the title of his later book indicates, what he came to defend was a *political*, rather than a *comprehensive*, liberalism.

Rawls lists a number of features of human interaction that explain why reasonable people can disagree: evidence is conflicting and complex; different weights can be attached to different considerations; concepts are vague; there are conflicts between different moral considerations, such as duties to family and duties to strangers; no society can contain a full range of values. He then goes on to define a 'reasonable conception of the good':

1. It entails the exercise of theoretical reason.
2. It entails the exercise of practical reason.
3. 'While a reasonable comprehensive view is not necessarily fixed and unchanging, it normally belongs to, or draws upon, a tradition of thought and doctrine'. It is not subject to 'sudden and unexplained changes, it tends to evolve slowly in the light of what, from its point of view, it sees as good and sufficient conditions' (Rawls, 1993: 59).

From the idea of reasonable pluralism Rawls offers an explanation of how citizens, from a variety of different reasonable comprehensive conceptions of the good can come to respect liberal political institutions. We develop an 'overlapping consensus': it is for citizens as part of their liberty of conscience individually to work out how liberal values relate to their own comprehensive conceptions, where a 'comprehensive conception' could be a religious belief system. Each reasonable comprehensive doctrine endorses the political conception from its own standpoint. Individuals work towards liberal principles from mutually incompatible comprehensive perspectives, and respect for those principles is built on the 'overlap' between them.

Rawls does not give concrete examples of how such an overlapping consensus can be achieved, so to illustrate his argument we provide an example of our own: how might Muslims embrace, from *within* their comprehensive conception of the good, liberal political principles? Some possible grounds are as follows:

- Islam has a long history of toleration of Jews and Christians, grounded in the belief that Islam is an aboriginal and natural form of monotheism, which incorporates the Prophets of the Jews and the Christians.
- So long as secular law is not incompatible with holy law (*Shariah*), then the former should be obeyed. There are arguments in Islam for obeying secular rulers.
- *Jihad* (exertion, struggle) has been misinterpreted: a believer is required to carry out *jihad* by 'his heart; his tongue; his hands; and by the sword'. *Jihad* can be an individual, spiritual struggle.
- 'Islam' is often defined as 'submission' or 'self-surrender'. Submission understood as self-imposed discipline is not incompatible with respect for human freedom – a person might *choose* to submit.
- For Muslims, behaviour is classified as: (a) required – includes prayer, alms-giving, fasting; (b) prohibited – theft, illicit sex, alcohol consumption; (c) recommended – charitable acts, additional prayers and fasts; (d) discouraged – might include unilateral declarations of divorce by men; (e) morally indifferent. From the perspective of respect for secular law, only (b) might raise difficulties – but much will depend on what penalties are imposed for prohibited acts.
- Requirements on women to cover themselves can be interpreted as symbolic – in the Arab–Islamic world there is huge variation in what is required of women. Men are also required to be 'modest'.

Each of these points can be contested, but it is at least plausible to argue that Muslims can be *politically* liberal. Other citizens – Christians, Jews, Hindus, atheists and so on – will, of course, produce different lists of reasons for endorsing liberal principles. The task is not to agree on a set of reasons – reasonable people will always disagree – but to converge on a set of institutions from diverse standpoints.

Edward Said: Critique of Orientalism

Said does not offer a positive model of multiculturalism, but rather a critique of Western views of 'the Orient'. Nonetheless, it is possible to discern in his writings claims about the value of culture that are relevant not only to relations between states and societies, but relations within particular political communities between different cultural groups. Said was hugely influential in the development of 'post-colonial' studies. That term denotes not simply what comes after colonialism, but rather it suggests a transformation of colonialism – the 'post' can be read in much the same way as the 'post' in 'postmodernism'.

Confrontation with alien cultures engenders dissonance – the inability to incorporate experiences into one's 'conceptual framework'. With the expansion of European empires in the nineteenth century there was a demand placed on the colonisers to 'make sense' of the 'other'. In his most famous book – *Orientalism: Western Conceptions of the Orient* (1991) – Said is concerned with the confrontation of European imperialists with a specific region, which itself is an imperial construction. The Orient was defined as the Arab–Islamic and Indian regions. Anthropologists and other scholars, whose work depended on the colonial enterprise, were forced to accept the kinship of the Orient and the Occident (Europe), and indeed the prior achievements of the former, among which were the technical innovations of ancient Egypt, the existence of complex urban societies, and the fact that the European languages were derived from the ancient Indian language Sanskrit. They had to acknowledge the close relationship between Islam, Judaism and Christianity, and the fact that the Christian 'Holy Lands' were located in the Orient, and that ancient Greek texts survived thanks to medieval Arab scholars (Said, 1991: 74).

Said argues that Orientalists adopted an 'objectifying' attitude to the Orient. While they accepted that Europe had its roots in the Orient, they claimed the achievements of the Orient had been taken over by Europeans. To use Marxist language, Europe was now the historical (or revolutionary) subject, whereas the Orient was static. Said describes the Orient as a (theatre) 'stage' affixed to Europe, with the 'locals' dressed up in costumes (Said: 63). And because Europe was now the historical subject, it could understand the Orient better than the 'Orientals'.

Post-colonialism is concerned with 'deconstructing' this binary opposition of subject (knower) and the object (known). In denying themselves, and seeking to be objective, the colonisers were less enlightened than those they sought to enlighten. In a later work, *Culture and Imperialism* (1993), Said argues that the 'other' (the colonised) does appear in French and British cultural life, and there is an implicit, although admittedly negative, recognition of the cultural (as well as material) dependence of the metropolitan centre on the 'periphery'. Joseph Conrad's *Heart of Darkness* is taken by Said as the most important literary example of this recognition, but novels, such as those of Dickens, which do not have an explicit imperial setting, recognise that empire structures the domestic context (Said: 13–14). Darkness, fear and instability are the themes, but this at least recognises the impenetrability of the 'other' – that which is not Western (Said: 33–4). The next step would be to acknowledge heterogeneity, which is distinct from pure negativity ('not us').

Where there might appear to be a more positive recognition of the 'Orient' is as the 'hidden self' of the West. The Romantic movement of the early nineteenth century was a reaction to the rise of scientific rationalism, but equally was a product of modernity. The Orient was a kind of storehouse for Romantic material (or a theatre stage, to use Said's analogy). But just as Romanticism implied controlled sensuality so the Orient was to be 'experienced' at a distance. The 'correct' attitude was melancholy: a sense of loss of sensuality. While the stress on Oriental sensuality appears superficially positive, in fact it reinforces the 'scientific' objectification of the Orientalists. Indeed, the more 'sensual' the Arabs were, the less 'rational' they were: sensuality went hand in hand with lawlessness and cruelty.

There are several general points to be gained from Said. First, although the world has been decolonised we are dealing with the legacy of empire, not merely in the obvious sense of global conflict and inequality, but in a deeper cultural sense:

there are structures of thought generated by colonialism that persist and which affect domestic politics. Second, the colonists' denial of their own culture persists in European countries. The 'majority community' may be conscious of its values, but not of their cultural pedigree – 'culture' appears to be what others possess. Third, we continue to use the language of modernisation: progress versus stasis. While Islamic society is often judged by quotations (in translation) from the Qu'rān and other holy texts, and by practices that are extinct in most parts of the Islamic world, Western society is not judged by a selective and uncontextualised reading of the Bible. In other words: 'they' haven't changed since 632, but 'we' have. An alternative version of this argument is that they have adopted our technology, but not our rationality.

One final point should be made about post-colonialism – if identity is important, then the colonial experience must be acknowledged as part of the identity of both coloniser and colonised. The desire in many parts of the colonised world to expunge that experience and seek a pure pre-colonial identity can be oppressive. Said recalls a meeting he had in the United States with an Arab Christian clergyman who was on a mission on behalf of Arab Protestants, of which Said himself was one. These communities had developed from the 1860s as a result of Christian proselytisation. Most converts were from the Eastern Orthodox Church. The cleric was concerned that the policy now (in the 1980s) was to disband these churches – withdraw financial support – and in the interests of Christian unity and survival encourage the followers to rejoin the Orthodox Church. The policy of the 1860s was now deemed a mistake. The cleric could see the point but felt aggrieved that a hundred years of experience was being bureaucratically wiped away.

Assessment: Identity, Reason and Freedom

We have presented a number of theories of multiculturalism: can any general conclusions be drawn from them?

(a) **Agency and identity** We argued in the section on Multiculturalism, Liberalism and Modernity that multiculturalists draw on the liberal conception of the human agent as a free being capable of shaping his or her identity, but criticise liberals for offering an 'empty' or 'a-cultural' conception of human agency. To varying degrees, the thinkers discussed in the previous section offer what they claim is an improved model of human identity and human agency.

(b) **Culture versus rationality** If culture is something we are born into and take for granted, then reason, which entails conscious evaluation and criticism, would appear hostile to culture. Again, insofar as liberalism stresses a rationalist approach to politics it is perceived as hostile to multiculturalism. Much of the work of multiculturalists is concerned with reconciling culture and reason. Although they offer very different conceptions of reason, for Tully, Rawls and Kymlicka the way we reason about just institutions is central to their defence of multiculturalism.

(c) **Freedom** Whereas liberals tend to discuss freedom in abstract terms, exemplified by charters of fundamental freedoms, multiculturalists contextualise freedom.

Certainly many of the thinkers we have discussed defend the traditional liberal freedoms, but they also argue that liberalism can be intolerant, and it is most often intolerant when it claims to be defending freedom. For example, Muslim women 'forced' to wear the *hijab* may claim that Western, non-Muslim women are not free if they are continually the object of the male sexualised gaze. Of course this claim can be challenged, especially when Muslim women are indeed forced to wear the *hijab*, but the claim is at least provocative: freedom is enjoyed *in a cultural context*. You can be formally free but oppressed by social mores.

(d) **Difference and equality** Both feminists and multiculturalists have forced liberals to re-evaluate their idea of equality. For liberals, human beings are morally equal, and that moral equality translates into a certain political equality, and a rather limited material equality. But men and women, as well as different cultural groups, may be morally equal, but they are still different – how we translate that conjunction of equality in difference into political principles and political institutions is a major challenge.

Multiculturalism – the New Wars of Religion?

We have argued that debates about cultural diversity suffer from a lack of conceptual clarity: religion, culture, race and ethnicity are run together. One justification for avoiding a sharp distinction between these phenomena is that discrimination can take many forms; the precise cause of discrimination can only be determined in context. Nonetheless, there is a difficulty that becomes most apparent in the distance between popular debates and academic debates about 'multiculturalism'. By 'popular debates' we mean discussions in newspapers, on radio, television and (perhaps) the internet; the models of multiculturalism discussed above are representative of the academic debate. Race and religion dominate popular debate, whereas culture, or cultural identity, is the focus of academic work. Sometimes academics do influence the wider debate: the most widely discussed contribution to that debate over the last decade has been Samuel P. Huntington's article 'The Clash of Civilizations?' (1993). Huntington argues that with the end of the cold war the 'great divisions among humankind and the dominating source of conflict will be cultural' (Huntington: 22). He lists seven current civilisations, and argues that there will be 'micro-conflicts' at the interface of these civilisations, and 'macro-conflicts' between power blocs for control of international institutions. The most significant conflict, according to Huntington, will be between Western and Islamic civilisations.

Huntington's thesis has, unsurprisingly, come under sustained attack, most especially for ignoring the cultural diversity that exists within societies characterised as belonging to a single civilisation. What is significant, however, is the influence of his article. The title has a slogan-like quality well suited to popular consumption. If Huntington is right then the post-cold war world is returning to something akin to the Wars of Religion of the sixteenth and seventeenth centuries, the settlement of which established the philosophical foundations of liberalism. It is not a picture of the world accepted by defenders of multiculturalism; for them, there are no monolithic 'civilisations' but complex social systems in which individuals form their identities from diverse sources. In this sense multiculturalism is not a return to the Wars of Religion but a critical development of the liberal ideology that emerged from those wars.

Summary

Multiculturalism emerged in the 1960s as a distinct area of academic debate, and over the following decades the language of 'cultural diversity' supplanted that of race and religion. Given the dominance of liberalism as an ideology, much discussion in the field of multiculturalism has revolved around the relationship between liberalism and multiculturalism, with the two standing in a complex relationship to one another. Multiculturalists reaffirm the values of freedom and equality but rearticulate these as equality in difference, and freedom in context. Although there are continuities with earlier debates over religious difference and toleration – debates that dominated political discourse in the seventeenth and eighteenth centuries – multiculturalism cannot be understood as simply a return to these earlier disputes, but rather multiculturalism is 'post-liberal', in the sense that it has absorbed the liberal emphasis on human self-expression, but challenges liberals to provide a more adequate understanding of self-expression, one that places much greater emphasis on cultural identity.

Questions

1. Does treating people equally mean treating them in the same way? Can you think of situations in which cultural difference may be a legitimate basis for difference in treatment?
2. Is it possible to 'pick and mix' cultural traits?
3. Is separatism the only way to respect cultural difference?
4. Is there a 'clash of civilisations'?

References

Benedict, R. (1935) *Patterns of Culture* London: Routledge & Kegan Paul.

Boas, F. (1940) *Race, Language, and Culture* New York: Free Press.

Conrad, J. (1995) *Heart of Darkness* (ed. D. Goonetilleke), Peterborough, Ontario: Broadview Press.

Geertz, C. (1993) *The Interpretation of Cultures: Selected Essays* London: Fontana.

Huntington, S. (1993) 'The Clash of Civilizations?', *Foreign Affairs* Summer 1993.

Kroeber, A. (1952) *The Nature of Culture* Chicago Ill.: Chicago University Press.

Kymlicka, W. (1989) *Liberalism, Community and Culture* Oxford: Clarendon Press.

Kymlicka, W. (1995) *Multicultural Citizenship* Oxford: Clarendon Press.

Macdonald, L. (1977) *Race Relations: The New Law* London: Butterworth.

Malinowski, B. (1965) *A Scientific Theory of Culture, and Other Essays* Chapel Hill: North Carolina University Press.

Mill, J.S. (1991) *On Liberty and other essays* (ed. J. Gray) Oxford: Oxford University Press.

Rawls, J. (1972) *A Theory of Justice* Oxford: Clarendon Press.

Rawls, J. (1993) *Political Liberalism* pbk edn New York: Columbia University Press.

Rushdie, S. (1988) *The Satanic Verses* London: Viking.

Said, E. (1991) *Orientalism: Western Conceptions of the Orient* Harmondsworth: Penguin.

Said, E. (1993) *Culture and Imperialism* London: Chatto & Windus.

Sharpe, E. (1983) *Understanding Religion* London: Duckworth.

Taylor, C. (1994) 'The Politics of Recognition', in A. Gutmann (ed.), *Multiculturalism: Examining the Politics of Recognition* Princeton, NJ: Princeton University Press.

Tully, J. (1995) *Strange Multiplicity: Constitutionalism in an Age of Diversity* Cambridge: Cambridge University Press.

Tylor, E. (1871) *Primitive Culture* London: John Murray.

Waldron, J. (1995) 'Minority Cultures and the Cosmopolitan Alternative', in Will Kymlicka *The Rights of Minority Cultures* Oxford: Oxford University Press.

Further Reading

A general book on the importance of culture in people's lives is Michael Carrithers, *Why Humans have Cultures: Explaining Anthropology and Social Diversity* (Oxford: Oxford University Press, 1992). Two fairly straightforward discussions of culture are provided by Geertz (1993) – read the first essay in the book – and Benedict (1935), Chapters 1–3. On religion, read Sharpe (1983). On the historical development of multiculturalism – or the 'politics of recognition' – read Taylor (1994). For various competing theories of multiculturalism you should read Waldron (1995); Tully (1995); Rawls (1993); Said (1991); see also Jürgen Habermas, 'Struggles for Recognition in the Democratic Constitutional State', in A. Gutmann (ed.) *Multiculturalism: Examining the Politics of Recognition*, Princeton: Princeton University Press, 1995 (and other essays in that volume).

Weblinks

Websites on multiculturalism – especially those originating from the United States – tend to be highly polemical. Nonetheless, they do provide a flavour of the passions aroused by the multiculturalism debate.

- A right-wing libertarian website against multiculturalism is: http://multiculturalism.aynrand.org/
- Kenan Malik attacks multiculturalism from a Marxist perspective: http://www.kenanmalik.com/essays/against_mc.html
- A US website dedicated to disseminating information on multiculturalism and with many links to other sites: http://members.aol.com/lacillo/multicultural.html
- UNESCO have an online journal, *International Journal on Multicultural Societies*: http://www.unesco.org/most/jmshome.htm
- A discussion of the Canadian Multiculturalism Act: http://laws.justice.gc.ca/en/C-18.7/

Chapter 15

Ecologism

Introduction

Ecologism has only emerged as a fully fledged ideology since the 1960s. As with all recent ideologies it has intellectual roots stretching back centuries, but the construction of a relatively autonomous set of ideas and prescriptions for action is a very recent occurrence. Ecologism should be distinguished from environmentalism – for environmentalists, concern for the environment is based primarily on concern about the consequences of environmental degradation on human beings, whereas for ecologists, something called 'ecology', or 'nature', is the source of value. It follows from this distinction that whereas environmentalism can be combined with other ideologies, ecologism is distinct. In terms of political practice, politicians from across the political spectrum have embraced the rhetoric, and sometimes the policies, of environmentalism.

Chapter Map

In this chapter we will:

- Distinguish **ecologism** from **environment-alism**.

- Outline the so-called 'ecological crisis'.

- Discuss the thought of two ecologists: Aldo Leopold and Arne Næss.

- Discuss the arguments of one – controversial – environmentalist: Garrett Hardin.

- Explore criticisms of ecologism.

Nuclear Power? Yes Please!

In the 1980s plastered on cars and on lapel badges was the German slogan around a smiley 'sun' face: 'Atomkraft? Nein Danke' ('Nuclear Power? No Thanks'). Central to the German Green movement – and virtually all Green movements – is the rejection of nuclear power as expensive, dangerous, and inextricably linked to the nuclear weapons industry. It therefore came as a shock to many Green activists when one of its leading theorists, James Lovelock – the man who had coined the word 'Gaia' to describe the mutual dependence of all life forms – came out in favour of nuclear power. Lovelock argued that the threat from global warming is now so great that 'nuclear power is the only green solution' (*Independent*, 24 May 2004). The 'great Earth system' – Gaia – is, he says, 'trapped in a vicious circle of positive feedback': extra heat from any source is amplified and its effects are more than additive. This means that we have little time left to act. The Kyoto Protocol, which aimed to cut omissions, is simply a cosmetic attempt 'to hide the political embarrassment of global warming'. If we had 50 years to solve the problem then it might be possible to switch from fossil fuels to 'renewables' such as wind and tide power, but realistically those sources will only make a negligible contribution to the world's energy needs over the next 20, or so, years. There is, Lovelock claims, only one immediately available source of energy which does not contribute to global warming and that is nuclear power. Opposition to nuclear power is based on an 'irrational fear fed by Hollywood-style fiction, the Green lobbies and the media'. These fears are, according to Lovelock, unjustified: 'we must stop worrying about minuscule risks from radiation and recognize that a third of us will die from cancer, mainly because we breathe air laden with "that all pervasive carcinogen, oxygen"'.

- Is Lovelock right? (for background information on nuclear power see weblinks)

Ecologism or Environmentalism?

Of the four chapters on 'new ideologies' in this book, this one has proved to be the most difficult for which to find an appropriate title. As we saw in Chapter 13, while there are feminisms the general label 'feminism' is broadly accepted by radical, socialist and liberal feminists. At least three possibilities suggest themselves for this chapter – ecologism, environmentalism and green (or Green) thought. And these differing possibilities carry distinct ideological implications. In the view of those who call themselves ecologists, environmentalism denotes an attitude compatible with almost all the competing ideologies. Environmentalists attach value to the 'environment' or 'nature' but only in relation to human consciousness and human concerns, and as such the environment is slotted in as a subordinate component of alternative ideologies, such as liberalism, socialism or feminism. Environmentalism is anthropocentric – that is, human centred. Ecologists, on the other hand, assert that 'nature' has intrinsic value, and that the task of ecologism is to engage in a critique of the anthropocentric world-view, which in socio-economic terms manifests itself as industrialism. Ecologism is 'eco-centred'. This does not mean that ecologists do not embrace values and perspectives derived from other ideologies, but rather those perspectives are assessed from the standpoint of the eco-system, or earth, as an irreducible and interdependent system. Whereas environmentalists share a post-Enlightenment belief in the uniqueness of the human perspective on the world – that is, they place human beings above, or outside, nature – ecologists challenge that philosophical position, maintaining that human life only has value insofar as it is a 'knot' in the 'net' of life, a net which connects together not only non-human animals, but non-sentient entities, such as trees, rivers and mountains. Indeed it is the net rather than the knots that is of ultimate value.

Students of politics are most likely to have encountered the political face of the **'green movement'** rather than be aware of the underlying philosophical differences within environmentalism, and one of our aims in this chapter will be to connect the philosophical ideas to the political movements (we discuss the rise of the Green movement in the section on green politics). The links are less direct than some writers on environmentalism recognise. To illustrate this, consider the idea of an 'environmental crisis' (discussed in the section of the same name). Many people maintain that industrialisation, urbanisation and population growth have either brought about, or threaten to bring about, irreversible changes to the natural environment such that the future of life on earth beyond more than one or two hundred years is in jeopardy. Some writers maintain that the difference between ecologism and environmentalism rests, in part, on attitudes to the seriousness of this crisis, with ecologists being very pessimistic, and environmentalists being more optimistic. There is some validity in this characterisation of this differing attitude, in that ecologists maintain that the causes of the crisis are not simply scientific– technical; the roots of the crisis lie in human attitudes to nature – we see nature as a resource to be 'exploited' for our benefit. However, a human-centred approach to the environment could also explain the crisis; without condemning human attitudes to nature it could be argued that environmental degradation is the collective consequence of rational individual behaviour.

Microbiologist and environmental theorist Garrett Hardin argued that overpopulation will have catastrophic consequences, and that food aid to the Third World should be ended so that population levels can be allowed to fall 'naturally' (his argument is discussed later in this chapter). Hardin is often thought of as an ecologist, and his misanthropic argument is used against ecologism, but, in fact, Hardin reasons from straightforwardly human-centred premises: human beings will suffer from overpopulation.

Although ecologism (also called '**deep ecology**') is the primary focus of this chapter, we will also consider environmentalism. We begin with a brief discussion of the idea that there is an environmental crisis. As suggested above, both ecologists and environmentalists accept such a notion, but they differ fundamentally over its causes, and its solution. After a brief consideration of Green politics, we discuss ecologism as a philosophical position, with the aim of connecting philosophy to politics. We analyse the writings of two of the most important figures in ecological thought: Aldo Leopold and Arne Næss. The third thinker we consider – Garrett Hardin – is hard to categorise as an ecologist, because his philosophical premises are clearly anthropocentric, but his proposed solution to what he regards as one of the fundamental causes of the ecological crisis – exponential population growth – has been so controversial that it is important to give it consideration. After a summary of ecologism, we discuss some major objections to it.

Environmental Crisis and Green Politics

Environmental Crisis

Most popular discussion of environmentalism – and ecologism – takes place within the context of a discussion of the so-called 'environmental crisis'. The first point to note is the singularity of the phrase: there is a crisis. This is controversial, for it may be that there is a series of distinct environmental problems. However, virtually all ecologists, and many environmentalists, argue that these problems are interconnected, and a coherent engagement with the environment must recognise this fact. Among the specific environmental problems are the following:

- **Global warming** This is acknowledged by most, but not all, scientists as the most serious environmental problem facing the planet. The earth's temperature is maintained by the 'greenhouse effect' – a layer of gases in the atmosphere traps a small percentage of the sun's radiation – but the burning of fossil fuels increases the greenhouse effect, with the result that sea levels will rise due to the melting of the ice caps, with some fairly obvious consequences for low-lying land areas. At a certain point in the process of global warming lifeforms will be threatened.

- **Resource depletion** Some resources, such as fish, are, with careful stewardship, naturally replenished; other resources, such as coal and gas, are not. Both types of resource are threatened by excessive demand and so overproduction (this raises the question of the 'tragedy of the commons', discussed in the section on Garrett Hardin).

- **Localised pollution** This may not cause a 'global crisis', but poor air in places such as Mexico City can have a debilitating effect on inhabitants.
- **Decline in species** Although the effects of species loss – or decline in bio-diversity – are unclear, many ecologists would argue that the loss of species is bad in itself, regardless of its wider impact. The use of agricultural chemicals and the genetic modification of crops are identified by some environmentalists as the cause of the decline in bio-diversity.
- **Nuclear War** This will not, of course, be a direct environmental problem unless nuclear weapons are actually used (although nuclear weapons testing has had environmental consequences). In the 1980s, when consciousness of the threat of nuclear war was much higher than it is today, scientists speculated that the use of intercontinental ballistic missiles could result in a 'nuclear winter': atmospheric pollution caused by dust, soot, smoke and ash would prevent the sun's rays from penetrating for a period of time long enough to eradicate most plant life and create a new ice age. Since the 1980s there has been a proliferation of states with nuclear weapons.

Students of political theory cannot be expected to be experts on the scientific causes of environmental problems, and the focus of this chapter is on the philosophical ideas behind ecology, many of which can be understood without reference to the 'environmental crisis'. However, the 'crisis' does raise interesting questions about the relationship between science and politics. Ecologists are critical of scientific rationality, and yet employ scientific evidence to support their arguments. We consider this apparent incoherence in a later section (Summary and Criticisms of Ecologism). Furthermore, while there is widespread distrust of scientists employed by multinational companies, and to a lesser extent by government agencies, scientists who speak on behalf of environmental groups enjoy a high level of trust.

Green Politics

Green political parties and movements emerged in the 1970s. In terms of political influence the most successful Green party is the German Green Party (Die Grünen/Bundnis 90). By 1982 they were represented in the parliaments of six of West Germany's regions (Länder), and they entered the Federal Parliament (Bundestag) in 1983, winning 5.6 per cent of the vote. In the following election their support rose to 8.3 per cent, and other parties began to adopt environmental policies. However, during the 1980s it became clear that there was a major schism between Realos (realists) and Fundis (fundamentalists); the former wanted power within the existing political system, while the latter challenged that system. Opposed to German unification in 1990, the Greens fell below the 5 per cent of the vote required for seats in the Bundestag (although their Eastern equivalent – Bundnis 90 – won 6 per cent of the Eastern vote, and thus seats). The internal dispute within the party was won by the Realos and the party – now in alliance with Bundnis 90 – grew in strength through the 1990s. In 1998 they formed a government with the Social Democrats. As of August 2005 they are still in power together, having been narrowly re-elected in 2002.

Environmental Movements

The Green movement encompasses more than just Green political parties – conservation and environmental pressure groups are also important. Indeed, as membership of political parties declines, so the membership of pressure groups increases. Figures from Britain indicate the importance of such groups, as shown in Table 15.1.

Table 15.1

Membership (in thousands)	1971	1991	1997	2002
Royal Society for the Protection of Birds	278	2,152	2,489	3,000
World Wide Fund for Nature	12	227	241	320
Wildlife Trusts	64	233	310	413
Friends of the Earth	1	111	114	119

Source: http://www.statistics.gov.uk/StatBase/ssdataset.asp?vlnk=6230&Pos=3&ColRank=2&Rank=272

The German Greens, as with other European Green parties, draws its strength disproportionately from young, public sector middle-class workers. One explanation that is often advanced for the rise of the Green movement is the emergence of 'post-materialist values': quality of life issues are more important than increasing income and enhanced career status. Such a view presupposes that a society has achieved a certain level of material comfort, and so the Green phenomenon may rest on a contradiction: the possibility of a Green politics depends on the generation of surplus goods and, therefore, the consumer society of which Greens are so critical.

Aldo Leopold and the 'Land Ethic'

It is argued that ecologism only emerged as a distinct ideology in the 1960s: prior to that there was no conscious movement around a distinct set of ideas (Dobson, 2000: 14–15). Aldo Leopold died in 1948, and so clearly, insofar as he was an ecologist, his ecologism was of a non-ideological kind. However, Leopold is important as a precursor of ideological ecologism. The essence of his 'land ethic' was that 'land' was an interdependent system, and not a commodity; human beings were part of the 'land community' and not masters of it; for human beings to understand themselves they must grasp the 'whole' of which they are a 'part'; and 'a thing is right when it tends to preserve the integrity, stability, and beauty of the biotic community . . . it is wrong when it tends otherwise' (Leopold, 1997: 150). What Leopold called 'land' was what later ecologists would call the eco-system, biosphere, Gaia, 'earth' ('Spaceship Earth'), and by 'community' Leopold meant an interdependent whole, the members of which were not simply human beings, or even all sentient beings, but all the life forms.

Biography   **Aldo Leopold (1887–1948)**

US conservationist, scientist and ecological activist and theorist, Leopold was born in Burlington (Iowa).

In 1909 he received the degree of Master of Forestry from Yale University, and then for the following 19 years he worked for the US Forest Service. He was first posted in New Mexico and Arizona, and then in 1924 transferred to the Forest Products Laboratory in Madison (Wisconsin).

In 1928 Leopold left the Forest Service to conduct game surveys of Midwestern states, funded by the Sporting Arms and Ammunition Manufacturers' Institute (the findings were published in 1931). Appointed a Professor of Game Management in 1933, the remaining 15 years of his life were divided between academic research, including field studies, and employment by the state on Conservation Commissions. Leopold's work of the 1930s was undertaken against the profound ecological crisis of the 'dust bowl' (1931–9), illustrated in John Steinbeck's novel *The Grapes of Wrath*, and graphically portrayed in the photographs of Dorothea Lange.

Underlying the land ethic was a controversial philosophical claim: from observation of the empirical world human beings can derive reasons for action. This violates Hume's 'naturalistic fallacy': claims about how people should behave cannot be generated from observational facts – the moral 'ought' cannot be derived from an observation of what 'is'. This is a recurrent problem with ecologism and we discuss it in more detail in Summary and Criticisms of Ecology. Another philosophical, or ethical, claim is that the history of morality is characterised by an 'expanding circle' of concern, whereby we now consider the ownership of other human beings – slavery – wrong, but we have not yet expanded the circle of concern to include the 'land'. The land ethic enlarges the boundaries of the community to include soils, waters, plants and animals. In fact Leopold links these two philosophical claims by arguing that morality has undergone an ecological evolution, suggesting that the moral 'ought' emerges over time from a growing realisation of what 'is'. Such evolution has its origins in:

> the tendency of interdependent individuals or groups to evolve modes of co-operation. The ecologist calls these symbioses. Politics and economics are advanced symbioses in which the original free-for-all competition has been replaced, in part, by co-operative mechanisms with an ethical content (Leopold 1987: 143).

The extension of ethics to land is an 'evolutionary possibility and an ecological necessity'. Certainly, Leopold argues, individual thinkers have condemned the abuse of the land, but 'society' has yet to embrace the land ethic. The conservation movement is the embryo of such social affirmation. Another important and influential claim was that human beings think they understand the mechanisms that underlie nature, whereas in fact they do not, with the implication that we should adopt a precautionary attitude to nature. In fact, in contemporary ecological thought this claim sits alongside the quite contradictory claim that science can 'prove' there is an ecological crisis.

Biography, p. 376

Leopold's land ethic was shaped by his experiences of state-led conservation of the 1930s and 1940s in the United States, and this led him to a salutary conclusion: respect for the land cannot be achieved if the state assumes sole moral responsibility for the environment. Rather, *individuals* must change their motivations, and this is a powerful and central claim of the ecological movement. Leopold noted that farmers accepted free public advice and technical assistance, and consequently progress was made with practices such as strip-cropping, pasture renovation and soil liming, but no progress was achieved against fencing woodland off against grazing, and none in preventing the ploughing and grazing of steep slopes. In short, the farmers accepted those remedial practices that were profitable, and ignored those which were beneficial to the 'community' as a whole – community in Leopold's wide sense – but damaged the farmers' profit margins. And increasing the level of environmental education is pointless without a change in attitudes and motivations – that is, without a recognition of obligations to the land. He observes that the existence of obligations is taken for granted when what is at issue are better roads or schools but 'their existence is not taken for granted, nor as yet seriously discussed, in bettering the behaviour of the water that falls on the land, or in the preserving of the beauty or diversity of the farm landscape' (Leopold: 145).

A difficulty which Leopold observes in moving from dominion over the land, driven by the desire for profit, to stewardship of the land, is that many members of the land community have no economic value: 'of the 22,000 higher plants and animals native to Wisconsin, it is doubtful whether more than 5 per cent can be sold, fed, eaten, or otherwise put to economic use' (Leopold: 145). But such plants and animals have, Leopold claims, 'biotic rights'. This would seem to entail a rejection of a human-centred attitude to the environment, but it is unclear whether this is really the case, with Leopold suggesting that if a private landowner were ecologically minded he would be proud to be the custodian of an eco-system that adds 'diversity and beauty' to his farm and community (Leopold: 146). And, furthermore, the assumed lack of profit in 'waste' areas has proved to be wrong, but only after the destruction of most of it.

To express the interdependence of nature Leopold uses the image of a pyramid, with a plant layer resting on the soil, an insect layer on the plants, a bird and rodent layer on the insects, and so on up through various animal groups to the apex layer, which consists of the larger carnivores. There exist lines of dependency between these layers, largely determined by the need for food and energy. Industrialisation has changed the pyramid in a number of ways. First, by reversing evolution: evolutionary change lengthened the food-chain through the emergence of more complex life forms; industrialisation shortens the chain by the elimination of both predators and of seemingly useless organisms. Second, by the exploitation, which puts geological, and other formations, to new uses, such as the generation of energy, and removes them from the 'natural chain'. Third, transportation disconnects the chain and introduces forms from one environment to a new environment, quite different one, and with sometimes unintended consequences. Leopold summarises the idea of the pyramid as an energy circuit in three basic ideas:

1. Land is not merely soil.
2. Native plants and animals keep the energy circuit open; others may or may not.
3. Man-made changes are of a different order than evolutionary changes, and have effects more comprehensive than is intended or foreseen (Leopold: 148).

But Leopold does not dogmatically assert that human-made changes necessarily threaten the continuation of life. He concedes that Europe has been transformed over the last two millennia, but that the 'new structure seems to function and to persist'; Europe, he concludes, has a 'resistant biota . . . its inner processes are tough, elastic, resistant to strain' (Leopold: 148). However, the correct perspective for an ecologist to adopt is global, and the earth as a whole, he maintains, is like a diseased body, where some parts seem to function well, but the whole is threatened with death. And, as with many ecologists, he identified population growth as a major cause of this 'disease':

> The combined evidence of history and ecology seems to support one deduction: the less violent the man-made changes, the greater the probability of successful readjustment in the pyramid. Violence, in turn, varies with human population density; a dense population requires a more violent conversion (Leopold: 149).

Conservationists fall into two groups, labelled by Leopold A and B: group A regards the land as soil and its function as a commodity, whereas group B regards the land as a biota, and its function as 'something broader', but 'how much broader is admittedly in a state of doubt and confusion' (Leopold: 149). While he may not have been aware of it, this distinction is an early statement of a divide which becomes clear after the 1960s – that between environmentalists and ecologists. Crucial to the coherence of ecologism is an explanation of that 'broader' function or value which troubled Leopold.

Arne Næss and 'Deep Ecology'

Arne Næss is credited with coining the contrasting phrases 'deep ecology' (more precisely: 'long-range deep ecology movement') and 'shallow ecology', with the spatial language intended to denote the depth of questioning of human values and reasons for action. To use John Rawls's language, deep ecology offers a comprehensive conception of the good for society and individuals, whereas shallow ecology offers a less-than-comprehensive, possibly merely political understanding of environmental values. Næss presents the idea of depth and comprehensiveness in the form of a table with four levels, with Level 1 being the most comprehensive, or 'deepest'.

Level 4	Actions	Individual behaviour.
Level 3	Policies	Particular policies carried out by governmental and non-governmental agencies.
Level 2	Platform principles	Packages of policies derived from an ideological standpoint or movement.
Level 1	Ultimate values	Grounded in, for example, a comprehensive philosophical or religious position.

Arne Næss (1912–)

A Norwegian, Næss was appointed to a university chair in philosophy at the age of 27, and continued as Professor of Philosophy at Oslo University until 1969.

Although his personal interests always included a love of the natural world – he is famous as a mountaineer, making the first ascent of Tirich Mir (7,690 metres) in the Hindu Kush in 1950 – his philosophical work on ecological theory, or what he called 'ecosophy', only really started after he resigned his professorship. But there are continuities with his pre-1969 work; that earlier work focused on semantics – a branch of linguistics – and Næss argued that the meaning of words must be recovered from their context. There is a parallel here with the interdependence of human beings in nature.

Næss argues that we do not have to agree on ultimate values in order to engage in deep ecological action; there is a process of moving up and down the stages, such that action can be guided by a plurality of different sets of ultimate values. We will explore the coherence of this idea shortly, but the point to make here is that the criticism that deep ecology is intolerant because it fails to respect the pluralism which exists in a modern society is not necessarily valid. Næss's emphasis on the plurality of ultimate values was, in part, born out of his experience in creating cross-cultural peace and ecological activist movements. As Næss argues:

> ecologically responsible policies are concerned only in part with pollution and resource depletion. There are deeper concerns which touch upon principles of diversity, complexity, autonomy, decentralization, symbiosis, egalitarianism, and classlessness (Næss, 1973: 95).

What Næss sought to do was develop a set of 'platform principles' (Level 2) – in other words, a 'manifesto', albeit a non-dogmatic one – around which people with diverse ultimate values can unite. Below are eight principles formulated by Næss and his friend and fellow deep ecologist George Sessions while out on a hiking trip in Death Valley, California:

1. The well-being and flourishing of human and non-human Life on Earth have value in themselves (synonyms: intrinsic value, inherent value). These values are independent of the usefulness of the non-human world for human purposes.
2. Richness and diversity of life forms contribute to the realisation of these values and are also values in themselves.
3. Humans have no right to reduce this richness and diversity except to satisfy vital human needs.

4. The flourishing of human life and cultures is compatible with a substantial decrease of human population. The flourishing of non-human life requires such a decrease.

5. Present human interference with the non-human world is excessive, and the situation is rapidly worsening.

6. Policies must therefore be changed. These policies affect basic economic, technological and ideological structures. The resulting state of affairs will be deeply different from the present.

7. The ideological change is mainly that of appreciating life quality (dwelling in situations of inherent value) rather than adhering to an increasingly higher standard of living. There will be a profound awareness of the difference between big and great.

8. Those who subscribe to the foregoing points have an obligation to directly or indirectly try to implement the necessary changes.

Biography, p. 379

Unlike Leopold, Næss was a trained philosopher, and so shows a greater awareness of the need for a credible philosophical basis for ecologism. Deep ecology requires an explanation of how particulars, such as individual animals, fit into the whole; Næss argues that part of the definition of an organism, such as a human being, is that it exists only in relation to something else. He uses the metaphor of the knot – a knot exists only as part of a net, and human beings are knots in the biospherical net (Næss, 1973: 95). Human beings are intrinsically valuable, but any statement of that value must make reference to the 'whole'.

Næss accepts that any realistic form of social organisation requires some 'killing, exploitation, and suppression' (Næss: 95). However, in principle, we should be biospherical egalitarians, meaning we should have deep respect for all forms of life – to restrict that respect to human beings is to mis-recognise humans, for the value we attach to each other must depend on a full understanding of who we are – 'knots in the biospherical net'. On this point ecologists and Marxists may find common ground, although Marxists are anthropocentric. Diversity enhances the potential for survival, and the chance of new modes of life; ecological diversity should translate into respect for cultural diversity. But diversity must be of the right kind – diversity due to class hierarchy is incompatible with the 'symbiosis' inherent in the biospherical net. This is important, because it is possible to read into nature hierarchy rather than equality; what Næss must, however, show is that mutual dependence really does imply equality. After all, there is a sense in which a master is dependent on his slave.

Deep ecologists, Næss argues, must fight pollution and resource depletion, and in this struggle they have found common cause with shallow ecologists, or environmentalists. But such an alliance can be dangerous because it distracts attention away from the comprehensive concerns ecologists should have. For example, if prices or taxes are increased in order to reduce pollution, then we need to know who will bear the cost – if it is the poor, then the egalitarianism implicit in the biospherical net is not being respected. Deep ecology favours 'soft' scientific research that limits disturbances to the environment, respects traditions, and is aware of our state of ignorance. Leopold also made reference to human ignorance, and as many writers on the ecological movement have noted this suggests affinities between ecologism and conservatism.

Conservatism, pp. 188–91

Autonomy and decentralisation are central to Næss's understanding of the forms of political organisation appropriate to deep ecology: 'the vulnerability of a form of life is roughly proportional to the weight of influences from afar, from outside the local region in which that form has obtained an ecological equilibrium' (Næss, 1973: 98). A self-sufficient community produces less pollution, and depletes fewer resources, than the existing inter-dependent world. But such a community is more democratic because the chain of decision making is much shorter – if decisions are made through a chain of authorities, such as local, national and supra-national, then if those decisions are made by majority vote the chances of local interests being ignored increase with the addition of every link in the chain.

Garrett Hardin and the Ethics of the Lifeboat

Garrett Hardin was a highly influential environmentalist. Although his arguments were neither original, nor profound, there are good reasons for discussing his work. First, he was concerned with a major issue for environmentalists: population growth (a secondary, but related, issue that concerned him was immigration to the developed world from the developing world). Second, he is sometimes, and quite erroneously, labelled an ecologist, as distinct from an environmentalist, and his arguments are quoted in political debates against ecologists. Third, he challenged one of the fundamental human rights – the right to procreate – and, more generally, his work raises important questions about global justice, questions to which we return in Chapter 18.

Hardin's most famous essay was 'The Tragedy of the Commons', which was based on a presidential address delivered at a meeting of the Pacific Division of the American Association for the Advancement of Science at Utah State University in June 1968. In the following 30 years it was reprinted in many collections, and Hardin himself revised it several times. The central problem is, by Hardin's own admission, not original; indeed, it is simply a statement of the Prisoner's Dilemma, which we discussed in Chapter 7. We are to imagine common lands on which herdsmen graze their cattle. So long as the numbers of herdsmen and cattle are low the commons will recover from the effects of grazing, new grass will grow, the cattle will be fed, and the herdsmen will make a living and so not starve. However,

Exercise, p. 172

Biography | **Garrett Hardin (1915–2003)**

An American, Hardin graduated in Zoology from Chicago University in 1936, and received a doctorate in Microbiology from Stanford University in 1941.

Most of his academic career was spent in the Department of Biological Sciences at the University of California, Santa Barbara, from where he retired as professor in 1978.

In his many works he sought to foster an interdisciplinary approach to environmental challenges, and was very much a 'public intellectual', debating issues such as abortion, population growth, food aid, nuclear power and immigration.

if the number of herdsmen and cattle grow – perhaps because population growth is no longer kept in check by war and disease – there will come a point at which the commons will not recover, and will indeed deteriorate to the point where even the original low level of grazing would not be supported. As we saw in our analysis of the Prisoner's Dilemma, even if an individual herdsman recognises the consequences of his actions – that is, can see clearly the 'tragedy' before him – it is in his interests to continue grazing and, in fact, to increase the number of cattle in order to compensate for the poorer yield.

Hardin makes a point that appears to echo those of deep ecologists: the harm from an individual action cannot be 'pictured' – the effects may not be discernible for years, and effects are, in any case, cumulative. Such is the case with the tragedy of the commons. Morality must take into account the full effects of an action; in Hardin's words, it must be 'system sensitive'. Without questioning the validity of Hardin's argument, it is important to distinguish his 'system' from that of Leopold or Næss – the long-term effects which concern Hardin are the effects on *humanity*. Hardin's argument, while concerned with environmental degradation, is thoroughly anthropocentric.

Almost all moral and political theorists have accepted that actions have to be assessed against their full consequences, so Hardin's argument is directed much more at popular moral beliefs, rather than at previous thinkers – it is doubtful that he is aware of the heritage of the arguments he propounds. Hardin argues that a popular morality focused simply on the rights of individuals, without regard to the 'system', will have catastrophic consequences; in particular, he objects to the United Nations declaration, as restated in the Declaration on Social Progress and Development (1969) (http://www.unhcr.ch/html/menu3/b/m_progre.htm) that 'parents have the exclusive right to determine freely and responsibly the number and spacing of their children' (Article 4):

> If each human family were dependent only on its own resources; if the children of improvident parents starved to death; if, thus, overbreeding brought its own 'punishment' to the germ line – then there would be no public interest in controlling the breeding of families. But our society is deeply committed to the welfare state, and hence is confronted with another aspect of the tragedy of the commons (Hardin, 1994: 334–5).

Hardin's comment makes reference to 'our society' – meaning the United States – and its commitment to the welfare state. The tragedy of the commons is, of course, a metaphor for the world's resources, and not every society has a welfare state. However, Hardin's audience is his own people, and the question of population growth is, for Hardin, closely linked to that of immigration. Since population growth is much higher in the developing world than in the developed world, migration from the former to the latter is a consequence of population growth. And Hardin has three fairly straightforward policy proposals: end the despoliation of the 'commons' insofar as this is within the power of the United States and other developed countries to do; stop food aid to the developing world; and severely restrict migration to the developed world.

We will say something about these proposals shortly, but we need to consider Hardin's underlying philosophical position. Hardin is not a philosopher, and so we have to engage in some speculation to capture his basic position, but it seems to amount to this: human beings are naturally selfish, or, at least, they are overwhelmingly concerned with their own survival. That some people are lucky to live in relatively wealthy societies and others in poor societies may be cause for a bad conscience, but it does not change the ethical situation. That most Americans are descended from people who 'stole' from Native Americans does not mean that they have an obligation to help the less fortunate:

> We are all the descendents of thieves, and the world's resources are inequitably distributed. But we must begin the journey to tomorrow from the point where we are today. We cannot remake the past. We cannot safely divide the wealth equitably among all peoples so long as people reproduce at different rates. To do so would guarantee that our grandchildren and everyone else's grandchildren, would have only a ruined world to inhabit (Hardin, 1974: 567).

Hardin employs the analogy of a lifeboat to illustrate his argument. Two-thirds of the world is desperately poor, while a third is relatively wealthy. Each of those wealthy nations can be likened to a lifeboat; in the ocean outside the lifeboat swim the poor of the world, who would like to clamber on board. If there are 50 people on a boat designed for 60, and 100 swimming in the water around the boat, what are we – where 'we' means those in the boat – to do? We could respond to the Christian call to be 'our brother's keeper' or the Marxist injunction to give to each 'according to his needs', but since all 100 are our brothers (and sisters) and all are equally in need, we have to choose: we could choose 10, which would leave us with no emergency capacity and would require us to explain why we did not admit the other 90, or we could take all 100, with the consequence that the boat will sink. Alternatively, each of the 50 could choose to sacrifice his or her life, but that altruistic act will not solve the global crisis.

The 'harsh ethics' of the lifeboat become harsher when population growth is taken into account. The people in the boat are doubling their numbers every 87 years; those swimming on the outside are doubling their numbers every 35 years. Hardin argues that it is misleading to talk about satisfying human needs, as if needs were minimal conditions, such as basic food and healthcare, which once met left a surplus to be distributed. Rather, because the satisfaction of needs has the effect of increasing the population, there is no end to the satisfaction of needs. The only 'ethical' response is to refuse to satisfy the needs by restricting immigration – stopping people getting on the lifeboat – and not giving food aid to those 'outside the boat'. A consequence of this harsh policy would be that countries, once solely responsible for their own well-being, would learn to manage, albeit after a great deal of suffering.

Summary and Criticisms of Ecologism

Summary of Ecologism

From our discussion of Leopold and Næss, and drawing on other ecological writings, we can summarise the key components of ecologism as follows:

1. The belief that there is something which can be called 'ecology' or the 'biosphere'; this is an interconnected whole on which all life depends.

2. The natural world, which includes all forms of life, has intrinsic value, and should not be used as an instrument to satisfy human wants; there is much debate within the ecological movement about the nature of this value, and we discuss this below. However, there is an intuitive sense that ecologism requires being 'in touch' with nature.

3. The quality of human life will be enhanced once human beings recognise 1 and 2: ecologism is not concerned to devalue human beings, but rather to get us to think about who we really are.

4. The structure of the natural world should be mirrored in the social and political world; the interdependence – but diversity – of the former translates into a commitment to a more equal society, respectful of difference.

5. To achieve ecological and social justice requires not simply a change in the social, economic, and political organisation of society, but a fundamental change in human motivation.

6. Ecologism is a distinct ideology, which sees in both liberalism (capitalism) and socialism a common 'enemy': industrialism. Industrialism *by definition* cannot be compatible with an ecological consciousness. For ecologists the earth is a physical object, with natural physical limits; industrialism, which is committed to economic growth, cannot respect the integrity and finitude of the earth.

7. Ecologists seek a 'sustainable society' – that is, one which is in tune with nature. In practical terms, this requires a reduction in consumption.

8. Although there is a division within deep ecology, a strong theme in ecological thought is distrust of 'technological fixes' – that is, a belief that advances in technology will overcome environmental problems.

Criticisms of Ecologism

To conclude the chapter we discuss the main alleged tensions, contradictions and incoherences in ecologism.

Ecologism has an Incoherent Value Theory

The central claim of ecologism is that there is value in the natural world that cannot be explained simply by reference to human wants, needs or consciousness: nature, or the environment, or the ecosystem has *intrinsic value*. The difficulty with this claim is that to say something has value is to make an evaluation, and such evaluation presupposes a capacity to evaluate, and only human beings possess such a capacity, therefore values are human centred.

An ecologist might respond by asking us to imagine a beautiful valley that no human being has ever seen – would something be lost if that valley ceased to exist? And if we conclude that something would be lost, then does that not show that value is independent of human consciousness? The difficulty is that the question asks us to *imagine* such a valley; while it is possible that a valley exists which no human eyes have ever seen, we nonetheless have the *concept* of a valley, and criteria for evaluating its beauty – after all, the artistic imagination entails the creation of something that does not 'really' exist. Perhaps, however, the ecologist is making a different claim: value does indeed depend on the human capacity to evaluate, but it does not follow that values are human centred. A distinction must be made between conative and cognitive explanations of value: if you think a mountain range is beautiful it may be because something in your emotional machinery triggers a positive reaction to it, or, alternatively, it may be because you think that the mountain range has features that any rational being can appreciate. The first explanation is conative, while the second is cognitive. The test of the difference is whether you can persuade another person that the mountains are beautiful – if you can then this suggests that the appreciation of such beauty is not reducible to your particular emotions. Lovelock makes an interesting comment in his article on nuclear power that we discussed at the beginning of the chapter: 'as individual animals we are not so special, and in some ways are like a planetary disease, but through civilisation we redeem ourselves and become a precious asset for the Earth; not least because through our eyes the Earth has seen herself in all her glory' (*Independent*, 24 May 2004).

If by 'intrinsic value' ecologists mean that the value of nature is not reducible to the emotions of individual human beings, then there are certain implications for ecologism. First, while it does provide a ground for environmental respect and protection, it still places human beings in a privileged position – although we cannot disprove the possibility, we have no reason to believe that non-human animals, let alone non-animal members of the 'biotic community', are capable of such appreciation of the natural environment. Second, if the 'natural world' has intrinsic – or cognitive – value, then the possibility exists that the created world also possesses intrinsic value, and where there exists a conflict between the two worlds it is not clear which should have the greater claim to protection.

An alternative strategy for placing value on the environment is to deny that a distinction exists between human beings and nature, such that it is meaningless to talk about *your* emotions or subjectivity, as distinct from that which is 'outside' you. If we collapse the difference between 'self' and 'other', where the other includes, for example, the mountain range that you are looking at, then it is unnecessary to talk about intrinsic value. However, it is difficult to understand what this extended self would be like, but more significantly, the *political* effect of accepting that such a self exists would be to internalise all the conflicts which presently exist between selves, understood in the narrow, everyday sense of individual self-conscious beings.

Ecologism cannot Bridge the Gap between Facts and Values (is and ought)

As we have seen, ecologists tend not to respect the distinction between facts and values, or 'is' and 'ought'. Of course, we should not accept uncritically the claim that the distinction cannot be bridged, and elsewhere we have addressed this challenge, but here we are concerned with ecologists' arguments. The approach adopted by many ecologists is to draw *analogies* between the natural world and the social world. Andrew Dobson offers the following (Dobson, 2000: 22):

Nature		Society and politics
Diversity	→	Toleration, stability and democracy
Interdependence	→	Equality
Longevity	→	Tradition
Nature as 'female'	→	A particular conception of feminism

We discuss below whether ecologism is, for example, tolerant, but the concern here is with the nature of ecological argument; in effect, we are being asked to look at nature, consider its intrinsic value, and draw conclusions about how we should behave to it, and to each other. The problem, which Dobson acknowledges, is that people can draw quite different conclusions from nature: interdependence can imply hierarchy rather than equality, and the supposed femininity of nature may imply 'natural roles' that restrict human autonomy. Dobson talks about the 'lessons from nature', but it is not simply that we disagree about the social implications of our observation of the natural world, but rather that there are no lessons – or, in more philosophical language, reasons for action – to be derived from such observation. This leads to the next objection, which also connects the first two objections together: the ecologists' conception of human reason.

Ecologism has an Incoherent Attitude to Human Rationality

It was argued that ecologists have to make some concession to human centredness: for nature to have intrinsic value there must exist beings capable of evaluation. But there is, arguably, a further concession to be made to anthropocentrism: the capacity to evaluate depends upon complex rational machinery that seeks to connect together different values, experiences and actions. Rationality depends on language and not simply a non-linguistic 'observation' of nature; when you, or Arne Næss, stand on the mountaintop and view the mountain range, your appreciation involves complex *and abstract* processes. Human beings' capacity to abstract from what confronts their senses is essential to their ability to believe on the basis of reasons, and to act from reasons. The idea of interconnectedness, which is a core doctrine of ecologists, is made possible by human reason; arguably, there is no interconnectedness in the world, except what the human mind connects together. This is not say that there is no physical world external to the mind, nor that its value depends on the subjective attitudes of individual human beings, but rather that the 'human mind', defined as a set of capacities shared by individual human beings, and made possible through language, is the means through which the world is viewed as interconnected.

More specifically, ecologists have an incoherent attitude to natural science. Without wishing to get too deeply into the philosophy of science, a major aspect of natural science is the acquisition of knowledge through repeatable experiments – experiments that must take place in a controlled environment (there are other understandings of natural science, and certainly natural science does not equate to the entire sphere of human reason). Science, so defined, necessarily abstracts from the 'particular', and seeks to acquire knowledge by finding something which is not unique to a particular thing – the individual rat in the laboratory is only of scientific interest insofar as its physiological or psychological behaviour is generalisable, that is, its behaviour must not be peculiar to that particular rat. This observation is not about the ethics of vivisection, but rather about how we acquire knowledge of the world: natural science is advanced through distance from nature, and not by being 'in touch' with nature. Yet at the centre of ecologism as a political movement is continual appeal to the 'scientific evidence' of environmental degradation – evidence acquired through a fundamentally anti-ecological rationality.

In part, the ambivalent attitude to natural science has its roots in the ecologists' conflation of science and technology, and, relatedly, of human rationality in general with a particular variant of it: instrumental rationality. Science developed in the early modern period as the result of changes in humans' understanding of their place in the world – only once the material world is seen as lacking in intrinsic spiritual qualities is it possible to treat it in an experimental way (Kuhn, 1962: 111–35). Technology, on the other hand, dates back to the earliest human activity – it is simply the marshalling of natural processes to serve human ends. Of course, advances in scientific understanding have aided technological advance, and many ecologists will argue that neither science nor technology are in themselves to be rejected, but rather it is the degree of intervention in, and alteration of, natural processes which is at issue. The danger with ecologism is that it fails to distinguish between human enquiry – the drive to understand the world – from human wants, that is, the desire to use the natural world for human ends. Human centredness is narrowly defined by ecologists as instrumental reason; nature is used as a means, or instrument, for human ends. But you do not need to be an ecologist in order to challenge instrumental reason; you can move completely within a human-centred view of the world and still raise *rational* objections to the idea that because we have the scientific knowledge to do something, such as clone human beings, then we should do it.

Ecologism Rests on a Naive Distinction between 'Nature' and 'Society'

Throughout this chapter we have operated with the distinction between 'nature' and 'society', or the natural world and the human world. This accords with the everyday sense that there is a distinction: imagine looking out of the window at a tree-lined street of apartment blocks. Human beings have constructed the apartments and planted the trees, but because the apartments function according to human design, whereas the trees, despite being planted in neat lines, develop according to processes understood, but not 'set in motion', by human beings, we reasonably enough say the trees are part of nature, and the apartments are part of the artificial, human world.

That distinction is valid, but difficulties arise for ecologists when they make further claims: (a) that the natural world forms an interconnected whole *set apart from* the human world, and on which the human world is dependent; (b) that the natural world has intrinsic value, whereas the human world does not. The interconnectedness–separateness thesis can be challenged in the following way: there is no part of the globe untouched by human activity, and therefore insofar as there are connections, these are between the two worlds. Of course, the ecological critique rests precisely on accepting as a fact that human beings have transformed the world, and for the worse! Their point is that we depend on the natural world, understood as a whole connected together through complex processes, such that the human world is secondary. This claim could be accepted by *environmentalists*: certainly, if we do not allow, say, fish stocks to be replenished because of over-fishing or marine pollution, there will be no fish in the supermarket, and no profits to be made from fish.

An *ecological* argument would require accepting not simply (a), but also (b): the natural world is separate and valuable in a way the human world is not. This is open to challenge. Venice is clearly one of the great human creations – a 'world heritage site' – built on a lagoon, and requiring considerable human intervention in the natural environment. That city, or at least the part of it most people understand as Venice, is under threat of sinking due to the combined effects of subsidence and rising sea levels; in addition, the lagoon is polluted through heavy industrial activity in the region. That there are natural processes at work, which are in part the result of a global environmental crisis, can be accepted by *environmentalists*, but that Venice itself has less value than naturally occurring phenomena is surely open to challenge. That, however, is the conclusion that an *ecologist* must draw.

The priority given to the natural world by ecologists rests in part on a 'hierarchy of needs', with physical reproductive needs at the base, and other needs, or 'wants', of lesser importance. In the aftermath of the 2001 outbreak of 'foot and mouth' disease in Britain there was a debate about whether the relatively generous compensation paid to farmers should be extended to hoteliers and other parts of the tourist industry that had been badly affected by the outbreak. A Green Party spokesperson argued that food production was 'more fundamental' to human beings than tourism. Behind this comment lay an image of British society as a self-subsistent food economy, where other human activities were somehow frivolous in comparison. Yet people working in the tourist industry were dependent on that income to satisfy *their* basic needs.

Ecologists sometimes suggest that we can have the benefits of the modern human world even if we remove the material conditions – industrialism – for modernity. Kirkpatrick Sale argues for a self-sufficient community, which does not engage in significant trade with other communities; such a community would ensure 'a wide range of food, some choices in necessities and some sophistication in luxuries, [and] the population to sustain a university and large hospital and a symphony orchestra' (Sale in Dobson, 2000: 118). But setting aside economic considerations about whether a low-trade world could sustain a high level of medical care, the social world that gives rise to relatively cosmopolitan institutions such as universities or orchestras has been one in which there is interaction between communities and cultures. Perhaps the argument is that we should preserve the cultural achievements of a modern industrial society, but without the costs; if that were Sale's point, then it would amount to a much more generous compliment to an industrial society than most ecologists are prepared to pay.

Ecologism either (a) Assumes a Naively Optimistic View of Human Nature, or (b) Requires an Unrealistic Transformation of Human Nature

If there is an environmental crisis, then what kind of response is required to overcome it? Presumably something has to change in terms of the relationship between human beings and nature. There are three possibilities: (a) changes in technology that conserve resources, slow down depletion or allow for economic growth without serious environmental consequences; (b) changes in the way we organise society, providing incentives or sanctions so as to alter behaviour; (c) changes in human motivation, which alter behaviour without requiring external incentives or sanctions. Ecologists are sceptical about (a), and prefer that (b), social and political changes, follow from (c), changes in motivation. It is significant that Hardin rejects (a) and (c) but endorses (b), arguing that only coercive measures will avert a global disaster.

A thread that runs through ecologism is that human behaviour in an industrialised society is bad for the environment, but also bad for human beings. This suggests that there is a 'real' human nature, which is fundamentally good, but it is distorted by human acquisitiveness, which is fed by, for example, advertising. Since the achievement of a sustainable society depends on a change in motivation, a great deal depends on the plausibility of this view of human nature. But, furthermore, ecologists must show that it is impossible to create and maintain a sustainable society without a change in motivation: technology will not fix environmental problems, and coercion is unacceptable and will lead to authoritarian regimes. Ecologists must argue, either that the real human nature will emerge fairly quickly as we move towards sustainability, perhaps because the human benefits of such a society will soon be apparent, or that changing human beings will be a major task. That task would be made easier if it could be shown that ecologism is a reasonable political doctrine – that is, one which people with diverse beliefs could accept.

Ecologism is a Religion, and as such Incompatible with the Value Pluralism of the Modern World

The last point brings us to a major objection raised, in particular, by liberals: ecologism, unlike environmentalism, is not simply a political programme, but requires individuals to endorse religious or spiritual beliefs that they might reasonably reject. Despite Arne Næss's insistence that ecologists can come together from a variety of different religious and philosophical perspectives, the ecological critique of industrialism identifies human motivation as the source of acquisitive attitudes, demands very significant changes in the way society is organised, and holds out the prospect of a reconciliation between human beings and nature that extends beyond political ideas. Most orthodox monotheists – Jews, Christians, Muslims – would interpret ecological ideas as a form of pantheism (earth as God) or panantheism (earth as part of God), standing against the metaphysical separation of God as creator from his creation. Many atheists would treat ecologism with the same suspicion that they treat other religions.

Summary

Ecologism's distinctiveness can be found in its emphasis on the interconnectedness of life on earth, and the demand for a fundamental change in human relations to nature – where nature, of course, is part of humanity, and humanity part of nature.

It offers a critique of both liberalism and socialism, and while recognising the important differences between those ideologies it finds commonalities: a commitment to economic growth that is incompatible with the finite nature of the earth. Humanity's ambitions exceed the resources of its home.

Questions

1. Are there major philosophical differences between environmentalists and ecologists?
2. Is ecologism compatible with democracy?
3. Is ecologism compatible with socialism?
4. Should an ecologist be concerned with animal rights?

References

Dobson, A. (2000) *Green Political Thought* London: Routledge.

Hardin, G. (1974) 'Living on a Lifeboat', *Bioscience* (24)10, 561–8.

Hardin, G. (1994) 'The Tragedy of The Commons' in C. Pierce and D. Ven de Veer, *People, Penguins and Plastic Trees: Basic Issues in Environmental Ethics* London: Wadsworth.

Kuhn, T. (1962) *The Structure of Scientific Revolutions* Chicago, Ill. and London: University of Chicago Press.

Leopold, A. (1994) 'The Land Ethic' in C. Pierce and D. Van de Veer, *People, Penguins and Plastic Trees: Basic Issues in Environmental Ethics* London: Wadsworth.

Næss, A. (1973) 'The Shallow and the Deep, Long Range Ecology Movements' *Inquiry* 16, 95–100.

Næss, A. and Sessions, G. 'Deep Ecology Platform' at www.deepecology.org/deepplatform

Further Reading

Dobson (2000) is the clearest introduction to Green political thought. Other useful discussions of ecological thought and practice include: John Barry, *Rethinking Green Politics: Nature, Virtue, and Progress* (London: Sage, 1999); Alan Carter, *A Radical Green Political Theory* (London and New York: Routledge, 1999); John Dryzek, *The Politics of the Earth: Environmental Discourses* (New York: Oxford University Press, 2005); Robyn Eckersley, *The Green State: Rethinking Democracy and Sovereignty* (Cambridge, Mass. and London: MIT Press, 2004); David Pepper, *Eco-socialism: From Deep Ecology to Social Justice* (London: Routledge, 1993). A good collection of the most important writings on ecologism is Andrew Dobson (ed.), *The Green Reader* (London: Deutsch, 1991). More philosophical are the following: John Benson, *Environmental Ethics: An Introduction with Readings* (London: Routledge, 2000); Robert Elliot (ed.), *Environmental Ethics* (Oxford: Oxford University Press, 1995); Robert Elliot and Arran Gare (eds), *Environmental Philosophy: A Collection of Readings* (Buckingham: Open University Press, 1983); Dale Jamieson (ed.), *A Companion to Environmental Philosophy* (Malden, Mass. and Oxford: Blackwell, 2003); Robin Attfield, *Environmental Philosophy: Principles and Prospects* (Aldershot: Avebury, 1994).

Weblinks

The following sites are 'theoretical' in orientation:

- A very extensive list of links: http://www.erraticimpact.com/~ecologic/
- A couple of websites (largely) hostile to ecologism and environmentalism: http://www.lomborg.com/ (Lomborg is author of *The Skeptical Environmentalist*, a book in which he questions the global warming thesis); http://www.environmentalism.com/

These sites are activist in nature:

- http://www.foe.co.uk/
- http://www.earthwatch.org/
- http://www.greenpeace.org/international/

On nuclear power:

- Environmentalists for Nuclear Energy (Lovelock is a member of this organisation, and the article discussed above can be found here): http://www.ecolo.org/
- World Nuclear Association (another pro-nuclear power body): http://www.world-nuclear.org/
- Union of Concerned Scientists (US organisation opposed to nuclear energy): http://www.ucsusa.org/clean_energy/nuclear_safety/index.cfm
- Swedish Anti-nuclear Movement: http://www.folkkampanjen.se/engfront.html

Chapter 16

Fundamentalism

Introduction

Politicians and the media speak more and more about the threat of 'fundamentalism' and how fundamentalism stands at odds with liberalism and democracy. But what is fundamentalism? How and why does it arise? Is it solely an Islamic phenomenon, or can other religions also have their fundamentalist proponents? Indeed, we will argue that all ideologies can be expressed in a fundamentalist fashion. What is the relationship between fundamentalism and the contemporary world?

Chapter Map

- **Fundamentalism** as a relatively new concept and more than a label.

- Fundamentalism as an ideology can be either secular or religious.

- Fundamentalism and 'fundamentals'. The contradictory relationship to modernity.

- The rejection of democracy and the propensity to violence.

- The relationship between Islam and fundamentalism. The link between fundamentalism and the Christian right in the United States. Fundamentalism in Israel.

- Huntington's 'clash of civilisations' and fundamentalism.

The Diversity of Fundamentalisms

A Palestinian boy runs in front of the controversial security barrier in Jerusalem, 5 January 2004.

You are poring over the newspaper one day and note the bewildering array of references to fundamentalism. There are chilling quotations from Osama Bin Laden. There is also a piece on the election campaign of the American president with emphasis on his concern to placate, and yet somehow distance himself from, Christian fundamentalists. Meanwhile the Israeli president is under fire for seeking to move any settlers out of (a few) Palestinian areas, and there is speculation as to whether he is doing this in order to maintain the other settlements that the international community deems illegal. His critics within Israel are labelled 'Jewish fundamentalists'. In the Business section of the paper there is a lively debate about globalisation with one of the contenders referring to 'market fundamentalism'. The paper seems to assume that the term 'fundamentalist' is self-explanatory, although it is clear that very different movements are being given the same label. Most are religious, but not all, and each is strongly opposed to the other.

- Is the concept of fundamentalism coherent? Consider whether the term applies to all religions, or to one religion in particular.

- It is often noted that in Enver Hoxha's (communist) Albania, religion was actually banned while portraits of the 'leader' peered out from every tree. Can someone committed to atheism, such as a Marxist, or a secularist, also be fundamentalist in character?

- Fundamentalists claim that they are seeking to restore the purity of their particular creed. Yet fundamentalism seems to be a reaction to change and modernity. Just what is the relationship between fundamentalism and contemporary life?

- We are continually being told that the world is becoming a global village. Has globalisation something to do with the rise of fundamentalism?

Label or Concept?

Fundamentalism is a relatively recent idea (although an old phenomenon). It relates to the interpretation of a creed that is intolerant of argument and debate, so that those who oppose a particular variety of fundamentalism are deemed 'enemies' and 'traitors'. Giddens, a sociologist who writes extensively on fundamentalism, comments that the term has only come into currency quite recently. As late as 1950 there was no entry for the word in the *Oxford English Dictionary* (Giddens, 1994: 6). This gives us an important clue as to its meaning, since although fundamentalists see themselves as looking to some kind of 'original' blueprint, the concept, as we will define it, is quite new and cannot be understood without analysing the pressures of the modern world.

Sidahmed and Ehteshami argue that fundamentalism is a label rather than a concept (1996: 14), and it is true that the term can be used in a dogmatic manner without thought being given as to what it might mean. But it will be argued here that the term can be a concept (i.e. something with a proper theoretical basis) and, therefore, it is not merely a descriptive but an evaluative term. Fundamentalism tells us what a creed looks like in such a way that it is unattractive to those who are open-minded. As with all political concepts, fundamentalism is both descriptive and evaluative, and the fact that the concept will be used negatively (as something to avoid), does not mean that we are not describing it as accurately as we can.

Fundamentalism (as are liberalism and secularism) is a contested category (i.e. it arouses controversy) but this does not make it so ambiguous that coherent exposition is impossible. We are not simply using the concept as a term of abuse: we are trying to expound it in as fair a way as we can.

Introduction, pp. xxxi–xxxvii

Fundamentalism and Religion

The term fundamentalism was first applied in a religious context at about the turn of the century, and referred to a defence of Protestant orthodoxy against the encroachments of modern thought. In the first decade of the twentieth century a series of 12 volumes entitled *The Fundamentals* was produced in the United States, containing 90 articles written by Protestant theologians. Three million copies were printed and distributed free of charge. But, as the *New Oxford Dictionary* points out, although one of the meanings of fundamentalism does relate to a strict and literal interpretation of the Bible by Protestants, the term, says the dictionary, can also be linked to any religion or ideology, 'notably Islam'.

Certainly, within religion, 'restorationist' movements in Christianity and Judaism show striking similarities to fundamentalist Islamic movements. Recent developments in Hinduism and Shinto also reveal commonalities with what is happening elsewhere (Kepel, 1994: 2–3). Moreover, fundamentalism can refer not only to any religion, but to any ideology; for example, reference is often made to 'market fundamentalism'. Any ideology, no matter how potentially tolerant, can be presented in fundamentalist terms, and therefore we cannot agree with the argument that the term relates essentially to understanding religion.

It is true that one fundamentalism feeds off another, and the construction of globalisation in fundamentalist terms has provoked a defensive religious fundamentalism as a response. The idea that the world has to conform to a view of liberty and democracy that stems from the White House in the United States – a fundamentalist kind of liberalism – has encouraged groups to espouse, for example, an Islamic fundamentalism in opposition.

Giddens comments that fundamentalism protects a *principle* as much as a set of doctrines, and hence can arise in religions such as Hinduism and Buddhism that had hitherto been ecumenical and tolerant. Fundamentalism, he adds, not only develops in religion but can arise in any domain of life subject to forces undermining traditional forms – whether this concerns the idea of nation, relations between people of different cultures, the structure of the family or relations between men and women. People feel threatened by these changes and look for ideas that attack the European Union, feminism, anti-racism, or whatever. This reaction need not (as our examples suggest) take a purely religious form. Secular ideologies may also be expressed in fundamentalist fashion. Think of the interpretation of French republicanism used to justify banning the headscarf among Muslim school girls. The neo-conservatives in the United States could be described as fundamentalists even though they do not subscribe to Islam, and militantly atheist regimes such as Stalin's Russia could be seen as treating Marxism in a fundamentalist fashion.

It is wrong, therefore, to assume that fundamentalism has to be religious in character, let alone Islamic, although veiled Muslim women and bearded Muslim men, book burners and suicide bombers have emerged, as Sayyid points out, as fundamentalist icons in Hollywood films, including, for example, *Not Without My Daughter* and *True Lies* (1997: 8).

Exercise

You live in a cosmopolitan city that has a large Muslim population. One day you pass a stall where people are handing out literature and you are surprised to see that freedom is regarded as a pernicious Western concept. When you suggest that the answer to the world's problems is 'more democracy', it is clear that those handing out the literature vigorously disagree and argue that only a return to 'true Islam' can save the world.

- Is this an accurate picture of the Islamic tradition? You have Muslim neighbours who seem quite liberal minded.

- Strong opposition by Islamic fundamentalists to Darwinism is expressed. Where else have you heard opposition to Darwin's theory of evolution?

- Your friend who hears this debate says that all religion is wrong, and this is why she is a convinced secularist. Can secularism be as intolerant and 'judgemental' as religious fundamentalism?

Fundamentals and Fundamentalism

Some writers suggest that fundamentalism merely involves a concern with the 'fundamentals' of a creed. This is far too broad a view of fundamentalism, and is also somewhat naive. It leads writers to describe as fundamentalist, mainstream groups that are pluralistic, democratic and inclusivist (Moussalli, 1998: 14).

A useful definition and observation is the following. Fundamentalism is a tendency that 'manifests itself, as a strategy or set of strategies, by which beleaguered believers attempt to preserve their distinct identity as a people or group'. This identity is felt to be at risk in the contemporary era, and these believers fortify it 'by a selective retrieval of doctrines, beliefs and practices from a sacred past'. These retrieved fundamentals are refined, modified and sanctioned in a spirit of shrewd pragmatism, as a bulwark against the encroachment of outsiders. The fundamentals are accompanied by 'unprecedented claims and doctrinal innovations'. These retrieved and updated fundamentals are meant to regain the same charismatic intensity today that (it is believed) was in evidence when the 'original' identity was forged from formative revelatory experiences long ago (Sidahmed and Ehteshami, 1996: 5).

Although fundamentalists hark back to a past that they seek to re-enact, this past is heavily doctored with mythology. The retrieval by fundamentalists (as was pointed out above) is 'selective' and 'innovatory'. Tariq Ali comments that fundamentalist Islamists chart a route to the past that, mercifully for the people of the seventh century, never existed (2002: 304). This is why it cannot be said that all Muslims are 'fundamentalists'. The leaders of fundamentalist movements are not theologians, but social thinkers and political activists.

It is often assumed that fundamentalists are genuinely concerned with resurrecting the fundamentals of a religious system. Hiro speaks of Islamic fundamentalists as releasing Islam from scholastic cobwebs and ideas imbibed from the West (Hiro, 1988: 1–2). But this, in our view, is not so. Fundamentalists are not conservatives trying to recover old truths. They want to remould the world in the light of doctrines that are quite new. Take the view that the regime in Saudi Arabia has of the Islamic religion. It can certainly be described as extremely conservative, but it is not fundamentalist. On the contrary, the gap between the wealthy few and the majority of salaried Saudis has been exploited by fundamentalist forces. It would be more accurate to say that conservative governments such as the regime in Saudi Arabia has provoked fundamentalism, rather than being fundamentalist itself. The fact that the royal family is pragmatic in its domestic and foreign policy and adopts a Western outlook and behaviour instigates the growth of fundamentalist tendencies as a reaction to it (Nehme, 1998: 277; 284).

Of course, terminology differs. Roy makes a distinction between an Islamism that is willing to get involved in social and political action in revolutionary fashion and a 'neo-fundamentalism' that is concerned simply with religious teaching (1999: 36). What Roy calls Islamists we call fundamentalists, and it is for this reason that we identify Islamic fundamentalism, for example, as a militant and anti-modernist movement that exploits Islam rather than seeks to defend its basic tenets. Muslims in general oppose violence and militancy: the Islamic University of Gaza may want people to return 'to our basics' (Jensen, 1998: 203), but it is not fundamentalist. Fundamentalists, as we define them, may claim a respect for fundamentals, but we should not overlook the cynicism, demagoguism (i.e. liberties taken with logic and reason) and 'selective retrieval' involved in their activity.

Modernity and Tradition

Ali describes religious fundamentalism as a product of modernity (2002: ix) and yet, as will become evident later, it is hostile to modernity. This is true of all fundamentalism, whether religious or secular. As Kepel points out, Christian fundamentalists seek not to modernise Christianity but to Christianise modernity, just as Islamic fundamentalists seek, he says, to 'Islamize modernity' (1994: 66; 2).

Fundamentalism is best described (forgive the apparent paradox) as a modern movement opposed to modernity. Fundamentalism is a product of modernisation – urban and intellectual in character. Fundamentalists use modern methods of propagating their ideas and recruiting adherents: what they attack are the emancipatory traditions, the belief in freedom, equality and self-government, that have characterised modern ideas since the Enlightenment. It is important to emphasise here the tension between form and content. Armstrong argues that fundamentalisms are 'essentially modern movements' that could take root in no other time than our own. They have absorbed, she says, the pragmatic rationalism of modernity that enables them to create an ideology which provides a plan of action (2001: viii; xiii).

But how can fundamentalism be *both* traditionalist and anti-traditionalist, modern and anti-modern? It is traditionalist in the sense that fundamentalists *claim* to be resurrecting traditions (although, as has been argued, such claims need to be taken with a healthy pinch of salt). But, as Giddens notes, the point about traditions is that you do not have to justify them – they normally contain their own truth, a ritual truth, asserted as correct by the believer (1994: 6). Fundamentalism arises in the novel circumstances of global communication (Giddens, 1994: 48), where traditions are being challenged, and these traditions cannot, it seems, be effectively defended in the old way. Hence the context is one of profound anti-traditionalism. We rather like Roy's description of Islamism (or what we call Islamic fundamentalism) as the *shariah* (the holy book dealing with law) plus electricity (1999: 52), while Armstrong speaks of fundamentalist movements having a 'symbiotic relationship' with modernity (2001: xiii).

The backdrop of fundamentalism is a globalised world in which cross-cultural communication has not only become possible but also obligatory. Fundamentalism accentuates the purity of a given set of doctrines, not simply because it wishes to set them off against other doctrines, but because it rejects the idea of debate and discussion with people who have different points of view. It is opposed to what Giddens calls a dialogic engagement of ideas in a public space (1994: 6). While fundamentalists reject the notion of a 'changing of places' essential to dialogue, the audience is nevertheless global. An imaginary tradition is championed in an aggressive, dogmatic and polarising way.

There is a curious love/hate relationship to the market. On the one hand, Osama Bin Laden T-shirts can be seen for sale in shops in Mozambique next to T-shirts with adverts for Coca-Cola emblazoned on them. Suya Mura is a traditional village in Japan that is publicised for its tourist potential (Giddens, 1994: 86–7). At the same time, fundamentalism Bin Laden-style rages against the wickedness and corruption of international capitalism. Modern technology, the internet and the Wall Street stock exchange are utilised in order to advance fundamentalist opposition to modernity – i.e. to liberal values.

Not surprisingly, many of those who challenge modernity are themselves products par excellence of this modernity. They have been through a secular education often with a bias towards technical disciplines, and they handle sacred texts in a way that challenges the conservatism of rabbis, (Muslim) ulemas or priests (Kepel, 1994: 4). Armstrong makes the point that whereas Westerners tended to see the Ayatollah Khomeini – the first ruler of Islamic Iran – as a throwback to the Middle Ages, much of his message and ideology was modern. He described Islam as 'the religion of those who desire freedom and independence. It is the school of those who struggle against imperialism' (Armstrong, 2001: 250; 256; see also Sayyid, 1997: 90). A very modernist formulation! Gray notes that radical Islamist views resemble European anarchism far more than they do Islamic orthodoxy (2003: 24; 79).

Ch 17:
Difference,
pp. 418–34

Indeed some writers even see a kind of postmodernism in fundamentalism. Brown speaks of it as a 'foundationalism without a grand narrative' (1995: 35). In other words, fundamentalism combines cosmopolitan relativism (Muslims are different) – hence there are no 'grand narratives' that many postmodernists say they dislike – with a dogmatic belief in rightness and wrongness – hence 'foundationalism'. Falk argues, for example, that politicised religion is a form of postmodern protest against the mechanisation, atomisation and alienation of the modern world (cited by Wolff, 1998: 50). But we would see postmodernism as a critique of modernism that goes beyond it, rather than an anti-liberalism which rejects democracy, the Enlightenment and universal promise. It is, therefore, better to speak of fundamentalism as an anti-modernism, rather than a **postmodernism**.

It is the deficiencies of modernity that produce fundamentalism. It has been said that the question of fundamentalism cannot be dissociated from the process of nation and state building and its failures. A fundamentalist is someone who has become conscious of the acute inequalities within and between countries, but who is also convinced that the current strategies of development will not succeed in alleviating them. Fundamentalism has developed in a situation where the state failed to provide the newly urbanised citizens with structures to replace the old communal ones. The alienated individual projects his frustrations on a world scale, seeking to create a community of believers who share a similar *Weltanschauung* (world outlook) (Zoubir, 1998: 127; 131–2).

It does not follow that, because fundamentalism is a kind of modernist reaction against modernity, we defend modernity. On the contrary, it is (as noted above) the failures of modernity that have created such an extreme and negative reaction. We are certainly not implying that liberalism or modernity itself is a desirable and natural 'norm'.

Fundamentalism, Democracy and Violence

The refusal of dialogue makes fundamentalism dangerous, for increasingly the use of violence is counter-productive and the only way of advancing humanity's interests is through argument and debate. By rejecting democracy, fundamentalism necessarily leads to **violence**.

Ch 1: The State, pp. 14–37

(Abstract) ethics, not democracy, is the watchword, and the value expected in the political domain is not liberty, but justice (Roy, 1999: 10–11). Choueiri, in his analysis of Islamic fundamentalism, comments that democracy is seen as a violation of God's sovereignty – the desires and opinions of secular majorities represent an outright usurpation of God's laws. Choueiri notes that in fundamentalist eyes, humanity has reverted to an age of ignorance. Some movements support democracy simply as a means to a non-democratic end (Choueiri, 1996: 20–1). As Ali Belhaj, star preacher for the Islamic Salvation Front in Algeria has put it, democracy is no more than a corruption or ignorance that robs God of his power and seeks to bestow this power upon his creatures (Kepel, 1994: 46).

Is it true that all forms of fundamentalism reject democracy? Kepel argues that the various movements of reChristianisation cannot reject democracy as an alien graft on their own system: they have to speak the language of democracy and this 'democratic constraint' influences what these movements actually say (1994: 197). Yet Armstrong cites a US fundamentalist who praises the early puritans for *opposing* democracy, and she refers to US fundamentalists who see democracy as a modern heresy to be abolished, and look towards the reorganisation of society along biblical lines (Armstrong, 2001: 273; 361). Moreover, as will be seen in Wilcox's (1996) analysis of the religious right, fundamentalist Christianity can also be militantly exclusivist and extol violence. Naturally, different fundamentalist movements are affected by their particular environment (the degree of poverty, unemployment and authoritarianism), and this accounts for their differential severity and harshness.

Nevertheless, the link between fundamentalism and the dislike for democracy applies generally, and explains the propensity by fundamentalists for violence. Thus the public and private violence of men against women – a gender fundamentalism – involves a refusal to communicate in situations in which patriarchal conditions are under challenge. There is no question of men imagining what it is like to be a woman, for differences are absolutised, and used to justify the domination over the 'other'. Similarly with the violence of what Giddens calls exclusionary ethnic groups (1994: 48): fundamentalisms of various kinds can act to sharpen up pre-existing ethnic or cultural differences. Whenever fundamentalism takes hold degenerate spirals of communication threaten where one antipathy feeds on another antipathy, hate is heaped upon hate (Giddens, 1994: 243; 245).

Violence, as we have argued elsewhere, involves a radical absence of common interest, so that the target of violence is seen as an enemy rather than a fellow human being. Active trust established through an acceptance of difference is the enemy of fundamentalism. By difference, Giddens means the opposite of what we have called 'division'. Dialogic democracy involves a recognition that everyone is different and this difference is a positive and unifying attribute (1994: 129). In a post-traditional age, he argues, nationalism stands close to aggressive fundamentalisms, embraced by neo-fascist groups as well as by other sorts of movements or collectivities (1994: 132). The point about fundamentalism, as it is conceptualised here, is that it is *new* so that, as Giddens points out, neo-fascism is not fascism in its original form – it is a species of fundamentalism steeped with the potential for violence (1994: 251).

What is Islamic Fundamentalism?

It is widely held that fundamentalism is a 'green threat' in the post-cold war world. The Islamic religion is seen as the new enemy to democracy, the United States and the West – a cancer destroying 'Western' values. But to conflate the Islamic religion with fundamentalism is itself a fundamentalist distortion of reality, intended to project all conflicts as a war either by or against Islam, some kind of resurrection of the crusades. It is a view held by the Christian right and extreme Zionists, and it involves a dramatic and unwarranted homogenising of Islam.

As Ali points out in his revealingly entitled *The Clash of Fundamentalisms,* the world of Islam has not been monolithic for thousands of years. The social and cultural differences between Senegalese, Chinese, Indonesian, Arab and South Asian Muslims are far greater than similarities they share with non-Muslim members of the same nationality (2002: 274). Roy even argues that Islamism has 'social-democratised' itself (1999: xi). A comparison between Zoubir's (1998) analysis of Islamic fundamentalism in Algeria and Robinson's (1998) assessment of the Muslim Brotherhood in Jordan demonstrates not only the diversity within Islam, but the necessary features that make up an Islamic *fundamentalism.*

Following the successful liberation war with France the state in Algeria, Zoubir points out, lost its legitimacy and its *raison d'être* in the eyes of a youthful and disenchanted population (1998: 132). Little was done to provide employment or housing for the young people who deserted the countryside for the shanty towns. The Algerian regime offered modernisation without secularisation, with a demagogic and equivocal position on religious and cultural issues. It was, and still is, corrupt and inefficient, and this has led to an identity crisis with disastrous consequences – an identity crisis that has been intensified by the defeat of Arab nationalism and the humiliations suffered by Arab regimes against Israel (1998: 133). Many mosques were built in Algeria and, were it not for their totalitarian conception, the fundamentalists could have provided the basis of a credible counter-hegemony programme along classic Gramscian lines. But whereas the Italian Marxist Gramsci urged the construction of a working-class hegemony or intellectual and moral supremacy based upon socialist values, fundamentalists in Algeria have sought an illiberal and anti-democratic domination. Many of the individuals who followed Nasser or Marx in the 1960s are fundamentalists today. Chaotic liberalisation of trade, and a cut in food subsidies and unemployment have all fed fundamentalism. Large segments of society have been marginalised, leading to widespread anger, despair, banditry and utter hatred towards the state and its clienteles (Zoubir, 1998: 139).

Robinson's study of Muslim brethren in Jordan and their party the Islamic Action Front (formed in 1992 when parties were legalised) is a study of Islamists who are not fundamentalists since, as Robinson points out, these organisations express their opposition to secularism in democratically permissible ways (1998: 173). A leader of the Muslim Brethren says: 'we have never believed in violence or intellectual terrorism' (1998: 182). But as it becomes more working class in composition and Palestinian influence increases, the Islamic Action Front has become increasingly divided (1998: 189). If inequalities continue to grow and the crisis in Israel/Palestine worsens, then this Islamic movement may turn to fundamentalism, not because it is Islamic, but because it will react negatively to a failing modernity.

Algeria not only offers a classic case study of the conditions that give rise to (Islamic) fundamentalism, but it also provides a model of how not to deal with the problem. Zoubir notes that the FIS (Islamic Salvation Front) emerged as the most mobilised and best-structured party in the country – it was legalised in 1989 despite its avowed opposition to republican principles (1998: 143–4). It looked certain to win the elections in 1992 when the army stepped in, cancelled the elections and banned the organisation. Since 1992 terrorism and banditry have plagued the country and successive governments have failed to regain a minimum level of trust and legitimacy (Zoubir, 1998: 154).

Ali argues that had the FIS been allowed to become the government then divisions beneath the surface would have come to the fore. The army could then have warned that any attempt to tamper with rights guaranteed by the constitution would not be tolerated (2002: 306). This would, at least, have put the argument squarely in favour of the concept of democracy that the FIS explicitly rejected. In fact, since the army's counter-productive action and the mutual escalation of terrorism it has engendered, faith in the FIS has also been eroded, as Zoubir points out, and the only concern by Algerians is civil peace, physical and economic security (1998: 157).

The comparison between the FIS in Algeria and the Islamic Action Front in Jordan is revealing. It not only shows that there is significant diversity between Islamic movements even in the Middle East, but reveals the kinds of conditions which need to be present before a fundamentalist movement can take root. Islamic ideology differs considerably from country to country or movement to movement. It delineates a wide spectrum of thought, from the transparently ultraconservative to a convolution of eclectic liberal ideas. It is thus inappropriate to categorise, as Bina puts it, all these movements as 'fundamentalist'. If applied indiscriminately the yardstick of fundamentalism runs counter to the very act of reconciliation of Islam with existing social formations that are, by necessity, transitory and historical (1994: 17–18). Adherence to Islam, as with other religious movements and movements in general, necessarily reflects the particular conditions in which fundamentalism takes root.

Nasser's Egypt had been a beacon of Arab progressivism. Nasser sought to destroy the Muslim Brotherhood and his government tried to turn the clerical graduates of the Islamic University of Al Azhar into mere transmission belts for his ideology. Nasser treated the Muslim Brotherhood with 'unexampled brutality' and those leaders who had not been hanged took refuge in oil sheikdoms in the Arabian Peninsular (Kepel, 1994: 18). In 1966 Sayyid Qutb, a member of the Brotherhood, was executed: his message, hugely influential, was that true Muslims should break with the existing world and build a real Islamic state (Kepel, 1994: 20). Armstrong quotes his comment that 'Humanity today is living in one large brothel! One only has to glance at its press, films, fashion shows, beauty contests, ballrooms, wine-bars, and broadcasting stations' (2001: 240). After the traumatic military defeat by Israel in 1967, Islamic orthodoxy began to gain increasing numbers of adherents. The sharp increase in the price of oil that followed the Arab–Israeli war of 1973 accelerated the flight from the countryside.

Sayyid Qutb (1906–66)

Born in a small town in Upper Egypt, Qutb moved to Cairo as an adolescent in order to further his education. He obtained his first job as an inspector in the Ministry of Education.

Qutb began to write in the late 1920s as a poet and literary critic, presenting social and political matters from a secular standpoint. By 1948, however, he adopted a more Islamic perspective, according to the limited knowledge of Islam that he had. *Social Justice*, his first Islamic book, was published in 1949.

After his return from a two-year study tour in the United States that ended in 1950, Qutb joined al-Ikhwan al-Muslimun (the Muslim Brotherhood), becoming one of their leading spokespeople. He sought to understand Islam in a new way, writing a *tafsir* (explanation) of the Qu'rān called *Fi Thilalil-Qu'rān* (In the Shade of the Qu'rān). Qutb was not interested in following the traditional approach of explaining the Qu'rān. He used his own opinions to expound the Qu'rān in a way that was over and above traditional sources. He treated the Qu'rān in ultramodernist fashion – as a work of art, not a repository of literal truth.

Qutb came up with a set of statements collected from all of the various Islamic sects that have sprung up since the earliest years of Islamic civilisation. He was influenced by the *Mu'tazili*/Sufi philosophical school of thought – a system of belief that runs completely contrary to the so-called 'Wahhabi' creed. His revolutionary ideology of *takfir* (excommunication) appealed to the youth who were increasingly critical of the Muslim Brotherhood. This accounts for Qutb's appeal to insurrectionary groups.

Qutb condemned the separation of the sacred from the secular in Christianity and warned that Islamic reformers threatened to create the same divide in Islam, preventing it from ordering all aspects of life according to the precepts of the Qu'rān. After his movement openly opposed the government of Jamal Abdul Nasser, Qutb spent the rest of his life in prison after 1954, except for a brief period in 1964–5. After being temporarily released Qutb was reapprehended, tried and executed for treason in 1966.

Yet in Egypt, as elsewhere, it is possible to be an Islamist without being a fundamentalist. Abul Fotouh, who is head of the Egyptian Medical Association and a leader of the Muslim Brotherhood, does not find the Western way of life at odds with Islam. 'At the end of the day', he comments, 'we have a set of common humanist values; justice, freedom, human rights and democracy' (*The Economist*, 2003: 6). However, Hammoud indicates that in Egypt it is the particular circumstances rather than the particular religion that have given rise to a fundamentalist opposition. The economic situation has led to increased inequality, productivity has decreased and unemployment has rocketed (Zoubir, 1998: 306). Fundamentalists in

Myths about Fundamentalism

- Fundamentalism is necessarily about religion.

- Fundamentalists seek to return to 'fundamentals'.

- Fundamentalists are hostile to all things modern.

- All Muslims are fundamentalists.

Egypt, as elsewhere, have begun to offer social and relief services that the modern state has signally failed to provide. The use of repression and emergency against opponents has helped to create a revolutionary opposition, and devastated confidence in notions of dialogue and consensus that are crucial to a democratic culture (1998: 329–31).

US Fundamentalism and the Religious Right

Anyone who thinks that fundamentalism is a purely Islamic phenomenon should pay some attention to the ideas and impact of Christianity in Italy (and France) or on the religious right in the United States. When US Christian fundamentalists Jerry Falwell and Pat Robertson declared that the attack on 11 September was a judgement of God for the sins of secular humanists, they were expressing a viewpoint not far removed from that of the Muslim hijackers (Armstrong, 2001: viii). In Italy, an organisation called the 'People's Movement' provided a valuable back-up resource for the Christian Democrats, although it reserved the right to campaign against any Christian Democrat suspected of harbouring secularist sympathies. Its weekly journal stigmatised secularised Christians as 'Catho-communists' (Kepel, 1994: 72–3). In France, an estimated 200,000 people have been involved with a charismatic revival, with supporters making common cause with those Islamic fundamentalists outraged by the 'Islamic veil' affair, where the state insisted that Muslim schoolgirls must dress in a secular fashion.

Fundamentalism (strictly defined) in the United States was rooted historically in the American South, and the depression of 1929 was seen 'as a sign of God's vindictive punishment on an apostate America as well as a sign of Christ's imminent return' (Kepel, 1994: 107). A poll in 1969 revealed that there were some 1,300 evangelical Christian radio and television stations, with an audience of about 130 million. Between 1965 and 1983 enrolment in evangelical schools increased sixfold, and about 100,000 fundamentalist children were taught at home. The enemy were 'secular humanists' who, fundamentalists alleged, sought to reduce the world to slavery (Armstrong, 2001: 267; 269; 272).

In Kepel's view, Reagan was elected in 1980 largely because he captured the votes of most of the evangelical and fundamentalist (using the term somewhat narrowly) electors who followed the advice of politico-religious bodies such as the Moral Majority. Just as the Islamic militants, the young US fundamentalists have had higher education (usually studying the applied sciences), and they have come from the large cities in the northern and southern states (Kepel, 1994: 8, 137).

Boston argues in his critique of Pat Robertson that Robertson's political unit, the Christian Coalition (launched in 1989) has a budget of $25 million with 1.7 million members and 1,600 local affiliates in all 50 states (1996: 16). Robertson owns the Christian Broadcasting Network (CBN) and, in his view, only Christians and Jews are qualified to run government. Not surprisingly, he and his movement deny the separation of Church and state. His support for Israel is premised on the assumption that he believes that Zionism in Israel will unwittingly contribute to the conversion of Jews to Christianity. In the 1980s he was a champion of South Africa's system of apartheid. The wealth of CBN can be seen from the fact that the

Network can clear between $75 and $97 million tax-free profit, and the political impact of Robertson's Christian Coalition is evident in Boston's contention that it holds the country's majority party, i.e., the Republicans, in a headlock (Boston, 1996: 132, 166, 183, 238).

Predictably the Christian Coalition, as with the Moral Majority before it, is also virulently anti-feminist in character (Wilcox, 1996: 9), and Coalition supporters follow the historic pattern of religious fundamentalists of keeping themselves apart from an impure world and (in their case) doctrinally impure Christians. Wilcox estimates that about 10–15 per cent of the public support the religious right, and there may be as many as 4 million members of the Christian Right and possibly 200,000 activists in politics (1996: 36; 71). The movement has always used the best technology available. In general, the Christian Right opposes any notion of compromise, and they tend to be intolerant of those with whom they disagree. They do not accept the civil liberties of liberals, although it is true that the more members of the religious right participate in conventional politics, the more reconciled to democracy they become (1996: 107–8; 111). For many, imposing Christianity on non-believers increases the odds that the souls of these hapless infidels will spend eternity in heaven. Fringe elements (in an interesting counterpart to Muslims who believe in a punitive version of the shariah) favour Mosiac law that would involve stoning sinners (1996: 125).

Some fundamentalists showed their contempt for US law by blockading abortion clinics and, in the words of Randall Terry, saw themselves as working for a nation 'not floating in an uncertain sea of humanism, but a country whose unmoving bedrock is Higher laws' (Armstrong, 2001: 360). As with fundamentalism elsewhere, there is a reaction against modernism that Christian fundamentalists believe will inevitably erode traditional values. As Wilcox points out, there is a small but significant trend to liberalism in the US public, and young Americans are far more liberal than the older cohorts they are replacing (1996: 144). Falk has analysed the increasing convergence of religion and politics as a growing adherence to postmodernism (1988), but although postmodernism challenges the separations and dualisms of the liberal tradition, fundamentalism does not.

For this reason, liberation theology is not fundamentalist at all, but seeks to challenge religious conservatism in exciting and innovative ways. It stands in contrast to what Falk himself calls a few islands of fundamentalist success that disclose the religious revision of modernism in an oppressive direction (1988: 380). It is not the rise of postmodern religion that is fundamentalist or cultist in character. It is rather movements that reject or merely negate modernism. The West, as Falk puts it graphically, has 'killed' God with its consumerist spirit (1988: 381) so that there has been a remarkable surge of fundamentalist religion in the last few decades (1988: 385). This is why it is problematic to speak of US fundamentalism as exhibiting, in Armstrong's words, postmodern tendencies, although she is right to note that it has 'a hard-line totalitarian vision' of the future (2001: 362).

Even in the 1980s it was clear that the 'coming out' of US fundamentalists in the form of the 'moral majority' and evangelical Christianity represented a determined assault on the modern lifestyle of 'secular' Christianity. The AIDS epidemic has been seen as a kind of objective confirmation of the fundamentalist

How to read:

Armstrong's *The Battle for God*

This is a very useful history of fundamentalism. The new preface should be carefully read and so should the introduction. Part One takes the story up to 1870, and can be skipped. Concentrate on Part Two. Chapter 5 'Battle Lines (1870–1900)' should be skim read, and so should Chapter 6 on 'Fundamentals'. Chapter 7 looks at developments between 1925 and 1960 and deserves a more careful read, while Chapters 8, 9 and 10 are important to an understanding of contemporary fundamentalism and require close attention. Although the book focuses on fundamentalism as a religious phenomenon, it does deal with Jewish, Christian and Muslim attitudes, and the after-word provides important insights into the role of religion in the modern world.

critique of modernism, and fundamentalists express their hostility to the preoccupation with means rather than ends associated with modernist solutions (Falk, 1988: 387). When Falk argues that a religion with postmodern strivings links emotion to reason and sees connections and relatedness as primary categories of knowledge (1988: 388), he demonstrates (however unwittingly) why the fundamentalism of the religious right in the United States cannot be seen in postmodernist terms. Indeed, what makes the religious right fundamentalist is the violence of its language and some of its practice (think of bombings against abortion clinics, for example), and the stark chasms it poses between the purists 'saved' and those whose lifestyle and values commit them to eternal damnation.

Jewish Fundamentalism and the Israeli State

A tiny minority of orthodox Jews in the 1920s began to see in Zionism – a belief that Israel represents a natural homeland for the Jews – a more holistic vision after the trauma and constrictions of exile, as Armstrong notes, and they were strongly opposed to secular Zionists. In the 1940s they established their own schools (2001: 259). Rabbi Yehuda, who led the Gahlet, an elite group within religious Zionist circles, declared that every Jew 'who comes to Eretz Israel [biblical Israel] constitutes . . . another stage in the process of redemption'. The war of 1967 in which Israel conquered the Golan Heights, the West Bank and the Gaza Strip was deemed proof that redemption was under way (Armstrong, 2001: 261, 263).

Kepel sees 1977 as a signpost year in which the dominant Zionist tradition was critically re-examined as Labour lost its first election in the history of Israel. Judaism was redefined in terms of observance and ritual (1994: 6). The war of 1973 ended in 'a psychological defeat for the Jewish state', and in the confusion and questioning of certainties there emerged the Gush Emunim (Bloc of the Faithful) that became the self-proclaimed herald for the re-Judaisation of Israel.

Four Facts about Fundamentalism

1. Fundamentalism is a concept rather than a label and it relates not simply to religion but to any ideology.
2. Although fundamentalism takes the form of a return to fundamentals, in fact fundamentalists are highly selective and innovative with regard to sacred texts.
3. Fundamentalism is a product of modernity and makes use of modern technology although it also rails against modernist ideas.
4. Fundamentalism espouses the use of violence to settle conflicts of interest, and is profoundly anti-democratic.

Gush Emunim was formed by a bloc of hawkish secularists and religious Zionists. It replaced the legal concept of the state of Israel with the biblical concept of the Land of Israel, and sought to plant more and more settlements in the occupied territories (1994: 140–1). The Zionist ideal needed to be renewed and fully realised. Israel was seen as a unique state that was not bound by international law (Armstrong, 2001: 280; 282).

After Rabbi Kook's death Gush Emunim split: a few identified the Palestinians as Amalekites, a people so cruel that God had commanded the ancient Israelites to slay them without mercy (Armstrong, 2001: 346). Terrorism was resorted to: Gush Emunin extremists were suspected of murdering students at the Islamic University of Hebron and making attempts on the lives of Palestinian mayors, and the organisation encouraged other groups to embrace the cause of re-Judaisation as well. Ultraorthodox groups began to recruit among university students and among Sephardic Jews, who were often immigrants from the Arab countries in which groups such as Gush Emunim had been quite unknown.

Religious parties represent such groups in parliament and they exercise real leverage on coalition governments. These groups argue for a sharp break between

Differentiating Religious Fundamentalisms

- *Islamic fundamentalism* is not the same as devotion to Islam. Fundamentalism arises in situations of severe social, political and economic dislocation, and as the portrait of the Egyptian Muslim Brotherhood reveals, Muslims can espouse liberal and democratic values.

- *US fundamentalism* expresses itself as a bigoted and intolerant Christianity. Its proponents have substantial resources, owning radio stations and targeting the Republican Party. US fundamentalism is anti-feminist, anti-Semitic and anti-Islam and it rejects modernity. Hence it is anti-modernist rather than postmodernist in character.

- *Jewish fundamentalism* takes the form of a religious orthodoxy that opposes secular Zionism and seeks an Israel that is not bound by international law and expands to its biblically ordained frontiers.

Biography **Osama Bin Laden (1957–)**

Born in Saudi Arabia to a Yemeni family. His father had made his fortune in the construction business and had close ties with the Saudi royal family. At school and university Bin Laden was a member of the Muslim Brotherhood.

When the Soviet Union invaded Afghanistan in 1979 he went to Pakistan and met Afghan rebel leaders who were resisting the occupation. He returned to Saudi Arabia to collect money and supplies for the Afghan resistance and eventually joined the fight himself. He opened a guest house in Peshawar as a stopping-off point for Arab mujahidin fighters. Eventually their numbers became so large that he built camps for them inside Afghanistan.

Bin Laden gave the umbrella group for his guest house and camps the name, al-Qaeda, Arabic for 'the base'. The jihad against the USSR and the Afghan government was supported by Saudi Arabia, Pakistan and the United States, and Bin Laden is alleged to have received training from the CIA. While in Afghanistan he founded the Maktab al-Khidimat (MAK), which recruited fighters from around the world.

After the Soviet withdrawal the 'Arab Afghans', as Bin Laden's faction came to be called, failed to receive the recognition that he felt they deserved, and an offer to create an army of mujahidin to defend the Saudi kingdom after the Iraqi invasion of Kuwait was turned down.

Bin Laden was particularly incensed by the stationing of US troops on Saudi soil. He returned to Saudi Arabia to work in the family construction business, but was expelled in 1991 because of his anti-government activities there. He spent the next five years in Sudan until US pressure prompted the Sudanese government to expel him, whereupon Bin Laden returned to Afghanistan. By the mid-1990s he was calling for a global war against Americans and Jews, and in 1998 he issued a fatwa that amounted to a declaration of war against the United States.

Two simultaneous bomb attacks against US embassies in Kenya and Tanzania followed a few months later. Although Bin Laden never acknowledged responsibility, those arrested named him as their backer. Experts say that Bin Laden is part of an international Islamic front, bringing together Saudi, Egyptian and other groups. It seeks the 'liberation' of Islam's three holiest places – Mecca, Medina and Jerusalem.

Bin Laden's organisation is believed not to be a tightly knit group with a clear command structure, but a loose coalition of groups operating across continents.

US officials say that his associates may operate in more than 40 countries across Europe and North America, as well as in the Middle East and Asia. According to the US State Department, his organisation was responsible for the bombing of the World Trade Center in 1973 as well as the atrocities of 11 September, and he is regarded as 'one of the most significant sponsors of Islamic extremist activities in the world today'. A video of him was released shortly before the US presidential election in 2004.

Jews and gentiles, with a demand for the strict observance of prohibitions and obligations. As with Protestant fundamentalists, devout Islamists or Catholic organisations such as Communion and Liberation, secularism is seen as suffocating by 'reborn' Jews, with the Enlightenment blamed for plunging humanity into 'a hostile sea of doubt' and cutting it adrift from 'firm moorings in a theocentric universe' (Kepel, 1994: 140–3). Some, such as the Russian émigré, Herman Branover who went to Israel in 1972, found Zionism and Israeli society intolerably secular. Nevertheless, even secular Zionists were held to be the unwitting bearers of a messianic redemption (1994: 147; 155).

Fundamentalism and the State

Some fundamentalists see the nation-state as an alien Western invention and look towards some kind of revolutionary international to cleanse the world of its imperfections. Yet the emphasis on violence and polarisation show that whether or not fundamentalists consciously

support the need for a state, their arguments are statist through and through. The view of opponents as enemies to be crushed by an organisation that monopolises truth and legitimacy projects in extreme form attitudes which exist even in the liberal state. Hence the ease with which the US president after '9/11' began to invert the sentiments of al-Qaeda, declaring that 'those who are not with us, are against us'.

While we are not suggesting that the state per se is a fundamentalist organisation, there is a continuity between the extolling of violence against enemies by fundamentalists and the use of force by the state. The same cynical, instrumental and ambiguous attitude towards modernity is evident in both, so that although they are different, fundamentalism – particularly if it can be blamed on a rogue state – is grist to the mill of the state's own contradictory identity. The cover of Tariq Ali's *The Clash of Fundamentalisms* shows a juxtaposition of Bush and Bin Laden that is both amusing and insightful.

An institution that links conflict with violence and seeks to justify monopolistic practices must operate in terms of divisions and dualisms which under pressure can easily become fundamentalist in character. The state, while not fundamentalist in itself, harbours fundamentalist leanings in its bureaucratic soul.

Stern religious observance is regarded by fundamentalists here, as elsewhere, as compatible with making use of the technology and apparel of the modern world. Gush Emunim received some support from the Israeli party Likud, but subsequently resorted to a terrorism that was officially denounced (1994: 161; 163). A plan to dynamite the mosques on the Temple Mount in Jerusalem was foiled by the Israeli secret service. Kepel finds striking similarities between these Jewish conspirators and the Islamic fundamentalist group that assassinated Sadat in 1981 – a process of re-Judaisation or re-Islamisation taken to extremes. Gush Emunim has a membership of some 50,000, most of them resident in the occupied territories (1994: 169–70). From the mid-1980s the ultraorthodox Jews (the haredim) became the most highly visible advocates of re-Judaisation, drawing support particularly from Sephardic Jews (1994: 178). The orthodox parties are able to wield substantial power. Although they receive only 15 per cent of the vote, they control several ministries and obtain large subsidies to strengthen their network of practising Jewish communities (Kepel, 1994: 180; 190). The Lubavitch believe that Israel should be cleansed of its Zionist accretions in order to become a 'Torahcracy' over the Land of Israel (i.e. Israel as projected in the Bible) (Kepel, 1994: 189). Hence they should, in our view, be regarded as extreme Zionists rather than anti-Zionists.

The assassination of Rabin, as did the assassination of Sadat, showed, as Armstrong points out, that two wars are being fought out in the Middle East. One is the war against Israel; the other is the war between the secularists and the religious (2001: 353).

The 'Clash of Civilisations': a Fundamentalist Thesis?

The link between fundamentalism and the state is well exemplified by Huntington's contention that globalisation is leading to a clash of civilisations. He explicitly identifies his position with the realist theory of international relations (1996: 185), and argues that the tools of realism – a state-centric view of the world which remains basically changeless – leads to an understanding of (violent) conflict in terms of cultural and what he calls 'civilisational' difference.

While he concedes that minorities in other cultures may espouse Western values – by which Huntington means the values of what he calls democratic liberalism – dominant attitudes in non-Western cultures range from widespread scepticism to intense opposition to Western values (1996: 184). Although almost all non-Western civilisations are resistant to pressure from the West – including Hindu, Orthodox, African and even Latin American countries – the greatest resistance to Western power has come from Islam and Asia (1996: 193).

Civilisations, Huntington argues, are the ultimate human tribes, and the clash of civilisations is tribal conflict on a global scale. Trust and friendship between the civilisations will be rare (1996: 206). He sees a deeply conflictual relationship (Huntington takes it for granted that conflict is always violent), not simply between Islamic fundamentalists and Christianity but between Islam itself and Christianity. Conflict is a product of difference. In civilisational conflicts, unlike ideological ones, kin stand by their kin (1996: 209–10; 217). Thus, the Gulf War is interpreted as a war between civilisations (1996: 251), and religion, in Huntington's view, is the principal defining characteristic of civilisation, so that what he calls 'fault-line wars' are almost always between people of different religions (1996: 253). At the global level, the clash is between the West and the rest. At the micro or local level, it is between Islam and others (1996: 255). The longer a fault-line war continues, the more that kin countries are likely to become involved (1996: 272).

Huntington takes the view that it is futile and counter-productive for countries to integrate their peoples. A multicivilisational United States, he argues, will not be the United States: it will be the United Nations. We must reject the divisive siren calls of multiculturalism (1996: 306–7; 310). Cultural identities inevitably collide in an antagonistic manner. 'We know who we are only when we know who we are not and often only when we know whom we are against' (1996: 21). Here is realism with a cultural twist! Nation-states are and will remain the most important actors in world affairs, but their interests, associations and conflicts are increasingly shaped by cultural and civilisational factors. Huntington has recently argued that the United States is now threatened by immigrants from Latin America who are altering the national identity of traditional America.

The Clash of Civilizations, it could be argued, is itself a kind of fundamentalism. But not only does it not arise from, it is staunchly opposed to the Islamic tradition. Huntington believes that human history is the history of civilisations (1996: 40).

Islamic civilisation in particular and non-Western culture in general are on the ascendant, and it is wrong to assume that with 'modernisation' the world becomes more amenable to Western values. In fact, he argues, the world is becoming more modern and less Western (1996: 78). Of course people are different, but for Huntington these differences can only lead to exclusion and antagonism. Thus he insists that religion posits a basic distinction between a superior in-group and a different and inferior out-group, and cultural questions (such as the mosque at Ayodhya or the status of Jerusalem) tend to involve a yes–no, zero sum choice. For self-definition and motivation, people need enemies (1996: 97; 130). Here is the core of a quasi-fundamentalism.

Of course civilisational differences are real and important, but Huntington is wrong to see them as a necessary source of antagonism. Abou El Fadl has rightly stressed the mixed lineage of civilisations (2003: 82). It is true that many Muslims are not convinced when the US attempts to present its demonisation of political figures such as the deposed Iraqi leader, Saddam Hussein, as something other than raw hostility to Islam per se. But it needs to be remembered that it was a US-led NATO that intervened in Kosovo to defend the human rights of people of Muslim faith against their Serbian (and Christian Orthodox) oppressors. This hardly fits the clash of civilisations thesis.

Huntington himself links what he calls 'Muslim assertiveness' to social mobilisation, population growth, and a flood of people from the countryside into the towns (1996: 102; 98). This is surely a social rather than a purely cultural explanation for antagonism. Moreover, only a realist schooled in state-centric analysis and rooted in US triumphalism could ignore the adverse effect of the insensitivity and arrogance of US policy makers upon others. It is not that the differences he speaks of are unimportant. Rather it is that he fossilises them, fails to see the contradiction between the 'culturalist' and sociological dimensions of his analysis and ignores the tensions within the so-called Western tradition between neo-liberal and social democratic strategies and values. His work is a good example of the way in which an extreme statism (with its conservative and superficial assumptions) can lead in the direction of fundamentalism. Divisions are taken for granted, so that it could be argued that there is a danger that the fundamentalism of the 'other side' is merely inverted rather than transcended.

Criticisms of Fundamentalism

- Fundamentalism differs from the state, but it is important to note the continuities. Fundamentalism seeks to monopolise the truth and use violence against enemies. So does the state. Of course fundamentalism is much more extreme than, say, the liberal state, but it takes to an extreme what are statist tendencies.

- Huntington's 'clash of civilisations' thesis is an example of a kind of academic quasi-fundamentalism that absolutises differences, and sees violent conflict in terms of cultural and 'civilisational' values. Instead of seeking to distinguish between, for example, liberal and fundamentalist Islamic doctrines, he treats Islam as a homogenous culture that is staunchly opposed to 'Western values'.

Summary

Fundamentalism is sometimes seen as a mere label. In our view it is more than this. It is a concept despite the fact that it is a relatively new idea. Although fundamentalism is often identified with religions, any ideology, no matter how secular, can take a fundamentalist form. Fundamentalism is not about the 'fundamentals' of a creed. Fundamentalists exploit the creeds they espouse in order to make them dogmatic, militant and violent in character.

Fundamentalists have an ambivalent attitude towards modernity. On the one hand they oppose it; on the other they not only make use of it, but fundamentalism can only be understood as part of the modern world. Fundamentalism sees deep divisions between the 'pure' and the 'contaminated'. It rejects dialogue and debate, and regards violence as the only way of tackling conflict.

It is wrong to assume that Islam is necessarily (or has a particular tendency to be) fundamentalist in character. Where Islamists turn to fundamentalism this is not because of their religion, but because of the particular circumstances in which they find themselves. Fundamentalism can take a Christian form. If we look at the Christian right in the United States, we see that not only are they wealthy, but they are politically influential and reject democratic values. In Israel Jewish fundamentalism has a love/hate relationship with Zionism. On the one hand, Jewish fundamentalists are concerned at the way in which some Zionists treat religion purely as a national identity rather than a sacred creed. On the other hand, they see the state of Israel as a first step towards building an Israel of biblical proportions.

The 'realism' of Huntington can be viewed as a kind of academic quasi-fundamentalism as a result of the author's contention that differences between civilisations necessarily lead to violence and antagonism.

Questions

1. Is fundamentalism simply about religion?
2. Is fundamentalism inherent in Islam?
3. Is the media treatment of fundamentalism fair?
4. Is fundamentalism a modern phenomenon?
5. How should democrats handle fundamentalists?

References

Abou El Fadl, K. (2003) '9/11 and the Muslim Transformation' in M. Dudziak (ed.), *September 11 in History* Durham, NC and London: Duke University Press, 69–111.

Ali, T. (2002) *The Clash of Fundamentalisms* London: Verso.

Armstrong, K. (2001) *The Battle for God* New York: Ballantine Books.

Bina, C. (1994) 'Towards a New World Order: US Hegemony, Client-States and Islamic Alternative' in H. Mutalib and H. Taj ul-Islam (eds), *Islam, Muslims and the Modern State* Basingstoke: Macmillan, 3–30.

Boston, R. (1996) *The Most Dangerous Man in America* New York: Prometheus Books.

Brown, W. (1995) *States of Injury* Princeton, NJ: Princeton University Press.

Choueiri, Y. (1996) 'The Political Discourse of Contemporary Islamist Movements' in A. Sidahmed and A. Ehteshami (eds), *Islamic Fundamentalism* Boulder, Col.: Westview Press, 19–33.

The Economist (2003) 'In the Name of God', 13 September.

Falk, R. (1988) 'Religion and Politics: Verging on the Postmodern' *Alternatives* XIII 379–94.

Giddens, A. (1994) *Beyond Left and Right* Cambridge: Polity Press.

Gray, J. (2003) *Al Qaeda and What It Means to be Modern* London: Faber & Faber.

Hammoud, M. (1998) 'Causes for Fundamentalist Popularity in Egypt' in A. Moussalli (ed.), *Islamic Fundamentalism* Reading: Ithaca, 303–36.

Hiro, D. (1988) *Islamic Fundamentalism* London: Palladin.

Huntington, S. (1996) *The Clash of Civilizations* New York: Simon & Schuster.

Jensen, M. (1998) 'Islamism and Civil Society in the Gaza Strip' in A. Moussalli (ed.), *Islamic Fundamentalism* Reading: Ithaca, 197–219.

Kepel, G. (1994) *The Revenge of God* Cambridge: Polity Press.

Moussalli, A. (1998) 'Introduction to Islamic Fundamentalism: Realities, Ideologies and International Politics' in A. Moussalli (ed.), *Islamic Fundamentalism* Reading: Ithaca, 3–39.

Mozaffari, M. (1996) 'Islamism in Algeria and Iran' in A. Sidahmed and A. Ehteshami (eds), *Islamic Fundamentalism* Boulder, Col.: Westview Press, 229–65.

Nehme, M. (1998) 'The Islamic-Capitalist State of Saudi-Arabia: The Surfacing of Fundamentalism' in A. Moussalli (ed.), *Islamic Fundamentalism* Reading: Ithaca, 275–302.

Robinson, G. (1998) 'Islamists under Liberalization in Jordan' in A. Moussalli (ed.), *Islamic Fundamentalism* Reading: Ithaca, 169–96.

Roy, O. (1999) *The Failure of Political Islam* London and New York: I.B. Tauris.

Salvatore, A. (1998) 'Discursive Contentions in Islamic Terms: Fundamentalism versus Liberalism' in A. Moussalli (ed.), *Islamic Fundamentalism* Reading: Ithaca, 41–73.

Sayyid, B. (1997) *A Fundamental Fear* London: Zed Books.

Sidahmed, A. and Ehteshami, A. (1996) 'Introduction' in A. Sidahmed and A. Ehteshami (eds), *Islamic Fundamentalism* Boulder, Col.: Westview Press, 1–15.

Wilcox, C. (1996) *Onward Christian Soldiers* Boulder, Col.: Westview Press.

Wolff, K. (1998) '*New* New Orientalism: Political Islam and Social Movement Theory' in A. Moussalli (ed.), *Islamic Fundamentalism* Reading: Ithaca, 41–73.

Zoubir, Y. (1998) 'State, Civil Society and the Question of Radical Fundamentalism in Algeria' in A. Moussalli (ed.), *Islamic Fundamentalism* Reading: Ithaca, 123–67.

Further Reading

- Giddens's *Beyond Left and Right* (referenced above) contains a very useful chapter on fundamentalism.

- Kepel's *The Revenge of God* (referenced above) contains invaluable material about religious fundamentalism.

- Moussalli's edited volume *Islamic Fundamentalism* (referenced above) is very useful and comprehensive.

- Wilcox's *Onward Christian Soldiers* (referenced above) provides a survey of the religious right in the United States.

- Huntington's *The Clash of Civilizations* (referenced above) is a real, if contentious, classic.

Weblinks

Quite good on the link between religion and fundamentalism:
http://www.vexen.co.uk/religion/fundamentalism.html

For the question of the market and fundamentalism, see:
http://www.opendemocracy.net/debates/article-2-95-1248.jsp

For a piece on fundamentalism as a concept, see:
http://www.shellier.co.uk/fundamentalism.htm

Part 4 Contemporary Ideas

What do we mean by a New Idea?

In the last part of this book we discuss five concepts: difference, human rights, civil disobedience, terrorism, and victimhood. To a significant extent difference, terrorism and victimhood owe their salience as political concepts to the emergence of the new ideologies discussed in Part 3, while human rights and civil disobedience are the product of changes within the liberal tradition of political thought. What distinguishes these four concepts from those discussed in Part 1 – state, freedom, equality, justice, democracy, citizenship – is their relatively recent emergence within political theory. Of course, the 'classical' ideas themselves have undergone change and much of our discussion in Part 1 focused on contemporary debates, but those debates revolved around 'problems' that emerged in the *earlier* phases of modernity. For example, the problem of state legitimacy and political obligation, the justification of property rights, arguments over the nature of the human agent, conflicts between freedom and equality, and debate about the nature of political authority and collective decision making.

The term 'problem' is used here in a precise, philosophical sense as a 'puzzle' that requires a solution, rather than everyday usage, which roughly defines a 'problem' as a fault, weakness or contradiction. An analogy from the world of music will illustrate what we mean: one of the 'great revolutions' in Western music took place in the first decade of the twentieth century. Although anticipated by nineteenth-century composers, Arnold Schoenberg (1874–1951) is normally credited with the first 'atonal' composition (that is, a work not composed in a key). Schoenberg did not set out to be a musical revolutionary, but rather he sought to save the tonal system; it was recognition that developments within tonality (such as chromaticism) had generated irreparable incoherences which led him to take those developments to their conclusion. In this sense Schoenberg had inherited musical problems – or puzzles – from his predecessors, such as Beethoven, Wagner and Mahler. To some extent political theory can be understood as an attempt to address problems inherited from preceding theorists, and the treatment by contemporary thinkers of classical concepts, or problems, is analogous to Schoenberg's engagement with tonality. The analogy should not be taken too far: music is a relatively self-contained art form, whereas political theory, by its nature, is an engagement with the empirical world, a world it cannot control but that it must interpret.

Political theory can best be thought of as involving two tracks: there is a body of theory, parallel to musical forms, that later theorists engage with and which 'newcomers' to the discipline may find strange and distant from the everyday world of politics, but there is also necessarily an engagement with that world of politics. We would argue that the two tracks are related, for changes in society will eventually work their way through to theoretical reflection, and this process is clear in the emergence of the new ideologies discussed in Part 3. But theorists must also maintain some distance from the world of politics, for otherwise they will be unable to distinguish the merely transitory and parochial from the significant. Without necessarily endorsing his wider philosophy, two observations from Friedrich Hegel are apt here: 'philosophy is time reflected in thought' and the 'the Owl of Minerva begins its flight at dusk'. Political thought must respect the particularity of history but in a way which does not reduce that particularity simply to a series of discrete events, and the Owl of Minerva – that is, understanding – may not emerge, or 'take flight', until we have achieved a necessary perspective on those events.

Biography, p. 19

Engagement with traditional problems of political theory, combined with social and political changes 'external' to the discipline of political theory, but to which political theorists must respond, can generate new problems. It is these new problems that justify separating out the classical and the new ideas. Take the concept of 'difference', which we discuss in Chapter 17: this can be understood either as a development of traditional liberal theorisation of the nature of the human agent, or as a radical shift towards a 'postmodern' perspective on humanity. As a continuation of liberal theory, the concept of difference is linked to identity: when liberals talk about human beings as naturally free and equal, what attributes attach to 'human being'? Do liberals allow for gender or cultural differences between human beings? Respect for identity involves recognising differences within the human subject – differences which mean that we may use different descriptions of ourselves in different situations. If, however, we take the idea of identity as a continually shifting phenomenon to its logical conclusion then we must necessarily empty identity of any 'essentialism'. This means you are what you choose to be and there are no 'grand narratives'. Gayatri Spivak, a literary theorist, argues that she, as a US-educated Asian Indian, cannot claim to speak on behalf of Indian widows, *satis*, who 'choose' to immolate themselves on their dead husband's funeral pyres, because individuals have experiences that cannot be reduced to a single language or 'narrative': feminists who claim there are experiences common to 'women' are not respecting the radical differences which exist between people. Without wishing to push the musical analogy too far, postmodernist (or post-structuralist) understandings of identity correspond to Schoenberg's radicalisation of tonal musical forms – the logic of tonality led to atonality, and the logic of difference leads to post-structuralism.

Ch 17: Difference, pp. 418–34

Other concepts discussed in Part 4 are more easily identified as continuous with traditional concepts, but they do, nonetheless, constitute a break with tradition. Consider human rights: early modern natural law theory appears at first sight the progenitor of human rights discourse. The idea that human beings have a moral status as children of God, or are implanted by God with a moral sense, does not seem entirely alien to the contemporary understanding of human rights as standards of behaviour owed to people simply by virtue of their humanity and thus transcending cultural particularity. But the shift from a theological to a secular justification renders the similarity between natural law theory and contemporary human rights theory superficial: human rights are grounded in the idea that the individual human being is a 'self-originating source of valid claims' against others, rather than being part of a natural, or cosmic, order. And the problem to which human rights are supposedly the answer is quite different to the problem to which natural law was a response: human rights function as a standard for international politics, whereas natural law was intended as a means of rejuvenating Christianity in the context of ecclesiastical corruption.

Ch 19: Civil Disobedience, pp. 460–84

Civil disobedience and terrorism can also be understood as responses to new problems. Indeed the two concepts dovetail together. Henry Thoreau is widely credited with writing the first work on civil disobedience (in 1849), but it is only after World War II that civil disobedience becomes a significant issue in political theory. We argue that although civil disobedience, that is, peaceful but illegal action, is possible in non-liberal societies – Gandhi's campaign against British rule in India being an example – it raises a special problem for a liberal society. Again, we use the word 'problem' in a precise sense, meaning a puzzle that demands a solution. The *puzzle* is this: we have special obligations to obey laws passed through the use of a democratic procedure, but that procedure can generate unjust laws which we have an obligation to disobey. This problem does not exist for a non-democratic society because there is no obligation to obey its laws, even if the laws themselves are 'just'. It follows that in a world where there are no liberal democratic societies civil disobedience will not be a prominent political issue (which is not to say that civil disobedience is not possible in such a world: repressive governments may be met with non-violent resistance). Until the twentieth century there were few, if any, fully liberal democratic societies – the denial of the vote to women ensured this was the case. Early modern theorists could think only in terms of rebellion or revolution, not civil disobedience.

Ch 18: Human Rights, pp. 436–58

Terrorism is related to civil disobedience, in that in part it is problematic when directed at liberal democratic societies. The differentiation of terrorism as one form of violence among other distinct forms is a consequence of the development of the liberal democratic value of peace: whereas pre-modern societies gloried in violence – think of the esteem attached to 'chivalry' – modern liberal societies stress the importance of peace and order. When liberal democracies use military force they claim to operate within rules of war. Terrorism is characterised as the absence of rules, hence the use of the word 'terror' (unfortunately, the use of an -ism – terrorism – implies it is an ideology rather than a concept, but really it is 'terror' that is the focus of discussion). We argue that the rather clichéd distinction expressed in the statement that 'one person's terrorist is another person's freedom-fighter' is not a useful one, and that the use of terror must be contextualised: against liberal democracies, where there exists a real possibility of political change, terror cannot be justified. In non-liberal societies, or where liberal societies are engaged in proxy wars, it is more difficult to draw a line between the justified and the unjustified employment of terrorist tactics. The point we make here is that the study of terrorism – both empirically in what is called 'terrorology' and ethically in political theory – is a relatively recent phenomenon, emerging under social and political conditions in which the classification of acceptable and unacceptable uses of violence has fundamentally changed.

Chapter 17

Difference

Introduction

In the period since the cold war there has been a substantial amount of interest in the concepts of 'identity and difference'. With the decline of a class analysis of politics writers have felt that the way people see themselves needs to be given much greater emphasis. This is particularly important where someone's identity diverges from the norm, and the fact that a person is black or gay or female or poor is deemed an attribute that needs to be taken into account when assessing the democratic quality of politics. How people see themselves is obviously linked to the way in which they differentiate themselves from others, so that the concept of difference is linked to the notion of identity and they are dealt with as a pair. Difference, it has been said, is 'a magic word of theory and politics radiant with redemptive meanings' (Hughes, 2002: 57).

Chapter Map

- A definition of difference: a monolithic and static view of a person's self awareness is in conflict with democratic norms.

- The postmodern view of 'différence' and its relation to the notion of difference.

- The use of the terms in feminist theory.

- The link between the concept of difference and the premises of liberal theory.

- The implications that difference has for the concepts of democracy and the state.

'A Protestant State for the Protestant People': Difference in Northern Ireland

A new Republican movement mural in West Belfast, 8 April 2004.

People in Northern Ireland have tended, since the founding of the statelet, to identify themselves in political and religious terms. A minority has seen itself as Catholic and Gaelic-Irish (sometimes called 'nationalist'), whereas the majority have identified themselves as Protestant and unionist – the latter term arising because they see themselves as loyal to the British crown and do not favour unification with the Republic of Ireland. These divisions led to Northern Ireland being, in Ian Paisley's rather chilling phrase, a 'Protestant State for the Protestant People', and the repression of the Catholics resulted in the British government in 1972 suspending the local parliament at Stormont and imposing direct rule. The Good Friday Agreement signed in 1998 has sought to encourage a new sense of identity and difference. Protestants were to try and understand the vulnerabilities and sensitivities of Catholics, and the nationalist minority were urged to put themselves in the position of unionists who were fearful of a united Ireland. A majority of the unionists appear to support Ian Paisley's Democratic Unionist Party, which sees identities in traditional terms, and is hostile to any sharing of power with Irish republicans, who have in the past espoused physical force as a solution to Northern Ireland's problems.

Imagine that you are a unionist who has lost relatives in one of the Provisional Irish Republican Army's (IRA) bombing campaigns. You are understandably suspicious of the fact that Sinn Fein – generally considered to be the political wing of the IRA – has signed the Good Friday Agreement and, as a result, former members of the IRA have taken part in the devolved executive that the Agreement set up and have become Ministers.

- Can you change your identity so that you are no longer a 'loyalist who hates Irish republicans', and regard yourself as a 'loyalist who understands where republicans are coming from'?

Now imagine that you are a republican who remembers the stories about parents, uncles and aunts who suffered at the hands of the unionist-minded paramilitary police, the B specials. You were personally traumatised in the late 1960s when loyalist terror gangs set fire to properties owned by nationalists. You detest the unionists and you feel that a united Ireland is only possible through the use of force.

- Can you change your hatred into an attitude of empathy so that you can see why unionists feel so hostile to republicans and identify so passionately with Britain?

Difference

Ch 14:
Multiculturalism,
pp. 350–68

The concept of difference can only be defined when you seek to establish your identity. A person's identity simply arises from how she sees herself (Alibhai-Brown, 2000: 123). Do you define yourself by your nationality – as say a Briton (or Scottish, Welsh or English) or a Norwegian, or a German; do you feel yourself defined by your religion – as a Jew, Christian, Muslim or whatever? Do you identify yourself by your gender, skin colour, region, class, sexual orientation etc? Normally the question of identity depends upon context.

If you are travelling outside of the UK, for example, your British nationality will be one you continually assert, whereas in Britain it may be an identity that you invoke much less frequently. If you are visiting a memorial for the victims of the Holocaust, you may feel that it is relevant to assert a Jewish identity; if a colleague is telling you about her sexual problems, then the fact that you are female and, say, gay becomes an identity that you wish to express, even though in other contexts this is an identity which may not require emphasis. A heated argument over the Iraq War may cause you to mention that you come from the Middle East and are a devout Muslim.

It is clear that having an identity only really arises as something of which you are aware when you wish to differentiate yourself from someone else. It is because your nationality is distinctive, or your gender, sexual orientation, religion, etc. is not universally held that your identity comes to the fore. This is why identity is always linked to difference. You are unlikely to assert your identity as a human being unless you are arguing about human rights or discussing the question as to whether animals suffer, since people by definition are human beings, and your human identity is not normally seen as a differentiating factor. This is why difference always implies identity, since to know who you are you must also know who you are not. Understandably people resent their identity being expressed in negative terms. Blacks under apartheid felt aggrieved at being referred to as 'non-whites': an identity that implies a deficiency or lack on the part of those thus labelled. It is said that while 'difference' is endlessly invoked in feminist theory it is often not defined (Hughes, 2002: 57).

The value of asserting identity arises because it is something all people have, even though people who have a dominant identity may think that it is something 'others' have and they do not. The word 'ethnic', for example, is frequently used about those who differ from the dominant norm, as in a situation in which whites in France say that they do not have an ethnic identity: this is something that belongs to others. Feminists feel aggrieved when the word 'man' is used as a synonym for humankind and are not reassured by the argument that 'man' includes women as well. Such identifiers echo earlier assumptions that the only people who really count are males, and therefore it seems appropriate to use 'man' in this all-embracing way.

In fact we all have an identity and we all have more than one. This means that everybody is different from everyone else. A number of crucial questions arise when teasing out the implications of our definition. Are some of our identities more important than others, or does it simply depend upon context? How do we resolve our differences? Do we regard 'others' as enemies that we have to repel, or partners to negotiate with? Under what circumstances do differences become an occasion for violence and war?

The Problem of the Dominant Identity

It is natural that people express an identity which is relevant to a particular context. What is problematic is the 'privileging' of a particular identity so that it becomes one which dominates all others. By this we mean that one identity is deemed dominant over a range of different contexts so that it is seen as far more important than other identities. Thus a nationalist could argue that national identity is more important than class or gender identity; a radical feminist would contend that being a woman is more important than being poor; a devout Christian could insist that her religious beliefs 'trump' her identity as a woman or the property she owns.

But why is having a dominant identity a problem? We would argue that if you have a dominant identity then it is more difficult to put yourself in the position of another. You are much more likely to see differences as attributes that threaten you, rather than as a natural part of everyone's identity. You arrange your own identities in strictly hierarchical fashion, so that, for example, the fact that you are a white, heterosexual man seems less important than the fact that you are, for example, Russian. You may be unaware of these other identities or you certainly downgrade them, and hence you are more likely to feel that other people with different identities have something wrong with them. Since you repress or de-emphasise your own different identities you will repress and respond hostilely to the differences of others.

Ch 13:
Feminism,
pp. 324–48

MacKinnon, a radical feminist, argues that difference is a secondary idea – difference, she says, is 'ideational, and abstract and false symmetrical' (1979: 219). This means that asserted differences may be unreal and relatively unimportant. Being a woman is thus more important than being black, a Catholic, lesbian or whatever. This, in our view, makes it difficult to empathise with those who are not women, or who prefer not to identify themselves in gender terms, or who link gender with questions of class, religion, ethnicity etc. Germaine Greer characterises men as women haters and, among the other unsavoury attributes that men have, she sees them as 'doomed to competition and injustice' (1999: 14; 287). But would she take this position if she did not privilege female identity in a way that downgrades all other identities? Surely some men are concerned with justice, while some women extol competition (to echo Greer's example): these facts come to light much more easily if being a woman is regarded as one identity among many, relevant in some contexts but not in others. Having a dominant identity makes toleration of others more difficult.

Biography,
p. 340

Proponents of a dominant identity may seek to exclude difference altogether. Gould gives the example of Habermas's notion of the public sphere, where he sees difference as 'something to be gotten past'. 'Diversity may be the original condition of a polyvocal discourse but univocity is its normative principle' (1996: 172). By this Habermas means that differences get in the way of the idea of human freedom and **emancipation**. Of course, regarding all people as human is important, but so is identifying the differences between them. In fact, the two go together. It is because as, for example, a Christian you see Muslims as human that you feel their differences should be respected and even celebrated. Gould finds it problematic that Habermas takes the view that in the public sphere 'the enhancing role of difference' is downgraded (1996: 173). It is true that differences result in conflict. But we should not regard conflict as necessarily involving violence. Conflict arises from our awareness of difference, and in a non-violent sense is part of agreement. Think about it. How can you have an argument with someone unless you also share certain assumptions?

Biography   Jürgen Habermas (1929–)

Between 1956 and 1959 Habermas worked as assistant to Theodor Adorno. In 1964 he was made Professor of Philosophy and Sociology at the University of Frankfurt and in 1971 he became co-director of the newly created Max Planck Institute for the Study of the Conditions of Life in the Scientific-Technical World. Habermas has been a key figure in directing and coordinating various research programmes and has influenced a wide range of empirical and historical studies.

His early work sought a 'reconstruction of historical materialism'. In it Habermas sought to mobilise all the intellectual resources of the twentieth century in order to redeem the nineteenth-century project of a science of society. In *Knowledge and Human Interests* (1968), his first major work, Habermas promotes the insight that interests inevitably play a role in determining the nature and shape of sociological (and indeed other scientific) investigation. He challenges the claim that science can be ethically neutral and purely technical. Habermas has drawn widely on empirical studies in sociology, anthropology, linguistics and psychology, but always with the aim of providing a modern, up-to-date version of 'human nature' as the basis for the progressive development and evolution of society. Habermas's work is justly claimed – by friend and foe – to be in direct continuity with traditions in social philosophy that stretch back to the beginnings of the Enlightenment.

His *Legitimation Crisis,* written in the early 1970s, argued that capitalism was experiencing severe problems but he declined to identify a social force which would advance an emancipatory solution to these problems. In 1981 he published *The Theory of Communicative Action* in which he maintained that a humane collective life depends on innovative, reciprocal and egalitarian everyday communication. But Habermas is condemned by his postmodern critics for maintaining a connection – however mediated – between questions of legitimation in science and the issue of legitimacy for political institutions. He is accused by Lyotard of presenting a 'grand narrative'. Being singled out for special treatment by postmodernists, Habermas has returned the compliment and is highly critical of what he sees as the irrationalist, nihilist and neo-conservative tendencies within postmodernism. He is deeply suspicious of its extreme scepticism.

Habermas's most sustained and substantial treatment of what he sees as the flaws and dangers of postmodernism is presented in his 12 lectures on *The Philosophical Discourse of Modernity* (1985). Habermas's mentor, Adorno, had held that the logic of modernity itself gave rise to domination. For Habermas, on the other hand, there is no historical necessity for *Zweckrationalität* (instrumental reason) to dominate the modern world.

Everybody has a different point of view, and therefore we should never assume that having things in common – 'sameness' – shuts out difference. Difference, whether of viewpoint, appearance, background, etc. is natural and necessary, and we should avoid thinking of it as problematic. If we do so, we will (even unthinkingly) privilege one identity and, in doing so, assert it as something that dominates others. Of course the idea of encouraging people to articulate their ideas in a public sphere is important but, as Gould asks, what of those who do not or cannot speak in public, 'who from inarticulateness, fear, habit or oppression are removed from participation in public life' (1996: 176)? We should help people to express and defend their differences – not regard difference as something to be ashamed of or to hide. It is true that France has a strong tradition of republicanism. But why should we interpret the separation of church and state in a way that prevents young Muslim women from wearing headscarves? After all, they are not insisting that everyone wears a headscarf: they merely want to display their difference.

Ch 5: Democracy, pp. 104–26

The assumption of a dominant identity threatens democracy since democracy requires that *all* seek to govern their own life. If we assume that certain identities are privileged, then those who differ will be excluded, and diversity will be crushed by uniformity.

Postmodernism/Post-structuralism and Difference

Introduction, pp. xxxi–xxxvii

Postmodernism or post-structuralism (we will use the terms synonymously) has become influential over the last 15 years. It challenges what it calls modernism, and the tendency of 'modernist' thinkers to see the world in opposites that exclude one another. One of these opposites is privileged, and the other downgraded. Thus, instead of seeing men and women as differences that imply one another – to know what a man is, you need to know what a woman is – modernists tend to regard one as more important than the other. Much of our own argument in this, as in other sections, has drawn upon postmodernist argument, and the rejection of 'dualism' follows from postmodern premises.

Postmodernists have written a good deal about difference, but what makes the postmodern view of difference contentious (in some of its formulations) is that it is often linked to an argument that denies progress, truth and emancipation. Because a person is different, the argument is that it is impossible to understand and sympathise with their view of the world. Difference is seen simply as dividing us, and the unity that makes this difference intelligible is ignored. Using difference in this way makes it impossible, in our view, to acknowledge dissimilarity in a way that shows respect for others and thus strengthens democracy. But many postmodernists are hostile to the idea of 'sameness' or unity, and this leads them to reject the very idea of emancipation – that everyone can govern their own lives albeit with different ideas and identities.

It is argued by Weedon that postmodernism represents a 'position', whereas post-structuralism is merely a method of critique that could be used in the struggle for change (Hughes, 2002: 65). If this is correct, then post-structuralism can avoid the pessimism, scepticism, relativism of which postmodernists are often accused. But whatever term we use, the notion of difference, as presented by Jacques Derrida, contains the idea that we should link dissimilarity with the need to defer meaning. For Derrida, the term 'différence' is a fusion of two senses of the French word 'différer' – to be different and to defer (Abrams, 1999: 57). The significance of a particular phenomenon can never come to rest in an actual 'presence' – by which is meant a language-independent reality. This is a complicated way of saying that we can never understand and empathise with a person's particular attributes, since all meanings are subject to infinite regress. Every phenomenon is different from every other and it is impossible to 'decide' what anything 'really' means. It is true that differences are infinite – try counting a person's differences, the colour of their eyes, their skin, their health, their religion, etc. – and you will soon find that you could go forever. But each of these differences can only be identified, because you yourself are a fellow human and, therefore, have something in common.

The idea that being different makes it impossible to have things in common reflects a sceptical view of the world so that no one can understand anyone else (or even themselves). This kind of scepticism is actually very old, and arises because reality or truth is seen as something that is static and unchanging. Once you discover that the world changes, and that what is here is gone tomorrow, you then deny that reality exists at all. All meanings are deemed arbitrary and purely relative to the language we use. Because meaning cannot be an unchanging absolute truth, it is then argued that it cannot be established at all, but must be 'deferred'. This, of course, makes it impossible to come to a position in which we show respect for diversity and insist that identities are multiple both between and within people. To respect diversity is to link it to something that we all share. If difference is interpreted in a way that excludes what we have in common – 'sameness' – then its real significance cannot be established.

But isn't this a rather airy-fairy argument that has no practical importance? Its importance arises from the assumption that we cannot, according to Derrida, distinguish between identities that have validity and those that do not. It is certainly true that differences can be used to discriminate and dominate, and post-structuralists are right to argue that one identity should not be privileged or, as we have said above, treated as dominant. Women, for example, are clearly different from men. But what does this undeniable difference mean? Does it mean that men are entitled to dominate women, and regard themselves as superior? Feminists have been understandably preoccupied with difference because they seek to argue that there is no justification for using differences between men and women as the basis for discrimination and exclusion. Women may be different from men, but in general they are no better and no worse. It does not follow, however, that the differences are all unreal, and that they are arbitrary social 'constructs'. As we argue in 'Ideas and Perspectives' see p. 425, the difference between men and women is *both* constructed socially and naturally based, and it would be wrong to argue that differences would have to be erased before domination ceases.

Post-structuralists sometimes reject what they call 'meta-narratives'. They see these as stories which want to be more than mere stories on the grounds that, in the words of Norris, they claim 'to have achieved an omniscient standpoint beyond and above all other stories that people have told so far' (cited by Hughes, 2002: 65). We all know of 'tall' stories, but these are things people say about themselves that are not true. In fact, all stories are a mixture of truth and falsehood because people are not gods. They are part of history and therefore, however authoritative people sound, future generations will always reveal parts of their story to be inadequate. This is a problem whether the story is about one group of people in particular or about the world as a whole. Why should we assume that 'grand narratives' are absolutely true (in a static and timeless sense) and then reject them? We should never have made this assumption in the first place. An evangelical Christian might, for example, regard the Bible as the source of timeless truth, but this is a fanciful assumption. We do not need to reject it with the same firmness that it is advanced, otherwise we simply turn the assumption inside out. To go beyond the assumption rather than simply invert it we need to see that, like all assumptions, it is a mixture of truth and falsehood.

To argue that differences have no meaning implies that there is no wider realm of reality by which we can distinguish between differences that are (relatively) 'true' and differences which are (relatively) 'false'. It is true that Indian people have darker skins than white Europeans but it is not true that one group is more intelligent than the other. If we make no distinction between beliefs and reality or concepts and objects, then how can we regard some differences as attributes to be

Ideas and Perspectives:

Sex and Gender

A good example of the problem of some post-structuralist treatments of difference is the question of sex and gender. Feminist theory has traditionally distinguished between the two by saying that whereas gender is historical and social, sex is natural and biological. The concern is to challenge the way in which natural biological differences between women and men have been linked to questions of power and domination so that it is argued by defenders of male domination that the biological differences between men and women justify discrimination and exclusion.

Of course, biological questions can be complicated by the fact that identities may overlap so that there are genuinely ambiguous individuals who are both men and women, or who wish to change from one sex to another. But broadly speaking we can argue that there should be gender equality and that biological differences, while 'relevant', have no causative significance in explaining why men may be deemed more powerful than women (Connell, 1987: 82–3; 139–40). The latter is a question of gender rather than sex. It is true that there is a linkage between sex and gender. In sexist societies, gender is reduced to sex so that biological difference is seen as a cause of discrimination, and women and men have different 'memories' based on this treatment. But even in a society where there was gender equality, one could still argue that biological differences would have social implications (Hoffman, 2001: 39). The fact that women give birth to children and are prone, for example, to breast cancer, will necessarily mean that different social patterns of behaviour are relevant to their well-being.

But while it is true that gender and sex are linked, it does not follow that the body is simply created through discourse and has a meaning that, in Shildrick's words, lies 'not in biological fact, but is constructed in and by representation' (Shildrick, 1997: 179). Clearly where sex is part of social activity it is gendered and its meaning reflects power relationships and cultural mores. But, as with hunger, sexuality is not wholly divorced from nature, and therefore there is a distinction between sex and gender which arises from the fact that one is a social construct and the other is not. There is certainly a link between sex and gender, but there is also a difference.

Biography   Jacques Derrida (1930–2004)

Born in Algiers of 'assimilated' Sephardic-Jewish parents. He was expelled from school because of growing anti-Semitism. In 1948 he enrolled at the Lycée Gauthier in Algiers to study philosophy, being strongly influenced by Sartre, Kierkegaard and Heidegger.

In 1949–50 he went to France, writing a Master's thesis on the philosophy of Husserl. In June 1956 he married, and became increasingly aware of the difficulties inherent in the encounter between philosophy and literature. In 1957–9 he taught for two years in a school for soldiers' children in Koléa near Algiers as his military service, and took up a teaching post in Paris.

In 1962 he wrote a translation of, and introduction to Edmund Husserl's *The Origin of Geometry*, and 1965 saw him teaching the History of Philosophy at the Ecole Normale Supérieure. He began his association with the journal *Tel Quel*, announcing the arrival of a new critical movement that questioned the claims of positivist literary theory and was influenced by semiology, Marxism, psychoanalysis and the structuralist 'sciences of man'.

In 1967 he published *Speech and Phenomena* (on Husserl), *Of Grammatology* and *Writing and Difference*, and a year later welcomed the student rising in Paris. In 1972 *Positions*, *Dissemination* and *Margins of Philosophy* was published. He divided his time between teaching in Paris and various US universities, including regular visiting appointments at Johns Hopkins and Yale. In 1973 *Speech and Phenomena* was published in English translation. In 1974 *Glas* appeared, Derrida's most 'literary' work to date, in the shape of an intertextual commentary on Hegel, Genet and the convergence of literature and philosophy. In 1975 he helped found GREPH (Groupe de Recherches sur l'Enseignment Philosophique), set up to examine institutional features of philosophy teaching and to challenge French government proposals to eliminate philosophy from the final-year lycée course.

In 1976 *Of Grammatology* was translated by Gayatri Spivak, with an important introduction. In 1980 *La Carte postale de Socrate à Freud et au-delà* appeared. In 1981 Derrida was arrested and imprisoned in Prague, where he had been running 'clandestine seminars', only to be released as a result of French government intervention. In 1982 he was named A.D. White Professor at Large at Cornell University. *Margins of Philosophy* was translated by Alan Bass, and Derrida appeared in the film *Ghost Dance*.

In 1983 Derrida was invited to play a coordinating role in the International College of Philosophy, a Paris-based communal venture intended to open up philosophy to non-academics, and in 1987 he took up an appointment as regular Visiting Professor at the University of California, Irvine. He published *The Truth in Painting*, and the English translation of *Glas* by John P. Leavey and Richard Rand appeared, together with a companion volume of textual exegesis and commentary.

In 1988 he was awarded the Nietzsche Prize, and his work began to attract massive attention. In 1992 he was awarded an honorary degree at Cambridge University despite bitter opposition. In 1994 he wrote about Freud and Foucault and published his *Spectres of Marx*.

celebrated and some alleged differences as attributes to be challenged? Post-structuralists sometimes reject the very distinction between a theory of knowledge (epistemology) and a theory of being (ontology), which means that it becomes impossible to distinguish genuine differences from false ones.

The truth is relative – different people see the world differently – but it is also absolute – there is a world of reality that enables us to prefer one concept to another. The word 'omniscient' (all knowing) in Norris's argument – that those who put forward meta-narratives subscribe to an omniscient standpoint – is all revealing, since it assumes that if something is not timelessly and purely true then it

Exercise

Three people identify themselves to you. The first is a nationalist who is staunchly opposed to the European Union and what he calls 'rule from Brussels'. The second is a feminist who describes herself as a democrat, black, Norwegian and of Asian origin. The third is a gay man who regards gayness as his main identity since it determines how people treat him, regardless of the fact that he is a man, likes football and lives in Bonn.

Clearly each of these persons has a distinct identity and differs from the others.

- Who has a dominant identity and who has an emancipatory identity?

- Who has a genuine identity and who has a false identity?

cannot be true at all. But, as Sandra Harding (a feminist philosopher) has argued, why should we take the view that, in giving up the idea that there is one static and divinely inspired truth, we must at the same time give up 'trying to tell less false stories'? We can aim to produce less partial and perverse representations about the world 'without having to assert the absolute, complete, universal or eternal advocacy of these representations' (Harding, 1990: 100). But if we reject the whole idea of 'representation' (i.e. that ideas 'represent' or reflect a world external to them), then it becomes impossible to use the term 'difference' critically.

Thus, to return to our example of women and men. They are different, but the differences do not justify discrimination, and this, as far as we can tell, is true. But in saying this, we could hardly deny that deeper insights lie ahead which will certainly alter the way in which this truth is presented. This is why we can say that such an assertion is *both* absolutely *and* relatively true. If it were simply absolutely true, then it would be a statement placed outside of human history. If it were just relatively true, then it would be confined in its scope to the moment we uttered it. By seeing the truth as absolute *and* relative, we are embracing a logic of 'both/and' rather than of 'either/or'.

Some identities are emancipatory, for instance that of a gay person striving for justice and recognition in a homophobic society. But some are not. Think, for example, of a gay person seeking medical treatment because they see their sexual differences as 'unnatural' and deviant. If we take the view that the politics of emancipation is itself to be rejected, then how can a discussion of identity and difference be linked to self-development and the self-government of all individuals? Difference ceases to be something we can evaluate (and if it is a real difference, something we can value), and becomes instead a source merely of mystification.

Feminist Theory and Difference

Clearly, the first feminists saw difference as something negative, because it was used to justify discrimination. When Locke or Rousseau spoke of female traits they spoke of differences that prevented women from being heads of households or taking part in politics. The liberal '**public/private**' divide was premised on the assumption that women's differences from men made them domestic creatures, suited to the private sphere but not to the public one. Wollstonecraft and J.S. Mill took the universal claims of liberalism which traditionally had applied only to men and argued that women were individuals too – they were just as rational and logical as men – and were therefore entitled to citizenship alongside men.

This notion is held by the Equal Opportunities Commission (EOC), an organisation set up in Britain to monitor and encourage the pursuit of equal opportunities. As far as women are concerned, the EOC seeks a society that 'enables women and men to fulfil their potential, and have their contributions to work and home life equally valued and respected, free from assumptions based on their sex' (Hughes, 2002: 41). In other words, the differences between men and women tend to be disregarded: the emphasis is upon what they have in common. They are equal, *not* different.

Cultural and radical feminists, influential during what may be called second-wave feminism (a feminism that took root in the late 1960s), reversed the earlier assumptions, valuing difference over equality. As Bohan has put it, 'the customary valuation of difference is turned on its head: women's ways of doing are revered, rather than demeaned' (Hughes, 2002: 47). Mothering was seen as the embodiment of virtue, and what was called maternal thinking should, it was argued, be extended to all spheres of public life. This position has led to separatism – not only the physical separation of women and men – but the cultural and intellectual separation as well. The very notion of 'objectivity' is identified as a male value, as is rationality. Adrienne Rich summed up the position succinctly: 'objectivity is male subjectivity'. As Barrett comments, 'men have one reality, women have another, and women's culture can be developed as a separate activity' (1987: 31). Experience is seen as something that differentiates men from women while uniting women against men.

Third-wave feminism – which is a feminism influenced by postmodernism – argues for a notion of difference that extends from differences between women and men to differences among women themselves. Feminism, it is argued, must break from the liberal view that if people are the same then they cannot be different, and if they are different, they cannot be the same. On this analysis, the second-wavers merely invert the first-wavers. Instead of arguing that women should be equal to men, they reject equality on the grounds that women are different from men. The feminists who have drawn critically upon postmodernism argue that one should cease to treat equality and difference as 'binary [i.e. exclusive] opposites'. To argue, as Brown does, that we should oppose the notion of gender equality on the grounds that 'equality presupposes sameness or equivalence' (cited in Hoffman, 2001: 41) is to accept uncritically the liberal view that we need to choose between equality and difference, whereas it could be argued that one without the other turns into its polarised opposite.

If we say that because white people are different from black people (as indeed they are, in appearance at least) they are unequal, and to be equal they must be the same, then arguably we violate both equality and difference. Equality is seen as something that suppresses difference – an unattainable goal since every individual is unique – and difference becomes something not to celebrate, but a justification for discrimination, and discrimination mystifies and misrepresents genuine differences. So that unless we link equality with difference we ride

How to read:

Hughes's *Key Concepts in Feminist Theory and Research*

It is difficult to find a work that deals with the question of difference in a readable fashion, but this has useful and relevant chapters. Skim read the introduction and Chapter 1 but read carefully Chapter 2 on equality and particularly Chapter 3 on difference, which contains a very helpful assessment of post-structuralism and postmodernism, and extends the question of difference into post-colonial theory. Chapter 4 on Choice and Chapter 5 on Care can be skim read. Chapter 6 on Time, though fascinating if one is looking at recent feminism, can be left out here, while Chapter 7 on Experience deserves a close read. Chapter 8 sums up the argument as a whole and should be skim read.

roughshod over both. Hartsock (1998: 60) distinguishes between difference as equality and difference as domination. We would go further and argue that when you dominate another you ignore his real differences and exploit a stereotypical and propagandist version of his identity. This is not a real difference but an imaginary one. In other words, unless difference is linked to equality it ceases to be a meaningful category.

Does this mean that women have nothing in common with each other, and therefore feminism itself is concerned with a category – 'women' – that does not exist? It is certainly true that women differ from one another: some are rich and some are poor; some are white and some are black; they have different sexual and linguistic identities etc. But they also have something in common. They are all subjugated by patriarchally minded men (and women); they are all subject to stereotypes, they all have biological differences that have social implications. This is why we argue, in the discussion on sex and gender, that the idea that differences disappear in an egalitarian society is wrong, because it assumes that equality excludes difference. In fact, each presupposes the other. To suggest that differences must take the form of 'oppressive gender hierarchies' (Hoffman, 2001: 41) is a liberal view that can take either a conservative patriarchal form (men are different from women – therefore they are justified in oppressing them), or a radical feminist form (women are different from men – therefore they should keep themselves apart). Why not argue that men and women are both the same and different? They are all human beings, entitled therefore to human rights and, as with all human beings, each is different from the other.

A feminism that chooses between equality *and* difference ends up unwittingly with a position of domination or separatism. Neither really advances the cause of women's emancipation.

Liberalism and Difference

Liberalism is historically significant because it is based upon what one of us calls elsewhere 'subversive abstractions' (Hoffman, 1988: 150). Liberalism argues that all individuals are free and equal, and it rests its case on these propositions as universal principles. This is subversive because it rejects medieval and authoritarian notions of a natural hierarchy that identifies people as inherently unequal with some explicitly entitled to dominate others. Liberalism ostensibly rejects 'differences' on the grounds that each of us is an individual who is the 'same' as the other.

The problem is of course that while these principles are undeniably subversive they are also *abstract* and, because they are abstract, repressive hierarchies come slithering in through the back door. The abstraction arises because people are seen as property – each individual has property over himself. Why is this abstract?

- It is abstract because it ignores the fact that people only become aware of themselves as individuals *in relation to others*. This means that property is both individual and social – the control that people have over their own bodies and their own objects arises because others cooperate.

- It is abstract because it is one-sided, and therefore ignores all the factors that make people what they are. It is true that individual drive and initiative are among the factors that mould us, but they are not the sole factors. Aspects of our social and natural environment also play their part.

- It is abstract because liberalism assumes that the relations between human and nature (i.e. *human nature*) take the form of an exchange between individuals through the market. This exchange takes away the particular facts of each person's context (whether they are rich or poor; men or women, etc.), and makes it appear that the parties to the exchange are the 'same'.

Why does abstraction allow repressive hierarchies to come slithering through the back door? Treating people as property may mean that they can actually be owned. Hence early liberals agreed with slavery, and Locke constructs an elaborate and thoroughly unconvincing argument to suggest that slaves are individuals who are captives in war – and instead of killing them their owners generously agree to allow them to live (1924: 127–8). Until the twentieth century liberals regarded individuals as men rather than women, since individuals were rational property owners, and women were seen as neither. Although property was supposedly produced by labour, in practice liberals allowed some to work for others. Whole countries could be owned as the property of those who made 'profitable' use of them, so that liberals until relatively recently supported colonialism and imperialism.

What abstraction does is to drive sameness and difference apart. Abstraction suppresses difference so that, because everyone is an 'individual', they are deemed to be all the same. In practice, of course, they are not, and therefore liberalism argues that inequalities are justified because the wealthy are energetic; men are rational; colonialists are 'civilised' etc. Liberalism either suppresses difference in the name of sameness (those who are not 'like us' must be excluded), or it suppresses sameness in the name of difference (because we are different, we are superior and have nothing in common with 'others'). One thing that liberalism cannot do is to celebrate difference, since this would imply that difference is something that is compatible with and in fact indispensable for sameness.

Robert Nozick, an extreme liberal, states in his *Anarchy, State, and Utopia*:

People generally judge themselves by how they fall along the most important dimensions in which they differ from others. People do not gain self-esteem from their common human capacities – self-esteem is based on differentiating characteristics: that's why it's self-esteem (cited by Ramsay, 1997: 94)

Democracy and the State

The analysis of identity and difference has important implications for our view of democracy and the state. If people are to govern their lives, then the differences they have need to be respected, so that they feel comfortable with their identity and able to participate in government.

Ch 2: Freedom, pp. 38–58

But what about differences that lead to intolerance and subjugation? Supposing it was argued that only Christians or Muslims could stand for office and vote, form political parties and be regarded as legitimate political actors, what would these differences mean for democracy? A useful guide here is Mill's harm principle. Differences that harm another's interest cannot be regarded as legitimate, and need to be subject to social and legal sanctions. It cannot be accepted that because someone is of a different gender, sexual orientation, religion, etc. that they cannot take part in the political process. We have argued above that to treat difference as justification for discrimination is to distort the concept. Recognising difference as part of a person's identity must imply that such difference is compatible with the differences of others.

What happens if a person's apparent difference leads them to harm themselves? It depends, it could be argued, as to whether this harm is reversible or not. A person may distinguish herself from another by drinking a substantial amount of alcohol on one particular day, and once she recovers from her hangover she suffers no long-term effects. But what happens if this is part of an addiction to drink that undermines a person's health, so that as a result of repeated drinking such a person cannot take part in political activity? This is a 'difference' that, in our view, is problematic, since it undermines self-development in a way that is potentially irreversible. While it may not be appropriate to employ legal sanctions against people who self-harm in such a way, social pressures are certainly justified since this kind of 'difference' hinders democratic activity. It is a pathology and not really a difference (as we have defined it), and whether it is harm irreversibly inflicted upon others or upon oneself it is problematic for democracy and requires social intervention to arrest it.

Advancing democracy makes it necessary that we distinguish authentic differences from pseudo-differences. Pseudo-differences are those used to justify discrimination and exclusion: we need to act against the latter, preferably through social sanctions, but through the use of physical force if all else fails. It could be argued that we 'discriminate' against children and unqualified people by imposing upon them various restrictions because they are 'different': who would like to be operated upon by someone who has not been properly trained as a surgeon? These are terminological points. In our view, acts to prevent harm do not count as 'discrimination' and therefore we are identifying relevant and thus genuine 'differences'. To refuse to allow a suitably qualified person to be a surgeon would be to exploit a 'pseudo-difference'. A democratic attitude towards difference must concern itself as to whether differences promote self-development or (we would call them pseudo-differences) prevent it.

The state is more contentious because whereas the notion of democracy as self-government is widely accepted (although its implications are not), the state is often seen as unproblematic in character. Yet an institution claiming a monopoly of legitimate force must threaten difference. The use of force to address conflicts of interest means that a person's identity is necessarily disregarded, and they become a thing. This may be the only way to tackle what we have called 'pseudo-differences', that is, the assertion of attributes that inflict harm. A person who feels that as a patriot they can attack others, throw bricks through their windows, etc. may need to be restrained through counter-force. Or a person who is different from others, let us say because he is gay, cannot be expected to suffer attacks on his person or his livelihood, and force may have to be employed against those who perpetrate the outrage. The point about force, whether it can be justified or not, is that it suppresses difference and its use by the state exhibits the same problem. Whether it is an attack on defenceless people by an authoritarian state, or a forceful seizure of criminals by a liberal state, the state necessarily crushes difference, since it is impossible to consider a person's attributes comprehensively when using force against them. What we mean by this is the following. Supposing force is used against a man who rapes a woman. The man might be a good gardener, able to repair cars, and very good with computers. None of these attributes are relevant because the man is deemed a rapist, and he must be locked up against his will. The other aspects of his personality are ignored. Such an abstract focus is inevitable when force is used.

Targeting an individual or group through the state makes it impossible to regard their differences positively, as attributes to be celebrated, and this is why states have to draw what postmodernists call 'binary distinctions' – distinctions in which someone wins and someone loses, 'differences' that are perceived in repressively hierarchical terms. The state is an institution that either obliterates or demonises differences. It treats its supporters as the 'same' and its enemies as different, and thus it disrupts the respect for difference that is crucial if people are to govern their own lives. This is why we need to distinguish between state and government. Government seeks to help people help themselves and, therefore, to use their distinct characteristics in a way that contributes towards development.

De Tocqueville on colonialism as an extinguisher of difference:

It is obvious that there are three naturally distinct, one might almost say hostile races. Education, law, origin, and external features too have raised almost insurmountable barriers between them; chance has brought them together on the same soil, but they have mixed without combining, and each follows a separate destiny.

Ch 1: The State, pp. 14–37

Among these widely different people, the first that attracts attention, and the first in enlightenment, power and happiness is the white man, the European, man par excellence; below him come the Negro and the Indian.

These two unlucky races have neither birth, physique, language in common; only their misfortunes are alike. Both occupy an equally inferior position in the land where they dwell; both suffer the effects of tyranny, and, though their afflictions are different, they have the same people to blame for them.

Seeing what happens in the world, might one not say that the European is to men of other races, what man is to the animals? He makes them serve his convenience, and when he cannot bend them to his will he destroys them . . . It is impossible to destroy men with more respect to the laws of humanity.

Democracy in America 1835/1966: 391; 421

Summary

It is important to clearly define difference, so that we can see that people differentiate themselves in terms of their distinct identity or identities. The problem with 'privileging' a particular identity is that it becomes dominant. The identities of others, or other identities within an individual, are downgraded and ignored, so that it is tempting to suppress these others.

The postmodern or post-structuralist view of 'difference' sometimes sees difference as something that cannot be resolved but must be endlessly 'deferred'. This is based upon a dualistic view of truth that is insupportable.

Feminism initially regarded difference as negative because it was identified with justification for discrimination. Second-wave feminists tended to invert this negativity so that female difference was seen as positive, separating men from women. Recent theorising has, however, sought to emphasise the importance of both sameness and difference. Liberalism is unable to celebrate diversity because its tendency to abstraction treats people as property. Either all are the same or all are different.

The state as an institution that tackles conflicts of interest through force divides people and, therefore, demonises difference and exalts sameness. It is unable to respect identity and thus acts in tension with democracy.

Questions

1. Does a person's identity revolve around one dominant feature?
2. Do you find the concept of 'différence' helpful?
3. Do you agree with the argument that liberalism is unable to handle the concept of difference?
4. What is difference?
5. Does the state facilitate the expression of difference among its inhabitants?

References

Abrams, M. (1999) *A Glossary of Literary Terms* New York and London: Harcourt Brace.

Alibhai-Brown, Y. (2000) *Who Do We Think We Are?* London: Allen Lane.

Barrett, M. (1987) 'The Concept of "Difference"' *Feminist Review*, 26, 29–41.

Connell, R. (1987) *Gender and Power* Cambridge: Polity Press.

Gould, C. (1996) 'Diversity and Democracy: Representing Differences' in S. Benhabib (ed.), *Democracy and Difference* Princeton, NJ: Princeton University Press, 171–86.

Greer, G. (1999) *The Whole Woman* London: Doubleday.

Harding, S. (1990) 'Feminism, Science and Anti-enlightenment Critiques' in L. Nicholson (ed.), *Feminism/Postmodernism* New York and London: Routledge, 83–106.

Hartsock, N. (1998) *The Feminist Standpoint Revisited and Other Essays* Oxford: Westview Press.

Hoffman, J. (1988) *State, Power and Democracy* Brighton: Wheatsheaf Books.

Hoffman, J. (2001) *Gender and Sovereignty* Basingstoke: Palgrave.

Hughes, C. (2002) *Key Concepts in Feminist Theory and Research* London: Sage.

Locke, J. (1924) *Two Treatises on Government* London: Dent.

Ramsay, M. (1997) *What's Wrong with Liberalism?* London and Washington: Leicester University Press.

Shildrick, M. (1997) *Leaky Bodies and Boundaries* London and New York: Routledge.

Tocqueville, de, A. (1966) *Democracy in America* London: Fontana.

Further Reading

- Carol Gould's 'Diversity and Democracy: Representing Differences' (referenced above) is a very stimulating treatment of the subject, and particularly valuable for its critique of the German philosopher Habermas.

- Barrett's 'The Concept of "Difference"' (referenced above) is a very useful survey of feminist treatments of this question.

- Abrams's *A Glossary of Literary Terms* (referenced above) is a useful book to consult for those who find reading Derrida in the original too daunting.

- Hughes's *Key Concepts in Feminist Theory and Research* (referenced above), discussed in this chapter, has a very valuable chapter on the question of difference.

- Paul du Gay has (along with several others) edited *Identity: a Reader* London: Sage, 2000, which contains valuable excerpts.

Weblinks

There is a very interesting paper by Barker on Race and Identity and Difference at:
http://www.psa.ac.uk/cps/1994/bark.pdf

For material on post-structuralism and difference, see:
http://homepages.gold.ac.uk/psrpsg/reviews/widder.html

Chapter 18

Human Rights

Introduction

A human right is an entitlement to treatment that a person enjoys simply by virtue of being a human being. Human rights are universal, meaning that possession of such rights is not contingent on belonging to a particular state or culture. Although the concept can be traced back to the eighteenth-century Enlightenment – the 'rights of man' – it is only in the twentieth century that a human right became a major concept in political discourse. The widespread ratification by states of the Universal Declaration of Human Rights, which was created in 1948, three years after the end of World War II, has changed world politics; although individuals are frequently denied their human rights, even by states purporting to respect them, the fact of the existence of human rights has shifted international politics from being based simply on nation-states' interest to one based on the recognition that individuals have claims against their own state. But human rights are open to the criticism that they are the product of a particular time and place – post-eighteenth-century Europe, or the West – and their 'imposition' is a form of imperialism. They can also be criticised for elevating individualism above collectivism, and 'negative' rights (to be left alone) above 'positive' rights (to a particular level of resources).

Chapter Map

In this chapter we will:

- Consider the modern discourse of human rights by reference to the Nuremberg trials of Nazi war criminals.

- Study human rights documents, and their philosophical implications.

- Analyse the concept of a right.

- Assess cultural relativist objections to human rights.

- Consider whether human rights can be extended to cover groups, and provide welfare.

Rough Justice?

Saudi Arabia has long been the target of criticism by human rights organisations such as Amnesty International. The country beheads murderers, rapists and drug smugglers. Other punishments include amputation of the right hand for theft, and flogging for selling alcohol. Saudi Arabia has one of the highest rates of execution in the world; beheadings are carried out in public. The condemned are not given notice that the execution will take place and the victim's family are often only informed after the event. Men, women and children are flogged in prisons and in public squares around the country, and there is no upper limit on the number of lashes judges can order.

The Saudi justice system is condemned not just for the perceived brutality of the sentences but also for the inequity of the legal procedures that result in those sentences. Criminal cases are heard by the General Sharia (Islamic Court), and the last stage of judicial review is by the 11-member Supreme Judicial Council. In cases of capital punishment the sentence must be approved by the Royal courts, which interpret the shariah (Islamic law). Many laws are vaguely worded. Prisoners allege that confessions were forced out of them by torture, and that they knew nothing of their case, and could not attend the trials, which are held in secret. Hearings last between five minutes and two hours. Defendants have no right to a lawyer, cannot call witnesses and are denied access to evidence. Wealthy Saudis and Westerners can bribe their way out of custody.

- If Saudi justice was administered fairly – that is, the accused had a lawyer, access to evidence, charges were clearly stated and an appeal was possible – would the punishments themselves be justified?

- Does the fact that, according to media reports, the majority of Saudis support the system of justice on grounds that it deters crime justify it?

- Should the fact that Saudi Arabia signed the United Nations Convention on Torture in 1997 make any difference to whether or not its justice system is valid?

- Does the fact that Saudi law is – it is claimed – based on Islamic law justify its justice system?

Human Rights after Nuremberg

A 'human right' can be defined as an entitlement to treatment a person has simply by virtue of being 'human', and as such human rights must be applicable irrespective of time and place. If we were to say that a person's rights are conditional on her being a citizen of a particular state, or belonging to a particular culture, then the rights would not rest simply on the fact of being a human being, and they would not be universal. This raises a difficulty for human rights discourse. The language of human rights is a modern phenomenon, traceable to the eighteenth-century Enlightenment, but only embodied in legal documents in the twentieth century. This suggests that human rights are culturally specific, that is, the product of a particular time (modern period) and a particular place (Western Europe). For critics of human rights the problem of cultural relativism is thought to be fatal – the alleged universalism of human rights simply masks a form of cultural imperialism.

There is no doubt that while human rights are claimed to be universal the widespread use of the concept is a relatively recent phenomenon. It is only with the formulation and signing of the Universal Declaration of Human Rights (hereafter referred to as the Declaration) (1948) that respect for human rights has become a significant consideration in domestic and international politics (that does not mean that human rights are, in fact, respected). And alongside the philosophical discourse and political rhetoric there has also developed a body of international human rights law and international legal institutions, such as the International Criminal Court (ICC) in The Hague (Netherlands). So there is a history to human rights. In the course of this chapter we will discuss whether the historicity of human rights undermines the claim made for their universality.

The Declaration was 'adopted and proclaimed' by the General Assembly of the newly formed United Nations on 10 December 1948. It was developed against the background of the war crimes trials known as the Nuremberg trials, which followed the defeat of Germany in May 1945. There were two sets of trials: those of the 'major war criminals', before the International Military Tribunal (1945–6), and those of the 'lesser war criminals' before the US Nuremberg Military Tribunals (1946–9). Among the 'lesser' criminals were medical researchers who had carried out barbaric experiments during the Nazi years (the so-called 'doctors' trial' took place in 1946–7). The Nuremberg process was criticised by some commentators as a series of show trials based on 'victor's justice'; after all, among the indictments were acts that had undoubtedly been carried out by the victorious Allies, such as the blanket bombing of cities. However, Nuremberg is significant for the study of human rights, in part because of its flaws, and, in part, because it introduced novel concepts. The legally significant features of the Nuremberg process were as follows:

• The indictment, or charges made against the defendants, were created *ex post facto* and were not related to the laws of Germany. The indictment contained four counts (types of charge): (a) conspiracy to wage an aggressive war; (b) planning, preparation and waging of an aggressive war; (c) war crimes, that included, for example, the mistreatment of prisoners of war; (d) crimes against humanity, which included the Holocaust.

- The compulsion defence – 'I was only obeying orders' – was removed.
- The *tu quoque* defence was removed – *ad hominem tu quoque* means 'at the person, you too' and effectively amounts to the defendant saying 'you committed the same crimes, so you have no authority to judge me'.
- The indictment made reference to violations of 'international conventions', but there is no citation of those conventions, with the implication that it was a loose term meaning the 'general standards of criminal law in civilised societies'.

Although the motivation among the leadership of the Allied powers to create the Nuremburg process was largely political, there was a moral consciousness at work, a consciousness that became stronger in later decades. Consequently, Nuremberg posed a problem: on the one hand there was a sense of what can be termed the 'objective wrongness' of what the Nazi regime had done that manifested itself as revulsion at the acts of those on trial. On the other hand, the trials seemed to depend on the creation of *post hoc*, or retroactive, laws. Retroactive laws violate the principle that there can be no crime without an antecedent law: if you do something that is legal at the time of doing it, then you should not be later prosecuted for that act. If retroactive laws are created then power is arbitrary. Other 'troubling' aspects of Nuremberg included the rejection of both the *tu quoque* and compulsion defences (we return to these problems later in the chapter). There has been considerable debate among legal and political theorists about the retroactivity problem; some theorists argue that German law was suspended at a point during the 1930s, and therefore the laws of Weimar Germany (1918–33) should form part of the basis of the indictment. Other theorists appeal to conventions, such as the prohibition on murder, which all right-thinking human beings, and all properly functioning legal systems, recognise as valid.

The point about Nuremberg is that German law of the Nazi period could not form the basis of the judgment, and so other laws or conventions, not rooted in a particular legal system, had to be used. And Nuremberg is not simply an interesting historical problem, because it has relevance for contemporary debates about human rights: if there are human rights as defined at the beginning of this section, then they are universal, and the universality extends across national boundaries and across times. The Nuremberg problem will not disappear when the last alleged Nazi war criminal has died, for it is fundamentally a philosophical problem: how can there be human rights if there are no laws embodying those rights? But if human rights only exist where there are laws stating those rights, then how can they be universal? The post-Nuremberg codification of human rights in the Declaration and the Genocide Convention (1948) helps to solve a legal problem, but not the political-philosophical one. To explain, the Declaration was (eventually) signed by the governments of most states, and through the force of treaty law human rights have been given legal validity. Had there been such a Declaration in the 1920s to which Germany had signed up, and that was not rescinded by the Hitler regime, then there would have been a clearer legal basis for Nuremberg (there was such a basis for the third count of war crimes: the Geneva Conventions of 1864, 1906 and 1929). However, this does not solve the philosophical problem: if a nation refuses to sign up to any human rights conventions does that mean it is not obliged to respect human rights?

Exercise

From what you know of the history of Hitler's regime and World War II consider the following questions:

• What was the underlying motivation for the Nuremburg trials?

• Should we be concerned that many of those on trial had not broken the laws of Nazi Germany (even if they had committed acts of extreme inhumanity)?

• Did it matter to the legitimacy of the trials that with regard to some of the charges the Allies themselves could have been deemed guilty?

This question – and the distinction between legal and philosophical problems – reveals an ambiguity at the heart of human rights discourse. When we use the term 'human rights' are we referring to a set of legal rights, or to moral rights, or, perhaps, to some form of political rhetoric that is based on neither legal nor moral grounds? If human rights equate to certain legal rights enjoyed by individuals through international law, then disputes about human rights will take place in a legal framework, by reference to legal documents and judgments. If, however, human rights are moral rights, then disputes are settled by reference to moral concepts and moral arguments. Put simply, as legal rights human rights are individual entitlements backed up by the force of law; as moral rights, they are individual entitlements supported by the force of argument. As tools of international politics, human rights are intended to secure certain outcomes: a state widely recognised as violating human rights may find itself shunned by other states and, consequently, its interests damaged. Many advocates of human rights rely on a mixture of treaty law and 'shame' to advance their cause. However, the political uses of human rights can generate cynicism. One of the justifications given for the bombing of Serbia in 1999 was that it was an 'exceptional measure to prevent an overwhelming humanitarian catastrophe', namely the mass deportation and killing of Kosovars. Yet the same description could be applied to the situation since 1995 in the province of Chechnya, where Russia has suppressed a breakaway movement, and engaged in a serious violation of human rights. The reasons for action in Kosovo and inaction in Chechnya is, in small part, logistical, but mainly the recognition of realpolitik: Russia has nuclear weapons.

The best approach for further study of the morality, legality, and politics of human rights is a consideration of human rights documents, and in the next section we focus on two: the Declaration, and the European Convention on Human Rights.

Human Rights Conventions

Literature on human rights tends to fall into two groups, with limited cross-over between them: human rights law and philosophical discussions of human rights. While respecting the difference between these approaches it is useful for students of political theory to establish the connections between them, because legality and morality are both important in debates about the relationship between the state and citizen. To this end we will look at two human rights documents: the Universal Declaration of Human Rights (Declaration), and the European Convention on Human Rights (Convention). There are important differences between these two documents, and the aim of our study is to draw out the philosophical and political implications of each document.

Universal Declaration of Human Rights (1948)

The Declaration consists of a Preamble and 30 articles. The Preamble asserts that the 'inherent dignity and of the equal and inalienable rights of all members of the human family is the foundation of freedom, justice and peace in the world'. Without specifying the events it acknowledges the 'barbarous acts which have outraged the conscience of mankind', and asserts that human rights must be protected through law.

The 30 articles are reproduced in summary form below. We have grouped them together for purposes of discussion; they are not, in fact, grouped in this way in the Declaration.

Article(s)	
1–2	Human beings should be treated equally, irrespective of personal characteristics or citizenship.
3	Right to life, liberty and security of person.
4–5	Prohibition on slavery, and on torture.
6–11	Equality before the law: equal protection by the state; right to an effective remedy for violation of one's rights; prohibition on arbitrary arrest and detention; right to a fair trial; presumption of innocence until guilt is proven; prohibition on retroactive laws.
12	Prohibition on arbitrary interference in private life.
13–14	Freedom of movement, including emigration; right to asylum in another country.
15	Right to nationality; prohibition on deprivation of nationality.
16	Right to marry; prohibition on forced marriage.
17	Right to own property; prohibition on arbitrary seizure of property.
18–20	Freedom of thought, conscience and religion; freedom of opinion and expression; right to peaceful assembly; prohibition on compulsion to belong to an association.
21	Right to political participation; equal access to public service; 'the will of the people shall be the basis of the authority of the government'.
22–26	Right to social security; right to work, and the free choice of employment; equal pay for equal work; right to 'just and favourable remuneration'; right to join a trade union; right to rest and leisure; right to an 'adequate' standard of living; 'motherhood and childhood are entitled to special care and assistance'; equal protection of children; right to education; right of parents to determine the kind of education their children receive.
27	Right freely to participate in the cultural life of the community.
28	'Everyone is entitled to a social and international order in which the rights and freedoms set forth in this Declaration can be fully realized'.
29	Everyone has duties to his or her community; the exercise of the above rights can only be limited in order to meet the 'just requirements of morality, public order and the general welfare in a democratic society'.
30	Nothing in the Declaration should imply that any state, group or person can engage in actions destructive of any of the rights and freedoms set out in it.

Several important points can be drawn from this document:

1. Although reference is made to the importance of legal protection, the document provides for no legal mechanisms, such as courts, to enforce human rights. And the linguistic style of the document lacks the precision a good legal document should possess.

2. Many of the rights themselves can be grouped: (a) rights that essentially amount to being left alone; (b) rights to participate in the political structure of the country, and to enjoy the protection of its laws; (c) rights to associate with people of your own choosing; (d) social rights, such as employment protection and a minimum level of resources. The first three groups clearly reflect the ethos of a liberal democratic society, whereas the last was a concession to the realities of power politics in the post-war period, where the Soviet Union was keen to stake out a distinct moral position, one that stressed social goods. (We discuss rights to welfare in the final section of this chapter.)

3. The rights are limited by articles 29 and 30, which talk of the duties of individuals – the reference to the 'requirements of morality' leaves open the possibility that the rights could be interpreted in significantly different ways in different cultures. (We discuss the 'cultural interpretation' of human rights in Relativism versus Universalism.)

European Convention on Human Rights (1950)

The European Convention on Human Rights – officially the Convention for the Protection of Human Rights and Fundamental Freedoms – was adopted in 1950 by the Council of Europe, an international organisation that began with 10 member states and now has 46 (www.coe.int). The Preamble to the Convention makes explicit its relationship to the Declaration by stating as its aim the 'collective enforcement of certain rights stated in the Universal Declaration'. There are, however, several important features that distinguish the Convention from the Declaration. These differences flow from the fact that the Convention is intended as a legal document, whereas the Declaration is a general statement of aspiration:

1. Many of the articles of the Convention are double-headed, meaning that the first part sets out the rights, but the second states a limitation on the right. For example, Article 10 is concerned with freedom of expression, but this is then limited by various considerations, including 'national security', 'public safety', 'protection of health and morals' and the 'protection of reputation'.

2. Section I of the document sets out the rights and freedoms of individuals, but Section II – which is about half the document – is concerned with the powers of the European Court of Human Rights, which was established by the Convention. Part III – 'Miscellaneous Provisions' – deals with various issues relating to the obligations of the contracting states.

3. The Convention has been amended – through 'protocols' – many times since its creation; in most cases this has entailed strengthening, or extending, the rights contained in it. For example, Protocol 6 (1983) restricted the use of the death penalty to times of war or national emergency; Protocol 13 (2002) prohibits the

Exercise

Imagine you are acting (as a lawyer) on behalf of someone (the appellant) making a legal appeal against his or her national government to the European Court of Human Rights. Your task is to construct a case based on the European Convention. Choose one, or more, of the following cases:

- An Irish woman is appealing against the Irish state's ban on abortion.

- A British gay man is appealing against the British state's refusal to enact same-sex partnership laws.

- A French Muslim woman is appealing against the French state's law prohibiting the wearing of 'conspicuous religious dress'.

Once you have constructed a case reverse roles and act as the legal representative of the respective states: your task is to argue that the Convention should not be extended to change the laws of those states.

You may find the European Court of Human Rights' website useful: http://www.echr.coe.int/. Click on 'Basic Texts' for a copy of the Convention.

death penalty in all circumstances (not all Council members have ratified Protocols 6 and 13 see http://www.worldpolicy.org/globalrights/dp/maps-dp-echr.html).

4. Although there is, unsurprisingly, a strong overlap between the rights contained in both documents, the Convention omits the 'social rights' (Articles 22–26) of the Declaration. Given that the 10 founding members of the Council were all Western European, this is unsurprising ('Eastern' states joined only after the collapse of state socialism in 1989 – Russia, for example, joined in 1996).

Why the Declaration and the Convention are Significant

The Declaration and the Convention are important in what they reveal about the nature and justification of human rights, and in the rest of this chapter we will pursue these further:

1. Human rights privilege certain values over others: there can be no doubt that human rights are individualist, in the sense that the integrity of the individual – her body and mind – and the choices she makes, are the object of protection. Certainly Articles 22–26 of the Declaration stress the social conditions for action, and they raise important questions that we consider in the section on Group Rights and Welfare Rights, but the 'core' human rights are individualist. This raises a couple of questions: do human rights do justice to the full range of values present in liberal democratic societies? Even if they do, can human rights be applied in societies built around a significantly different set of values? These questions are addressed in the next two sections.

2. The differences between the two documents are interesting and important and raise the issue of what happens to the concept of a human right when we try to

apply it in a concrete legal-political situation: must a human right be a legal right? Even if a human right need not be a legal right might it not be that the only human right worth having is one that can be enforced in law? This raises the Nuremberg question: can we have rights that are not recognised in any legal document?

3. Rights will conflict – rights can conflict with one another, and they can conflict with certain duties. A system of rights must, therefore, be compossible, that is, the rights must be mutually possible. Furthermore, rights must be 'actionable', meaning that the fulfilment of the right cannot require impossible actions. To use a slightly silly example, if you have 100 people, and 50 oranges, then you cannot give each person a right to an orange, or, at least, a whole orange. The Convention strives for compossibility and actionability.

We have approached the concept of human rights by looking at actual documents rather than abstract philosophical arguments. However, to test the coherence and validity of human rights it is necessary to move to a more abstract level of discussion. In the following section we consider the concept of a right – that is, any right, not simply a human right – and consider its philosophical implications. Above all we are concerned with the implication that human rights are individualist, and cannot reflect the full range of values that are present even in a liberal democratic society (we return to this issue in the last section, when we consider (a) group, or cultural rights, and (b) welfare rights). In the section entitled Relativism versus Universalism we extend this objection by considering whether human rights can have validity in non-liberal democratic societies. This entails consideration of what is called the universalism-relativism debate: are there universal moral values, or are such values relative to a particular culture?

What are Rights?

What we want to establish in this section is what the concept of a right presupposes about the nature of the right-holder, and his relationship to other right-holders. In other words, what does a system of rights tell us about the nature of human beings, and their relationship to one another in society? The standard starting point for a discussion of the concept of a right is the scheme set out by legal theorist Wesley Hohfeld.

Categorising Rights: Hohfeld's Scheme

Hohfeld (1923) was not interested in human rights, but rather his aim was to categorise rights as they were used in a domestic legal system, and in particular in his own country, the United States, and other common law countries, such as England (1923). All rights, Hohfeld argued, are relationships: if Jane has a right to something, then there is something that Sam must do, *or refrain from doing*. So the basic idea of a right is an 'advantage' relative to another person, or group of people (that 'group' could be everybody else). Hohfeld argues that there are two kinds of relationship at work in the holding of a right: jural opposition and jural correlation.

Since it would unnecessarily complicate the discussion to talk about opposition, we will simplify Hohfeld's scheme and consider only correlation – that is, what other people must do if Jane's right is to be respected. Hohfeld sets out four relationships of correlation, which we can take to be four different types of right (claims, privileges, powers, and immunities):

RIGHT-HOLDER:	Claim	Privilege	Power	Immunity
OTHER PEOPLE:	Duty	No-claim	Liability	Disability

1. **Claim** If Jane possesses a claim (or claim-right) she is in a position legitimately to demand something from another person, or group of people. That other person (or those people) is (are) under a duty to perform the demanded action. For example, if Jane books a flight then she has entered into a contract with the airline company that they will supply a seat on a specified flight – Jane has a claim against the airline company, and were the airline not to supply the seat, Jane could take action in law, which is what is meant by saying that rights are 'actionable'. The claim to the seat was established because Jane exercised another kind of right – a power – when she entered into the contract. However, claims need not be the result of a contract. (We discuss the significance of this later.)

2. **Privilege** (sometimes called a **liberty**) Of all the four types of right this is the most misunderstood. Some writers prefer to talk of liberty (or freedom), rather than privilege, and argue that the correlative to a liberty is a 'duty not to interfere'. They are partially correct: Hohfeld should have called them liberties, but there is no correlative duty. A liberty simply entails the absence of duty (a 'no-claim'): you are free to do whatever you are not under a duty to do. But that does not mean that other people are under a duty not to interfere in your actions: a world of liberties is, in Hobbesian terms, a state of nature. In fact what are termed fundamental freedoms in human rights documents tend, on closer inspection, to be claims, or powers, or immunities.

3. **Powers** A power entails the ability to create legal relationships. For example, the right to marry is a power that, when exercised, alters your legal relationships: through your actions you alter your legal relationship to the person you marry, and also your relationship to those outside the marriage contract. You cannot marry anyone else unless powers of annulment are first used, and you gain taxation benefits and so alter your relationship to the state. It is through powers that many – but not all – claims are created.

4. **Immunities** To possess an immunity is to be in a position to resist the powers of others. Immunities exist, most often, where there are different levels of legal authority, such as a legislative authority which creates and destroys rights, and a judicial authority that upholds a constitution. The immunities created in a constitution exist to insulate the individual from the powers of the legislature: an immunity *disables* the legislature from exercising powers that would change your legal position. Immunities are often misleadingly referred to as 'fundamental liberties', but must, in fact, be immunities, since liberties are not intrinsically resistant to alteration as a result of legislative action. An example of an immunity would be the 'right to nationality', which amounts to your state being 'disabled' from changing your civil status – put in everyday language, it cannot strip you of your citizenship.

The significance for human rights of Hohfeld's scheme will become clearer when we look at the relationship between the different types of rights, but before doing that it is worth seeing whether we can categorise the rights listed in the Declaration under these headings. In fact, it is very difficult. For example, Article 6 states that 'everyone has the right to recognition everywhere as a person before the law'. That Article is so broad that it could entail a claim against the state, or imply a power to do certain things, or could act as a block on the state changing your legal position, meaning that you possess an immunity. One of the differences between the Declaration and the Convention is that the latter can be more easily broken down in terms of these rights. However, even that document leaves a great deal open about what legal relationships are at work. And we need to know about these relationships to understand the character of human rights, and address the question of whether human rights preclude other important values and principles.

Will Theory versus Benefit Theory

Hohfeld's study was analytical: he wanted to lay out the different forms of rights. He was not interested in explaining the underlying connections between them (he thought claims were 'rights proper', but did not justify this). Since many human rights are, in fact, bundles of Hohfeldian rights, it is important to consider how the Hohfeldian rights connect together. Indeed, as suggested above, the rights contained in human rights documents are very broad in scope, and it may be that different judges will interpret them in very different ways. 'Theories of rights' attempt to connect up the different Hohfeldian rights; some writers assume that a theory must reduce the different Hohfeldian rights to a single right. This is a mistake: what a theory should do is explain the relative importance of each type of right. The two most important theories of rights are benefit theory (also known as interest theory) and will theory (also known as choice theory):

- Benefit theory singles out a claim as the most important kind of right. A right-holder is somebody who benefits, or is intended to benefit, from the performance of a duty. Physical protection would be an example of a claim – you have a *claim* to physical protection, and the state, insofar as it is capable of doing so, has a *duty* to prevent you being physically harmed.
- Will theory singles out powers as primary. A right-holder is someone who is in the position to control the performance of a duty through the exercise of powers. The example of Jane's purchase of a seat on a flight would be an example of powers as primary – to acquire the seat she must exercise a power, and by so doing she acquires a claim.

Benefit theory takes rights to be the way in which *interests* are protected – which is why some theorists prefer the term 'interest theory'. The right-holder need not be in a position to assert his/her/its rights. Will theory stresses *agency*: rights are things we use to control our lives and relationships with other people. Consequently, a will theorist would be much more restrictive about who can have rights. It would be too simplistic to associate benefit/interest theory with the political left, and will theory with the right, but it is the case that those on the left who want to express egalitarian principles in the language of rights will tend to stress interests rather than agency.

The significance of this debate for human rights can be described in terms of depth versus breadth. For a will theorist rights are not broad but they are deep, because if the scope were broadened then rights could be more easily overridden (to 'override' a right is legitimately to set it aside because it conflicts with another, more important, right, or with another principle; the overriding of a right should not be confused with the violation of a right, which is the illegitimate non-recognition of that right). For example, if there is a human right to hold (private) property, but no human right to a minimum level of subsistence, then the property right will not come into conflict with any claim to subsistence. This is not to say that the restriction of human rights to property holding precludes a claim to subsistence, rather it means that the property right 'trumps' the claim to subsistence. On a will theory of human rights, the range of activities and states of being protected by human rights is narrower than on a benefit theory of human rights. Benefit theory permits a greater range of values, but at the price of weakening rights. To summarise the discussion of this section: if the 'rights and freedoms' set out in human rights documents are to be applied to concrete situations then it is necessary to break them down into Hohfeldian rights, which, given that privileges (liberties) are problematic, amounts to three types of right: claims, powers and immunities. The degree to which human rights can encompass the full range of values of a society depends to some extent on which of the Hohfeldian forms is taken to be of primary importance.

Relativism versus Universalism

So far we have talked about the concept of a right and about the historical origins of human rights documents and mechanisms of enforcements. What we have not discussed is the justification of human rights. We assume that the *fact* of law does not necessarily *justify* a law. Once we accept this we are forced to confront the cultural relativism thesis, which can be stated thus:

> Values have to be understood as part of a complex whole; that complex whole is 'culture'. When discussing the universal applicability of 'human rights' we must take into account the impact that they will have on particular cultures. For some cultures those rights express central values, for others they may, with some revision, be compatible with that culture, but for others they may be wholly inappropriate and damaging.

Cultural relativism does not necessarily entail the rejection of morality: the Declaration may be valid for certain cultures. What cultural relativists challenge is the claim to universal application. This raises the question whether a relativist can endorse some form of human rights. One possibility is to distinguish 'state' and 'culture': the Council of Europe is composed of more than 45 states, but it could be argued that there is a single European culture, which has its roots in Christianity (medieval Europe was often referred to as 'Christendom'). Similarly the Islamic world is composed of many states bound together by Islamic culture (it might also be argued that the Arab world, as part of the wider Islamic world, is a distinct culture). If we endorse the distinction between state and culture then it might be possible to talk of trans-national standards of treatment. Those standards would allow a distinction to be made between two types of rejection of human rights: (a) *violation* of culturally accepted human rights by a particular regime; (b) *legitimate rejection* of human rights on cultural grounds. For example, it could be debated whether Saudi Arabian penal policy, such as the amputation of hands, is grounded in Islamic teaching and Arab custom, or whether it simply serves the interests of the Saudi state to have such an apparently draconian form of punishment.

This argument, while plausible, is difficult for a defender of human rights to embrace. As we suggested in the first section of this chapter, human rights are rights that individuals have by virtue of their humanity. The 'cultural argument' makes rights, or any other standard of treatment, contingent on a person's culture. While there may be a role for culture in the justification, formulation and implementation of human rights, the radical 'culturalism' that forms the basis of the cultural relativism thesis is incompatible with a defence of human rights. We need then to consider arguments against cultural relativism or, put another way, arguments for universalism. We set out three types of argument in favour of the universality of human rights – it may be that none of these arguments work, and that we need to return to cultural relativism thesis. The arguments are presented primarily to stimulate reflection on the universalism–relativism debate.

Intuition and Moral Consensus

Jack Donnelly, in his book *Universal Human Rights in Theory and Practice*, defends what he terms weak cultural relativism, which entails strong universalism. Weak cultural relativism assumes that human rights are universally applicable but allows that 'the relativity of human nature, communities and rules checks potential excesses of universalism'. Strong cultural relativism holds that culture is the principal source of the validity of a right or rule, and 'at its furthest extreme, strong cultural relativism accepts a few basic rights with virtually universal application but allows such a wide range of variation that two entirely justifiable sets of rights might overlap only slightly' (Donnelly, 2003: 90).

The looseness of the language of the Declaration Donnelly regards as a strength. The Declaration is a general statement of orienting value, and it is at this level – and only at this level – that a moral consensus exists. For example, Articles 3–12 'are so clearly connected to basic requirements of human dignity, and are stated in sufficiently general terms, that virtually every morally defensible contemporary form of social organization must recognize them' (Donnelly: 94). Below we discuss the 'rational entailment' argument, of which there are several versions, but the central idea is that certain standards of treatment can be derived from the conditions which humans require for action, and as such a society cannot deny those standards without also denying the preconditions for its own existence. Donnelly's statement has the appearance of such an argument, but in fact he then goes on to appeal to human intuition. By 'intuition' is meant a strong sense of, or belief in, the rightness or wrongness of something, but without the ability to give a complete explanation of that sense or belief. Donnelly identifies the intuition that people should be treated in a certain way irrespective of their culture by means of a question:

In twenty years of working with issues of cultural relativism, I have developed a simple test that I pose to sceptical audiences. What rights in the Universal Declaration, I ask, does your society or culture reject? Rarely has a single full right (other than the right to private property) been rejected (Donnelly: 94).

He recalls a visit to Iran in 2001, where he posed the above question to three different audiences. In all three cases discussion moved quickly on to the issue of freedom of religion, and in particular to atheism, and to apostasy by Muslims, which the Declaration permits, but Iran prohibits. Donnelly observed that the discussion was not about freedom of religion, but rather about Western versus Islamic interpretations of that right (we discuss freedom of religion in the final section of this chapter).

Particular human rights are like 'essentially contested concepts' in which there are differing interpretations but strong overlap between them. So long as 'outliers' are few, we can talk about a consensus around human rights. Such 'outliers' would be cultures that do not accept a particular human right. The fact that increasing numbers of states are prepared to sign up to the Declaration, and to later, and more specific, United Nations conventions Donnelly takes to be evidence of a dynamic consensus in favour of human rights. He also observes that when Western states criticise non-Western states for apparently barbaric practices that criticism is sometimes accompanied by a serious lack of self-awareness; in 1994 18-year-old American Michael Fay was convicted by a Singaporean court of vandalising hundreds of thousands of dollars worth of property. He was sentenced to three months in jail, required to pay a fine and, most controversially, was condemned to six strokes of the cane (the cane would leave permanent scars). There was widespread condemnation in the United States. Donnelly tersely observes that President Clinton, while condemning the sentence 'failed to find it even notable that in his own country people are being fried in the electric chair' (Donnelly: 99).

To sum up, Donnelly's observations are interesting, but two points are problematic. First, an intuition in favour of human rights at best indicates that there may be something underlying those rights which is, in some sense, universal. But if this is so then it should be possible to move beyond intuition and provide reasons for respecting human rights. Second, the fact that *states* have signed up to human rights conventions does not entail *cultural* agreement: human rights must be recognised as valid by large parts of the populations of states, and not simply by the leadership. In many states the governing elites are disconnected from their peoples, and although states may be considered the main actors with regard to human rights, respect for such rights does depend on popular recognition.

International Hypothetical Contract

The fact that increasing numbers of states are prepared to sign up to human rights conventions does not in itself amount to an argument for the universality of human rights, but it may provide an element in an argument. In Chapters 4 and 7 we discussed the idea of the social contract, which has been a device used by liberal political theorists to justify state power. Our discussion focused on the 'domestic' use of the contract: political theorists such as Hobbes, Locke, Rousseau and Rawls were concerned with the relationship of the individual to the state. This contrasts

pp. 170–1

with an 'international contract', which is a contract not between individual human beings but between states. We also made a distinction between a quasi-historical contract, whereby we could imagine that people could have agreed contractually to create a state, and the hypothetical contract in which the contractors are 'idealised' and the 'contract' is a thought experiment rather than an imagined historical event.

Interestingly enough, whereas defenders of the historical contract do not claim that there was actually an agreement to enter the state – they claim simply that it was imaginable – international legal institutions can plausibly be described as the product of an agreement between the member states of the international community: agreements to create international institutions. Of course, there is not a single 'moment' of agreement, for the ratification of a convention can take place over decades. Furthermore, there has never been an international agreement to create a single state; such an agreement would constitute the dissolution of all existing states. The closest the international community has come to the creation of a single, multi-national global power has been the formation of the United Nations with the commitment by member states to provide military personnel to enforce international law.

The problem of enforcement may be thought a serious deficiency of international law, and one that can only be remedied through the creation of a single state. However, there is a considerable body of international law, such as commercial law, which states respect without recourse to a global enforcement agency. As Locke argued, enforcement, while important, is not the main deficiency evident in the state of nature, for a more significant deficiency is the absence of a body capable of interpreting, and indeed determining, the law. Even if all states subscribed to the Declaration, its wording is so general as to require a third-party judgement on its meaning. In practice, the United Nations effectively 'contracts out' the interpretation of human rights to bodies such as the European Court of Human Rights. The general point to make is that a hypothetical international contract differs from a domestic one in that its object is not the creation of a world state that will enforce human rights, but rather it is a device for creating a charter of human rights and associated multinational institutions. States will not then be able to violate human rights on grounds of disagreement about their interpretation, and will have incentives – such as the desire for reputation – to respect them.

Rawls and the International Hypothetical Contract

pp. 86–7

John Rawls extends his theory of 'domestic' justice to the international sphere in his book *The Law of Peoples* (1999). The underlying aim of that book is to outline the just foreign policy of a liberal society: when is intervention in the affairs of another state justified? And what duties do liberal societies have to non-liberal ones? Although that aim is quite narrow, in the course of the book Rawls does present an argument intended to show that non-liberal, non-Western societies can respect human rights. Although he does not use these terms with great precision Rawls makes a distinction between three types of society or 'people':

• **Liberal societies,** such as those which (largely) respect human rights conventions, and the conventions of war.

- **Decent non-liberal societies,** of which there can be several variants, but the one type Rawls discusses possesses a 'decent consultation hierarchy' (hereafter referred to as *decent societies*).
- **Outlaw states** – states that violate the law of peoples, by, for example, waging aggressive wars or engaging in serious violations of human rights. (There are also *burdened societies*, where socio-economic conditions make respect for international law difficult.)

Rawls applies the idea of the original position and the veil of ignorance to international law, but there are some significant differences between how these devices are used in Rawls's theory of (domestic) justice, and his law of peoples. These are best summarised as a table:

Domestic Justice	Law of Peoples
Individual human agents are in the original position.	Representatives of peoples are in the original position.
Agents are denied knowledge of their particular conceptions of the good, e.g. their religious beliefs.	Representatives have knowledge of their conceptions of the good, e.g. the predominant religion of their society
There is one process whereby principles of justice are selected.	There are two 'runs': (a) liberal societies agree; (b) decent hierarchical societies agree.

Liberal societies agree among themselves on a 'law of peoples', and then decent societies endorse those same principles (Rawls argues that liberal democratic societies, by their nature, will tend to respect the human rights of their own peoples and the sovereignty of other peoples). The law of peoples consists of eight principles: mutual recognition of each people's independence; honouring of agreements; legal equality of peoples; duty of non-intervention (except in the case of dealing with outlaw states and grave violations of human rights); right to self-defence; respect for human rights; respect for the rules of war; duty to assist peoples living under conditions that prevent them from becoming just (liberal) or decent societies. The law requires of liberal societies that they do not seek to change the fundamental character of a decent society.

Democratic Peace

This is the theory that liberal democracies do not go to war with one another, preferring instead to settle their disputes through negotiation. Immanuel Kant is credited with offering an early version of the theory in his essay 'Perpetual Peace' (published 1795, in Kant, 1996: 317–51), where he argued that 'commerce' (trade) established bonds between peoples, and gave them a material interest in maintaining peace, even where the interests of states conflicted, and, furthermore, the legal traditions of liberal states led them to value arbitration over violence. The Democratic Peace argument was given renewed force with empirical and theoretical studies by Michael Doyle (1997) and Bruce Russett (1994). Doyle studied all wars since 1800 and found no case of two liberal democracies going to war against one another. Obviously, the credibility of the claim depends on how democracy is defined, but the argument is at least plausible.

Democratic
Peace, p. 451

To understand how a decent society could endorse the law of peoples, and consequently why a liberal society should 'tolerate' a decent society, we need to know the characteristics of the latter. Rawls argues that it is peaceful in that it pursues its interests through trade and diplomacy. The domestic laws of a decent society should be guided by 'common good conception of justice', meaning that while it may not grant the freedoms to individuals enjoyed in a liberal society, in a fundamental sense all citizens are treated equally. There should exist a 'decent consultation hierarchy', which permits the possibility of dissent (the Arab–Islamic concept of Shura would be one example of a consultation hierarchy). Importantly, the common good conception of justice entails respect for human rights, including the right to life, liberty (freedom from slavery and forced labour), personal property and equality before the law. Although a decent society may not permit apostasy and proselytisation, it must accord a degree of religious freedom to minorities, and because that right is limited it must also allow citizens to emigrate. The fundamental philosophical point Rawls makes about human rights is that they should not depend on a particular conception of the human agent as autonomous, but rather 'human rights set a necessary . . . standard for the decency of domestic political and social institutions' (Rawls, 1999: 80).

Human rights fulfil three roles: (a) they are a necessary condition of a regime's legitimacy; (b) they determine the limits of sovereignty – the law of people prohibits intervention in the affairs of another state except when that state is violating human rights; (c) they set a limit on the pluralism among peoples. Even if Rawls is correct in arguing that a decent society can respect human rights, are there any grounds for believing that they will do so for reasons other than state interest? Do they respect human rights for the 'right reasons', or because such respect is useful to establishing a reputation in international politics? A similar argument could be applied to the international behaviour of liberal states, but the difference between liberal and non-liberal societies is that human rights are deeply embedded in the culture of the former. Even if the leaders of liberal societies are cynical in their use of human rights rhetoric in international politics – intervening in Kosovo but not Chechnya – they may well (largely) respect human rights in their domestic political systems.

Rational Entailment

The 'rational entailment' argument identifies certain conditions for the existence of social order and from those conditions maintains that there are certain standards of treatment which all societies should respect. The argument can take two forms – empirical and logical. The empirical version observes actual societies and claims that the long-term survival of a society depends on the recognition of human rights. This version has only limited plausibility – many societies function without respect for human rights; it is somewhat more plausible to maintain that human rights-respecting societies are more successful than human rights-violating ones, where success is measured by economic growth and political stability. The logical version does not deny that social life is possible without human rights, but rather that a human rights-violating society cannot justify its own political and legal organisation without falling into contradiction. In Chapter 3 we discussed the citizenship laws of

pp. 69–70

Nazi Germany which effectively stripped Jews of their citizenship and opened the way for serious violation of their human rights – ultimately, the right to life. Legal theorist Lon Fuller argued that Nazi law could not respect certain principles internal to law, such as the prohibition on non-retroactivity. Fuller is not suggesting that Nazi Germany did not 'function', but rather that it could not justify its laws; implicit in Fuller's argument is a belief in human rights, to which he is offering a logical entailment defence. Of course, a society can simply choose not to justify its actions – although that is surprisingly rare – but refusal to engage in the justification process does not undermine the logical entailment argument.

Jürgen Habermas offers the best contemporary statement of logical entailment. Before we get to his defence of human rights against cultural relativism, it is necessary to set out briefly Habermas's rather complex theory of social change. If we define 'culture' as the 'taken-for-granted horizon of expectations', then under conditions of modernity culture is 'threatened' by rationalisation in the form of money (or the market) and bureaucratic power – relations between human beings become consciously instrumental, rather than implicit and 'taken for granted'. There is a diminution of trust. Many theorists, especially in the German philosophical tradition in which Habermas has been formed, are pessimistic about the consequences of modernity. However, Habermas argues that the emphasis on instrumentalisation – or what he calls 'systemic rationality' – ignores the positive achievements of modernity, expressed in 'communicative rationality' (Habermas, 1984: 8–22). The growth in consciousness of human rights is one of the achievements of communicative rationality.

What does Habermas mean by 'communicative action'? People engage in speech acts: person A *promises* to meet person B on Thursday, *requests* B stop smoking, *confesses* to find B's actions distasteful, *predicts* it will rain. Implicit in each speech act is an offer or claim. In the first two cases A is making a claim to normative rightness, in the third case a claim to sincerity, and in the final case a claim to truth. B can contest all three such 'validity claims' (Habermas, 1984: 319–28). The success of each speech act depends upon both parties orienting themselves to principles of reason that are not reducible to individual intentions: in addressing B person A treats her as an end in herself. The validity claims are implicit in all human action, that is, they are universal. This seems a promising basis for defending universal human rights against the challenge of cultural relativism. However, the validity claims are abstract from everyday life, and so to redeem them requires appeal to a stock of culturally specific values. That means the content of human rights is dependent on culture.

One way to address this problem of cultural dependence is to maintain that politics is a dialogue, in which people bring to bear their different cultural perspectives, such that what emerges from the dialogue is something pluralistic yet coherent. For example, Muslims may be criticised by Western feminists for projecting a patriarchal conception of gender relations. By engaging in dialogue Muslims may reform their view of women's rights, but Westerners might also be obliged to recognise the deficiencies in their own understanding of family relations, by, for example, acknowledging the costs entailed in the commodification of sex in a liberal society.

Habermas argues that there is a tradition in Anglophone legal and political theory of conceiving of the state as grounded in the protection of individual 'private' rights – rights derived from the market contract model. Hobbes is the *locus classicus* of this conception of individual–state relations. If we operate with such a theory then it is inevitable that individual rights will be a threat to cultural reproduction; in effect, increasing reliance on rights would be another example of the systemic rationality eroding the lifeworld. We are then left with a choice: either we assert the primacy of individual rights at the expense of cultural interaction, or we maintain the authority of the collective over the individual. Private rights entail the assertion of personal autonomy, but they ignore the other half of the concept of autonomy – public autonomy:

> from a normative point of view, the integrity of the individual legal person cannot be guaranteed without protecting the intersubjectively shared experiences and life contexts in which the person has been socialized and has formed his or her identity. The identity of the individual is interwoven with collective identities and can be stabilized only in a cultural network that cannot be appropriated as private property any more than the mother tongue itself can be (Habermas, 1994: 129).

The implication of Habermas's argument is that universal human rights are, contrary to Rawls's theory, grounded in human autonomy, but that human autonomy itself has a collective dimension which must take into account cultural interpretations of human rights. Legality is central to the realisation of human rights, and Habermas's theory of law bears some resemblance to Fuller's: law is not reducible to the assertion of will – people are not simply subjects of law – but the formation of law is a discursive process. The legal realisation of human rights will inevitably involve 'local interpretation' – for example, Muslim societies will interpret human rights differently to Western societies – but human beings are bound together through discourse, and discourse presupposes a conception of the human agent as autonomous.

Group Rights and Welfare Rights

In an earlier section (What are Rights?) we raised the problem of the value range of human rights: to what extent can human rights encompass the full range of values in a society? In this final section we address this question by considering two specific kinds of right – group rights and welfare rights.

Group Rights

So far the discussion has implied that it is individual human beings who have human rights. The first question to ask is, can collective entities have rights? At this stage we are not concerned with human rights, but rather with the conceptual issues raised earlier. It is certainly the case that in law, both domestic and international, rights are attributed to collective entities, such as firms or states, for these are individuals in the sense that they have an identifiable – individuated – good which can be secured through rights. Indeed, in English commercial law publicly limited companies are described as 'artificial persons'. So there is no conceptual problem in talking about collective rights (or group rights); what is at issue is whether a right can be asserted by a group against the state on grounds analogous to those by which individual human beings assert their human rights.

pp. 360–1

In his book *Multicultural Citizenship* (1995) Will Kymlicka discusses the right to religious freedom, and identifies three elements to this right: (a) freedom to pursue one's (existing) faith (practice); (b) freedom to seek new adherents to that faith (proselytisation); (c) freedom to renounce one's faith (apostasy). He also makes a distinction between internal restrictions and external protections, arguing for the latter against the former: we enjoy a 'group right' insofar as we as individuals are protected against wider society. It follows from this that the right to religious freedom must contain all three elements. Traditionally, in Muslim countries only the first element is respected, and the implication of Rawls's argument is that a decent hierarchical society can be said to respect human rights even if it restricts religious freedom to that element. (It should be said that, historically, Muslims have shown much greater tolerance of religious minorities, such as Jews and Christians, than has been the case in Christian Europe with regard to its religious minorities.)

Does Kymlicka's argument amount to a defence of group rights as human rights? Not really, because the right to religious freedom is held by the individual. Those who argue that human rights are 'individualistic' will not be convinced by Kymlicka's understanding of group rights, for there exists a possible conflict between the right and what it seeks to protect: religion. Religion is a collective activity and can only be sustained as a collective activity, but the individual right to freedom of religion implies that as individuals we stand back from a religious community and assess its value for us. It might be, of course, that after reflection we affirm 'our' religious belief, but this implies that only cultures compatible with reflection and revision of belief are capable of recognising the human right to religious freedom. (We discuss the conflict between individual and group rights in more detail in Chapter 13.)

Welfare Rights

In discussing the Universal Declaration of Human Rights we noted that Articles 22–26 were concerned with 'social rights', and that these rights were dropped from the European Convention. In 1969 the United Nations proclaimed the Declaration on Social Progress and Development, which sets out in more detail principles and objectives for international development. The question is whether it makes sense to talk of welfare rights as human rights, or whether development can only be an aim or aspiration subordinate in moral status to respect for what might be termed the 'negative rights' to be left alone (such rights are not strictly negative for they require action by states).

Defenders of the 'right to development' argue that there are socio-economic conditions to 'negative rights'. To assess this claim we need, first of all, a definition of 'development'. Development could mean either: (a) the right of a *state*, or a *community*, to a certain level of resources, or (b) the right of an *individual* to a certain level of resources. If the individual holds the right (in Hohfeld's language: claim), then who has the corresponding duty: that individual's own state, or rich states, or the international community? If states have the right to development then that would imply that the only relevant issue of wealth distribution is between states, whereas if individuals have the right then the distribution of wealth within a particular state is morally relevant. In fact, it is clear from the 1969 Declaration that the UN took the individual to be the bearer of the right:

> Development is a comprehensive economic, social, cultural and political process, which aims at the constant improvement of the well-being of the entire population and of all its individuals on the basis of their active, free and meaningful participation in the development and in the fair distribution of benefits resulting therefrom.

The human right to development raises a number of philosophical problems. First, as we have argued, rights must be both compossible and actionable, meaning that a set of rights must constitute a coherent whole and they must take a form in which a remedy can be obtained when a person complains that his human rights have been violated. The requirements of development may well result in the setting aside of certain fundamental 'negative' rights, for example, a society that wishes to control urban growth may seek to control freedom of movement and choice of occupation, so that a problem of compossibility arises. A right to development cannot be actionable in the way that violations of negative rights can be: it is significant that many societies have ratified laws on asylum, and largely respect those laws, but those same societies make it clear that they do not accept economic migrants. Second, the right to development may entail significant intervention in the social, economic and political organisation of other states; certainly, violation of negative rights can justify intervention, but violation of such rights is often clear, whereas the failure of a state to ensure the fair distribution of resources within its boundaries is a much less clear violation, and external intervention may be 'open-ended'.

Summary

The fundamental philosophical debate around human rights is concerned with their alleged 'parochialism': that is, their origins in a particular culture. That something has a history does not, in itself, invalidate its claim to universality, but there is a particular problem about human rights even in those cultures from which they emerged: critics argue that human rights place a great moral weight on individual autonomy to the detriment of other values, such as welfare and community. For defenders of human rights, the increasing spread of human rights discourse indicates a welcome development in humanitarian moral consciousness; for opponents, human rights go hand in hand with the growing power of Western liberalism. We can apply the discussion of this chapter to human rights in Saudi Arabia: against Donnelly, the fact that Saudi Arabia has signed up to human rights conventions guarantees neither that its legal institutions are fair, nor that its punishments are proportional. For Rawls, the Saudi regime would not constitute a 'decent hierarchical people', and for Habermas there is a link between the procedural injustice of the regime and the extremity of its punishments.

Questions

1. Why should states respect human rights?
2. If it can be shown that human rights discourse emerges from a Western tradition does this undermine the claim that they are universal?
3. Is the exercise of human rights compatible with respect for the environment?
4. Is the 'right to welfare' coherent?

References

Convention for the Protection of Human Rights and Fundamental Freedoms (European Convention on Human Rights): http://www.echr.coe.int/Convention/webConvenENG.pdf.

Donnelly, J. (2003) *Universal Human Rights in Theory and Practice* Ithaca, NY: Cornell University Press.

Doyle, M. (1997) *Ways of War and Peace* New York: Norton.

Habermas, J. (1984) *The Theory of Communicative Action*, Vol. 1: *Reason and Rationalization of Society* London: Heinemann.

Habermas, J. (1994) 'Struggles for Recognition in the Democratic Constitutional State', in A. Gutmann (ed.), *Multiculturalism: Examining the Politics of Recognition* Princeton, NJ: Princeton University Press.

Hohfeld, W. (1923) *Fundamental Legal Conceptions as Applied in Judicial Reasoning* New Haven, Conn: Yale University Press.

Kant, I. (1996) *Practical Philosophy* (ed. M. Gregor), Cambridge: Cambridge University Press.

Kymlicka, W. (1995) *Multicultural Citizenship: A Liberal Theory of Minority Rights* Oxford: Clarendon Press.

Rawls, J. (1999) *The Law of Peoples* Cambridge, Mass. and London: Harvard University Press.

Russett, B. (1993) *Grasping the Democratic Peace* Princeton, NJ: Princeton University Press.

Universal Declaration of Human Rights: http://www.un.org/Overview/rights.html.

Further Reading

It is important to be clear about the nature of *rights* before venturing into a discussion of *human* rights – a good introduction is Peter Jones, *Rights* (Basingstoke: Macmillan, 1994). General discussions of human rights include: Maurice Cranston, *What are Human Rights?* (New York: Taplinger, 1973) and Ellen Frankel Paul *et al.* (eds), *Human Rights* (Oxford: Oxford University Press, 1984). More intellectually demanding are: Alan Gewirth, *Human Rights: Essays on Justification and Applications* (Chicago, Ill: University of Chicago Press, 1982); R. J. Vincent, *Human Rights and International Relations* (Cambridge: Cambridge University Press, 1986). On the issue of cultural relativism read Simon Caney and Peter Jones (eds), *Human Rights and Global Diversity* (London: Frank Cass, 2001); Jane Cowan *et al.* (eds), *Culture and Rights: Anthropological Perspectives* (Cambridge: Cambridge University Press, 2001), and from the above references Donnelly (2003), Habermas (1994) and Rawls (1999). On collective rights see Judith Baker (ed.),

Group Rights (Toronto, Ont: University of Toronto Press, 1994), and on welfare rights see Robin Attfield and Barry Wilkins (eds), *International Justice and the Third World: Studies in the Philosophy of Development* (London: Routledge, 1992).

Weblinks

There are many excellent human rights resources on the web:

- From a more legal perspective:
  http://library.kent.ac.uk/library/lawlinks/human.htm

- The other sites are a mix of theory, law and advocacy:
  Human Rights Resource Center: http://www.hrusa.org/
  Human Rights Education Associates: http://www.hrea.org/
  Human and Constitutional Rights: http://www.hrcr.org/
  Amnesty International: http://www.amnesty.org/
  Human Rights Watch: http://www.hrw.org/

Chapter 19

Civil Disobedience

Introduction

Civil disobedience is the non-violent breaking of a law on moral grounds. While there were theorists of civil disobedience in the nineteenth and early twentieth centuries, and the theory may be applicable to non-democratic societies, this chapter focuses on post-World War II discussion of civil disobedience in a liberal democratic society. Although few people may ever engage in civil disobedience in their lifetimes it is not a peripheral concept, for the justification of civil disobedience touches on the moral basis of majoritarian democracy. Whereas in the pre-modern and early modern periods political theory was concerned with the right to rebel, the fundamental question raised by civil disobedience to a modern audience is this: how is it possible to have a general respect for the rule of law and yet break specific laws?

Chapter Map

In this chapter we will:

- Distinguish civil disobedience from legal protest, revolution, and 'mere criminality'.

- Discuss whether we have a special obligation to obey democratically agreed laws.

- Analyse one of the most influential philosophical discussions of civil disobedience – that advanced by John Rawls.

- Apply that theoretical discussion to a case study: the Civil Rights Movement in the United States.

- Discuss Martin Luther King's justification of the Civil Rights Movement.

Protest and Survive?

Peace campaigners demonstrating at RAF Greenham Common air base, 12 December 1982

In 1981 a group of women set off on a march from Cardiff (Wales) to Greenham Common, a British–American airbase located about 60 miles (100 kilometres) west of London, where Cruise Missiles (guided missiles with nuclear warheads) were to be sited. Once there, they established the 'Greenham Common Women's Peace Camp', and for the next two years they attempted to disrupt construction work – which included the building of missile silos – at the base. Despite their efforts the missiles arrived in November 1983. However, the Peace Camp remained for the rest of the decade, and indeed some women continued there until 2000. There were frequent arrests, resulting in fines and, in a few cases, imprisonment. The local council made repeated attempts to evict the protestors. The 1987 Intermediate-range Nuclear Forces (INF) Treaty signed by the United States and the USSR resulted in the removal of the missiles from Greenham Common. By 1991 all the missiles had gone; in 1992 the US Air Force left, soon followed by their British counterparts. The women who remained after 1992 claimed they were now making a symbolic protest against all nuclear weapons. At the heart of the anti-nuclear protests – which took place across Western Europe in the early 1980s – was a belief that if they did not engage in peaceful law-breaking (civil disobedience) then humanity was doomed: the slogan of the British organisation, the Campaign for Nuclear Disarmament (CND) was 'protest and survive', an ironic comment on the title of a 1960s British government guide to citizens on how to survive a nuclear attack: 'Protect and Survive'.

- Were the Greenham common protestors justified in breaking the law?

Civil Disobedience and Law-breaking

In this chapter we are concerned with justifications for civil disobedience, and naturally it makes sense to start with a definition of 'civil disobedience'. However, as we shall see, definition and justification are closely related, so that a particular definition implies a certain understanding of the role civil disobedience plays in the political system. What we offer here is an initial definition, which will require further clarification: civil disobedience is morally justified law-breaking, *normally* intended to change a particular law or policy. Civil disobedience has then these components: (a) it involves breaking the law – it is not simply legal protest; (b) there are moral reasons justifying the action; (c) the aim is to change a law or policy; it is not intended to bring down an entire political system – civil disobedience is not revolution.

Of all the concepts discussed in this book, civil disobedience is among a relatively small group where theory and practice are closely related, and indeed where some of the most important theorists of the concept have been its practitioners. American Henry David Thoreau (1817–62) is credited with offering the earliest theory of civil disobedience. Thoreau was imprisoned for refusing to pay a tax that was intended to fund what he regarded as an unjust war by the United States against Mexico. In his essay 'Civil Disobedience' (1849), Thoreau argued that an individual had a moral duty to break an unjust law – you should, he suggests, 'let your life be a counter-friction to stop the machine' (Thoreau, 1991: 36). In other words, civil disobedience was intended to obstruct the implementation of immoral policies. Thoreau's argument was highly influential. Mahatma Gandhi (1869–1948) read 'Civil Disobedience' while in prison, and developed both its theory and practice in his struggle against British rule in India. It was also from a prison cell that Martin Luther King, Jr. wrote what became known as the 'Letter from Birmingham City Jail' (1963), a plea to fellow church leaders to accept the legitimacy of non-violent law-breaking in pursuit of equal rights for US citizens. We will discuss King's argument in some detail in the final section of this chapter. Our concern is primarily with the role of civil disobedience in a liberal democratic society, and for that reason we focus on theorists who locate their discussions of civil disobedience within a wider political theory. We apply that theoretical discussion to Martin Luther King, Jr. and the Civil Rights Movement.

Law-breaking

Criminals break laws, and so do people who engage in civil disobedience. How then do we distinguish the civilly disobedient from the merely criminal? In part, the distinction will rest on *how* the law is broken, in part on *why* it is broken. Before discussing the 'how' and the 'why' it is worth reflecting on the questions in the exercise on page 463.

Reasons for breaking the law fall into four categories, although the fourth is a sub-category of the third:

1. **Individual self-interest:** a law is not in the individual's interests.
2. **Group interest:** a law is not in the interests of a particular group.
3. **Morality:** a law is morally wrong.
4. **Justice:** a law is unjust.

Exercise

Consider three cases of law-breaking, where:

1. you have broken a law on grounds of self-interest;

2. you have broken a law because you considered the law morally wrong;

3. you have broken a law in the process of protesting against something you consider to be morally wrong.

If you have never broken a law on one or all of these grounds, then imagine cases where you might break the law!

Now ask yourself the following questions – taking each of the above cases in turn (paying special attention to the distinction between cases of type 1 and type 2):

- How did you break the law – was it a public act, or did you evade detection?

- Did you feel guilty about breaking the law?

- Did you consider your actions selfish?

- Do you believe you were morally *justified* in breaking the law?

- Were you morally *obliged* to break the law?

- Was the law widely respected – if not, did that make a difference to your attitude?

All defenders of civil disobedience would reject the first category as justifying law-breaking – to break the law simply because it does not suit your interests is to engage in a criminal act. The second category is more complex. Marx argued that it was in the interests of a particular group, the working class, to overthrow the capitalist system and that as a result a classless society would be created. It follows that it is in the long-term interests of *all* human beings that the working class should succeed. But Marx advocated the complete transformation of society – that is, *revolution* – and not merely the removal of certain laws. And there could for Marx be no appeal to morality, for morality is the product of existing, capitalist, society.

Civil disobedience, as distinct from revolution, must appeal to moral ideas accessible to those who support the existing laws. The willingness of the civilly disobedient to accept the penalties for their law-breaking assumes that the 'oppressors' can be moved by their actions. Consequently, most theories of civil disobedience rest on the third and fourth categories. But, as we will see, there is an important distinction between breaking a law because you judge it immoral, and breaking it because you believe it is unjust.

Although self-interest is not a justification for civil disobedience, self-interest might well be a motivating factor. For example, the segregation laws operative in the southern states of the United States before the 1960s damaged the interests of *individual* blacks and blacks as a *group*. But this does not invalidate the claims of people such as Martin Luther King, Jr. that he and other blacks were morally justified in breaking the law.

Civil Disobedience and Political Obligation

Although there is debate among political theorists about the kinds of moral reasons that can justify civil disobedience, there is general agreement that civil disobedience implies political obligation. Laws are broken by people who have a respect for the law. To grasp this we need to distinguish political obligation from legal obligation and social obligation:

- **Legal obligation** Laws are by definition obligatory. If you dispute whether you are under a legal obligation to do something, such as pay a certain tax, then the issue can be settled by reference to a statute, or some other publicly stated legal judgment.
- **Political obligation** The question of whether a person has a *moral* obligation to obey the law cannot be settled by pointing to a statute or legal judgment – we need extra-legal arguments to determine whether a moral obligation exists. The term 'political obligation' *normally* means the moral obligation to obey the law (but see the next point).
- **Social obligation** Some political theorists widen the concept of political obligation to include moral obligations not enforced by law. For example, it might be argued that adults in the United Kingdom have a moral obligation to vote; however, while it is a legal requirement to register to vote, it is not a legal requirement to vote. In Australia, in contrast, voting is required by law. We will restrict the term 'political obligation' to the question of obedience to law, so that it does not arise with regard to voting in the United Kingdom, but it does in Australia. (Whether we decide to vote or not may be relevant to political obligation narrowly defined as obedience to law – we discuss this issue below in relation to Peter Singer's argument about participation.)

p. 172

There are different arguments for political obligation, but the Prisoner's Dilemma is useful as a way of organising our thoughts about obligation and disobedience. The resolution of the dilemma entails an agreement to cooperate, where such cooperation will be enforced by the state. That resolution is threatened by free-riders, who seek to enjoy the benefits gained from cooperation while evading the costs. The image of the free-rider is of the person who breaks the law out of self-interest. However, there are morally motivated free-riders: submission to the state involves not only giving up self-interest but also a degree of moral judgement. It is this which underlies the claim that civil disobedience is only justified if it appeals to certain kinds of moral reasons – reasons shared by (most) fellow citizens.

Civil Disobedience and Democracy

Democracy and Obedience

Civil disobedience plays a special role in democracy, because it not only indicates the moral limits of majority rule, but also forces us to reflect on the justifications *for* majority rule. For that reason it is important to consider the relationship between civil disobedience and democracy. While many people living in a liberal

Biography **Peter Singer (1946–)**

Born in Melbourne, Australia, in 1946, Singer is best known for his book *Animal Liberation* (1975), which argues that discrimination on the grounds of species is no more justified than race or gender discrimination. Singer defends a form of utilitarianism. One conclusion he draws is that 'active euthanasia' – which includes what some critics prefer to call infanticide – can be justified. The book under discussion here – *Democracy and Disobedience* – was an early work, and appears somewhat unconnected with his later, better-known works. However, the roots of his utilitarianism can be seen in *Democracy and Disobedience*: each person's views should count equally.

democracy consider violating the laws of a non-democratic regime to be not only permissible but praiseworthy, they consider it wrong to break democratically agreed laws. Sometimes the objection to civil disobedience in a democracy is revised when people reflect on particular cases, but there remains a core conviction that democracy is special. Peter Singer provides a philosophical defence of this view in his book *Democracy and Disobedience* (1973). Singer uses a very artificial example to illustrate his argument; however, its artificiality helps to bring out the main lines of the argument.

Oxford University is a collegiate university, with most living and teaching centred around the individual colleges. Singer asks us to imagine that each college is equivalent to a state, and the colleges taken together represent the world system of states. The undergraduates in a college form what Singer calls the Association. Students cannot opt out of membership of the Association. A student could transfer to another college at the university, but she would be obliged to join *its* Association. Of course, she could leave the university, but we are to imagine that the whole world is Oxford University, so that short of death there is no possibility of leaving. The Association of each college has been in existence for as long as anybody can remember – if there was ever a point at which it was set up, the records have been lost. The Association charges a subscription from each student, and we can take this to be equivalent to taxation. At this point we come to alternative ways of making decisions on how much to charge and what the money is spent on:

- **The Leader** Some time ago one student who is now the Leader decided that decision making was inefficient, and the decisions arrived at were stupid. He would now make the decisions, albeit guided by the interests of the other students. If anyone objected they would have to fight it out with the Leader's friends, who were the best fighters in the Association.

- **Democracy** Decisions are taken by a majority vote of all members of the Association. At the meetings all members are free to speak, subject to some essential procedural requirements, such as an agreed time limit on speeches. Meetings are conducted fairly, and the votes are calculated correctly. (There is a third model – the 'Senior Member' – but its introduction would unnecessarily complicate the present discussion.)

We assume that under each model decisions have been made without too much dissension – of course, some students will have found themselves on the 'losing side', but they have accepted whatever decisions have been made. However, an issue arises that causes serious dissension. The Association uses some of the subscription money to buy newspapers that are for general use in the common room, and must not be taken away. One day, it is decided that the common room should take a new paper, *The News*. One member of the Association – the Dissenter – objects to this newspaper, arguing that it is racist, and that other members of the Association, less attuned to the paper's bigotry, will be influenced by it to the detriment of the few black students in the college. Consider now the two models:

- **The Leader** The Dissenter asks the Leader to reconsider his decision, but the Leader is unmoved. The Dissenter 'takes things into his own hands' by getting up early each morning and removing the paper before the others have had a chance to read it.
- **Democracy** It had been agreed by majority vote, and after lengthy debate, that the common room would take *The News*. The Dissenter found himself in a minority. At the next and later meetings he attempts to get the decision reversed, but it becomes clear that a majority wants to take the paper. On realising this, the Dissenter behaves in the same way as under the other model: he removes the paper.

With regard to the Dissenter the initial question that Singer poses is not whether he has moral reasons for removing *The News*, but whether the fact that under the Democracy model there are special reasons for not removing it, reasons which do not exist under the Leader model. Participation is the key difference between democratic and non-democratic systems:

> the Dissenter, by voluntarily participating in the vote on the question of whether *The News* should be ordered, understanding that the purpose of the election is to enable the group to reach a decision on this issue, has behaved in such a way as to lead people reasonably to believe that he was accepting the democratic process as a suitable means of settling the issue (Singer, 1973: 50).

Democratic decision making is a 'fair compromise' between people who have conflicting moral views.

Fair Compromise

Singer distinguishes between 'absolute fairness' and a 'fair compromise'. Fair compromise is fairness *given certain conditions*. To illustrate the distinction between absolute fairness and fair compromise he gives a couple of examples (the second involves a certain amount of gender-stereotyping, but it is Singer's example and not ours!):

- Two people claim a sum of money, and a judge is appointed to adjudicate between them. Although she can be sure only one has a legitimate claim, she cannot establish which one has the claim, and so divides the money up 50/50. This is a fair compromise. An example of an unfair compromise would be to flip a coin.
- A husband and wife argue over who should do night-time baby duties. The husband says he works all day and so should have an unbroken night of sleep, whereas the wife claims she attends to the baby all day, and so should have a break at night. A fair compromise would be to alternate duties. An unfair compromise would be for the wife to do weekday nights, and the husband weekends.

The point about a fair compromise is that a person can still feel that the decision – to split the money, or to alternate baby duties – is 'unfair' in an 'absolute' sense, but that under the circumstances it is fair. As Singer argues with regard to the Dissenter: 'to disobey when there already is a fair compromise in operation is necessarily to deprive others of the say they have under such a compromise. To do this is to leave the others with no remedy but the use of force' (Singer: 36).

Singer argues that while we cannot consent – either explicitly or tacitly – to the procedure itself, we can consent by our actions to the decisions made under it. Singer borrows a concept from law to express the moral bindingness of participation: estoppel. He quotes an English judge – Lord Birkenhead: 'Where A has by his words or conduct justified B in believing that a certain state of affairs exists, and B has acted upon such belief to his prejudice, A is not permitted to affirm against B that a different state of facts existed at the same time' (Singer: 51). An everyday, non-legal example would be the British convention of buying a round of drinks in a pub (bar): if four people go to the pub and the first person buys four pints of beer, and then the second person does so, and then the third person likewise, the fourth, who has accepted three pints, can reasonably be expected to buy a round. She has not consented to the rule or convention of buying a round, but her acceptance of the three pints has affected the behaviour of her three friends.

Singer anticipates the objection that the Dissenter can avoid being bound through estoppel simply by not participating in the democratic process. He argues that the notion of a fair compromise generates not only an obligation to accept the decision of the majority, but also to participate in the process: it is not reasonable to sit it out. If you sit it out and then find the decision made is unacceptable you cannot have grounds for refusing to accept the decision, because you were unreasonable in prejudging the decision. People who do not vote can have no complaint against the decisions made by those who do.

Problems with Democracy

Singer's defence of obedience to a democratically agreed law is an 'all things being equal' defence. He does not argue that we should *always* obey such law. Although he does not discuss situations in which civil disobedience is justified, some of the more obvious ones are dealt with below:

(a) In a representative democracy – Singer's example was of a direct one – the elected representatives will not necessarily mirror the social, ethnic and gender composition of the electorate. The fact that elected assemblies often do not mirror their electorates is not in itself a justification for disobedience. However, if it can be shown that a particular group – for example working-class women – has not had its interests communicated then Singer's participation argument is invalidated.

(b) Most voting systems do not take into account the intensity of a person's preferences. A minority may feel *very strongly* about an issue, but they are outvoted by an *apathetic* majority. Civil disobedience can be a means by which not only are views communicated but the *intensity* of those views are made apparent.

(c) Some people find themselves in a permanent minority. This is exacerbated if electoral politics is based on one dominant social characteristic. For example, in Northern Ireland voting is largely along religious lines. In the period 1922–73 there existed a devolved parliament in Northern Ireland with the Protestant Unionists in the majority (although a significant number of Catholics voted for Unionist parties, at least in the early years). The continuous exclusion of Catholics led to the civil rights movement of the 1960s, which was influenced by the US Civil Rights Movement.

(d) Some people are denied the vote. The largest group is children. Their interests are affected by legislation over which they have no control. Civilly disobedient actions undertaken by children are rare but, arguably, groups of adults representing the interests of children could be justified in engaging in civil disobedience on their behalf.

(e) It could be argued that animals have interests and that these are clearly affected by the democratic process. Although nobody would seriously suggest that cats and dogs should be given votes, there might be a duty of care on human beings, and that duty must be articulated. Some notable examples of civil disobedience have been based on concern for animal welfare; in Britain, there has been a long-running campaign against the use of animals in what are seen by some as unnecessary experiments.

(f) The decisions made today will affect future generations. The justification given for some acts of civil disobedience against the building of roads and airports is that fossil fuel emissions exacerbate global warming, which will have catastrophic consequences for future generations.

The implication of the above points is that democracy can on occasion break down, but that it can also be 'fixed'. The more radical challenge lies in the rejection of majority decision making: a person may believe that a law is simply wrong, and no amount of institutional reform can create a situation in which the majority 'makes it right'. For example, defenders of animal experimentation for medical purposes will maintain that they have given due weight to non-human animals as beings worthy of moral respect, but that human beings have greater moral claims. Opponents of such experiments will disagree, and maintain that actions such as breaking into laboratories and releasing animals is justified on moral grounds. It is very difficult to find common ground between these two positions.

We live in a pluralistic society in which there is not only conflict between different individual and group interests, but also between different moral conceptions. The stability and legitimacy of the political system requires some agreement on moral principles. There need not be agreement on all moral issues – after all, liberalism has its roots in the recognition of pluralism – but there must be some agreement. In the next section we reconsider the arguments of Rawls, who does provide an account of that shared morality, but also justifies civil disobedience.

Rawls: Civil Disobedience and Conscientious Refusal

Rawls's discussion of civil disobedience has been highly influential because among writers on civil disobedience. His account is unusual in locating the defence of civil disobedience in a wider political theory. For Rawls the issues raised by civil disobedience go to the heart of the moral basis of democracy.

The Context

We discussed Rawls's work in Chapter 4: as the title of his most important work – *A Theory of Justice* (1972) – implies, Rawls sets out a conception of a just society. Most of *A Theory of Justice* is concerned with what Rawls calls ideal theory; that is, he assumes for the purposes of his argument that people comply strictly with the principles to which they have agreed. He departs from this assumption in one relatively short section of the book – the discussion of civil disobedience. It is only in a society where there is partial, rather than strict, compliance with the principles of justice that civil disobedience has a role. This is because civil disobedience is an appeal to the majority – to its 'sense of justice'. The majority is being asked to respect principles that it implicitly accepts. In a (fully) just society there would be no need for civil disobedience and in an unjust society there is no sense of justice to which you can appeal.

It may occur to you that Rawls's theory is just that – *his* theory. But what Rawls is trying to do is articulate what he believes is latent in the culture of a liberal democratic society: we do believe that people have rights; that there should be a social minimum (although maybe not the difference principle); that those who hold power should be accountable. The aim of a theory of justice is to create a 'model' by which we can analyse those beliefs – we do not just invent principles of justice; this is why the original position is a thought experiment. In a later book, *The Law of Peoples* (1999), Rawls addresses questions of international justice. The primary motivation for writing that book was to provide a way of assessing the legitimacy of the foreign policies of liberal democratic societies. This is germane to the present discussion, for civil disobedience has often been directed at what are perceived to be unjust wars.

pp. 450–2

Obligation to Obey the Law

Rawls begins his discussion with an apparently paradoxical claim: we have a duty to obey unjust laws, but we are also morally entitled, and possibly have a duty, to disobey unjust laws. To understand this we need to consider the structure of Rawls's theory. The principles of justice are chosen from a position in which people are morally equal – the original position. But the chosen principles are fairly general in nature – they do not take the form of constitutional rights, or concrete laws, and *laws* are the object of civil disobedience.

There are several stages between the agreement to principles of justice and the creation of laws, and what happens between these stages is crucial to our understanding of Rawls's argument for civil disobedience. Rawls sets out a four-stage sequence for the production of law, as shown in Figure 19.1.

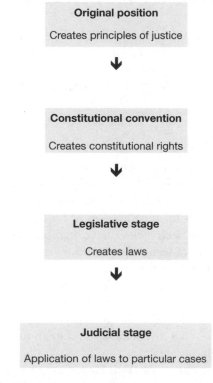

Figure 19.1 Creating Law

pp. 85–90

We are already familiar with the original position. Individuals are required to choose principles of justice behind a veil of ignorance: not only are they denied knowledge of their individual identities but also of their particular societies. Rawls argues that rational individuals would choose two principles, which roughly speaking can be summarised as: (1) an equal set of basic liberties, and (2) the guarantee of a social minimum. Once the principles are chosen we need to apply them to real societies. We are to imagine a constitutional convention in which members are denied knowledge of their own identities, but have knowledge of their society. Delegates at the convention are charged with producing a constitution that conforms to the two principles of justice. The convention is imaginary, or hypothetical; although many countries have had something like a constitutional convention – the United States being the obvious example – the exercise can also be applied to a country such as the United Kingdom, which has an uncodified constitution.

Rawls's treatment of the next stage – the legislative – is somewhat unrealistic. He imagines the 'ideal legislator' to be a person who passes statutes that conform to the constitution, but from the standpoint of denial of knowledge of his or her identity. A more realistic view would be that as we move down the sequence of stages the 'veil of ignorance' is progressively lifted, such that at the constitutional stage the delegates know their society but not their individual identities, and at the legislative stage they know both their societies and their identities. If we accept this revision to Rawls's four-stage sequence, then what happens at the legislative stage is a battle for votes, organised by political parties in a majoritarian electoral system. Obviously the danger is that what has been chosen at the first two stages – the principles of justice and the constitution – are jettisoned at the legislative stage in favour of the straightforward clash of competing interests, and the oppression of the minority by the majority. In reality, in a developed liberal democracy this does not happen: politicians usually operate with a sense of justice, and in framing legislation elected representatives quite often ignore the majority of their electorate, and pass laws protective of minority groups. A realistic model of the legislator is a person who is 'cross-pressured': she needs to get elected and re-elected and so cannot ignore the often illiberal views of the electorate, but at the same time she is moved by institutionally embodied principles of justice.

It is at the fourth – judicial – stage that Rawls thinks we have complete knowledge of the facts. This stage entails the application of rules, or laws, to particular cases by judges and administrators, and the following of rules by citizens. The possibility of injustice arises at this stage and therefore also scope for civil disobedience. Given our criticism of Rawls's description of the third – legislative – stage, it would simplify the discussion if we combined the third and fourth stages, and simply called it the legislative stage.

With this sequence of stages now in place we can return to the paradox of conflicting obligations. First, how can we have an obligation to obey unjust laws? At the first stage – the original position – we know that principles of justice must be embodied in a constitution, and constitutions provide the framework for law-making. We also know that people are in conflict with one another, and so laws will never be passed unanimously – there will always be winners and losers. What is required is a decision-making rule that is acceptable to all. It is highly unlikely that anything other than majoritarianism would be chosen in the constitutional convention. The danger is that the majority will sometimes pass unjust laws – laws which, for example, deny equal rights to minority groups. Therefore, we have a conflict:

- The principle of majority rule is effectively endorsed from stage one, which is a standpoint of moral equality, and therefore of justice.
- Majority rule will sometimes generate unjust laws.

If an individual felt entitled and, perhaps, obliged to break every law he deemed unjust, then majoritarian democracy would collapse, and in the process so would the possibility of a just society. The question, or challenge – 'what if everyone did that?' – can always reasonably be asked of someone engaged in civil disobedience.

Rawls argues that the original position argument only works if we assume that we have a moral duty to create and uphold just institutions – this is a 'natural duty' in the sense that it precedes the choice of particular principles of justice. This means: we 'enter' the original position not knowing what principles we will choose, *but committed to respecting whatever principles are chosen*. We do not choose principles but then refuse to live by them.

The natural duty to create and uphold just institutions amounts to respecting the real difficulties of 'operationalising' principles, and so not disobeying every law you think is unjust. On the other hand upholding justice also means resisting injustice. What civil disobedience then involves is making a judgement not between just and unjust laws but between *different types of unjust laws*. One suggestion Rawls makes for determining the point at which civil disobedience is justified is the degree to which a particular group bears the burden of injustice. If a group finds itself habitually, rather than occasionally, the victim of injustice then there are grounds for civil disobedience. The black community in the southern states of the United States up until the civil rights legislation of the 1960s is an obvious example.

The Nature and Role of Civil Disobedience

Given the fact that in a just society decisions will be made by majority vote – subject to many checks and balances – the possibility of civil disobedience arises for Rawls only in a democratic society:

> At what point does the duty to comply with laws enacted by a legislative majority (or with executive acts supported by such a majority) cease to be binding in view of the right to defend one's liberties and the duty to oppose injustice? This involves the nature and limits of majority rule. For this reason the problem of civil disobedience is a crucial test for any theory of the moral basis of democracy (Rawls, 1972: 363).

The leading idea behind Rawls's theory of civil disobedience is that in breaking the law *the civilly disobedient are addressing, or appealing to, the sense of justice of the majority*. All the other points that Rawls makes, including the important distinction he makes between civil disobedience and conscientious refusal, lead back to this idea.

Rawls sets out a number of conditions on civil disobedience:

1. **Injustice must be clear** What is unjust is determined by the principles of justice. Of the two, breaches of the first principle – equal liberty – are likely to be much clearer than denial of the second – guarantee of a social minimum (the difference principle). For example, to deny a class of adults the right to vote on grounds of their ethnic or religious identity, or their gender, would be clear infraction of the first principle. It is not only a clear injustice, but its remedy – granting the equal right to vote – is easy to grasp. On the other hand, significant economic inequality is much less *obviously* unjust, and the solution to the claimed injustice is not apparent.

2. **It involves breaking the law, rather than simply testing it** Some laws are broken in order to force a judicial judgment, but this does not constitute civil disobedience. As we will see this might rule out classifying significant aspects of the struggle against segregation in the southern states as civil disobedience.

3. **It need not involve breaking the law, which is the object of civil disobedience** Laws are broken in the process of engaging in civil disobedience, but they need not be the direct object of the civilly disobedient action. For example, in order to protest against an unjust war, you might sit down in the middle of the road, thus violating traffic laws, but it is not the traffic laws that are the target of the action (you will probably accept that it makes sense to have laws which prohibit people sitting down in the road!).

4. **It must be a public act** Civil disobedience is a communicative act – the majority is being given 'fair notice' that a law is unjust. The communicative act consists not simply in the transmission of information – that could be achieved through covert action – but in getting the majority to understand that the civilly disobedient are making an appeal. Indeed, there is a distinction between communicating something to the majority, and *appealing* to it.

5. **It must be non-violent and must not constitute a 'threat'** The reasoning behind this is similar to that behind (4) – the civilly disobedient want the majority to change the law for the right reason, namely because it is unjust and not because they fear the consequences of maintaining the law. Rawls could be criticised for naivety: one group may be genuinely non-violent and non-threatening, but their actions could be unintentionally threatening insofar as they make the majority aware of the existence of other, less peaceful, groups. The shadow of Malcolm X and the Nation of Islam was always behind that of Martin Luther King, Jr. Furthermore, it is not obvious that *non-violent* obstruction undermines the appeal to a sense of justice, and most campaigns have involved the deliberate *inconveniencing* of the majority.

6. **The civilly disobedient accept the penalties for law-breaking** Once again, the reasoning behind this point is that the civilly disobedient are appealing to, rather than threatening, the majority. Willingness to accept the penalties for law-breaking – that is, not resisting arrest – demonstrates sincerity. Such behaviour may embarrass the majority, who must ask themselves whether they really want to punish, often in a draconian fashion, clearly peace-loving people.

7. **Even if laws are seriously unjust, civil disobedience must not threaten the stability of the political system** The thinking behind this requirement is that a situation might arise where there are a number of groups justifiably engaged in civil disobedience, but the conjoint effects of their actions threaten the stability of the political system. In such a situation groups must show restraint. Although it is rather unrealistic, Rawls suggests that civilly disobedient groups might come to an agreement whereby groups take it in turns engaging in civil disobedience. One might wonder whether a political system that provokes so much civil disobedience is even 'partially' just, but he may have in mind the United States in the 1960s, when there were civil rights actions *and* anti-Vietnam War actions.

8. **Civil disobedience takes place within 'fidelity to law'** This underwrites the entire project of civil disobedience. The civilly disobedient do not seek to bring down the existing system, but rather they seek to strengthen it by removing

injustice, such that the system will win the loyalty of all citizens. In this sense the civilly disobedient demonstrate fidelity – or faithfulness – to the law.

We round off our outline of Rawls's theory with a discussion of his distinction between civil disobedience and conscientious refusal.

Conscientious Refusal

A distinction can be made between disobedience on general moral grounds, and disobedience on the narrower – but still moral – ground of injustice. Rawls's aim in *A Theory of Justice* was to articulate a morality – a 'theory of justice' – appropriate to the political sphere. That political morality leaves open many other areas of morality. Conscientious refusal may be grounded in that political morality, but it need not be; it may be based on 'religious or other principles at variance with the constitutional order' (Rawls, 1972: 369). The clearest modern example of conscientious refusal is objection to military service, either for general pacifist reasons or because of opposition to a particular war. Rawls argues that such objections cannot be *automatically* accepted, for justice requires on occasion that people be prepared to defend – by force of arms – the political system. However, he concedes that the spirit of pacifism accords with the values underlying a just society – it is rare for nearly just societies to go to war against one another (this is the so-called 'democratic peace argument'). He also argues that an unjust war – a war that violates the laws of peoples – can quite properly be the object of civil disobedience.

p. 451

Conscientious refusal cannot be an appeal to the sense of justice of the majority. The danger with conscientious refusal is that it undermines the political order by substituting individual moral judgement for the collective judgement of society. An example would be the refusal to pay taxes that go towards the development and maintenance of nuclear weapons. It is possible that most people are 'nuclear pacifists' – while they might believe that a just war with conventional weapons is possible, the use of nuclear warheads represents a hugely disproportionate response to the aggression of another country. But, amongst nuclear pacifists, a majority might judge that the *threat* to use – rather than actual use of – nuclear weapons is better than submission to a foreign power. Of course, a nuclear power has to convince the putative enemy country that it really will use the weapons, and so there is an element of subterfuge, as well as risk, behind deterrence theory which seems at odds with the transparency one expects of a just society. Nonetheless, there can be reasonable moral disagreement, such that the will of the majority should prevail.

Another important distinction between civil disobedience and conscientious refusal is that the latter may entail a greater 'introversion' than the former: a significant strand in conscientious refusal is the striving for moral integrity, that is, a feeling that *regardless of the consequences* you cannot support a law or policy. Insofar as conscientious refusal is a form of 'moral purity' it is in tension with civil disobedience, which looks 'outwards' towards the majority, and appeals to it to change. The idea of moral purity is central to Gandhi's *satyagraha*, which means an 'insistence on truth'. Because *satyagraha* is the moral basis of civil disobedience it is often – erroneously – translated as civil disobedience. One final point: conscientious refusal is not incompatible with civil disobedience because an individual might be *motivated* by her non-political moral beliefs, but still attempt to communicate in the language of justice to the majority.

Martin Luther King, Jr. and the Civil Rights Movement

The aim of this final section is to apply the theoretical discussion of the previous section to a case study of civil disobedience: Martin Luther King, Jr. and the Civil Rights Movement in the United States in the 1950s and 1960s. There are several reasons why we have chosen this: (a) it is the most famous example of civil disobedience and the one that influenced Rawls (*A Theory of Justice*, published in 1971, was written during the period of the Civil Rights Movement); (b) it is now close to 40 years since the main objectives of the movement were achieved, so we can assess its impact – from a Rawlsian perspective this is important, because if civil disobedience is an appeal to the majority to remove injustice *and so strengthen the political system*, then we need to see whether this was a result of the movement.

Biography   Martin Luther King, Jr. (1929–68)

Born into a family of pastors – his grandfather was the minister at Ebenezer Baptist Church in Atlanta, his father succeeded him, and Martin Luther acted as an assistant minister – he attended segregated public (state) schools in Georgia, going on to graduate with a BA degree (1948) from Morehouse College, and to undertake theological training at the racially mixed Crozer Theological Seminary.

With a fellowship from Crozer he enrolled in graduate studies at Boston University, receiving a doctorate degree in 1955. It was while he was at Boston that he met his future wife Coretta Scott, who, after King's death, wrote an account of their life together: Coretta Scott King, *My Life with Martin Luther King, Jr.* (London: Hodder & Stoughton, 1970).

In 1954 King became pastor of Dexter Avenue Baptist Church in Montgomery (Alabama) and a member of the executive of the influential National Association for the Advancement of Colored People, and as such spearheaded the bus boycott in Montgomery. During the boycott King was arrested and his house bombed, but the effect was to make King the undisputed leader of the Civil Rights Movement.

In 1957 he was elected President of the Southern Christian Leadership Conference. In the 11 years between 1957 and 1968 King travelled over 6 million miles, spoke over 2,500 times, wrote five books and numerous articles. His most famous speech – the 'I Have a Dream' address – was delivered at the culmination of a march of 250,000 people on Washington DC. He was the youngest man to be awarded the Nobel Peace Prize (1964). On the evening of 4 April 1968, while standing on the balcony of his motel room in Memphis (Tennessee), King was assassinated. Congress passed legislation in 1983 making the third Monday in January 'Martin Luther King Day', a nationwide holiday.

This biography is adapted from that produced when King was awarded the Nobel Peace Prize: http://nobelprize.org/peace/laureates/1964/king-bio.html

Historical Background to the Civil Rights Movement

The Civil Rights Movement has its roots in the struggle for emancipation from slavery in the nineteenth century. There were sporadic slave revolts before 1860, but it was during the civil war of 1861–5 that the struggle for emancipation become a central focus of American life. During the civil war, the Northern and Western states of America had remained within the Union, while the 11 Southern states formed the Confederacy (the 11 were: Alabama, Arkansas, Florida, Georgia, Louisiana, Mississippi, North Carolina, South Carolina, Tennessee, Texas, Virginia). After President Abraham Lincoln issued the Emancipation Proclamation (1862), slavery became the main issue dividing 'North' (Union) and 'South' (Confederacy). But it is important to stress the constitutional struggle behind the issue of slavery, because this underlay the political debate in the 1950s and 1960s.

The 10th Amendment (the 10th article of the Bill of Rights) guarantees states' rights: 'the powers not delegated to the United States by the Constitution, nor prohibited by it to the States, are reserved to the States respectively, or to the people'. The 'states' rights' argument tended to be used by whichever bloc was in the minority: in the earlier nineteenth century the (minority) anti-slave states of New England asserted states' rights to prohibit the holding of slaves against the majority slave states. When the balance tipped in favour of anti-slavery, the now-minority slave states asserted their rights to maintain a social institution – slavery – which they held to be central to their life and culture.

The Union defeated the Confederacy and in 1866 Congress passed the Civil Rights Act (which followed the 13th Amendment to the Constitution, abolishing slavery), which declared that all persons born in the United States were citizens and so entitled to 'full and equal benefit of the laws'. However, white Southerners, while forced to accept the abolition of slavery, used state power – through the Democratic Party – to deny newly emancipated blacks their voting rights, educational opportunities and other benefits 'of the laws'. The so-called 'Reconstruction' (1865–77) was a failure. So by the beginning of the twentieth century most blacks in the South had lost the right to vote, and there was widespread *legally enforced* segregation of education, transport and other services. In the first half of the twentieth century American blacks were divided over the correct tactics to adopt against discrimination: Booker T. Washington (1856–1915) advocated abandoning politics in favour of economic advancement; W.E.B. Du Bois (1868–1963) founded the National Association for the Advancement of Colored People (NAACP), which demanded full equality in accordance with the US Constitution; after World War 1 Marcus Garvey (1887–1940) advocated separation from white society, and even emigration to Africa.

The Civil Rights Movement

After World War II – ostensibly a war against racism in which many thousands of black servicemen had fought – the pressure for change increased. We will focus on particular events and tactics, rather than provide a narrative; several of the books (Further Reading) and websites (Weblinks) provide useful timelines.

Discrimination was so widespread – deeply institutionalised – in the South that it is difficult to pinpoint particular laws that were the object of civil disobedience.

However, among the more blatantly discriminatory laws were: the denial of the right to vote (through a wide range of mechanisms); segregated schooling; segregated services, such as seats on buses and places at 'lunch counters'; denial of entry to many facilities, such as libraries, cinemas and swimming pools; denial of places at colleges and universities; illegitimate restrictions on the right to protest; failure on the part of the police to protect blacks against violence from white racists such as the Ku Klux Klan.

Not all the actions of the civil rights activists would fall under the category of 'civil disobedience'. In fact, three strands can be discerned: (a) legal protests and actions, such as the Montgomery bus boycott (although, in fact, such actions soon became 'illegal' as legal devices were deployed against the participants); (b) actions through the courts, using or testing federal law against state law; (c) acts of peaceful law-breaking – that is, civil disobedience – such as refusing to obey police orders to disperse, and sitting at segregated lunch counters, where the proprietors could appeal to state law to enforce segregation. It is extremely important to understand how the Civil Rights Movement took place within a context of constitutional conflict, which mirrored the federal versus states conflict of the nineteenth century. Repeatedly, the federal level attempts to force desegregation on the South. Here are some key examples (federal level in bold):

- 1954: *Brown* v. *Board of Education of Topeka*: **Supreme Court** determines that segregation in public schools is unconstitutional.
- 1957: Nine black students are blocked from entering the formerly all-white Central High School, Little Rock, Arkansas. **Federal troops** sent in to protect the nine.
- 1961: James Meredith becomes first black student to enrol at the University of Mississippi; violence erupts and **President Kennedy** sends in 5,000 **federal troops**.
- 1963: 24th Amendment to the **Constitution** abolishes the poll tax, which had been used to prevent blacks registering to vote.
- 1964: **Congress** passes the Civil Rights Act – the most radical civil rights legislation since the 1866 Civil Rights Act.
- 1965: **Congress** passes the Voting Rights Act.
- 1965: **President Johnson** issues Executive Order 11246, enforcing affirmative action.
- 1967: *Loving* v. *Virginia*: **Supreme Court** rules that the prohibition on interracial marriage is unconstitutional.
- 1968: **Congress** passes another Civil Rights Act, this time outlawing discrimination in the sale, rental and financing of housing.

The laws that were the object of civil disobedience were state laws rather than federal laws; in general, the federal level was on the side of the Civil Rights Movement. We now consider some specific actions undertaken by civil rights activists: bus boycotts and freedom rides; sit-ins at lunch counters and other segregated spaces; marches, particularly on electoral registration offices.

Bus Boycotts

In romanticised accounts of the Civil Rights Movement the refusal of Rosa Parks to give up her seat for a white passenger is often taken as the starting point of the

Civil Rights Movement. On 1 December 1955 Parks got on a bus in Montgomery (Alabama), and sat in the fifth row with three other blacks in the 'coloureds' section' of the bus. After a few stops the front four rows filled up, and a white man was left standing; custom dictated that there could not be 'mixed' rows, so all four would be required to move; three of them complied but Parks refused. She was subsequently arrested. Significantly – from the perspective of civil disobedience – the charge was unclear: when a black lawyer tried to find out, the police told him it was 'none of your damn business'. (Legal theorist Lon Fuller argued that valid law must have certain characteristics, among which is clarity.)

pp. 68–70

It should be said that Parks's action was not entirely spontaneous; the Civil Rights Movement had been looking for a suitable 'victim' to publicise the issue of bus segregation and provoke a widespread boycott, and her action was not really the start of the Movement. There had been previous attempts to bring about a boycott. The boycott was effective, but the authorities then sought legal devices to end it: they required cab drivers to charge a minimum 45 cents per journey (black drivers had been charging 10 cents – the price of a bus ticket; the pro-boycott organisation, the Montgomery Improvement Association (MIA) (headed by Martin Luther King, Jr.), then instituted a 'private taxi' scheme); a very old law prohibiting boycotts was used, and King was arrested; liability insurance on the 'private taxis' was not granted. Eventually a *federal* court decided that such segregation was unconstitutional, and this was confirmed by the Supreme Court.

Freedom Rides

In 1947 the Congress of Racial Equality (CORE) set out to test the Supreme Court's 1946 ruling that segregation on interstate transportation was unconstitutional by sitting in 'whites only' seating. The so-called 'journey of reconciliation' met heavy resistance and was not a success. In 1961 the same strategy was adopted, but this time other court rulings had reinforced the claim for desegregation, and the campaign was better organised: white civil rights activists would sit in 'blacks only' seats and also use blacks only facilities at rest stops, and black civil rights activists would do the reverse on the same buses and at the same stops. They met a great deal of resistance, including mob violence and mass arrests. Ultimately they succeeded in getting the Interstate Commerce Commission to outlaw segregation. From the perspective of Rawls's criteria for civil disobedience, the freedom rides are a grey area: the *political* aim of the action was to shame President Kennedy, who was perceived at the 1960 election to be sympathetic to civil rights, but who on taking office in January 1961 was much cooler about tackling the Southern states. The *legal* aim was to test the Supreme Court's 1946 ruling. It is a matter for debate whether *testing* a law constitutes civil disobedience.

Sit-ins

The strategy here was very similar to the freedom rides: groups of black students would challenge segregation by sitting at 'whites only' lunch counters and wait until they were served; once served they moved to the next shop. There was also an element of boycott: the Woolworth's chain had segregated counters in the South, but mixed counters in the North – there was a boycott of New York shops designed to force the company to desegregate its entire chain. At first, the sit-ins met with little resistance – the students were not served, but neither were they harassed. But a white reaction did build up, with white youths attacking the activists, and the police then arresting the (peaceful) activists. A common tactic of the activists was for one group to be ready to take the place of the arrested group, with the consequence that the jails would soon fill up and the machinery of justice grind to a halt. Again, from our perspective this is interesting: Rawls says that civil disobedience must not only be non-violent – and the sit-ins certainly were non-violent – but also non-coercive. Arguably, incapacitating the justice system is coercive. Also, relatedly, and again contra Rawls, the reason why many actions, including the bus boycotts, worked was not because the majority became aware of injustice, but because their interests were damaged – pressure came from bus companies and stores to desegregate.

Electoral Registration Campaigns

The biggest 'flashpoint' was over voter registration. In principle, blacks could vote, but the Southern states found numerous ways to make it difficult for them to register as voters: there were few registration offices in black areas; opening hours were highly restricted; potential voters were intimidated with the connivance of the authorities – photographs were taken and employers informed; there was often a tax (poll tax) for registration; there were literacy qualifications (although many blacks were better educated than the officials).

The most famous, or infamous, set of events took place in 1965 at Selma (Alabama). In 1963 just 1 per cent of blacks in Selma were registered to vote. After winning the Nobel Peace Prize (December 1964) King decided that Selma should be the focus of a campaign. After various marches, arrests, and considerable violence on the part of the authorities, events came to a head on 7 March 1965 with a march across Edmund Pettus Bridge in Selma (Pettus was a Confederate General) where protestors were met by police and state troopers, who ordered them to disperse. They then attacked the protestors; pictures of their actions were transmitted across the world. What followed was complex, involving decisions such as whether to accept legal injunctions on marches, but eventually the Voting Rights Act (1965) was passed, with the number of registered black voters rising from 23 per cent in 1964 to 61 per cent in 1969. Although it is clear that the Civil Rights Movement affected the general political debate, it is a matter of debate whether *individual* campaigns, such as that at Selma, was causally responsible for *particular* pieces of legislation, such as the Voting Rights Act. We now turn to King's justification of his actions.

Martin Luther King, Jr. 'Letter from Birmingham City Jail' (1963)

King's Letter was addressed to fellow – mainly Southern white – clergymen, some of whom had criticised King's campaign of civil disobedience. Given that Rawls argues civil disobedience is an appeal to the majority, it is important to recognise the *two* audiences King addresses: the clergy are the explicit addressees, but the majority of US citizens are the implicit addressees. Although he does not separate them out we can discern both Christian and secular arguments in the Letter; of course, the great majority of Americans define themselves as Christian, but King communicates awareness that Christian arguments are not sufficient to justify civil disobedience. In setting out King's argument, we follow his narrative of events. Obviously his account should not be treated uncritically, but since our prime concern is with how he justified his actions from his perspective, the veracity of the historical details can be left to historians.

King sets out 'four basic steps' in a campaign of civil disobedience (King, 1991: 69):

1. the collection of facts to determine whether injustice is 'alive';
2. negotiation;
3. self-purification;
4. direct action.

The action that resulted in King's imprisonment – and the occasion for the Letter – were illegal demonstrations in Birmingham, Alabama. These were directed against the 'whites only' and 'no coloreds' signs in shops, the segregated restaurants (lunch counters), and the deliberate negligence of the police in investigating 18 bombings of black homes and churches over the previous six years. With regard to the first step, there was little doubt that Birmingham had one of the worst records on civil rights in the South.

The next step was to negotiate before engaging in civil disobedience. There were attempts to get the shopkeepers to remove their signs. Promises were made but not honoured. A mayoral election in March 1963 between the reactionary Bull Connor and moderate – but still segregationist – Albert Boutwell resulted in the latter's victory, but because the three-man commission that had run Birmingham, and included Connor, refused to stand down, there was no movement on removal of discrimination. Negotiation had failed. The next step was 'self-purification'. This must be distinguished from what we identified as the 'introversion' that sometimes characterises conscientious refusal. The aim of self-purification is to ascertain whether the protestors will be able to endure violence without reacting violently. To this end, workshops on non-violent protest were held.

Finally, we come to the act of civil disobedience. King argues that one of the aims of civil disobedience is to 'create such a crisis and establish such creative tension that a community which has constantly refused to negotiate is forced to confront the issue' (King: 71). The new Mayor Boutwell might be persuaded that resistance to desegregation was futile. It could be argued – and King was aware of this – that the effectiveness of civil disobedience rests on the existence of a violent alternative to it. Those engaged in civil disobedience need not intend to communicate this message for this message to be communicated through their actions. In 1963 the widely perceived 'alternative' to Martin Luther King, Jr. was Malcolm X's Muslim movement (see his biography box). Indeed King cites this movement in his Letter, arguing that if civil rights activists are dismissed as 'rabble rousers' and 'outside agitators' then millions of blacks 'out of frustration and despair, will seek solace and security in black nationalist ideologies, a development that will lead inevitably to a frightening racial nightmare' (King: 77).

Biography	Malcolm X (1925–65)

Born Malcolm Little, in Nebraska in 1925, the son of a Baptist minister, Malcolm X – he rejected the 'slave name' Little in favour of X, which denoted his lost African name – became a leading figure in the black separatist movement, a movement that advocated violence to end discrimination, although there is a debate about whether Malcolm X himself ever advocated violence.

While in prison (1946–53) he converted to Islam and joined the Nation of Islam (NOI). He was credited with increasing that NOI's membership from 500 in 1952 to 30,000 in 1963. Disillusioned with NOI, in 1964 he formed the Muslim Mosque and went on pilgrimage to Mecca. His experiences of meeting a wider range of whites persuaded him that integration was possible. He was assassinated by NOI followers in 1965.

Websites: http://www.cmgww.com/historic/malcolm/index.htm
http://www.brothermalcolm.net/mxcontent.html
http://www.malcolm-x.org/

Responding to the question how it is possible to obey some laws but disobey others, King argues that there are just laws and unjust laws:

> an unjust law is a human law that is not rooted in eternal and natural law. Any law that uplifts human personality is just. Any law that degrades human personality is unjust. All segregation statutes are unjust because segregation distorts the soul and damages the personality. It gives the segregator a false sense of superiority, and the segregated a false sense of inferiority (King: 73).

In expanding on this distinction King cites the Christian 'church fathers' Augustine (354–430) and Aquinas (1225–74), Jewish philosopher Martin Buber (1878–1965), and Protestant theologian Paul Tillich (1886–1965). It may appear that King is appealing to a particular moral conception, drawn from Judaism and Christianity, rather than a *political* morality. Three points should be made. First, so long as the underlying appeal extends beyond your own particular conception of what is ultimately valuable, which for King is rooted in Christian teaching, then enlisting Christian (and Jewish) thinkers – Augustine, Aquinas, Buber, Tillich – is legitimate. In effect, King is saying 'I am a Christian, but you do not have to be a Christian to recognise the injustice I describe'. Insofar as we interpret King's argument for civil disobedience to be based on his Christian beliefs it might be thought he is engaged in what Rawls terms conscientious refusal, but conscientious refusal is not incompatible with civil disobedience – a person, such as King, can be motivated by a secular political morality *and* a Christian morality. What would be problematic is to appeal only to a non-political morality.

Second, the letter was written to Christian clergy, so the Christian references are unsurprising. Third, King goes on to restate the argument in secular language:

> An unjust law is a code that a majority inflicts on a minority that is not binding on itself. This is difference made legal. On the other hand a just law is a code that a majority compels a minority to follow that it is willing to follow itself. This is sameness made legal (King: 74).

He gives a couple of examples, the first of which is problematic. Because the state of Alabama had denied blacks the right to vote they could not be bound by its laws. The danger with this argument is that even if blacks had voted, being in a minority they might have been subject to discriminatory laws. A rather better example is the denial of police permits to demonstrate: King accepts that there should be controls on demonstrations, but objects to the misuse of permits to deny civil rights activists the possibility of peaceful protest, while opponents of civil rights can protest unhindered. (We could also add that peaceful protestors were arrested, while their white attackers were let free; that prisoners were often released into the hands of the Ku Klux Klan; and that the right to choose who to serve in a shop or restaurant was asserted as a right when whites wanted to discriminate, but choosing to boycott buses was deemed illegal.)

King argues that a sign of the good faith of the civil rights activists is that they break the law openly and are willing to accept the penalties for law-breaking. These are, of course, on Rawls's list of conditions for civil disobedience. And finally, as if to underline the stabilising power of civil disobedience, King concludes his Letter with the following statement:

> One day the South will know that when the disinherited children of God sat down at lunch counters they were in reality standing up for the best in the American dream and the most sacred values in our Judeo-Christian heritage, and thusly, carrying our whole nation back to those great wells of democracy which were dug deep by the founding fathers in the formulation of the Constitution and the Declaration of Independence (King: 84).

What makes the Civil Rights Movement an important example of civil disobedience is that in philosophical terms it took place in the space between the constitution and lower-level law. This may also, however, raise some definitional difficulties. The most visible aspect of the civil rights struggle was the clash between supporters and opponents of equal rights in the streets, on the buses and at the 'lunch counters'. But behind that struggle was another: a struggle between federal law and constitutional judgements on the one side, and the Southern states on the other. It is notable that when defenders of segregation organised themselves politically – at elections – they adopted the banner of States' Rights: the rights of the states against the president, Congress, and Supreme Court. Civil disobedience was made possible by: (a) the existence of a (basically) just constitution, and (b) the refusal at a lower level of law-making to respect the constitution. It could be argued that what the civil rights activists were doing was appealing, not to the majority of fellow Americans, but to the judiciary; in effect, they were forcing test cases for the legitimacy of state law. On the other hand, it might be maintained that it was through elected representatives in Congress – representatives of 'the majority' – that the great strides forward in civil rights were made.

The failure of the Civil Rights Movement to change Southerners' attitudes is revealed in the Congressional voting figures for the Civil Rights Act (1964). In the Senate, the Democrats divided 46–21 in favour (69 per cent in favour) and the Republicans were 27–6 in favour (82 per cent). All Southern Democratic Senators voted against. In the House of Representatives, the Democrats divided 152–96 in favour (61 per cent) and the Republicans 138–34 in favour (80 per cent). Of the Southern Democratic Congressman 92 out of 103 (89 per cent) voted against.

Summary

Civil disobedience may seem a marginal political issue, given that most citizens do not engage in it. However, the arguments for and against civil disobedience go to the heart of the moral basis of democracy and, in particular, the only viable form of democracy in a modern society: representative majoritarian democracy. While Rawls's theory of civil disobedience does not really hold up when it is tested against historical reality it provides a very useful framework within which to assess both the grounds, and the limits, of majoritarian democracy. More generally, the development of the concept of civil disobedience grew out of, but also represents a critique of, early liberal theories of political obligation; civil disobedience implies that human beings should retain a degree of moral autonomy vis-à-vis the state.

Questions

1. Does the fact that a law was passed through a democratic process give us a special reason for obeying it?
2. Can a person who engages in civil disobedience give a coherent answer to the accusation that 'if everybody did that, there would be a collapse in social order'?
3. Is there a valid distinction between civil disobedience and conscientious refusal?
4. Was the US Civil Rights Movement really an example of civil disobedience?

References

King, Jr. M.L. (1991) 'Letter from Birmingham City Jail' in H.A. Bedau (ed.), *Civil Disobedience in Focus* London: Routledge.
Rawls, J. (1971) *A Theory of Justice* Oxford: Oxford University Press.
Rawls, J. (1999) *The Law of Peoples* Cambridge, Mass. and London: Harvard University Press.
Singer, P. (1973) *Democracy and Disobedience* Oxford: Clarendon Press.
Thoreau, D. (1991) 'Civil Disobedience' in H.A. Bedau (ed.), *Civil Disobedience in Focus* London: Routledge.

Further Reading

There is not an extensive literature on civil disobedience (although civil disobedience is often implicitly discussed in the context of political obligation). Nonetheless, the following are useful: H.A. Bedau (1991) contains 'classic' texts on civil disobedience. Another edited collection by Bedau is: H.A. Bedau, *Civil Disobedience: Theory and Practice* (New York: Pegasus, 1969). Two further studies are Chaim Gans, *Philosophical Anarchism and Political Disobedience* (Cambridge: Cambridge University Press, 1992) and Leslie Macfarlane, *Political Disobedience* (London: Macmillan, 1971). For some books on the Civil Rights Movement see: Adam Fairclough, *To Redeem the Soul of America: the Southern Christian Leadership Conference and Martin Luther King, Jr.* (Athens, Geo. and London: University of Georgia Press, 1987); David Garrows, *Protest at Selma: Martin Luther King, Jr., and the Voting Rights Act of 1965* (New Haven, Conn. and London: Yale University Press, 1978): John Salmond, *My Mind Set on Freedom: A History of the Civil Rights Movement, 1954–68* (Chicago, Ill: Ivan R. Dee, 1997).

Weblinks

Most websites on civil disobedience are activist oriented, but these can be interesting because they provide guidance on carrying out civilly disobedient acts – it is useful to compare this advice with Rawls's checklist:

- ACT-UP (gay rights organisation):
  http://www.actupny.org/documents/CDdocuments/CDindex.html

- Peace campaigners: http://www.activism.net/peace/nvcdh/

- Animal rights campaigners: http://www.animal-law.org/library/pamphlet.htm

- Fathers4Justice (a British-based group campaigning for fathers' access to their children): http://www.fathers-4-justice.org/

Chapter 20

Terrorism

Introduction

Since 11 September 2001, when the World Trade Center and part of the Pentagon were demolished through terrorist attacks, the question of terrorism has been widely debated in the media and elsewhere.

Just what is terrorism? Can a terrorist be coherently distinguished from a guerrilla or freedom fighter? An analysis of terrorism is particularly important, given the fact that authoritarian regimes may find it convenient to label all manifestations of opposition as 'terrorist' in nature. Why does terrorism arise? And above all, what we can do about it? It is important that we try to understand terrorism, not as a way of condoning it but because we will never be able to eradicate terrorism unless we understand it – its sources, its *raison d'être* and its apparent justifications.

Chapter Map

- The liberal tradition and **terrorism**. The traditional view of the state as an institution that is not itself terrorist.

- Salmi's distinction between four types of violence, and a critique of Salmi's position. The distinction between political violence and terrorism proper.

- Marx, Lenin and Mao's view of terrorism. The problem of a general theory of terrorism.

- The roots of terrorism.

- The link between terrorism and the state. The problem of US policy towards terrorism.

9/11 and its legacy

The World Trade Centre burning after the hijacked aircraft hit on 11 September 2001

Everyone can remember where they were when September 11th happened. There was saturation media coverage, and it was clearly the worst terrorist outrage anyone could recall since World War II. There was a sense of total unreality as a second plane collided with the tower of the World Trade Center not long after the first plane had struck. Thousands of people were already at their desks in both towers, while some 80 chefs, waiters and kitchen porters were working in a restaurant on the 106th floor. Many who worked for firms located in the crash zone were killed instantly. Those on the floors above the collisions were already doomed, their escape routes cut off by fire. And then the news about the Pentagon. Overall, the estimated death tolls reached 3,030 with 2,337 injuries. Al-Qaeda was blamed for the atrocities, and there was a sense at the time that this was a truly historic event. Everything that has happened since then, the wars on Afghanistan and Iraq, the passing of anti-terrorist legislation, the establishment of the internment camp at Guantanamo Bay, has confirmed that this was an event with enormous repercussions. It has brought the question of terrorism into everyone's consciousness.

Politicians and ordinary people alike condemned the atrocity. But why did it happen?

- Is the very attempt to understand the events of '9/11' an act of thoughtless condonation, or is understanding crucial to an effective way of responding to the action?

The act was denounced as 'evil'.

- Is this a useful category for characterising terrorist outrages, or is the notion of evil unable to get to grips with the reasons why such an event happened?

What did the terrorist action achieve? Clearly it obtained massive publicity.

- But did it make it easier or more difficult to implement policies that would tackle the causes of the problem?

Liberalism and the Question of Violence

We normally define terrorism as the use of political violence against individuals or the functionaries of the state. But it is clear that violence can be used against the state (and thus individuals) which would not be regarded as terrorism, so that we need to be clear when the use of such violence is regarded as 'terrorist' and when it is not.

Definitions of terrorism necessarily contain reference to acts of violence, and what makes terrorism a negative term is that violence itself is seen as negative. Indeed, it is defined in one recent volume as 'a type of political depravity which unfortunately has become commonplace' (Harmon, 2000: 2). The generalised opposition to violence comes out of the liberal tradition.

Biography, p. 171

In the *Leviathan* written by Thomas Hobbes (1588–1679) there is an emphasis upon avoiding war and establishing a commonwealth based on consent. No covenant can be valid that exposes a person to 'Death, Wounds, and Imprisonment' (Hobbes, 1968: 169). Here is the view that force or violence negates freedom, and although Hobbes allows freedom to be consistent with fear and necessity, it cannot be reconciled with force. Indeed, so concerned is Hobbes with the problem of force and the individual's natural right to avoid it, that (unlike Locke) he takes the view that an individual is not bound to fight for the state (Hoffman, 1998: 46).

Biography, p. 176

Locke (1632–1704) likewise argues that only when someone is not under the 'ties of common law of reason', can 'force and violence' be deployed (Locke, 1924: 125). It is true that Locke justifies slavery as a state of war continued between a lawful conqueror and captive (1924: 128), so that even if force can be lawful (a point to which we will return), the liberal tradition sees a conflict between violence and freedom, violence and rights.

The notion of terrorism becomes possible only when violence is seen in negative terms. Whereas pre-modern thought regarded violence as a sign of human empowerment – hence the positive evaluation of the warrior – liberalism argues for a world in which market exchanges are defined as activity that has banished violence. Thus the praise for terrorism, which is offered by Sheikh Azzam, reputedly the teacher of the Saudi terrorist, Osama Bin Laden, cannot be squared with the liberal tradition. The notion that terrorism is some sort of an obligation in the Muslim religion is not only a dubious reading of Islam: it implies a legitimacy for violence which the liberal tradition cannot accept, at least as the criterion of a free person.

It is true that Hobbes refers to the force of the state as 'terror' (Hobbes, 1968: 227), but the use of the term is atypical. It is much more common to refer to the use of force by the state, and terror used by the enemies of a state who resort to what is seen as illegitimate violence.

The State and Terrorism

The liberal tradition often distinguishes between force and violence – and thus force and terrorism. State terrorism refers to states that sponsor terrorism, not the state per se as an organisation that uses terror.

Lacqueur, who has written numerous works on the question of terrorism, argues that Iran has sponsored the Hizbullah group in the Lebanon, and it has extended support to Shi'ite groups in Afghanistan and Palestinian groups such as the Islamic Jihad. Iraq under Saddam Hussein, he argues, has been much more cautious in its support for terrorist groups, but it did provide some shelter to the remnants of the Abu Nidal group and the People's Liberation Front for Palestine (Lacqueur, 2003: 223–5).

Although we think that there is a strong case for using force and violence as synonyms, Johnston sharply distinguishes the two on the grounds that violence is force that violates some moral or legal norm, so that we can differentiate between, say, police force and criminal violence. He argues that it is important to combine confrontation and conciliation, reason and force in combating violence, and he identifies terrorists as criminals (Johnston, 1993: 16–17). It is true that criminals do not necessarily see themselves as acting politically, whereas terrorists do.

The argument is that because the force of the state is authorised and limited to specific purposes, it cannot be considered 'violent', and therefore the notion of terror and terrorism has to be restricted to those who oppose the state. Miller comments that 'it is a well-entrenched feature of our language that to describe an action as an act of violence is to condemn it forcefully' (Miller, 1984: 403). Wilkinson contends that it is 'sheer obfuscation' to imagine that one can theorise about terrorism in a value-free way (1979: 101).

In Miller's view, the force/violence distinction only applies when laws are general; when they are enacted in advance of behaviour they seek to control; when they do not discriminate between persons on irrelevant grounds, and the penalties are standardised and applied impartially (1984: 404). Violence is unpredictable and irregular. It is for this reason that the political theorist Petit argues that only when force is used in an arbitrary way is freedom is compromised (Petit, 1997: 302). A non-arbitrary use of force, that is the working of a liberal state, governed by a constitution, does not make you unfree, so that Petit's argument is that the force of a constitutional state does not lead to domination, and therefore should not be regarded as violence.

An Assessment of Salmi

Salmi, a development economist from Morocco, has written an important work entitled *Violence and Democratic Society*. In it he defines violence as an act that threatens a person's physical or psychological integrity (Salmi, 1993: 16), and he distinguishes between four categories of violence.

- *direct* violence involves deliberate attacks that inflict harm (kidnappings, homicide, rape, torture). This would certainly embrace terrorism. But Salmi distinguishes between direct and

- *indirect* violence when, he argues, violence is inflicted unintentionally as in cases of *violence by omission* when, say, inaction contributes to starvation or genocide (as in Roosevelt's failure to intervene in 1942 against Hitler's final solution) (1993: 18). This indirect violence may also take the form of what Salmi calls *mediated* (1993: 19) violence that occurs when individuals or institutions produce goods or trade in weapons of war which (again unintentionally) damage the health and environment of others. Salmi's third category relates to what he calls

- *repressive violence* (1993: 20), when people are derived of their political, civil, social or economic rights, while
- *alienating violence* (1993: 21) – his fourth category – embraces the kind of oppression (ethnic and male chauvinism, racism, hostile acts of homophobia, opposition to AIDS sufferers, etc.) that undermines a person's emotional, cultural and intellectual development. What are we to make of these categories, and their link to the question of terrorism?

It seems to us problematic to characterise direct violence as merely one form of violence among others. For this is the violence that deserves our immediate attention since it prevents people from (even in a formal sense) governing their lives. Salmi estimates that between 1820 and 1970 (after the Napoleonic war through to the Vietnam conflict) some 68 million people died as a consequence of 'direct' violence, and this is the form of violence that, as the public rightly perceives, is the pressing problem (Salmi, 1993: 47). Whereas inaction (as in Salmi's second category) may be categorised as an evil, it cannot be said to constitute violence per se, although it may certainly be the *cause* of violence.

Again, what Salmi calls *repressive* and *alienating violence* may lead to direct violence, but until it does it cannot be called violence (and thus terrorism) as such, although as with the so-called indirect violence of unemployment it certainly harms people and should be condemned. Violence, as we see it, should be restricted to the infliction of deliberate physical harm: a case could certainly be made for incorporating abuse as violence where it leads to physical pain of the kind expressed through depression etc. But violence becomes too broad a category if it is linked to any kind of pressure that affects someone's 'integrity' if by that is meant their capacity to act in a particular way.

For the same reason we would resist the argument of Bourdieu, a radical French social theorist, that violence can be symbolic or 'structural' (Bourdieu, 1998: 40, 98). Clearly, verbal and other forms of non-physical aggression are *linked* to violence, but we would prefer to distinguish between the causes of violence and violence itself. We will later challenge the notion that the liberal state uses only force and not violence, but we take the view that violence is best defined as the intentional infliction of physical harm.

But although all terrorism is violent, not all violence even against the state is terrorism.

Distinguishing between Political Violence and Terrorism

It is our view that when political violence is used in conditions in which no other form of protest is permissible, then it would be wrong to call it violence. Miller argues that 'violence may be permissible in dictatorships and other repressive regimes when it is used to defend human rights, provoke liberal reforms, and achieve other desirable objectives' (Miller, 1984: 406). Such violence should not be called terrorism, and the Thatcher government was wrong to describe the African National Congress (ANC), which resorted to violence (among other tactics) against the apartheid regime, as terrorist in character. The US government saw the ANC as one of the most notorious terrorist groups at the time. The point is that the ANC only resorted to violence as a response to the actions of a regime that banned the organisation and imprisoned its leaders.

Brian Bunting, a South African who has written widely on the anti-apartheid struggle, has documented in detail the laws passed in the period of 'grand apartheid' under Dr Verwoerd that, among other things, prevented peaceful protest. He cites the comment of Umkhonto we Sizwe (the ANC aligned Spear of the Nation) on its birth in 1961 where it talked about carrying on the struggle for freedom and democracy 'by new methods' that 'are necessary to complement the actions of the established national liberation organizations' (Bunting, 1969: 216). The ANC was no more terrorist than the partisans and liberation movements that fought against the Nazis during World War II. We would therefore disagree with the inclusion of the ANC in Harmon's glossary of terrorist groups (Harmon, 2000: 281). The violence employed by the ANC was regrettable, and it is worth noting that grisly 'neck-lacing' of those seen as regime collaborators (when individuals had old car tyres placed around their necks and these were then set ablaze with petrol) was a practice that the ANC never officially supported. The ANC is better described as a democratic rather than a terrorist movement. Chomsky (2003: 61) speaks of the French partisans using 'terror' against the Vichy regime, but although he intends by this example to expose what he considers to be the hypocrisy of the United States, violence against illiberal systems should not be described in these terms.

Biography, p. 504

To argue that using political violence against an illiberal state is not terrorist is better than arguing that one can be both terrorist and freedom fighter. This is not to say that the use of political violence in conditions in which it cannot be labelled terrorist is not problematic. We should be careful not to idealise political violence. Movements that resort to violence inevitably commit human rights abuses as well, and anyone who thinks that liberation movements are purely and simply a 'good' thing ought to see how, in contemporary Zimbabwe for example, the use of political violence can leave a legacy of authoritarianism and brutalisation. Reports from human rights groups have noted that in the first half of January 2004 there were 4 deaths, 68 cases of torture and 22 kidnappings, with much of the violence carried out by youths from the ruling ZANU-PF party (http://news.bbc.co.uk/1/hi/world/africa/1780206.stm).

In a moving work, *The Soft Vengeance of a Freedom Fighter* (1991) Sachs, a leading supporter of the ANC, a human rights lawyer and now a judge in South Africa, recalls the anguish he felt when he heard reports that Umkhonto we Sizwe were to target white civilians in the struggle to liberate South Africa. Having lost the sight of one eye and his right arm as the result of a car bomb in Maputo in Mozambique in 1988 (the work of agents of the South African security forces), Sachs feared that a free South Africa might come to consist largely of one-eyed and one-armed people like himself. He was hugely relieved to hear reports that his organisation was not planning to escalate violence in a way that would plunge South Africa 'in an endless Northern Ireland or Lebanon type situation, where action becomes everything and politics gets left behind' (Hoffman, 1994: 22). His anxiety eloquently testifies to the fact that violence remains a dangerous process even when it is (justifiably) used against illiberal states, and cannot be called terrorist in character.

Terrorism, Ambiguity and the Liberal State

If political violence can be justified when a state is explicitly authoritarian and denies its opponents any channel of legal change (as in apartheid South Africa), it becomes terrorism when employed against a liberal state. The liberal state, as we have already suggested, is distinctive in its opposition to force or violence as a method of settling conflicts of interest. This is why, under pressure, the liberal state has conceded rights to wider and wider sections of the community, and it promotes in the main a culture of self-reliance and universal freedoms. The opponents of the party in power are entitled to use, as Wilkinson (an academic expert on terrorism) points out, the normal channels of democratic argument, opposition and lobbying through political parties, pressure groups, the media and peaceful protest (Wilkinson, 1979: 40).

Ch 10:
Anarchism,
pp. 238–61

Given the fact that the liberal state uses as its legitimating norm the notion that its laws are *authorised*, the use of violence against the liberal state is certain to be counter-productive. Groups such as the June 2nd movement and the Baader Meinhof group grew out of the West German student movement of the 1960s, and were hostile to the liberal state, believing that it merely represented big business. The bombings that they embarked upon succeeded only in provoking the state to tighter security policies with substantial public support. As Harmon points out, the motivating philosophy in the case of violence against liberal societies is often one of anarchism, and violent outrages do not advance, but rather set back, the cause of democracy. The movement against the Vietnam War (1965–1973) created, in addition to a legitimate and sensible protest movement, small numbers of terrorists such as the Weathermen, who attacked the officials and property of the state (Harmon, 2000: 6).

Terrible ironies accompany the use of violence in liberal states. Take, for example, attacks by animal rights activists on the directors of companies believed to be involved with testing on animals. These movements justify the most appalling suffering of humans (who are also a kind of animal as well), and actions such as these are invariably used by the media to diminish public sympathy for the animal rights cause. Is the destruction of property rather than individuals to be seen as terrorist in nature?

There are two problems here. The first is that the use of violence against property can easily (if unintentionally) harm individuals who are protecting such property, and the illegal nature of the act can have adverse political consequences. We would describe violence against property as 'soft' terrorism since in most circumstances peaceful forms of protest can create a change in opinion and would be more productive. But breaking the law per se does not count as terrorism, and in the movement in Britain against the Poll Tax in the late 1980s widespread public support was created for acts of defiance. The Poll Tax or Community Charge was calculated according to the number of people inhabiting a house rather than the value of the property itself. In general, it could be argued that violence against property is likely to be counter-productive and set the struggle for democracy back. The cause is invariably overshadowed by the damage caused, and so the content of the protest is lost.

The use of violence in liberal societies is always inclined to be ideologically ambiguous. Lacqueur argues with some justification that groups of the extreme 'left' often merge with, and become indistinguishable from, groups of the far right. Anti-Semitism may characterise terrorists who claim emancipation as their objective, and Lacqueur poses the question: 'Is Osama bin-Laden a man of the left or right? The question is, of course, absurd' (2003: 8). But why? It is true that the extreme left can merge with the extreme right – but the distinction between left and right is still useful. Anti-liberalism can easily be right wing in character, but it depends upon whether this infringement of liberal values is resorted to as an attempt to emancipate humanity or privilege a particular group. The kind of Islamic fundamentalism that al-Qaeda espouses is right wing, not simply because it is authoritarian but because it opposes (even in the future) democracy, female emancipation, toleration etc. It is impossible to be a left-wing anti-Semite, although one can certainly be critical of the state of Israel and therefore be an anti-Zionist. Anti-Semitism is a particularistic creed (i.e. it does not espouse the freedom of all humans) and can therefore be legitimately characterised as a right-wing doctrine. Ideological ambiguity arises when logically incompatible elements are mixed together and whether something is of the extreme right or the extreme left depends upon the overall judgement we make of the 'mix'.

Box, p. 406

Is Colonel Qaddafi, the current leader of Libya, a man of the left and right? He is a mixture but his nationalist chauvinism would tend to make him more right than left wing, although we would accept that authoritarian methods can be presented in the name of emancipation. As Harmon notes, his work extolling the virtues of a third way between capitalism and communism was, in the early 1990s, eagerly distributed by the British National Front (2000: 10). The point about terrorism is that the use of violence by the left in conditions of liberal democracy can easily become linked to terrorism of the right, as in the 'critical support' that some Trotskyite groups gave to the Iranian leader Ayatollah Khomeini and the reactionary Taliban.

What are more difficult to categorise are movements such as the IRA that (unlike the Red Brigades of Italy) enjoy a real base of popular support. Why? O'Day warns against the danger of forcing 'Irish terrorism into a strait jacket' (1979: 122). In Northern Ireland, the whole nature of the state has been problematic in liberal terms, and it is difficult, if not impossible, to envisage a minority becoming a majority, because of the nationalist divide. A liberal society can only operate to isolate extremists and advocates of violence if it offers meaningful political rights and the prospect of constitutional change. If this does not occur then we have a classic 'tyranny of the majority' scenario that promotes illiberal values and institutions, as Northern Ireland dramatically demonstrated particularly before 1972 when the police force was partisan and unionists won seats in local elections through manipulating the electoral boundaries. Writing in 1979, O'Day can still speak of the 'deep-seated Catholic grievances' of the nationalist minority in the North (1979: 129). The fact that the Provisional IRA has called a ceasefire with the Good Friday Agreement of 1998, and its political wing has become more preoccupied with simply propagating republican values, suggests that its terrorism was complicated by the popular support it enjoyed and the fact that it did not operate in a conventional liberal state.

O'Day comments that popular support 'may be passive, but it is, nonetheless, real and important' (1979: 124). The 1921 Treaty that partitioned Ireland was seen by republicans as a cynical exercise by the British that created, in the place of the historic nine county Ulster, a six county statelet with a contrived Protestant majority. O'Day speaks of the IRA as having 'enduring appeal'. In O'Day's judgement, much of the Irish activity is 'less properly described as terrorism than a particularly unpleasant form of violence springing directly from the grievances of an oppressed minority or the frustration of the young and unemployed' (1979: 126–7, 132).

Marx on the Problem of Terrorism

Ch 9: Socialism, pp. 208–37

We have characterised Marxism as a mixture of post-liberal and anti-liberal views, views that build on liberalism and views which are authoritarian in character. The question of what counts as violence is all important here, since if capitalism itself is seen as a form of violence then Marxists would appear to condone counter-violence even in a liberal society, and this, in our argument, would make Marxism sympathetic to terrorism.

Some argue that, for Marx, death caused by indifference and neglect 'are as much a part of human violence as the violent acts of revolutionaries' (Harris, 1973–4: 192). Now there is no doubt that Marxist violence can be readily justified in conditions where workers either do not have a vote or the franchise is fraudulent. But Harris's argument is questionable. For, Marx does not regard the exploitation of labour by capital as violent, and in *Capital* he argues it is 'dull compulsion' of the relations of production that subjects labour to capital. It is not normally violence or force. The *Communist Manifesto* argues that when workers destroyed imported goods, smashed machinery and set factories ablaze, they failed to understand that it is the relations of production that need to be changed, not the instruments of production (Marx and Engels, 1967: 89). Random acts of violence are unhelpful and misguided.

It is true that Marx and Engels in the *Address of the Central Authority to the [Communist] League* speak of the fact that the communists 'must compel the democrats to carry out their present terrorist phrases' encouraging popular revenge against hated individuals or public buildings (Marx and Engels, 1978: 202), but this was said in the throes of violent revolution against an autocratic system and cannot be taken as an endorsement of violence against a liberal state. What makes Marx sceptical about terrorism in general is that it rests upon a belief in an abstract will, not in the maturation of material conditions. This is why he comments in *On the Jewish Question* that the belief that private property can be abolished through the guillotine as in the reign of terror by the Jacobins, is naive and counter-productive (Marx and Engels, 1975: 156). (The Jacobins were radicals who resorted to terror in the later phases of the French Revolution of 1789.)

Ch 9:
Socialism,
pp. 208–37

The problem of terror arises in Marxism from the belief in the inevitability of revolution. Revolution invariably involves violence, and if such violence is directed against a liberal society it counts as terrorism. Moreover, the idea that the use of violence is purely tactical and arouses no problem of morality ignores the difficulty which violence creates in a liberal society.

The Leninist and Maoist Position on Terrorism

In countries such as Tsarist Russia (1696–1917) the use of violence against particular individuals was deemed counter-productive by the Bolsheviks. Indeed it was labelled terrorism both by its propagators and critics. What made such violence harmful was that it did not advance the cause of anti-Tsarism. Thus the killing of Tsar Alexander II (who had come to power in 1881) created, as Lacqueur points out, a backlash and was used to justify more severe policies on behalf of the regime. In the same way, the upsurge of democratic forces that compelled the Tsarist government to introduce a new constitution lost its impact when, as a result of 'terrorist' attacks in 1906, these concessions were withdrawn.

Ch 10:
Anarchism,
pp. 238–61

The problem here is that the attacks on particular figures are premised upon a flawed analysis of the political process. Many of the terrorists and champions of political violence, past and present, have been motivated by an anarchist philosophy that extols abstract will-power, and has little regard for broadening and deepening a popular movement opposed to a repressive regime. Marx and Engels condemned the Fenians – the Irish Republican Brotherhood – in London, not because the two revolutionaries did not sympathise with the cause of Irish freedom, but because they felt that blowing up people in London would not strengthen this cause. Even under repressive regimes, where political violence can be justified, terrorist-type violence, the killing of individuals and, worse, civilian bystanders, can be counter-productive and lead to political marginalisation.

Biography,
p. 223

What is however problematic is Lenin's view that violence is normally necessary, and raises no ethical dilemmas. To describe the Bolsheviks as the 'Jacobins of contemporary Social Democracy' and to cite with approval Marx's comment that 'French terrorism' involved a settling of accounts with absolutism and feudalism in a 'plebian manner' (Hoffman, 1984: 56) implies that violence is acceptable in, it seems, almost any context. For Lenin, it is an integral part of politics. To define a dictatorship – even the dictatorship of the proletariat – as authority untrammelled by laws and based directly on force (Lenin, 1962: 246), is to condone the use of violence by the post-liberal state and, it would seem, even against the liberal state. Such violence would, in the analysis adopted here, be regarded as terrorism.

Ch 1: The State,
pp. 14–37

It is surely revealing that Sorel, the French anarcho-syndicalist, at the end of his *Reflections on Violence,* has a hymn of praise to Lenin as a 'true Muscovite' because of his propensity to use violence (Sorel, 1961: 281). Sorel's own rather mystical deification of violence places him closer to the fascists (1961: 23), but it is instructive that he was an admirer of Lenin. Rosa Luxemburg was to express her anxiety over the dictatorial methods and 'rule by terror' that Lenin and Trotsky adopted after the October revolution.

Biography,
p. 222

Georges Sorel (1847–1922)

Born in Cherbourg and, after receiving a private education there, attended the Ecole Polytechnique, where he distinguished himself in mathematics. He entered the Civil Service as an engineer and retired after 25 years, then promptly took up writing, and through innumerable books established his place as a major social critic.

He published nothing before he was 39. In *Le proces de Socrate* (1889) and *La ruin du monde antique* (1894, 1901) he argued that a strong moral structure rested upon a sturdy family, a warrior mentality, and an 'epic state of mind' rooted in myth. He became a socialist in 1892, and in his work on the natural sciences argued that increasingly nature is an artificial construct, and it is absurd to think that an overarching natural science is possible. Workers overcome their own 'natural natures' through acting heroically.

In 1906 he wrote – to give it its title in English – the *Social Foundations of Contemporary Economics* – in which he praised Marx but dismissed his notion of class conflict as 'inevitable' and the argument that life for workers would become increasingly miserable. He was particularly hostile to the idea that violent conflict would come to an end in a higher communist society.

In *The Illusions of Progress* written in 1908 he linked the idea of progress with decadence, and felt that the notion of dialectical progress in Marx's writings would sap the vitality of workers' organisations and subject them to an aristocracy of politicians and state functionaries. He became a syndicalist, taking the view that workers' organisations ought to act through strikes and direct action rather than through conventional political involvement. Myths, he argued, were ideas that steeled people with certainty and moral purpose, and he famously spoke of the 'myth' of the general strike.

He elaborates this point in his *Reflections on Violence* that first appeared in 1908. Here he speaks of the 'social poetry' that sustains moral energy. After 1908 he became pessimistic about the future of the workers' movement, and until 1914 he thought that royalism could provide the moral inspiration needed for action. He showed some sympathy for fascism, and it is said that his passion for revolutionary activity in place of rational discourse made him influential in shaping the direction of fascism, especially in Mussolini's Italy. In his final years he welcomed the Russian Revolution in the hope that it would bring about self-governing workers' councils.

Mao Zedong's notion of guerrilla war draws upon classical Chinese writings and stresses the need to attack an enemy (which is numerically superior) at its weakest points (Schram, 1967: 156). What is new in Mao's formulation is the emphasis upon the need politically to win the confidence of the poor peasantry – a strategy which appears to contradict the notorious Maoist formulation that political power stems from the barrel of a gun. Mao's execution of 'enemies' becomes problematic in terms of the analysis here, when force is unleashed during his political opponents, particularly during the Cultural Revolution, and it is only after the establishment of state power that he can be regarded as a terrorist rather than a freedom fighter.

What we have called the anti-liberal elements within Marxism – in particular the notion of class war and revolution – create support for a political violence

How to read:

Sorel's *Reflections on Violence*

This is a classic text that sets out Sorel's support for violence and the myth of the general strike. You need to concentrate on those chapters that deal with Sorel's views of violence in particular (although if you were concerned about his defence of syndicalism – revolutionary trade unionism – you would concentrate on other chapters). You can skip the introductory letter to Daniel Halevy – a French historian – but his 'Introduction to the First Publication' is worth a careful read. Chapter 1 deals with his evaluation of Marxism and socialism and therefore, for purposes of the argument, can be left out. Chapter 2, which deals with what Sorel sees as the pacifist attitudes of the middle classes, deserves a careful read, as does Chapter 3 on 'Prejudices Against Violence'. Note that each chapter contains a brief summary at the top that is worth perusing. Chapter 5 on the 'Political General Strike' can be skipped, but Chapter 6 on the ethics of violence is worth reading carefully. Chapter 7 and Appendix 1 can be skipped, but Appendices 2 and 3 deserve a careful read, since the latter contains Sorel's revealing assessment of Lenin.

that can become terrorist in character. It is true that Marxism does not support the view (which Frantz Fanon, an Algerian revolutionary, endorsed), that violence is somehow an ennobling and 'cleansing' process. Fanon argues that violence 'frees the native from his inferiority complex and from his despair and inaction; it makes him fearless and restores his self-respect' (Fanon, 1967: 74). This kind of view sees the terrorist as a person without normal relationships: they are wedded to the Struggle or Revolution, not to family and friends. This view is inherent, it could be argued, in violence, and therefore on the surface of things would seem opposed to Marxism's methodology (Marxism speaks of individuals entering into relations with one another). Nevertheless, Marxism does contain aspects that facilitate the use of violence, and thus terrorism, in liberal and socialist societies.

A General Theory of Terrorism?

Lacqueur argues that there will perhaps never be an authoritative guide to terrorism because there is not one terrorism, but a variety of terrorisms: what is true for one does not necessarily apply to the others (2003: 8).

Lacqueur is certainly right to stress that terrorism takes many different forms. In the nineteenth century terrorism was linked to struggles for national independence and social justice, and sought to avoid civilian casualties. In the twentieth century this has changed, and the most disturbing feature of what has been called the 'new terrorism' is the way in which no distinction is made between functionaries of a particular regime and ordinary civilians. The IRA tried to give warnings for its attacks; so does ETA (the Basque Euskadi Ta Azkatasuna) – al-Qaeda does not. A recent analysis of the Middle East describes suicide bombing as a 'new terrorism' (Azzam, 2003: 10). A clear distinction, therefore, needs to be made between 'traditional' terrorism that regarded civilian deaths as 'regrettable', and the terrorism of groups such as al-Qaeda which specifically targets ordinary people.

But while distinctions need to be noted, it has to be said that variety is common to all movements and 'isms'. Movements such as socialism and concepts such as democracy are also extremely variegated – terrorism is no different. Lacqueur insists that terrorism, 'more perhaps than most concepts', has generated widely divergent interpretations (2003: 232), but there seems to be no reason why this should be so. Of course, it is complicated by the fact that the term has now (mostly) acquired a distinctively pejorative tone but concepts such as democracy have acquired, as we have pointed out, a distinctively positive connotation.

While the search for a 'general theory' needs to be sensitive to difference and variety, it is possible to argue the case for a definition of terrorism while stressing the complexity and heterogeneous nature of the phenomenon. When Lacqueur takes the view that 'the search for a scientific, all-comprehensive definition is a futile enterprise' (2003: 238), his problem arises because he assumes that such a definition must be beyond controversy and counter-argument. An impossible demand! He in fact goes on to provide a working definition – 'the systematic use of murder, injury, and destruction, or the threat of such acts for political ends' – which is perfectly acceptable provided we add that such violence is employed in liberal or post-liberal societies. The use of violence to challenge and remove an authoritarian or explicitly anti-liberal regime cannot be called terrorism.

Lacqueur also argues that what makes a general theory impossible is the fact that there is not 'one overall explanation' of the roots of terrorism (2003: 22). But this argument rests upon a false juxtaposition between the general and the particular: certainly a theory of terrorism is complex and there are many factors involved. But this is true of all theory. It is a reflection of a complex world, infinite in its particularity. The general can only express itself through the particular, and when we come to present our own 'general theory' it is clear that multiple factors are necessarily involved.

It has been argued that, on the one hand, we should 'perhaps' think of terrorisms rather than terrorism, thus freeing ourselves from the tyranny of the search for an all-embracing and universally acceptable definition. On the other hand, the term 'terrorism' is still used in the singular (Gearson, 2002: 22).

The Roots of Terrorism

There is certainly no simple explanation for terrorism, but finding its roots can only help to provide some guidance to this complex phenomenon. Terrorism is not necessarily to be found in the harshest regimes, since highly efficient dictatorships can make political violence extremely difficult, whereas it is a sad fact of life that regimes, which are either democratic or partly democratic, have become much more vulnerable to terrorist attack. Regimes that appeared democratic at the outset of terrorist attack may cease to be so – such as the Uruguayan crushing of the Tupamaros – after the threat has been dealt with (Friedlander, 1979: 235).

Lacqueur argues that while poverty is a factor it should not be exaggerated: very poor countries may see civil unrest and even civil war, but not terrorism. The followers of terrorism might be poor, whereas the leaderships are wealthy and middle class: 'terrorism rarely occurs in the poorest and richest countries, especially if these happen to be small societies in which there is little anonymity; between these extremes, terrorism can occur almost anywhere'. He cites Kofi Annan, Secretary-General of the UN, to the effect that the poor suffer enough: why add to their misery by branding them potential terrorists (Lacqueur, 2003: 16; 18)? Alongside poverty must be added national and ethnic conflict, although this kind of conflict has not been evident in some countries in which terrorism has occurred. It is useful to distinguish between the 'symptoms' and 'causes' of terrorism (von Hippel, 2002: 25). No strategy can be successful that simply addresses itself to the symptoms, and ignores the reasons as to why terrorism arises. Just as it is difficult to define terrorism, it is also difficult to locate terrorism's roots, but what can be said is that terrorism arises because people cannot 'change places'. This is not because people are different, since we are all different from one another – in terms of our age, occupation, gender, outlook etc. There are a multiplicity of factors involved in an inability to change places: significant disparities in wealth; religious intolerance; bitterness and despair; and the prevalence of a 'blame' culture that helps to convert differences into divisions. When these divisions are not understood, and no realistic strategy exists for overcoming them, we can have terrorism.

The problem with the Lacqueur analysis is that it sees terrorism as insoluble. 'It stands to reason', he argues, 'that if all mankind were to live in small countries, preferably in small cities, and if all human beings were well off, there would be less violence, be it crime or terrorism. But there is no reason to assume that violence would disappear altogether' (2003: 15). Lacqueur seeks to argue that terrorism per se is ineradicable. It is clear that no factor, on its own, will do the trick. Removing the problem posed by the state of Israel, eliminating world poverty, tackling repression and injustice, reducing the frustration which inequality engenders, addressing a culture that glorifies war, would clearly help to reduce terrorism. But it would be foolish, indeed, to imagine that any particular factor, or even taking them together, would eliminate terrorism. The way in which, for example, former colonies had their boundaries drawn – dividing linguistic and ethnic groups in arbitrary fashion – has stored up appalling problems that will take decades to resolve. But why should we assume that terrorism will always exist?

To argue, as Laqueur does, that 'there are no known cures for fanaticism and paranoia' (2003: 10) is to suggest that psychological problems lie outside of social relationships and cause terrorism. We know, for example, that depression and mental illness can arise from problematic family relationships and these are often linked to aggressive, authoritarian and patriarchal attitudes. Psychological problems have their roots in social relationships. To suggest that terrorism will always be with us because it is a complex phenomenon is to generalise from the contemporary world in a way which creates fatalism and despair. The point is that in a world in which poverty, national and ethnic injustices, patriarchal policies and practices were being tackled, people would be better able to 'change places' than they are at the moment. A reduction in terrorism implies logically that terrorism can be eliminated, since there is no evidence that it is part of human nature to murder, maim and destroy for political reasons.

Von Hippel is more positive than Lacqueur. She notes that strong authoritarian states – such as Egypt, Algeria and Saudi Arabia – may also provide conditions for terrorism, just as the collapse of states, such as the Sudan and Somalia may provide a breeding ground. She concedes that 'sharpening the focus on root causes' can lead to 'politically awkward situations and policy choices'. Nevertheless, these need to be addressed if 'the counterterrorist campaign is to succeed' (Von Hippel, 2002: 38). It is difficult to eradicate terrorism, but the problem is not in principle insoluble.

The Problem of Terror and the State

Ch 1: The State, pp. 14–37

We have already cited Hobbes's comment that the state uses terror to maintain order. 'Perhaps it is time', Friedlander argued in 1979, 'to terrorize the terrorists' (1979: 232). It seems to us that built into Weber's definition of the state is an emphasis on the use of violence to settle conflicts of interest, and therefore it can only be plain prejudice to assume that the state cannot or does not use terror against its enemies. Von Hippel concedes that 'no state has a complete monopoly on organized violence' (2002: 30) and as we have pointed out in the chapter on the state, states claim a monopoly which they cannot and do not have.

There is a good deal of confusion in this area. On the one hand, one writer seems to think it necessary to separate terrorism from the monopolistic use of violence claimed by states, and sees terrorism as the work of sub-national groups or non-state entities. On the other hand, he says that during the 1930s terrorism became 'a state monopoly' 'reminding observers that enforcement terrorism has been much more destructive than agitational terrorism' (Gearson, 2002: 11; 15). The reference to 'enforcement terrorism' surely implies that states can and do exercise terror.

Lacqueur sees the argument that states use force as a 'red herring', although he concedes that the terrorism exercised by states has caused far more victims than the terrorism exercised by small groups. He gives the example of Nazi Germany and Stalinist Russia (2003: 237), and, it is important to note, even liberal states use force against those who are deemed to break the law. This force can be characterised as terrorism. The terrorism of the liberal state is usually implicit since attempts are made to regulate and limit the use of force by state functionaries. But this terrorism becomes explicit when states (such as the current Israeli state) espouse policies of assassination against their opponents. It is true that there is a difference between the terrorism of small groups and the terrorism of the state (2003: 237). But the fact remains that while the use of force can under certain circumstances be justified, it can never be legitimate. We may have to use terror against those who will not respond to mere social and moral pressures, in order to create a breathing space in which constructive policies cementing common interests can be employed. In other words, we need to pay careful attention to the context in which terrorism is used. The leader of the Palestinian group Hamas has stated recently that he regretted the death of women and children in suicide bombings, and declared that if the international community supplied his organisation with F-16s and helicopter gunships they would attack the military forces of Israel with those instead.

Ch 1: The State,
pp. 14–37

States, in general, claim a monopoly of *legitimate* force so that the use of force to tackle conflicts of interest has to be authorised, and in liberal states this means (as noted above) that force is legally regulated and formally limited. Two further things can be said about the violence of the state. The first is that it is often a response to violence from within the community, and a stateless society is only desirable if social order is secured through what have been called elsewhere, governmental sanctions. Where government is relatively weak then a state is important since it seeks, however partially, to secure a monopoly of force. And second where it is impossible to arbitrate and negotiate around conflicts of interest, the violence of the state is justifiable, although, as argued elsewhere, this must be on the grounds that the use of violence is the only way to provide a breathing space to enable policies to be implemented that will cement common interests. Present violence can only be vindicated if it diminishes future violence.

Nevertheless, the point is that states use terror against terror, violence against violence, and this is a risky and undesirable business. It may be provisionally justified in the sense that under the circumstances there is no other way to create a framework for policies to create common interests. But the elimination of terrorism must address the question of the state: otherwise we normalise and naturalise violence. The belief that the state is permanent may lead to the argument that terrorism is here to stay. If states use violence against individuals, why should this not be described as terrorism?

Schultz, Secretary of State under Reagan (US President 1980–9), argued that terrorism had to be dealt with by force and violence – not by mediation and negotiations, which were seen as a sign of weakness (Chomsky, 2003: 48). We made the point in Chapter 1 that violence is becoming easier and easier to inflict. The same is obviously true of terrorism, as a part of this violence. It is also worth noting that the nature of war itself is changing: as Freedman points out, we have moved over the past century from a situation in which '90 per cent of the casualties of war were combatants to one where 90 per cent are civilians' (2002: 48). The use of violence is becoming more and more costly in character, while becoming easier and easier to inflict.

The Force/Violence Distinction and the Analysis of Terrorism

In characterising the force of the state as violence and thus terrorist, we are not denying the differences that exist between formal and informal terrorism. Indeed a general definition of terrorism presupposes, as argued above, the acknowledgement of serious and significant differences. But simply because two forms of a movement or institution are different, this does not mean that they do not also have something in common.

The argument by Johnston that states use force, whereas criminals and terrorists use violence (1993: 16–17) is unpersuasive, since with the best will in the world it is impossible to limit force. Force by its nature always goes to extremes. State functionaries are not saints: their job – this is particularly true in the case of members of the armed forces – may be to injure and even kill, and it would be naive to think that this is possible in a way which is always proportionate and

Ch 1: The State,
pp. 14–37

regulated. The same objection holds for Petit's argument that it is only when force is used in an arbitrary way that freedom is compromised. He equates the law with the force of the state (1997: 302), but why can we not have laws based upon social sanctions, so that offenders are punished but not in a statist manner? Of course this is only possible when people can identify with one another, but these are the kinds of sanctions that are used in everyday life in thousands of institutions which enforce rules and regulations against those who breach them. Petit's argument is that the use of force only makes you unfree when this force is arbitrary.

But how can force be non-arbitrary? The use of force even when it is regulated and supposedly limited has an irreducibly arbitrary element since you cannot treat a person as a thing (which is what force involves) without an element of arbitrariness. How do you know the way in which the person upon whom the force is inflicted will respond? The perpetrator of force must be ready to act suddenly and unpredictably, so that the notion of arbitrary force is a 'pleonasm', that is force cannot be other than arbitrary. Petit acknowledges the problem when he concedes that criminal law processes often terrorise the innocent as well as the guilty and in practice, if not ideally, fines and prison sentences can be exposed as domination (1997: 154). It is true that non-arbitrary force is an 'ideal', but it is the kind of ideal that the state can only undermine as an institution claiming a monopoly of force.

Petit argues that many people, responsive to ordinary norms, may not be so responsive if they knew that there was no great sanction attendant on breaking the norms (1997: 154). But this, it could be argued, is wrong. Force, while transitionally necessary in a world where negotiation cannot work, weakens norms, creates resentment and undermines rather than consolidates responsiveness to norms. Petit takes the view that arbitrary interference involves a high level of uncertainty – there is no predicting when it will strike (1977: 85). This is surely a problem inherent in force itself.

To argue that the goal of the state is the promotion of freedom as non-domination (Petit, 1997: ix), can only be naive, given the fact that the state as an institution involves arbitrariness and thus domination. Petit contends that if the welfare and the world-view of the public are taken into account then the act of law or state is not arbitrary (1977: 57). It is certainly true that a 'democratic' state is less arbitrary than an explicitly authoritarian one, but what makes the state inherently arbitrary is its use of force.

In the same way, the political theorist Dagger (1997: 94) does not recognise that forcing a person to be free is not simply a Rousseauian paradox: it is inherent within the state itself. Dagger, as does Petit, sees dangers in the criminal law but argues that while civic virtue is a positive good, punishment may be a necessary evil (1997: 79). The point is that state is here to stay. This surely is the nub of the problem. Whether liberalism is accepted (as it is by Dagger) or rejected (by Petit in favour of republicanism, a view that individuals should participate in politics), terrorism can never be eliminated if we continue to rely upon an institution claiming a monopoly of legitimate force.

Chomsky has spoken of the 'unmentionable but far more extreme terrorism of the powerful against the weak' (2003: 7), but such an analysis is only possible when we see the state as an institutional expression of terrorism itself. It is true that if powerful states would stop participating in terrorism, that would reduce the amount of terrorism in the world by an enormous quantity (2003: 20). Taking the official US government's definition of terrorism – the use of violence to achieve political, religious or other ends through intimidation – are we not entitled to ask whether Israel's invasion of the Lebanon was not a 'text book example' of terrorism thus defined (Chomsky, 2003: 52)?

The Significance of 9/11

Nothing that has been argued so far suggests that force should not be used when innocent civilians are cruelly and heartlessly destroyed as happened on September 11th. But the point is that using terror against terrorism is dangerous and can easily be counter-productive, for remember that, according to our critique, the state itself is a terrorist that uses terror against terrorism. This is always a risky business.

Chomsky argues that the current leader of the 'War against Terror' is the only state in the world that has been condemned by the World Court for international terrorism (2003: 50). Friedlander describes terrorism as war and 'combating it is also war' (1979: 237), but might this kind of posture lead to the kind of laws that alienate not only civil libertarians, but citizens generally? Terrorism has been defined in the PATRIOT Act passed in October 2001 in the United States in such a way that it could incorporate simple acts of civil disobedience.

Howard Zinn in his *Terrorism and War* contends that US foreign policy has promoted and provoked terrorism. He cites a Defence Science Board that acknowledges the link between US involvement in international situations and the increase in terrorist attacks (2002: 9). His argument is that if you look at the death and indiscriminate bombing which has occurred then it is impossible to avoid the conclusion that, for example, 'we are terrorizing Afghanistan' (2002: 11). He argues that 'we have to broaden our definition of terrorism, or else we will denounce one terrorism and accept another' (2002: 16). We must allow for the extension of the concept of terrorism to the state itself. He insists that to understand terrorism is not to justify it, and to identify terrorism simply with the fanaticism of individuals is superficial.

Zinn warns that there is a reservoir of possible terrorists among all those people in the world who have suffered as a result of US foreign policy (2002: 17). Not only can a policy of terrorism against terror be counter-productive, but it can also heighten inequalities at home and abroad. The infant mortality rate in the United States is one of the worst in the world and now it is likely to increase (Zinn, 2002: 19). The country spends $350 billion on being a military superpower; yet $101 billion could save 8 million lives in the poorer countries of the world (2002: 18). War ravages civil liberties: even in 1979 it was argued that 'part of the cost of protecting the public against terrorist violence is the reduction of individual rights in a free society' (Friedlander, 2002: 234). But the US public sees anyone who looks Middle Eastern, Arab or Muslim as a potential terrorist. War undermines the pursuit of truth, and encourages domestic imitators. McVeigh, who was a veteran of the Gulf War, described the children he killed in the Oklahoma bombing as

Ideas and Perspectives:

Terrorism and '9/11'

James Hamill, in a recent analysis of the Iraq War, comments that an animosity has been consolidated that 'may contain within it the seeds of a future terrorism' (2003a: 326). The ideological right, he argues, had long held the view that overwhelming force should be deployed regardless of international legal norms, and September 11th legitimised these ideas. They were expressed in a document in September 2002 outlining national strategy, and although attempts to establish a link between Iraq and Bin Laden's al-Qaeda were 'unsuccessful', the policy of dismantling weapons of mass destruction via regime change was pressed (2003a: 328). Iraq provided the old-fashioned, inter-state conflict that made the 'war against terrorism' more concrete and tangible. This strategy document is seen as embodying a 'Bush doctrine' of comparable importance to the 'Truman doctrine' of 1947 that sought 'containment' of the Soviet Union (Kurth, 2002: 404).

Dr Hans Blix, head of the UN Monitoring Commission, has attacked the US and Britain for planning the war well in advance, and contended that they were fabricating evidence against Iraq to legitimise the campaign (Hamill, 2003a: 330). Hamill provides a detailed argument to show that the armed action was in defiance of the UN Charter, and describes the action as 'a war in search of a pretext' (2003b: 9). Hamill's fear is that the launching of an illegal war will foster a climate in which more young people throughout the Arab world will become receptive to the crude anti-Western rhetoric of terror groups (2003b: 100). It will increase rather than diminish the impact of Bin Laden-style extremism, and encourage states to accelerate their own programmes to develop nuclear capability (2003b: 11–13).

Biography · Noam Chomsky (1929–)

Born in Philadelphia, Pennsylvania. His undergraduate and graduate years were spent at the University of Pennsylvania where he received his PhD in linguistics in 1955. During the years 1951 to 1955 Chomsky was a Junior Fellow of the Harvard University Society of Fellows. While a Junior Fellow he completed his doctoral dissertation on 'Transformational Analysis'. The major arguments of the dissertation appeared in *Syntactic Structure* (1957). This formed part of a more extensive work, *The Logical Structure of Linguistic Theory*, which was published in 1975.

Chomsky joined the staff of the Massachusetts Institute of Technology in 1955 and in 1961 was appointed full professor in the Department of Modern Languages and Linguistics. From 1966 to 1976 he held the Ferrari P. Ward Professorship of Modern Languages and Linguistics. In 1976 he was appointed Institute Professor.

In 1958–9 Chomsky was in residence at the Institute for Advanced Study at Princeton, NJ, and in the following years he delivered a number of key memorial lectures. He has received honorary degrees from many universities. He is a Fellow of the American Academy of Arts and Sciences and the National Academy of Science, and has received a number of honours both for his contribution to linguistic theory and his work for peace.

He has visited many countries in South America, the Middle East and Asia, arguing passionately that the United States has caused destruction and misery in its foreign policy. He is particularly concerned with the way in which the media in the United States and Western Europe projects what he sees as a superficial and misleading view of US policy, and he seeks in his campaigning work and writing to develop a radical critique of these policies.

'collateral damage', while the factory bombed in the Sudan on the orders of President Clinton produced not nerve gas, but pharmaceuticals (Zinn, 2002: 21).

Zinn finds that since September 11th an atmosphere has been created in the United States in which it becomes difficult to be critical of US foreign policy (2002: 62). It has been said that the United States now has a national strategy that trumpets freedom in the abstract but subordinates it to counter-terrorism in practice (Daalder *et al.*, 2002: 411). It is difficult to see how the terrorism of the weak cannot be defeated by the terrorism of the strong. Kurth speaks of 'a dialectical and symbiotic connection, perhaps an escalating and vicious cycle' between Islamic terrorism and US empire (2002: 404). Imaginative policies are needed that seek to address the root causes of terrorism, the poverty, insecurity, lack of self-esteem, injustice, inequality, etc. underlying the frustration and anger which expresses itself in terrorist form. Inverting terrorism cannot eliminate it. As Daalder *et al.*, put it pithily, 'unless the United States closes the gap between its words and its deeds, it risks fuelling the very threats that imperil its security' (2002: 411).

Summary

Terrorism uses violence, but the liberal tradition is the first to see violence in the political process as a phenomenon to be condemned. The predominant view is that it is wrong to see the state itself as a terrorist organisation. States may sponsor terrorism, but terrorism is best identified as the use of violence against the state, and terrorists as those who act on its behalf.

Salmi has distinguished between four types of violence. Only his notion of direct violence involves physical force. The other concepts – indirect violence, repressive violence and alienating violence – use the notion of violence too broadly and fail to make the crucial distinction between violence and the causes of violence. The distinction between political violence and terrorism proper is a crucial one. When people are denied political and legal rights they may resort to political violence. This violence may be problematic (even counter-productive) but it should not be described as terrorism. Terrorism only arises when political violence is directed against liberal states. Those opposing liberalism might be of the left or the right, or take a position that is ideologically ambiguous.

Marx generally identifies capitalist exploitation as 'coercive' (constraining would be a better term) rather than violent in character, and regards violence as justifiable where states deny political rights. Lenin, on the other hand, appears to justify violence even against liberal states. Despite argument to the contrary, terrorism can be defined in general terms even though (as are all movements) it is certainly a variegated and heterogeneous phenomenon. It is only possible to eradicate terrorism if we can analyse its roots, although they may be extremely varied and multiple in character.

States, it could be argued, use terror to tackle conflicts of interest, so that the problem of terrorism is connected to the problem of the state. Without recognising this, counter-terrorist measures (as US policy demonstrates) can make a bad situation even worse.

Questions

1. Is it possible to distinguish between a terrorist and a freedom fighter?
2. What role does the liberal tradition play in defining terrorism?
3. Should we speak of terrorisms rather than terrorism?
4. Is it correct to regard the state itself as a terrorist institution?
5. Do you agree with the argument that the recent war on Iraq has exacerbated rather than reduced the problem of terrorism?

References

Azzam, M. (2003) 'Weapon of the Weak' *The World Today*, August/September.

Bourdieu, P. (1998) *Acts of Resistance* Cambridge: Polity Press.

Bunting, B. (1969) *The Rise of the South African Reich* rev. edn Harmondsworth: Penguin.

Chomsky, N. (2003) *Power and Terror* New York: Seven Stories Press.

Daalder, I., Lindsay, J. and Steinberg, J. (2002) 'Hard Choices: National Security and the War on Terrorism' *Current History* 101 (659) 409–13.

Dagger, R. (1997) *Civic Virtue* Oxford: Oxford University Press.

Fanon, F. (1967) *The Wretched of the Earth* Harmondsworth: Penguin.

Freedman, L. (2002) 'The Coming War on Terrorism' in L. Freedman (ed.), *Superterrorism: Policy Responses* Malden Mass. and Oxford: Blackwell, 40–56.

Friedlander, R. (1979) 'Coping with Terrorism: What is to be Done?' in Y. Alexander *et al.* (eds), *Terrorism: Theory and Practice* Boulder, Col.: Westview, 231–45.

Gearson, J. (2002) 'The Nature of Modern Terrorism' in L. Freedman (ed.), *Superterrorism: Policy Responses* Massachusetts: Blackwell, 7–24.

Hamill, J. (2003a) 'The United States, Iraq and International Relations', *Contemporary Review* 282, 326–33.

Hamill, J. (2003b) 'The United States, Iraq and International Relations', *Contemporary Review* 283, 7–15.

Harmon, C. (2000) *Terrorism Today* London: Frank Cass.

Harris, J. (1973–4) 'The Marxist Conception of Violence', *Philosophy and Public Affairs* 3, 192–220.

Hobbes, T. (1968) *The Leviathan* Harmondsworth: Penguin.

Hoffman, J. (1984) *The Gramscian Challenge* Oxford: Basil Blackwell.

Hoffman, J. (1994) *Is Political Violence Ever Justified?* Leicester: Centre for the Study of Public Order, University of Leicester.

Hoffman, J. (1995) *Beyond the State* Cambridge: Polity Press.

Hoffman, J. (1998) *Sovereignty* Buckingham: Open University Press.

Johnston, S. (1993) *Realising the Public World Order* Leicester: Centre for the Study of Public Order, University of Leicester.

Kurth, J. (2002) 'Confronting the Unipolar Moment: The American Empire and Islamic Terrorism', *Current History* 101 (659), 414–20.

Lacqueur, W. (1987) *The Age of Terrorism* Boston, Mass.: Little, Brown.

Lacqueur, W. (2003) *No End to War* New York and London: Continuum.

Lenin, V. (1962) *Collected Works* Vol. 10 London: Lawrence & Wishart.

Locke, J. (1924) *Two Treatises of Civil Government* London: Dent.

Marx, K. and Engels, F. (1967) *The Communist Manifesto* Harmondsworth: Penguin.

Marx, K. and Engels, F. (1975) *Collected Works* Vol. 3 London: Lawrence & Wishart.

Marx, K. and Engels, F. (1977) *Collected Works* Vol. 9 London: Lawrence & Wishart.

Marx, K. and Engels, F. (1978) *Collected Works* Vol. 10 London: Lawrence & Wishart.

Miller, D. (1984) 'The Use and Abuse of Political Violence', *Political Studies* 37(3), 401–19.

O'Day, A. (1979) 'Northern Ireland, Terrorism and the British State', in Y. Alexander *et al.* (eds.), *Terrorism: Theory and Practice* Boulder, Col.: Westview, 121–35.

Pettit, P. (1997) *Republicanism* Oxford: Oxford University Press.

Sachs, A. (1991) *The Soft Vengeance of a Freedom Fighter* London: Paladin.

Salmi, J. (1993) *Violence and Democratic Society* London: Zed.

Schram, S. (1967) *Mao Tse-tung* Harmondsworth: Penguin.

Sorel, G. (1961) *Reflections on Violence* New York: Collier.

Volpp, L. (2003) 'The Citizen and the Terrorist' in M. Dudziak (ed.), *September 11 in History* Durham and London: Duke University Press, 147–62.

Von Hippel, K. (2002) 'The Roots of Terrorism: Probing the Myths' in L. Freedman (ed.), *Superterrorism: Policy Responses* Malden Mass. and Oxford: Blackwell, 25–39.

Wilkinson, P. (1979) 'Terrorist Movements' in Y. Alexander *et al.* (eds.), *Terrorism: Theory and Practice* Boulder, Col.: Westview, 99–117.

Wilkinson, P. (1986) *Terrorism and the Liberal State* Basingstoke: Macmillan.

Zinn, H. (2002) *Terrorism and War* New York: Seven Stories Press.

Further Reading

- Lacqueur's *No End to War* (referenced above) is comprehensive and authoritative. Lacqueur has written a huge amount on terrorism, and this is his most recent volume.

- Miller's 'The Use and Abuse of Political Violence' (referenced above) contains some very useful insights into the question.

- Von Hippel's 'The Roots of Terrorism: Probing the Myths' (referenced above) offers a perspective that is both interesting and challenging.

- Hoffman's 'Is Political Violence Ever Justified?' *Social Studies Review,* 4(2) 1988, pp 61–2 is a brief and contentious 'polemic' on the problem.

- Salmi's *Violence and Democratic Society* (referenced above) contains a challenging analysis as to what violence is and how we might identify it.

- Wilkinson's *Terrorism and the Liberal State* (referenced above) provides a very good overview from one of the country's leading academic authorities on the subject.

Weblinks

For the problem as it is seen in Britain: http://www.homeoffice.gov.uk/terrorism/

For a detailed source that enables you to visit numerous sites: http://uk.dir.yahoo.com/society_and_culture/crime/types_of_crime/terrorism/

For a useful survey of terrorism by Halliday, see:
http://www.opendemocracy.net/debates/article-2-103-1865.jsp

For a useful guide to different sources and organisations:
http://www.psr.keele.ac.uk/sseal/terror.htm

For a critique of US reactions to '9/11', see:
http://www.guardian.co.uk/comment/story/0%2C3604%2C1036571%2C00.html

Chapter 21

Victimhood

Introduction

We live in a society in which it has become increasingly common for people to think of themselves as victims. In the USA feminism has sometimes been characterised as 'victim feminism'. We want to argue that 'victimhood' is one of the newer concepts that political thinkers ought to tackle, since it involves the question of the state, conflict resolution and the problem of violence. To espouse victimhood is not the same as being a victim. We will argue that victimhood arises when a person who may be a victim, believes that nothing can be done to rectify their situation or expects others to come up with a solution that they cannot conceive themself. Victimhood is a pathology, by which we mean a negative situation that paralyses a person's capacity to act on his own behalf.

Chapter Map

- The relationship between victims and violence. The difference between being a victim and espousing victimhood.

- The link between the concept of **victimhood** and the concept of power.

- Women as the victims of victimhood. The question of punishment and legal redress in the analysis of victimhood.

- Victimhood, dualism and emancipation.

- The South African Truth and Reconciliation Commission and the liberal critique of victimhood.

- Contract and victimhood.

- Victimhood and denial.

'Arbeit Macht Frei'

The gate at Dachau concentration camp bears the infamous motto *Arbeit Macht Frei* (Work Brings Freedom)

Imagine you are in Nazi Germany during World War II. The death camps are at work as part of the so-called 'final solution'. Jews can be heard saying that if they ever get out alive, they will never speak German again, since the German people have inflicted unspeakable horrors upon them. Nazi camp attendants tell themselves that the Jews aren't human and would destroy the Third Reich if they were not exterminated. Residents living outside Dachau see the smoke rising from the camp and can smell the gas, but prefer to believe that it is inorganic rubbish that is being burned and insanitary clothing that is being purified.

It is clear from this example that the Jews are the victims, the Nazis their tormentors, and the residents unwilling to face the grim truth about what is happening in their neighbourhood.

- How justified is the view that the Nazis represent Germany as a cultural and national identity, although this is the Nazis' ultra-nationalist claim?

- The Nazi camp attendants see the Jews as non-human and a threat to their national identity: why are they unable to see that they and the Jews possess a common humanity?

- The residents sense that something appalling is taking place in their vicinity. Why don't they face reality and do something about it?

- Although each party plays a different and conflicting role, what do the responses we have depicted have in common?

Victims and Violence

In all relationships, power is involved and, therefore, there will be those who are relatively disadvantaged. But the term 'victim' is used to describe a person or group who have been subject to violence or general misfortune. Violence is itself defined as the direct or indirect infliction of physical harm. Victims are people who deserve our sympathy and concern, and although victims of violence are a particular problem, the notion of a victim is wider than this. Men and women who are beaten by their partners are victims; so are people who are attacked by others. In a world in which large numbers of people are killed, maimed or harmed by others, it would be untenable to deny the existence of victims.

By violence, we do not simply mean the direct infliction of physical harm by sticks and stones. We also mean the indirect infliction of physical harm, which arises from abuse, the kind of insecurity that causes pain and depression, torment of a kind that destroys a person or a people's sense of self-worth. Not all forms of harm stem from violence, as we have defined it. It is tempting, but wrong, to identify unemployment, or poverty or destitution as 'structural violence' since violence implies an *intention* to inflict harm. It arises when people cannot change places, and a person or people are treated as *things* or objects by the perpetrator of the violence. Certainly, the recipients of violence deserve to be characterised as victims, and this can be the violence of a brigand or the state, since we have argued elsewhere that violence by the state is still violence, however much it may claim **legitimacy**, authorisation and legality.

Ch 20: Terrorism, pp. 486–509

But what of people who suffer? Those who suffer as a result of the unintentional harm inflicted upon them, like poverty or destitution, unemployment or diseases (which may arise through a failure to provide resources or medicine to tackle them), are also victims and they too deserve our sympathy and concern. Honderich has demonstrated recently the dramatic inequalities that characterise the world today. The worst off tenth has about two or three per cent of what there is. In a place like Mozambique the worst off have this share of what is a very small total, and this affects the distribution of freedom and power, respect and self-respect, health and mortality. The worst tenth of the population in Africa have lifetimes of about 30 years (Honderich, 2002: 22; 18).

Clearly, we can speak of victims of poverty, starvation and deprivation just as we can speak of victims who are tortured, 'disappear', step on landmines, are thrown into prisons, or are blown to pieces by mechanised instruments of war. We can also speak of people who suffer from ill health (that is not obviously caused through neglect or inequality) as victims say of cancer and heart disease. They are victims because they suffer, and they deserve our compassion.

In short, there is an infinity of categories of people whom we can call victims.

What is Victimhood?

Victimhood is a pathology. It involves the belief that being a victim renders a person or group powerless, a mere object, lacking in agency and thus the capacity to exert independent action. We will argue later that victimhood arises from a mistaken view of power.

Victimhood is seen here as something that is different from the existence of victims. It is true that people need to see themselves as victims (or have been victims in the past) in order to embrace victimhood, but the two are not the same. Victimhood involves a belief that the violence exerted against an individual or group or the suffering they experience, is tragically unavoidable. Victimhood induces a righteous inactivity or a futile retaliation that makes a bad situation worse. Where **violence** is involved, it sees this as a product of differences. Hence victimhood is ideological in the sense that it rests upon falsehood, illusion and above all, a view that the misfortune is 'natural' in the sense that it cannot be changed or ameliorated. Proponents of victimhood argue that the person suffering should simply accept their fate and/or make the perpetrator suffer as they have.

Ch 17: Difference, pp. 418–35

Victimhood arises when victims cannot understand why violence has been exerted against them, or why they are in difficult and sometimes degrading circumstances. It is true that the purveyors of victimhood are aware of who is tormenting them where such harm is intentionally inflicted – Jews in the Holocaust camps could point to Nazi soldiers and camp guards; men and women can identify partners who attack them; children are painfully aware that particular adults are abusing them. Oppressed individuals or an oppressed group invariably know who are depriving them of their basic human rights. Moreover, it is obvious to the cancer sufferer what is causing the pain.

But victimhood arises because the knowledge of a person's plight is superficial and thus misleading. Tormentors, for example, are stereotyped, by which we mean they are subject to a process of generalisation that distorts reality. 'Explanations' are offered which suggest that the violence is inexplicable, so that the causality asserted is imaginary and misleading. A person suffering from a disease, may believe that it is the will of their creator which causes them pain, and there is nothing which can be done about it.

Jews who are afflicted with victimhood believe that the Nazis are evil because they are Germans. Women assume that men, rather than aggressive partners, are to blame for their oppression; blacks imagine that because their tormentor may be white, whiteness itself creates hostility to black people. This is why we argue that difference should not be seen as the problem. It is true that in many cases tormentors are strikingly different from their victims – but these differences in themselves do not provide a rational explanation for the oppression and discomfort. They do, however, provide a convenient way of 'rationalising' the suffering inflicted. The problem with victimhood is that it is plausible but ultimately misleading. It is tempting for a woman who has been mistreated by male partners, to seek a life that shuns men: but this is futile since it assumes that men are inherently aggressive and sexist, and can never change.

Victimhood 'naturalises' the violence and pain that victims suffer, by assuming that such violence and suffering is inevitable and unavoidable. Nothing can be done about it. Hence victimhood paralyses agency in that it promotes a belief that victims are powerless to resist their oppressor in meaningful and realistic ways, or act in ways that might alleviate, if not eradicate, their symptoms. Victimhood, insofar as it espouses resistance, believes that salvation can only come from 'outside' – from a protector who will punish their tormentor, a benevolent spiritual force, or an external agency that rescues the victim who is unable to act on her own behalf.

Victimhood and Power

Part 1: pp. 2–12

Victimhood assumes that power can only be purely negative or purely positive. It is one-sided in its view of human relationships, and victimhood rests upon a polarized and dualistic view of social interaction.

As we pointed out in our first chapter, in pre-modern times (i.e. in slave-owning or medieval societies), power is seen as positive in the sense that it is identified through a person or group's contribution to the community in which they live. To exercise power is to strengthen relationships with others so that power is identified in communal and relational terms. This notion of power has one major drawback. It ignores the role of the individual – his or her personal interests – and sees power in repressively hierarchical terms. To exercise power is to enact a particular role, and this role is something that is preordained by forces beyond the control of an individual or a group. Power is exercised not by individuals but by priests, lords, men, Christians, Greeks, etc. The community is hierarchically defined both internally as well as externally. Men exercise power over women just as lords exercise power over peasants: power is naturalised, and although proponents of positive power argue that such power should be benevolent and sociable, in many cases repression is involved. It is true that slavery can be sustained only as a relationship if slaves accept the rule and role of their masters, but force and domination is crucial to sustaining pre-modern power relationships, even though this repression and force appears nowhere in the concept of power.

A notion of positive power 'on its own' (as it were) can only generate a sense of victimhood since those on the receiving end of 'positive power' may be tempted to regard the violence used against them, or the suffering they have to endure as somehow preordained, just as those exercising violence feel that 'nature' has compelled them to act in this way in order to sustain their particular roles. For this reason, the rise of an explicitly theorised concept of negative power represents an important step forward in political theory. The negative view of power is part of the liberal tradition that arises in Europe in the seventeenth century, and takes the view that power is something to be used against nature, other individuals in general, and the state in particular. It is worth noting that what makes the seventeenth-century thinker, Hobbes, a liberal and an exponent of negative power is his view that everyone is first and foremost an individual, and although the state has absolute power over the individual he may refuse to comply with the state where his interest (and in particular his right to life) is threatened.

Power is negative because it is deemed to be an activity *against* others. People no longer enact preordained roles. They behave as individuals and seek to defend their self-interest: this is not immoral or ungodly. Self-interest is deemed 'natural' and in the eyes of Protestantism historically, individualism is in accordance with the creator's wishes. It is not difficult to see that negative power 'on its own' also feeds into the notion of victimhood. The classical liberal tradition seeks to justify action as necessary to an individual's survival, so that victims of violence may see violence and suffering as the result of 'natural' aggressiveness which either must be accepted, or rebutted by becoming a 'natural' aggressor oneself.

In reality, notions of 'roles' and hierarchically defined relationships come in through the back door so that Locke, for example, a seventeenth century

Exercise

Four people confront you. One is a woman who has been raped; the second is a man suffering from lung cancer; the third is a former soldier who is suffering from severe psychological problems; while the fourth is a homeowner whose house has been burgled by a black intruder.

- The first notes that the man who attacked her has a problem with women that probably goes back to his childhood, although she feels that he should be punished.

- The second feels that the cancer has resulted from the failure of his wife and doctor to take proper care of him.

- The third takes the view that war is a dangerous and unpredictable business and hopes that his children will never have to fight in armies.

- The fourth feels that the burglary demonstrates that black people can never be trusted and should be encouraged to leave the country.

Clearly all four are victims. Which of the four demonstrate attitudes of victimhood?

exponent of individual rights, deems men to be naturally stronger than women and therefore the 'natural' leaders of households. Even J.S. Mill in the nineteenth century links his concern with individual development with a belief that Indians, for example, are children who require dictatorial control from paternal Europeans. The problem with the concept of negative power is that it inverts pre-modern notions of positive power: it does not transcend them. Hence in its one-sided rejection of community and relationships, it perpetuates a notion of victimhood. The notion of negative power is classically expounded by Hobbes who sees power as power *over* another. Power is tied to exclusion, and the body is seen as something that the individual owns as part and parcel of their private property. This notion, although viable as part of a wider theory of power, is untenable on its own. It generates the abstraction, atomism and **dualism** that the ideology of victimhood requires. Liberalism, it might be said, perfects victimhood by postulating in its classical form the concept of the isolated individual unrelated to anyone else: it cannot transcend it.

Introduction, p. xxxiv

Ronai warns that the power dichotomy must not be inverted (1999: 140): the discourse of victim/perpetrator corresponds to naive and one-sided versions of positive and negative power. 'The language of victimhood', she comments, 'is disempowering' (1999: 152). Power is not a static quality that individuals either do or do not possess. It is always negotiated, always provisional, always in motion (Marecek, 1999: 176). It is neither solely positive or simply negative, but *both*.

Are Women Victims?

Radical feminism in particular portrays women as victims of male oppression. Wendy Brown has rightly warned against 'paralyzing recriminations and toxic resentments parading as radical critique' (Brown, 1995: xi). It is not that women do not suffer: victimhood presupposes that they have no guarantees of political redress (1995: xii). Radical feminists 'blame' men and assume that women are impotent or, as we shall see, must rely upon the state and the law as their 'protector'.

Brown identifies victimhood with one-sided attacks on liberalism. She cites Nietzsche's view of freedom as the *will* to assume responsibility for oneself. Contrary to the liberal argument, freedom does not elude power, but involves a power that enhances the individual's capacity to act (1995: 25). Victimhood tends to a 'moralising politics' that codifies injury and powerlessness. It seeks not power or emancipation for the victim, but the revenge of punishment so that the perpetrator is hurt as much as the victim. Politics becomes reduced to punishment (1995: 27). In Nietzsche's view, as Brown points out, morality springs from and compensates powerlessness; powerlessness is invested with the Truth, while power inherently distorts (1995: 46). Instead of indulging in recrimination, she argues, we need to engage in struggle.

Central to Brown's argument is the notion of *ressentiment* (revenge) that produces an effect (rage, righteousness) that overwhelms the hurt. It also produces a culprit responsible for the hurt, and a site of revenge to displace the hurt (a place to inflict hurt as the sufferer has been hurt). The late modern liberal subject literally seethes with *ressentiment*. Such an identity becomes 'invested in its own subjection'. Again, she quotes Nietzsche: 'I suffer: someone must be to blame for it' (1995: 68–73).

A particular target of her argument is the radical feminist, MacKinnon. 'There's no way out', is the most frequent response among students to MacKinnon's work. MacKinnon's account of sexual antagonism is utterly static. Men are depicted as a homogeneous whole that oppresses women, and women are seen as a similarly homogeneous group. What can be done about it? Because MacKinnon sees women as subject to victimhood, she eliminates the very dynamic of social change on which Marx, say, counted for emancipatory practice. The oppressed have no inner resources for the development of consciousness or agency. MacKinnon's critique of sexism becomes an implicitly positivist, conservative project. Its 'victims' need protection rather than emancipation. There is an unrelieved past, present and future of domination. Women are relentlessly victimised by their gendered construction. We must curtail and regulate, rather than emancipate. Not freedom, but censorship; more rights to sue for damages, better dead-bolt locks on the doors (Brown, 1995: 92-4). For MacKinnon, the 'solution' is to single out pornography as the essential manifestation of sexism, and to deal with pornography through the proposed ordinances giving women the right to sue for damages. This argument brings to the fore the authoritarian character of MacKinnon's position.

Feminism must find a way that sees women as victims, but avoids victimhood through developing strategies that give women the power and confidence to make inroads into male domination, to act in a way that increases agency and self-determination. A feminist and female therapist interviewed by Marecek declared: 'I think we need to view ourselves as responsible adult human beings who are learning hopefully to make choices and figure things out for ourselves a little better' (Marecek, 1999: 171). Naomi Wolf describes 'victim feminism' as a set of beliefs 'that cast women as beleaguered, fragile, intuitive angels' (Atmore, 1999: 191). Although this is a one-sided presentation of a one-sided position, it is

Friedrich Nietzsche (1844–1900)

Born in Prussia, he was educated at an elite school near Naumburg, and in 1864 he became a student of theology and philology at the University of Bonn. In the following year he continued his studies at the University of Leipzig, and in 1869 was appointed professor of classical philology at the University of Basel.

In 1870 he served as a volunteer medical orderly in the Franco-Prussian war, and two years later he published *The Birth of Tragedy* where he argued that tragedy played a central role for the ancient Greeks in maintaining their certainty about life. The book was dedicated to the composer Richard Wagner, and called into question much of the received wisdom about ancient Greece.

However, he broke with Wagner, and in 1879 he resigned from the University. He spent the next ten years of his life in southern Switzerland and northern Italy, and in 1883 he began work on *Thus Spoke Zarathustra*. In 1886 he wrote *Beyond Good and Evil*, and a year later he published *On the Genealogy of Morals*. His argument in the latter centres on the moralities of slave and master but he regards the triumph of slave morality as the internalisation of oppression. In 1888 he wrote *Ecce Homo*, which was published posthumously in April 1908.

He became insane in 1889 and spent the last 11 years of his life in the care of his mother and sister. Although the Nazis made use of his work, they did so fallaciously since Nietzsche opposed nationalism as a futile attempt to prevent the disintegration of the modern state. He did, however, anticipate a war 'such as no-one has ever seen'.

certainly true that the dualistic thinking that underpins this kind of position is contrary to a feminism that takes women seriously.

Dualism, Women and Victimhood

Brown argues that in the case of MacKinnon, a single socially pervasive dualism structures totality, the divide between men and women. Her dualisms and absolutes articulate a profound late modern anxiety (Brown, 1995: 95). The point has a wider philosophical relevance.

The notion of victimhood presupposes that there is an unbridgeable chasm between friend and enemy, truth and falsehood. Hence it makes a political resolution of conflicts – a resolution based on conciliation and compromise – impossible. The victim not only suffers, but as already noted, the only 'solution' is to make the 'other' suffer as well. Instead of going beyond the notion of a victim, the victor must become a victim if 'justice' is to be secured. It is commonplace to encounter parents whose children have been murdered, and who want revenge and the guilty party to be punished as severely as possible. It is an understandable reaction, but it is wholly futile, for how will severe punishment either bring their child back to life, or make the perpetrator into a better person? Bitterness prevails over reason, and the dualism between victor and victim remains, albeit in an inverted form.

To transcend victimhood, it is crucial to understand why a person suffers and what can be done about it. It is understandable that when a woman is raped, she wants the perpetrator punished, but such a reaction cannot in itself be said to solve the problem, any more than hanging stopped people stealing sheep in the eighteenth century. A culture needs to be developed (and this requires a radical change in the distribution of resources) in which the identity of both parties changes, so that men view women as friends and equals, not as prey and targets. Overcoming dualism is both a philosophical and eminently practical task, for men and women will never be able to change places if the material circumstances of each makes stereotyping seem plausible. Overcoming dualism involves cementing a common interest, so that differences can be resolved through negotiation, and the use of the state becomes redundant.

Ch 1: State, pp. 14–37

The danger with rights for victims, as Brown argues, is that they can entrench a dualism between the ideal and reality, so an unbridgeable chasm between the two exists. Rights, she argues, mystify as well as provide entitlements. There is a danger, she argues, that the same device that confers legitimate boundary and privacy, can leave the individual to struggle along, in a self-blaming and depoliticised universe. Her concern is that asserting rights can mystify the powers that construct, buffet and position the individual (Brown, 1995: 126–8). Asserting rights *can* perpetuate a sense of victimhood.

MacKinnon uses the notion of rights to expose and redress inequalities that arise in liberal societies and are sometimes presented abstractly – as part of 'nature' – which we simply have to accept. Women are wholly identified, as Brown points out, with sexual victimization (Brown, 1995: 131). Rights are certainly valuable, but their limitations must be seen. They endow you with an entitlement, but they leave open the question as to how you are going to make this entitlement a reality. 'On their own' they can lead to victimhood, unless the person demanding rights begins to assert a real agency that seeks to realize them as vehicles of emancipation (1995: 133). Gray warns that we should not see rights abstractly: 'as theorems that fall out of theories of law or ethics'. They are judgements about human interests 'whose content shifts over time as threats to human interests change' (Gray, 2000: 113).

How to read:

Brown's *States of Injury*

This is a valuable book that deals with the theme of this chapter. The preface outlines the arguments to be adopted and deserves a careful read. The introduction can be skim read, but Chapter 2 (Exposures and Hesitations) is important. This contains a useful critique of postmodernism, and material from Nietzsche where Brown identifies Nietzsche's critique of 'slave morality' with what we have called the pathology of victimhood. Chapter 3 (Wounded Attachments) is also important and needs to be digested. Chapter 4 is useful for an understanding of feminism, but in the context of victimhood can be skim read. Chapter 5 is also worth reading carefully and the comments on Marx are of particular interest. Chapter 6 (Liberalism) should be skim read and the last chapter (for purposes here) can be skipped.

Human Rights and Victimhood: The South African Truth and Reconciliation Commission (TRC)

Wilson, in his *The Politics of Truth and Reconciliation in South Africa* (2001), evaluates the attempt by the Truth and Reconciliation Commission (TRC) to encourage the forsaking of revenge (2001: xix). The TRC was established in 1995 one year after an African National Congress (ANC) government had been elected to power. Past injustices were to be redressed on the basis of a need for understanding, not vengeance; reparation, not retaliation. The notion of *ubuntu* became a key notion in the immediate postapartheid order. It was explicitly counterposed to victimisation. Former Archbishop Desmond Tutu who chaired the commission, took the view that the African understanding of justice is restorative. It sees justice as a force that is concerned not so much to punish but to restore a balance that has been knocked askew (Wilson, 2001: 8–12).

The South African TRC had a wider remit than the Uruguayan or Chilean truth commissions – it could name individuals concerned and grant amnesties. Wilson argues that while the Report of the TRC chronicled acts of a devastating kind, its methods were flawed. It urged reconciliation in a context that meant amnesty for violators of human rights (2001: 97–9).

It brought individual suffering into a public space where it could be collectivised and shared by all (2001: 111). It linked this individual suffering to a national process of liberation, and argued that victims should forgive perpetrators, and abandon any desire for retaliation (2001: 119). The Commission espoused a Christian argument about forgiveness, with Tutu contending that redemption 'liberates the victim' (2001: 120). Punitive retribution was characterised as illegitimate 'mob justice', while loyalties and identities were to be created that had not existed before (2001: 129; 131).

This attempt to avoid victimhood seems admirable, but the problem is that the TRC sought an ethic of forgiveness in the context of past and present savage conflicts of interest, conflicts involving torture, killing, and the most grisly forms of repression. As Wilson points out, the white community in South Africa seemed indifferent or plainly hostile to the work of the Commission (2001: 155), and there was insufficient emphasis upon the murderous character of apartheid and the inequalities that it embodied. The right to punish was to be given up in a situation in which the grossest violations of human rights had occurred.

A punitive view of justice was simply dismissed in a situation where it seemed to make sense, and the amnesties granted to state-killers during the apartheid period (who had rather cynically come to the TRC to 'confess') served, in Wilson's view, to deepen rather than reduce polarisation (2001: 161). Cohen notes that South Africans are particularly cynical about the apparent ease with which some of the worst perpetrators have adopted the rhetoric of the 'new South Africa' as if the past never existed (Wilson, 2001: 132). There was a feeling that grievances and pain were not really addressed. Certainly, this was not done by the TRC's grand vision of reconciliation (2001: 171; 175). Little wonder that the TRC proved to be peripheral to the lives of those in townships wracked by revenge killings. Wilson particularly instances the killings that have continued in places like Sharpeville (2001: 187).

Biography	Desmond Tutu (1931–)

Born in Klerksdorp, Transvaal (as it was then). His father was a teacher, and he himself was educated at Johannesburg Bantu High School. After leaving school he trained first as a teacher at Pretoria Bantu Normal College and in 1954 he graduated from the University of South Africa.

After three years as a high school teacher he began to study theology, being ordained as a priest in 1960. The years 1962–6 were devoted to further theological study in Britain leading up to a Master of Theology. From 1967 to 1972 he taught theology in South Africa (he was a lecturer in Lesotho between 1970 and 1972) before returning to England for three years as the assistant director of a theological institute in London. He published an African Prayer Book and between 1978 and 1980 he published sermons, press statements, speeches and articles in a volume entitled *Crying in the Wilderness: The Struggle for Justice in South Africa*. He was elected a Fellow of Kings' College in 1978 and in the same year received an honorary doctorate from the General Theological Seminary in the United States. He was involved with the World Council of Churches, attending the Fifth Assembly in Nairobi in 1975 and the Sixth Assembly in Vancouver in 1983.

In 1975 he was appointed Dean of St Mary's Cathedral in Johannesburg, the first black to hold that position. From 1976 to 1978 he was Bishop of Lesotho, and in 1978 became the first black General Secretary of the South African Council of Churches. Tutu is an honorary doctor of a number of leading universities in the United States, Britain and Germany.

From 1985 to 86 he was Bishop of Johannesburg, becoming Archbishop of Cape Town a year later. In 1985 he was awarded the Nobel Peace Prize in Oslo, Norway for his quest for a non-violent end to apartheid. Under his leadership, the church in South Africa became immersed in the political struggle. He has written widely on the problem of hope and suffering, and contributed to a volume entitled *God at 2000*. He wrote a foreword to Charlene Smith's book on Mandela, and in 1994 he published *The Rainbow People of God: The Making of a Peaceful Revolution*. He co-authored *Reconciliation: The Ubuntu Theology of Desmond Tutu* with Michael Jesse Battle, and wrote *Some Evidence of Things Seen: Children of South Africa* with Paul Alberts and Albie Sachs.

During the investigation of the Truth and Reconciliation Commission that he chaired, he declared that he was 'appalled at the evil we have uncovered'. 'Listening to all the pain and anguish, you take it into yourself in many ways ... maybe one day you will sit down when you think of all those things and you will cry'.

South Africa has one of the world's most liberal constitutions but also one of the highest indexes of socio-economic inequality. It is a society where 50 per cent of the population is classed as living in poverty. The low level of reparations for victims provided by the government and the generous amnesties granted to perpetrators strengthened the view that the TRC's version of human rights violated perceived, everyday principles of justice (2001: 194; 200). Wilson shows, through a detailed analysis, how justice in the township of Boipatong is implemented in a way that emphasises retribution rather than reconciliation. This is seen as creating legitimacy for legal institutions – that such justice can achieve many of the aims of peaceful coexistence sought by advocates of reconciliation and forgiveness (2001: 201). Pure reconciliation was equated by township dwellers with weakness on issues of social order, as being soft on criminals and apartheid-era murderers. In places like Boipatong where there are local courts, vengeance is regarded as more predictable and routinised (2001: 212).

It is not that the TRC were wrong to address the problem of victimhood with its gory philosophy of an eye for an eye and tooth for a tooth. The case against the notion of victimhood is compelling, and Wilson (like Brown) quotes both Nietzsche and Weber who identify the desire for punishment with vengeance and an abstract moralism that condemns without attempting to understand (Wilson, 2001: 159). But the TRC in its opposition to local informal courts whose procedures were often arbitrary and which inflicted lashings upon wrongdoers, failed to distinguish between the kind of vengeance which takes the form of unregulated killings and counter-killings, and *retribution* which though often motivated for a desire for revenge, dispenses a punitive justice by what Wilson calls 'more institutionalized types of mediation and adjudication' (2001: 162). Without an element of retribution, (even) postapartheid state legality is often perceived by township residents to be alien to the 'community' (2001: xx).

Wilson concludes with the view that while human rights that stress reconciliation are important, they cannot entirely define the common good of the community as it exists in South Africa today (2001: 224). The problem with the TRC, in other words, was the adoption of an abstract liberal critique of victimhood – not one that takes account of specific circumstances and sees the need to move slowly and gradually beyond the notion of punishment. The point has to be made, as we have argued in our chapter on the state, that transcending the notion of victimhood presupposes a diminution of the kind of dreadful crimes which inevitably give rise to the demand for vengeance. In one of the most violent societies of the world – with a population brutalised by apartheid and hundreds of years of racist oppression – the movement beyond victimhood requires imaginative transitions and multiple stages of a complex and democratic-oriented kind. To imagine that abstract invocations of human rights will bring out calmness and forgiveness is simply naive.

Is Contract an Answer to the Problem of Victimhood?

Victimhood arises, it might be argued, because individuals and groups lack a contract between themselves or with the state. The notion of contract represents both the strengths and weaknesses of the liberal tradition. The great strength of contract is that it enshrines a norm of equality and individuality. To enter into a contract with another, we have *in some sense* to change places. Ancient and medieval thought has no notion of contract (in the modern sense) because it has no notion of equality and individuality. Hence liberals wax lyrically over the transition from status to contract – from a situation in which people have different roles within a preordained and repressive hierarchy, to one in which people supposedly follow their self-interest and freely exchange their goods and services with others.

Would victims be helped if they entered into contracts, symbolically or in reality, with those who were to victimise them? The weakness of contract is that the equality and freedom enshrined in contracts is formal and not real. By this we mean that contracts in themselves do not address the problem of social position and power: they concern themselves with a formal equality that ignores real disparities in wealth, esteem, confidence, education, etc. The labour contract in a capitalist society equalises the position of those who have wealth with those whose situation is such that they must work for another. The marriage contract equalises the position of one partner who has power and resources and (in many cases) another partner who lacks confidence, self-esteem and an ability to break with traditional deference. The prostitution contract (which utopian socialists likened with some justification to the marriage contract) involves an exchange that 'permits' one party to abuse another. Because the equality in this particular contract is so formal as to appear positively fraudulent, most societies outlaw prostitution albeit in hypocritical and one-sided ways.

Just as we need a conception of power that is negative *and* positive, so we need a concept of contract that seeks to translate egalitarian aspirations into an egalitarian reality. The signing of contracts represents a step forward in the sense that both parties seem to recognise themselves in each other. If Israelis and Palestinians could see themselves as contractual partners, that would represent important progress. But if contract is not simply to be a device in which the powerful legitimate their attacks upon the powerless, we need to move beyond the formal and towards the real. This is not to say that we will ever reach a position in which we can say 'everyone is finally equal'. We are only now becoming aware of the way in which mental health and cultural disabilities like dyslexia negatively affect freedom and willpower. The formality involved with the institution of the contract invites us to be aware of (and act to reduce) the gulf between benevolent theory and less than wholly benevolent practice.

This is why the institution of contract is often seen as a solution to the problem of victimisation. In fact, the institution of contract can promote victimhood. If a contract legalises and legitimates exploitation, then it is not only compatible with the creation of victims, but it becomes the central device by which people are impoverished and abused in the contemporary world. It is true that the victims of victimhood might reject the very idea of contract, on the grounds that because contracts can mask exploitation, they are worthless. This makes it all the more crucial that we understand the limitations of the liberal tradition while building upon its strengths. We should neither reject contract nor idealise the idea of contract. The victims of victimhood throw the baby out with the bathwater.

There is an analogy with the question of contract and discourse on human rights. Both are valuable, but both are limited. They abstract from real circumstances, and therefore to understand the problem of victimhood, we need to address the context that creates the passivity, resignation and moralism. Dickenson has argued that contractual relations do not have to be unequal and oppressive, though many feminists have thought them to be so (Dickenson, 1997: 64). Contract, she argues, give women authentic subjecthood, but her argument assumes that parties to a contract can be 'genuinely equal' (1997: 174). This is precisely the problem. For the notion of contractual equality involves an abstract attitude that ignores difference.

We prefer Virginia Held's arguments that the notion of humans as contractors is inappropriate for 'morality in general' (Held, 1993: 196) i.e. morality conceived in a concrete fashion, for as she points out, 'contracts must be embedded in social relations which are non-contractual' (1993: 204). Thus, to take the example used above: a woman who contracts as an 'equal' with a man, may have low self-esteem and lack confidence and independent resources. Individualistic liberal conceptions are a useful device as long as we do not overlook the fact that we are abstracting from reality (1993: 219).

Victimhood and Denial

Victimhood – whether of the victim or victimiser – leads to denial. Cohen identifies denial as a personal or collective amnesia, a forgetting of what happened, whether we are talking about genocide and the atrocities that arise from ethnic hatreds, or the perpetration of abuse. In Cohen's view, there is no need to invoke conspiracy or manipulation to understand such cover up (Cohen, 2001: 12).

Cohen is interested not simply in those who suffer and those who cause this suffering. He is also interested in the response of those who hear about or witness an atrocity and do nothing. Observers, he notes, may share a zone of denial with victims – the refusal to acknowledge a truth which seems too impossible to be true (2001: 14). Bystanders may be similar to perpetrators: they want to believe that they themselves will not become victims of random circumstance and that somehow the victims deserve their fate (2001: 16). When asked about British arms being used in massacres in East Timor, Alan Clark, then British Defence Minister, replied: 'I don't really fill my mind much with what one set of foreigners is doing to another' (2001: 20).

The problem needs to be politically analysed. When a victim seeks to understand critically and rationally their plight, it is then easier for such a person or group to overcome residual denial, self-blame, stigma or passivity, and to seek appropriate intervention. It also becomes correspondingly harder for the offender to offer denials ('She asked for it') that have much chance of being accepted (Cohen, 2001: 52). 'They started it' is the primeval account for private violence. The offender's claim to be the 'real' victim (as in the ethnic cleansing that characterised the break up of former Yugoslavia) may refer to short-term defence and provocation, but in political atrocities, denial of creating victims is likely to be ideologically rooted in historically interminable narratives of blaming the other (2001: 96). The victims, it is said, bring torment on themselves, as in Golda Meir's reproach that Arabs made nice Israeli boys do terrible things to them. A Serb soldier speaks of the Battle of Kosovo (which took place in 1389!) as if it happened the week before. Groups are

Marx

The political state, in relation to civil society, is just as spiritual as is heaven in relation to earth... None of the supposed rights of man ... go beyond the egoistic man, man as he is, as a member of civil society; that is, an individual separated from the community, withdrawn into himself, wholly preoccupied with his private interest, and acting in accordance with his private caprice.

('On the Jewish Question' in Tucker (ed.) *The Marx-Engels Reader* London and New York: Norton, 34; 43.)

Ideas and Persectives:

Victimhood and the State

Victims can espouse victimhood by resorting to the state to 'protect' them. Resort to the law (in a statist sense) becomes a substitute for taking action to tackle the problem in a meaningful way. For in state-centred societies, the role of the law is to punish and restrict; it cannot empower and transform.

Brown gives the example of an ordinance in a US city against discrimination in housing on the basis of 'sexual orientation, transsexuality, age, height, weight, personal appearance, physical characteristics, race, color, creed, religion, national origin, ancestry, disability, marital status, sex, or gender' (1995: 65). Such an ordinance, she points out, fails to tackle the problem of poverty and destitution – those who need shelter but cannot afford to obtain it – and assumes in liberal fashion that all have resources. The problem is seen as a formal one – the problem of discrimination. In our view, such an ordinance is not useless but it would be naive to imagine that it empowers those whose differences extend to the ability to buy.

The victims of victimhood see the state as a substitute for empowerment and agency. Of course, people who have suffered may campaign to change the law or influence the state, and such activity will enhance rather than diminish their sense of agency. It is the privatised reliance upon the law and the state to protect and compensate an aggrieved party that signals a manifestation of victimhood. As Brown points out, the state and the law become neutral arbiters of injury (1995: 27).

The state and statist law is taken at face value – they are seen in Hobbesian terms as a substitute (and 'representative') for the will of an individual. The state claims a monopoly of power while the individual has none, and the use of violence by the state against the perpetrator is regarded as a solace to the aggrieved individual.

The notion that the state is 'neutral' and there to defend the powerless individual by punishing their tormentor, perpetuates that sense of powerlessness and impotence which are central to the ideology of victimhood. Cohen points out that one of the reasons why 'bystander states' do not intervene when atrocities occur, is that they believe that 'the nation-state is not a moral agent with moral responsibilities' (2001: 162) – a prejudice that lies at the heart of Machiavelli's analysis of the modern state.

The argument is that relying upon the state in a passive and uncritical way is problematic. Of course, where the state is pressurised to change its policies so that it promotes solutions that are thoughtful and innovative, then the state can assist in combating victimhood. For example, a parent whose child has been killed by a drunk driver, might simply blame the perpetrator and demand a draconian penalty, or in addition the parent might ask the police to remind people who serve alcohol in bars, that it is illegal (and irresponsible) to sell alcohol to persons who are driving and who have already had a few drinks. The latter response would still leave parent (and their child) victims, but it would help the person to resist victimhood.

so enclosed in their 'own circle of self-righteous victimhood' that they cannot learn from anybody outside themselves (2001: 96–7).

Victims are said to be lying and cannot be believed because they have a political interest in discrediting the government. Or 'denial magic' is invoked: the violation is prohibited by the government and so could not have occurred (2001: 105). But not all those who claim to be victims, are necessarily victims. Cohen argues that the notion of repressed memory syndrome (RMS) – often invoked to argue that parents have sexually abused their children – is questionable. The victim, at painful psychic cost, stigmatises the accused (2001: 122).

Victims can also embrace self-denial like the Jews in Germany in the 1930s (2001: 141). Perpetrators, victims and bystanders can, indeed, normalise (in the sense of 'get used to') the most unimaginable horrors. This progressive accommodation may even be essential for atrocities to take place (2001: 188). Victims, as well as perpetrators and bystanders, can suffer a victimhood that leads them to deny suffering and abuse. What makes the concept of victimhood so relevant in today's world is that current versions of identity politics are based on collective identity as *victims*. There is a trend that encourages competition about which group has suffered the most (2001: 290).

The State, Mutuality and Dualism

Cohen argues that the free-market version of globalisation allows a 'post-modern forgetting' to supplement older, more ideological forms. Thus, the traditional Turkish denial of the Armenian genocide is supplemented by a discourse of mindless relativism, a mechanical repetition of the idea that every claim must be untrue – there must always be another point of view (Cohen, 2001: 244). In this way, victims, perpetrators and bystanders are encouraged to veil the enormity of the past. But the problem here lies with the state: a relativist version of postmodernism is linked to victimhood because it facilitates a numbing reconciliation to the status quo.

We have argued that victimhood involves a passive acceptance of the violence inflicted by tormentors, or an imaginary solution to the problem that rests in practice upon a belief that the violence is inexplicable and somehow 'natural' in character. Under the influence of victimhood, victims see the world in the same way that tormentors do. They assume that violence is the result of 'fate' – forces over which they have no control – and whereas tormentors appear as the beneficiaries of these beliefs, victims suffer pain and indignity as a consequence. The state acting as a substitute for the agency of the individual or group, mystifies the mutuality involved in the perpetrator/victim exchange.

Indeed, it is perfectly possible for the victim to become a tormentor. In fact what makes victimhood pathological is that 'victims' easily slip into the position of perpetrators, and since the purveyors of victimhood see violence and suffering as natural and inevitable, they find it impossible to defend themselves except by resorting to the violence from which they have suffered. If the state cannot inflict the violence on their behalf, they do themselves! Criminals have frequently suffered abuse in their own past, and it is impossible to understand the psychology of tormentors without noting that they too subscribe to the notion of victimhood, even if, in reality, others are the victims, and not themselves. Today's victim easily becomes tomorrow's tormentor, since victimhood rests upon an inversion of a repressive 'relationship', rather than its transcendence. Repression remains: we do not go beyond it.

It is true that perpetrators appear to be dynamic and interventionist, whereas the victims seem passive and fatalistic. But these differences are illusory. The tormentor is no more in control of her destiny than the victim. Indeed, the tormentor seeks to vindicate the violence he inflicts upon others, by invoking the status of victim. Nazis saw themselves as the victims of international forces which humiliated Germany; abusive men may have actually suffered abuse themselves, often at the hands of women, and hence see women in general as legitimate targets of their wrath. Unionists in Northern Ireland will recall the horrors of Irish republican violence, and Czechs may justify their hatred of Romanies in terms of the attacks on property that the latter supposedly perpetrate. One cannot understand the extraordinary and tragic acts of violence by the Israeli state against Palestinians without some knowledge of the Jewish experience of the Holocaust.

The ease with which victims and tormentors 'change places' shows that victimhood is a pathology that unites both parties in a deadly and self-destructive embrace. It is true that victims deserve our sympathy in the way that tormentors do not. But victimhood merely perpetuates the violence and suffering involved, whether it is the aggressive violence of the tormentor, or the righteous violence of the victim. In one sense, victims and tormentors *relate* to one another when, under the influence of victimhood, they see the 'other' as inhuman.

But a relationship, as we define it, involves taking responsibility for activity and seeking to understand 'others' in a rational manner. Violence, we would argue, destroys relationships, because through violence, people see one another as mere objects, and hence act against the enemy in the same way that they would act against non-human entities. Indeed, part of the discourse of victimhood involves presenting the 'other' as non-human – as objects to be crushed, not as humans to be changed.

A **dualism** between victims and the 'other' – in our terminology, a division, not a difference – arises with victimhood, and the state employs the language of victimhood to justify its violence. The target of state force is an enemy, evil, inexplicably immoral and thus fully deserving of their fate. The language of abstract moralism ties in with the notion of vengeance: the other must pay for their crimes, she must suffer as the victim has suffered. The state can and does 'victimise' its enemies so that the victims of victimhood are perpetuated in a deadly cycle of violence and counter-violence.

The ideology of 'victimhood' can only be transcended when people have sufficiently cohesive common interests that they can 'change places': the state as the institutionalised expression of victimhood then becomes redundant.

In the last analysis, victimhood expresses itself as a form of self-violence and self-hatred, since the inability to understand why the other has acted in an aggressive way, leads to shame and 'guilt'. Wives who are beaten by their partners, may believe that they deserve such violence, since they are worthless individuals who cannot satisfy their partners' 'needs'. As 'wives', they might subscribe to the view that they are naturally disadvantaged by impersonal and inevitable structures which nobody can change.

A relational position, as we have defined it here, involves avoiding the polarising 'either/or' approach, associated with modernity and the liberal tradition. Indeed, it is precisely this notion of 'those who are not with us, are against us' which expresses disdain for the 'both/and' logic that lies at the heart of a consistent relational position. A relational view of the world accepts that people are both different and the same, but in a way which enhances the capacity for action and self-determination. Mutuality instead of being negative and self-contradictory, becomes positive and empowering.

Victimhood involves an illicit generalisation of the other which makes this positive changing of places impossible. Under the influence of the ideology of victimhood, it is impossible to understand that tormentors not only see themselves as victims, but that an aggressive attitude in one regard may coexist with human or positive attributes in other respects. Nazis, for example, banned smoking (albeit in highly authoritarian fashion) from public places while condoning horrendous experiments on Jews. The project to create a 'purer' world is always dangerous if this 'purity' is seen in abstract and absolutist terms. It is wrong to assume that 'all Germans are Nazis'. Tormentors are not homogenously evil – they invariably have redeeming features.

None of this means that victims should never use violence or retaliate against tormentors. After all, victims have legitimate self-interests to defend, and they may find it impossible to defend themselves without a protective use of violence. But violence, however provisionally necessary it may be in conditions where people simply cannot change places positively, always destroys relationships. Moreover, violence can easily generate an ideology of victimhood, and this is why it is an extremely dangerous form of activity to undertake or condone.

Freedman puts the point well when he comments that 'victim status is becoming a prized commodity in international politics, because it is a means by which a group with no capacity of its own can acquire powerful external allies' (2002: 48). Not only are these allies usually states, but such an attitude is inherently *statist* in character. Victimhood does disservice to the plight of victims. It perpetuates and aggravates the problems which victims face. Victims, we have argued, are those subject to violence or because their straitened circumstances leaves them prey to exploitation and abuse. Tackling victimhood can only be a long-term process – as we saw in relation to the problems facing a postapartheid South Africa. It involves the transcendence of dualism, a negative and self-destructive mutuality, and indeed, the state itself.

Summary

Victims are not simply people afflicted by violence; a person can be legitimately called a victim when her life is unintentionally harmed, or she suffers from illness. It is crucial to distinguish between being a victim and espousing victimhood. Victimhood arises when a victim is unable to understand the real causes of his woes and ascribes an imaginary causality to the suffering concerned.

When we approach the question of power in a one-sided way, seeing it either as solely positive or negative, then we embrace victimhood itself. Women are often the victims of oppression, but they embrace victimhood when they see this oppression as something that they cannot resist and prevent. A desire simply to punish tormentors and resort to the external sanctions of the law, reflects the kind of impotence associated with victimhood.

The temptation to see action in dualistic terms is also a hallmark of victimhood. The notion of rights must be tied to a meaningful action to tackle the problem, otherwise rights themselves can lead to victims espousing victimhood. The South African Truth and Reconciliation Commission sought to tackle the evils of apartheid without creating a sense of victimhood. But it demonstrates the danger of ignoring the particular context in which crimes are committed and how victimhood can only be avoided if resources are provided and judgements reached that deal with grievances expressed.

Contract in itself is not an answer to the pathology of victimhood, since contract can unwittingly reinforce, rather than detract from, a sense of victimhood. Contract can play a positive role when its abstract limitations are grasped. Denial is central to victimhood. The tormentor rationalises his wrongdoing, and the bystander finds imaginary reasons for her inactivity. It could be argued that the concept of victimhood is tied to the state as an institution that seeks to justify force by demonising its opponents.

Questions

1. Can one be a victim without espousing victimhood?
2. Is a sense of victimhood inevitable when violence is involved?
3. Should those who victimise others be punished?
4. Can it be said that the person who victimises another is also a victim?
5. Consider the efficacy of the following responses by a victim: (a) Resort to state-enforced law; (b) asserting rights that have been trampled upon; (c) acting in concert with others to ensure that the victimisation does not reoccur.

References

Atmore, C. (1999) 'Victims, Backlash and Radical Feminist Theory' in S. Lamb (ed.), *New Versions of Victims* New York and London: New York University Press, 183–211.

Brown, W. (1995) *States of Injury* Princeton NJ: Princeton University Press.

Cohen, S. (2001) *States of Denial* Cambridge: Polity Press.

Dickenson, D. (1997) *Property, Women and Politics* Cambridge: Polity Press.

Freedman, L. (2002) 'The Coming War on Terrorism' in L. Freedman (ed.), *Superterrorism: Policy Responses* Massachusetts: Blackwell, 40–56.

Gray, J. (2000) *Two Faces of Liberalism* Cambridge: Polity Press.

Held, V. (1993) *Feminist Morality* Chicago, Ill. and London: University of Chicago Press.

Honderich, T. (2002) *After the Terror* Edinburgh: Edinburgh University Press.

Lamb, S. (ed.) (1999) *New Versions of Victims* New York and London: New York University Press.

Marecek, J. (1999) 'Trauma Talk in Feminist Clinical Practice', in S. Lamb (ed.), *New Versions of Victims* New York and London: New York University Press, 158–82.

Ronai, C.R. (1999) 'In the Line of Sight at *Public Eye: In Search of a Victim*' in S. Lamb (ed.), *New Versions of Victims* New York and London: New York University Press, 139–57.

Wilson, R. (2001) *The Politics of Truth and Reconciliation in South Africa* Cambridge: Cambridge University Press.

Further Reading

- Lamb's *New Versions of Victims* (referenced above) is a useful read. Look particularly at the essays by Atmore, Marecek and Ronai.

- Wilson's *The Politics of Truth and Reconciliation in South Africa* (referenced above) is a valuable assessment of the South African Commission.

- Cohen's *States of Denial* (referenced above) contains fascinating material that is relevant to the problem of victimhood.

How to read, p. 518

- Brown's *States of Injury* (referenced above) is a real classic.

- Nietzsche's *On the Genealogy of Morals* New York: Vintage 1969 is worth dipping into.

Weblinks

There is tantalising reference to a school on the theme of 'beyond victimhood' in http://www.corrymeela.org/Residential/winter school 99.html

Questions of power and superiority are dealt from a religious point of view in http://www.fpireland.org/part1.htm

Interesting thoughts on the Middle Eastern problem, and its bearing on victimhood: http://www.redress.btinternet.co.uk/thinkpiece.htm

Conclusion

One of the questions that interests students of **politics** is the relationship between studying politics as an academic discipline and the practice of politics in the world outside. We thought that it might be useful to tackle this question by way of concluding this volume.

Academic Political Theory and Politics

What makes concepts political is that they respond to conflicts that arise in the world of practice. Academic political theory should address itself to the kind of issues that politicians themselves raise, and which are part and parcel of public debate.

We have already noted, in the discussion about ideologies, the problem of trying to treat **politics** in a purely neutral manner as though it was a study of mere behaviour or an analysis of words. But it does not follow from a critique of what came to be called 'apolitical politics' that academic political theory has no differences from the kind of political theory which appears in party manifestos and in the speeches of politicians.

The fact that academic political theory has something in common with the theory of the publicist and propagandist does not mean that it does not also have something which is different from everyday discourse. Academic political theorists write for individuals who are either academically trained or who are anxious to educate themselves in a systematic and coherent way. Academic political theory is not primarily geared towards convincing an audience of the ideological correctness of its position. Its task is to stimulate rather than persuade, so that rhetoric is curtailed in favour of logic, and sober evidence is offered in place of extravagant emotion. It is not the task of the academic political theorist to exhort people to undertake a particular course of action at a particular time and particular place. Although thinking about a problem is crucial to solving it, this is not the same as actually organising people to implement a solution.

Academic political theory can and should seek to raise the tone of public political debate. Good causes can be strengthened by good arguments, while party positions and publicist writing provide challenging points of reference to make academic political theory more relevant and useful. There is nothing wrong in Thatcher making use of Hayek's work on the free market, even if (in our judgement) both were mistaken! Academic political theory differs from the theory of the public political world, but it is still *political* in character because, despite these differences, it has common features.

We hope that the mix of classical and new political ideas and ideologies has shown the relevance of theory to political practice, and that when you read the newspaper, see a TV programme or follow the arguments of a text, you will be better placed to make up your own mind as to the wider significance of the positions reported or championed.

Glossary

Abstraction   A conceptual and practical process that mystifies and conceals underlying social relationships.

Affirmative action   The apparent departure from equal treatment in order to help disadvantaged groups. Affirmative action is also known as reverse discrimination or positive discrimination.

Anarchism   A theory that seeks to abolish the state, but adopts statist tools of analysis and hence enjoys no success.

Atomistic   An approach that treats individuals and entities in purely discrete terms and ignores the relationships between them.

Authority   An exercise of power in which the moral status of the person exercising the power comes to the fore and is seen as legitimate.

Behaviouralism   An argument that sees human and natural activity as similar, and hence asks that the study of politics be presented as a 'natural science'.

Capitalism   A system of production that divides society into those who can hire the services of others, and those who are compelled to work for an employer.

Caste society   A society in which wealth and other goods are distributed according to some notion of natural inequality.

Citizen   A person able to govern their own life. Citizenship is an emancipatory situation towards which we move, but can never actually reach.

Civic nationalism   The view that nations can be held together by civic ties, such as willingness to participate in legal and political institutions. The alternative view is ethnic nationalism.

Civil disobedience   Law-breaking on moral grounds.

Class   An identity that divides people based upon economic, social, regional, religious, gender, ethnic and other differences.

Coercion   A concept and practice that is close to, but not the same as, force. Coercion involves a threat to use force where this force is credible.

Communitarianism   A theory that stresses that all people belong to communities and can only identify themselves in relations with others.

Consent   Uncoerced acceptance of something, such as state authority.

Conflict   A clash of interests that can be tackled through violence, but only resolved through non-statist pressures. Conflicts of the latter kind are inevitable and arise from the fact that we are all different from one another.

Conservatism   An ideology which is sceptical about reason: because human beings have limited rational capacities they must rely on tradition to guide them.

Constraint   A natural or social pressure that ensures we do something that we had not intended to do.

Contestability   A concept that points to the fact that an idea is controversial, or can be challenged.

Contractarianism   A stream of liberal thought that imagines the state to be the product of a decision between individuals to agree to submit to it. Contractarianism implies individuals consent to the state.

Culture   The often taken-for-granted web of social relations which encompasses many domains of experience, shapes a person's character, and may provide him or her with a set of values by which to live.

Deep ecology   A form of ecologism, stressing both the interdependence of nature, and the need for fundamental human change; it is contrasted with 'shallow ecology', which is essentially environmentalism.

Democracy   A society in which people govern themselves.

Difference   Identifications that separate people and inevitably cause conflict to arise.

Division   Differences that undermine common interests and necessitate the use of force.

Dualism   A gulf between two entities, conceptual or real, that is impossible to cross. It points to a divide rather than a difference.

Ecologism   An ideology centred around 'ecology', stressing the interdependence of all forms of life.

Egalitarianism   A type of political theory which makes equality a fundamental concept.

Emancipation   The capacity of people to act freely, and thus govern their own lives.

Environmentalism   A movement which highlights the importance of preserving the earth's natural resources and guaranteeing a fair share of those resources for future generations. Unlike ecologism it can be combined with many different ideologies.

Equality   Treating 'like cases alike'; different types of equality depend on how we define what is meant by 'like cases' (see legal equality and equality of opportunity).

Equality of opportunity   The equalisation of the opportunity to acquire certain things, or, at least, guaranteeing that each person has a specified chance of acquiring those things.

Essentialism   An attitude that stresses the importance of one determining attribute and ignores all others.

Ethnic nationalism   The view that nations are held together by ethnic ties (*see* ethnicity). The competing view is **civic nationalism**.

Ethnicity   The identification of a culture with tangible, visual symbols and signs such as dress, food, or religious observance.

Fascism   A movement or political and social system that rejects parliamentary democracy, bans other political parties and movements, is hostile to the ideas of the Enlightenment and liberalism, and is particularly opposed to socialism and Marxism.

Feminism   A theory that works for the emancipation of women.

Force   A pressure that undermines the agency of individuals by physically harming them.

Freedom (or **liberty**)   The absence of constraint, or, alternatively, the existence of choice.

Free-riding   Gaining the benefits of cooperation without paying the price. This problem is central to the resolution of the Prisoner's Dilemma.

Fundamentalism   A belief in an ideology that is dogmatic, allows no debate, and holds to the absolute truth of the doctrine espoused.

Genocide   The attempt to destroy an entire ethnic or racial group; genocide can take place without mass murder – mass sterilisation is a form of genocide.

Globalisation   A linkage between peoples of the globe that enables them to understand and empathise with one another.

Goodness (or **goods, the good**)   That which is worth pursuing – 'goods' need not be moral goods: a sharp knife is 'good' for killing people. The 'good' (singular) denotes a view of the world, such as a religion. (*See also* **rightness**).

Government   The resolution of conflicts of interest. It can occur at every level in society; it is inherent in social relationships, and needs to be contrasted with the state.

Green movement   The organised political expression of either ecologism or environmentalism.

Harm   Damage to somebody or something; normally, damage to a person's fundamental interests.

Hierarchy   An asymmetrical linkage that is inherent in relationships. It is normally assumed to be repressive, but it need not be.

Human rights   Entitlements to treatment which it is claimed individuals have simply by virtue of being human.

Humanitarian intervention   Military intervention in order to prevent the serious violation of human rights.

Identity   The sense of belonging to something or of sharing an attribute, such as religious belief, gender or ethnicity, with other people.

Ideology   A set of beliefs that are tied to either defending, placing demands upon or bringing about a state.

Individual   A person who is separate from others but who finds their identity through relating to these others.

Intuition   The sense that something is right and wrong, despite the inability to articulate reasons for that view. Much political theory entails appeal to intuitions.

Justice   Distributive justice is concerned with the fair distribution of the 'benefits' and 'burdens' of cooperation (retributive justice is a quite separate concept – it is the idea that a punishment should 'fit' a crime).

Law   A norm passed by a specific procedure and recognised as binding. A law does not necessarily need force as a sanction.

Legal equality   Each person has the right to a fair trial, and sanctions, such as imprisonment, are similar for all people.

Legal moralism   The view that the law should be used to enforce moral beliefs or practices – opponents of legal moralism do not reject morality, but argue that non-harmful acts should not be illegal.

Legitimacy   Power that has been authorised through an appeal to a wider constituency.

Liberalism   An ideology that takes freedom (or liberty) to be a fundamental value; it also regards individuals as naturally equal, although natural equality is, for many liberals, compatible with significant material inequality.

Libertarianism   A form of liberalism which takes private property rights to be of fundamental importance.

Liberty   *See* **freedom**.

Linguistic analysis   A view that theoretically challenging problems are problems arising from the use of language.

Market   A mechanism that enables exchanges to occur, but in a way which conceals the real power that people possess.

Marxism   A theory whose potential for emancipation is undermined by notions of class war, revolution and dictatorship.

Meritocracy   A society in which wealth, and other goods, are distributed according to innate ability.

Modernity   A term that denotes the onset of the liberal period so that modernism is used as a synonym for liberalism.

Momentum concept   A concept that has a potential for freedom and equality, but whose progress is infinite, and therefore can never be realised.

Monopoly   A process or agent that dominates a collectivity demanding an ultimate loyalty from its subjects.

Morality   A system of beliefs that emphasises the rightness or wrongness of an activity or process.

Multiculturalism   The existence of a number of cultures in a single political system; alternatively, an ideology which recognises that fact as important or values such diversity.

Nation   A collective, normally territorial, entity which commands allegiance. Some theorists argue that nations are the product of modernity, others claim they are 'primordial' or perennial.

Nationalism   An ideology that takes the nation to be of fundamental value.

Natural   A process that is developmental. What is natural is therefore susceptible to historical change.

Naturalism   A doctrine which treats the natural in a static and ahistorical way. It assumes that what exists at the present can never change.

Neoconservatism   An American stream of conservatism that stresses natural rights and the importance of resisting what it sees as tyranny.

Order   A stability in the possession of things; security against violence and a trust in others that promises will be kept.

Paternalism   Intervention to restrict a person's freedom on the grounds that it is in his or her interests.

Patriarchal   A static concept and practice that enshrines male domination. Patriarchy need not be pursued by biological men.

Perennialism   A body of theory concerned to explain the rise of the nation. Perennialists claim that nations predate modernity, although nationalism – consciousness of nationhood – is modern.

Political obligation   The moral obligation to obey the state. Many political theorists, especially anarchists, question whether political obligation is possible.

Politics   A public process that involves resolving conflicts of interest. Politics is undermined by force, and is inherent at every level in all societies.

Post-liberalism   A theory that accepts liberalism but goes beyond it, by extending liberal values to all individuals and thus challenging the need for a state.

Postmodernism   A theory that goes beyond modernism and therefore challenges the dualisms and one-sidedness expressed in the modernist tradition.

Power   The capacity to exert pressure on a person or group so that they do something they otherwise would not have done.

Prejudice   Used in a specific sense by conservatives to mean judging the right action by appealing to habit and experience rather than to rational analysis.

Pre-modern   A theory and practice that has yet to obtain the institutions and to support the values of liberalism (or modernism).

Private   The sphere of life in which conflict is imperceptible or embryonic.

Private property   The division of material goods according to which individuals have an entitlement to a certain good, and can exclude other people from its use.

Public   The sphere of life in which conflict is manifest and has to be resolved.

Race   A concept used to categorise people according to how they look (phenotypical similarity).

Radicalism   An approach that seeks to examine the roots of a phenomenon, disparaging rival approaches as superficial in character.

Reconstruction   The reworking of concepts so that an alternative to the status quo is charted.

Relational   An approach that stresses that individuals and collectivities only find their identity in relationships with one another.

Relationship   A linkage that is vitiated by force but whose mutuality is necessarily hierarchical in character and sustained by coercion and constraint.

Relativism   The rejection of **universalism**: moral norms are dependent on a cultural context.

Religion   An organised system of belief and practice centred around an idea of 'holiness' – that is, something outside historical experience.

Revolution   A fundamental transformation of something: revolutions can be social, economic, intellectual and political.

Rightness   That which is obligatory: for example, you should keep your promises. A person can do the right thing for bad reasons, so rightness must be distinguished from goodness.

Rights   Entitlements in law or simply as part of morality that do not involve harming oneself or others.

Slavery   A term that embraces people who are unfree and are the property of others. Although chattel slavery – the explicit and legal ownership of people – has largely died in the contemporary world, the term can be applied analogously to people who have to work for or are wholly dependent on others.

Socialism   An ideology that asserts society is of equal importance to the individual, and it can therefore be regulated publicly in the interests of the individual.

Society   A group of people who relate to one another for specific purposes. Societies exist at all levels.

Sovereignty   The ability to govern one's own life: sovereignty is an absolute concept that can only express itself in particular historical circumstances.

State   An institution that claims a monopoly of legitimate force for a particular territory. This claim makes it contradictory and paradoxical.

State sovereignty   The claim by supporters of the state that the state has ultimate and final legitimate force over a particular society.

Static concept   One that is divisive in character and cannot, therefore, be reconstructed.

Statism   An approach that creates or accepts divisions and thus the need for force to tackle them.

Terrorism   The use of political violence in situations in which people have reasonable avenues of peaceful protest.

Totalitarianism   A movement or system that aspires to control every aspect of society in an authoritarian manner. It therefore rejects liberalism and democracy.

Toleration   The willingness to allow other people to behave in ways of which we disapprove. The first major historical form of political toleration was religious toleration.

Universalism   The belief that there are moral codes or values binding on all people, irrespective of culture. The alternative position is cultural or ethical **relativism**.

Utilitarianism   A stream of liberal thought that maintains political institutions should maximise the overall level of utility in society. Utilitarians disagree about the definition of 'utility', but possibilities include pleasure, happiness and preference-satisfaction.

Victimhood   A belief, usually from victims, that their plight is caused by themselves or others who must be blamed and punished as a substitute for actively seeking the roots of their problem.

Violence   A synonym for force.

Will   A capacity to exercise choice as an agent.

Index

Page references in *italics* denotes glossary entry
Page references in **bold** denotes biography entry

T